P9-CKE-736

Thinking and Deciding, Third Edition

Thinking and Deciding has established itself as a required text and important reference work for students and scholars of human judgments, decisions, and rationality. In this, the third edition, Jonathan Baron delves further into many of the key questions addressed in the previous editions. For example, how should we think? What, if anything, keeps us from thinking that way? How can we improve our thinking and decision making? Baron has also revised or expanded his treatment of topics such as risk, utilitarianism, Bayes's theorem, utility measurement, decision analysis and values. By emphasizing decision making, Baron has made *Thinking and Deciding, Third Edition,* more relevant to researchers in applied fields, such as medicine, business, public policy, and law, while maintaining its appeal to graduate and undergraduate students.

Jonathan Baron is Professor of Psychology at the University of Pennsylvania. He is the author of *Morality and Rational Choice* and *Judgment Misguided* and the editor of *Teaching Decision Making to Adolescents* and *Psychological Perspectives on Justice* (with Barbara Mellers).

Thinking and Deciding

Third Edition

Jonathan Baron
University of Pennsylvania

CAMBRIDGE UNIVERSITY PRESS
Cambridge, New York, Melbourne, Madrid, Cape Town, Singapore, São Paulo

Cambridge University Press
32 Avenue of the Americas, New York, NY 10013-2473, USA

www.cambridge.org
Information on this title: www.cambridge.org/9780521650304

© Cambridge University Press 2000

This publication is in copyright. Subject to statutory exception
and to the provisions of relevant collective licensing agreements,
no reproduction of any part may take place without
the written permission of Cambridge University Press.

First published 1998
Second edition published 1994
Third edition published 2000
7th printing 2007

Printed in the United States of America

A catalog record for this publication is available from the British Library.

Library of Congress Cataloging in Publication Data

Baron, Jonathan, 1944–
Thinking and deciding / Jonathan Baron. – 3rd ed.
    p.   cm.
Includes bibliographical references and indexes.
ISBN 0-521-65030-5 (hard). – ISBN 0-521-65972-8 (pbk.)
1. Thought and thinking.   2. Decision-making.   I. Title.
BF441.B29   2000
153.4'2 – dc20   93-46230
                                                           CIP

ISBN   978-0-521-65030-4 hardback
ISBN   978-0-521-65972-7 paperback

Cambridge University Press has no responsibility for
the persistence or accuracy of URLs for external or
third-party Internet Web sites referred to in this publication
and does not guarantee that any content on such
Web sites is, or will remain, accurate or appropriate.

Contents

Preface   **xiii**

I   THINKING IN GENERAL   1

1   What is thinking?   **5**
Types of thinking   6
The search-inference framework   6
Thinking about beliefs 12
How do search processes work? 14
Knowledge, thinking, and understanding 17
    Naive theories 17
    Understanding 22
Conclusion 29

2   The study of thinking   **31**
Descriptive, normative, and prescriptive 31
Methods for empirical research 34
    Observation 34
    Computer models and artificial intelligence 43
    General issues 43
Development of normative models 47
Descriptive models and heuristics 49
Development of prescriptive models 50
Conclusion 51

3   Good thinking: The nature of rationality   **53**
A normative view 53
Rationality 55
    The meaning of rationality 55
    Rationality and luck 56
    Objections to rationality 57

Rationality and emotion   59
Rationality and belief   62
    Rational belief formation   62
    Self-deception   63
    Beliefs as a cause of desires   65
Are people ever really irrational?   66
Conclusion   66

4 Logic   67
What is logic?   67
Types of logic   70
Difficulties in logical reasoning   72
Mental models   74
Logical errors in hypothesis testing   78
    The four-card problem   78
    The error as poor thinking   79
    Resistance to instruction   80
    Dual processes and rationalization   81
    Content effects   82
Extensions of logic   84
Conclusion   87

II PROBABILITY AND BELIEF   89

5 Normative theory of probability   93
What is probability?   96
    The frequency theory   97
    The logical theory   98
    The personal theory   99
Constructing probability judgments 102
    Probability as willingness to bet 102
    Comparison with a chance setup 103
Well-justified probability judgments 104
Evaluating probability judgments 106
    Calibration 106
    Scoring rules 107
Bayes's theorem 109
    An example from medicine 109
    Formulas for Bayes's theorem 111
    Why we should accept Bayes's theorem 114
    Why frequencies matter 115
    When Bayes's theorem is useful and when it isn't 117
    A digression: Coincidences 118

Another digression: The Monty Hall problem 119
Use of Bayes's theorem in expert systems 120
Conclusion 123

6 Descriptive theory of probability judgment   125
Accuracy of probability judgments 125
Frequency judgments 126
Calibration and inappropriate extreme confidence 127
Improving calibration by conditional assessment 132
Heuristics and biases in probability 134
The representativeness heuristic 134
The gambler's fallacy and "probability matching" 139
The availability heuristic 141
Subadditivity 144
Hindsight bias 145
Averaging 146
Conclusion 147

7 Hypothesis testing   149
Hypotheses in science 150
An example from medicine 150
Testing scientific hypotheses 153
The psychology of hypothesis testing 156
Concept formation 157
Congruence bias 159
Information bias and the value of information 166
Utility and alternative hypotheses 170
Conclusion 171

8 Judgment of correlation and contingency   173
Correlation, cause, and contingency 173
Accuracy of judgment 176
Attentional bias 176
Attentional bias in judging correlation 176
Attentional bias in judging contingency 179
Effect of goals on illusion of control 181
Effects of prior belief 182
Illusory correlation 183
Personality traits 183
Prior belief and attentional bias 186
Understanding theory and evidence 187
Conclusion 189

9 Actively open-minded thinking   **191**
  Examples of actively open-minded thinking 192
  Myside bias and irrational belief persistence 195
      The order principle, the primacy effect, and total discrediting 197
      The neutral-evidence principle 200
  Effect of active open-mindedness on outcomes 203
  Determinants and related phenomena 204
      Beliefs about thinking 204
      Distortion of beliefs by desires 206
      Related results 211
  Factors that moderate belief persistence 213
      Elastic justification 213
      Value conflict 213
      Accountability 214
      Stress 215
      Groupthink 216
  Conclusion 218

III DECISIONS AND PLANS   **219**

10 Normative theory of choice   **223**
  Expected-utility theory 227
  Why expected-utility theory is normative 232
      The long-run argument 232
      The argument from principles 233
      An alternative principle: Tradeoff consistency 237
  The utility of money 238
  Conclusion 243

11 Description of choice under uncertainty   **245**
  Bias in decisions under uncertainty 246
      Neglect of probability 246
      Preference reversals 247
      The Allais paradox 248
  Prospect theory 250
      Probability: the pi function 251
      Utility: The Value function and framing effects 255
      Extending prospect theory to events without stated probabilities . . 259
  Rank-dependent utility theories 260
  Emotional effects of outcomes 263
      Regret and rejoicing 263
      Disappointment and elation 265
      The role of regret in decisions 266

Rationality of regret and disappointment in decision making 267
The ambiguity effect 268
Ambiguity and "unknown probability" 269
Rationality of the ambiguity effect 270
Aversion to missing information 271
Ambiguity and adjustment of probability 273
Uncertainty and reasons for choice 273
Conclusion 274

12 Choice under certainty   **277**
Single-mindedness 277
Compatibility and evaluability 280
Response mode compatibility 281
Evaluability and joint versus separate evaluation 281
Effects of the options available on choice 282
Intransitivity of preferences 283
Elimination by aspects 284
Asymmetric dominance 287
Compromise 288
Mental accounting 288
The status quo (endowment) effect 288
Omission bias 291
Emotional effects of the reference point 292
Opportunity costs 293
Positive and negative attributes 294
Integration and segregation 295
The sunk-cost effect 297
Mental budgets and underinvestment 300
The reference price 301
Conclusion 302

13 Utility measurement   **303**
Decision analysis and related methods 303
The Oregon Health Plan 304
Decision analysis versus cost-benefit analysis 306
The measurement of utility 310
Utility measurement as prediction 310
Direct versus indirect judgments 311
Simple direct judgment and the analog scale 313
Difference measurement 314
Standard gambles 316
Time tradeoff and person tradeoff 320
What counts in health utility? 322
Adaptation and point of view 323

Other methods involving matching and comparison 324
Contingent valuation (CV) 327
Disagreement among measures 330
Conclusion 333

14 Decision analysis and values   **335**
Fundamental versus means values 336
Discovering values 337
Objectives of hiring a new faculty member in psychology 338
Conjoint measurement 340
MAUT as a type of decision analysis 343
Rules and tradeoffs 350
The value of human life 352
Teaching decision analysis 354
Conclusion 355

15 Quantitative judgment   **357**
Multiple linear regression 358
The lens model 361
The mechanism of judgment 368
Do people really follow linear models? 368
Impression formation 370
Averaging, adding, and number of cues 371
Representativeness in prediction 373
Anchoring and underadjustment 375
Classification 376
Functional measurement and conjoint analysis 378
Conclusion 380

16 Moral thinking   **381**
Morality and utility 382
The logic and illogic of moral judgments 383
Imperatives and the naturalistic fallacy 383
The fallacy of relativism 384
Utilitarianism as the normative theory 386
Maximizing expected utility for everyone 387
Interpersonal comparison 389
Rights theories 392
Deontological rules 394
Rule utilitarianism 396
Biases in moral judgment? 399
Acts and omissions 400
Other possible biases 401
Can intuitions be values? 403
Conclusion 405

17 Fairness and justice   **409**
   The study of fairness and justice 410
   Equity theory: the desire for justice 411
   Utilitarianism and fairness 413
   Intuitions 417
   Heuristics and self-interest 425
   Negotiation 426
   Conclusion 431

18 Social dilemmas   **433**
   Laboratory versions 434
      Prisoner's dilemma 435
      Effects of repetition 436
      N-person prisoner's dilemma 436
   Normative and prescriptive theory 438
   Motives in social dilemmas 441
      Altruism 442
      Competition 444
      Fairness, equality, and envy 445
      Fear and greed 446
   Trust 450
   Voters' illusions 452
   Thoughtlessness 455
   Solutions to social dilemmas 455
      Experimental approaches 456
      Social reform 459
   Conclusion 460

19 Decisions about the future   **463**
   The choice of personal goals 465
   Good reasons for sticking to plans 467
   Bad reasons for sticking to plans: Biases 468
   Discounting 470
      Economic theory of discounting 470
      Normative theory of discounting 473
      Descriptive data on discounting 474
      The rationality of personal discounting 479
   Self-control 480
      Why we need self-control 481
      Methods of self-control 481
   Emotions and time 484
   Adaptation, contrast, and heuristics 485
   Morality, prudence, and personal plans 487
   Conclusion 488

20 Risk   **489**

Normative theory 490
    Public control of risk 491
    Private insurance 494
    Investment and entrepreneurs 494
Risk regulation and the intuitions that support it 495
    The psychometric approach 496
    Voluntary versus involuntary 498
    Known versus unknown 499
    Catastrophic versus individual 500
    Proportions versus differences 500
    Individual versus statistical 502
    Natural versus artificial 503
    Omission versus commission 504
    Zero risk 505
    Intuitive toxicology and naive theories 506
Intuitions about tort law 507
Insurance and protective behavior 508
Investors and entrepreneurs 511
Individual and sex differences 514
Conclusion 516

References   **519**

Author Index   **555**

Subject Index   **563**

Preface

The third edition of this book represents a major shift of focus. The first edition (1988) began with the idea of providing relevant background to those who wanted to teach thinking and decision making in schools. It was also intended as a basic text for undergraduate psychology students. In the intervening years, the second purpose was achieved to some extent, although other books have come along that have also filled this need. *Thinking and Deciding* tended to be used more in advanced undergraduate and beginning graduate courses, and as a reference work. The first purpose, to my knowledge, was not achieved at all. On the other hand, I found my book on the shelves of many colleagues in medicine, where it was used as a kind of basic introduction for people who wanted to do research in medical decision making. It was also familiar to scholars in business, law, and public policy, in the same way.

I have thus decided to go with the flow, and decreased the emphasis on thinking in general while adding more about decision making, of a sort that might be useful to researchers in applied fields such as medicine, business, public policy, and law. Although it is now primarily directed at graduate students in these fields (or physician-researchers, who must educate themselves), I intend to keep using it in my own undergraduate course. The students seem to like it.

The book retains many of the features of the first two editions:

1. Knowledge about thinking and decision making has been scattered among a number of different fields. Philosophers, psychologists, educators, economists, decision scientists, and computer scientists all have different approaches to the theory of thinking and decision making. The approach represented in this book represents my own effort to draw together some of the key ideas about thinking from these different disciplines into a unified theory. Much of this theory is not original or new. If it were either of these, I would not be so confident that it is basically correct.

2. I retain the idea that all goal-directed thinking and decision making can be described in terms of what I call the *search-inference framework*: Thinking can be described as inferences made from possibilities, evidence, and goals that are discovered through searching.

3. I also argue that one main problem with our thinking and decision making is that much of it suffers from a lack of *active open-mindedness*: We ignore possibilities, evidence, and goals that we ought to consider, and we make inferences in ways that protect our favored ideas.

In the course of this book, I apply these ideas to the major concepts and theories in the study of thinking. I begin, in part I, with general considerations: the nature of rationality; methods for studying thinking; and logic. Part II is concerned with belief formation, which is a form of thinking in which the goal of thinking is held constant. In this part, I introduce probability theory as a formal standard. Part III concerns decision making, including the making of decisions about personal plans and goals, and decisions that affect others, such as those that involve moral issues or matters of public concern. This part introduces utility theory, which formalizes many of the ideas that run throughout the book.

Although the approach is broad, some things are left out. I deal here with thinking, as a purposive activity — as a way of choosing actions, beliefs, and personal goals — not as an experience. I also exclude such highly skilled behavior as speaking and understanding language. Such skills can help us think, and thinking well can help us to acquire them, but these skills in themselves do not fit into the framework.

Many people have provided useful comments and other assistance. For the first two editions, Judy Baron, Kathie Galotti, and anonymous reviewers each gave useful advice about several chapters. Other chapters or sections were helpfully read by George Ainslie, Dorrit Billman, Colin Camerer, Allan Collins, Deborah Frisch, John C. Hershey, Joel Kupperman, and David Messick. Many students brought errors to my attention. Christie Lerch, as an editor for Cambridge University Press, provided the final, most demanding, most detailed, and most helpful set of criticisms and constructive suggestions concerning all levels of writing and organization.

The third edition has benefited greatly from extensive comments by Peter Wakker, Craig Fox, Howard Kunreuther, and Robin Gregory, and less extensive but still helpful comments from Paul Slovic, Peter Ubel, Judy Baron, and David Baron. David Baron has also helped, in all editions, with formatting, figures, and general computer advice. The book was formatted using LATEX, and figures were drawn with Systat, Metapost, and a couple in raw PostScript.

I am also grateful to many colleagues who have influenced my thinking over the years, including Jane Beattie, Colin Camerer, Deborah Frisch, John C. Hershey, Howard Kunreuther, David Perkins, Ilana Ritov, John Sabini, Mark Spranca, and Peter Ubel.

Part I

THINKING IN GENERAL

Part I is about the basics, the fundamentals. Chapters 1 through 3 present the concepts that underlie the rest of the book. Chapter 1 defines thinking, introduces the main types of thinking, and presents what I call the search-inference framework for describing thinking. Chapter 2 introduces the *study* of thinking and decision making, including the three types of questions we shall ask:

1. The *normative* question: How should we evaluate thinking? By what standards?

2. The *descriptive* question: How do we think? What prevents us from doing our best thinking?

3. The *prescriptive* question: What can we do to improve our thinking and decision making, both as individuals and as a society?

These three questions define the content of the book. We can ask them about every topic. The third chapter introduces a theory of the nature of *good* thinking and of how we tend to think poorly. By using the normative theory to evaluate our actual thinking, we can know how it must be improved if it is found wanting. In this way, we can learn to think more *rationally*, that is, in a way that helps us achieve our goals.

Chapter 4 briefly introduces the study of logic. This is an older tradition in both philosophy and psychology. It is of interest because it has, from the time of Aristotle, taken roughly the approach I have just sketched. Logic provides a standard of reasoning. Although people often reason in accord with this standard, they sometimes depart from it systematically. Scholars across the centuries thus have asked, "How can we help people to think more logically?"

normative - should do

Prescriptive - can do to move from Descriptive to normative

Descriptive - actually do

Chapter 1

What is thinking?

Beginning to reason is like stepping onto an escalator that leads upward and out of sight. Once we take the first step, the distance to be traveled is independent of our will and we cannot know in advance where we shall end.

Peter Singer (1982)

Thinking is important to all of us in our daily lives. The way we think affects the way we plan our lives, the personal goals we choose, and the decisions we make. Good thinking is therefore not something that is forced upon us in school: It is something that we all want to do, and want others to do, to achieve our goals and theirs.

This approach gives a special meaning to the term "rational." Rational does not mean, here, a kind of thinking that denies emotions and desires: It means, *the kind of thinking we would all want to do, if we were aware of our own best interests, in order to achieve our goals.* People want to think "rationally," in this sense. It does not make much sense to say that you do not want to do something that will help you achieve your goals: Your goals are, by definition, what you want to achieve. They are the criteria by which you evaluate everything about your life.

The main theme of this book is the comparison of what people do with what they should do, that is, with what it would be rational for them to do. By finding out where the differences are, we can help people — including ourselves — to think more rationally, in ways that help us achieve our own goals more effectively.

This chapter discusses three basic types of thinking that we have to do in order to achieve our goals: *thinking about decisions, thinking about beliefs,* and *thinking about our goals themselves.* It also describes what I call the *search-inference frame-work,* a way of identifying the basic elements in all of these thinking processes.

Types of thinking

We think when we are in doubt about how to act, what to believe, or what to desire. In these situations, thinking helps us to resolve our doubts: It is purposive. We have to think when we *make decisions*, when we *form beliefs*, and when we *choose our personal goals*, and we will be better off later if we think well in these situations.

A *decision* is a choice of action — of what to do or not do. Decisions are made to achieve goals, and they are based on beliefs about what actions will achieve the goals. For example, if I believe it is going to rain, and if my goal is to keep dry, I will carry an umbrella. Decisions may attempt to satisfy the goals of others as well as the selfish goals of the decision maker. I may carry an extra umbrella for a friend. Decisions may concern small matters, such as whether to carry an umbrella, or matters of enormous importance, such as how one government should respond to a provocation by another. Decisions may be simple, involving only a single goal, two options, and strong beliefs about which option will best achieve the goal, or they may be complex, with many goals and options and with uncertain beliefs.

Decisions depend on beliefs and goals, but we can think about beliefs and goals separately, without even knowing what decisions they will affect. When we think about *belief*, we think to decide how strongly to believe something, or which of several competing beliefs is true. When we believe a proposition, we tend to act as if it were true. If I believe it will rain, I will carry my umbrella. We may express beliefs in language, even without acting on them ourselves. (Others may act on the beliefs we express.) Many school problems, such as those in mathematics, involve thinking about beliefs that we express in language only, not in actions. Beliefs may vary in strength, and they may be quantified as probabilities. A decision to go out of my way to buy an umbrella requires a stronger belief that it will rain (a higher probability) than a decision to carry an umbrella I already own.

When we decide on a *personal goal*, we make a decision that affects future decisions. If a person decides to pursue a certain career, the pursuit of that career becomes a goal that many future decisions will seek to achieve. When we choose personal goals by thinking, we also try to bind our future behavior. Personal goals of this sort require self-control.

Actions, beliefs, and personal goals can be the results of thinking, but they can also come about in other ways. For example, we are born with the personal goal of satisfying physical needs. It may also make sense to say that we are born holding the belief that space has three dimensions. The action of laughing at a joke does not result from a decision. If it did, it would not be a real laugh.

The search-inference framework

Thinking about actions, beliefs, and personal goals can all be described in terms of a common framework, which asserts that thinking consists of *search* and *inference*. We search for certain objects and then we make inferences from and about them.

Let us take a simple example of a decision. Suppose you are a college student trying to decide which courses you will take next term. Most of the courses you have scheduled are required for your major, but you have room for one elective. The question that starts your thinking is simply this: Which course should I take?

You begin by saying to a friend, "I have a free course. Any ideas?" She says that she enjoyed Professor Smith's course in Soviet-American relations. You think that the subject sounds interesting, and you want to know more about modern history. You ask her about the work, and she says that there is a lot of reading and a twenty-page paper. You think about all the computer-science assignments you are going to have this term, and, realizing that you were hoping for an easier course, you resolve to look for something else. After thinking about it yourself, you recall hearing about a course in American history since World War II. That has the same advantages as the first course — it sounds interesting and it is about modern history — but you think the work might not be so hard. You try to find someone who has taken the course.

Clearly, we could go on with this imaginary example, but it already shows the main characteristics of thinking. It begins with doubt. It involves a search directed at removing the doubt. Thinking is, in a way, like exploration. In the course of the search, you have discovered two possible courses, some good features of both courses, some bad features of one course, and some goals you are trying to achieve. You have also made an inference: You rejected the first course because the work was too hard. *options*

We search for three kinds of objects: possibilities, evidence, and goals.

Possibilities are possible answers to the original question, possible resolutions of the original doubt. (In the example just given, they are the two possible courses.) Notice that possibilities can come from inside yourself or from outside. (This is also true of evidence and goals.) The first possibility in this example came from outside: It was suggested by someone else. The second came from inside: It came from your memory.

Goals are the criteria by which you evaluate the possibilities. Three goals have been mentioned in our example: your desire for an interesting course; your feeling that you ought to know something about recent history; and your desire to keep your work load manageable. Some goals are usually present at the time when thinking begins. In this case, only the goal of finding a course is present, and it is an insufficient goal, because it does not help you to distinguish among the possibilities, the various courses you could take. Additional goals must be sought.

I use the term "goal" throughout this book, but it is not entirely satisfactory. It evokes images of games like soccer and basketball, in which each team tries to get the ball into the "goal." Such goals are all-or-none. You either get one or you don't. Some of the goals I discuss here are of that type, but others are more like the rating scales used for scoring divers or gymnasts. This is, in a way, closer to the fundamental meaning, which is that the goals are criteria or standards of evaluation. Other words for the same idea are criteria, objectives, and values (in the sense of *evalu*ation, not the more limited sense referring to morality). Because all these terms are misleading in different ways, I will stick with goals. At least this term conveys the sense that, for most of us, goals have motivational force. We *try* to achieve them.

Evidence consists of any belief or potential belief that helps you determine the extent to which a possibility achieves some goal. In this case, the evidence consists of your friend's report that the course was interesting and her report that the work load was heavy. The example ended with your resolution to search for more evidence about the work load of the second possibility, the American history course. Such a search for evidence might initiate a whole other episode of thinking, the goal of which would be to determine where that evidence can be found.

In addition to these search processes, there is a process of *inference*, or *use of evidence*, in which each possibility is strengthened or weakened as a choice on the basis of the evidence, in the light of the goals. Goals determine the way in which evidence is used. For example, the evidence about work load would be irrelevant if having a manageable work load were not a goal. The importance of that goal, which seems to be high, affects the importance of that evidence, which seems to be great.

The objects of thinking are represented in our minds. We are conscious of them. If they are not in our immediate consciousness, we can recall them when they are relevant, even after an episode of thinking resumes following an interruption. The processes of thinking — the search for possibilities, evidence, and goals and the use of the evidence to evaluate possibilities — do not occur in any fixed order. They overlap. The thinker alternates from one to another.

Why just these phases: the search for possibilities, evidence, and goals, and the use of evidence? *Thinking is, in its most general sense, a method of finding and choosing among potential possibilities, that is, possible actions, beliefs, or personal goals.* For any choice, there must be purposes or goals, and goals can be added to or removed from the list. I can search for (or be open to) new goals; therefore, search for goals is always possible. There must also be objects that can be brought to bear on the choice among possibilities. Hence, there must be evidence, and it can always be sought. Finally, the evidence must be used, or it might as well not have been gathered. These phases are "necessary" in this sense.

The term *judgment* will be important in this book. By judgment, I mean the *evaluation of one or more possibilities with respect to a specific set of evidence and goals*. In decision making, we can judge whether to take an option or not, or we can judge its desirability relative to other options. In belief formation, we can judge whether to accept a belief as a basis of action, or we can judge the probability that the belief is true. In thinking about personal goals, we can judge whether or not to adopt a goal, or we can judge how strong it should be relative to other goals. The term "judgment," therefore, refers to the process of inference.

Let us review the main elements of thinking, using another example of decision making, the practical matter of looking for an apartment. "Possibilities" are possible answers to the question that inspired the thinking: Here, they are possible apartments. Possibilities (like goals and evidence) can be in mind before thinking begins. You may already have seen one apartment you like before you even think about moving. Or possibilities can be added, as a result of active search (through the newspaper) or suggestions from outside (tips from friends).

Goals are criteria used for evaluating possibilities. In the apartment-hunting example, goals include factors such as rent, distance from work or school, safety, and design quality. The goals determine what evidence is sought and how it is used. It is not until you think that safety might be relevant that you begin to inquire about building security or the safety of the neighborhood. When we *search for goals*, we ask, "What should I be trying to do?" or "What is my purpose in doing this?" Can you think of other criteria for apartments aside from those listed? In doing so, you are searching for goals. We also often have a *subgoal*, a goal whose achievement will help us achieve some other goal. In this example, "good locks" would be a subgoal for "safety." Each possibility has what I shall call its *strength*, which represents the extent to which it is judged by the thinker to satisfy the goals. In decision making, the strength of a possibility corresponds to its overall desirability as an act, taking into account all the goals that the decision maker has in mind.

Evidence is sought — or makes itself available. Evidence can consist of simple propositions such as "The rent is $300 a month," or it can consist of arguments, imagined scenarios, or examples. One possibility can serve as evidence against another, as when we challenge a scientific hypothesis by giving an alternative and incompatible explanation of the data. Briggs and Krantz (1992) found that subjects can judge the weight of each piece of evidence independently of other pieces.

Each piece of evidence has what I shall call a *weight* with respect to a given possibility and set of goals. The weight of a given piece of evidence determines how much it should strengthen or weaken the possibility as a means of achieving the goals. The weight of the evidence by itself does not determine how much the strength of a possibility is revised as the possibility is evaluated; the thinker controls this revision. Therefore a thinker can err by revising the strength of a possibility too much or too little.

The *use of the evidence* to revise (or not revise) strengths of possibilities is the end result of all of these search processes. This phase is also called *inference*. It is apparent that inference is not all of thinking, although it is a crucial part.

The relationship among the elements of thinking is illustrated in the following diagram:

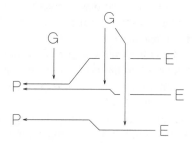

The evidence (*E*) affects the strengths of the possibilities (*P*), but the weight of the evidence is affected by the goals (*G*). Different goals can even reverse the weight of a piece of evidence. For example, if I want to buy a car and am trying to decide between two different ones (*possibilities*), and one of the cars is big and heavy (*evidence*), my concern with safety (a *goal*) might make the size a virtue (*positive weight*), but my concern with mileage (another *goal*) might make the size a detriment (*negative weight*).

The following story describes the situation of a person who has to make an important decision. As you read it, try to discover the goals, possibilities, evidence, and inferences:

A corporate executive is caught in a dilemma. Her colleagues in the Eastern District Sales Department of the National Widget Corporation have decided to increase the amount they are permitted to charge to their expense accounts without informing the central office (which is unlikely to notice). When she hears about the idea, at first she wants to go along, imagining the nice restaurants to which she could take her clients, but then she has an uneasy feeling about whether it is right to do this. She thinks that not telling the central office is a little like lying.

When she voices her doubts to her colleagues, they point out that other departments in the corporation are allowed higher expense accounts than theirs and that increased entertainment and travel opportunities will benefit the corporation in various ways. Nearly persuaded to go along at this point, she still has doubts. She thinks of the argument that any other department could do the same, cooking up other flimsy excuses, and that if all departments did so, the corporation would suffer considerably. (She makes use here of a type of moral argument that she recognizes as one she has used before, namely, "What if everyone did that?") She also wonders why, if the idea is really so harmless, her colleagues are not willing to tell the central office.

Now in a real quandary, because her colleagues had determined to go ahead, she wonders what she can do on her own. She considers reporting the decision to the central office, but she imagines what would happen then. Her colleagues might all get fired, but if not, they would surely do their best to make her life miserable. And does she really want them all fired? Ten years with the company have given her some feelings of personal attachment to her co-workers, as well as loyalty to the company. But she cannot go along with the plan herself either, for she thinks it is wrong, and, besides, if the central office does catch them, they could *all* get fired. (She recalls a rumor that this happened once before.) She finally decides not to go above the company's stated limit for her department's expense accounts herself and to keep careful records of her own actual use of her own expense account, so that she can prove her innocence if the need arises.

In this case, the *goals* were entertaining clients in style; following moral rules; serving the interests of the corporation; being loyal to colleagues; and avoiding punishment. The *possibilities* were going along, turning everyone in, not going along, and not going along plus keeping records. The *evidence* consisted of feelings and arguments — sometimes arguments of others, sometimes arguments that our executive thought of herself.

Initially the executive saw only a single possibility — to go along — but some evidence against that possibility presented itself, specifically, an intuition or uneasy feeling. Such intuitions are usually a sign that more evidence will be found. Here, the executive realized that withholding evidence was a form of lying, so a moral rule was being violated. With this piece of evidence came a new *goal* that was not initially present in the executive's mind, the goal of being moral or doing the right thing. She sought more evidence by talking to her colleagues, and she thought of more evidence after she heard their arguments. Finally, another possibility was considered: turning everyone in. Evidence against this possibility also involved the discovery of other relevant goals — in particular, loyalty to colleagues and self-protection.

The final possibility was a compromise, serving no goals perfectly. It was not as "moral" as turning her colleagues in or trying to persuade them to stop. It might not have turned out to be as self-protective either, if the whole plot had been discovered, and it was not as loyal to colleagues as going along. This kind of result is typical of many difficult decisions.

This example clarifies the distinction between *personal goals* and *goals for thinking*. The goals for thinking were drawn from our executive's personal goals. She had adopted these personal goals sometime in the past. When she searched for goals for her thinking, she searched among her own personal goals. Many of her personal goals were not found in her search for goals, in most cases because they were irrelevant to the decision. Each person has a large set of personal goals, only a few of which become goals for thinking in any particular decision.

The examples presented so far are all readily recognizable as decisions, yet there are other types of thinking — not usually considered to be decision making — that can be analyzed as decision making when they are examined closely. For instance, any sort of inventive or creative thinking can be analyzed this way. When we create music, poetry, paintings, stories, designs for buildings, scientific theories, essays, or computer programs, we make decisions at several levels. We decide on the overall plan of the work, the main parts of the plan, and the details. Often, thinking at these different levels goes on simultaneously. We sometimes revise the overall plan when problems with details come up. At each level, we consider possibilities for that level, we search for goals, and we look for evidence about how well the possibilities achieve the goals.

Planning is decision making, except that it does not result in immediate action. Some plans — such as plans for a Saturday evening — are simply decisions about specific actions to be carried out at a later time. Other, long-term plans produce personal goals, which then become the goals for later episodes of thinking. For example, a personal career goal will affect decisions about education. Thinking about plans may extend over the period during which the plans are in effect. We may revise our plans on the basis of experience. Experience provides new evidence. The goals involved in planning — the criteria by which we evaluate possible plans — are the personal goals we already have. We therefore create new goals on the basis of old ones. We may also decide to give up (or temporarily put aside) some personal goals.

We may have short-term plans as well as long-term plans. When we are trying to solve a math problem, we often make a plan about how to proceed, which we may revise as we work on the problem.

Thinking about beliefs

The search-inference framework applies to thinking about beliefs as well as thinking about decisions. When we think about beliefs, we make decisions to strengthen or weaken possible beliefs. One goal is to bring our beliefs into line with the evidence. (Sometimes we have other goals as well — for example, the goal of believing certain things, regardless of their fit with the evidence.) Roughly, beliefs that are most in line with the evidence are beliefs that correspond best with the world as it is. They are beliefs that are most likely to be *true*. If a belief is true, and if we hold it because we have found the right evidence and made the right inferences, we can be said to *know* something.[1] Hence, thinking about beliefs can lead to knowledge.

Examination of a few types of thinking about belief will show how the search-inference framework applies. (Each of these types is described in more detail in later chapters.)

Diagnosis. In diagnosis, the goal is to discover what the trouble is — what is wrong with a patient, an automobile engine, a leaky toilet, or a piece of writing. The search for evidence is only partially under the thinker's control, both because some of the evidence is provided without being requested and because there is some limitation on the kinds of requests that can be obeyed. In particular, the import of the evidence cannot usually be specified as part of the request (for example, a physician cannot say, "Give me any evidence *supporting a diagnosis of ulcers*," unless the patient knows what this evidence would be). In the purest form of diagnosis, the goal is essentially never changed, although there may be subepisodes of thinking directed toward subgoals, such as obtaining a certain kind of evidence.

Scientific thinking. A great deal of science involves testing hypotheses about the nature of some phenomenon. What is the cause of a certain disease? What causes the tides? The "possibilities" are the hypotheses that the scientist considers: germs, a poison, the sun, the moon. Evidence consists of experiments and observations. Pasteur, for example, inferred that several diseases were caused by bacteria, after finding that boiling contaminated liquid prevented the spread of disease — an experiment. He also observed bacteria under a microscope — an observation.

---

[1] For a more complete introduction to these concepts, see Scheffler, 1965. We shall also return to them throughout this book.

Science differs from diagnosis in that the search for goals is largely under the thinker's control and the goals are frequently changed. Scientists frequently "discover" the "real question" they were trying to answer in the course of trying to answer some other question. There is, in experimental science, the same limitation on control over the evidence-search phase: The scientist cannot pose a question of the form "Give me a result that supports my hypothesis." This limitation does not apply when evidence is sought from books or from one's own memory.

Reflection. Reflection includes the essential work of philosophers, linguists, mathematicians, and others who try to arrive at general principles or rules on the basis of evidence gathered largely from their own memories rather than from the outside world. Do all words ending in "-ation" have the main stress on the syllable "a"? Does immoral action always involve a kind of thoughtlessness? In reflection, the search for evidence is more under the control of the thinker than in diagnosis and experimental science; in particular, thinkers can direct their memories to provide evidence either for or against a given possibility (in this case, a generalization). One can try to think of words ending in "-ation" that follow the proposed rule or words that violate it. One can try to recall, or imagine, immoral actions that do or do not involve thoughtlessness. In reflection (and elsewhere), new possibilities may be modifications of old ones. For example, after thinking of evidence, a philosopher might revise the rule about immorality: "All immorality involves thoughtlessness, except _____." Reflection lies at the heart of scholarship, not just in philosophy but also in the social sciences and humanities.

Insight problems. Much of the psychology of thinking concerns thinking of a very limited sort, the solution of puzzle problems. For example, why is any number of the form ABC,ABC (such as 143,143 or 856,856) divisible by 13?[2] These are problems whose solution usually comes suddenly and with some certainty, after a period of apparently futile effort. Many are used on intelligence tests. Essentially, the only phase under the thinker's control at all is the search for possibilities. Often, it is difficult to come up with any possibilities at all (as in the 13 problem). In other cases, such as crossword puzzles, possibilities present themselves readily and are rejected even more readily. In either case, search for evidence and inference (acceptance or rejection) are essentially immediate, and the goal is fixed by the problem statement. It is this immediate, effortless occurrence of the other phases that gives insight problems their unique quality of sudden realization of the solution.

Prediction. Who will be the next president of the United States? Will the stock market go up or down? Will student X succeed if we admit her to graduate school? Prediction of likely future events is like reflection, in form, although the goal is fixed. The evidence often consists of memories of other situations the thinker knows about, which are used as the basis of analogies — for example, student Y, who did succeed, and who was a lot like X.

Behavioral learning. In every realm of our lives — in our social relationships with friends, families, colleagues, and strangers, and in our work — we learn how

---

[2]Hint: What else are such numbers also divisible by? Another hint: What is the smallest number of this form? Another hint: A and B can both be 0. Another hint: Is it divisible by 13?

our behavior affects ourselves and others. Such learning may occur without thinking, but thinking can also be brought to bear. When it is, each action is a search for evidence, an experiment designed to find out what will happen. The evidence is the outcome of this experiment. Each possibility we consider is a type of action to take.

This kind of learning can have much in common with science. Whereas science is a "pure" activity, with a single goal, behavioral learning has two goals: learning about the situation and obtaining immediate success or reward in the task at hand. These goals frequently compete (Schwartz, 1982). We are often faced with a choice of repeating some action that has served us reasonably well in the past or taking some new action, hoping either that it might yield an even better outcome or that we can obtain evidence that will help us decide what to do in the future. Some people choose the former course too often and, as a result, achieve adaptations less satisfactory to them than they might achieve if they experimented more.

An example of behavioral learning with enormous importance for education is the learning of ways of proceeding in thinking tasks themselves — for example, the important strategy of looking for reasons why you might be wrong before concluding that you are right. The effectiveness of thinking may depend largely on the number and quality of these thinking strategies. This, in turn, may (or may not) depend on the quality of the thinking that went into the learning of these heuristics.

The results of behavioral learning are beliefs about what works best at achieving what goal in what situation. Such beliefs serve as evidence for the making of plans, which, in turn, provide personal goals for later decisions. For example, people who learn that they are admired for a particular skill, such as telling jokes, can form the goal of developing that skill and seeking opportunities to display it.

Learning from observation. This includes all cases in which we learn about our environment from observation alone, without intentional experimentation. As such, it can include behavioral learning without experimentation — namely, learning in which we simply observe that certain actions (done for reasons other than to get evidence) are followed by certain events. It also includes a large part of the learning of syntax, word meanings, and other culturally transmitted bodies of knowledge.

The distinctive property of learning by observation is that the evidence is not under the thinker's control, except for the choice of whether we attend to it or not. By contrast, Horton (1967, pp. 172–173) has suggested that one of the fundamental properties of *scientific* thinking is active experimentation: "The essence of the experiment is that the holder of a pet theory does not just wait for events to come along and show whether or not [the theory] has a good predictive performance. He bombards it with artificially produced events in such a way that its merits or defects will show up as immediately and as clearly as possible."

How do search processes work?

All of these types of thinking involve search. Search for possibilities is nearly always present, and search for evidence or goals is often included as well. The critical aspect of a search process is that the thinker has the goal of finding some sort of mental representation of a possibility, a piece of evidence, or a goal.

Search is directed by the goals, possibilities, and evidence already at hand. Goals provide the most essential direction. If my goal is to protect the walls in my house from my child's scribbling, I seek different possibilities than if my goal is to teach my child not to scribble on walls. Possibilities direct our search for evidence for them or against them, and evidence against one possibility might direct our search for new ones.

There are two general ways of finding any object: *recall* from our own memory, and the use of *external aids*, such as other people, written sources (including our own notes), and computers. External aids can help us overcome the limitations of our own memories, including the time and effort required to get information into them. As I write this book, for example, I rely extensively on a file cabinet full of reprints of articles, my own library, the University of Pennsylvania library, and my colleagues and students. I rely on my memory as well, including my memory of how to use these tools and of who is likely to be able to help with what.

Thinking is not limited to what we do in our heads. The analogy between thinking and exploration is therefore not just an analogy. When an explorer climbs up a hill to see what lies beyond, he is actually seeking evidence. Moreover, libraries, computers, and file cabinets make us truly more effective thinkers. When we try to test people's thinking by removing them from their natural environment, which may include their tools and other people they depend on, we get a distorted picture (however useful this picture may be for some purposes).

Because thinking involves search, there must be something for the search to find, if thinking is to succeed. Without *knowledge*, or beliefs that correspond to reality, thinking is an empty shell. This does not mean, however, that thinking cannot occur until one is an expert. One way to become an expert is to think about certain kinds of problems from the outset. Thinking helps us to learn, especially when our thinking leads us to consult outside sources or experts. As we learn more, our thinking becomes more effective. If you try to figure out what is wrong with your car (or your computer, or your body) every time something goes wrong with it, you will find yourself looking up things in books and asking experts (repair people, physicians) as part of your search for possibilities and evidence. You will then come to know more and to participate more fully in thinking about similar problems in the future. It is often thought that there is a conflict between "learning to think" and "acquiring knowledge"; in fact, these two kinds of learning normally reinforce each other.

What we recall (or get from an external aid) may be either an item itself or a rule for producing what we seek. For example, the "What if everybody did that?" rule is not by itself evidence for or against any particular action, but it tells us how to obtain such evidence. When we solve a problem in physics, we recall formulas that tell us how to calculate the quantities we seek. Rules can be learned directly, or we can invent them ourselves through a thinking process of hypothesis testing or reflection. (The use of rules in thinking can be distinguished from the use of rules to guide behavior. We may *follow* a rule through habit without representing it consciously.)

Recall or external aids may not give us exactly what we want, but sometimes an item suggests something else more useful. We may transform what we get in a variety of ways to make it applicable to our situation (Bregman, 1977). This is the important mechanism of *analogy*. To see the role of analogies in thinking, try thinking about a question such as "Can a goose quack?" or "How does evaporation work?" (Collins and Gentner, 1986; Collins and Michalski, 1989). To answer the first question, you might think of ducks. To answer the second, some people try to understand evaporation in terms of analogies to things they already know. The escape of a molecule of a liquid might be analogous to the escape of a rocket from the earth. The conclusion drawn from this analogy is that a certain speed is required to overcome whatever force holds the molecules in the liquid. Some people conclude that the force to be overcome is gravity itself. (In fact, gravity plays a role, but other forces are usually more important.) *surface tension*

Notice that analogies, as evidence for possibilities, need different amounts of modification depending on their similarity to the possibility in question. In the 1980s, an analogy with the U.S. military experience in Vietnam was used to argue against military intervention against Communists in Nicaragua. Later the same analogy was used (unsuccessfully) to argue against military intervention in Somalia. The analogy was more distant in the latter case, because Communists were no longer the enemy. The appeasement of Hitler at Munich has been used repeatedly to support all sorts of military interventions, some closely related, some not so close.

When an analogy requires modification, the person may need to think about how to make the necessary modification. For example, the lesson of Munich may be that fascists should not be appeased, or it could be that one's enemies should not be appeased. Likewise, if you know how to find the area of a rectangle, how should you apply this knowledge to finding the area of a parallelogram? Do you multiply the base by the length of the sides next to it, or do you multiply the base by the height? For rectangles, both yield the same result. Evidence can be brought to bear about which of these possibilities serves the goal.

Standards for the use of analogies as evidence have changed over the centuries in Western science (Gentner and Jeziorski, 1993). Modern analogies — such as Rutherford's analogy between the structure of the atom and the structure of the solar system — are based on common relations among elements of two domains: the sun (nucleus) is more massive than the planets (electrons) and attracts them, so that they revolve around it. Relations between an element of one domain and an element of the other — such as the fact that the sun gives off electrons — are irrelevant to the goodness of the analogy. By contrast, alchemists made analogies with shifting bases, according to superficial appearance rather than relations among elements. Celestial bodies were matched with colors on the basis of appearance (the sun with gold; the moon with white) but also on the basis of other relations (Jupiter with blue because Jupiter was the god of the sky). For metals, the sun was matched with silver on the basis of color, but Saturn was matched with lead on the basis of speed (Saturn being the slowest known planet, lead being the heaviest, hence "slowest," metal). Alchemists also thought of some analogies as decisive arguments, while modern scientists think of them as suggestions for hypotheses to be tested in other ways, or as means of exposition.

Young children's analogies are more like alchemists' than like modern scientists'. When asked how a cloud is like a sponge, a preschool child answered, "Both are round and fluffy," while older children and adults are more likely to point out that both hold water and give it back. This is one of many areas in which standards of reasoning may be acquired through schooling.

Knowledge, thinking, and understanding

Thinking leads to knowledge. This section reviews some ideas about knowledge from cognitive psychology. These ideas are important as background to what follows.

Naive theories

Naive theories are systems of beliefs that result from incomplete thinking. They are analogous to scientific theories. What makes them "naive" is that they are now superceded by better theories. Many scientific theories today will turn out to be naive in the light of theories yet to be devised. Theories develop within individuals in ways that are analogous to their development in history.

For example, certain children seem to hold a view of astronomy much like that of some of the ancients (Vosniadou and Brewer, 1987). They say, if asked, that the earth is flat, the sun rises and passes through the sky, perhaps pushed by the wind, and so on. Unless the children have been specifically instructed otherwise, these are natural views to hold. They correspond to the way things appear, and this is the reason the ancients held them as well.

When the wonders of modern astronomy are first revealed to them, these children will at first modify their structure as little as possible, so as to accommodate the new information. For example, one child (according to an anecdote I heard) learned dutifully in school that the earth goes around the sun. When asked later where the earth was, he pointed upward, answering, "Up there, going around the sun." This earth he had learned about could not be the same earth he already knew, which, after all, was obviously flat and stationary. Another child (described by Piaget, 1929, p. 236) had been taught about the cycle of night and day and the rotation of the earth. She had been told that when it was night in Europe (where she lived), it was day in America. Not wanting to give up her idea of a flat earth, she now reported, when asked, that there was a flat-earth America underneath the flat-earth Europe, and that at night the sun dropped below the European layer to shine on the American layer.

Vosniadou and Brewer (1987) point out that when the modern view is finally adopted, the change is truly radical. First, the concepts themselves are replaced with new concepts. For instance, whereas some young children believe that the sun is alive, sleeps at night, and could stop shining if it wanted to, older children learn that the sun is a star like the others that shine at night. Second, the relationships among the child's concepts change. The earth is no longer physically at the center of the universe; the light from the moon is understood as related to the positions of the earth and sun. Finally, the new system explains different phenomena. It explains the relationship between sun, moon, and stars, but *not* the relationship between sun, clouds, and wind (which might have been understood as being interrelated in the old system). This last point is of interest because it suggests that something is lost by adopting the new system — not just the innocence of childhood, but also a way of understanding certain things. The appearance of the earth as being flat and of the sun as being much smaller than the earth now become mysteries. Eventually, these things too will be explained, of course. In sum, as children adopt adult astronomy there are changes of belief that are as radical as those that have occurred in history, from the system of ancient astronomy to the system of Copernicus.

Just as children have naive theories of astronomy, children and adults seem to have naive theories in other subject areas, such as physics, which must be replaced, sometimes with great difficulty, in order for a person to learn a modern scientific theory. Often these naive theories correspond to systems proposed by early scientists such as Aristotle. (We shall see in the last two parts of this book that there may also be naive theories of judgment and decision making, theories held by most adults.)

Clement (1983), for example, found that students who had taken a physics course held a theory (sometimes even after they had finished the course) about physical forces that was similar to one held by Galileo in his early work but that later both he and Newton questioned. The students believed that a body in motion always requires a force to keep it in motion. In contrast, we now find it more useful to suppose that a body keeps going unless it is stopped or slowed by some force. Of course, wagons and cars *do* require force to keep them going, but that is because they would otherwise be slowed down by friction.

Clement asked his subjects what forces were acting on a coin thrown up into the air, during the time it was rising but after it had left the thrower's hand. Most students (even after taking the course) said that there was a force directed upward while the coin was rising, in addition to the force of gravity pulling the coin down. This view fits in with the "motion implies force" theory that the students held. Physicists find it more useful to suppose that there is only one force, the force of gravity, once the coin is released.

Clement also asked the students about the forces acting on the bob of a pendulum while the pendulum is swinging. Many students said that there were three forces: (1) the force of gravity, pulling the bob straight down; (2) the force of the string, pulling the bob directly toward the point where the string was attached; and (3) a force acting in the direction in which the bob was moving, as shown in the following diagram. A modern physicist would say that the third force is unnecessary to explain the motion of the bob.

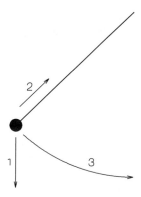

In another series of studies, McCloskey (1983) asked undergraduates, some of whom had studied physics, to trace the path of a metal ball shot out of a curved tube at high speed, as shown in the following illustration. The tube is lying flat on top of a surface; therefore the effect of gravity can be ignored. Many of the subjects, including some who had studied physics, said that the path of the ball would be curved. In fact, it would be straight. McCloskey argues (on the basis of interviews with subjects) that these students held a theory in which the ball acquires some sort of "impetus," a concept something like the mature concept of momentum, except that the impetus can include the curvature of the path. A similar theory was apparently held during medieval times.

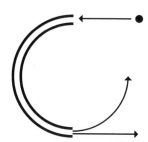

Roncato and Rumiati (1986) showed subjects a drawing like the following,[3] which shows two bars, each supported by a cable from the ceiling, attached to a pivot through the bar, around which the bar could turn freely. The thicker lines under each bar are supports. What happens when the supports are carefully removed? (Think about it.) Most subjects thought that the first bar would become horizontal and the second bar would remain tilted (although perhaps at a different angle). They seemed to think that the angle of the bar would indicate the discrepancy between the weight on the two sides, as a balance scale would do. In fact, the first bar would

[3] Reproduced with the authors' permission.

not move. (Why should it?) The second would become vertical. Perhaps this naive theory results from reliance on a false analogy with a balance.

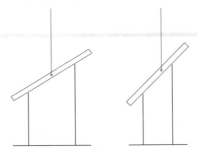

Another of McCloskey's studies involved asking subjects to trace the path of a ball after it rolls off the edge of a table. One incorrect answer is shown in the following illustration, along with the correct answer. Subjects seem to think that the impetus from the original force takes a little time to dissipate, but that once it does, gravity takes over and the ball falls straight down (much like movie cartoon characters, who usually look first, then fall). In fact, the momentum from the original push keeps the ball moving at the same speed in the horizontal direction, and the path changes direction only because the downward speed increases.

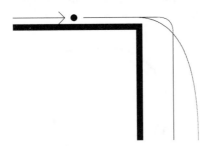

McCloskey (pp. 321–322) argues that these naive theories are not entirely harmless in the real world:

> An acquaintance of ours was recently stepping onto a ladder from a roof 20 feet above the ground. Unfortunately, the ladder slipped out from under him. As he began to fall, he pushed himself out from the edge of the roof in an attempt to land in a bush about 3 feet out from the base of the house .... However, he overshot the bush, landing about 12 feet from the base of the house and breaking his arm. Was this just a random miscalculation, or did our acquaintance push off too hard because of a naive belief that he would move outward for a short time and then fall straight down?

It is also possible that naive theories have some advantages. Kempton (1986) has found that people in the United States tend to hold two different theories of home heat control. The physically correct theory for the vast majority of homes in the United States is the *feedback theory*. By this theory, the thermostat simply turns the heat on and off, depending on the temperature. As one Michigan farmer put it, "You just turn the thermostat up, and once she gets up there [to the desired temperature] she'll kick off automatically. And then she'll kick on and off to keep it at that temperature." By this theory, it does no good to turn the thermostat way up to warm up the home quickly. People who hold this feedback theory tend to leave the thermostat set at a fixed value during the day.

Many people hold a different view, the *valve theory*. By this view, the thermostat is like the gas pedal of a car. The higher you turn it up, the more heat goes into the house, and the faster the temperature changes. People who hold this theory turn the thermostat way up when they come into a cold house, and then, if they remember, turn it down after the house warms up. The valve theory may well lead to wasted fuel, but it does give people a simple reason why they ought to turn the thermostat down when they are out of the house: less fuel will be used when the setting is lower.

The feedback theory is technically correct, as can be ascertained by looking inside a thermostat; however, it has some serious drawbacks. First, the valve theory does a better job than the basic feedback theory of explaining certain phenomena. In many homes, thermostats do need to be set higher to maintain the same feeling of warmth when it is very cold outside. This is easily explained by the valve theory, but in the feedback theory other concepts must be invoked, such as the fact that some rooms are less well heated than others and that some of the feeling of warmth may come from radiant heat from the walls and ceiling. Likewise, it may be necessary to turn the thermostat up higher than normal when entering a cold room, because the walls and furniture take longer to come to the desired temperature than the air does, and the room will still feel cold even after the air (which affects the thermostat) has reached the desired temperature.

Second, the feedback theory does not easily explain why it is a good idea to turn the heat down when one is out of the house. One valve theorist felt that the heat should be turned down when one is out, but, she said, "My husband disagrees with me. He ... feels, and he will argue with me long enough, that we do not save any fuel by turning the thermostat up and down .... Because he, he feels that by the time you turn it down to 55 [degrees], and in order to get all the objects in the house back up to 65, you're going to use more fuel than if you would have left it at 65 and it just kicks in now and then." Now the husband's reasoning here is physically incorrect. The use of fuel is directly proportionate to the flow of heat out of the house, and this, in turn, depends only on the temperature difference between the inside of the house and the outside. Thus, the house loses less heat, and uses less fuel, when it is at 55 degrees Fahrenheit than when it is at 65 degrees; but, as Kempton notes, the physically correct argument requires a more abstract understanding than most people typically achieve. If they act according to the valve theory, they may actually save more energy than if they act in terms of a rudimentary feedback theory, such as that held by the husband in this example.

We might be tempted to suppose that the valve theory is maintained by its functional value in saving fuel rather than by the ready availability of analogies with other valves (accelerators, faucets) and by its explanatory value. This conclusion does not follow. To draw it, we would need to argue that the functional value of the valve theory *causes* the theory to be maintained (Elster, 1979). Are people really sensitive to the amount of fuel they use? People's beliefs sometimes are for the best, but, as McCloskey argues, sometimes they are not.

This example is a particularly good illustration of naive theories, because it seems likely that the subjects have actually thought about how thermostats work. They have had to face the issue in learning how to use them. In the previous examples from college physics, it is not clear that the subjects really "had" any theories before they were confronted with the problems given them by the experimenters. They may simply have constructed answers to the problems on the spot. The fact that their answers often correspond to traditional theories simply reflects the fact (as it would on any account) that these theories explain the most obvious phenomena and are based on the most obvious analogies. After all, balls thrown with spin on them keep spinning; why should not balls shot out of a curved tube keep curving as well?

The home heat-control theories seem to provide yet another example of restructuring (assuming that some people change from the valve theory to the feedback theory). Like the Copernican theory of astronomy, the fully correct theory requires new concepts, such as the concept of heat flow over a temperature difference and that of radiant heat. The theory establishes new relationships among concepts, such as thermostat settings and heat flow. It also explains different phenomena, such as the fact that the house temperature stays roughly at the setting on the thermostat.

Understanding

Students and their teachers often make a distinction between *understanding* something and "just memorizing it" (or perhaps just not learning it at all). Everyone wants to learn with understanding and teach for understanding, but there is a lot of misunderstanding about what understanding is. The issue has a history worth reviewing.

Wertheimer and Katona

Max Wertheimer (1945/1959), one of the founders of Gestalt psychology in the early part of this century, is the psychologist who called our attention most forcefully to the problem of understanding. Wertheimer's main example was the formula for finding the area of the parallelogram, $A = b \cdot h$, where A is the area, b is the base, and h is the height. Wertheimer examined a group of students who had learned this formula to their teacher's satisfaction. On close examination, though, they turned out not to understand it. They could apply it in familiar cases such as the following parallelogram:

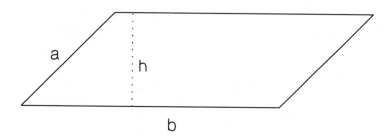

But they refused to apply the formula to new cases, such as a parallelogram depicted standing on its side, which had not been among the original examples that they had studied:

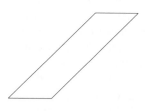

They also were given other new cases (which Wertheimer called "*A* problems") that followed the same principle: A rectangle was made into another figure by re-moving a piece from one side and attaching it to the opposite side, as shown in the following diagram, just as a parallelogram can be made into a rectangle by cutting a triangle from one side and moving it to the other side (without changing *A*, *b*, or *h*). Some students did indeed apply the formula to such cases, multiplying the base by the height to get the area, but these same students usually also applied the formula to other problems showing figures that could *not* be turned back into rectangles by moving a piece around (*B* problems). In sum, learning without understanding was characterized either by lack of transfer of the principle to cases where it applied or by inappropriate transfer to cases where it did not apply.

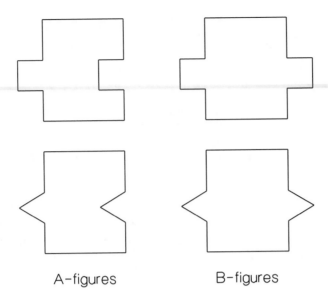

A-figures   B-figures

In contrast to these students, Wertheimer reported other cases of real understanding, some in children much younger than those in the class just described. Most of the time, these children solved the problem for themselves rather than having the formula explained to them. They figured out for themselves that the parallelogram could be converted into a rectangle of the same area without changing b or h. One child bent the parallelogram into a belt and then made it into a rectangle by cutting straight across the middle. Wertheimer does not insist that understanding arises only from personal problem solving, but he implies that there is a connection. When one solves a problem oneself, one usually understands why the solution is the solution.

Learning with understanding is not the same as discovery by induction. Wertheimer (pp. 27–28) made this philosophical point concretely by giving the class the values of a (the side other than the base), b, and h from each of the following problems (with parallelograms drawn) and asking the students to compute the area of each parallelogram:

a	b	h	Area to be computed
2.5	5	1.5	7.5
2.0	10	1.2	12.0
20.0	1 1/3	16.0	21 1/3
15.0	1 7/8	9.0	16 7/8

Wertheimer describes what happened:

> The pupils worked at the problems, experiencing a certain amount of
> difficulty with the multiplication.

Suddenly a boy raised his hand. Looking somewhat superciliously at the others who had not yet finished, he burst out: "It's foolish to bother with multiplication and measuring the altitude. I've got a better method for finding the area — it's so simple. The area is $a + b$."

"Have you any idea why the area is equal to $a + b$?" I asked.

"I can prove it," he answered. "I counted it out in all the examples. Why bother with $b \cdot h$. The area equals $a + b$."

I then gave him a fifth problem: $a = 2.5$, $b = 5$, $h = 2$. The boy began to figure, became somewhat flustered, then said pleasantly: "Here adding the two does not give the area. I am sorry; it would have been so nice."

"*Would it?*" I asked.

I may add that the real purpose of this "mean" experiment was not simply to mislead. Visiting the class earlier, I had noticed that there was a real danger of their dealing superficially with the method of induction. My purpose was to give these pupils — and their teacher — a striking experience of the hazards of this attitude.

Wertheimer also pointed out that it is difficult or impossible to understand a principle that is "ugly" — that is, not revealing of certain important relationships in the matter to which it refers. An example would be a formula for the area that reduced to the simple formula only by some algebraic manipulation:

$$A = \frac{(b - h)}{(1/h - 1/b)}$$

Another way to put this, perhaps, is that the process that leads to understanding will fail to learn what cannot be understood. This process is unlikely to accept falsehood, even when propounded by authority, because falsehood is usually incomprehensible.[4] Of course, many facts are essentially arbitrary, so that "understanding," in the sense in which we are using the term, is impossible. A statement such as this — "The Battle of Hastings was fought in 1066" — must be accepted without understanding.

Katona (1940), a follower of Wertheimer, made several additional observations concerning the relation between understanding and learning. Katona taught subjects how to solve different kinds of problems under various conditions, some designed to promote understanding and others designed not to do so. Certain of his problems concerned rearranging squares made of matchsticks so that a different number of squares could be made from the same number of matchsticks with a minimal number of moves. For example, make the following 5 squares into 4 squares by moving only 3 sticks:

[4]Scheffler (1965) makes related arguments.

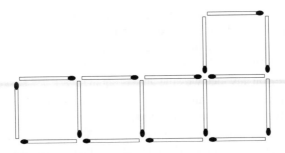

The "no understanding" groups simply learned the solutions to a few such problems. The "understanding" groups were given a lesson in the relationship between number of matches, number of squares, and the number of matches that served as the border between two squares. The most efficient way to decrease the number of squares is to eliminate squares that share sides with other squares, so that the resulting squares touch only at their corners. For example, the square in the lower right is a good one to remove. You can then build a new square on top of the second by using the bottom of the second square for the top side of the new one. Groups that learned with understanding of the common-side principle were able to transfer better to new problems, and they even "remembered" the solutions to example problems more accurately after a delay, even though these examples were not part of the lesson itself. The difference between Katona's demonstrations and Wertheimer's is mainly in the fact that subjects could see immediately whether they had solved Katona's problems or not, so they did not propose false solutions. Hence, Katona did not observe inappropriate transfer of the sort observed by Wertheimer.

Katona also pointed out that learning with understanding was not the same as learning with "meaning." Two groups were asked to memorize the number 5812151-92226. One group was given a meaning for the figure: They were told that it was the number of dollars spent in the previous year by the federal government. This group recalled the figure no more accurately than a group told nothing about the figure's meaning. A third group, however, which discovered the inner structure of the number (a series starting with 5, 8, 12, and so forth) did recall it more accurately.

What is understanding?

What does understanding mean? Can we reduce understanding to knowing certain kinds of things? If so, what kinds? One possibility, suggested by Duncker (1945, p. 5) is that "[knowledge of] the functional value of a solution is indispensable for the understanding of its being a solution." By "functional value," Duncker means the means–end, or subgoal–goal, relationship. For example, the parallelogram problem can be solved through the subgoal of making any nonrectangular parallelogram into a rectangle.

The idea that understanding involves knowledge of purposes or goals goes far toward explaining understanding. It helps us, for example, to see why the term "understand" is relative to some context, purpose, or goal. We can have partial understanding of some idea when we know the relationship of the idea to some goals but not others. For example, before I read a revealing article by Van Lehn and Brown (1980), I thought that I fully understood decimal addition. I found, however, that I was unable to answer a rather obvious question about decimal addition: "Why do we carry (regroup), rather than simply add up the numbers in a column whatever the sum (possibly putting commas between columns)?" Why do we not write the sum of 15 and 17 as 2,12? The reason given by Van Lehn and Brown is that if we wrote totals in this way we would violate the "cardinal rule" of our number system, the requirement that each quantity have a unique representation. This rule can be seen as a major goal — or purpose — that we have imposed on ourselves in the design of our number system. Even before I learned this, however, my understanding of some of the purposes of carrying was complete; for example, I did know that one reason for carrying, as opposed to simply writing a single digit and forgetting about the rest, was to "conserve quantity" – another (more crucial) goal imposed in the design of the number system.

Perkins (1986) suggests that there is somewhat more to understanding than knowing purposes. Understanding, Perkins states, involves knowing three things: (1) the structure of what we want to understand; (2) the purpose of the structure; and (3) the arguments about why the structure serves the purpose.

First, we must know the *structure* of the thing to be understood, the piece of knowledge, or what we shall (for reasons given shortly) call the *design.* We must know a general description of the design. Typically, this description refers to other concepts already known (or understood) for the relevant purpose. For example, $A = b \cdot h$ may be described *with reference to* the concepts "formula" (presumably already understood), "equality," and "variable." A full description would also indicate that b represents the base and h the height. Appropriate interpretation of the description is, practically always, facilitated by the use of at least one *model* or example in which the interpretation is given for a specific case.[5]

Second, we must know the *purpose*, or purposes, of the design: for example, to find the area of the parallelogram. The purpose also refers to still other concepts, such as "area" and the concept of "purpose" itself. So far, Perkins's theory fits well with the idea that the critical part of understanding is knowing purposes.

The third part of understanding, and the part that is new, is the group of *arguments* that explain how the design in fact serves the purpose. These arguments consist of other facts and beliefs. For example, in the case of the parallelogram, one argument explaining why the formula gives the area is that the parallelogram has the same area as a rectangle of the same base and height. Subsidiary arguments are relevant to each of these points: sameness of area, sameness of base, and sameness of height.

Perkins originally developed his theory for designs in general rather than knowl-

[5]The danger here is that the interpretation will be too closely associated with a single model. The students described earlier who could not apply the formula to a parallelogram turned on its side might have been suffering from such an overly narrow description of the design, rather than from a more complete failure of understanding.

edge in particular. A "design," as Perkins uses the term, is anything whose structure serves a purpose. It may be invented by people or it may evolve. In Perkins's theory, buttons, forks, and hands are designs; rocks and rainbows are not. Consider a pencil. One of its *purposes* is to write. Perhaps you have a wooden pencil with you (a *model*) that you can use to examine the *structure* of a pencil. What are the *arguments*? The pencil is soft, so that it can be sharpened (another purpose). The wooden shaft is (usually) hexagonal, so that the pencil does not roll off the table when you put it down (still another purpose). The pencil has an eraser on the end, so that .... What other purposes might be served by the pencil's design? With this question, we can also criticize the ordinary pencil. It wears out. How can we change the design to prevent this? (The mechanical pencil.) Keep at it, and you will be an inventor, a designer.

Perkins's important insight was that *his* design — his theory of design — applied to knowledge as well: Hence the title of his book, *Knowledge as Design.* We can think of just about any kind of knowledge this way. The decimal system that we all labor over in elementary school is quite an impressive design — far superior, for example, to the Roman system of calculation. The theories and concepts discussed in this book, and in many other academic subjects, are also designs. Often the purpose of such designs is to explain something. In mathematics, designs often have the purpose of helping us to measure something.

The nature of arguments may be understood by thinking of them as *evidence* (defined as part of the search-inference framework). In thinking about the area of the parallelogram, for example, a student might simultaneously search for possibilities (possible formulas — perhaps ones already known that might be applied); evidence (properties of the figure that might provide a clue); and goals (actually subgoals, assuming that our student does not question the utility of the basic task itself). She might discover the formula for the rectangle (a possibility); the evidence that the parallelogram is visually similar to a rectangle (which would increase the strength of this possibility – for some students, perhaps increasing it enough that search would stop here); and the subgoal of making the parallelogram into a rectangle. This subgoal would in turn initiate a new process of thinking, inside, as it were, the main process.

By this account, a student understands the formula $A = b \cdot h$ when he has learned the following facts:

- The *purpose* is to find the area.

- The *design* is to use the rectangle formula, replacing one side of the parallelogram with the height.

- One *argument* is based on the subgoal (subpurpose) of making the parallelogram into a rectangle.

- The *design* for this subpurpose is to move the triangle from one side to the other.

- An *argument* for this subdesign is that when we do this, the area is unchanged.

- Another *argument* is that the base is unchanged and the height is unchanged.

Sometimes the things we are asked to learn are not well supported and can be improved or replaced. The strategy of thinking as we learn is likely to encourage the discovery of such deficiencies. Students who insist on understanding do not learn simply because they are told that such and such is the truth. They resist false dogma. If they are given a questionable generalization to learn (such as the claim that totalitarian states never become democratic without violence), they will think of their own counterexamples (such as Chile).

Perkins's analysis of understanding in terms of purposes, designs (and models), and arguments has several implications. First, this theory calls attention to the relationship between understanding and the use of evidence. Understanding involves knowing what is a good argument. We must have certain standards for this, and these standards are likely to change as we become more educated. A young child often accepts an argument if it is merely consistent with the possibility being argued. An older child, in accepting the argument, often also insists that the argument be *more* consistent with this possibility than with some other possibility. It appears that understanding must be renewed as we become more sophisticated about arguments. There seem to have been no child prodigies in philosophy. This domain, by its nature, insists on the highest standards of evidence and therefore cannot be understood at all in an immature way.

Perkins's theory, like Wertheimer's, is also a remedy for a common misconception about the nature of understanding that is exemplified in the work of Ausubel (1963) and many others. The essence of Ausubel's theory is the idea that new knowledge becomes meaningful when relationships are established between new knowledge and old. Although Ausubel specifies that relationships must not be arbitrary in order for learning to count as meaningful, he fails to define "arbitrary relationships" with sufficient clarity to rule out mnemonically learned relationships (that is, relationships learned through special memorization techniques) that might hinder the acquisition of true understanding in Wertheimer's sense. Relationships of the sort indicated by Ausubel, for example, can just as easily be used to learn a falsehood (such as a formula stating that the area of a parallelogram is the sum of the lengths of the sides) as to learn the correct formula. Ausubel omits any consideration of purpose or of evidence that a given element serves a purpose. These latter restrictions, as we have seen, seem to be required to account for Wertheimer's demonstrations — particularly his argument that the process of learning with understanding resists the learning of falsehoods.

Conclusion

Thinking can help us to make decisions that achieve our personal goals, to adopt beliefs about which courses of action are most effective, and to adopt goals that are most consistent with our other goals (including the general goal of being satisfied with our lives). In the rest of this book, we shall be concerned primarily with the properties of thinking that make it useful for these purposes. Like any goal-directed activity, thinking can be done well or badly. Thinking that is done well is thinking of the sort that achieves its goals. When we criticize people's thinking, we are trying to help them achieve their own goals. When we try to think well, it is because we want to achieve our goals. Thinking leads to understanding, which is the best way to improve naive theories, but no guarantee that further improvement is impossible. The best defense against baloney is to ask about the purpose and the arguments.

Chapter 2

The study of thinking

Descriptive, normative, and prescriptive

Here is a problem: "All families with six children in a city were surveyed. In 72 families, the *exact order* of births of boys (*B*) and girls (*G*) was G B G B B G. What is your estimate of the number of families surveyed in which the *exact order* of births was B G B B B B?"

Many people give figures less than 72 as their answers, even if they believe that boys and girls are equally likely (Kahneman and Tversky, 1972). Apparently they feel that the second sequence, which contains only one girl, is not typical of the sequences they expect. In fact, if you believe that boys and girls are equally likely, your best guess should be exactly 72.✗ This is because the probability of each sequence is $1/2 \cdot 1/2 \cdot 1/2 \cdot 1/2 \cdot 1/2 \cdot 1/2$ or $1/64$, the same in both cases. In other words, the two sequences are equally likely. (If you do not believe this, consult a textbook of probability theory.) What makes this problem tricky is that the first sequence looks more like the kind of sequence you might expect, because it has an equal number of boys and girls, and the sexes alternate fairly frequently within the sequence.

This problem can help us illustrate three general *models*,[1] or approaches to the study of thinking, which I shall call descriptive models, prescriptive models, and normative models.

Descriptive models are theories about how people normally think — for example, how we solve problems in logic or how we make decisions. Many of these models are expressed in the form of *heuristics, or rules of thumb,* that we use in certain situations. In the probability problem that I just described, the heuristic used is to judge probability by asking, "How similar is this sequence to a typical sequence?" (see Chapter 6). Because the sequence G B G B B G is more similar to the typical

---

[1] The term "model" comes from the idea that one way to understand something is to build a model of it. In this sense, the game of Monopoly is a model of real estate investment. In this book, the term "model" is used loosely to mean "theory" or "proposal." Sometimes, however, the models will be more detailed — for example, computer models or mathematical models.

✗ Assuming # family with 6 children >> 72

sequence than B G B B B B, the former is judged more likely. Another heuristic is the "What if everyone did that?" rule for thinking about moral situations, and another is the use of analogies in making predictions.

•   Unlike many other fields of psychology, such as the study of perception, where the emphasis is on finding out "how it works," much of the study of thinking is concerned with how we *ought* to think, or with comparing the way we usually think with some ideal. This difference from other fields is partly a result of the fact that we have a considerable amount of control over how we think. That is not so with perception. Except for going to the eye doctor once in a while, we have very little control over how our visual system works. To answer the question "How do we think?", we also have to answer the question "How do we *choose* to think?" The way we think is, apparently, strongly affected by our culture. Such tools as probability theory, arithmetic, and logic are cultural inventions. So are our attitudes toward knowledge and decision making. Thus, the way we think is a matter of cultural design. To study only how we happen to think in a particular culture, at a particular time in history, is to fail to do justice to the full range of possibilities.

Part of our subject matter is therefore the question of how we *ought* to think. If we know this, we can compare it to the way we *do* think. Then, if we find discrepancies, we can ask how they can be repaired. The way we ought to think, however, is not at all obvious. Thus, we shall have to discuss models or theories of how we ought to think, as well as models of how we do think. Models of how we ought to think will fall, in our discussion, into two categories: prescriptive and normative.

Prescriptive models are simple models that "prescribe" or state how we ought to think. Teachers are highly aware of prescriptive models and try to get their students to conform to them, not just in thinking but also in writing, reading, and mathematics. For example, there are many good prescriptive models of composition in books on style. There may, of course, be more than one "right" way to think (or write). There may also be "good" ways that are not quite the "best." A good teacher encourages students to think (or write) in "better" ways rather than "worse" ones.

Prescriptive models may consist of lists of useful heuristics, or rules of thumb, much like the heuristics that make up many descriptive models. Such heuristics may take the form of "words to the wise" that we try to follow, such as "Make sure each paragraph has a topic sentence" or (in algebra) "Make sure you know what is 'given' and what is 'unknown' before you try to solve a problem." In studying probability, one might learn the general rule "All sequences of equally likely events are equally likely to occur." Knowing this rule would have saved you the effort of calculating the answer to the problem about the families with six children.

To determine which prescriptive models are the most useful, we apply a *normative model*, that is, a standard that defines the best thinking for achieving the thinker's goals. For probability problems like the one concerning the birth order of boys and girls, the normative model is the theory of probability. By using the theory of probability, we could prove that the rule "All sequences of equally likely events are equally likely to occur" always works.

Normative models evaluate thinking and decision making in terms of the personal goals of the thinker or thinkers. For decision making, the normative model consists of the policy that will, in the long run, achieve these goals to the greatest extent. Such a model takes into account the probability that a given act (for example, leaving my umbrella at home) will bring about a certain outcome (my getting wet) and the relative desirability of that outcome according to the decision maker's personal goals (see Chapter 10). It is not enough simply to say that the normative model *is* the decision that leads to the best outcome (carrying an umbrella only when it will rain). We need a way of evaluating decisions at the time they are made, so that we can give prescriptive advice to the decision maker who is not clairvoyant.

You might think that the best prescriptive model is always to "try to use the normative model itself to govern your thinking." This is not crazy. Performing musicians often listen to their own playing as if they were an audience listening to someone else, thus applying their best standards to themselves, using such evaluation as feedback. Likewise, in some cases, we can evaluate our own thinking by some normative model. This approach has two problems, though. First, although it may be possible to evaluate a musical performance while listening to it, the application of normative models to thinking and decision making is often time consuming. A normative model of decision making may require calculations of probabilities and desirabilities of various outcomes. (For example, in deciding whether to take an umbrella, I would have to determine the probability of rain and the relative undesirability of carrying an umbrella needlessly or of getting wet.) Because we value time, the application of normative models is self-defeating. If we spend time applying them, we insure that we will violate them. For most practical purposes, people can do better by using some simple heuristics or rules of thumb (for example, "When in doubt, carry the umbrella") than by making these calculations. Even if the calculations sometimes yielded a better choice than the choice that the heuristics would yield, the difference between the two choices in desirability usually would be too small to make calculation worthwhile as a general policy.

The second problem with attempting to apply normative models directly is that we sometimes may do better, according to these models, by aiming at something else. For example, we shall see that people tend to be biased toward possibilities they already favor. These same biases will affect any attempt to apply some normative model. For example, they may affect judgments of probability. So it may be necessary to bend over backward to avoid such effects.

In short, normative models of thinking specify an ideal standard. The idea is to figure out what kind of thinking would bring us closest to achieving our personal goals, or the personal goals we would have "on reflection" — that is, after thinking about them carefully and well. Descriptive models specify what people in a particular culture actually do and how they deviate from the normative models. Prescriptive models are designs or inventions, whose purpose is to bring the results of actual thinking into closer conformity to the normative model. If prescriptive recommendations derived in this way are successful, the study of thinking can help people to become better thinkers.

Methods for empirical research

The development of descriptive models is the business of psychological research. A great variety of methods can help us in this task. Some involve observation of people (or animals) in their usual activities. Other methods involve construction of artificial situations, or experiments.

Observation

When we observe, we collect data but do not intervene, except insofar as necessary to get the data. Sometimes we can get interesting data literally by observing and recording what people do in a natural setting. Keren and Wagenaar (1985), for example, studied gambling behavior by observing blackjack players in an Amsterdam casino over a period of several months, recording every play of every game. Observations of behavior in real-life situations do not encounter the problems that may result from subjects trying to please a researcher; however, there are other problems. Goals in the real world are often complex, and it is difficult to "purify" the situation so as to determine how a subject would pursue a single goal. For example, a subject in a hypothetical gambling experiment can be instructed to imagine that his goal is to win as much as he can, but Keren and Wagenaar (1985) found that in real life gamblers were often as concerned with making the game interesting as with winning.

Process tracing

Many methods attempt to describe thinking by tracing the *process* of thinking as it occurs. These methods are not concerned with the subject's conclusion, but with how the conclusion was reached, that is, the steps or "moves" that led to it. Ideally, it would be nice to have a mind-reading machine that displays the subject's thoughts on a television set, in color images and stereophonic sound. Until such a device is invented, we must make do with less direct methods.

One method in this category involves the use of computers and other apparatus to record everything that subjects look at, and for how long, while performing an experiment (e.g., Payne, Bettman, and Johnson, 1988). This method has been used for studying decisions about apartments. The subject is asked to read a table giving data on various apartments. Each column represents an apartment and each row gives figures on matters such as rent, size, and distance from work. If the subject scans across the rent row first and then seeks no other information about the apartments with the highest rent, we can infer that she has eliminated those apartments on the basis of their high rent. To use this method effectively, the experimenter must be clever in setting up the experiment, so that such inferences can be made.

Perhaps the simplest and most direct method for process tracing is to give a subject a task that requires thinking and ask the subject to "think aloud," either while doing the task or as soon afterward as possible. What the subject says is then a *verbal think-aloud protocol*, which a researcher can analyze in many ways. This method has been in almost continuous use since the nineteenth century (Woodworth and Schlosberg, 1954, ch. 26, give some examples).

To get a feeling for this method, try reading the following puzzle problem; then stop reading, and think aloud to yourself as you try to work out the answer. Remember that your task is to do the problem and to say out loud, at the same time, what is going on in your mind, *as it happens*.

Problem: Examine the following three-by-three matrix. Notice that the lower right-hand corner of the matrix is blank. What symbol belongs in that corner?

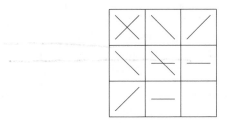

Here is an example of a verbal protocol in which someone is thinking about this problem. (The different moves are numbered for later reference):

1. Let's see. There's an X, a tilted X, and a bunch of lines – diagonal lines along the top and left side, and horizontal lines in the lower right.

2. It looks like there ought to be another horizontal line in the lower right.

3. That would make a nice pattern.

4. But how can I be sure it's right?

5. Maybe there's a rule.

6. I wonder if the X has something to do with the diagonals. The X is really just the two diagonals put together.

7. That doesn't help me figure out what goes in the lower right.

8. Oh, another idea. Maybe there's two of each thing in each row.

9. Yes, that works. The X is there because there have to be two left diagonals and two right diagonals in the top row. And it works for the columns too.

10. So I guess there has to be a dash and a right diagonal together in the bottom right.

This example is fairly typical. It reveals to us that the thinker is making a search for possibilities, evidence, and goals. Now here is an analysis of the same verbal protocol, describing each step in terms of the search-inference framework:

1. The subject spends some time simply seeking evidence, without any idea about the answer (that is, without being aware of any possibilities for it).

2. A possibility is found for the answer.

3. Evidence is found in favor of the possibility. (Some subjects would stop here, making an error as a result of failing to search further.)

4. Further search for evidence.

5. The subject sets up a subgoal here. The original goal was to say simply what kind of symbol went in the lower right-hand corner. The new goal is to find a rule that will produce the pattern. The search for goals and subgoals — as if the subject said to himself, "Exactly what should I be trying to do?" — is an important, and often neglected, part of thinking.

6. Here is a possibility about the rule, suggested by the evidence that "X is two diagonals put together." It is not a complete possibility, however, for the idea that X has something to do with the diagonals does not say exactly what it has to do with the other diagonals in the matrix. So this possibility, because it is incomplete, sets up a subgoal of making it complete.

7. In this problem, the possibility and the subgoal are put aside because the subject cannot find a way in which they help to satisfy the goal of finding a rule. This failure is a kind of evidence, and the subject uses this evidence to weaken the possibility in question.

8. Another possibility for the rule is found (not unrelated to the first).

9. Evidence for this possibility is sought and found.

10. The subject returns to the original goal of figuring out what goes in the lower right, a task quickly accomplished once the subgoal of finding the rule is achieved.

This analysis shows how the search-inference framework enables us to categorize the moves that a thinker makes in the course of thinking. Notice that a given move can belong to two different categories, because the move may have two different functions; for example, in move 6, the same object is both a possibility and a new subgoal. A given phase in an episode of thinking can contain other episodes of thinking, which can contain others, and so on. For example, the task of searching for the goal might involve trying to understand the instructions, which might involve searching for possibilities and for evidence about the meaning of words such as "matrix" (if one did not know the meaning already). As an exercise, you might find it useful to generate another verbal protocol of your own thinking about some problem and analyze it in this way.

Psychologists have developed a great variety of other methods for analyzing think-aloud protocols. (Ericsson and Simon, 1980, review a number of these.)

Different approaches use different *units of analysis*. Some investigators allow the system of analysis itself to define the unit: I did this in the example just given, using as units the categories of the search-inference framework. Other investigators divide the protocol into linguistic units, such as sentences. Others use time measurements, dividing the protocol into 5- or 10-second units and analyzing what is happening (or not happening) in each unit. Approaches also differ in the categories used. The method of analysis is closely linked with the investigator's own goals and the theoretical or practical questions that led to the work.

Despite the extensive use of this method, many doubts have been raised over the years about its adequacy:

1. Some mental processes do not produce much that is accessible for conscious report. Or the processes may go by too quickly for the subject to remember them.

2. The instruction to think aloud may induce subjects to think differently than they ordinarily would. For example, they could think less quickly because of the need to verbalize everything. Verbalization could interfere with thinking, or it could help by forcing thinkers to be more careful. Both of these results have been found, but it has also been found that in many tasks verbalization has no apparent effect (Ericsson and Simon, 1980).

3. Verbal protocols might be misleading with respect to the underlying determinants of the subjects' behavior. For example, suppose that you are deciding whether to buy a used television set, and you say, "The picture is nice, but the sound isn't very good, and $200 is too expensive. I'll keep looking." One might infer from this that you are following a rule that you should not pay more than $200, no matter what. Although this may be true, it may instead be true that you would be willing to pay more if the sound quality were good enough. You may be trading off quality against price, even though you do not express this in your verbalizations (Einhorn, Kleinmuntz, and Kleinmuntz, 1979).

4. Subjects may be unable to explain how they reached a certain conclusion. For example, in an experiment done by Nisbett and Wilson (1977), passersby in a shopping mall were asked to compare four nightgowns and rate their quality. Most subjects gave the last nightgown they examined the highest rating, regardless of which of the four it was, but all subjects attributed their rating to some property of the nightgown itself rather than to its position in the sequence.

Ericsson and Simon (1980) argue that this last sort of demonstration does not shed any light on the validity of verbal reports, because there is a difference between reporting *what* one is thinking (as in the matrix problem) and explaining the *causes* of one's conclusions. Asking subjects to infer a cause requires that the subjects take the role of scientists, which they may not be able to do. If the subjects simply report their experiences instead of inferring causes, then they cannot be accused of making an error.[2]

Ericsson and Simon argue that verbal reports sometimes provide a quite reliable method for discovering how thinking proceeds. In particular, they assert, "thinking" aloud is useful when there is relevant information to be reported that is in the subject's "working memory" (or immediate consciousness). An example would be the information reported in the matrix task. In such cases, performance is found not to be affected by the requirement to think aloud, and what subjects do is consistent with what they say.

More generally, as Ericsson and Simon point out, verbal reports are just one kind of investigative method. Any method of investigation has defects, and these defects are more serious in some cases than in others. When possible, a good investigator will try to use a variety of methods to check the results from one against the results from another.

Interviews

Sometimes researchers interview subjects extensively. Some interviews are like questionnaires, because the interviewer simply reads the questions and the subjects answer them. Interviews give the opportunity to ask follow-up questions or let the subjects explain their answers at greater length. A useful idea is the *structured interview*, which is essentially a set of questions to be answered, with the assumption that the interviewer will ask follow-up questions until the subject gives a satisfactory answer to each question, or gives up. Compared to strict questionnaires, interviews have the advantages of making sure that the subjects understand the questions and answers each as it is intended. They also allow subjects to explain their answers. The disadvantage is that they provide an opportunity for the interviewer to influence the answers.

Use of archival data

Another method for process tracing is the use of historical records of decisions made by groups. Janis (1982), for example, studied group decision making by reading records of how President Kennedy and his advisers made the policy decisions that led to the Bay of Pigs fiasco in 1961. This method is useful when the records are very complete, as they are in this case.

Another application of this is the measure of "integrative complexity" (Schroder, Driver, and Streufert, 1967; Suedfeld and Rank, 1976; Suedfeld and Tetlock, 1977). Using this method, Tetlock measured the complexity of speeches by U.S. senators (1983a) and personal interviews given by members of the British House of Commons

---

[2]It is not even clear that the subjects in Nisbett and Wilson's experiments made an error at all. If a subject said she liked the last nightgown she examined because of its texture, she could be correct, even though it is also true that she liked it because it was the last: The fact that it was the last might have caused her to like its texture.

(1984). Integrative complexity is scored on a scale of 1 to 7. The scoring takes two dimensions into account, "differentiation" and "integration," although only the latter dimension is reflected in the name "integrative." In Tetlock's examples (1983a, p. 121), a score of 1 is given to a statement that expresses only a one-sided view, neglecting obvious arguments on the other side, thus failing to "differentiate" the two sides. For example,

> Abortion is a basic right that should be available to all women. To limit a woman's access to an abortion is an intolerable infringement on her civil liberties. Such an infringement must not be tolerated. To do so would be to threaten the separation of Church and State so fundamental to the American way of life.

A score of 3 is given when the statement is differentiated — that is, when it includes arguments (evidence or goals) for both sides:

> Many see abortion as a basic civil liberty that should be available to any woman who chooses to exercise this right. Others, however, see abortion as infanticide.

A score of 5 or higher is given when the person making the argument succeeds in "integrating" opposing arguments, presenting a reflective statement about the criteria by which arguments should be evaluated:

> Some view abortion as a civil liberties issue — that of the woman's right to choose; others view abortion as no more justifiable than murder. Which perspective one takes depends on when one views the organism developing within the mother as a human being.

Tetlock found that moderate leftists got the highest scores, and he interpreted this in terms of the fact that this group was constantly facing issues that put their values in conflict, such as the goals of equality and economic efficiency, which conflict in such questions as whether the rich should be taxed to help the poor (thus reducing economic incentive but increasing equality).

Hypothetical scenarios

Another way to learn how people think or make decisions is to observe the conclusions that people draw or the decisions they make. The investigator then makes inferences from the effects of relevant variables on these responses. (A "variable" is anything that we can measure, label, or manipulate.) Investigators strive both to capture the phenomenon of interest and to control the effective variables, so that they can determine which variables do what.

Sometimes we observe people making real decisions, or what they think are real decisions. Real decisions may involve money that is actually paid at the end of an experiment. Social psychologists often stage realistic deceptions, which the subjects think are real. Most of the studies of decision making described in this book ask subjects what they would do in hypothetical situations. The disadvantage of hypothetical questions is that the results may not tell us much about what people would actually do in the real world. For example, in answering the hypothetical question, people may tell us that they would do what they think *we* (the researchers) would *want* them to do — not what they would really do. This is called a "social desirability" effect. (This is not a serious problem if the experimenter is *interested* in the subjects' views about what is the best decision.)

An advantage of using hypothetical situations for a study is that the researchers can extensively manipulate the situation to find out what variables are affecting the subject's responses. Another advantage is that the experimenter can easily ask subjects for justifications or explanations. Justifications and explanations can suggest new hypotheses for study, provide evidence bearing on other hypotheses, and provide evidence that subjects understand (or fail to understand) the situation as the experimenter intended. Hypothetical situations are also useful in telling us how subjects would respond to situations that are novel to them, and situations that are difficult to stage in the laboratory. Finally, hypothetical decisions may be just as useful as real ones for finding out how people think about certain types of problems.

Training studies

One way to test a prescriptive theory about thinking is to try improve it through instruction and then show some effect of the instruction on something else. This avoids the problem of looking for correlations between good outcomes and good thinking. Such correlations can result when the outcomes and the thinking are both influenced by the same factors, such as general mental ability. Training studies can use a control group, which is not trained, so that any later differences between the trained group and the control group can be ascribed to the training. Another advantage of these studies is that it often leads to a promising educational technique.

Transfer of learning is the effect of learning in one situation on learning or behavior in a very different situation. If we are teaching *thinking*, transfer is essential. Because thinking (as defined in this book) is what we do *when we do not know what to choose, desire, or believe*, thinking will be most essential in situations that we have not encountered before. Can teaching of thinking transfer? A number of studies suggest that it can.

Some studies have examined the effects of certain courses on reasoning about judgments and decisions. Schoemaker (1979) found that students who had taken a statistics course gave more consistent answers to questions involving choices of gambles. Students who had not taken the course were also more likely to bid more than the maximum amount that could be won in order to play a gamble in which money could be won, and more likely to require more money than the maximum loss in order to play a gamble in which money could be lost.

Fong, Krantz, and Nisbett (1986, experiment 4) found that statistical training transfers to solving everyday problems involving statistical reasoning. Half of the men enrolled in a college statistics course were interviewed by telephone at the beginning of the course, and the other half were interviewed at the end. The interview (conducted by a woman experimenter) ostensibly concerned sports and began with questions concerning sports controversies (such as what colleges should do about recruiting violations) in order to hide the fact that the basic concern was with statistics. Then subjects were given questions concerning such matters as why the winner of the Rookie of the Year award in baseball usually does not do as well in his second year as in his first. A nonstatistical response might be "because he's resting on his laurels; he's not trying as hard in his second year." A statistical response (based on the principle of regression to the mean in numerical prediction explained in Chapter 15) would be "A player's performance varies from year to year. Sometimes you have good years and sometimes you have bad years. The player who won the Rookie of the Year award had an exceptional year. He'll probably do better than average his second year, but not as well as he did when he was a rookie." Students gave more good statistical answers of this sort at the end of the course than at the beginning. Therefore, these students did transfer what they had learned to cases where it is relevant.

Nisbett, Fong, Lehman, and Cheng (1987) carried out other studies in which they examined the effects of various kinds of university instruction on statistical, logical, and methodological reasoning. The researchers measured statistical reasoning by asking subjects to suggest explanations of certain facts, such as that the Rookie of the Year typically does not do as well in his second year or that "a traveling saleswoman is typically disappointed on repeat visits to a restaurant where she experienced a truly outstanding meal on her first visit" (p. 629). Each fact could be explained either in terms of nonstatistical factors ("Her expectations were so high that the food couldn't live up to them") or statistical ones ("Very few restaurants have only excellent meals, odds are she was just lucky the first time"). Subjects were given credit here for mentioning the statistical explanations as possibilities (which they were, whether the other explanations were also true or not).

To measure methodological reasoning, the researchers asked subjects to comment on flawed arguments. One item (from a newspaper editorial) argued for the learning of Latin and Greek on the grounds that students who had studied these languages in high school received much higher than average scores on the Verbal Scholastic Aptitude Test.[3] Another item concerned a claim that the mayor of Indianapolis should fire his police chief because crime had increased since the chief began his tenure in office.[4] Logical reasoning was measured with problems of the sort to be discussed in Chapter 4.

---

[3] Subjects were scored as giving correct responses if they pointed out that students who studied Latin and Greek in high school were unusually competent and would probably do well on the test even without studying these languages.

[4] Subjects were scored as correct if they pointed out the potential relevance of crime-rate increases in other cities over the same period.

Nisbett and his colleagues found that logical reasoning, as measured by their test, did not improve from the beginning to the end of two introductory college courses in logic (one emphasizing formal logic, the other emphasizing informal fallacies). It did not improve as a result of two years of graduate school in chemistry, either. Logical reasoning did improve, however, as a result of two years of graduate school in law, medicine, or psychology. The researchers suggest that these three fields emphasize logical reasoning to some extent. This improvement was found in two different kinds of studies, one in which students just beginning graduate school were compared to students who had just completed their second year, and the other in which the same students were tested at the beginning and the end of their first two years of graduate training.

Statistical and methodological reasoning showed a somewhat different pattern. The largest improvement by far occurred among psychology students, probably because training in such things as the use of control groups is an important part of graduate work in psychology. Methodological reasoning also improved with medical training, which places some emphasis on the conduct and interpretation of medical research, but there was essentially no improvement from training in either law or chemistry.

Lehman and Nisbett (1990) found that undergraduate training can have similar effects. Courses in the social sciences affected mostly statistical and methodological reasoning. Courses in the natural sciences (including mathematics) and humanities affected mostly logical reasoning. These studies together provide further evidence that appropriate education, in which certain methods of reasoning are explicitly emphasized, can have general effects on the tendency to use these methods in everyday problems unrelated to the areas in which the methods were taught. They also indicate that some of these effects can be specific to certain methods.

Training studies are not perfect either. Some aspect of the training may be effective, other than the aspect intended. Really both correlational and experimental (training) studies are useful, and to some extent they make up for each others' flaws.

Experimental economics

Much of the research described in this book is closely related to research in economics. Economists develop normative models, and some of those models are the same as those considered here. Traditionally, economists have assumed that people follow normative models, or, at least, that those who use economic theory would do well to assume that people are rational. (If you assume that people are irrational, rational people may find a way to take advantage of your assumptions.) Some economists, however, have tried to test economic theory in the laboratory, using methods much like those of psychology. They are called experimental economists. (See Kagel and Roth, 1995, for an overview.)

In this book, I make no distinction between the work of experimental economists and the work of other researchers. Economic experiments are relevant to many issues discussed here. But the work does have a kind of characteristic approach. First, economists tend to be suspicious of verbal reports or judgments that have no consequences for the subjects. They tend to look at choices, and they provide real consequences to subjects in the form of payoffs, typically money.

More importantly, experimental economics derives its hypotheses from economic theory, and it assumes that this theory is meant to be universally descriptive of human behavior. The theory should therefore apply in the laboratory as well as in real markets. This is an ambitious assumption, but one that is worthy of our attention. If economic theory is universally true in this way, it could help explain other social phenomena, such as politics, crime, and sexual behavior. It is thus important to find out how the simplest assumptions of economic theory must be modified in the light of human psychology.

Computer models and artificial intelligence

Some of the most important contributions to the descriptive theory of thinking have not come from observation of people thinking but rather from attempts to make computers think. Simon (1969) has argued that much of the conduct of thinking is not determined by the peculiarities of human psychology but by the nature of the task. If, for example, we want to understand how people play chess, we would do well to try to build a chess-playing computer. It may not play chess exactly the way that people do, but it will tell us a lot about what kind of thinking is possible.

Such attempts have two different goals. One is to try to program the computer to do the task in the way that people do it. The computer program then becomes an embodiment of a particular theory about thinking.[5] The purpose of such an effort is to find out whether a certain type of theory can possibly account for a certain kind of behavior and to refine the theory itself by observing the difficulties that arise when we try to make it work.

Another goal is to forget about trying to make the computer perform as we do but simply try to make it do its best. At first it may seem surprising that this approach has also yielded important insights about human thinking. It is less surprising when we reflect on Simon's view about the importance of the task itself in determining how thinking is done.

There are no perfect methods for development of descriptive theory. On the other hand, imperfect methods may be informative enough. Medical scientists who develop new treatment methods often proceed on the basis of imperfect research. Similarly, educators and decision scientists can develop new ways to improve thinking and decision making on the same basis.

General issues

A few general issues arise repeatedly in discussions of research on judgment and decision making.

[5] This is the approach taken by Newell and Simon (1972) and by J. R. Anderson (1976).

intra   *inter*

Within-subject versus between

Often a research wants to examine the effect of some manipulation on a judgment. For example, consider the "outcome bias" experiments of Baron and Hershey (1988). The idea was to show that ratings of the quality of a decision were affected by the outcome of that decision, even though the judge knew everything that the decision maker knew at the time. Subjects made judgments about hypothetical scenarios in which, for example, a surgeon decided to do an operation, with a known probability of success, and the operation either succeeded or not. Subjects judged the surgeon to be a better decision maker when the operation succeeded. One way of doing this experiment is to present the two outcomes next to each other. When this is done, very few subjects think that the outcome matters. They understand that using the outcome is a judgment made in hindsight and that the surgeon knew only the probability of success.

Another way to do the experiment is to present the two conditions (success and failure) to different subjects. This is called a between-subject design, and the first method is called within-subject. In this kind of research, these two methods answer somewhat different questions. The within-subject method asks what subjects think they should do. In this case, it asks whether they think that outcome ought to matter. The between-subject method asks whether people are affected by success versus failure when they are unaware that the difference is being manipulated. This is more like the real-world situation.

Subjects think that success-failure should not matter, yet they are affected by it in a between-subject design. This seems to be a clear demonstration of a violation of a normative model, since the subjects themselves endorse the normative model that outcome should not matter. At the very least, the subjects are being inconsistent with their own judgments. But what of those few subjects who show the effect even in a within-subject design? Can they too be said to be violating a normative model?

The purpose of normative models is to evaluate how well people are achieving their own goals. Given this purpose, it is possible for a person to have an incorrect opinion about the normative model itself. So subjects who think that outcome should matter could in fact be violating a normative model. As I shall argue in the next section, normative models are not justified by pointing to common opinion. They must be defended directly. The defense could be wrong, but that does not imply that it should not be attempted. I thus conclude that errors (that is, departures from a normative model) in a within-subject design can still be true errors. But they are errors in what subjects think they ought to do, not necessarily in what they do when presented with one case at a time. Of course, people generally try to do with they think they should do, so errors found in within-subject designs are likely to be present in between-subject designs as well.

Within-subject designs often show smaller effects, but the effects are easier to detect statistically. For example, a subject's judgment of a surgeon's decision will depend on many factors that characterize that subject, such as her attitude toward surgery in general. When each subject judges only one case, some subjects will rate the success condition to be worse than other subjects' ratings of the failure condition. On the average, subjects may rate the success condition higher, but many subjects will be needed to show that this difference is not the result of random variation. When each subject evaluates both cases (success and failure), these extraneous factors are constant. Only a few subjects may be needed to show an effect, because no subjects will rate the failure condition higher than the success condition. If as few as five subjects rate the success condition higher, with none rating the failure condition higher, this is unlikely to be due to random variation. (The probability of such a result is 2^{-5}, or .031, low enough to meet the usual standard of statistical significance.)

It is often of interest to compare both kinds of designs. They tell us different things. Frisch (1993) has compared several effects in this way. In some cases, the effects are found in both within-subject and between-subject designs. In other cases, mostly the latter.

One design captures some of the advantage of within-subject and between-subject designs. This is to make up several cases, differing in details. For example, Case 1 could be about an appendicitis operation, Case 2 about heart surgery, and so on. Each case has a success and a failure condition, S and F. Then present each subject with half the cases in their S form and half in their F form. The other half of the subjects get the forms switched. Thus, one group of subjects gets 1S, 2F, 3S, 4F, 5S, 6F, and so on, and the other group gets 1F, 2S, 3F, 4S, and so on. No subject sees the S and F form of the same case, so the subjects would be responding to each case without comparing it to its partner. But, with enough cases, we can find each subject's average S rating and average F rating. Because each subject does both kinds of ratings, many of the extraneous factors will be constant. We can even extend this design by presenting the first group of subjects with 1F, 2S, etc., *after* doing 1S, 2F, etc. With enough cases, subjects won't remember their earlier responses.

Sampling

Researchers from different traditions have very different approaches to the sampling of subjects. Sociologists and public-opinion researchers go to great lengths to draw random samples from some population, such as the adult citizens of some particular nation. Psychologists often use what others call (somewhat derisively) "convenience samples," such as students enrolled in an introductory psychology course.

When you want to say something about a particular population, you need to sample that population in a representative way. You must choose respondents at random and try to get them all to respond. If they do not respond, you must try to show that the ones who did not respond would not have answered differently from the ones who responded. Much research has been done on how this should be done (Dillman, 1978).

Little of the research described in this book is concerned with any particular population. It is concerned with people in general. The studies are designed to demonstrate some effect, such as the outcome bias just described. Then further studies are done to analyze the effect. All that is required for these studies is some group of subjects who show the effect in question. Most researchers are not very interested in the prevalence of the effect.

Arguably, if the population of interest is human beings, and if we are reasonably optimistic about the future, most human beings have not yet been born. It is thus impossible to sample them randomly. Although this point is sort of a joke, there is a serious part to it. Efforts to sample some particular nation are misdirected if we are really interested in a broader population. If we want to make sure that our results are not due to some idiosyncrasy of our sample, a general way to do this is to examine very different samples, particular people from different cultures. Often cultural comparisons can be enlightening in other ways.

Of course, differences among people are of interest for many reasons. If some people show a bias and others do not, we can look for both causes and effects of these differences. Cultural differences enlighten us about the range of human possibility. Individual differences may result from education, sub-cultural differences, or genetic differences. They may affect people's success or failure in achieving various goals. Research on differences among people is based on correlations, that is, observation of differences rather than experimental manipulation. Because of this, it is often difficult to determine what the cause of some difference is, or whether it is responsible for some effect. For example, sex differences could result from genetic or environmental causes. Still, such research is often useful.

The recent growth of the Internet has provided new opportunities for recruiting subjects. As more and more people around the world get access to the World Wide Web, for example, it has become possible not only to recruit convenience samples on the Internet but also to recruit specialized samples, such as cancer patients or citizens of India. Even the convenience samples tend to be more varied than the college students typically used in research. It is possible to test for effects of age, for example, which varies very little among students. The articles in Birnbaum's (2000) book discuss methods for doing research on the Web and report findings about such research. In general, Web subjects are not much different from student subjects, or other samples, in their results.

Incentives

Experimental economists typically put people in real situations, in which payoffs depend on subjects' responses. They argue that asking people what they would do is less useful than observing what people actually do. Studies that compare hypothetical and real choices that involve money typically find small differences — which may result from differential attention to certain features of the real situation — but the same effects (Irwin et al., 1992; Camerer, 1995; Beattie and Loomes, 1997). In no case has anyone ever found an effect for hypothetical choices that is not found for real choices, or vice versa.

Some of the worry about hypothetical choices is that they are too far removed from reality. Two points can be made in reply. First, in some cases, we are interested in how people think rather than just in what they do. This is not an idle interest, because knowing how people think can help us persuade them to think and act differently, if they should. Economists call such persuasion "cheap talk," but much of child rearing and education takes exactly this form.

Second, the argument about unreality is true, but it is true of experiments that use real money too. Demonstrations of any effect in the laboratory are not enough to show that the effect is important in the real world. For example, take the case of the outcome bias described earlier, in which we judge decision makers according to their good or bad luck rather than the quality of their decision making. This bias could cause us to hold people responsible for events they could not control. In order to find out whether it is really important, though, we need to go beyond the laboratory and look for examples where this might have happened in the real world, such as in lawsuits. Discovery of such cases does not settle the issue either. In the real world, we lack the control of extraneous variables that is possible only in the laboratory. But both kinds of demonstrations together can give us sufficient confidence to act, if action is otherwise warranted.

Development of normative models

The study of thinking, as we have seen, involves the comparison of actual judgments and decisions to some normative standard of what they ought to be. We cannot answer the question of what they "ought" to by observing what they are, through gathering descriptive information. The whole point is to evaluate our judgments and decisions, to see if they can be improved. We cannot do this if we adopt a standard of evaluation that we know in advance will tell us that nothing is wrong.

Where, then, do normative models come from? This is a hard question, but it has some possible answers. One answer is implicit in the discussion of within-subject versus between-subject experiments. Normative standards are whatever people take them to be. If you think that luck should not affect your judgments of someone else's decision-making ability, and if luck does affect your judgment, then you are inconsistent with your own standard. This is a minimal definition of normative models. People may well disagree on their standards, so we will have different normative models for different people. Also, we will have no guidance for people who are genuinely puzzled about what their standard ought to be.

We might try to save this perspective by using some sort of criterion of what is "generally accepted." Thus, if most people accept the idea that luck shouldn't matter, we should feel safe in evaluating others according to that standard. General acceptance is an unclear standard, though. Of the various normative models discussed in this book, most people accept logic, fewer accept probability, fewer still accept expected-utility theory, and fewer still, probably a minority of those who have thought about it, accept utilitarianism. Yet, I shall argue for all these standards. The majority can be wrong, and the majority *has been* wrong repeatedly throughout history with respect to moral issues in particular. (This must be true. Once most people thought that slavery was fine. Now practically nobody thinks this.) There must be some other way of settling the issue other than appeal to general acceptance. Without any other way, general opinion would self-reinforcing.

Another approach is "reflective equilibrium." Rawls (1971, p. 47) argued that moral philosophy could follow the model of linguistics, as developed by Noam Chomsky. Chomsky argued that we develop a theory of grammar on the basis of our intuitions about what is grammatical. By "intuition," I mean a judgment made directly without looking for reasons. Our intuition tells us that the sentence "The apple fell off the table and then they broke" is wrong, so we think that there is a rule about agreement of pronouns and the nouns they stand for. On the other hand, the sentence "The subject read the item, and then they responded" isn't so bad. (It avoids the need for "he or she.") In this case, the typical copy editor would decide that the rule wins, and they would declare this to be ungrammatical. In some other case, grammarians might allow an exception to the rule, explicitly. Rawls argues that we can do philosophy like this. We go back and forth between our intuitions and a theory of our intuitions, declaring the intuitions to be wrong only when we decide that the theory is too good to mess up.

This view of normative theory is widely accepted. Notice, though, that it contains a hidden assumption, which is that a system underlies our intuitions and the system has a claim to truth. This assumption makes sense in linguistics. Language, we may assume, evolved to fit our psychological makeup. The basic psychological principles of language are expressed in grammar. Languages that go against these rules are, thus, in a sense, wrong. Yet, in matters of decision making, especially those that involve morality, we cannot assume that the psychological principles that lie behind our thoughts are the best ones. At least we must be open to the possibility that they are not.

Our intuitions are not infallible. A conflict between intuition and principle does not always mean that the principle is wrong, for there may be other relevant arguments, or there may be no better alternative. Although most of our intuitions about thinking and decision making are probably held for good reason, some of them probably are not. They could simply be the results of exposure to certain cultural standards, or they could have been formulated by individuals and used uncritically for so many years that they have come to be accepted as truth. Although most people in our culture agree that killing and stealing are wrong, for example, we disagree strongly about whether premarital sex, abortion, or euthanasia are right or wrong. When there is disagreement, somebody's intuition must be wrong.

Often, as in the problem about the six children presented at the beginning of the chapter, intuition yields easily to convincing arguments such as those based on mathematics. These arguments frequently concern the purpose of the normative model in question, for example, having accurate beliefs. In other cases the arguments for some principle are less comprehensible or less compelling, than are, say, mathematical arguments about probability theory, but the arguments may still be correct. Intuitions are often useful evidence in philosophical reflection, but they are not the last word.

I shall take the view that normative models result from imposing an analytical framework on reality and working out the implications of that framework. Arithmetic is an example. Why do we think that one plus one is two? It is not a fact about the world, but of a system that we impose on the world whether the world fits or not. When we watch raindrops fall on a windowpane, we often see that they merge. One raindrop plus one raindrop can make one big raindrop, not two. You may be tempted to say that this isn't fair. We say it isn't fair because drops falling on top of each other do not count as "addition." We do not apply the framework this way. But why not? The answer is that, once we have adopted the framework, we force the world into it. Drops falling on top of each other doesn't count exactly because, if it did, we would have to give up the framework. If we have to do too much forcing, or exclude too many things, then the framework seems less useful, and we look for another one. But once we have adopted a framework, we can deduce conclusions from it, just as many of the conclusions of mathematics can be deduced from a few simple principles of sets and arithmetic, principles that we impose on the world.

I will use a similar kind of imposed framework in analyzing decisions. For example, I will analyze some decisions into options, unknown states of the world, and outcomes. Once we adopt this framework, many normative conclusions will follow. Arguments about normative models should be about the applicability of such frameworks, as opposed to alternatives.

Many people find the idea of normative models bothersome. They think that, if most people violate some model in some situation, then the model could not be truly normative in that situation. The majority cannot be wrong, they think, and we should adjust the normative model to fit what people do. There *is* a point to this argument. People who tried to develop normative models *have* made mistakes, and a normative model is more likely to be a mistake if most people violate it than if most follow it, so a lack of fit with behavior is first-blush evidence that something might be wrong with the application of the model to the situation in question. We should look carefully for such errors. But the evidence is only first blush. We cannot adjust the model just because it doesn't fit behavior, or we risk undercutting its entire purpose, which is to determine how our behavior goes against our own goals, so that we can achieve our goals better. The point here is not to evaluate behavior, it is to improve it. We would not know what "improvement" is without a standard that is separate from behavior.

Descriptive models and heuristics

Two types of descriptive models are common in the study of decisions. One type involves mathematical models, much like those used in physics, chemistry, or economics. For example, in Chapter 11, we shall discuss a descriptive model of decision making for people told the probabilities of various outcomes of a decision. The model says that people do not use the probabilities as given but, instead, transform them according to a certain function. The form of the function explains many of the discrepancies between the normative model and actual decisions.

Another type is to describe judgment and decisions in terms of heuristic methods. Our modern concept of heuristic methods was devised by George Polya, an eminent mathematician born in Hungary in 1887, who moved to Stanford University in 1940. There he began the task of trying to set down what he had learned over the years about the *methods* of mathematics, as distinct from its content. His first book on this subject, *How to Solve It* (1945), brought into common use the term "heuristic," an adjective originally meaning "serving to discover." The term is often used in the expression "heuristic method" or simply as a noun meaning "heuristic method." The use of heuristics, or heuristic methods, constitute "heuristic reasoning," which Polya defines (p. 115) as "reasoning not regarded as final and strict but as provisional and plausible only, whose purpose is to discover the solution of the present problem." Heuristic methods are likely to help solve many different problems, but no one can specify exactly when each method will help.

Polya's heuristics can be understood as suggestions to facilitate more extensive search for useful possibilities and evidence. They encourage active open-mindedness in mathematical problem solving. An example, is: Could you imagine a more accessible related problem? Suppose you were asked to solve the equation:

$$x^4 - 13x^2 + 36 = 0$$

If you use this heuristic, the attempt to think of a related problem might make you think of an ordinary quadratic equation, which (let us suppose) you know how to solve. You might then see that you could make this problem into the simpler one by letting $y = x^2$, which changes the equation into an ordinary quadratic equation in y. Once the values of y are found, the values of x can be determined.

Beginning with Kahneman and Tversky (1972) researchers have used the idea of heuristics to explain departures from normative models. The problem described at the very beginning of this chapter is an example. The idea captures much of the theorizing in this field. People develop heuristics exactly because they are often useful. But the use of these heuristics leads to biases. The question is whether we can learn better heuristics, or other ways around the problems they cause. That is the prescriptive question.

Development of prescriptive models

If the basis of descriptive models is observation and the basis of normative models is reflection, then the basis of prescriptive models is design. Methods of thinking — such as logic, legal argumentation, and scientific method — were invented and are now passed along as part of our culture. The normative and descriptive findings discussed in this book point to the need for other methods of bringing our thinking closer to the normative standard. As new methods are invented, ways of spreading them through a society must be invented as well. The most direct way of doing this is through schools. Many prescriptive models take the form of heuristics that can be taught.

New methods can be designed for computers as well as people. Computers are powerful tools that can extend our powers of thinking and decision making. In order to use them to improve our thinking, however, we need to know just how our thinking needs to be improved.

Conclusion

The study of thinking goes back at least to Aristotle and other Greek philosophers, who attempted to codify the rules of good thinking (in the form of logic), to describe what goes wrong with our thinking in daily life, and to propose ways of guarding against the errors we tend to make. In the last century, this speculative approach has been supplemented with the scientific study of thinking. We no longer have to rely on our experience alone. We must not, however, let ourselves get carried away with the power of science. It cannot tell us how we ought to think ideally, nor how we can best approximate this ideal. A scientist cannot "discover" what *good* thinking is: That is still a matter for philosophy and design. In this spirit, the next chapter puts forward a general prescriptive model based on the search-inference framework.

Exercise: Making a think-aloud protocol

Produce a think-aloud protocol for one of the problems given in the footnote — don't look yet — by making notes on your thoughts as they occur to you. Resist the temptation to read the problem you are to think about until you are ready with pencil and paper in hand. Transcribe your notes (adding explanations when necessary to make them comprehensible). Aim for one or two pages (if typed double spaced). Remember to record all of your thoughts.[6]

Finally, in the margin of your transcription, classify the moves you made in terms of the search-inference framework (ch. 1), using the following code (which you may modify, as long as you describe your modifications):

SP — search for possibilities
SG — search for goals
SE — search for evidence
P — possibility recognized (stated)
G — goal recognized
E — evidence recognized
I — inference made (evidence used, conclusion drawn)

---

[6]   A. Why is it hotter in the summer than the winter?
B. What work (if anything) should be given to the entering Freshman class to read and discuss as part of its orientation?
C. Write a poem (or at least start one).
D. Successive squares (0, 1, 4, 9, ...) differ by successive odd numbers (1, 3, 5, ...). Can this rule be generalized?

Chapter 3

Good thinking: The nature of rationality

In the case of any person whose judgment is really deserving of confidence, how has it become so? Because he has kept his mind open to criticism of his opinions and conduct. Because it has been his practice to listen to all that could be said against him; to profit by as much of it as was just, and expound to himself ... the fallacy of what was fallacious.

John Stuart Mill (1859)

A normative view

The purpose of this chapter is to introduce a coherent normative model for thinking. I shall design the model to reflect what we want it to do: help us think in the way that best achieves our personal goals. I shall then make some assumptions about where thinking most often departs from this normative model, descriptively. These assumptions lead to a general prescriptive theory of thinking.

The best kind of thinking, which we shall call *rational thinking*, is whatever kind of thinking best helps people achieve their goals. If it should turn out that following the rules of formal logic leads to eternal happiness, then it is "rational thinking" to follow the laws of logic (assuming that we all want eternal happiness). If it should turn out, on the other hand, that carefully violating the laws of logic at every turn leads to eternal happiness, then it is these violations that we shall call "rational." When I argue that certain kinds of thinking are "most rational," I mean that these help people fulfill their goals. Such arguments could be wrong. If so, some other sort of thinking is most rational.

Using the search-inference framework of Chapter 1, let us consider how our best thinking is done. Take decision making. We do not achieve our goals best if we

53

neglect some of them as we are evaluating the "possibilities." If, for example, in choosing a college course to take as an elective, I forget to consider the difficulty of the course, I may choose a course that is too hard. Other things being equal, the more goals I consider, the better my decision is likely to be.[1] (Of course, other things usually are not equal. Time may be short, and it takes time to search for goals. Let us come back to that later.)

Likewise, we do not achieve our goals best if we neglect possibilities that might achieve them better than the one we adopt. Even if Political Science 101 would serve my goals best, I cannot choose it if I do not think of it. Good thinking requires a thorough search for possibilities — other things being equal.

For the same reason, we must search thoroughly for evidence. The more I find out about the college courses I am considering, the more likely I am to pick one that does in fact satisfy my goals. We must also seek evidence in a way that is most helpful in finding the possibility that best achieves our goals. We must not seek evidence for any other reason. In particular, we should not seek evidence because we know it will turn out to favor possibilities that are already strong in our minds. If I seek evidence only about the good qualities of a course I am thinking of taking — because I want my initial hunch to be right, for example — I will miss the evidence about its bad qualities.

We must use evidence in a way that best achieves our goals, not in any other way. Again, we should not use evidence in a way that favors possibilities that are already strong, just because we want them to be the ones ultimately chosen. We should be willing to change if the evidence points that way.

There is a problem with the idea that more search is always better. The search for possibilities, evidence, and goals takes time and effort. If our search is lengthy, eventually a point may be reached at which the effort is not worthwhile, in terms of achieving our goals. One of our goals is not to spend our whole life lost in thought. Sometimes, when a quick decision is required, our goal is to think quickly. If registration ends tomorrow, I must pick a course now, making do with the possibilities and evidence at hand. Thus, we must balance the benefit of thorough search against the cost of search itself. Ordinarily, search is most useful at the beginning of thinking, and there is a "point of diminishing returns" beyond which search is no longer useful (Baron, Badgio, and Gaskins, 1986).

The real danger is not in thinking too little, then, but rather in behaving as though we had great confidence in conclusions that were reached with little thought. We should not make momentous decisions on the basis of unexamined beliefs, and we should not express strong confidence in hasty conclusions that fly in the face of conclusions reached by others who have thought much more.

In sum, good decision making involves *sufficient search* for possibilities, evidence, and goals, and *fairness* in the search for evidence and in the use of evidence (Baron, 1985b, 1991). Search is "sufficient" when it best serves the thinker's per-

---

[1] In the case of thinking about beliefs, the goal is usually fixed (as described in Chapter 1), so search for goals is less important.

sonal goals, including the goal of minimizing the cost of thinking. Search and inference are "fair" when they are not influenced by factors other than the goals of the thinking itself. Good decision making also requires use of the best methods of inference. We can think about these methods themselves.

This normative model of thinking is not very helpful as a practical, prescriptive model. In order to arrive at a prescriptive model, we ought to find out where people depart from the normative model. Then we can give practical advice to correct these departures, as well as whatever other advice will help people do their best thinking. In Chapter 9, I shall argue that people typically depart from this model by favoring possibilities that are already strong. We must thus make an effort to counteract this bias by looking actively for other possibilities and evidence on the other side. I call this *actively open-minded thinking*.

One comment before going on. It is possible to reflect on one's goals in life. Therefore, what achieves one's goals as they *are* may not achieve them as they *will be* after one thinks about them. We can still call the thinking good, though, if it takes into account a person's goals as they are.

Another thing we should note is that rational thinking can be defined relative to a person at a given time, with a given set of beliefs and goals. People may think rationally on the basis of irrationally formed beliefs. For example, if I believe (a delusion) that the Mafia is pursuing me, I might still make rational decisions for coping with that situation. Similarly, people who pursue irrational goals may do poor thinking about their goals, but, given their goals, they may still do good thinking about how to achieve them. If my goal is to escape from the Mafia, I may pursue it well or badly.

Rationality

Rationality concerns the methods of thinking we use, not the conclusions of our thinking. Rational methods are those that are generally best in achieving the thinker's goals. It is true that when we say someone is "irrational," we usually disagree with this person's conclusion — but we disagree in a particular way. We think that better methods ought to have been used in reaching that conclusion. When we call someone "irrational," we are giving advice (to this person or anyone else who listens) about how he ought to have thought.

The meaning of rationality

Rationality is, therefore, not the same as accuracy, and irrationality is not the same as error. We can use good methods and reach erroneous conclusions, or we can use poor methods and be lucky, getting a correct answer. There are even cases — such as thinking about one's life goals — where, although there is no reasonable standard of "correctness," we can still speak of rationality and irrationality.

Rationality is a matter of degree. It makes sense to say that one way of thinking is "more rational" or "less rational" than another. Also, there may be no single "best" way of thinking. There may be several ways of thinking that are indistinguishable in terms of their value in helping people achieve their goals, but still better than many other ways of thinking.

A useful theory of rational thinking, such as the one I have begun to outline here, ought to provide advice to people that they can follow. It does no good to try to teach people by saying, "Be correct!" or "Make good decisions!" That is like telling investors to buy low and sell high. This advice only tells people what their goals are, not how to achieve them. An appropriate response to such advice is, "Gee, thanks."

We can speak of the rationality of social institutions and of whole societies, as well as the rationality of individuals. Again, the criterion is whether these groups make collective decisions in ways that achieve the goals of their members, taken together. Such social decisions are affected both by the practices of institutions and cultures — the way they are organized for decision making — and by the decisions of individuals within those groups. We can therefore judge the rationality of individual decision making from the group's point of view as well as from the point of view of the individual's own goals. The judgments made from these two points of view need not always agree.

Rationality and luck

In discussing rational decision making, we must distinguish between good decision making and good outcomes. A *good decision* is one that makes effective use of the information available to the decision maker at the time the decision is made. A *good outcome* is one that the decision maker likes. Such an outcome can result from a good decision, but it can also result from good fortune, following a bad decision. Of course, the whole point of good thinking is to increase the probability of good outcomes (and true conclusions), but many other factors affect outcomes aside from good thinking. Some of these have to do with good thinking on earlier occasions. Others have to do with luck — factors beyond the person's control (hence, beyond any general advice we could give).

If we want to promote good decision making, we should ensure that people do the best they can with what is knowable. We cannot insist on clairvoyance. Prudently made investment decisions can lead to surprising losses. A decision to perform surgery could have been a rational one, even if the patient is the one in a thousand who dies on the operating table from that operation. In offering advice or instruction on good decision making, it does not do much good to say, "Do whatever achieves a good outcome." When we think a decision was badly made, we try to learn some lesson from it for our future decisions. If we think a decision was well made but turned out badly, there is no lesson to be learned. In such a case, we may need to make special efforts to emphasize the quality of the decision, lest the unfortunate outcome dissuade us from our good decision-making practices.

Similarly, when we judge how well a decision was made, we must bear in mind the possibility that well-made decisions turn out badly. Of course, when a decision turns out well, it is more likely to have been well made than if it turned out badly. (We do not appoint commissions of inquiry to study the causes of good outcomes.) Still, people do tend to judge decisions by their outcomes even when they know everything that the decision maker knew, as though decision makers were held responsible for their luck (Baron and Hershey, 1988).

These comments apply to belief formation, as well as to decision making. In general, good thinking leads us to true beliefs, but it can mislead us, and poor thinkers can hit on the truth by chance.

Objections to rationality

The definition of rationality as "the kind of thinking that helps us achieve our goals" answers a number of objections to the concept of rationality as a guide and dispenses with some caricatures of the concept.

First, rationality is not the same as cold calculation of self-interest. Many people think of rationality as exemplified by Dr. Strangelove (in the Stanley Kubrick film), whose single-minded devotion to winning a nuclear war enabled him to think quite coolly about the annihilation of most of the rest of humanity.

Rational thinking need not be cold. Emotions, in fact, are one type of evidence. A bad feeling about a choice is a reason not to make it — although not an overriding reason. Often, bad feelings are signals that some more tangible reason will reveal itself with further search. Even when the more tangible reason does not reveal itself, it may be rational to give uneasy feelings some weight, for the reason may still be there, even though we do not know what it is.

The seeking of pleasant emotions and the avoidance of unpleasant ones are surely goals that most people have (and would want to have, after thinking about their goals). Because these goals are things we want, we often think about how to achieve them.

Moreover, rationality need not be self-interested. Moral goals, including concern for the feelings of others, surely are among the goals we have and ought to have. More generally, rationality does not need to be single-minded; single-mindedness corresponds to the failure to search for more than one goal. The political leader who worries only about maximizing the Gross National Product is not the one who is rational. The rational leader is, rather, the one who worries about such things as people's feelings, the satisfaction of their desires, in all their variety (and in the long run).

Nor is rational thinking the same as thinking too much. When people really think rationally, the amount of thinking that they do is appropriate to the situation, insofar as possible. Rational thinkers, we have said, are moderate.

A more serious objection to rationality, some claim, is that it stands in the way of commitment, which is sometimes necessary. Apparently, President Richard Nixon of the United States believed that the most effective way of preventing a first strike by the Soviet Union was to maintain a powerful nuclear arsenal. Nixon appeared to be a madman, who was crazy enough to respond to a nuclear attack even at the risk of destroying civilization. The best way to appear to be mad in this way is to be mad in fact.

Another way to state this objection more generally is to argue that the ultimate objectives of rational decision making (decisions that best serve our goals) are not achieved by *trying* to make rational decisions but by trying to achieve some other goal — such as patriotism — which, by itself, is not necessarily always rational. In some cases, that is, rational thinking is *self-defeating* (Parfit, 1984). Like trying to "be spontaneous," trying to be rational may ensure that we cannot succeed in doing so. This objection does not undercut the idea of rationality as such. It does, however, imply that people might be better off not *knowing* about rationality and not trying to achieve it.

This approach, in my view, endangers the survival of rationality in a society. If rational thought is useful at all, then it must be maintained as a practice. Parents must teach it to their children, teachers must teach it to their students, and people must respect each other for their rationality. If the practice of rational thought is not to be lost, some group of people, at least, will have to maintain it. If that group is not to be an entire society, then it will have to be some sort of elite that perpetuates itself from generation to generation. This is not a foolish idea. It has been tried before in history, and it is still being tried. It is clearly inconsistent, however, with the ideal of an open society, in which all are given the tools and the opportunity to participate in decisions that affect them. Suppression of the teaching of rationality can therefore interfere with the existence of an open society itself. Without an elite that makes all important decisions, there is no way to ensure that people will make decisions that serve their own goals except by teaching them to think rationally.

A final objection to the concept of rationality is the claim that rational thinkers cannot be happy. By this argument, happiness requires a certain amount of self-deception. If one questions one's beliefs too closely, one may discover that one is not as successful, competent, or well liked as one thought. This is consistent with Alloy and Abramson's finding (1979; discussed in Chapter 7) that depressives correctly perceive their lack of control. Perhaps if we all correctly perceived the world, we would all be depressed.

It is true that some of us maintain an overly rosy view of ourselves through a kind of irrationality, in which we ignore the evidence against our rosy views. We convince ourselves that everything is just dandy, without asking whether it could be better. Many people may live their entire lives this way, happy as clams. If rational thinking were defined as whatever led to happiness, we might well have to change our view of what rational thinking is. Instead of respect for evidence, neglect of evidence might turn out to be rational.

In my view, happiness does not require such irrationality. Often, the happiness that results from irrationally formed beliefs goes along with irrationally formed goals. For example, people who think that they are universally liked often have the goal of being liked by everyone. Although it is surely rational to want to be liked, it is, for most people, hopeless to try to be liked by *everyone*. A balanced, rational view of how things actually are needs to be combined with a balanced, realistic view of how they ought to be, if we are not to be disappointed. If one's goals are as rationally formed as one's beliefs about how well one's goals are being achieved, accurate beliefs need not be disappointing. If I desire to be liked by *most* of the people I meet, I probably will not need to deceive myself in order to convince myself that this goal is being achieved reasonably well.[2]

Rationally formed beliefs have other advantages. On reflection, the combination of accurate beliefs and realistic goals may be more desirable than the combination of irrational beliefs and unrealistic goals, even though both combinations are capable of making us happy for the moment (and perhaps for longer, if we are lucky).

Rationality and emotion

Rationality is often contrasted with emotion. If we think of "emotion" as a way of making decisions *without thinking*, then this contrast is reasonable. Sometimes it pays to think. We have already seen, however, that emotions enter into thinking itself in a variety of ways. In particular, we noted that emotions can serve as evidence and that the creation or avoidance of certain emotions can serve as goals of behavior, and therefore as goals of thinking. Let us look a little further into the relation between emotion and rationality.

What is emotion? Roughly, we can take an emotion to be "a state that is subjectively experienced as pleasant or unpleasant, that drives or motivates certain kinds of behavior specific to the emotion, and that tends to be elicited by a certain kind of situation." Anger, for example, is usually unpleasant. In extreme anger, our muscles tighten and our hearts pound; we are more inclined to strike out; we want to hurt certain people or to see them hurt. Anger is typically induced by what we consider unfair treatment (of ourselves or of others). Fear, while also unpleasant, is induced by danger. Fear can increase our belief that harm will occur, and it can reduce our tendency to adopt risky options. Other emotions are elation, sadness, embarrassment, pride, regret, and rejoicing. Some emotions are related to moral behavior in particular, such as guilt feelings, anger, and empathic sadness or joy. The situations that induce emotions, as well as their effects on behavior, can differ from person to person. Likewise, people may use the same term for an emotion in different ways. (Sabini, 1992, has an interesting discussion of emotions.)

Much of our behavior seems to be designed to let us feel desirable emotions. The way we do this is often indirect. The first parachute jump, researchers tell us, evokes terror followed by relief. After a few jumps, however, the terror decreases, and the relief becomes euphoria that may last for days (Solomon & Corbit, 1974). A single extremely positive experience (such as winning the state lottery), on the other hand, can *reduce* the capacity to experience future pleasures, and vice versa

---

[2]Practically all of the "irrational beliefs" mentioned by Ellis (for example, 1987) as causes of psychological disturbance take the form of goals that are impossible to achieve.

(Brickman, Coates, and Janoff-Bulman, 1978). Direct attempts to induce pleasant emotions, then, are sometimes self-defeating. Many desirable emotions are essentially by-products of actions taken for other reasons (Elster, 1983).

Although emotions can serve as goals, they are certainly not the *only* goals we strive to achieve in our behavior. If you find this hard to believe, consider the fact that many people strive for goals that will not be reached until after their own deaths and thus cannot possibly give them any future emotional experience. They put money aside for their children's inheritance, or they work for long-term causes in their old age, perhaps even knowing that their death is near. It may even be that the desire for emotional experiences plays a very unimportant role in the major goals of most people. Some Buddhists systematically strive to eliminate emotions, on the grounds that, on the whole, they are just not worth it (Kolm, 1986).

Emotions are to some extent unavoidable, but they are also partly under our control. Many actors can induce or suppress emotions in themselves almost on cue. Some people try to reshape their character — often with the help of therapists — so that their emotional responses change. Moreover, emotions often have undesired effects; for example, teachers who get angry at their students may fail to teach well, as a result. Emotions can also have desired effects, as when the emotions of athletes make them try harder.

Are emotions rational? When emotions are *not* under our control, this question makes no more sense than asking whether the knee-jerk reflex is rational. Even if we decide that we do not like this reflex, there is nothing we can do about it, so the question is empty. If emotions are *partly* under our control, however, we can at least think about whether we should try to control them. (We could want them to be stronger or weaker.) The decision about whether or not to try may be made well or badly, like any decision. In thinking about whether to try to control our emotions, we must consider the cost of the effort, which may be substantial. It could be better to live with a slightly mixed-up emotional system than to spend years in therapy trying to fix it. On the other hand, therapy for some kinds of undesirable emotional responses, such as phobias, could be well worth the effort involved (see Beck, 1976).

Emotions may help us achieve our goals in the long run, even when they seem to prevent us from achieving our goals in the short run (Frank, 1988). For example, suppose that you are in an experiment called the "ultimatum game," in which another subject is instructed to make you an offer of some part of $20. You know that if you accept the offer, then she gives you the amount offered and keeps the rest of the $20 for herself. If you refuse the offer, then neither of you gets any money. Now suppose that she offers $1. Would you accept? Most people would not (Thaler, 1988), even though it would be in their short-run interest to do so. (They would gain a dollar.) Very likely, an offer of only $1 out of $20 makes people angry, and this causes them to reject it. Now if the other subject knows that you are the sort of person who will hurt yourself in order to hurt someone who has made you an unfair offer, she will make you better offers in the future (e.g., $10). So a short-run loss can ensure long-run gains. Displaying your anger at an unfair offer (if only by rejecting it) is a way to maintain this kind of reputation. If people see that you are in the grip of an emotion, they will know that you mean it.

Because of the long-run advantages, people with such emotions may have reproduced more in the past, so emotions may have been maintained by natural selection (Frank, 1988). Although emotions can have this sort of benefit, and may well have had it while the human species was evolving, the same emotions can lead to harm in other cases, as when anger — combined with biased judgment of what is fair — prevents people from negotiating an agreement to end a conflict.

Our knowledge of our emotions can become part of our thinking itself. For example (Chapter 11), in thinking about risky choices such as buying stock, we could take into account the regret we would feel if the value of the stock were to go down after we bought it. We could think of this emotion of regret as a risk we take in addition to the financial loss itself. If we know that we usually cannot control this emotion but are bothered by it, our unwillingness to feel so much regret could give us a good reason not to buy the stock, even if we were willing to take the risk on financial grounds alone. On the other hand, we may know that we can control this emotion. If the stock goes down, some people are able to avoid the feeling of regret by telling themselves (truthfully, perhaps) that the risk was worth taking, even though the venture did not work out. Control of emotion, therefore, can be a rational choice in its own right.

The emotions we have — and those we expect to have — can be influenced by our beliefs in a variety of respects. For example, if you come to believe that smoking is morally wrong, you will get less pleasure from smoking, you will feel more guilty from smoking, and you will (after you quit) be more likely to get angry at smokers. You will also anticipate these emotions, and that anticipation will affect your decisions. For example, in order to avoid anger, you will not go to a restaurant that has no section for nonsmokers. Sometimes these effects of anticipated emotions can become disabling: Fear of having a panic attack keeps some people from going out in public (Chambless and Gracely, 1989), even when the panic itself is caused by clearly exaggerated fears of heart attacks or other unlikely misfortunes (Cox, Swinson, Norton, and Kuch, 1991).

Changing people's beliefs can change both their emotions and their anticipation of these emotions. Thus, a woman's panic attacks may perhaps be reduced by convincing her that her heart palpitations do not (as she thought) indicate an incipient heart attack (Salkovskis and Clark, 1991). Likewise, when a children's vaccine can cause death from side effects that rarely occur, some people say they would decide not to vaccinate a child because they fear the guilt feelings that would result if their child died from the vaccine, even if the vaccine reduced the overall risk of death. These people would change their decision if they were convinced that vaccination was the morally right thing to do under these conditions. They would then worry more about the guilt feelings that would result if their unvaccinated child died from the disease (Baron, 1992).

Can emotions *make* us think irrationally? Janis and Mann (1977) present a number of cases in which this seems to occur. They show, for example, that people experiencing fear often do not think effectively about how they can deal with the real danger that causes the fear. It may be misleading, though, to call such an effect "irrational." Once the emotion is present, its effect on thinking could be unavoidable. If there is nothing to be done about the effect, it is empty to call it irrational. If there is any irrationality, it may be in failing to control the emotion itself, or in failing to shape one's character so that panic does not easily occur.

In sum, the relation between rational thinking and emotion is more complex than a simple contrast between the two, once we stop using the term "emotion" as a substitute for the word "irrationality." We need to think about emotions in the psychological sense in which I have been using the term, as states with certain causes and effects. Emotions — in this sense — are often the goals of our decisions. They also affect our decisions in ways that are sometimes desired and sometimes undesired. They may help us in the long run, even if they hurt us in the short run. They may make us behave more morally, or less morally, than we would without them. They can impair thinking itself, but, in moderation, they can also help it.

Rationality and belief

When we form beliefs, we generally have the goal of believing what is true. We therefore look for beliefs that fit the evidence we have. When we have time to think thoroughly and openly, we look for evidence against beliefs we are considering — that is, evidence that they are not true — and we seek alternative beliefs. Chapter 9 argues that such thinking — which is "actively open-minded" — is a good prescriptive method to counteract the biases that favor pre-existing beliefs.

Rational belief formation

In general, then, actively open-minded thinking is most likely to lead to true beliefs. In addition, when we cannot be sure that a belief is true, good thinking will ensure that our *confidence* in the belief is in proportion to the evidence available. Appropriate confidence is, in most cases, a more realistic goal than certainty.

The main advantage of true beliefs, or beliefs that we hold with appropriate confidence, is that they allow us to make better decisions, decisions more likely to achieve our goals. This is illustrated most clearly in the discussion of probability and utility theory in Chapters 5 and 10, where we shall see that coherent and consistent probability judgments are the ones most likely to give us good results. The same point may be made more generally, even when numerical probabilities are not at issue. If our confidence depends appropriately on the evidence we have, we will take the calculated risks that we ought to take, and when action requires certainty, we shall hold back if we cannot be certain.

There may well be other reasons to have rationally formed beliefs. We could have the goal of pursuing truth "for its own sake," regardless of the help it gives us in making decisions. There is surely nothing irrational about having such a goal.

Self-deception

Although our goal in belief formation is usually to believe the truth (or to have appropriate confidence), sometimes it would seem better to believe what is false. It might therefore be more rational sometimes to think in a way that leads to false beliefs. This amounts to self-deception. Although self-deception can at times be best, at other times it lies behind the most insidious forms of irrationality, as when people convince themselves that some idea of theirs is right, despite the evidence against it.

What is self-deception? To some, the idea implies that we really have two selves — the "deceiver" (perhaps the unconscious), who knows the truth, and the "deceived." The deceiver must have some reason to carry out his deception. For example, he might want the deceived to feel that she has been right all along. (The deceived might find changing her mind to be painful, and the deceiver might be sympathetic.)

Although this idea of a dual self has its appeal, it is not needed to explain self-deception. All I need to do to deceive myself is to do something in order to control my belief, without being aware that I have done it. For example, the philosopher Pascal argued (see Chapter 10) that one ought to try to believe in God, since if God exists and one does not believe, one might be damned, and this is too big a risk to take. Pascal felt that someone who understood this argument could voluntarily become a believer by honestly trying to live the Christian life. In doing this, one would eventually, through studying the Bible and associating with other Christians, come to believe in Christianity and in the Christian God. Eventually one would very likely forget that the whole thing was inspired by the ulterior motive of avoiding eternal damnation.

All that is necessary for self-deception, then, is that when we form our belief we do not take account of the fact that self-deception has occurred. If we do, it will not work. If we keep in our minds the fact that we began to go to church only because we were afraid of hell, we will not be so easily persuaded by what we hear there.

Our beliefs are manipulated more frequently than Pascal's rather extreme example suggests. If you go to law school and become a lawyer, you will very likely come to believe that lawyers are good people who serve a valuable function in society (even if you go to law school for some other reason, without believing this at the outset). Similarly, if you have a child, you will very likely come to believe in the frivolity of those who voluntarily remain childless. Any course of life you choose, in other words, is likely to affect your beliefs. If you want to control your beliefs, then, you can do so by choosing your course of life for that purpose. On a more mundane level, some people set their clocks 5 minutes fast, in order to get to work on time — hoping to deceive themselves, if only for a panicky moment, into thinking that time is short, so they will get off to work quickly.

Can self-deception ever be rational? On the one hand, self-deception seems to be one of the major means we have for maintaining (at times with great confidence) false and harmful beliefs. If we want to believe that smoking is harmless, for example, we can make ourselves believe this by seeking evidence in favor of our belief and ignoring evidence against it. We must be sure not to take fully into account the fact that we have done these things, for, if we do, we will see that the evidence we use was as good as useless, "cooked" to order. It might as well have been made up.

This kind of biased search can become so much a matter of habit for some people that they do not know that they behave this way. Perhaps they formed the habit unconsciously, because it was more comfortable. If they never questioned their beliefs, they never had to suffer the pain of changing them.

It is difficult to know how many of our beliefs are maintained in this way. If you wonder about a particular belief, try to think about it in an actively open-minded way over a period of time. This is the only cure for self-deception, and it is a cure that has few undesirable side-effects, even for those who did not really have the disease.

Self-deception is thus clearly irrational, in some cases. It is almost necessarily a part of poor thinking. If people *know* that their thinking is poor, they will not believe its results. One of the purposes of a book like this is to make recognition of poor thinking more widespread, so that it will no longer be such a convenient means of self-deception.

On the other hand, in certain cases we can be reasonably sure that the benefits of self-deception outweigh the costs:

1. We can sometimes manipulate our own behavior to our benefit through self-deception. A simple case is one already described, setting one's clock ahead in order to get to work on time. Similarly, the behavior of liars may be more convincing if they believe the lies they tell. If they can make themselves believe their lies, they will be more effective. Actors, of course, deliberately try to deceive themselves in order to act more convincingly. Loyal spouses may maintain their belief that their spouse is the best one for them by never "experimenting" with other possibilities.

2. Beliefs can affect goals, particularly the strength of the goals; therefore, we may deceive ourselves in order to control our goals. Athletes may convince themselves that they are likely to win, in order to make themselves undergo the rigors of training or take the risks that they must take in playing. The potential cost here is that the effort and risk will be futile and hopeless, but again, the benefits might outweigh this. On the other hand, some people convince themselves that their goals are unattainable in order to avoid the anguish of trying to attain them (Elster, 1983).

3. Beliefs themselves can make us happy or unhappy, and sometimes the beliefs that make us unhappy have no compensating advantages. It can be reasonable not to want to be told that one is dying from an incurable disease, especially if one would only continue to live one's life as best one could. Workers who are subject to occupational hazards sometimes convince themselves that the risks are minor (Akerlof and Dickens, 1982), avoiding the stress of worrying about them. In general, it seems reasonable not to want to know bad things that we cannot do anything about.

From a _normative_ point of view, whether self-deception should be attempted in a given case depends on the balance of costs and benefits in that case. From a prescriptive point of view, it may be wise to try to seek the truth as a general rule. First, self-deception is often unnecessary. There are other ways of getting to work on time besides setting the clock ahead. Marital fidelity and bliss do not necessarily require the belief that one's spouse was the best possible choice.

Second, self-deception can have harmful effects. For every athlete who can win by "psyching herself up" for an important match, there are countless other average athletes who convince themselves that they will make it to the Olympics and waste years trying. (They may then tell themselves it was all somehow worthwhile, thus continuing the deception.) Excessive self-esteem can result in optimistic self-deception that leads, in turn, to excessive risk taking. In a video-game experiment with monetary prizes, subjects with high self-esteem generally performed better and chose targets that they were capable of achieving. In an "ego threat" condition, however, all subjects were told, "Now if you are worried that you might choke [lose your nerve] under pressure or if you don't think you have what it takes to beat the target, then you might want to play it safe and just go for two dollars." In this condition, subjects with high self-esteem tried for the larger prize and, in the end, made less money than those with lower self-esteem (Baumeister, Heatherton, and Tice, 1993).

Finally, if we get the idea that it is OK to deceive ourselves, we may well overdo it, because cases in which self-deception is irrational can be hard to recognize. When we overdo it, we are prevented from knowing the truth even when we want to. A person who has been ill but who has said to his doctor, "If it's really bad, don't tell me," may not be able to be truly reassured if his doctor tells him that he will indeed recover. In extreme cases, habitual self-deceivers may wake up one day in terror, not knowing which of their beliefs are real. Those who set out on the path of self-deception should proceed with caution.

Beliefs as a cause of desires

Beliefs can produce a "sour grapes" effect. When something seems impossible or difficult for us to attain, we _want_ it less. Sometimes this is rational: If we can adjust our desires to reality, we will be happier. Changing our belief is irrational, though, when we are too easily persuaded to give up a goal that we could achieve (Elster, 1983).

Whether this effect is rational or not, it seems to occur. Harris (1969) asked subjects to rate the desirability of a number of phonograph records, one of which they would be given at the end of the experiment. Then subjects were told that a certain record would not be given away, and the ratings were done again. The excluded record was given lower ratings than it had been given when it was a possible goal. We might call this the "Pangloss effect," after Dr. Pangloss, the "sage" in Voltaire's _Candide_, who, after each tragic episode in the story, explains at great length why it was "all for the best."

Are people ever really irrational?

Much of the research described in this book involves attempts to show that people do not follow normative or prescriptive models — that is, they do not think in the best way. We are tempted, when reading about such studies, to come to the defense of the researchers' subjects. After all, calling someone "irrational" is not nice, especially if it is a false accusation.

Sometimes we attempt to defend these subjects by arguing that the behavior in question is functional — that it serves some purpose other than "rationality." If people are illogical, for example, perhaps it is because they "want" to be and feel better when they behave this way, or because illogic leads them to a "deeper" truth.

There are indeed situations in which people can be rational while appearing to be irrational. The theory of rationality that is used to judge their thinking may be wrong, or some important goal (such as the subject's emotions) may have been neglected in applying the theory of rationality.

On the other hand, we cannot assume that people always have good reasons for appearing to be irrational. People can really be irrational sometimes. In this book I shall assume that the "burden of proof" is not on one side or the other. This is because I shall also assume that our main interest is in helping people to think better (or to maintain those aspects of good thinking that they already use). Therefore, the two kinds of mistakes that we can make — deciding falsely that others are or are not irrational — are both costly ones. If we falsely conclude that people are *irrational* in some way, we may waste our effort in trying to help them — and we may even make them worse. If we falsely conclude that people are rational when they are not, we lose an opportunity to help them. (Of course, to paraphrase Pogo, "them" is "us.")

For every argument of the form "If we're so irrational, how did we ever get to the moon?", there is another argument of the form "If we're so rational, how come we [pick your favorite complaint about the world situation or about people]?" It is, in a way, from our point of view, a cause for optimism to discover biases and irrationalities, for we can teach people to avoid them. If the errors of humanity — collective and individual — cannot be prevented, our future is precarious.

To conclude, the purpose of the research discussed in this book is not to give grades to the human race or to Western culture. History gives the grades. Our job is to try to figure out *why* the human race is getting C's rather than A's — and whether anything can be done about it.

Conclusion

The idea of rationality presented in this chapter, and developed in the rest of the book, is not an arbitrary standard that some dictator of the mind is trying to impose on the world. It is a standard that we would all want to meet because we want to achieve our own goals. If you think I am wrong, you must argue that the standards I propose do not help us achieve our goals. All of this follows from the idea that the purpose of thinking is to achieve our goals.

Chapter 4

Logic

Nothing is better than eternal happiness.
A ham sandwich is better than nothing.
Therefore, a ham sandwich is better than eternal happiness.

[handwritten: 2 meanings of Nothing — no.thing / having no thing]

Nickerson (1986)

Past writers (for example, Arnauld, 1662/1964) have taken formal logic as a normative model of thinking. Today, people sometimes use the word "logical" as if it simply meant "reasonable" or "rational." Logic has influenced education — where it served as the basis for the teaching of thinking for centuries — and it has provided us with much of our language for talking about thinking: "premise," "assumption," "contradiction."

Today logic has lost its central place as the normative model for thinking. But the development of logic and its psychology provide an example of the approach emphasized here, which compares human reasoning to normative models. Because logic is so old, it is not often challenged as a normative model. Errors in logical reasoning are generally accepted as errors or biases. Later I will discuss models that are not (yet) so well accepted. Claims about bias may seem more questionable. All claims, of course, are questionable, but we must remember the example of logic before we conclude that the whole enterprise is so tenuous as to be meaningless.

What is logic?

Matthew Lipman has written a series of philosophical "novels" to introduce children in elementary and secondary schools to philosophical thinking. In one of these, *Harry Stottlemeier's Discovery* (1974; say the name aloud and think of a famous Greek philosopher), Harry is daydreaming in class. Suddenly he hears the teacher asking him whether Halley's comet is a planet, and he struggles to come up with an

67

answer. He reasons that all planets go around the sun; Halley's comet goes around the sun; therefore, Halley's comet must be a planet, so he answers yes.

Later, when the immediate embarrassment has passed, Harry and his friends reflect on why he was wrong. They notice that true sentences (sentences stating a truth) beginning with "all" usually become false when they are reversed: Compare "All dogs are animals" with "All animals are dogs," or compare "All planets are things that go around the sun" with "All things that go around the sun are planets." Harry conjectures that this is true of all sentences, but a friend points out that true sentences beginning with the word "some" can be switched around and remain true (and false ones can remain false). For example, "Some women are artists," "Some artists are women" (both true); "Some dogs are mice," "Some mice are dogs" (both false). Harry and his friends discover that this is also true for sentences beginning with "no": "No women are artists," "No artists are women" (both false); "No dogs are mice," "No mice are dogs" (both true).

What are Harry and his friends doing here? One answer (Popper, 1962, ch. 9) is that they are engaged in a kind of *reflection* (as defined in Chapter 1). They are trying to formulate generalizations about the truth and falsity of expressions in language. The generalizations are expressed in terms of the *form* of the expressions. For example, one rule is that if the statement "No X are Y" is true, then the statement "No P are Q" is also true. This rule does not depend on what we plug in for P and Q. It is like many laws in mathematics, such as $x + y = y + x$, which is also true regardless of the values of x and y. Of course, reflection of this sort is successful only if the search is thorough or if the thinkers are lucky in coming up with informative examples.

The *evidence* for this reflective enterprise consists of our own knowledge of the truth or falsity of various statements, plus our understanding of the words in question. It might be said that we understand the terms only because we already *know* the laws of logic, so that all we are doing is discovering what we already know. However, let us be skeptical about this claim for a while. Perhaps we understand the terms without knowing the laws of logic.

When we reflect on the truth and falsity of expressions, we try to draw conclusions that are *always* true. For example, it may *usually* be true that "when some A's are B's and some B's are C's, then some A's are C's" (for example, "Some men are scientists"; "Some scientists are New Yorkers"; "Some men are New Yorkers"), but it is not *always* true ("Some men are scientists"; "Some scientists are women"; "Some men are women" ?!). This rule, then, is not one of the laws of logic. In fact, we might conclude instead that nothing follows at all from an expression that contains two *some*'s.

Logicians study the behavior of arguments laid out in a certain form: a list of *premises* and a *conclusion* that may or may not follow from the premises. An argument laid out in this way is called a *syllogism*. When a syllogism is *valid*, the conclusion follows from the premises. That is, if the premises are assumed to be true (whether they are actually true or not), the conclusion must be true. When a syllogism is *invalid*, the conclusion can be false even if all the premises are true. The validity of syllogisms depends on their form, not on the specific terms used in them. We can use letters such as P, Q, L, or M to stand for specific terms. If the syllogism is valid, no matter how we replace the letters with actual terms, it will be impossible for the conclusion to be false if the premises are true.

Consider another example:

> An L can be an M.
> An M can be an N.
> Therefore an L can be an N.

Is this a valid syllogism? Is the conclusion always true whenever the premises are true? How can you tell? Try to think of examples. "A man can be a scientist"; "A scientist can be a New Yorker"; "A man can be a New Yorker." So far, so good; but remember (from ch. 3) that good thinkers try to find evidence against a possibility as well as evidence in its favor. Try to find an example that shows the rule is *false* — that is, a *counter*example. What about substituting "men," "scientists," and "women," for L, M, and N, respectively, just as we did before? "A man can be a woman?" Aha! The syllogism is invalid; the proposed rule is false. Did you know that before? Was it part of your knowledge of the word *can*? Hmm.

Let us try another one (told to me by P. N. Johnson-Laird):

> A is to the right of B.
> B is to the right of C.
> Therefore A is to the right of C.

Sounds good. This must be part of what we mean by "to the right of." Or is it? Imagine three people — A, B, and C — sitting around a circular table. Indeed, A may be on B's right, and B on C's right, but A would have to be on C's left. This rule is wrong as well. We discovered that it was wrong by constructing what Johnson-Laird calls a *mental model* of a situation. The mental model served as a counterexample. This example makes it much more plausible (to me, anyway) that when we reflect on the laws of logic we are not simply discovering what we already know. Before I heard Johnson-Laird give this example, I judged that this rule was true, and I was prepared to use it to make inferences. (Luckily for me, he did not ask me to bet on it.)

As a final example, let us consider a syllogism that is one of the bugaboos of logic students:

> If A then B.
> B.
> Therefore A.

(In the shorthand form used by philosophers, here "A" means "A is true"; "B" means "B is true"; and so forth.) What happens if we substitute words for the letters?

> If it rains, Judy takes the train.
> Judy took the train today.
> Therefore it rained.

Again, this sounds good, but, clearly, Judy might also take the train if it snows. The conclusion would not always follow, so the syllogism is invalid.

The word "if," used in these statements, actually seems to have two meanings in ordinary speech. In the *conditional* meaning, the statement "If A then B" means that B will be true if A is true and that B will be possible also if A is not true (for example, "if it snows"). In the *biconditional* meaning, the same expression means that B will be true only if A is true and not if A is false. In this case, whenever the statement "If A then B" is true, the statement "If B then A" will be true as well. The implication works both ways; hence the term "biconditional." Mathematicians often use the phrase "if and only if" to indicate a biconditional meaning.

In ordinary speech, the meaning intended is usually clear from the context. Suppose I say, "If you don't shut up, I'll scream!" You would be surprised if I screamed anyway after you shut up. Here, the natural interpretation is the biconditional, not the conditional. If the biconditional interpretation were meant, then the argument "If A then B. B. Therefore A" would be valid.

Why, then, do logicians usually insist that the word "if" be interpreted in the conditional sense? Because this is more conservative. If you do not know which sense is intended, you had better not draw the conclusion that A is true (in the bugaboo syllogism just discussed), because you might be wrong. On the other hand, suppose the statement is this: "If A then B. A." Here you *can* infer B, no matter which sense is intended.

For the same reason, logicians take the statement "Some X are Y" to be consistent with the possibility that "All X are Y," even though we would never say that some X are Y if we knew that all X are Y. The point is that we might say that some X are Y when it is true that all X are Y and we do not know it yet. (In a new city, we might notice that some taxis are yellow; it might be that all are.) Therefore, the argument "Some X are Y. Therefore, some X are not Y" is not valid. It is not always true.

In sum, logic is a *normative model* of inference, arrived at by *reflection* about arguments. The study of logical reasoning is a good example of the comparison of actual reasoning to normative models.

Types of logic

Logicians have developed several systems of rules. Each system concerns arguments based on certain terms.

The system of *propositional logic* is concerned with the terms "if," "and," "or," and "not." The last example about Judy and the train was in this system. Here is a more complex example of a valid argument that uses propositional logic:

If there is an F on the paper, there is an L.
If there is not an F, there is a V.
Therefore, there is an F or there is a V.

The system of *categorical logic* is concerned with membership in categories. It concerns the behavior of arguments with the words "all," "some," "none," "not," and "no." This is the type of logic most intensively discussed by the Greek philosopher Aristotle, the main inventor of formal logic, and the type most studied by psychologists. Here are two examples of valid arguments of this type:

All A's are B's.
All B's are C's.
Therefore all A's are C's.

Some A are B.
No B are C.
Therefore some A are not C.

The system of *predicate logic* includes both propositional and categorical logic. It includes relations among terms as well as class membership. A "predicate" is anything that is true or false of a term or set of terms. In the sentence "A man is a scientist," the word "scientist" is considered a "one-place predicate," because it says that something is true of the single term "man." In the sentence "John likes Mary," the word "likes" is considered a "two-place predicate," because it describes a relation between two specific terms. In predicate logic, we can analyze such questions as this: "If every boy likes some girl and every girl likes some boy, does every boy like someone who likes him?"

Other systems of logic extend predicate logic in various ways. For example, *modal* logic is concerned with arguments using such terms as "necessarily" and "possibly." The idea is not simply to capture the meanings of English words as they are normally used but also, as in the "if" example described earlier, to develop formal rules for particular meanings, usually the most conservative meanings. No sharp boundary separates modern logic from "semantics," the part of modern linguistics that deals with meaning. (In the next chapter, we shall examine other extensions of logic to informal reasoning.)

The various systems of logic I have listed constitute what I shall call "formal" logic. These systems have in common their concern with validity, that is, the drawing of conclusions that are absolutely certain from premises that are assumed to be absolutely certain. (The next chapter considers "informal" logic.)

If we view formal logic within the search-inference framework, we see that formal logic is concerned with the rules for drawing conclusions from evidence with certainty. That is, it is concerned only with inference, the use of evidence. It says nothing about how evidence is, or should be, obtained. Formal logic, therefore, cannot be a complete theory of thinking. Moreover, formal logic cannot even be a complete normative theory of inference, for most inferences do not involve the sort of absolute certainty that it requires.

Nonetheless, logic may be a partial normative theory of inference. Each system of logic has its own rules that specify how to draw valid conclusions from a set of evidence, or *premises*. These rules make up the normative model. Within logic, there are many such systems of rules, and often there are many equivalent ways of describing the same system. These rules are the subject matter of logic textbooks.

For each system of logic, we can ask whether people actually make inferences in a way that is consistent with the rules of logic. When we do think logically, we can ask how we do it. It is not necessarily by following the rules as stated in logic textbooks. When we do not, we can ask why not and whether the problem can be corrected.

For propositional logic, there is considerable evidence that people (at least adults) have learned to follow many rules that correspond directly to some of the major argument forms. For example, consider the following syllogisms (from Braine and Rumain, 1983, p. 278):

1. There is a G. There is an S. Therefore there is a G and an S.

2. There is an O and a Z. Therefore there is an O.

3. There is a D or a T. There is not a D. Therefore there is a T.

4. If there is a C or a P, there is an H. There is a C. Therefore there is an H.

These inferences are so obvious (once we understand the words) that no thinking seems to be required to evaluate their truth. Moreover, we seem to be able to draw more complex inferences by stringing these simple ones together. For example, evaluate the argument "If there is an A or a B, there is a C. There is a B or a D. There is not a D. Therefore there is a C." This argument combines forms 3 and 4 in the list. Braine and Rumain (1983) and Rips (1983) review and report a number of studies of such reasoning. It is possible to predict the difficulty of evaluating an argument by figuring out which of the basic arguments from propositional logic must be put together in order to make it up. This approach to the study of logic has been called *natural logic* or *natural deduction*. The name reflects the idea that certain forms of argument are just as easy for most of us to use and understand as speaking. Researchers have been particularly interested in finding out how we have acquired these abilities. Studies of children suggest that some of them are slow to appear, developing only as children mature (Braine & Rumain, 1983).

Difficulties in logical reasoning

The natural-logic approach sometimes works for propositional logic, but it does not seem to work for categorical logic. First, categorical syllogisms seem to be much harder. Moreover, the difficulties are of a different sort. In most problems in propositional logic, we either see an answer right away or we puzzle over the problem, sometimes solving it, sometimes not. In categorical reasoning, we almost always come up with an answer, but the answer very often turns out to be wrong. Consider this very difficult example (from Johnson-Laird & Bara, 1984): Given the statements

> No A are B.
> All B are C.

what can you conclude about A and C? Most people conclude that no A are C, but this is wrong. (I will explain why later.)

Several researchers have tried to explain why categorical syllogisms are sometimes so difficult. A very early attempt was that of Woodworth and Sells (1935), who proposed that the premises of syllogisms create an "atmosphere" that affects the conclusion that is drawn. When subjects hear "Some A are B; some B are C," they naturally think, "Some A are C," even though this is wrong. The same is true of "No A are B. No B are C. Therefore no A are C." The atmosphere effect does explain a number of such errors, but not all of them (Johnson-Laird, 1983, pp. 72–76). It is also not a complete theory, because it fails to explain how anyone ever gets the right answer to these problems.

Another account of errors is that of Chapman and Chapman (1959), who pointed out that subjects often "convert" one of the premises. If the premise says that all A are B, they infer that all B are A as well. Subjects therefore reason: "All A are B. Some C are B. Therefore some C are A." This is wrong because the C's that are B's might not be A's. Some evidence in support of this account comes from a study by Ceraso and Provitera (1971). In this study, errors were reduced by restating the problem in a way that explicitly warned the subjects against conversion. They were told, for example, "All A are B, but some B might not be A."

Chapman and Chapman also theorized that subjects reason probabilistically. Instead of giving conclusions that must always be true (which is what they are asked for), subjects give conclusions that are likely to be true. Hence, when given "Some A are B. Some B are C," subjects conclude that some A are C, which is indeed likely to be true but is not always true.

The most radical account of errors in syllogistic reasoning is that of Henle (1962), who maintained that all such errors are not truly errors of logic but of understanding or interpretation. Henle points out that subjects sometimes act as though they are being asked about the truth of a conclusion, rather than whether it follows from the premises. They do not assume that the premises are not to be questioned. In other words, they *fail to accept the logical task.*

Some of the clearest examples of this phenomenon are found in studies of cultures without widespread schooling. Here is an example (from Scribner, 1977, p. 490) in which a nonliterate Kpelle (West African) rice farmer is interviewed:

> All Kpelle men are rice farmers.
> Mr. Smith is not a rice farmer.
> Is he a Kpelle man?

> *Subject*: I don't know the man in person. I have not laid eyes on the man
> himself.
> *Experimenter*: Just think about the statement.
> *S*: If I know him in person, I can answer that question, but since I do not
> know him in person I cannot answer that question.
> *E*: Try and answer from your Kpelle sense.
> *S*: If you know a person, if a question comes up about him you are able
> to answer. But if you do not know the person, if a question comes
> up about him, it's hard for you to answer it.

What is really interesting about this case is that the farmer is *using* a syllogism much like the one he is refusing to answer (Johnson-Laird, 1985, p. 315):

> If I do not know an individual, then I cannot draw any conclusion about
> that individual.
> I do not know Mr. Smith.
> Therefore I cannot draw any conclusion about Mr. Smith.

The main difference between the two syllogisms (aside from the minor difference in form) is that the subject accepts the premises of the second but is unwilling to accept the premises of the one that he is given as a basis for reasoning. Scribner suggests that even a few grades of schooling may teach people to reason in the "genre" of formal logic, in which the premises must be accepted. This may occur even though formal logic is not ordinarily taught. Students could learn this early, Scribner suggests, from doing verbal problems in arithmetic. Even first-graders are sometimes asked to assume that "Bill has 3 pencils and gets 2 more." Students learn quickly that when they are asked how many pencils Bill has, "I don't know Bill" is not the sort of answer the teacher expects.

Young children in the United States, in one experiment, failed to accept the logical task, much as the farmer did (Osherson and Markman, 1974–1975). When asked, "Is it true that this poker chip [concealed] in my hand is either red or not red?", most young children answered, "I don't know; I can't see it." The children did not seem to think of trying to answer the question on the basis of its form alone. (Other evidence indicates that they understood the meaning of the question.)

Henle (1962) points to a number of other errors, such as misinterpreting a premise (as in Chapman & Chapman's conversion), slipping in an additional premise, and omitting a premise. Although she argues that these are errors in logic and that reasoning proceeds correctly once these errors are made, it is not clear what she thinks a true error in logic would be.

Mental models

Johnson-Laird and his colleagues (Johnson-Laird & Steedman, 1978; Johnson-Laird, 1983; Johnson-Laird & Bara, 1984) proposed a different approach to logical reasoning, based on the idea of mental models. This approach applies to categorical syllogisms and perhaps to other types. In essence, the idea is that we try to form a mental model of the situation expressed in the premises and derive a tentative conclusion by examining the model. If we are sufficiently careful thinkers, we then try to find an alternative mental model, according to which the tentative conclusion we have drawn would not be true. If we fail to find such a counterexample, we assume that our conclusion is correct. This theory explains both how we succeed in obtaining correct answers and why we sometimes fail.

Let us first see how the theory works for a simple example:

> All artists are beekeepers.
> All beekeepers are chemists.

To complete such a syllogism, we imagine some sort of mental model. For example, we might imagine a few artists (indicated by A's) and a few beekeepers (B's), with some sort of tag to indicate which are the same person:

$$A \ = \ B$$
$$A \ = \ B$$
$$(B)$$

The (B) at the end indicates that there might be a beekeeper who is not an artist. (We do not have to use exactly this kind of mental model. We might, for example, imagine an A circle inside a B circle.) We then make the same kind of mental model for the beekeepers and chemists (C's). Finally, we combine the two mental models:

$$A \ = \ B \ = \ C$$
$$A \ = \ B \ = \ C$$
$$(B) \ = \ C$$
$$(C)$$

We can then "read off" the conclusion that all artists are chemists. We can fool around with this model, eliminating the (B) or the (C), and the conclusion will still hold. If we try to think of another model, we will not be able to. There is only a single model for this syllogism.

Consider now the syllogism beginning

> Some A are B.
> Some B are C.

For this syllogism, many people come up with the following model:

$$A \ = \ B \ = \ C$$
$$(A) \ \ \ \ (B) \ \ \ \ (C)$$

That is, they imagine that some of the A's are B's and some of *these* B's are C's. If they stop here, they will conclude that some A's are C's, a common error. If they seek an alternative model, they may come up with this one:

```
A    =    B
(A)       B    =    C
         (B)       (C)
```

That is, the B's that are C's need not be the same B's that are A's. Since there is no single conclusion consistent with both models, the subjects conclude correctly that nothing follows at all from these two premises.

Now let us consider the syllogism that we examined earlier, beginning:

> No A are B.
> All B are C.

There are three models to consider here:[1]

1.			2.			3.		
A			A			A	=	(C)
A			A	=	(C)	A	=	(C)
B	=	C	B	=	C	B	=	C
B	=	C	B	=	C	B	=	C
		(C)			(C)			(C)

(Here the horizontal line under the A's indicates separation, as in the premise "No A are B.") In model 3, all of the A's are C's. Subjects often conclude that no A are C. It is apparent that this conclusion is consistent only with the first of the three models. The only conclusion consistent with all three models is that some C are not A, and this is the correct answer.

We see that one reason for mistakes in dealing with syllogisms is that subjects sometimes draw a conclusion based on a single model, and fail to consider alternative models, especially models that are inconsistent with their conclusion. If we think of models as "evidence" and the conclusion as a "possibility," this kind of error is an example of failure to seek evidence against a favored possibility, a basic source of poor thinking. The same can be said when subjects consider two models, but not a third model, although this error is less extreme. Johnson-Laird and Steedman (1978) and Johnson-Laird and Bara (1984) were able to predict the relative difficulty of different syllogisms, and the errors that are made, by assuming that many subjects fail to consider more than a single model. The most difficult syllogisms tend to be those that require consideration of three alternative models.

Johnson-Laird (1983) has also found that the models people form seem to be "directed," that is, the order of the terms in each premise makes a difference. Syllogisms are easiest when the first term of the conclusion is the first term in the first premise and the second term in the conclusion is the second term in the second premise (in the order: A–B, B–C, therefore A–C). It is as though the premises had to be diagrammed in left-to-right order, with the B's of the first premise next to the B's of the second premise, before the subject could combine them. When the subject must reverse one

---

[1] It is assumed here that there is at least one A, one B, and one C.

of the premises, the task is more difficult. Because the order of the terms is called the "figure," this effect is called the "figural effect." This effect can be seen when the difficulty of a syllogism depends on the order in which the terms are presented. For example, given

> Some A are B.
> All B are C.

almost all subjects conclude, correctly, "Some A are C." However, given

> Some B are A.
> All B are C.

many subjects say, "No valid conclusion," even though "Some B are A" means the same as "Some A are B." Those subjects who are correct in the second form are also more likely to state the conclusion as "Some C are A," possibly because they have switched around the "arrows" in their mental model of the second premise. The figure seems to affect both the difficulty of the problem and the way in which the conclusion is expressed.

Ability to solve categorical syllogisms is affected both by the tendency to consider alternative models and by the figural effect. Subjects who have the greatest difficulty are often unable to put together even a single model, especially when the premises are not in the most convenient order (that is, A–B, B–C). These subjects find the problem particularly hard when one of the premises must be turned around. Other subjects do not find the problem hard when only a single model must be considered, almost regardless of the figure, but do have trouble with multiple-model problems.

Galotti, Baron, and Sabini (1986) found support for this analysis. Subjects were selected according to their scores on a test of syllogistic reasoning. Subjects were asked to give an initial answer under time pressure, and a final answer without pressure. It was thought that the initial answer might be based on a single model of both premises, and that the final answer in good reasoners (high scorers) would result from consideration of alternative models inconsistent with the initial conclusion. Good reasoners were in fact more likely to correct answers that were initially incorrect, especially on problems in which "nothing follows," which always involved more than a single model. Good reasoners also took about twice as much time as poor reasoners between initial and final answers. (The two groups were about equal in the time spent on initial answers.) Apparently, those who were good at the task were more thorough in their search, and possibly more self-critical as well. They seemed (in think-aloud tasks) to search for models that were inconsistent with their initial conclusion.

The mental-model approach can be extended to both predicate logic and propositional logic. Consider the following examples of predicate logic:

1.   None of the A's is in the same place as any of the B's.
     All of the B's are in the same place as all of the C's.

2.   None of the A's is in the same place as any of the B's.
     All of the B's are in the same place as some of the C's.

Problem 1 easily leads to the conclusion "None of the A's is in the same place as any of the C's." A single model is required for this: AAA / BBBCCC. (The slash separates the different places.) If a single model of the second problem is constructed, an incorrect conclusion might be drawn. Specifically, the model AAA / BBBCC / CC might yield the conclusion "None of the A's is in the same place as any of the C's." The correct answer requires consideration of a second model, AAACC / BBBCC. The answer is, "None of the A's is in the same place as some of the C's." Johnson-Laird, Byrne, and Tabossi (1989) found that subjects made more errors on predicate-logic problems requiring two models than on those requiring one model.

Propositional logic can also be analyzed with models (Johnson-Laird, Byrne, & Schaeken, 1992). Consider the following premises:

June is in Wales, or Charles is in Scotland, but not both.
Charles is in Scotland, or Kate is in Ireland, but not both.

Each premise requires two models, but when the premises are combined only two models remain, one corresponding to "June is in Wales, and Kate is in Ireland," the other to "Charles is in Scotland." So the conclusion is "June is in Wales, and Kate is in Ireland, or Charles is in Scotland, but not both." If the premises are changed so that "but not both" is changed to "or both," then each premise has three models, and many more models are required for a conclusion.[2] In general, problems that require more models are more difficult.

Logical errors in hypothesis testing

The four-card problem

Suppose you are given the following four cards. You are told that each card has a letter on one side and a number on the other. Thus, the first two cards have numbers on the other side, and the last two have letters.

You are given the following rule, which may or may not be true of all four cards:

If a card has a vowel on one side, then it has an even number on the other side.

---

[2]A correct conclusion is that any two of the three statements (one about each person) could be true, or all three, or Charles could be in Wales. ?

Your task is "to name those cards, and only those cards, that need to be turned over in order to determine whether the rule is true or false" (Wason, 1968b). Think about this before going on.

Most subjects give as their answer A only, or A and 4. A few answer A, 4, and 7. Very few answer A and 7. Can you discover the right answer on your own? Try it before reading on. Here is a hint: One set of subgoals is to find out whether *each card* is needed. How would you determine whether each card is needed?

You might think of the following idea: Imagine each possible result you could find by turning over each of the cards, and ask yourself whether the rule could be true if the result were found. For the first two cards you would ask, "Could the rule be true if the number on the other side were even? If it were odd?" For the last two cards you would ask, "Could the rule be true if the letter on the other side were a vowel? What if it were a consonant?" If the rule could be true no matter what is on the other side, you do not need to turn over the card.

If you try this approach, you will find that you *do* need to turn over the A card, because if there is an odd number on the other side, the rule is false. You do not need to turn over the K. One surprise (for some) is that you do not need to turn over the 4. Whether the letter on the other side is a vowel or a consonant, the rule could still be true. (The rule does not say anything about what should happen when there is a consonant.) A second surprise (for some) is that you *do* need to turn over the 7. There could be a vowel on the other side, and then the rule would be false.

What has interested psychologists about this problem is that it seems easy, but it is actually hard. Subjects frequently give the wrong answer, while stating (if asked) that they are sure they are correct. Why is this problem so hard? What causes the errors? A large literature has grown up around this problem, and the results seem to illustrate some interesting facts about human thinking.

The error as poor thinking

First, some evidence suggests that the error here is in part a failure to search for evidence and subgoals — in particular (1) the subgoal of determining the relevance of each card; (2) the possibility of determining the relevance of each possible result of turning over each card; and (3) the evidence from whether these results could affect the truth of the rule. In sum, the error results from insufficient search. This hypothesis is supported by the finding that performance improves if subjects are asked to consider only the last two cards, the 4 and the 7. They are more likely to choose the 7 and less likely to choose the 4. When the task is made more manageable by cutting it down, the subjects are perhaps inclined to think more thoroughly about the two remaining cards (Johnson-Laird and Wason, 1970).

In an extension of this experiment, the same researchers gave subjects the task of testing the rule, "All triangles are black." Each subject was given a stack of 15 black shapes and 15 white shapes. The subject could ask to inspect a black shape or a white shape on each trial, for up to 30 trials. After each shape was selected, the experimenter told the subject whether or not it was a triangle. It is apparent here that the black shapes are not relevant, just as the 4 is not relevant in the card problem. If a black shape is selected, the rule ("All triangles are black") could be true, whether the shape is a triangle or not.

All subjects selected all of the white shapes eventually: They realized that these shapes were indeed relevant. Also, most of the subjects *stopped* selecting black shapes (which were irrelevant) even before they found a black shape that was not a triangle. (A black shape that was not a triangle would make them realize that black shapes were irrelevant.) Very likely, the repeated trials gave the subjects a chance to think about their strategy, and they realized that black shapes were irrelevant even before they were forced to this realization. No subject ended up selecting all of the black shapes.[3]

Resistance to instruction

Although subjects can be helped, there is also considerable evidence of resistance to instruction. Possibly this resistance is a result of subjects' biased commitment to their initial answers. They ignore evidence against them because they want them to be correct. (A way to test this would be to give the instruction before the subject gives any answer; this has apparently not been tried.) For example, Wason (1977) reports an experiment in which subjects were faced with clear evidence that they had made an error, yet the subjects persisted in holding to their initial answer.

In the experiment, each card contained a circle or nothing in the middle, and a border or nothing around the edge. The rule to be evaluated was this: "Every card with a circle on it has a border around it." Subjects were shown the following four cards:

1.   Circle in middle, edge covered up
2.   No circle in middle, edge covered up
3.   Border around edge, middle covered up
4.   No border around edge, middle covered up

The question is to decide which cards must be uncovered in order to test the rule. The right answer here is cards 1 and 4. Card 4 must be looked at because the rule would be false if there were a circle. At a critical point in the experiment, the border of card 4 is uncovered, and the subject sees that the card has a circle in the middle. Here is an example of what one subject, an undergraduate taking advanced mathematics, who had chosen cards 1 and 3, said to the experimenter about her choice:

---

[3] An alternative account of the effect of cutting down the problem to two kinds of cards and of spreading it out over several trials is that these changes decrease the load on working memory. The problem as originally presented may simply be too complex to be thought about all at once. An argument against this account is that there is nothing to stop subjects from trying to overcome such memory limits by doing for themselves what the experimenters do for them, that is, thinking about cards one by one. In general, the limits imposed by working memory can be overcome by the use of more time-consuming strategies. Therefore, although performance might improve if working memory were larger, it might also improve if subjects simply thought more.

> *Experimenter*: Can you say anything about the truth or falsity of the rule
> from this card [card 4, with the cover removed, revealing a circle]?
> *Subject*: It tells me [the rule] is false.
> *E*: Are you still happy about the choice of cards you needed to see?
> *S*: Yes.
> *E*: Well, you just said this one makes it false.
> *S*: Well, it hasn't got a ... border on it, so it doesn't matter.

Several other subjects continued to deny that card 4 was relevant, even after they had admitted that it actually proved the rule false when it was uncovered. Apparently they were simply failing to use the very powerful evidence that was staring them in the face. If they were to use it, it would cause them to change their original selection.

Dual processes and rationalization

If these examples show a bias in the *use* of evidence, another set of experiments suggests a related bias in the *search* for evidence. In a series of studies carried out by Evans and his collaborators (reviewed in Evans, 1982, ch. 9), it has been found that when subjects are asked to give *reasons* for their choices of cards, the reasons given often seem to be rationalizations that they thought of afterward to explain their choices rather than true determinants of the choice. Evans has made this point dramatically by arguing that reasoning involves "dual processes," one that actually draws conclusions and another that rationalizes the conclusions after they are drawn.[4]

The best evidence for this comes from experiments in which the actual determinants of the choice of cards seem to have nothing to do with the reasons that subjects give. Instead the choices of cards seem to be determined by an elementary process of *matching* to the elements of the rule. When subjects given the following cards are asked to test the rule "If there is a B on one side, then there will be a 3 on the other side," they seem to choose the B and 3 cards simply because they are both mentioned in the rule itself.

How do we know that this is the actual determinant of the choice? One very clever way to tell is to change the rule so that it becomes "If there is a B on one side, then there will *not* be a 3 on the other." If subjects are simply matching, they will still choose the B and 3 cards. Now, however, these are the right answers. This time, the 3 card is relevant, because, if there is an A on the other side, the rule is false.

---

[4] Surely this point may be made too strongly. After all, some people do succeed in solving even the four-card problem, and many people do change their mind on the basis of reasons (evidence, goals, new possibilities). The important aspect of Evans's point is that the determinants of the conclusions we draw are, all too often, not fully rational, in terms of being sensitive to the results of a search process.

In fact, subjects tend to choose the B and 3 cards whether the rule is stated in the original, affirmative form or in the new, negative form. When they are asked to justify their answers, however, their justifications are correct only for the negative form. One subject (from Wason and Evans, 1975) who chose the 3 card justified this choice in the negative task by saying, "If there is a B on the other side, then the statement is false." This, of course, is perfectly correct. The same subject, however, immediately after doing the negative task, chose the 3 card for the affirmative task as well. Here, the justification was "If there is a B on the other side, then the statement is true." This, of course, is beside the point.

The same subject did not choose the 6 card for either rule. Again, for the negative rule, the subject gave a correct justification for not choosing the 6 card: "Any letter may be on the other side; therefore [there is] no way of knowing if the statement is true." (If only the subject had applied this argument to the 3 card!) In the affirmative condition, however, the subject justified not choosing the 6 card as follows: "If numbers are fairly random, then there may be any letter on the other side, thereby giving no indication unless the letter is B." Again, the subject could have chosen this card and justified it in the same way as the 3 card was justified for the negative rule.

In sum, subjects' justifications tend to be correct when they have chosen the correct cards, and incorrect when they have chosen the incorrect cards. Yet the justifications seem to play little role in determining the choice itself, for the choice remains much the same whether the rule is stated affirmatively or negatively. It would appear that the justification is indeed after the fact, that it is the result of a search for evidence *in favor* of a decision already made.

Content effects

Performance in the four-card task is affected by the content of the rules. (See Evans, 1982, ch. 9, for a review.) The clearest effects concern bureaucratic rules. Johnson-Laird, Legrenzi, and Legrenzi (1972) showed adult subjects in England a drawing of sealed and open stamped envelopes and asked them, "Which of the following envelopes must you examine to test the rule: If a letter is sealed, then it has a 5d stamp on it?"[5]

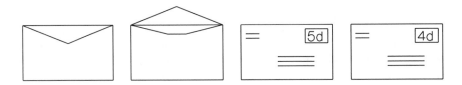

These subjects had an easy time figuring out that one had to check the closed envelope and the 4d envelope in order to test this rule. However, when Griggs and Cox (1982) attempted to replicate this experiment using college students in the United

[5]A "5d" stamp is a stamp worth 5 pence.

States, there was no difference between the envelope condition and a control condition with abstract materials (like the original four-card task described earlier). The American students were helped, however, when they were asked to imagine themselves as police officers whose job it was to test the rule "If a person is drinking beer, then the person must be over 19 years of age." In this case, most students understood that the people to check are those drinking beer (to find their age) or those 19 or under (to see whether they are drinking beer).

These results indicate that the mere concreteness of the envelope condition did not help to make the problem easier. Rather, thinking was helped either by familiarity with the actual situation, by analogy with a similar known situation, or by a general rule for reasoning about permissions (Cheng, Holyoak, Nisbett, and Oliver, 1986). Cheng and her colleagues call such a general rule a "pragmatic inference schema." It is in between a rule of formal logic and an analogy to a specific example. We may think of it as a heuristic that leads to conformity with a formal rule in a certain kind of situation.

Another possibility is that performance is helped when subjects can *understand* the rule testing. (Here I use the word "understand" in the sense discussed in Chapter 3.) When the testing of the rule has a purpose — to detect violators — subjects may understand better, and discover more easily, the arguments in favor of a certain "design" for testing the rule. One source of the difficulty of the original task may have been the subjects' lack of understanding of the task, which, in turn, resulted from the lack of a purpose, other than the arbitrary purpose provided by the experimenter.

Exercises on mental models in syllogisms
The purpose of these exercises is to help you understand the strengths and limitations of Johnson-Laird's theory as an account of your own performance in solving difficult syllogisms.

A. What conclusion can you draw from each of the following pairs of premises? Remember, the possible conclusions are:
  All A are C.
  All C are A.
  Some A are C (or, equivalently, some C are A).
  No A are C (or no C are A).
  Some C are not A.
  Some A are not C.
  No conclusion possible.
Explain how you reached your answer for each syllogism; use diagrams if you wish. Here are the syllogisms:
  1. No B are A. Some C are B.
  2. Some B are not A. Some C are B.
  3. No A are B. All B are C.
  4. No B are A. Some B are C.
  5. Some B are not A. Some B are C.

B. What form(s) did your mental models take? Do you think that it was a form that would represent "Some A are B" as different from "Some B are A" (and/or "No A are B" as different from "No B are A")?

C. On which items, if any, did you consider more than one mental model? Can you count the models you considered?

Extensions of logic

A limitation of formal logic as a normative model of thinking is that it deals only with conclusive arguments. Few of the rational conclusions that we draw in daily life can be made with such absolute certainty as the conclusion of a logical syllogism (even when we can be sure of the premises). For example, it does not follow logically, from the fact that smokers are much more likely to get lung cancer than nonsmokers, that smoking causes lung cancer, but one would be a fool to insist on a *logically* conclusive proof before concluding that smoking is dangerous to your health. If logic could be made more relevant to everyday reasoning, it would be far more useful.

Toulmin (1958) tries to account for the structure of all arguments, not just those treated by formal logic. He suggests that arguments have a basic structure (illustrated in the following diagram) that includes four basic elements: *datum, claim, warrant,* and *backing*.

For example, consider the argument "Harry was born in Bermuda. So, presumably, Harry is a British subject." The *datum* (fact) here is that Harry was born in Bermuda. The *claim* is that he is a British subject. The *warrant* here is not explicitly stated, but if it were, it would be, "A man born in Bermuda is usually a British subject." The *warrant* is the *reason why the claim follows from the datum*. Just as the claim can be introduced with "so" or "therefore," the warrant can be introduced with "since" or "because." Harry's birth bears on his citizenship *because* people born in Bermuda are usually British subjects. Finally, the *backing* is the *justification for the warrant*, the reason we accept it. Here, the backing consists of the various laws pertaining to British citizenship.

Notice that the word "presumably" had to be inserted in the argument. Toulmin calls this a *qualifier*. The qualifier indicates that there are conditions under which the conclusion does not follow. Qualifiers are necessary with certain kinds of warrants. In this case, there are various reasons why Harry might not be a British subject, even though he was born in Bermuda.

Toulmin adds a final element, the *rebuttal* (of the claim), which consists of the reasons why the claim might *not* hold. The rebuttal can be introduced with the word

Table 4.1: Some types of warrants.

Warrant type	Definition of type	Example
Meta	Based on the process of problem solving	Solving a problem requires defining the constraints of the problem.
Governmental	Based on general knowledge of the way governments function	Ministries of governments solve central problems slowly.
Logical	Based on general logical reasoning or common sense	If an approach is unsuccessful, it should be abandoned.
Psychological	Deriving from general rules of human behavior	People work harder when they are given incentives to work.
Analogical	Based on reasoning from what is known about a different system to conclusions about the target system	In Latin America, the peasants find extralegal ways to obtain money; this is probably true in the USSR.

Source: Adapted from J. F. Voss, S. W. Tyler, and L. A. Yengo, "Individual Differences in the Solving of Social Science Problems," in R. F. Dillon and R. R. Schmeck (Eds.), *Individual Differences in Cognition* (New York: Academic Press), Vol. 1, p. 213.

"unless." In the case of Harry, the rebuttal would be, "unless both of Harry's parents were aliens, or Harry became an American citizen, or ...." The rebuttal gives the reasons why the qualifier is necessary. The rebuttal is like a warrant, but it argues against the claim rather than in favor of it. Just as the warrant justifies the claim, the rebuttal justifies the qualifier. Thus, the complete structure of an argument can be diagrammed as follows:

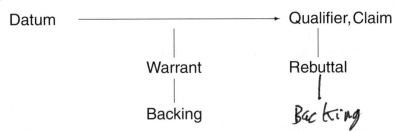

Warrants are of different types. Some warrants are specific to certain topics, such as law, science, mathematics, human behavior, or plumbing. In law, warrants can consist of laws and precedents set by previous cases. In science, they can be previous findings, analogies, and accepted laws.

Voss, Tyler, and Yengo (1983) applied Toulmin's scheme to actual reasoning in social sciences. They asked experts on the Soviet Union, and others, to discuss the problem of how to improve Soviet agriculture. Some of the kinds of warrants they discovered are listed in Table 10.1. For example, the psychological warrant about incentives might be used to justify a claim that certain Soviet workers would work harder with incentives, based on the datum that they are not now given incentives. That datum, in turn, might be a claim that was reached in a different argument. Of course, qualifiers such as "probably" or "presumably" would have to be inserted.

Formal syllogisms illustrate a kind of warrant. For example, consider a syllogism much like those discussed earlier in this chapter:

> Anne is one of Jack's sisters.
> All of Jack's sisters have red hair.
> So, Anne has red hair.

Here, the first premise ("Anne is one ...") is the datum; the second premise ("All of Jack's sisters ...") functions as the warrant; and the conclusion ("So ...") is the claim. Note that no qualification is necessary here. (There are other kinds of warrants, such as those used in mathematics, that do not require qualification.) Moreover, the claim follows by virtue of the meaning of the statements. We can paraphrase the second premise as "Any sister of Jack's can be taken to have red hair." In such cases, we can replace the "So ..." with "In other words, ..." The claim is practically a restatement of the warrant, with the particular term ("Anne") substituted for the general term ("All of Jack's sisters"). Toulmin calls this sort of syllogism _analytic,_ meaning, roughly, that the claim follows from an analysis of the premises.[6]

Note that even the syllogism just given can have different meanings, depending on the *backing* of the warrant. The backing is not stated in formal syllogisms, but it does matter. For example, the original syllogism would be valid if the backing were "Each of Jack's sisters has been checked individually and found to have red hair." Suppose, however, the backing were "All of Jack's sisters have previously been observed to have red hair." Now the syllogism is not analytic, and a qualifier is needed:

> Anne is one of Jack's sisters.
> All of Jack's sisters have red hair (a statement backed by the fact that
> they have previously been observed to have red hair).
> So, presumably, Anne has red hair (unless she dyed her hair, her hair
> turned white, etc).

The rebuttal, the reason for the qualifier, is the clause beginning with "unless."

In sum, we might say that formal logic is concerned with some of the arguments that require no qualifiers. Toulmin expands the design of logic by admitting other kinds of warrants, and he suggests a more detailed study of the various kinds of warrants used in different fields of knowledge. He wants to know what acceptable warrants have in common across fields and how they differ from field to field.

---

[6]The term "analytic" is usually contrasted with "synthetic," but Toulmin prefers the term "substantive" as a contrast.

Now let us see if we can restate Toulmin's design in terms of the search-inference theory. Toulmin's *datum* clearly corresponds to a *piece of evidence*. When possibilities are suggested by evidence, we can say that a *claim corresponds to a possibility*. If no qualifier is required, the evidence is sufficient to make that possibility acceptable, and thinking can stop right there. If qualifiers are required, other evidence and other possibilities can be considered. When possibilities are already present, evidence may strengthen them or weaken them through the same kind of warrant.

Toulmin thus calls attention to the need for warrant in informal reasoning. When somebody says, "The weather forecast said it will rain, so, presumably, it will snow," the statement sounds odd because it is difficult to imagine a warrant that connects the datum (the forecast) and the claim (snow). Likewise, in thinking, the effect of a piece of evidence on a possibility depends on a warrant.

The search-inference framework goes beyond Toulmin in that it describes thinking as involving (typically) more than one possibility. Toulmin can incorporate other possibilities only as rebuttals. If we are trying to determine Harry's citizenship, for example, evidence that he was born in Bermuda does support the possibility that he is British. A thorough thought process would, however, consider other possibilities, such as United States or Canadian citizenship, and other evidence, such as the fact that he has a Texas accent. Rather than making rebuttals part of the basic argument, we might think of alternative possibilities as the general rebuttal, "unless some other possibility is better."

Moreover, the view of thinking as selecting among possibilities for certain purposes or goals calls attention to the fact that the usefulness of warrants depends on goals. The datum that a Cadillac is heavier than most cars does not imply that I ought to buy one if my only goal is fuel economy, but it does if my only goal is safety. Although Toulmin's approach is sensitive to this role of goals, it is limited in being concerned only with inference, not with search.

Conclusion

Formal logic, by its very nature, is not a complete theory of thinking. Because logic covers only inference, it cannot help us to understand errors that result from insufficient search. When we treat logic problems as examples of problems in general, however, they do serve as good illustrations of the effects of certain types of poor thinking: the failure to consider alternatives to an initial conclusion or model and the failure to seek counterevidence.

The theories of everyday reasoning that best describe human inferences are those that are most consistent with the search-inference framework. These theories allow that good inferences do not have to be certain and can admit qualification. Once the idea of uncertainty is admitted, the "goodness" of an argument depends on the relative weight of arguments for and against a possible conclusion and on the relative support that the evidence gives to this possibility as opposed to others. The theories of inference discussed later in this book all take this view.

Part II

PROBABILITY AND BELIEF

Practically all thinking involves beliefs in some way. We make decisions on the basis of beliefs about the outcomes of each option. If I want to drive to the city, I choose my route according to my beliefs about speed and safety. When we think about the strengths of our goals, such as the relative importance of speed and safety, we do this as well on the basis of beliefs, for example, beliefs about what it would feel like to have an automobile accident. Beliefs themselves can be the objects of thought. I can think about how much the construction on the expressway is likely to slow me down, given that it is Saturday afternoon. (Is there a sports event in town?)

Part II explores three major approaches to the analysis of belief formation: probability theory, the theory of hypothesis testing, and the theory of correlation. It concludes with a chapter on biases in belief formation in general.

Probability theory (Chapter 5) is a normative theory for evaluating numerically the strengths of our beliefs in various propositions. Like logic, it is a theory of inference, but unlike logic, it concerns degrees of belief rather than certainty. In Chapter 6, we shall see that our belief strengths, as manifest in our judgments of probability, violate this normative model seriously. It is not just that our numbers are not exactly correct. They are often systematically out of order. We believe that one event is more likely than another when the rest of our beliefs imply the opposite. We can take steps to guard against these violations. Actively open-minded thinking can help. When probability judgments are very important, computers can help us as well.

The theory of hypothesis testing (Chapter 7) concerns the selection of evidence: asking the right question to find out how much to believe some hypothesis. If we ask questions well, we can make inferences from their answers that bring our beliefs into line with the available evidence as efficiently as possible. Scientists try to do this when they design experiments, and physicians try to do it when they order tests. Again, we shall find certain biases that cause us to depart from the normative model. Some of these biases can be ameliorated by actively open-minded thinking, especially by considering other hypotheses than those we favor.

Chapter 8 deals with beliefs that concern the correlation between two variables. We tend to perceive data as showing correlations when we already believe that we will find a correlation. Chapter 9 shows that this distorting effect of prior belief occurs throughout our thinking, and the chapter also explores the causes of this bias and the conditions under which it occurs. The existence of this bias is the main justification for my claim that we need to remind ourselves to be open to new beliefs and evidence against our old ones: Our natural tendency is often the opposite.

Chapter 5

Normative theory of probability

O fortune
Like the moon
Everchanging
Rising first
Then declining;
Hateful life
Treats us badly
Then with kindness
Making sport with our desires,
Causing power
And poverty alike
To melt like ice.

Translation of anonymous twelfth- or thirteenth-century Latin
lyric, set to music by Carl Orff, to begin *Carmina Burana*,
completed in 1936.

Our theory of thinking is intended to help us choose among actions and beliefs. Making such choices obviously often involves estimating the likelihood that various events will occur in the future. Will it rain tomorrow? Will I get the job I applied for? Probability theory is a well-established normative theory that deals with such estimates.

The ancient Egyptians played games of chance that involved calculation of probabilities, but the development of modern probability theory began only in the seventeenth century (Hacking, 1975). In part, this development was inspired by the practice of town governments raising money by selling annuities. Miscalculation of the chances of living to various ages left some towns bankrupt. One person who helped solve the problem of how to figure the price of annuities so that the seller makes a profit was Edmund Halley (also famous for discovering the comet that bears

93

his name and for persuading his friend Isaac Newton to publish his work on planetary orbits).

Also in the seventeenth century, Blaise Pascal and others recognized that probability theory was relevant to everyday beliefs and decisions, not just to games of chance and other repeated events. Our interest in probability derives from this fact. I must point out, however, that the idea that probability is relevant to everyday beliefs is one view among others. We shall discuss these other views later in this chapter.

We shall think of *probability* here as *a numerical measure of the strength of a belief in a certain proposition* – for example, the belief that it will rain today or the belief that my sore throat is due to streptococcus. (A "proposition" is a statement that can be true or false. Propositions can concern future events, but they can concern present states or past events as well.) By convention, probability ranges from 0 to 1, where 0 means that the belief in question is certainly false — it will not rain — and 1 means that it is certainly true — it will rain. A probability of .5 means that it is equally likely to rain or not rain. Probability can also be expressed as a percentage, a fraction, or as an *odds* ratio — the ratio of the probability of a proposition being true to the probability of its being false. A probability of .75 is the same as 75%, or 3/4, or 3 to 1 odds — because the probability of the proposition's being true (.75) is three times its probability of being false (.25).

We shall use the term *probability judgment* to indicate the assignment of a number to a belief.[1] The process of probability judgment includes evaluation of the evidence relevant to the belief in question, if any such evaluation occurs. When I judge the probability that the Democrats will win the next U.S. presidential election, I engage in a process of search and inference before I assign the number. If, however, I have just gone through that process, I can assign a number to the resulting belief with no further thinking about the issue itself.

The mathematical theory of probability is a normative theory of inference. It specifies how the probability of one belief should depend on the probabilities of other beliefs that serve as evidence for or against the first belief. If the probability that it will rain is .8, then the probability that it will not rain has to be .2. If the probability of precipitation is .8 and the probability of all forms of precipitation other than rain is .3, then the probability of rain is .8 − .3, or .5. We shall see that a few simple rules determine the relation between the probability of one belief and the probabilities of other, related beliefs.

Part of our interest in the normative theory of belief stems from the role of belief in decision making. The strength of our beliefs in various consequences of our actions is and should be an important determinant of our decisions. Our belief about the probability of a certain kind of accident will determine what safety precautions we take or what kind of insurance we purchase. In Chapter 10 we shall see how probabilities can be incorporated into the theory of decision making.

Although probability judgments are useful for making decisions, they concern

---

[1] Other authors sometimes use the terms "probability assessment" and "probability assignment" for the same process.

belief only, allowing the users of such judgments to attend to the goals they have at the time. A weather forecaster tells us the probability of rain, rather than giving us direct advice about whether to carry an umbrella, because our goals may differ. Some of us care more about getting wet than others. Similarly, an individual may make probability judgments at one time without knowing what goals and options will be present later, when the judgments are used.

What is the relation between this theory and everyday thinking? First, bear in mind that probability theory is a *normative* model, not necessarily a prescriptive one. That is, it is a standard by which we can evaluate the relationships among our beliefs, but it is not necessarily something we should *try* to follow.

How can we apply this standard? Our beliefs do not come with numbers assigned to them, so we cannot simply read off the numbers to determine whether they follow the theory. One way of applying the standard is to ask whether we can *assign* probabilities to beliefs in a way that follows the rules. All of our beliefs are held with various degrees of certainty. Some (such as my belief that $2 + 2 = 4$) are, for all practical purposes, absolutely certain. Others (such as my belief that every even positive integer is the sum of two primes, or my belief that the Democrats will win the next election) are less than completely certain. Suppose we can compare our beliefs in degree of certainty. For any two beliefs, we can say which is more certain. If we can do this, then we can assign numerical probabilities to the beliefs. We could do this in many different ways, except that we would have to assign 1 to beliefs that were certain to be true and 0 to beliefs that were certain to be false, and we would have to make sure that we assign higher numbers to beliefs that were held with greater certainty. To determine whether a set of beliefs meet the normative standard, we could ask whether there is *any* way of assigning numbers to them so that the rules of probability theory are followed. We shall see that this cannot be done in some cases.

Another way to determine whether a set of beliefs conforms to the model is to use actual numbers. We can give people numerical probabilities and ask them to make inferences from them about other numerical probabilities, as we did in the problem concerning six-children families at the beginning of Chapter 2. (We assumed there that the probability that the next child born will be a boy was .5.) In doing experiments of this sort, we cannot always assume that people know how to assign probabilities to their beliefs in the best way. Sometimes we can set up the experiments so that our conclusions do not depend on this assumption. In other cases, we are interested in people's understanding of the normative theory itself, or in their ability to translate their beliefs into probabilities that are useful to others.

The ability to express beliefs numerically is a useful one when decisions are made by people who draw on the expertise of others. If you are trying to decide whether to undergo a surgical procedure, you might ask your surgeon how likely it is that the procedure will succeed. Likewise, military leaders can ask their intelligence officers about the likelihood of success of an attack, and political leaders can ask the same question about a peace initiative. In many such cases, information is provided verbally ("very likely"), but numerical probabilities are also used sometimes. Weather forecasters — the experts we rely on when we make our own decisions about umbrellas and outings — use numerical probabilities routinely ("30% chance of snow").

In sum, we can study numerical probabilities for three reasons. First, they can tell us about the rationality of belief — its conformity to a normative model — as long as we are careful not to assume that our subjects know how to assign numbers in a way that comes closest to the normative model. Second, we can study people's understanding of the normative model itself. Such an understanding can be useful to people who want to think carefully about the relationships among certain sets of their beliefs, such as physicians trying to diagnose a disease. Third, because probabilities are used to communicate belief strengths, we can study the accuracy of communication.

What is probability?

At the outset, one might ask whether probability judgments are really "judgments" at all. Aren't they much more objective than that? Crapshooters who know that the probability of snake eyes is $1/36$ are not making a judgment; they are using the result of a mathematical calculation. Surely the weather forecaster and the surgeon are doing something like that too — or are they? How do we tell whether a probability judgment is correct? Is there an objective standard?

The question of what it means to say that a probability statement is "correct" has been the subject of competing theories, and the disagreement continues today. I would like to begin this discussion by doing some reflective thinking about the three major theories that bear on this issue (see Savage, 1954; Hacking, 1975; von Winterfeldt & Edwards, 1986).

The question of when probability statements are correct has two sub-questions: (1) How should we *make* or *construct* well-justified probability judgments? For example, when is a surgeon justified in saying that an operation has a .90 probability of success? (2) How should we *evaluate* such judgments after we know the truth of the matter? For example, how would we evaluate the surgeon's probability judgment if the operation succeeds, or if it fails?

These are not the same question. I may be well justified in saying that a substance is water if I have observed that the substance is odorless and colorless, with a boiling point of 212 degrees Fahrenheit and a freezing point of 32 degrees Fahrenheit. I would find that I had been wrong in hindsight, however, if the chemical formula of the substance turned out to be XYZ rather than H_2O (Putnam, 1975). In the case of water, we accept the chemical formula as the ultimate criterion of correctness, the ultimate evaluation of statements about what is water and what is not. We would still consider people to be well justified if they judged the substance to be water on the basis of its properties alone, even if our evaluation later showed that their judgment had been incorrect.

We shall discuss three theories. The first says that probability statements are about *frequencies*, the second says that they are about *logical possibilities*, and the third says that they are *personal judgments.* The frequency theory gives the same answer to the construction question as to the evaluation question, and so does the logical theory. The personal theory gives different answers.

The frequency theory

According to the frequency theory, probability is a measure of the relative frequency of particular events. By the simplest, most literal form of this theory, the probability of a smoker's getting lung cancer is simply the proportion of smokers who have gotten lung cancer in the past. According to this theory, unless a probability statement is based on such a proportion, it is meaningless and should not be made. If a probability statement differs from the observed relative frequency, it is unjustified and incorrect.

This theory runs into trouble right away. It would certainly make life difficult for weather forecasters. What could they possibly mean when they say that the probability of rain is 50%? They might mean "On days like today, it has rained 50% of the time in the past," but obviously they do not really mean this. Besides, if they did, they would have the problem of saying in what way the days they had considered were "like today." If these days were like today in being December 17, 1993, then there is only one such day, and the probability of rain would either be 1 or 0, and we will not know which it is until today is over or until it rains (whichever comes first). If those other days were like today in being December 17, regardless of the year, a simple record of past years would suffice for forecasting, and we could save a lot of money on satellites and weather stations. If those other days were like today in the precise configuration of air masses, then, once again, there probably were not any such days except today. The problem is thus that any event can be classified in many different ways. The relative frequency of the event, compared to other events in a certain class, depends on how it is classified.

The true frequency theorist might agree that weather forecasters are being non-sensical when they give probability judgments. But the problems of the theory do not end here. Suppose I flip a coin, and it comes up heads 7 out of 10 times — not an unusual occurrence. What is the probability of heads on the next flip? The simple frequency view would have it that the probability is .7, yet most of us would hold that the probability is .5, because there is no reason to think that the probabilities of heads and tails are different unless we have some reason to think that the coin is biased. The simple frequency view flies in the face of strong intuitions. That by itself is not reason to give it up, but it surely is reason to look seriously at some of the alternatives.

Some have attempted to save the frequency view from this last objection by modifying it. They would argue that probability is not just the observed frequency, but rather the limit that the observed frequency would approach if the event were repeated over and over. This seems to take care of the coin example. We think that the probability of heads is .5 because we believe that if we continued to flip the coin over and over, the proportion of heads would come closer and closer to .5.

Why do we believe this, though? We have not actually observed it. This approach already gives considerable ground to the view that probability is a judgment, not simply a calculation of a proportion. Moreover, this view does not deal with the weather-forecasting example. Most of us intuitively understand what the forecaster is trying to do. A theory of probability that disallows this activity is a strange theory indeed, and once again we are compelled to look for alternatives.[2]

The logical theory

The logical theory of probability is the theory usually assumed in most introductory treatments of probability, especially with respect to card games and dice. The theory is useful when we can define a set of logically equivalent, or *exchangeable*, propositions. The evidence for each of these propositions is the same, and any two of them can be exchanged without affecting our beliefs in their truth, so their probabilities must be the same. Typically, when we make calculations in card games, we regard every card remaining in a deck as equally likely to be drawn, because the only evidence we have for any particular card is simply that it is somewhere in the deck and we have exactly this evidence for each of the cards.

The logical theory reached fruition in the work of a philosopher, Rudolph Carnap (1950). Very roughly, his idea is that the probability of proposition x is the proportion of exchangeable "possible worlds" in which x is true. In theory, one can list all of the possible worlds by taking every combination of the truth and falsity of all of the "atomic propositions," those propositions that can be true or false but cannot be expressed in terms of other propositions. The idea of possible worlds is used to justify the conventions of probability for exchangeable events. For example, the set of possible worlds in which I draw an ace from a deck of cards is exchangeable with the set of all possible worlds in which I draw a king.

Suppose I flip three coins. We generally think of the three flips as exchangeable, because we think that the order does not matter, and we think that the names we give to the coins do not matter either. There are eight compound events (three-flip units) that can be made up of these basic, exchangeable propositions: HHH (heads, heads, heads), THH (tails, heads, heads), HTH, HHT, TTH, THT, HTT, and TTT. In half of these compound events, the first coin comes up heads; hence, the probability of this event is $1/2$. In $1/4$ of these worlds, the first two coins come up heads; hence the probability of both of these events is $1/4$, and so on. Of course, each of these events corresponds to an infinite set of atomic possible worlds.

Like the frequency view, the logical view holds that probability is objective — that is, it is something that can be known. When two individuals give different probability judgments, at most one can be correct. As in logic, once the premises are

[2]Another, more subtle, argument (from Hacking, 1965) against this view is that some sequences may have no limit. Consider the sequence HTTHHHHTTTTTT .... In this sequence, H is followed by enough T's so that there are $2/3$ T's, then T is followed by enough H's so that there are $2/3$ H's, and so on, alternating. If you were dropped into the middle of the sequence somewhere, it would be reasonable to think that your chance of landing on a T would be .5, yet this sequence has no limit.

accepted, the conclusion follows. The assumptions here concern exchangeability.

An advantage of the logical view is that it solves the problem raised by the coin. It explains quite well why we believe that the probability of a coin's coming up heads is 1/2.

A disadvantage is that it is usually impossible to find exchangeable events. I cannot sensibly enumerate equally likely possibilities in order to calculate the probability of rain tomorrow, in the way that I would enumerate the possible poker hands in order to calculate the probability of a flush. Therefore, like the frequency theory, the logical theory renders many everyday uses of probability nonsensical. When I want to evaluate my physician's judgment of the probability that I have strep throat, it does not help to ask about the proportion of possible worlds in which I would have it. Likewise, the logical view is ordinarily useless as a justification for making probability judgments, except in textbook (or casino) cases of "fair" (perfectly unbiased) coins and roulette wheels.

The personal theory

The personal view of probability differs from the others in seeing probability as a personal judgment of the likelihood of a proposition or event rather than an objective fact (Savage, 1954). By this view, a probability judgment can be based on any of one's beliefs and knowledge, including knowledge about frequencies or about the set of logical possibilities, but including other knowledge as well. Different people have different beliefs and knowledge, so two reasonable people might differ in their probability judgments. Thus, a physician may be justified in saying that a particular smoker has a .20 probability of getting lung cancer, even though the relative frequency of lung cancer among smokers is .40. The patient in question might, for example, have lungs that look healthy on an X-ray film. Some other physician might be justified in saying that the probability was .30. Even if two people both had all of the relevant beliefs and knowledge for a given case, their judgments might still differ, although, as we shall see, we would not expect their judgments to differ by much.

The personal view makes the important distinction between the well-justified construction of probability judgments and their evaluation. The constructive part of the theory provides a normative theory (and in some cases a prescriptive theory) for our *thinking* about probability judgments. Probability judgments are not simply waiting in our heads to be pulled out when needed. Good thinking about probability judgments can help us both with forming beliefs consistent with our evidence and with assigning numerical probabilities to those beliefs.

The evaluation of probability judgments becomes more difficult when we accept the personal view. According to the other theories, a probability judgment can be evaluated in terms of frequencies or exchangeable events. By the personal theory, it is possible for one judge to be better than another, even if both make well-justified judgments. We need a way of assessing a judge's track record. (We shall find one, later in this chapter.)

The main advantage of the personal view is that it applies more widely. It allows us to make probability judgments about anything, even unique events such as who will win the next United States presidential election. It therefore allows us to use our feelings that certain propositions are more likely to be true than others, even though we cannot justify these feelings in terms of relative frequencies or exchangeable events.

An apparent disadvantage of the personal view is that with this theory we have difficulty explaining why we ought to pay attention to knowledge of frequencies (for example, of the occurrence of diseases). If 40% of the last 10 million smokers have developed lung cancer, it seems wrong to believe that a particular, randomly selected smoker in this group has a 2% probability of developing lung cancer. Later, in the section on Bayes's theorem, we shall explore the reasons why the personal view does require us to attend to relative frequencies, even if we are not ruled by them.

Personalists take seriously the idea that probability judgments are always possible, even when one does not know anything about frequencies or exchangeable events. In some cases, personalists must appeal to the *principle of insufficient reason*: If there is no reason to expect one event to be more likely than another, then we should consider the two events to be equally likely. If a shuffled deck of cards is placed before us, we have no reason to believe that any particular card is more likely to be drawn than another, so we must assign a probability of $1/52$ to each card. This principle essentially incorporates the logical view (when it applies) into the personal view: If we have no reason to believe one proposition more than another, the events should be treated as exchangeable.

The principle of insufficient reason is controversial. The problem is that it can lead to different probability judgments, depending on how we define a "proposition" or an "event." Suppose you come into my laboratory, and I show you an opaque urn full of marbles. I ask you the probability that the next marble I draw from the urn will be black. You might reason that (given the usual colors for marbles) each marble is either black or not black and that you have no reason to favor one or the other, so the probability must be $1/2$. Or you might reason that each marble is either black, white, gray, red, orange, yellow, green, blue, indigo, or violet, and, again, you have no reason to favor one or the other of these, so the probability of black is $1/10$.

The personalist can make two different replies to this problem. One is that probability, like logic, is dependent on the assumptions one makes. The two lines of reasoning just described make different assumptions about what the possible events are. Probability judgments can yield different results for different assumptions. One must choose one's assumptions carefully and then regard one's conclusions as subject to change if the assumptions change.

The second reply is that we never really need to make probability judgments from this sort of ignorance. When you come into my laboratory, you actually know a fair amount about marbles. You have seen a lot of them, and you have some idea of the variety of colors. You also know something about psychologists and how likely they are to try to pull some trick on their subjects. You can put all of this knowledge together to make an informed judgment of the probability that the marble will be black. (I would guess about 1/4, because I think black marbles are more common than other colors and that psychologists are far less likely to pull tricks than is commonly assumed.)

These replies do not settle the issue, which is one of great current interest. Many have felt that the real solution to the problem is to invent new theories of probability (for example, Shafer, 1976; Shafer and Tversky, 1985). The replies do allow us to proceed on the assumption that the personal view is at least a reasonable one.

In general, then, the personal view takes both relative frequency and logical analysis to be useful in the construction of probability judgments, but it allows us to consider other factors as well, such as our understanding of how things work and our judgment of the extent to which frequency data are relevant. Because of this more liberal attitude toward the basis or justification of probability judgments, this theory offers no single, simple method for well-justified construction of probability judgments, as each of the other theories does. Many different methods can be well justified.

The personal theory makes a clear distinction between the well-justified construction of probability judgments and their evaluation. The basis of this distinction is that complete evaluation can be done only after we know which propositions are true (or which events occurred). This after-the-fact evaluation tells us which of the many well-justified methods for constructing probability judgments work best.

What of the view that probability statements are objective? We do speak of them that way. We can say, "I thought that the probability of a major earthquake in California next year was 5%, but now I know that it is really 10%." What could we mean? According to the frequency and logical theories, we cannot mean much. (By these theories, though, it would make sense to say: "I thought that the probability of tossing three heads in three tries was 1/4, but now I know that it is 1/8.") According to the personal theory, saying "I know the probability is 10%" is really a shorthand for saying, "I have now constructed my probability judgment based on what I take to be the best evidence." For example, I have heard that this is what the experts say. But someone who had another good method for estimating probability might "know" that the probability is 12%. Such judgments remain personal.

Does true probability exist? According to the personal theory, the only true probabilities are 0 and 1. A proposition is ultimately true or false; an event will happen or not. It is (technically) meaningless for a forecaster to say, "The probability of rain is between .4 and .6." It will rain or not. The forecaster's statement is at best an expression of reluctance to put a number on her own degree of belief.

There is, though, a way of expressing the idea of true probability in Bayesian terms (Brown, 1993). Suppose that the forecaster has a standard way of proceeding in making a forecast, and she hasn't finished yet. She has looked at the radar and the satellite photos, but she has not yet looked at the output of the two computer models that she usually consults. Her statement could then refer to the degree of belief that she will have after she gets the standard data. It is a prediction of her own judgment, and its possible range. This kind of analysis makes even more sense when the standard data are statistical. For example, it would make sense to say "The probability of winning the point if you get the first serve in, in a grand slam tournament, is between .6 and .8." You would say this before you looked up the numbers. As we shall see later, the numbers need not dictate your final belief about the probability, but they have a way of narrowing it down pretty sharply. Notice, though, that such judgments could change even if all that "standard" data are available. If we learn that the player in question has a very powerful first serve, then we would raise our probability. If we learn that he has a sore shoulder, we would lower it.

In sum, we can, within the personal theory, assign a meaning to "true probability" so that it is something other than 0 or 1, and so that we can talk about its range. But we can do this only with respect to some assumption about what the standard data are.

Constructing probability judgments

According to the frequency theory and the logical theory, probability statements are reflections of objective facts in the world. According to the personal view, probability statements are judgments, and probability judgments need to be constructed by appropriate methods.

Probability as willingness to bet

What should we be trying to do when we make a probability judgment? Many theorists have argued that we should think about our personal willingness to bet that the proposition in question is true. Surely, the probability of a proposition should be one of the determinants of our willingness to act as though the proposition were true — to "bet on it" (see Chapter 10). In addition, the idea that probability can be defined in terms of a tendency to take action ties the concept of probability closely to observable behavior. However, the idea that probability judgments can be constructed by thinking about our willingness to bet has drawbacks.

Ramsey (1931) argued that if we believe that the probability of an event is .5, this amounts to saying that we are equally willing to bet on the event's happening as on it not happening. To take a more complicated case, suppose I value $3 three times as much as I value $1. Suppose you ask me the probability that it will rain tomorrow, and I say that I would be willing to bet, at 3-to-1 odds, that it will. This means that I would be willing to accept $1 if it does rain, on condition that I would pay $3 if it does not. Moreover, I would be just as willing to do the opposite, to pay $1 if it rains or accept $3 if it does not. According to the betting interpretation of probability, this means that my subjective probability of rain is .75. I would regard it as three times as likely to rain (.75) as not to rain (.25).

Over a long series of making such bets, based on this same degree of belief, I would come out even, winning and losing the same amounts, if my judgments corresponded to the relative frequencies of the events. If I collect $1 every time the .75-probability event happens and pay $3 every time the .25-probability event happens, then, out of 100 events, I will collect about $75 for the more frequent event and pay out about $75 (25 times $3) for the less frequent event. This fact may help to make clear the use of the concept of betting in the measurement of probability. In sum, by this view, the way to construct personal probability judgments is to ask ourselves what odds we would consider fair. (We shall return to the connection between the personal view and relative frequencies.)

It is not clear that thinking about bets is the best way to elicit probability judgments (Shafer, 1981). We think about probabilities, and, more generally, the strengths of our beliefs, because our probability judgments help us to make decisions. We often do not know what decision to make until we think about the strengths of our beliefs about the consequences of the various options before us. We cannot consult our decisions to determine what we believe, because we need to know what we believe in order to make our decisions.

Comparison with a chance setup

The idea of betting, however, can be useful in the task of explaining to judges (for example, experts) what their task is when we ask them to make probability judgments. We need not use anything as difficult to think about as betting odds. Instead, we can ask judges to compare the situation to some sort of device with known probabilities, what Hacking (1965) calls a *chance setup*, such as an honest roulette wheel or a game with a "spinner" (a pointer that spins). For example, suppose I want to assess my probability judgment, made in 1993, that a Republican would win the U.S. presidency in 1996. Instead of thinking about what sort of odds I would be willing to take in a bet, I might simply imagine a spinner, like the one shown here:

I might ask myself which is more likely: that a Republican will win or that the point of the spinner will land in the shaded part of the circle. I adjust the size of the shaded part until I am unable to say which is more likely. My probability judgment, when I have finished this adjustment, is the size of the shaded part (as a proportion of the whole). In practice, it would be a good idea to try this several times, sometimes starting with a small area and adjusting upward, sometimes starting with a large area and adjusting downward. Such techniques as this are used routinely in the formal analysis of decisions (Chapter 10).

The chance-setup approach to probability assessment is consistent with the gambling approach. If I thought that the point of the spinner was more likely to land on the shaded part, I would be more willing to bet on that outcome. If I thought that it was less likely to land there, I would rather bet that a Republican would become president than that the point of the spinner would land on the shaded part. Although this approach helps judges understand the significance of probability judgments for action, it is important that they also understand the fact that they can construct their probability judgments by thinking about the evidence for their beliefs rather than by thinking about what choice they are inclined to make before they think about the evidence at all.

Well-justified probability judgments

Are there rules or constraints that will help in constructing probability judgments? If there are, these rules may serve as reasons we can give for our judgments, when we are asked to justify them, as well as methods for constructing them.

Surely some of these rules have to do with the use of evidence, part of the search-inference process. If you have more evidence for x than for y, you should assign a higher probability to x. If you get additional evidence for x, your probability judgment for x should increase. In probability theory to date, little has been said about such rules.

Other constraints on probability judgments have to do with the need for *coherence* among judgments concerning various propositions. This means that our probability judgments must obey the rules of probability *as a mathematical system*. Related judgments must "cohere" according to these rules. The basic rules that define the concept of coherence are the following:

- It is certain that any proposition will be either true or false. Hence, the probability of a proposition's being true, plus the probability of its being false (called the probability of the *complement* of the proposition), must equal 1. A probability of 1 represents certainty.

- Two propositions, A and B, are *mutually exclusive* if they cannot both be true at the same time. If you believe that A and B are mutually exclusive, then $p(A) + p(B) = p(A \text{ or } B)$: That is, the probability of the proposition "either A or B" is the sum of the two individual probabilities. If we assume that "It will rain" and "It will snow" are mutually exclusive propositions (that is, it cannot both rain and snow), then the probability of the proposition "It will rain or it will snow" is the sum of the probability of rain and the probability of snow. This rule is called *additivity*.

- The *conditional probability of proposition A given proposition B* is the probability that we would assign to A if we knew that B were true, that is, the probability of A conditional on B being true. We write this as $p(A/B)$. (Note that the slash means "given," not "divided by.") For example, $p(\text{king/face card}) = 1/3$ for an ordinary deck of cards (in which the face cards are king, queen, and jack).

- The *multiplication rule* says that $p(A \& B) = p(A/B) \cdot p(B)$. Here $A \& B$ means "both A and B are true." For example, if the probability of a person being female is .5 and the probability of a female's being over 6 feet tall is .02, then the probability of being a female over 6 feet tall is p(tall & female) = p(tall/female) $\cdot$ p(female) = (.02) $\cdot$ (.5) = .01. Or, p(king & face card) = p(king/face card) $\cdot$ p(face card) = $(1/3) \cdot (3/13) = 1/13$. This is a special case, because a king must be a face card.

- In a special case, A and B are *independent*. Two propositions are independent for you if you judge that learning about the truth or falsity of one of them will not change your probability of the other one. For example, learning that a card is red will not change my probability that it is a king. In this case, we can say that $p(A/B) = p(A)$, since learning about B does not change our probability for A. The multiplication rule for independent propositions is thus $p(A \& B) = p(A) \cdot p(B)$, simply the product of the two probabilities. For example, p(king & red) = p(king) $\cdot$ p(red) = $(1/13) \cdot (1/2) = 1/26$.

Such rules put limits on the probability judgments that are justifiable. For example, it is unjustifiable to believe that the probability of rain is .2, the probability of snow is .3, and the probability of rain *or* snow is .8. If we make many different judgments at one time, or if our past judgments constrain our present judgments, these constraints can be very strong. As a rule, however, these constraints do not determine a *unique* probability for any proposition. Reasonable people with exactly the same evidence can still disagree.

In practice, the constraints can be useful in checking probability estimates. You can often estimate probabilities in different ways, and then use these rules to check them. If you think that the probability of precipitation other than rain and snow is zero, and if you judge the probabilities of rain as .2, snow as .3, and precipitation as .8, then you know your judgments disagree, and you can use this fact to adjust them.

One consequence of rules 1 and 2 is that the probability of mutually exclusive and exhaustive propositions must add up to 1. ("Exhaustive" means that the propositions considered are the only possible ones.) Psychological research has shown that people can easily be induced to violate this rule. Robinson and Hastie (1985) asked subjects to read mystery stories. At several points in the stories, evidence was revealed that implicated or ruled out one character or another as guilty of the crime. At each point, subjects were asked to indicate the probability that each of the characters was guilty. The probabilities assigned to the different subjects added up to about 2 for most subjects, unless the subjects were explicitly instructed to check the probabilities to make sure that they added up only to 1. When one character was ruled out, the probabilities for the others were not usually raised so as to compensate, and when a clue implicated a particular suspect, the probabilities assigned to the others were not usually lowered. (Later, we shall see many other violations of the rules.)

The rules of coherence can help us to construct probability judgments by giving us a way to check them. To return to the mystery, for example, if we regard the probability that the butler did it as .2, the neighbor as .3, and the parson as .8, we know, from the fact that the figures add up to more than 1, that something is wrong (unless the parson *is* the neighbor) and that we have reason to think again about the relation between these numbers and the evidence we have for the propositions in question. (Of course, coherence alone cannot tell us which numbers we ought to adjust.) The rules can also help us to decide which of two probability judgments is better justified, by examining the consistency of each of the judgments with other judgments.

Although the coherence requirement plays an important role in the construction of probability judgments, it is still reasonable to ask how such judgments should be related to the evidence we have for them. If, in terms of the search-inference framework, we think of probability judgments as "strengths" assigned to "possibilities," we can ask how these strengths ought to be dependent on the weight of the evidence. As yet, little has been said about this, although the work of Collins and Michalski (1989, summarized in Chapter 4) provides one approach.

Evaluating probability judgments

Let us turn now to the question of how probability judgments are to be evaluated, according to the personal theory. First, the criteria for well-justified construction, particularly coherence, can be used for evaluation as well. If a person's probability judgments are not coherent, for example, they cannot all be correct. At least one of them must be incorrect. There are two additional criteria that may be applied after the truth is known — that is, after it is known whether the event in question occurred or not: calibration and scoring rules.

Calibration

Suppose that I am a weather forecaster. On several different days, I say that there is a 75% probability of rain that day. On some of those days it does rain, and on some it does not. If my probability judgments are *well calibrated*, the proportion of these days on which it rains should be 75%, over the long run. It should also rain on 100% of the days for which I say there is a 100% probability, 50% of the days for which I say there is a 50% probability, and so forth. If my judgments are perfectly calibrated, in the long run, these kinds of proportions will match exactly.

Note that my judgments can be coherent without being calibrated. For example, I can say that the probability of heads is .90 and the probability of tails is .10. These two are consistent with each other, but not with the facts. If my judgments are perfectly calibrated, however, they must also be coherent, for whenever I say that the probability of rain is 75%, I must also say that the probability of no rain is 25%.

Good calibration helps in making decisions. If the weather forecast is so poorly calibrated that the probability of rain is really 1.00 when the forecast says .25, I will get wet, if I regard .25 as low enough so as not to require an umbrella.

Calibration is a *criterion for evaluation* of probability judgments, not a method for making them. Calibration serves as a criterion in hindsight, after we know what happened. In principle, calibration could be assessed for judgments based on frequencies or on the logical view, but this would be superfluous. If the assumptions going into the judgments were correct, calibration would have to be perfect, and we would know what the probability judgments were without asking a judge.

It may seem that calibration is related to the frequency view of probability. In a way it is. Calibration certainly captures the idea that we want our probability judgments to correspond to something about the real world, which is perhaps the major idea behind the frequency view. By the personal view, however, a judgment can be justifiable even before the frequency data are in. For the frequency view, the judgment is meaningless unless the data are in. In addition, a personalist would argue that calibration, though always desirable, is often impossible to assess. When someone predicts the probability of a nuclear-power plant explosion, there are simply not enough data to assess calibration.[3]

Scoring rules

We encounter certain problems in using coherence and calibration to evaluate probability judgments. Coherence does not take into account what actually happens. A judge can make completely coherent judgments and still get all of the probabilities exactly backward. (When such a judge said .80, the observed probability was .20; when the judge said 1.00, the event never happened.) Moreover, the idea of calibration does not tell us how to measure *degree* of miscalibration. A set of probability judgments is either calibrated or not; however, degrees of error surely make a difference.

More important, calibration ignores the *information* provided by a judgment. A weather forecaster's predictions would be perfectly calibrated if they stated that the probability of rain was .30 every day, provided that it does actually rain on 30% of the days. Such a forecast would also be coherent if the forecaster added that the probability of no rain was .70. These forecasts would be useless, however, because they do not distinguish days when it rains from days when it does not rain.

Is there some way of assigning a single score to a set of probability judgments, indicating everything we want to know about the accuracy of the judgments in the set? If we had such a measure, we could use it to compare the effectiveness of different judges or methods in specific situations, such as weather forecasting or medical diagnosis. As yet, nobody has discovered a uniquely best measure. Part of the field of mathematical probability, however, is concerned with the design of *scoring rules*, which are essentially formulas for evaluating the overall accuracy of a set of probability judgments (Lindley, 1982; von Winterfeldt & Edwards, 1986).

[3] It is an important empirical question whether we can assess a judge's calibration *in general*, so that we could draw conclusions about the judge's calibration in one area from calibration in another. The answer to this question, however, has nothing to do with the question of whether judgments are in principle justifiable in the absence of frequency data.

Table 5.1: Probability judgments made by two hypothetical weather forecasters

A's judgment	B's judgment	Outcome
.90	.80	Rain
.90	.80	Rain
.10	.00	No rain
.50	.40	No rain
.80	.90	Rain

These formulas use the same information that is used in judging calibration: a list of probability judgments coupled with the information about what actually happened.

Here is an example of a *quadratic scoring rule*. We look at p_i, the judgment for each of these outcomes. (The i refers to the i'th outcome; i is 1 for the first outcome, 2 for the second, and so on.) If the judge is doing a good job, p_i should be high when the event occurs and low when it does not occur. We set up the score so that a low score is good and a high score is bad (as in golf); a perfect score is 0. When the event does not happen, we look at p_i. When the event happens, we look at $1 - p_i$. The reason the rule is called "quadratic" is that we square these quantities before adding them up. Thus, the score will equal the sum of $p_i{}^2$ for outcomes that do not occur and the sum of $(1 - p_i)^2$ for outcomes that do occur.

Suppose we look at two weather forecasters' predictions of rain. Table 5.1 shows the data: probability judgments made by two judges, A and B. By the quadratic rule, the score for judge A would be: $(1 - .90)^2 + .10^2 + .50^2 + (1 - .80)^2$, which equals .31. The score for judge B would be $(1 - .80)^2 + .00^2 + .40^2 + (1 - .90)^2$, which equals .21. Because it is better to have a lower score, judge B seems to be a better forecaster. (Of course, four predictions are really too few to give a clear estimate.)

Certain scoring rules are called *proper*. This means that a judge should try to give her best estimate, if she wants the highest score possible.[4] The quadratic scoring rule is proper, and it has other advantages as well.[5] Other scoring rules, however, such as the fourth power instead of the square, are also proper. In general, there is no uniquely best scoring rule. If possible, in practical applications, it is helpful to devise a scoring rule specifically for the application at hand.

➤   Scoring rules are of considerable interest at present because of recent advances in the use of expert systems for calculating probabilities. In such systems, human experts enter basic knowledge into a computer program. For example, if the program is to provide the probability of each of several diseases for a specific patient, a physi-

---

[4]An example of an *im*proper scoring rule is to take the absolute value instead of the square. In this case, the judge can score as high by raising judgments to 1.00 if they are over .50 and lowering them to 0 if they are under .50 as by telling the truth, on the average.

[5]If we think that there is some critical value of a probability for making a decision, and if this critical value is equally likely to occur anywhere in the interval from 0 to 1.00 inclusive, then the quadratic scoring rule estimates the expected cost of incorrect decisions.

cian might put into the computer probabilities of the symptoms of different diseases. The program uses various rules, such as Bayes's theorem (described shortly) to calculate the probability of each disease from a list of the patient's symptoms. Whatever the application, it is usually possible to design several different expert systems for the same task, and it is often helpful to compare designs in terms of their results. Scoring rules are exactly what is needed to make such comparisons.

In sum, a good scoring rule serves as an overall summary of the relation between probability judgments and actual events. The rule is affected by the degree of miscalibration, and it takes information into account as well. There is no unique best scoring rule. To some extent, the way we score a probability assessor depends on why we want the probability judgments.

Bayes's theorem

An especially interesting consequence of the coherence requirement is Bayes's theorem. It is this theorem that explains how frequency information is relevant to probability judgment within the personal theory. But it is mainly about how to infer $p(H/D)$ from $p(D/H)$. It turns out that you need other information in order to reverse a conditional probability in this way.

An example from medicine

Let us begin with a simple but realistic example (based on Eddy, 1982). Suppose that you are a physician. A woman in her thirties comes to you, saying that she has discovered a small lump in her breast. She is worried that it might be cancerous. After you examine her, you think — on the basis of everything you know about breast cancer, women with her kind of medical history, and other relevant information — that the probability of cancer is .10 — that is, 1 in 10.

You recommend a mammogram, which is an X-ray study of the breast. You know that in women of this type who have cancer, the mammogram will indicate cancer 90% of the time. In women who do not have cancer, the mammogram will indicate cancer falsely 20% of the time. We can say that the *hit rate* is 90% and the *false-alarm* rate is 20%.[6] The mammogram comes out positive. What is the probability that the woman actually has cancer? Try to answer this by yourself (intuitively, without calculating) before going on.

Many people say that the probability is 90%; many others say that it is over 50%. Even some medical textbooks make this mistake (Eddy, 1982). Let us see what it would actually be, if our probability judgments are coherent. First, let us simply calculate it carefully; later, I shall explain a general formula for this sort of calculation.

---

[6]In medicine, the term *sensitivity* is used, instead of "hit rate," and *specificity* means 1–(false-alarm rate); the "specificity" of this test is 80%. I shall stick with "hits" and "false alarms," because they are the terms generally used in psychology.

Suppose that there are 100 women of this type, and the numbers apply exactly to them. We know that 10 of them have cancer and 90 do not. Of the 90 with cancer, 20% will show a positive mammogram, and 80% will not. Of the 10 that do have cancer, 90% will show a positive mammogram and 10% will not. Thus we have the following:

No cancer and positive mammogram	$90 \cdot .20$	$= 18$
No cancer and negative mammogram	$90 \cdot .80$	$= 72$
Cancer and positive mammogram	$10 \cdot .90$	$= 9$
Cancer and negative mammogram	$10 \cdot .10$	$= 1$

Because the patient had a positive mammogram, she must fall into one of the two groups with a positive mammogram. In the combined group consisting of these two groups, there are 27 patients. Of these 27 patients, 9 have cancer. Thus, the probability that our patient has cancer is 9/27, or .33. It is far more likely that she was one of those without cancer but with a positive result than that she really had cancer. Of course, a .33 chance of cancer may well be high enough to justify the next step, probably a biopsy, but the chance is far less than .90.

Another very useful way of describing situations like this is to draw a "tree" diagram, like the following. In this type of diagram, the number on each branch of the tree is the probability of taking that branch, given that one has gotten as far as the "root" of the branch in question (the roots are on the left). To compute the probability of getting to the end of a branch, on the right, you multiply all of the probabilities along the way. (This is illustrated in the equations at the right side of the diagram.) This kind of diagram helps you to think of all of the possibilities. It is especially useful when the probabilities of the various branches are influenced by different sorts of factors, so that some of these probabilities might be constant over a variety of circumstances that affect the others. For example, to a first approximation, the factors that affect $p(\text{cancer})$, such as the patient's age, do not affect $p(\text{positive/cancer})$ or $p(\text{positive/no cancer})$. These conditional probabilities are roughly constant for various groups of patients.

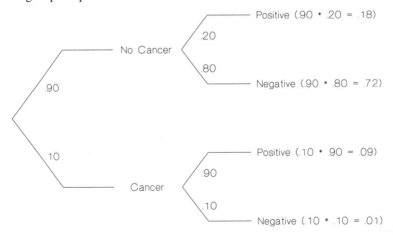

Formulas for Bayes's theorem

Let us now see how this sort of problem can be described by a general formula, derived algebraically from the rules of coherence and other assumptions.[7] In the medical example, if we use H to indicate the hypothesis (possibility) that the patient has cancer and D to indicate the datum (fact, evidence) of a positive test result, we would have the values $p(H) = .10$; $p(D/H) = .90$; $p(D/\tilde{}H) = .20$. The two conditional probabilities say that the probability of the datum, given that the hypothesis is true, is .90 and the probability of the datum, given that the hypothesis is false ($\tilde{}H$), is .20. (The expression $\tilde{}A$ means "not A" or "A is false," for any proposition A. $p(\tilde{}A)$ is therefore "the probability that A is false.")

What we want to know in this case is $p(H/D)$. That is, we know that D is true, and we want to use this evidence to revise our probability judgment for the disease. Because we know that D is true, we can *conditionalize* on D. In other words, we can look at the probability of H in just those cases where D is known to be true — that is, the 27 patients.

We can calculate $p(H/D)$ from the multiplication rule, $p(H \& D) = p(H/D) \cdot p(D)$, which implies:

$$p(H/D) = \frac{p(H \& D)}{p(D)} \tag{5.1}$$

In our example, $p(H \& D)$, the probability of the disease and the positive test result together, is .09 (9 out of 100 cases), and $p(D)$, the probability of the test result is .27 (9 cases from cases who have cancer and 18 from cases who do not, out of 100 cases. This is what we concluded before: The probability of cancer is $1/3$, or .33.

Why is this formula correct? Recall that the conditional probability of H given D is the probability that we would assign to H if we knew D to be true. If we think of probability as a proportion of cases, then we want to know what proportion of the cases with D also have H. This is just the number of cases with D and H divided by the number with D.

Formula 1 expresses an important implication of the multiplication rule: our judgment of the conditional probability of A given B — our judged probability of A if we learned that B were true — should be equal to the ratio of our judgment of the probability of A and B to our judgment of the probability of B.

Formula 1 does not help us much, because we don't know $p(H \& D)$. But we do know $p(D/H)$ and $p(H)$, and we know from the multiplication rule that $p(D \& H) = p(D/H) \cdot p(H)$. Of course $p(D \& H)$ is the same as $p(H \& D)$, so we can replace $p(H \& D)$ in formula 1 to get:

$$p(H/D) = \frac{p(D/H) \cdot p(H)}{p(D)} \tag{5.2}$$

Formula 2 is useful because it refers directly to the information we have. In the example, p(D/H) is .90, and p(H) is .10, except for $p(D)$. But we can calculate that

[7]We shall not discuss the mathematical details here. They are found in many textbooks of probability.

too. There are two ways for D to occur; it can occur with H or without H (that is, with $\tilde{}H$. These are mutually exclusive, so we can apply the additivity rule to get:

$$
\begin{aligned}
p(D) &= p(D \& H) + p(D \& \tilde{}H) \\
&= p(D/H) \cdot p(H) + p(D/\tilde{}H) \cdot p(\tilde{}H)
\end{aligned}
$$

This leads (by substitution into formula 2) to formula 3:

$$
p(H/D) = \frac{p(D/H) \cdot p(H)}{p(D/H) \cdot p(H) + p(D/\tilde{}H) \cdot p(\tilde{}H)} \tag{5.3}
$$

Formulas 2 and 3 are called *Bayes's theorem*. They are named after Rev. Thomas Bayes, who first recognized their importance in a theory of personal probability (Bayes 1764/1958). In formula 3, $p(H/D)$ is usually called the *posterior probability* of H, meaning the probability after D is known, and $p(H)$ is called the *prior probability*, meaning the probability before D is known. $p(D/H)$ is sometimes called the *likelihood* of D.

Formula 3 is illustrated in Figure 5.1. The whole square represents all of the possible patients. The square is divided, by a vertical line, into those patients with cancer, on the right (indicated with $p(H) = .1$), and those without cancer (indicated with $p(\tilde{}H) = .9$). The height of the shaded region in each part represents the conditional probability of a positive test result for each group, $p(D/H) = .9$ and $p(D/\tilde{}H) = .2$, respectively. The darker shaded region represents the possible patients with cancer and positive results. Its area (.09) represents the probability of being such a patient, which is the product of the prior probability (.1) and the conditional probability of a positive result (.9). Likewise, the area of the lighter shaded region (.18) represents the probability of being a patient with a positive result and no cancer. Possible patients with positive results are in the two shaded regions. It is apparent that the darker shaded region occupies $1/3$ of the two shaded regions together.

Still another version of Bayes's theorem is expressed in formula 4:

$$
\frac{p(H/D)}{p(\tilde{}H/D)} = \frac{p(D/H)}{p(D/\tilde{}H)} \cdot \frac{p(H)}{p(\tilde{}H)} \tag{5.4}
$$

This form is derived by using formula 1 to calculate $p(H/D)$ and $p(\tilde{}H/D)$ and then dividing one by the other. Notice that the right side of the equation in formula 4 is just

$$
\frac{p(D \& H)}{p(D \& \tilde{}H)}
$$

since $p(D \& H) = p(D/H) \cdot p(H)$ and $p(D \& \tilde{}H) = p(D/\tilde{}H) \cdot p(\tilde{}H)$.

Formula 4 is expressed in terms of odds rather than probabilities. In our example, the odds of cancer are 9/18. The term to the left of the equals sign in formula 4 is the

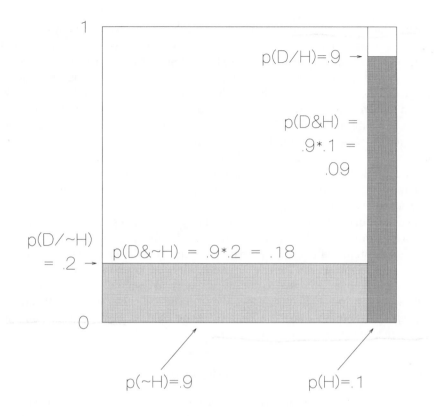

Figure 5.1: Graphic illustration of Bayes's theorem.

odds of the hypothesis's being true given the datum D; this is called the *posterior odds*. To the right of the equals sign in formula 4 are two fractions. The one on the right is the *prior odds* of the hypothesis, the odds before the datum is known. In our example, this is .10/.90, or 1/9. The other term is the *diagnostic ratio, the probability of the datum (D), given that the hypothesis is true, divided by the probability of the datum given that the hypothesis is false*. An advantage of this form of Bayes's theorem is that it is sometimes easier to assess the diagnostic ratio than to assess the two likelihoods that make it up.

This version also makes clear the two main determinants of the posterior odds: the prior odds and the diagnostic ratio. The posterior odds is simply the product of these two. Substituting the numbers from our example, we have

$$\frac{.09}{.18} = \frac{.90}{.20} \cdot \frac{.10}{.90}.$$

The important point is that the posterior probability should depend on two things: what the evidence says (the diagnostic ratio), and what we believed before we got the evidence (the prior odds). As we shall see, this is not always obvious.

Here is an exercise in which Bayes's theorem is used to construct a probability judgment. It is Sunday morning at 7 A.M., and I must decide whether to trek down to the bottom of my driveway to get the newspaper. On the basis of past experience, I judge that there is an 80% chance that the paper has been delivered by now. Looking out of the living room window, I can see exactly half of the bottom of the driveway, and the paper is not in the half that I can see. (If the paper has been delivered, there is an equal chance that it will fall in each half of the driveway.) What is the probability that the paper has been delivered? The footnote has the answer.[8]

We should bear in mind the *purpose* of Bayes's theorem. It allows us to construct judgments of the probability of some hypothesis (here, that the paper has been delivered) given some data that we have observed (the absence of a view of the paper), on the basis of judgments about the probability of the data given the hypothesis and about the prior probability of the hypothesis. It is often possible to bypass the use of Bayes's theorem and judge the probability of the hypothesis given the data directly. I could have done this in the case of the newspaper. Even in such cases, however, Bayes's theorem can be used to construct a "second opinion," as a way of checking judgments constructed in other ways. We shall see in Chapter 6 that the theorem can provide a particularly important kind of second opinion, because direct judgments are often insensitive to prior probabilities.

Why we should accept Bayes's theorem

Bayes's theorem is a consequence of the four rules of coherence we have stated. Why should we accept these rules? In Chapter 10 we shall see that these rules are a mathematical consequence of expected-utility theory, a theory of decision making that defines how we can best achieve our goals when we make decisions under uncertainty about their outcomes (Chapter 10), but there are other reasons, of a more abstruse (but no less important) sort.

Cox (1946, and 1979, pp. 132–142) has also shown that the four principles can be mathematically derived from two simpler assumptions about the relative strength of beliefs and from the laws of set theory (a form of the logic of propositions and categories discussed in Chapter 4). One assumption is that once the strength of our belief in a proposition A is fixed, the strength of our belief in $\sim A$ can take only one value, for any proposition A. Our belief that it will not rain depends on our belief that it will rain, and vice versa. If our belief in rain increases, our belief in no rain must decrease.

The second assumption is that the strength of our belief that both A and B are true is determined once two other belief strengths are fixed: the strength of our belief

---

[8]The prior probability is of course .80. If the paper has been delivered, there is a .50 probability that I will not see it in the half of the driveway that I can see. Thus, $p(D/H) = .50$, where D is *not* seeing the paper. If the paper has *not* been delivered ($\sim H$), $p(D/\sim H) = 1$. So, using formula 3, the probability of the paper's having been delivered is $\frac{.50 \cdot .80}{.50 \cdot .80 + 1 \cdot .20}$, or .67. If I want the paper badly enough, I should take the chance, even though I do not see it.

in B and the conditional strength of our belief in A given B (that is, the strength of our belief in A if we were to find that B is true). A and B can stand for any propositions.[9] Our belief that a patient has *both* a sore throat and the flu can have only one strength once we have fixed the strength of our belief that the patient has the flu and the strength of our belief that the patient has a sore throat *if* he has the flu.

These are weak assumptions, because they do not say *what* function a belief should be of other beliefs. It is difficult to imagine how they could be wrong if we try to quantify the strengths of our beliefs. Cox shows, however, that any set of belief strength that conforms to his assumptions must also conform to the principles of coherence we have stated.[10] Cox concludes that probability is the only sensible way of representing belief strengths. [11]

Of course, this is a normative argument. It does not imply that we should try to assign numbers to our beliefs. It does imply that if we do try to assign numbers there are severe limits on how we can do it without violating some very basic assumptions.

Why frequencies matter

Now let us return to the question of why probability judgments – and the beliefs they express — should be influenced by relative frequencies: That is, just what is wrong with believing that a randomly selected smoker's chance of getting lung cancer is .01 when 200 out of the last 1,000 smokers have gotten lung cancer? It seems that there is something wrong, but the personal view, as described so far, has trouble saying what, as long as a person's probability judgments are consistent with each other, that is, coherent. The personalist's answer is that indeed it is impossible to criticize a person for any honest belief, as long as it is consistent with his other beliefs. The more information there is about relative frequency, however, in general, the closer the person's belief must come to what that information says. This is a result of the requirement of coherence itself. Specifically, Bayes's theorem implies that a probability judgment must get closer to the observed relative frequency as the number of observations gets larger.

The argument supporting this conclusion is mathematical. I shall not go through the whole argument, but here is a simple case. Suppose that there are 10 balls in an urn. Each ball is either white or black. You want to estimate the proportion of white balls. To help you do this, I draw a ball out of the urn, show it to you, and put it back. (I sample the urn "with replacement.") Then I do this again, and again. Suppose that

---

[9]Of course, A and B can be reversed, so that the belief in A and B is determined by the belief in A and the belief in B given A. Also, Cox does not quite state this assumption this way, because he regards all probabilities as conditional. He says that our belief in $(A$ and $B)/C$ is determined by our belief in $A/(B$ and $C)$ and our belief in B/C, where the slash indicates a conditional belief.

[10]More precisely, Cox shows that any set of belief strengths that conforms to his assumptions can be transformed into a coherent set by an exponential function. This limitation is not important for the issue at hand, however, because the exponent is fixed, and the exponential function preserves the rank ordering of probability assignments.

[11]Heckerman (1988) extends Cox's argument, showing other advantages of probability.

after 100 draws, 71 of the balls have been black. What do you think the proportion of black balls is? Most people will say that 0.70 (7 out of 10) is most likely.

If we apply Bayes's theorem to this situation, we first note that there are 11 possible hypotheses about the proportion of white balls (0, 0.10, 0.20, ..., 1.00). Each hypothesis has a *prior probability*, before any balls are drawn. The only requirement for the prior probabilities is that they all add up to 1.00. I shall also assume that none of them is zero (in cases like this, it would be unreasonable to rule out anything without evidence).

After we draw a sample of balls, the probabilities of the hypotheses — now *posterior probabilities* — change. To calculate the posterior probability of each hypothesis, we need to know the likelihood of our getting the same sample given the hypothesis; that is, we need to know $p(D/H)$. If the likelihood is high, that hypothesis will become more probable, relative to others.

Now the likelihood of a sample of 71 black balls out of 100 balls, given a hypothesis of 0.70, is fairly high. Thus, after the sample has been drawn, the probability of this hypothesis will increase, relative to others. The likelihood of finding 71 black balls in a sample of 100 balls, given, say, a hypothesis of .10, however, is extremely low, so the probability of this hypothesis will decrease after the sample has been drawn. In general, the posterior probabilities of some hypotheses will be higher than the prior probabilities of these hypotheses, and the posterior probabilities of other hypotheses will be lower. The greatest proportionate increase will occur for those hypotheses that come closest to the sample itself.

The larger the sample, the larger these effects become. The likelihood of 7 balls out of 10 being black, given a hypothesis of 0.50, is not especially low. The likelihood of 70 out of 100 is much lower, and the likelihood of 700 out of 1,000 is minuscule. (The probability of any specific number becomes smaller, in fact. The important point is that it becomes smaller faster for those hypotheses distant from the sample.) Thus, the larger the sample, the more probable the hypothesis closest to the sample proportion. When the sample is small, differences among people's prior probability judgments will excuse fairly substantial differences among their posterior probability judgments. As the sample becomes larger, it becomes more and more difficult to excuse such differences. The differences in the prior probability judgments would themselves have to be enormous. This is why the Bayesian personalist thinks that frequencies are relevant to probability judgment and belief formation.

This is not an unreasonable view. Take coin flips, for example. Our prior belief about the proportion of "heads" for a coin taken out of our pocket, as we noted earlier, is that proportions near .50 are very likely. Finding that 7 out of 10 flips came out heads would not change our beliefs much, because our prior probability for .50 is so much higher than our prior probability for, say, .70. If 700 out of 1,000 flips of a coin came up heads, however, we would begin to think that it was a trick coin, as improbable as we had thought that was at the outset. If 700,000 out of 1,000,000 flips came up heads, that would practically remove all doubt. We would be practically certain that we had a trick coin.

In sum, the personal view is able to account for our belief that relative frequency matters. It also explains why relative frequency sometimes does not matter very much, that is, when we have strong prior beliefs that the relative frequency is in a small range (for example, the relative frequency of heads will be close to .50). Although the personal view allows individual differences in judgment, it also asserts that the larger those differences, the less likely it is that they are the result of honest differences in prior probability judgments rather than simple errors.

We can think of the personal theory as a pair of designs, one for constructing judgments and the other for evaluating them. The main argument for the personal theory is that it allows us to assess probabilities when we need them — that is, for making decisions — using all of the information we have available.

More exercises on Bayes's theorem[12]

1. What is the probability of cancer if the mammogram is negative, for a case in which $p(\text{positive}/\text{cancer}) = .792$, $p(\text{positive}/\text{benign}) = .096$, and $p(\text{cancer}) = .01$? (Hint: The probability that the test is negative is 1 minus the probability that it is positive.)

2. Suppose that 1 out of every 10,000 doctors in a certain region is infected with the AIDS virus. A test for the virus gives a positive result in 99% of those who are infected and in 1% of those who are not infected. A randomly selected doctor in this region gets a positive result. What is the probability that this doctor is infected?

3. In a particular at-risk population, 20% are infected with the virus. A randomly selected member of this population gets a positive result on the same test. What is the probability that this person is infected?

4. You are on a jury in a murder trial. After a few days of testimony, your probability for the defendant being guilty is .80. Then, at the end of the trial, the prosecution presents a new piece of evidence, just rushed in from the lab. The defendant's blood type is found to match that of blood found at the scene of the crime, which could only be the blood of the murderer. The particular blood type occurs in 5% of the population. What should be your revised probability for the defendant's guilt? Would you vote to convict?

5. (Difficult) You do an experiment in which your hypothesis (H_1) is that females score higher than males on a test. You test 4 males and 4 females and you find that all the females score higher than all the males (D). The probability of this result's happening by chance, if the groups did not really differ (H_0), is .0016. (This is often called the level of statistical significance.) But you want to know the probability that males and females *do* differ. What else do you need (other than more data), and how would you compute that probability?

When Bayes's theorem is useful and when it isn't

Students who finally understand Bayes's theorem often try to apply it when it is not appropriate or when it is not needed. The theorem is typically useful when H, the hypothesis, corresponds to a cause of the observed datum D. In this case, it is easy to think about, or gather statistical evidence about, the probability that H leads to D,

[12] Answers are at the end of the chapter.

that is, $p(D/H)$. For example, it may be easier to think about the probability of fever (D) given appendicitis (H), than the probability of appendicitis given fever. Statistical evidence about $p(D/H)$ is particularly easy to collect when many factors affect $p(H)$ and few factors affect $p(D/H)$. This is often true of medical tests such as mammograms. The probability of cancer (H) is affected by age and many other factors, but the probability of a positive mammogram given cancer ($p(D/H)$ is affected by relatively few factors and can often be assumed to be the same for everyone.

A case where we cannot use Bayes's theory straightforwardly is one in which we have different sources of opinion about $p(H)$. We can think of these as $p(H/D_1)$, $p(H/D_2)$, and so on. The problem is that we have both D_1 and D_2, and these two probabilities do not agree. A typical example is one in which two expert judges disagree. If one physician says that the probability of the disease is .8 and another says it is .6, we might regard these as two sources of data, which must be put together.

There is no one right way to do this that applies in all cases. This problem of "reconciling" discrepant probabilities has a large literature.[13] Lindley, Tversky, and Brown (1979) discuss one interesting approach to this problem, which draws on Bayes's theorem indirectly. Roughly, and briefly, the idea is to consider the conflicting reports as data, as I suggested in the last paragraph. We imagine that there is some "true probability" of H. Let us call it $\mathcal{P}$. We think about the conditional probability of each report, given $\mathcal{P}$, namely, $p(D_1/\mathcal{P})$ and $p(D_2/\mathcal{P})$. We also have a prior probability for each possible value of $\mathcal{P}$. We then apply Bayes's theorem to get the posterior probability $p(\mathcal{P}/D_1 \ and \ D_2)$. That is:

$$p(\mathcal{P}/D_1 \ and \ D_2) = \frac{p(D_1 \ and \ D_2/\mathcal{P}) \cdot p(\mathcal{P})}{p(D_1 \ and \ D_2)}$$

We can then find the expected value of $\mathcal{P}$. Various simplifying assumptions help make this practical. The same method can be used with a single probability assessor making assements in several different ways. (For another way of reconciling such incoherent probabilities, see Osherson et al., 1997.)

A digression: Coincidences

Several everyday phenomena and puzzle problems can be understood better in the light of Bayes's theorem. One of these is the feeling of coincidence. You have this feeling when you think of someone and then read her obituary, or when you sit down in a dark cinema and then realize that you are sitting next to someone you know and haven't seen for years. Events like these seem too improbable to be just chance.

When you try to calculate "the probability of this event," you run into a small problem. The question is what "this event" actually is. Is it sitting next to this particular person in this particular theater on this date? Or is it sitting next to someone you know in some theater on some date? Notice that the latter is a much more inclusive

---

[13]The rest of this chapter is more advanced, and less detailed, than what came before. It is intended as a guide for further study.

event, and much more probable. But the more inclusive event, if it happened, would probably cause you to think that it was a coincidence. Perhaps the real event is the feeling of surprise. We may feel surprised because we focus on too small a class of events that would count as surprising (Falk, 1981–2). As Martin Gardner (1972) put it, "It is easy to understand how anyone personally involved in a remarkable coincidence will believe that occult forces are at work. You can hardly blame the winner of the Irish Sweepstakes for thinking that Providence has smiled on him, even though he knows it is absolutely certain that someone will win." Finding a coincidence is like shooting an arrow and then drawing the target circle around it.

Gardner's comment calls attention to another feature of coincidences, which is that they implicitly involve two hypotheses (Horwich, 1982). One is that nothing unusual is happening, that the event is just chance. The other is that something unusual is happening, such as divine intervention or some other supernatural force. We are surprised when such alternative hypotheses seem to be supported. This is why we are not surprised when we sit next to someone whose name happens to be Harry Smith, even though this is roughly just as improbable as sitting next to someone we know. After all, the person we sit next to probably has *some* name. Although this particular name is unlikely, there is no alternative explanation of it. If H_1 is the alternative hypothesis and H_0 is the just-chance hypothesis, we are surprised because $p(D/H_1)$ is greater than $p(D/H_0)$. Note, however, that $p(H_1)$ may still not be very high.

Another digression: The Monty Hall problem

Here is a well known problem, often called the Monty Hall problem, after the host of the TV show "Let's make a deal" (Nickerson, 1996).

> Suppose you're on a game show, and you're given a choice of three doors. Behind one door is a car; behind the others, goats. You pick a door, and the host, who knows what's behind the doors, offers to open a second door, which has a goat. After that, you can switch to the third door, or you can stay with your original choice. Do you have a better chance to win the car if you switch?

Another way of looking at this question is to ask whether the host can provide useful information, in the sense we've been discussing. If you do no better by switching, then he cannot.

Let us say that A is the door you pick first, and B and C are the two other doors. We can use Bayes's theorem to analyze the probabilities before and after the door is opened.

If you don't ask the host to open a door, your chance of winning is 1/3. The car has an equal chance of being anywhere. You don't know which door the host would open if he opened a door.

Suppose you ask the host to open a door, and he opens B, revealing a goat. What is the probability of this datum D_b given the three hypotheses, H_a, H_b, and H_c?

$p(D_b/H_a) = 1/2$. If the car were in A, he would pick one of the other two doors at random.

$p(D_b/H_b) = 0$. If the car were in B, he wouldn't pick it.

$p(D_b/H_c) = 1$. If the car were in C, he would have to pick B, since he's not going to pick A or the door with the car.

Now we can apply Bayes's theorem to calculate $p(H_c/D_b)$, that is, the probability that the car is in C, given that the host has opened B.

$$p(H_c/D_b) = \frac{p(D_b/H_c) \cdot p(H_c)}{p(D_b/H_a) \cdot p(H_a) + p(D_b/H_b) \cdot p(H_b) + p(D_b/H_c) \cdot p(H_c)}$$

Notice that the denominator is $p(D_b)$, since these are all three ways that D_b can arise, and they are mutually exclusive.

Substituting numbers:

$$p(H_c/D_b) = \frac{1 \cdot (1/3)}{(1/2) \cdot (1/3) + (0) \cdot (1/3) + (1) \cdot (1/3)} = \frac{1/3}{1/6 + 1/3} = 2/3$$

So your chance of winning is 2/3. The same argument applies if the host picks door C. We would call that D_c instead of D_b. Hence, asking the host to open the door increases your chance of winning by 1/3, whether he picks B or C.

The trick here is to realize that the host will not pick the door with the car, so, by opening one door, he is telling you something. He is telling you one place where the car is not to be found. That leaves two others, but they are not equally likely, since you have already eliminated one of the two others from the ones he could have picked. He is telling you which of the two remaining doors doesn't have the car.

Perhaps this problem has a general lesson: We need to think about how our information gets to us, as well as what it is on its face.

Use of Bayes's theorem in expert systems

Bayes's theorem has been used extensively in expert systems, including one that helps geologists look for mineral deposits   (Duda, Hart, Barrett, Gashnig, Konolige, Reboh, & Slocum, 1976), and many that provide probabilities for medical diagnosis (for example, Schwartz, Baron, and Clarke, 1988).[14] The basic idea is most easily explained in the case of medical diagnosis.

Suppose that we are trying to determine the probability of two diseases, H_1 and H_2, and that there are four possible symptoms that a patient might have, S_1, S_2, S_3.

[14]Many systems use "certainty factors" and "belief functions" instead of probabilities. Some of the early workers who designed these systems were suspicious of probability theory, for a variety of reasons (including their ignorance of its philosophical and mathematical basis). Some of these systems, particularly those using certainty factors, can lead to nonsensical conclusions. One way of fixing such systems to avoid such conclusions made them equivalent to probability theory (Heckerman, 1986). In the case of belief functions, however, the dispute with probability theory seems more serious. For additional reading, see Charniak (1983); the symposium in *Statistical Science*, 1987, 2 (1); and Baron (1987).

and S_4. We ask an expert to tell us the probability of each symptom's being observed, given each disease, or $p(S_j/H_i)$. Now let s_j be whatever is observed about S_j (present, absent, or unknown). Thus the conditional probability of s_j given H_i is $p(S_j/H_i)$ if S_j is observed to be present and $1 - p(S_j/H_i)$ if S_j is observed to be absent.[15] Now suppose we observe that some symptoms are present and others are absent. If we know the conditional probability of the whole list of observed symptoms, given each disease, or $p(s_1 \& s_2 \& \ldots /H_i)$, this is a likelihood in Bayes's theorem. If we know, in addition, the prior probability of each disease for a given patient, $p(H_i)$, we can apply Bayes's theorem.

The difficulty here is this: How do we calculate the probability of a whole *list* of symptoms, given each disease? One way to do this is to assume that the symptoms are *conditionally independent*. That is, *if* the patient has a given disease, the knowledge that a patient has one symptom does not affect the probability that the patient has any other symptom. The symptoms are independent *conditionally* on a patient's having the disease. If we can make this assumption, then the probability of a list of observed symptoms, given the presence of each disease, is just the product of the probabilities of the individual symptoms given the disease. Thus, $p(s_1 \& s_2 \& \ldots /H_i) = p(s_1/H_i) \cdot p(s_2/H_i) \cdot \ldots$ We can represent the situation with the following diagrams, where the S's represent the symptoms and the D's represent the diseases:

In real life, however, the assumption of conditional independence for symptoms usually does not make sense. (This was one of the reasons that early workers despaired; they thought this assumption was necessary.) For example, appendicitis usually causes an inflammation of the intestines, which, in turn, causes nausea and anorexia (loss of appetite). Even if we know from other evidence that a patient has appendicitis, we also know that once the symptom of nausea appears anorexia is also more likely. Anorexia and nausea are *not* conditionally independent, given appendicitis.

The most common way to solve this problem (Charniak, 1983) is to develop a more adequate model of the situation. Instead of thinking about diseases and symptoms, we add at least one additional level, often called the level of *pathstates*. The

---

[15]We assume here that all relevant symptoms have been asked about. If a symptom has not been asked about, the probability of knowing what we know about it — namely, that it is either present or absent — is 1, so $p(s_j/H_i) = 1$.

pathstates are caused by the diseases, and the symptoms are caused by the path-states. Pathstates are conditionally independent, given disease; and symptoms are conditionally independent, given pathstates. We get a tree like the one in the following diagram. Here P_1, P_2, and P_3 represent pathstates and a, b, and c represent conditional probabilities of the lower state given the state immediately above.

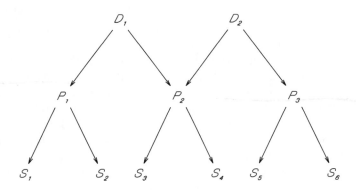

With a tree like this, it is easy to calculate the probability of a given set of symptoms, as long as each line (branch) on the tree has been assigned a probability and as long as we know the prior probability of the disease. To get some idea of how this is done, consider only the probabilities labeled a, b, and c in the tree diagram; these are, respectively, $p(P_1/D_1)$, $p(S_1/P_1)$, and $p(S_2/P_1)$. Considering only this part of the whole tree, the probability of S_1 and S_2 together, given D_1, would be $a \cdot b \cdot c$. This is because the probability of the pathstate P_1 given D_1 is a, and if the pathstate is present, the probabilities of the symptoms are b and c, respectively. Because the symptoms are independent, given the pathstate, we can multiply their probabilities. (For more details, see Kelly & Barclay, 1973; Duda, Hart, and Nilsson, 1976; Pearl, 1982; and Schwartz, Baron, and Clarke, 1988.)

Computers make complex calculations easy, and it may seem as though all we need to do, in order to construct an expert system, is develop the best possible normative theory and then program a computer with it. We must remember, however, that expert systems are truly *systems*. They are not only computer programs: rather, they are computer programs, plus their justifications, plus (most important) procedures for eliciting probabilities from *people* (experts). Experts must be given the best opportunity to use their knowledge, and, if necessary, they must be helped to think about it in the most useful way. Thus, expert systems are prescriptive solutions to practical problems. They are not necessarily just realizations of a normative model. In particular, we need to do more descriptive research, to find out what kinds of structures are most suited for elicitation of personal probabilities from experts and to determine the extent to which expert opinion and frequency data can each be relied upon. The design of expert systems depends as much *on the psychology of experts as on the mathematical possibilities.*

Conclusion

The theory of probability describes the ideal way of making quantitative judgments about belief. Even when we simply judge which of two beliefs is stronger, without assigning numbers to either belief, the one we judge to be stronger should be the one that is more probable according to the rules of probability (as applied to our other beliefs). Let us now turn to the psychological research in this area to find out how people ordinarily make judgments of these types. The difference between the normative theory (described in this chapter) and the descriptive theory (Chapter 6) will suggest some prescriptive improvements.

Answers to exercises:

1. $p(\text{neg}/\text{ca}) = .208$, $p(\text{neg}/\text{ben}) = .904$, $p(\text{ca}) = .01$

$$
\begin{aligned}
p(\text{ca}/\text{neg}) &= \frac{p(\text{neg}/\text{ca})p(\text{ca})}{p(\text{neg}/\text{ca})p(\text{ca}) + p(\text{neg}/\text{ben})p(\text{ben})} \\
&= \frac{(.208)(.01)}{(.208)(.01) + (.904)(.99)} = .0023
\end{aligned}
$$

The lesson here is that negative results can be reassuring.

2. $p(\text{aids}) = .0001$, $p(\text{pos}/\text{aids}) = .99$, $p(\text{pos}/\text{no aids}) = .01$

$$
p(\text{aids}/\text{pos}) = \frac{(.99)(.0001)}{(.99)(.0001) + (.01)(.9999)} = .0098
$$

3. $p(\text{aids}) = .20$, $p(\text{pos}/\text{aids}) = .99$, $p(\text{pos}/\text{no aids}) = .01$

$$
p(\text{aids}/\text{pos}) = \frac{(.99)(.20)}{(.99)(.20) + (.01)(.80)} = .96
$$

The lesson here is that tests can be useful in at-risk groups but useless for screening (e.g., of medical personnel).

4. $p(\text{guilt}) = .80$, $p(\text{match}/\text{guilt}) = 1.00$, $p(\text{match}/\text{innocent}) = .05$

$$
p(\text{guilt}/\text{match}) = \frac{(1.00)(.80)}{(1.00)(.80) + (.05)(.20)} = .988
$$

5. You know $p(D/H_0) = .0016$, but you must make a judgment of the prior $p(H_1)$, which is the same as $1 - p(H_0)$ and of $p(D/H_1)$. The latter depends on how big you judge the effect would be. Then

$$
p(H_1/D) = \frac{p(D/H_1)p(H_1)}{p(D/H_1)p(H_1) + p(D/H_0)p(H_0)}.
$$

The difficulty of specifying the unknown quantities helps us understand why Bayesianism is unpopular among statisticians.

Chapter 6

Descriptive theory of probability judgment

How closely do most of us follow the normative theory when we make probability judgments? Until the late 1960s, it was thought that even people with little experience did reasonably well at it intuitively. Since then, psychologists have found that we do poorly at making probability judgments — in systematic ways. It is not just that our judgments are erroneous. Our judgments are erroneous because we attend to variables that we should ignore and ignore variables to which we should attend. Misleading heuristics, naive theories, and the basic processes that cause poor thinking contribute to these errors. Luckily, research has shown that with practice and education to correct such errors, we can improve our probability judgments and become very good judges indeed.

Accuracy of probability judgments

How accurate are our probability judgments? To answer this question, let us use the normative standards we developed in Chapter 5. First, we ask whether we are sensitive to information about frequencies when such information is available. (Of course, from a personal point of view, probability judgments ought only to approximate relative frequencies, but when judges use frequency information to revise their personal probabilities, it surely helps them to perceive that information correctly.) Second, we ask about calibration. We shall cover both frequency judgments and calibration in this section. A third way of assessing accuracy is to assess coherence. Several results discussed later in the chapter demonstrate systematic biases that cause incoherence (like the study of Robinson and Hastie, 1985, mentioned in Chapter 5).[1]

---

[1] A fourth method is to apply scoring rules to probability judgments, but this method has not been used much as a research tool.

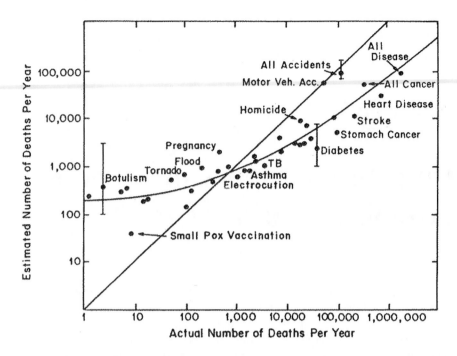

Figure 6.1: Subjects' estimates of the frequency of various causes of death as a function of actual frequency. From S. Lichtenstein, P. Slovic, B. Fischhoff, M. Layman, and B. Combs, "Judged frequency of lethal events," *Journal of Experimental Psychology: Human Learning and Memory*, (1978): *4*, 565. Reprinted by permission of the first author, and of M. G. Morgan and M. Henrion, who redrew the figure.

Frequency judgments

How good are people at assessing frequencies? A number of studies have found that when people are asked to judge frequencies of events that they have some experience with, they underestimate very high frequencies and overestimate very low ones. For example, Attneave (1953) asked subjects to estimate the relative frequency with which various letters of the alphabet occur in ordinary written English. What percentage of all of the letters in a newspaper, for example, are *a*'s, *e*'s, and so forth? Subjects tended to overestimate low probabilities (*z*'s) and underestimate relatively high ones (*e*'s). A similar effect was observed by Lichtenstein, Slovic, Fischhoff, Layman, and Combs (1978) when subjects were asked to judge the frequency with which various dangers caused deaths in the U.S. population today. The actual frequencies range from a death rate of 0 for smallpox, to heart disease, which has a rate of 360,000 per 100,000,000 people per year. A plot of the data from this study is shown in Figure 6.1.[2]

These results are not really so surprising when we think about the effect of inaccuracy itself on numerical probability estimates. Errors of any sort tend to push numbers toward the middle of the probability scale. For example, an error in judging the probability of death from smallpox (0) can go only in one direction — up, since subjects do not give numbers less than 0 as answers. There is more for us to learn from this study of Lichtenstein and her colleagues, however, and we shall return to it.

These results imply that we tend to overestimate the probability of very infrequent or unlikely events, such as accidents in nuclear-power plants or rare diseases. (Later in this chapter, however, we shall consider biases that tend to make such estimates too *low*.)

Calibration and inappropriate extreme confidence

How well calibrated are most people's probability judgments? One way to test this is to ask for confidence intervals. A confidence interval is a numerical interval within which a certain quantity has a certain probability of falling. If we estimate some quantity (such as what the Dow Jones Industrial Average will be tomorrow) and then give an "interval" around that estimate such that the true value has, say, a 90% chance of falling within the interval, we have provided a "90% confidence interval" for that quantity. Subjects typically give confidence intervals that are too small (Alpert and Raiffa, 1982) — a kind of overconfidence effect. This kind of demonstration works with almost anything. If the students in a class try to put a 95% confidence interval around the age of the teacher, usually more than 5% of the intervals are too small. If the intervals were the right size, then about 1 in 20 intervals should be too small. Perhaps people underadjust, once they have determined their initial best estimate, or anchor. They may fail to think of a sufficient number of reasons why their initial estimate could be substantially wrong.

Adams and Adams (1960) asked subjects to make various kinds of probability judgments — for example, subjects were asked to spell a word and then to indicate their *confidence* that they were correct as a probability figure (using percents). When subjects said that they were "100% certain" that they were correct, they were actually correct about 80% of the time. When their confidence was 80%, they were correct about 55% of the time. In general, subjects were overconfident. Although their mean confidence was 72%, their mean accuracy was 57% on the words used. Only at the very lowest probabilities, from 0% to 20%, were subjects underconfident. For example, when subjects indicated 0% confidence in a spelling (certain to be wrong), they were actually correct about 12% of the time. This pattern of results is shown in Figure 6.2.

[2]Geometric means of subjects' responses are used in this graph in order to avoid undue influence by subjects who gave very high numbers. Subjects were given the correct answer for "motor vehicle accidents" as a standard.

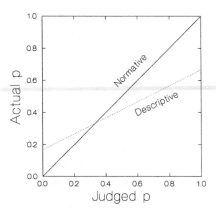

Figure 6.2: Typical pattern of results for a subject's judgment being correct as a function of the subject's confidence that the judgment is correct.

Researchers have found this pattern of results — general overconfidence, especially when confidence is high, but underconfidence when confidence is low — in a great variety of tasks (Lichtenstein, Fischhoff, and Phillips, 1982, provide a review). Sometimes the effects were not as pronounced as in the graph in Figure 6.2. For example, subjects do not deviate from good calibration quite as much when they are asked to recognize correct spellings rather than to produce them (Adams and Adams, 1960). In other cases, though, overconfidence is extreme. In one cross-cultural study, subjects answered a general-knowledge questionnaire with items such as "When did the People's Republic of China join the U.N.: 1971 or 1972?" or "What is the capital of New Zealand: Auckland or Wellington?" Subjects also indicated their confidence as a probability. All of the items had two choices for answers, so subjects could score 50% correct by guessing; a confidence level lower than 50% was therefore never warranted. College students from Hong Kong and Malaysia were correct only about 65% of the time when they said that they were 100% certain of being correct. (The probability judgments of Indonesian students were even more poorly calibrated.) British students' answers were considerably better calibrated; they scored about 78% correct when they said that they were 100% certain. These differences are not the result of differences in knowledge about the questions: Rather, the British subjects were more cautious, using the 100% category far less often, so that they were more likely to be correct when they did use it. The researchers suggested that cultural differences affect the way that people think about probability (Wright,   Phillips, Whalley, Choo, Ng, Tan, and Wisudha, 1978; see also Wright and Phillips, 1980).

Fischhoff, Slovic, and Lichtenstein (1977) examined a number of possible explanations of the basic finding of overconfidence for high-confidence judgments. They used items like those employed by Wright and his colleagues (for example, "Absinthe is: a liqueur or a precious stone?"), as well as other kinds of items — for example, items in which subjects had to indicate which cause of death was more common in the United States (for example, appendicitis, or pregnancy, abortion, and childbirth taken together).

They noted that the probability scale is limited at the top. It does not allow people to go beyond 100%, so any error may tend to make people give a spuriously large number of 100% judgments. To test this theory, they asked subjects to express their judgments as odds instead of percentages. It then became impossible to indicate 100% confidence, for that would correspond to infinite odds. This helped a little, but the basic effect was still present.

Fischhoff and his colleagues also considered as a possible explanation of overconfidence the possibility that people have little idea what probability means: "People's inability to assess appropriately a probability of .80 may be no more surprising than the difficulty they might have in estimating brightness in candles or temperature in degrees Fahrenheit. Degrees of certainty are often used in everyday speech (as are references to temperature), but they are seldom expressed numerically nor is the opportunity to validate them often available" (p. 553).

This argument does not explain all the results. Even if people do not have a good feeling for what "80% confidence" means, they do have a good idea of what 100% confidence means: It clearly means absolute certainty — no chance at all of being incorrect — yet the overconfidence phenomenon is still found with 100% judgments.

In addition to the finding of overconfidence at 100%, another finding suggests that overconfidence is not merely a result of misuse of the probability scale. People themselves are willing to act on their judgments. Fischhoff and his colleagues asked the subjects whether they would be willing to play a game. After making the confidence judgments (still using odds for their estimates), the subjects were told (p. 558):

> Look at your answer sheet. Find the questions where you estimated the odds of your being correct as 50 to 1 or greater.... We'll count how many times your answers to these questions were wrong. Since a wrong answer in the face of such high certainty would be surprising, we'll call these wrong answers "your surprises."

The researcher then explained:

> I have a bag of poker chips in front of me. There are 100 white chips and 2 red chips in the bag. If I reach in and randomly select a chip, the odds that I will select a white chip are 100 to 2, or 50 to 1, just like the odds that your "50 to 1" answers are correct. For every "50 to 1 or greater" answer you gave, I'll draw a chip out of the bag.... Since drawing a red chip is unlikely, every red chip I draw can be considered "my surprise." Every time you are surprised by a wrong answer ..., you pay me $1. Every time I am surprised by a red chip, I'll pay you $1.

Of course, since the subjects' confidence was usually *greater* than 50 to 1, they stood to come out ahead if their estimates were well calibrated. Of 42 subjects (people who responded to an advertisement in a college newspaper) 27 agreed to play the game. (Several other subjects agreed when the payment for a red chip was raised.) In one experiment, the game was not actually played. If the game had been played — because of the overconfidence effect — subjects would have lost an average of $3.64 per person (assuming that 1 out of every 51 chips drawn was red). Only 3 out of 36 who agreed to play would have won any money. In a second experiment, subjects were told that the game would actually be played. Of 19 subjects, 13 agreed to play, and all 13 lost money. (Of course, the experimenter did not really take the money. Because he knew about the overconfidence phenomenon, that would have made the experiment a con game.) These results show that if the subjects did not know how to use the probability scale or the odds scale, they did not *know* that they did not know. (Now *you* know!)

The general finding of overconfidence must be qualified by an additional fact. Probability judgments are not very sensitive to the amount of knowledge that subjects have about the test items in question (Lichtenstein and Fischhoff, 1977). For example, two tests were constructed, one using difficult items and one using easy items. (All items concerned general information.) On the difficult test, the mean percentage correct was 62%, but the mean confidence rating was 74%. On the easy test, however, the mean percentage correct was 80%, although the mean confidence rating was 78%. Notice that the mean confidence ratings did not differ much for the two tests, although the mean scores did differ. As a result, although subjects were overconfident on the difficult items, they were underconfident on the easy items; they did not seem to realize how easy the items were. Even on the easy test, however, subjects were still overconfident when they gave extremely high confidence ratings: For 100% ratings, the actual percentage correct was about 93%. Thus, subjects are not *always* overconfident. Rather, it might be said that they are always overconfident *when they express extreme confidence.* More generally, it might be said that confidence ratings are not affected as much as they should be by the amount of knowledge that the subject has about the type of item or about the particular item. To put it another way, the calibration curve is not as steep as it should be.

Is it humanly possible to be well calibrated? Is the overconfidence effect the result of a bias or a limitation on our ability? We do not know the answer to this in general. We do know the answer for expert judges who make probability judgments every day as part of their work. The answer is that such people can be amazingly well calibrated.

Murphy and Winkler (1977) studied the calibration of some 25,000 weather forecasts made in the Chicago area over a 4-year period ending in 1976. Since 1965, weather forecasts have included probability information for rain, snow, and other conditions. Weather forecasters use a variety of information, including statistical tables of events of past years, but they do make their predictions on the basis of personal judgment; weather forecasts are made by people, not computers. Murphy and Winkler found that calibration was nearly perfect. When the forecasters said that there was a 100% chance of rain, it rained about 98% of the time, and so on down the line.

This does not mean that the forecasts were always very informative. Again, if you know that it rains on 1 out of every 10 days, your forecasts can be perfectly calibrated if you give .10 as the probability of rain, every day. Of course, this is not what the forecasters did.

Most important, this result shows that overconfidence can be overcome. Whatever their accuracy in predicting the weather itself, weather forecasters are extremely accurate in assessing the confidence that should be placed in their own predictions. Quite possibly they learn this from years of feedback.

Research has demonstrated that a major cause for the phenomenon of "overconfidence when confidence is high" is a bias that I have emphasized earlier: the tendency to seek evidence in favor of an initial belief, as opposed to evidence against it. Koriat, Lichtenstein, and Fischhoff (1980) gave subjects the same sort of two-alternative questions used in the studies described earlier and asked for confidence judgments. Some subjects were asked to give reasons *for* and *against* their favored answer before assigning a confidence judgment. Other subjects gave only *for* reasons, others *against* reasons, and others none at all (as in the original studies). The overconfidence phenomenon was reduced (but not completely eliminated) in those subjects who were asked for both *for* and *against* reasons and in those subjects who were asked for *against* reasons alone. Apparently subjects were failing to think of such criticisms on their own, without the explicit instruction to do so. Subjects who were asked to give *for* reasons did not differ from the control group that gave no reasons at all. Apparently subjects think of *for* reasons on their own, without prompting.

In a related study, Hoch (1985) asked graduating business students, just beginning their search for jobs, to assign probabilities to various outcomes of their job search, such as "What is the probability that your starting salary *will* exceed $ _____ ?" or "What is the probability that you *will* receive more than ____ job offers by the end of the school year?" Actual data were collected on the same subjects at the end of the school year from computer records of the placement office. Subjects generally had been overconfident, although they were more overconfident when asked about high salaries as opposed to low ones, and about few offers as opposed to many. Subjects who were told to think of reasons why the event in question might not occur showed less overconfidence than subjects not told to generate reasons. (For the low-salary or few-offer events, there was little effect: Subjects did *not* become *under*confident when asked to think of "against" reasons; therefore thinking of "against" reasons did not simply decrease probability estimates whether they were accurate or not.) Subjects who were told to think of reasons why the event *might occur* showed the same overconfidence as subjects not told to generate reasons. As in the study by Koriat and his colleagues, subjects seem to generate reasons on their "favored" side without being told, but they do not tend to generate reasons on the other side so thoroughly. Here, the "favored" side is the optimistic one; uninstructed subjects seem to be generating reasons in favor of something they would like to be true.

In sum, one reason for inappropriately high confidence is failure to think of reasons why one might be wrong. Such inappropriate confidence could, in turn, cause a person to stop searching for alternative possibilities, leading to insufficient thinking.[3]

A second reason for overconfidence is that people may base their confidence on the apparent implication of the evidence they have, without first asking how credible that evidence is. Griffin and Tversky (1992) told subjects that coins, when spun, did not necessarily fall heads 50% of the time. Subjects were told that a coin fell on one side 60% of the time and were asked how confident they would be that it was heads, on the basis of differently sized samples with different proportions of heads. Confidence judgments were excessively influenced by the proportion of heads in the sample (the direction of the evidence), and not enough by the size of the sample (the credibility or weight of the evidence). For example, according to Bayes's theorem a sample of 19 heads and 14 tails should lead to the same posterior probability of "bias toward heads" as a sample of 5 heads and 0 tails, but confidence was higher with the smaller sample (92.5%) than with the larger (60%). By analogy, more overconfidence is found when subjects know less about a topic. Subjects were more overconfident in predicting the behavior of someone else in a game than in predicting their own behavior. They seemed to ignore the fact that their evidence about the other person was weaker than their evidence about themselves. In general, the direction of the evidence is more salient than its weight or credibility, and subjects may not search beyond the direction.

Improving calibration by conditional assessment

Here is an exercise to improve probability judgment for personal probabilities. The idea is to estimate each probability two ways. One way is a direct judgment. The other way is a calculation from other judgments. After doing both, you can reflect on the two and pick your final judgment. It is as if you make yourself into two different people, for the purpose of getting a second opinion. The second opinion might even be better than the first.

> The next time you take a trip by airplane, what is the probability that you will sit next to someone who knows someone who you know (E)?
>
> First estimate the probability directly, $p(E)$.
>
> Now think of two mutually exclusive and exhaustive ways this might happen, for example, departing the place where you live (D) and arriving at it (A). Estimate the probability that your next trip will be each of these [$p(D)$, $p(A)$], and the probability of the event in question in each case, $p(E/D)$ and $p(E/A)$. Then compute an overall probability $p(E/D)p(D) + p(E/A)p(A)$ (as described in the last chapter). A tree diagram might help:

[3]Gilovich (1991) explores the implications of this problem for judgments and decisions in everyday life.

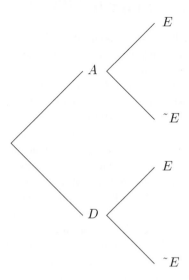

Notice, by the way, that this tree is like computing the denominator of Bayes's theorem, in the last chapter. D and A here correspond to H, the hypothesis, and $\tilde{\ }H$, the complement of the hypothesis. There we were asking about the probability of the data.

Can this procedure help? To find out, Kleinmuntz, Fennema, and Peecher (1996) gave subjects tasks questions like the following:

Background: What is the probability that more than 840 institutions granted MBA degrees in the U.S. in 1990?

Conditional 1: Suppose you knew for sure that more than 840 institutions granted the MBA degree in What is the probability that more than 53,600 MBAs graduated in 1990?

Conditional 2: Suppose you knew for sure that less than 840 institutions granted the MBA degree in 1990. What is the probability that more than 53,600 MBAs graduated in 1990?

The researchers calculated a second probability assessment from the two Conditional assessments. They compared this to the Background assessment. The computed assessment was better calibrated. In part, this was because the computed assessments were less extreme, hence less subject to the overconfidence of extreme probability judgments. The researchers did not ask subjects to think of their own conditioning events, but this study gives us reason to think that doing that and paying attention to the results would make probability judgments more accurate.

Heuristics and biases in probability

The first good evidence of biases in probability judgments came from studies of children. Older children answer probability questions according to frequency rather than relative frequency (Piaget and Inhelder, 1975). For example, they prefer to bet on an urn with 9 winning chips out of 100 rather than an urn with 1 out of 10, and they think they are more likely to win that way. Piaget and Inhelder thought that this error largely disappeared by mid-adolescence, but adults sometimes make the same error (Denes-Raj and Epstein, 1994). Thus, adults continue to be influenced by frequency even when they know that relative frequency is relevant.

The rules of probability define coherence. A good way to ask whether our probability judgments are coherent is to study the *inferences* that we make from some probabilities to others. For example, in the mammogram example in Chapter 5, you were asked to infer the probability that a woman patient had cancer from a few other probabilities. In the 1960s, Daniel Kahneman and Amos Tversky began to study such inferences. They were able to demonstrate consistent errors, or biases. Moreover, they suggested that these biases could be explained in terms of certain heuristics that the subjects were using to make the inferences.

The representativeness heuristic

Consider the following problem (Tversky and Kahneman, 1982, p. 156, from an earlier unpublished study):

> A cab was involved in a hit and run accident at night. Two cab companies, the Green and the Blue, operate in the city. You are given the following data:
>
> (a) 85% of the cabs in the city are Green and 15% are Blue.
>
> (b) A witness identified the cab as Blue. The court tested the reliability of the witness under the same circumstances that existed on the night of the accident and concluded that the witness correctly identified each one of the two colors 80% of the time and failed 20% of the time.
>
> What is the probability that the cab involved in the accident was Blue rather than Green?

Try to answer this intuitively before reading on. Did you notice that this problem is analogous to the mammogram problem? The question there was whether the patient had cancer; the issue here is whether the cab was Blue. The prior probability here is .15, because that is the proportion of Blue cabs in the city. Instead of a mammogram, we have a witness's report. The witness's "hit" rate is .80 and his "false-alarm rate" is .20. If we apply Bayes's theorem, formula 4, we get:

$$\frac{p(H/D)}{p(\tilde{H}/D)} = \frac{p(D/H)}{p(D/\tilde{H})} \cdot \frac{p(H)}{p(\tilde{H})} = \frac{.80}{.20} \cdot \frac{.15}{.85} = \frac{12}{17}$$

Thus, $p(H/D)$ is $12/(12 + 17)$, or .41. Most subjects, however, say that the probability is over .50, and many say that it is .80. They think that the cab is more likely to be Blue than Green, but the correct inference from the information presented is the reverse.

Why do we make such errors? Perhaps subjects misunderstand the idea of conditional probability. They are told that the probability of the witness's reporting Blue, given a Blue cab, is .80, but when asked later what they were told, they often say they were told that the probability of a Blue cab, given that the witness reports Blue, is .80 (D. Davis, personal communication). This mistake is similar to the conversion error in logic (Chapter 4), in which subjects seem to confuse the statement "All A are B" with the statement "All B are A." This mistake will account for those subjects who say that the probability of the cab's being Blue was .80, but many subjects, without going as high as .80, still give probabilities over .50.

Kahneman and Tversky (1972) proposed another mechanism for this effect, the *representativeness heuristic*. "A person who follows this heuristic evaluates the probability of an uncertain event, or a sample, by the degree to which it is: (*i*) similar in essential properties to its parent population; and (*ii*) reflects the salient feature of the process by which it was generated" (p. 431). The representativeness heuristic may be based on "the degree of correspondence between a sample and a population, an instance and a category, an act and an actor, or, more generally, between an outcome and a model" (Tversky and Kahneman, 1983, p. 295). In the taxicab problem, the data about the witness seem to be salient, or striking, for most subjects. The subjects think that the courtroom testimony is generated in a way that is like the way in which the test results with the witness were generated. (These were the results that led to the 80% figure.) The proportion of Blue cabs in the city does not appear to these subjects to be very important, although it is.

→ To help subjects notice this proportion, Tversky and Kahneman (1982) gave it a *causal* role in the accident. They replaced item *a* in the taxicab problem with this item: "(a') Although the two companies are roughly equal in size, 85% of all cab accidents in the city involve Green cabs and 15% involve Blue cabs." Subjects given this version were more likely to pay attention to the prior probability. This was indicated by their giving lower probability estimates.

The bias caused by the representativeness heuristic can be illustrated in a number of other problems. Kahneman and Tversky (1973) asked one group of subjects to estimate the *proportion* of first-year graduate students in the United States in nine different fields (business administration, computer science, engineering, humanities and education, law, library science, medicine, physical and life sciences, and social science and social work). Subjects judged computer science to be the second smallest (7% of all graduate students) of the nine fields, with social science and social work the second largest (17%). (These judgments were realistic at the time the study was done, around 1970.) These proportions constitute the prior probabilities, which are often called the *base rates*, before any additional evidence about a particular graduate student is provided.

Another group of subjects was given the following personality sketch of a first-year graduate student (1973, p. 238):

> Tom W. is of high intelligence, although lacking in true creativity. He has a need for order and clarity, and for neat and tidy systems in which every detail finds its appropriate place. His writing is rather dull and mechanical, occasionally enlivened by somewhat corny puns and by flashes of imagination of the sci-fi type. He has a strong drive for competence. He seems to have little feel and little sympathy for other people and does not enjoy interacting with others. Self-centered, he nonetheless has a deep moral sense.

The subjects were asked to judge how *similar* Tom W. was to the typical graduate student in each of the nine fields. The subjects considered Tom to be most similar to computer-science students and least similar to social-science and social work students. These similarity ratings correspond to the representativeness of the sketch of each of the categories.

A third group was told that the sketch of Tom had been written by a psychologist, on the basis of projective tests, when Tom was a senior in high school. This group of subjects was asked to rank the nine different fields according to the *probabilities* of Tom's being in them. The rankings matched almost perfectly the rankings given by the similarity group. Tom was considered to be most likely to be studying computer science and least likely to be studying social science or social work. The probability ratings were not related at all to the prior probabilities. When subjects are asked to make a probability judgment, they apparently base it entirely on their beliefs about similarity, or representativeness, and not at all on their beliefs about prior probability. (It can be assumed that this group of subjects would have given the same prior probability and similarity ratings as the other groups; all groups were drawn from the same population of respondents to an advertisement in a college newspaper.) This neglect of prior probability leads to systematic errors in ranking the fields in probability, that is, in saying which of two fields was more likely. The error is therefore not just a matter of not assigning the right numbers to beliefs.

These same results were obtained even when subjects were told that the personality description was written when Tom was in the 9th grade, on the basis of an interview with a counselor, and even when the subjects were told that this sort of evidence is not very useful. These results were found again in another type of study in which subjects were actually given the prior probability information. Once again, it was ignored, and probability judgments were determined by similarity. Only when subjects were given no evidence at all on which to base a similarity judgment did they make use of their beliefs about prior probability.

Psychologists themselves make this kind of mistake. Langer and Abelson (1974) showed a film of an interview to a group of psychoanalysts and a group of behavior therapists. Half of the members in each group were told that the young woman being interviewed was a student who had asked for psychotherapy. The other half were told that the student had volunteered for a psychological research project and that the interview was conducted by the researcher as part of the project. All subjects (the analysts and behavior therapists) were asked to judge whether the student interviewed was neurotic. The two subgroups of the analysts gave different judgments as a function of what they were told; they were more likely to rate the student as neurotic if they were told that she had sought psychotherapy than if they were told that she was a volunteer in an experiment. The behavior therapists gave the same rating of neuroticism, no matter what they were told.

Langer and Abelson concluded that the analysts were "biased" by what they had been told about the student and that the behavior therapists were not biased. Davis (1979) does not agree that the analysts were biased. He argues that the analysts were simply sensitive to the prior probabilities, whereas the behavior therapists were not. Surely a student who asks for psychotherapy, Davis claims, is more likely to be neurotic than the average subject in a research project. Unless one believes that the interview provides perfect information, like a diagnostic test or a witness that is always right (an impossibility), one ought to supplement the information from the interview with other information at one's disposal, such as the fact that a student had asked for psychotherapy. If anyone made an error here, Davis concludes, it was the behavior therapists, for neglecting the information about the student. Ironically, Davis points out, Langer and Abelson themselves made the same error, for they too judged the information about prior probabilities to be irrelevant.

An example that has practical meaning for college students is the use of various kinds of information on an individual's background, such as the prestige of the college a student attended or the student's social or ethnic origins, in the prediction of success in graduate school or in a job. The argument from Bayes's theorem is that such facts are often relevant. If students with a certain kind of social and cultural background are more likely to do well in graduate school or jobs than students from some other background, then that aspect of background should be used, if we seek the most accurate possible prediction. If we simply ignore group membership (when it is statistically relevant), members of disadvantaged groups can be expected, on the average, to perform less well than members of advantaged groups. Such neglect of group membership therefore constitutes a kind of special consideration for members of disadvantaged groups. There are, of course, excellent social reasons why we should try to help disadvantaged applicants by giving them special consideration, but when we do this we are pursuing other goals than picking the applicants who can be expected to perform best. The special consideration that results from simply neglecting group membership might be too much, too little, or the wrong kind of consideration, in view of these other goals. (Part III of this book discusses many aspects of decision making that are relevant to policy issues of this sort.)

Another apparent effect of the representativeness heuristic, aside from the neglect of information about prior probabilities, is the _conjunction fallacy_. Tversky and Kahneman (1983, p. 297) gave subjects the following description:

> Linda is 31 years old, single, outspoken and very bright. She majored in philosophy. As a student, she was deeply concerned with issues of discrimination and social justice, and also participated in anti-nuclear demonstrations.

Subjects were then asked to rank the following items in terms of probability:

> Linda is a teacher in an elementary school.
> Linda works in a bookstore and takes Yoga classes.
> Linda is active in the feminist movement. [F]
> Linda is a psychiatric social worker.
> Linda is a member of the League of Women Voters.
> Linda is a bank teller. [B]
> Linda is an insurance salesperson.
> Linda is a bank teller and is active in the feminist movement. [B and F].

The critical items here are those that I have marked *F* ("feminist"), *B* ("bank teller"), and *B and F*; the other items are fillers, designed to disguise the issue. Of course, subjects rated F as very probable and B as very unlikely. However, they rated "B and F" as more probable than B alone. This result was found even when the subjects who rated B were not the same as the subjects asked to rate "B and F" or F, so it does not seem that subjects misunderstood "bank teller" to mean "bank teller but not feminist." The subjects who rated B alone heard no mention of feminism.

Of course, the requirement of coherence in probability judgments makes this choice impossible. The set of people who are both bank tellers and feminists cannot be larger than the set of female bank tellers. These sets would be the same only if every female bank teller were an active feminist.

What the subjects do seem to be doing, once again, is judging probability according to representativeness, or similarity. Although the description given was not judged (by other subjects) as very representative of women bank tellers, it was judged to be *more* representative of women bank tellers who are feminists. (See Tversky and Kahneman, 1983, for other examples and an interesting discussion.) This error leads to an incorrect ordering of probabilities. It, therefore, concerns the strengths of beliefs themselves, not just our ability to assign numbers to beliefs.

A simpler form of the conjunction fallacy can be found in children. Agnoli (1991) asked children questions such as "In summer at the beach are there more women or more tanned women?" or "Does the mailman put more letters or more pieces of mail in your mailbox?" Tanned women and letters are more representative, and most children, even seventh graders, judged these as more likely than the more inclusive set.

Is use of the representativeness heuristic irrational? If so, how? In everyday reasoning, it is not necessarily irrational to use similarity in our judgments. In many cases, there is little else we can rely on as a guide to the interpretation of a piece of evidence. In the taxicab problem and the other problems just discussed, however, other relevant information is either provided or readily accessible in memory. In these cases, subjects seem to be overgeneralizing a heuristic that is typically useful, the heuristic of judging probability by representativeness. From a prescriptive point of view, we need to ask whether subjects can learn to take other information into account, that is, whether they can learn more specific heuristics. The rate of errors in the conjunction fallacy, at least, can be substantially reduced by brief instruction in the logic of sets (Agnoli and Krantz, 1989). Such instruction is also effective in the simpler version used with children (Agnoli, 1991). It thus appears that people are capable of learning other heuristics, in at least some cases in which the representativeness heuristic often leads to error.

In situations in which very careful thinking is required, such as medical decisions potentially involving life and death, the evidence we have seen suggests that formal calculations may be worthwhile. Even the best thinking — unaided by mathematics – may give inferior results.

The gambler's fallacy and "probability matching"

Another kind of error possibly related to the use of the representativeness heuristic is the *gambler's fallacy*, otherwise known as the *law of averages*. If you are playing roulette and the last four spins of the wheel have led to the ball's landing on black, you may think that the next ball is more likely than otherwise to land on red. This cannot be. The roulette wheel has no memory. The chance of black is just what it always is. The reason people tend to think otherwise may be that they expect the *sequence* of events to be representative of random sequences, and the typical random sequence at roulette does not have five blacks in a row.

The gambler's fallacy, or something like it, may affect people's behavior when they must make choices concerning repeated events. In a typical experiment on this question, Peterson and Ulehla (1965) asked subjects to roll a die with four black faces and two white faces and to predict (for monetary reward) which face would be on top after each roll. Subjects should know that the die had no memory, so that it was more likely to come up black each time, no matter how many times black had come up in a row. But many subjects persisted in predicting white some of the time, especially after a long run of blacks. This phenomenon was called "probability matching" because people (and some animals, in similar tasks) approximately matched the proportion of their responses to the probabilities of success. For example, they would choose black 2/3 of the time. But this is only a rough approximation, and individual subjects differ substantially.

Such behavior does not seem to result from boredom. Gal and Baron (1996) asked subjects about hypothetical cases like this and found that many subjects believed in the heuristic they were using, in much the way in which subjects believe in naive theories of physics. In one case, for example, a die was rolled and the task was to bet which color would be on top. A subject said, "Being the non-statistician I'd keep guessing red as there are 4 faces red and only 2 green. Then after a number of red came up in a row I'd figure, 'it's probably time for a green,' and would predict green." Another subject seemed aware of the independence of successive trials but still wanted to leave room for an intuitive attachment to a heuristic: "Even though the probability of green coming up does not increase after several red — I always have a feeling it will. Red is the safe bet but intuition will occasionally make me choose green.... I know that my intuition has nothing to do with reality, but usually they coincide."

Children and young adolescents exhibit a more extreme form of this behavior, in which they think of probability as largely irrelevant to decision making. For example, in an interview study of young adolescents, Baron, Granato, Spranca, and Teubal (1993) asked a question about whether we should wear seat belts. The next question was, "Jennifer says that she heard of an accident where a car fell into a lake and a woman was kept from getting out in time because of wearing her seat belt, and another accident where a seat belt kept someone from getting out of the car in time when there was a fire. What do you think about this?" Many subjects responded like the following two:

> A: Well, in that case I don't think you *should* wear a seat belt.
> Q: How do you know when that's gonna happen?
> A: Like, just hope it doesn't!
> Q: So, should you or shouldn't you wear seat belts?
> A: Well, tell-you-the-truth we should wear seat belts.
> Q: How come?
> A: Just in case of an accident. You won't get hurt as much as you will if you didn't wear a seat belt.
> Q: OK, well what about these kinds of things, when people get trapped?
> A: I don't think you should, in that case.

> A: If you have a long trip, you wear seat belts half way, ...
> Q: Which is more likely?
> A: That you'll go flyin' through the windshield ...
> Q: Doesn't that mean you should wear them all the time?
> A: No, it doesn't mean that.
> Q: How do you know if you're gonna have one kind of accident or the other?
> A: You don't know. You just hope and pray that you don't.

These subjects simply did not ask themselves whether the probabilities of the two outcomes were relevant. Gal and Baron (1996) found similar response patterns with dice in adolescents.

The availability heuristic

People often judge probability by thinking of examples. Consider the following problem (Tversky and Kahneman, 1973, p. 211): Which is more likely, that a word in English starts with the letter K or has K as its third letter? The sensible way to try to answer that is to think of examples of words. This is the *availability heuristic*. Most people find it easier to think of words that start with K than words with K as their third letter, so they say that the former is more probable. Actually, the latter is more probable. Tversky and Kahneman assert that we think otherwise because our memory of spellings tends to be organized by initial letters.

➤ The same researchers give another example (Tversky and Kahneman, 1983, p. 295): What is the probability that a seven-letter word randomly selected from a novel would end in *ing*? What is the probability that such a word will have *n* as its sixth letter? When different groups of subjects were asked these questions, the probability estimates were higher for *ing* than for *n*. Of course, the former instances are included in the latter instances, so the former instances cannot be more frequent. Here, the conjunction fallacy is produced by the availability heuristic. The words ending in *ing* are more available because the suffix *ing* is a better retrieval cue than a single letter; subjects think of words more quickly when given this cue than when given the other.

Recall the study that Lichtenstein and her colleagues made (1978) of judgments of the frequency with which different dangers caused death in the United States (Figure 6.1). We have already noted that subjects tended to overestimate the frequency of low-probability events, and vice versa. Lichtenstein and her colleagues found, however, that there was another important determinant of errors in estimation: the frequency with which dangers were mentioned in newspapers. For example (taking into account the effect of frequency itself), tornadoes and electrocutions — which are almost always reported in the paper – are overestimated. Deaths resulting from smallpox vaccinations and many common diseases such as asthma are underestimated; these things are usually not reported.

Researchers have also demonstrated the effects of the availability heuristic in subjects' use of probability trees. When experts try to assess the probability of an event's occurring — let us say an engineer wants to predict the probability of a catastrophe in a nuclear-power plant — they often use such tree diagrams as a way of trying to ensure that they have considered all of the possibilities. By breaking such a problem down in this way, we can obtain a more accurate probability assessment.

To take a more familiar example, however, consider the following list of categories of the things that can prevent a car from starting:

Battery charge too low	Starting system defective	Fuel system defective	Ignition system defective	Other engine problems	Mischief or vandalism	All other problems
Faulty ground connections .... Terminals loose or corroded .... Battery weak	Switches defective .... Transmission not in "park" .... Seat belt problem .... Faulty starter motor .... Starter drive defective	Insufficient fuel .... Excess fuel (flooding) .... Defective choke .... Defective air filter	Coil faulty .... Distributor faulty .... Spark plugs defective .... Defective wiring between components	Oil too thick .... Pistons frozen .... Poor compression	Theft or breakage of vital part (such as battery) .... Siphoning of gas .... Disruption of wiring	

Each of the sub-possibilities listed can be further subdivided. For example, "faulty ground connection" can be subdivided into "paint," "corrosion," "dirt," and "loose connections." Fischhoff, Slovic, and Lichtenstein (1978) presented this "tree" (with lines between each main possibility and its sub-possibilities, and with all of the sub-sub-possibilities), to a group of automobile mechanics and asked for probability estimates for the major branches (such as "Battery charge too low"). Subjects assigned a mean probability of .078 to the last category, "All other problems." A similar group of mechanics was then given the tree with two of the branches pruned, those involving the starting and ignition system. The subjects using the unpruned tree had assigned mean probabilities of .195 and .144 to these two branches, respectively. In the pruned tree, the problems that these branches represented should go under "All other problems," and the probability for that category should therefore increase from .078 to .078 + .195 + .144, or .468. The actual mean probability assigned to "all other problems" by the group with the pruned tree was .140, a slight increase but not big enough.

When something is not represented in our analysis, we tend not to think of it. This effect may weigh on the other side of the debate about nuclear-power plants from the other effects we have been considering. Availability of frightening news stories, such as those about the Three Mile Island and Chernobyl accidents, as well as overestimation of the frequency of such accidents (which very rarely occur), may tend to lead to overestimates of risk, but failure to consider what information might be omitted from the analysis may lead to underestimates. Most nonexpert estimates of accident risk are based on just this sort of analysis. People tend to underestimate the probability of "All other problems."[4]

---

[4] A well-known professor of decision theory — after lecturing on fault trees for cars not starting – went to the parking lot to find that his own car would not start. After checking all the branches of the tree that

Availability is also affected by personal experience. When we do something with another person, we may remember our own point of view more vividly than we remember the point of view of the other person — a point of view we may not even experience. Ross and Sicoly (1979) asked husbands and wives to estimate the extent to which they were responsible for a number of activities, such as cleaning the house, making breakfast, and causing arguments. Ratings of the two spouses for the same activity tended to differ. Each spouse tended to think that he or she was more responsible than the other spouse thought. As a result, the total responsibility added up to more than 100%. For example, if a husband thought that he was 60% responsible for causing arguments, and the wife thought that she was 60% responsible, that would add up to 120%. This effect held for the negative items (such as causing arguments) as well as the positive ones. In a second study, the same effect was found when basketball players were asked to estimate the extent to which the members of their own team, rather than their opponents, were responsible for "turning points" in their games.

Availability of examples can be affected by mood, and this effect, in turn, can affect probability or frequency judgments. E. J. Johnson and Tversky (1983) gave college students descriptions of various events, written like newspaper stories, to read. They then asked the students to estimate the frequencies with which 50,000 people would experience certain dangers (such as traffic accidents, fire, and leukemia) within a 1-year period. When the newspaper story concerned the violent death of a male undergraduate — for example, in a fire – estimates of *all* risks increased, whether or not they were similar or identical to the event in question. The same kinds of increases occurred when the story was simply a sad one about a young man who had just broken up with his girlfriend while undergoing other stresses from his family and his job. When the story was a happy one about a young man who experienced positive events — getting into medical school and doing well on a difficult examination — frequency estimates decreased.

The kinds of availability problems described so far cannot be called "irrational" when they occur in everyday life. It would, in most cases, take an unreasonable amount of effort to avoid the effects of memory organization or of the information we are given by others. In many cases, these effects could be avoided only with the use of systematic data analysis of the sort done by scientists. Most of the time, availability is probably as good a guide as we can expect, when systematic data are not available. In extremely important decisions, however, such as those that affect many people, it is worthwhile to take every precaution we can imagine to avoid error. In such decisions, the danger of availability effects is a good reason for us to rely on systematic data collection and analysis — rather than our own hunches — when numerical data are available.

he could check without the help of a mechanic, he finally called a towing service. As the car was about to be towed away, he noticed that the car was not his. His car started without trouble, after he remembered where he had parked it.

Subadditivity

The availability and representativeness heuristics often work in similar ways to raise (or lower) the judged probability of some category of events. When members of a category are highly available, the judgment will be raised. When the description of a subcategory is similar to (representative of) that of a larger category, the subcategory will be judged as more probable if the larger category is assumed. Availability or representativeness may increase if a description is more explicit.

For example, subjects in one experiment judged that the probability of death from cancer in the United States was 18%, the probability of death from heart attack was 22%, and the probability of death from "other natural cause" was 33%. Other subjects judged that the probability of death from a natural cause was 58%. Natural causes, of course, are made up of exactly cancer, heart attack, and other causes. But the sum of those three probabilities was 73%, not 58%. This kind of result is observed consistently (Tversky and Koehler, 1994). In another example, subjects wrote down the last digit of their social security number and estimated the proportion of married couples in the United States with exactly that many children. The sum of the proportions for 0, 1, 2, and 3 children was 1.45. Of course, it must be less than one, because some couples have more than 3.

The last two results can be explained in terms of availability of examples. Representativeness may also play a role. In another study in this series, physicians evaluated the probability of various outcomes of a case description about a patient admitted to the emergency ward. The overall judged probability that the patient would survive was lower than the sum of probabilities assigned to several ways in which this could happen. The general phenomenon is called _subadditivity_, because the judged probability of the whole is less than the probabilities of the parts. The fault tree experiment described above is another example of subadditivity.

Subadditivity is also found in frequency judgments of the sort required by surveys. For example, answers to questions like "How often in the past month have you felt embarrassed?" are usually lower than the sum of answers to "How often in the past month have you felt embarrassed about something you said?" and "How often in the past month have you felt embarrassed about something someone else said?" (Mumford and Dawes, 1999).

The same mechanisms may underlie an effect of familiarity on probability judgment. More familiar events are more available. We thus find it easier to think of reasons why these events will happen, and reasons why they won't happen. Fox and Levav (2000) asked students at Duke University which of two events was more likely. One was "Duke men's basketball beats UNC [University of North Carolina] men's basketball at Duke's Cameron Indoor Staduim in January 1999," and the other was "Duke men's fencing beats UNC men's fencing at Duke's Cameron Card Gym in January 1999." Duke students are much more familiar with basketball than with fencing. Seventy-five percent of the students thought the basketball victory was more likely. Other students answered identical questions, but with Duke and UNC switched. Forty-four percent of the students sait that a UNC victory in basketball was more likely than a UNC victory in fencing. Of course, 44% plus 75% is larger than 100%, and only one such game would be played. Thus, familiarity with basketball led subjects to think of the basketball event as more likely than the fencing event, no matter which basketball event was described.

Hindsight bias

Another cause of distortion that is observed in everyday reasoning can be more easily avoided. This is illustrated in the phenomenon of *hindsight bias*. Fischhoff (1975) asked subjects to read true historical accounts of incidents with which they were unfamiliar, drawn from history books as well as personal psychological case histories. One scenario concerned the battle between the British forces and the Gurkhas (from Nepal) on the northern frontier of Bengal in 1814. Subjects were asked to assign numerical probabilities to the major possible outcomes: British victory; Gurkha victory; military stalemate with no peace settlement; or military stalemate with a peace settlement. The history provided was consistent with any one of these outcomes.

Some subjects were told the outcome: The British won. These subjects were asked to rate the probability of the various outcomes as they would have if they had not been told the true outcome. The mean probability that these subjects assigned to the true outcome was .57. Other subjects were not told the outcome. They rated the probability of a British victory as only .34. Evidently, subjects who were told the outcome could not avoid what they knew in hindsight.

Similar results have been obtained from many other kinds of studies. Fischhoff (1977) give subjects two-choice questions concerning general knowledge, like those used in the studies of confidence described earlier in this chapter. Some subjects were told the answers and were asked what probabilities they would have assigned to these answers had they not been given them. Once again, these probabilities were higher than those assigned to the same items by other subjects who had not been given the answers. It appears that people tend to underestimate how much they have learned from being told something. They tend to think they knew it all along.

Slovic and Fischhoff (1977) presented subjects with descriptions of scientific experiments. In one experiment some blood from a rat that had just given birth was injected into another female rat. The question was whether the second rat would exhibit maternal behavior. Some subjects, the hindsight group, were told that the first time this experiment was done, the rat did exhibit the behavior. They were asked to estimate the probability that all of the next 10 rats would replicate this initial result. Other subjects, the foresight group, were asked how they would answer this question *if* the experiment worked on the first rat. The hindsight group gave higher proportions. For this experiment, the hindsight subjects gave a mean probability of .44, and the foresight subjects gave a mean probability of .30.

In a second study, subjects were asked to give reasons why the study worked out the way it did *and* how they would explain the result if it came out the *other* way. These instructions reduced the effect. The same kind of instructions were effective in reducing hindsight bias among a group of neuropsychologists who were asked what probabilities they would have assigned to various possible diagnoses of a case if they had not been told the answer (Arkes, Faust, Guilmette, and Hart, 1988). The hindsight bias here was the tendency to assign higher probabilities to the diagnosis they were told was true. When they were asked to give a reason for each possible diagnosis, the bias was reduced. Apparently, when subjects are given the "answer," they think of reasons why this answer must be correct. They fail to think of reasons why it might be incorrect, reasons that might occur to them if they were asked to estimate the probability of the outcome without knowing how it had turned out.

This effect seems to be an example of one of the major biases described in Chapter 3, a tendency to search for evidence in a biased way — in particular, to search for evidence that favors a possibility that is already strong. Telling people the answer is a way to make that possibility strong. Telling them to think of evidence on the other side is a way to reduce the bias.

Averaging

Birnbaum and Mellers (1983) presented subjects with a task very much like the taxicab problem. Subjects were asked to estimate the probability that particular used cars would last for three years. They were told the prior probability figures for cars of the same model and year, for example, 30% probability of lasting for three years. For most problems, subjects were also told that a judge had examined the car and had pronounced it in "good shape" (or, in other problems, in bad shape). Subjects were also given statistical information about the reliability of the judge; for example, they might be told that the judge had correctly identified 60% of the cars that would last for three years and 60% that would not. Each subject was given several problems of this type, so that the subject's sensitivity to prior probabilities and diagnostic evidence (what the judge said about the car) could be determined by comparing the conditions with different values of these quantities.

Subjects were generally sensitive to both prior probabilities and diagnostic evidence. (Previous studies have found that prior probabilities are not totally neglected when subjects are given several problems with different prior probabilities rather than just one problem.) The results when prior probabilities were very high (.90 probability of lasting) or very low (.10 probability) were especially interesting. Take the case in which the prior probability is .90; the judge says the car is in good shape; and the judge is correct 60% of the time for good cars, and 60% for poor cars. By Bayes's theorem, the probability that the car will last is slightly higher than .90. The odds are:

$$\frac{p(H/D)}{p(\tilde{}H/D)} = \frac{p(D/H)}{p(D/\tilde{}H)} \cdot \frac{p(H)}{p(\tilde{}H)} = \frac{.60}{.40} \cdot \frac{.90}{.10} = \frac{27}{2}$$

Hence, the probability is $27/(27 + 2)$ or .93. Even though the evidence from the judge is poor, it adds a little to what the prior probabilities indicate.

Subjects typically give a value considerably *lower* than .90 under these circumstances (and a value higher than .10 when the prior probability is .10 and the judge says the car is in bad shape). When they are given the prior probability alone, they use it. They say that the probability is .90, for a prior probability of .90 (and .10, for a prior probability of .10).

What they seem to be doing is *averaging* the information they are given. (See Chapter 15 for another example of averaging.) This leads them to weigh the evidence from the judge in the wrong direction. Averaging can result from a kind of anchoring-and-adjustment process in which subjects anchor on one probability (for example, the prior probability) and adjust in the direction of the other (for example, the diagnosticity of the judge's opinions). Lopes (1987a) found that subjects can be easily taught to avoid this error by thinking, first, about the direction in which each piece of evidence should change their probability judgment and, second, about how much their judgment ought to move toward a probability of 1 or 0.

Conclusion

This chapter examined a number of biases in probability judgment and the heuristics that seem to cause them. How might we interpret these biases and heuristics from the point of view of *prescriptive* theory? How serious are they? Is it irrational to neglect prior probabilities when estimating posterior probabilities?

Cohen (1981) has argued that the rules of probability are not normative, because no one has presented a good argument explaining why we should follow them. Violations of the rules, according to Cohen, are wrong only from the point of view of the rules themselves, as though we had violated the rules of a game. I argued in chapter 5 that the rules are not arbitrary and can be justified by arguments concerning their suitability to their purpose.

The view at the opposite extreme (which perhaps no one holds) is that probability theory is both normative and prescriptive, so that any violation of it is a clear instance of irrationality. A counterexample to this extreme view is that some effects of the use of the availability heuristic are prescriptively justifiable even though they are normatively incorrect. To avoid these effects — at least in the laboratory tasks where they are found – would require much more time than it is reasonable for a person to spend. (Of course, for more important decisions, the extra time would be well spent.)

Von Winterfeldt and Edwards (1986) argue that many violations of probability theory are real and potentially serious but are not "irrational"; rather they are simply the result of ignorance — of our not having learned certain methods of mathematical calculation or estimation (like the heuristic that Lopes taught her subjects). This view could certainly account for the biases involved in averaging. The errors in averaging observed in the laboratory show only that a knowledge of probability theory does not develop on its own without instruction. The results are no more a sign of irrationality than it would be if we demonstrated that most people cannot solve problems in physics. We cannot expect them to, because they have not had a course in physics yet. People's willingness to make probability judgments despite their lack of training suggests that they are using a "naive theory," like the naive theories of physics discussed in Chapter 1. Evidence of bias in averaging is evidence of a need for education — but the kind of education in question is specific to probability.

The important aspect of this view is its claim that biases are specific to calculations with numerical probabilities, as opposed to thinking or belief formation in general. It is, in my opinion, irrelevant to questions of rationality whether a bias results from mere ignorance or from something else (such as, perhaps, unwillingness to use rational methods even after learning how to use them). Rational methods are those methods of thinking that help people achieve their own goals (or the goals they ought to have). The most important of these methods are those that can be used in all thinking. If an irrational bias that affects all thinking — such as the lack of active open-mindedness — results from ignorance about rational thinking itself, the bias is still irrational, because it prevents people from achieving their goals. Therefore, the important part of Von Winterfeldt and Edwards's argument is that the biases are specific to numerical calculation.

That view holds for averaging but not for all the biases. Some of the ones that we have observed reflect two central biases that prevent good thinking in general: insufficient search, or the failure to consider alternative possibilities, goals, and additional evidence; and favoritism toward initially favored possibilities. These central biases seemed to be involved in overconfidence and in hindsight bias. They may be involved in representativeness bias as well, since information about prior probabilities could be a neglected source of evidence against initial conclusions. If people thought more thoroughly about what evidence was needed, they could take prior probabilities into account, whether or not they received special instruction in probability. Likewise, if people thought critically about their own heuristics, by looking for cases in which the heuristics are misleading, they could learn what these cases are and what other heuristics are more useful. These central biases partly account for other more specific biases, because they stand in the way of the learning that might correct them.

For most people, however, special instruction, as well as good thinking, is required to learn about probability theory. Probability is already taught as part of school mathematics. When our naive theories can have harmful effects, more systematic instruction may be warranted. Such instruction could include such topics as the relevance of prior probabilities and the dangers of hindsight, availability, and extreme confidence.

Chapter 7

Hypothesis testing

Data! Data! Data! I cannot make bricks without clay.

Sherlock Holmes

A hypothesis is a proposition that we evaluate, or test, by gathering evidence concerning its truth or, more generally, its probability. A physician trying to explain a patient's illness forms hypotheses about the patient's disease and then tests these hypotheses by asking the patient questions and ordering various tests. A scientist trying to explain the cause of a disease also forms hypotheses and tests them by doing experiments or by gathering other sorts of evidence (such as statistics about the incidence of the disease).

Hypothesis *testing*, the topic of this chapter, is the selection of the evidence, the asking of questions. The physician must decide what questions to ask, and the scientist must decide which data to collect. Hypothesis testing is that part of the search-inference process in which the thinker searches for evidence that can strengthen or weaken various possibilities. Each possibility is a possible answer to some question (goal) that inspired the search for hypotheses: What is wrong with the patient? What causes this disease?[1]

Hypothesis testing is important in everyday life and in other professions as well as in medicine and science. Children may learn the meanings of words by testing hypotheses. When we solve a test problem from Raven's Progressive Matrices (Chapter 2), we gather evidence to test some hypothesis about the rule. We try out a command on a computer in order to test some hypothesis about what the command does. Clinical psychologists test hypotheses in the same way physicians do, and, of course, detectives test hypotheses all the time.

Hypothesis testing is an essential part of actively open-minded thinking because it involves putting our beliefs to the test of evidence. The very act of testing a favorite hypothesis requires that we be open to the possibility that it is incorrect (if we are

---

[1] The term "hypothesis testing" is used in statistics to refer to making inferences from data. That is a different question.

willing to make the correct inference from counterevidence) and that we challenge our hypotheses actively rather than waiting passively for couterevidence to come along (Popper, 1962; Horton, 1967).

Before we can test hypotheses, we must have them in mind. Hypothesis formulation is the search for possibilities to test. A good hypothesis answers the original question, can be tested by gathering additional evidence, and is consistent with the evidence at hand. A scientist must try to think, simultaneously, of good hypotheses and good experiments to test them. Sometimes we collect evidence in the hope that it will suggest a hypothesis – as Sherlock Holmes did so well – rather than to test a hypothesis that we have in mind.

This chapter is concerned with the normative, descriptive, and prescriptive theory of hypothesis testing. The theory of probability – coupled with a simple theory of decision making – turns out to provide a good normative model. Departures from this model suggest certain prescriptive heuristics: considering alternative hypotheses and looking ahead by asking what we will do with the information we seek when we get it.

Hypotheses in science

An example from medicine

A classic case of hypothesis testing in science, which illustrates how vital this process can be, was the work of Ignaz Philipp Semmelweis on the causes of childbed fever, or puerperal fever (Hempel, 1966), a disease that is now known to bear a large responsibility for the high mortality rate for new mothers that was a fact of life, in Europe and the United States, until the late nineteenth century. Semmelweis's work was done in the 1840s, before the acceptance of what we now call the "germ theory" of disease and the use of antisepsis. The Vienna General Hospital had experienced a very high rate of deaths from puerperal fever for several years (over 10% in some years) among women who had just given birth in the First Maternity Division. The prevalence of the disease in the Second Maternity Division was much lower (around 2%).

Semmelweis, a physician in the First Division, set out to discover the cause. He excluded a number of hypotheses on the basis of evidence already at hand. For example, he reasoned that the epidemic could not be the result of overcrowding, because the First Division was less crowded than the Second. (Women tried to avoid it.) Most other possible factors, such as diet and general care, were identical in the two divisions. One difference was that in the First Division, deliveries were done with the mothers on their backs during delivery, and in the Second, on their sides. Semmelweis could not imagine how this could matter, but he ordered that all deliveries be done with mothers on their sides – to no avail. Another hypothesis was that the disease was psychologically transmitted by the priest, when he passed through the wards of the First Division (with a distinctive bell to indicate his presence) in order to administer the last rites to a dying patient. The hypothesis was that this demoralized the other patients, already weakened by childbirth, and caused their deaths. Semmelweis induced the priest to enter the wing by a roundabout route without his bell, so that he would not be noticed. Again, there was no change. New mothers still died.

A colleague of Semmelweis's died of an infection received from a scalpel that had been used to perform an autopsy. Semmelweis noticed that the colleague's symptoms resembled those of puerperal fever. It occurred to him that deliveries in the First Division were done by medical students and physicians who often had just performed autopsies, whereas deliveries in the Second Division were done by midwives. He hypothesized that "cadaverous matter" – material from the corpses that stuck to the students' hands – might be the cause of the disease. To test this hypothesis, he induced the students and physicians to wash their hands in a solution of chlorinated lime, which he thought would remove the cadaverous matter, before delivering babies. This succeeded. The incidence of puerperal fever was sharply reduced, to the level of the Second Division.

Following this great success, on one occasion Semmelweis and his colleagues examined a woman in labor who suffered from a festering cervical cancer and then proceeded to examine twelve other women without washing their hands, confident that they could do no harm, since the first woman was alive. Eleven of the twelve others died of puerperal fever. This tragedy convinced Semmelweis to broaden his hypothesis to include "putrid living matter" as well as cadaverous matter. (Semmelweis himself was later to die accidentally in a similar way.)

Of course, Semmelweis was still not quite right. As we know today (after the laborious testing of many other hypotheses by many scientists), bacteria were the problem. Students and interns transferred the bacteria from the corpses of women who had died of the puerperal fever to women who were not yet infected. Semmelweis did not end the disease, because there were other paths by which the bacteria could be transmitted. Of course, Semmelweis's work was by no means in vain. It led others, such as Pasteur, more directly to the germ theory, and it saved many lives along the way. Incorrect hypotheses may still be of considerable value, both in practical terms and in narrowing the search for further hypotheses.

Semmelweis's work illustrates nicely how hypothesis testing often works. To use the terms of the search-inference framework, a hypothesis is a *possibility*. The hypothesis usually concerns a possible *cause* of some event. Roughly, a "cause" is an event or state whose presence or absence would make the event in question occur or not occur, if the hypothesized cause could be manipulated.[2]

In the simplest sort of hypothesis testing, we imagine some result that would definitely be obtained if the hypothesis were true, and we look for that result. For example, Semmelweis's hypothesis that the position of delivery was important implied

---

[2]Often, causes cannot be manipulated. When we say that the shape of the moon's orbit is "caused," or determined, by the earth's gravity, we cannot test this by removing the gravity and seeing what happens. Still, to say that the orbit is determined by gravity is to make a claim about what *would* happen if we could remove the gravity. Note also that the term "cause," as used here, includes partial causes, or influences.

that changing the position would reduce the incidence of the disease. This result was not found, so that hypothesis was eliminated. His hypothesis that cadaverous matter caused the disease implied that hand washing would help. Because it did help, the hypothesis was accepted.

This simple method has its dangers. When a predicted result is found, we must still be wary of the possibility that there are *alternative explanations.* An alternative explanation is another hypothesis – aside from the one we are testing – that is also consistent with a result. In fact, Semmelweis discovered an alternative (and better) explanation of the cadaverous-matter hypothesis, and we have now accepted a still-better alternative: The cause was microorganisms specific to the disease in question. Alternative explanations are one of the bugaboos of science.

Despite the existence of alternatives to the cadaverous-matter hypothesis, Semmelweis still succeeded in his original goal of reducing the incidence of the disease. We test hypotheses because of some goal, and when that goal is achieved, the presence of alternative explanations can become a matter of curiosity rather than substance. For Semmelweis, the main goal was to find a cure for the disease. (Of course, the pursuit of alternative explanations in this case was not a matter of mere curiosity. Although hundreds of lives were saved, even more were saved with each new step in medical knowledge.)

In science, the worst situation – which happens all too often – is to do an experiment to test some hypothesis, have the experiment succeed, and then discover that we have overlooked a plausible and important alternative hypothesis that could have been eliminated if only a different experiment had been run. For example, if Semmelweis had tested his delivery-position hypothesis by asking the midwives to do all of the deliveries (rather than by asking the students to use the position that the midwives used), he would not have known whether the delivery position or something else was at fault. If he had then changed the students' methods, expecting an immediate cure, he would have been surprised to find no improvement. In general, the way to avoid such surprises is to anticipate alternative explanations in advance, before doing an experiment – especially when the experiment is expensive or time-consuming.

A second danger is that a hypothesis will be falsely rejected because of a bad experiment. Suppose Semmelweis had tested his hypothesis by asking the students to examine their hands to make sure they were clean, and if not, rinse them off in a basin of water instead of chlorinated lime. This experiment would very likely have failed, and Semmelweis might have falsely concluded that transmission of material on people's hands had nothing to do with the disease. The same situation would have come about if chlorinated lime had not turned out to kill bacteria.

Any experiment involves additional assumptions other than the hypothesis itself: for example, the assumption that the chlorinated lime (or water) would remove the offending substance. If the experiment fails, the hypothesis is not necessarily disproved, for some other assumption may be at fault. The best experiments are those in which the key assumptions are very likely to be true. For example, we have a great deal of evidence that high temperatures kill bacteria. If we boil an object that we suspect is contaminated for an hour and find that it is still capable of transmitting disease, we conclude that the disease is not bacterial, yet the bacterium in question may turn out to be an oddity, a type that can withstand high temperature.

In the early stages of scientific inquiry, scientists must stumble around in the dark, using methods that are still untested in order to establish facts, which, if they are established, validate the methods themselves.

Testing scientific hypotheses

Much of the literature in the philosophy of science is concerned with the normative and prescriptive theory of hypothesis formulation and testing. In science, hypotheses are often derived from *theories*, which are coherent explanations of several different phenomena. Newton's theory of gravitation, for example, explains the motions of the moon and the planets, and the trajectories and acceleration of bodies in free fall near the earth. A new hypothesis derived from this theory is that gravitational force is reduced at the tops of mountains.

The work of Karl Popper has had an especially important influence on our thinking about theories and how they are tested (see Popper, 1962, especially ch. 1). Popper wanted to carry out a "rational reconstruction" of scientific practice: That is, he wanted to look at the actual practice of scientists and describe it in the most "charitable" way. He assumed that scientists were often rational, and he tried to use this assumption to discover the nature of rationality in science.

Popper was particularly interested in trying to distinguish the method of formulating theories in the more successful sciences, such as modern physics (especially Einstein's theory of relativity), from the method used in what he considered questionable sciences, including the psychoanalytic theories of Adler (for whom Popper had worked for a time) and Freud and the political theory of Marx. Popper criticized these latter theories for their apparent capacity to explain any result or observation. When some Freudians or Marxists were given counterexamples to their favored theories, he said, they always had some explanation of why the counterexample was not a good one. At worst, they would accuse their critic of bias, terming it "resistance" or "false consciousness."

In contrast, Popper noted, Einstein's theory of relativity made a strong prediction about the exact angle at which a beam of starlight would be bent as it passed by the sun. If the angle had been anything other than predicted, Einstein would have had to admit that his theory was incorrect, but the prediction was accurate. Einstein's theory, in contrast to Freud's or Marx's, was therefore *falsifiable* – that is, capable of being proved false by an experiment or observation. Moreover, Einstein's theory was a great advance, because the prediction was *risky*: In terms of the other theories accepted at that time, the angle that Einstein's theory predicted was considered extremely unlikely.

Popper therefore concluded that sciences advance successfully by making theoretical statements that are "bold conjectures" and then trying to refute them (falsify them) through experiment or observation. Those conjectures that survive the attempts to refute them become accepted theories, such as the theory of relativity, but they are never finally "proved," since they can always be refuted in the future (just as Newton's theory was partly refuted by the success of Einstein's).

Popper's theory set the agenda for reflection about the prescriptive theory of science. Subsequent philosophical writers have criticized Popper's argument, qualifying it in important respects. "Bold conjectures," they point out, are often wrong, especially if the theory that predicts certain observations is unlikely to be true. Popper's theory does better as an account of successful theory formulation in hindsight than as a prescription for scientific practice. The procedure he advises is not very practical: It is a little like telling a scientist, "Take a wild guess, *and be right!*"

John Platt (1964) suggested that scientists should try to play the game "Twenty Questions"[3] with nature using a more conservative strategy, which he called "strong inference." Rather than making a bold (unlikely) conjecture, the scientist should divide the possible hypotheses about some phenomenon roughly in half and then try to rule out one of the halves. When we play Twenty Questions, we usually begin with some question like "Is it alive?" If the answer is positive, we then ask, "Is it animate?" Each question divides the possibilities roughly in half. Likewise, in real science, we might ask whether a disease is transmitted by an organism. If the answer is yes, we might ask whether the organism is bacterial, and so on. Platt argues that this method, which he called "strong inference," is more efficient than asking "boldly" whether the disease is caused by a spirochete (when there is no reason to think that it is).

Another difficulty with Popper's theory is that it assumes that hypotheses can be falsified. Platt's theory has this assumption as well, for it assumes that one half of the hypotheses or the other will be eliminated by a good question. We have already seen that this assumption may be too idealistic to serve as a prescriptive theory for scientific practice. It is rarely, if ever, true that a scientific theory can be refuted by any one observation or experiment. Usually it is possible – with more or less plausibility – to find some reason why the experiment was not a good test of the hypothesis. In some cases, like the case of rinsing the hands in a basin of water, the experiment may truly be a poor one.

Imre Lakatos (1978) attempts to answer this criticism by arguing that most scientific theories have a "core" of crucial claims, along with a "periphery" of claims that can be changed as needed. A particular hypothesis involves both core and peripheral claims. If the hypothesis is rejected by an experiment, we can reject the peripheral claim and keep the core. For example, he says, the core of the Ptolemaic theory of astronomy was the claim that the sun and the planets revolve around the earth. Over the years, many peripheral claims (about "epicycles," or orbits within orbits) had been added, subtracted, and modified, in order to explain the fact that the planets seemed at times to reverse direction relative to the stars. The core of the

---

[3] In this game, one person thinks of something (a person, object, or animal, for example), and the other tries to discover what it is by asking no more than twenty questions, to which the answers given are only yes or no. The "scientist" may guess the word at any time, but if she is wrong, she must give up for that word.

Ptolemaic theory was protected by these modifications. When Copernicus showed how the planetary motions could be explained more simply by assuming that the earth and the planets revolved around the sun, no crucial experiment or potential observation was known that could be used to demonstrate which of the two theories was superior. The Copernican theory won out, according to Lakatos, because this theory was more *progressive* as a program for research; one could ask and answer more questions within it than within the Ptolemaic theory. When Kepler assumed the Copernican theory was true, for example, he was able to show that planets moved in elliptical orbits, and Newton, in turn, showed how these ellipses could be explained by the inverse-square law of gravity.

For Lakatos, then, a theory is useful if it generates valuable research. Lakatos's view implies that theories cannot be compared directly with one another, to determine their closeness to truth or their probability. We can compare theories only in hindsight, after we have seen what research they generated. Again, this view is not useful advice to practicing scientists, unless they can foresee the future.

We could, however, use probability theory (as we do with other hypotheses) to evaluate the effect of experimental results on hypotheses. By asking about the effect of various results on our hypotheses before we do an experiment, we can determine the value of the experiment before we do it. To find how the probability of a scientific hypothesis changes when we obtain an experimental result, we would assign a prior probability to each hypothesis, $p(H)$. Observations and experimental results would constitute the data, the D's. After assigning a likelihood to each datum given each hypothesis, $p(D/H)$, we could then use Bayes's theorem to calculate the posterior probability of the hypothesis, $p(H/D)$. The data cannot, in science, be expected to raise the probability of a hypothesis precisely to 1 or lower it precisely to 0. Other things being equal, however, a good scientific experiment would be one with potential outcomes that have a high probability, given some hypothesis, and a low probability given others. If we obtain such a result, our probabilities for the various hypotheses would change greatly, and we would, therefore, have learned a lot.

Probability theory would constitute part of the *normative* theory of science. The other part of the normative theory would be the theory of decision making, which is explored in Part III.[4] The theory is normative but not necessarily prescriptive. Although scientists can, and sometimes do, calculate probabilities as specified by this theory, they can probably do nearly as well by following certain prescriptive rules of thumb, which we shall discuss shortly.

This normative theory can help us to understand why the prescriptive advice of Popper and Platt, on how to formulate and test scientific hypotheses, is good advice when it is possible to follow it. For Popper, a good result (D, datum) is one that has a probability of 1, given the hypothesis being tested (H), and a very low probability given any other hypothesis ($\tilde{\ }H$). If the critical result is found, the probability of H

---

[4]This view – that the normative theory of science consists of probability theory and decision theory – is advocated by Horwich, 1982, especially pp. 1–15, 51–63, and 100–136. I expressed my own support for it earlier in *Rationality and Intelligence*, 1985b, ch. 4.

increases considerably, because the diagnostic ratio is so high.[5]

For Platt, a good *experiment* is one that seeks a result with a probability of 1, given one set of hypotheses, H_1, and a probability of 0, given some other set H_2; H_2 is the same as $\tilde{}H_1$ (everything not in H_1). If the result is found, we know that the truth is in H_1; if not, we know that the truth is in H_2. Moreover, Platt specifies that the sets should be chosen so that $p(H_2)$ and $p(H_1)$ are about .5. By this choice of hypotheses to test, we can ask the fewest questions to determine exactly where the truth lies – that is, in which sub-hypothesis of H_1 or H_2.

More generally, however, we should look for results in which the conditional probabilities for results, given the important hypotheses, differ greatly. Whether we seek results with probabilities of 1 or 0 will depend to some extent on why we need to know and how sure we need to be. We do not always need absolute certainty in order to take some practical action or in order to accept some scientific theory as very likely true, for the purposes of planning our next experiment. A good heuristic to keep us on the trail of such results is this: "Be sure to consider alternative hypotheses." If our planned experiment or observation cannot distinguish the hypothesis of interest from the alternatives, it is not a good experiment. If no experiment can do so, our hypothesis is untestable, and we ought to re-examine our goal in formulating it.

Sometimes, results that are predicted by a new hypothesis, but improbable otherwise, are already known but not noticed before the new hypothesis is stated. For example, astronomers before Copernicus knew that retrograde motion of planets (opposite to their usual direction through the stars) occurred only when the planets were high in the sky at midnight (hence opposite the sun). This fact was implied by Copernicus's theory. In Ptolemy's theory, it was an unlikely coincidence. It was not taken as evidence against Ptolemy's theory, though, until a better alternative was found (Lightman and Gingerich, 1991). According to probability theory, this is reasonable: the fact that evidence is improbable given a hypothesis does not weaken the hypothesis unless the evidence is more probable given some alternative.

The psychology of hypothesis testing

A traditional theory in psychology (Bruner, Goodnow, and Austin, 1956), now largely discredited, holds that knowing a *concept* amounts to knowing how to classify some instance as a member of a certain category. It was argued, moreover, that we classify instances on the basis of *cues*. For example, in card games, knowing the concept "spade" amounts to knowing how to classify cards as spades or nonspades. In this case, there is a single relevant cue, the shape of the little symbol in the upper left-hand corner of each card. The concept "seven," in cards, is based on a different

[5]Popper would disagree with this account, because he regards probability as a poor criterion of the value of a theory. He argues that the "most probable" theory is always the least interesting, citing, as an example, a noncommittal statement such as this: "The light will be bent some amount, or possibly not at all." He does not, however, consider a *change* in the probability of a hypothesis as a criterion of the value of a *result*, which is what is argued here.

cue – the number printed in the corner (or seven symbols in the middle of the card). Cues are also called *attributes* or *features* of things.

Concept formation

In some cases, the theory holds, a concept is characterized by a *conjunction* of cues or features: that is, by all of them together, an "and" relationship. The concept "seven of spades" is characterized by both the shape of the symbol *and* the number. A "bachelor" is characterized by the features "unmarried, male, adult." In other cases, a concept is characterized by a *disjunction* of features: that is, one of several features, an "or" relationship. A "face card" (in some card games) is either "a card with a picture" or "an ace." "Earned income" consists of "wages, salaries, tips, commissions, etc."

According to the traditional view in psychology (which is by no means well accepted today), we ordinarily learn concepts by testing hypotheses about the cues or features. Consistent with this view is the finding that young children, while they are first learning the meaning of words such as "dog," often make mistakes that appear to be based on incorrect hypotheses that they have not yet eliminated by critical tests or evidence. A young child might first suppose that the word "dog" refers to any four-legged animal. Only by trying the word out on cows and being corrected does the child discover that this hypothesis is incorrect. Similarly, one child used "ba-ba" to refer not only to herself but to other people, and the cat as well (Ingram, 1971); her concept was defined by the single feature of animacy. At some point she observed that adults used the word "baby" to refer only to creatures that were small and human as well as animate. When testing a hypothesis about the meaning of a word, a child often has to wait for evidence provided by other people. Adults do not always provide feedback when a child uses a word incorrectly, so, the theory claims, it is difficult for children to carry out experiments to actively test their hypotheses. Bruner and his colleagues also distinguished between "deterministic" and "probabilistic" cues.

Given this view of concepts, psychologists hoped to improve their understanding of how we learn concepts by asking subjects to learn artificial concepts in the laboratory. Bruner, Goodnow, and Austin performed a classic set of experiments using this design (1956). In most of their experiments, the stimuli were cards (special ones, not an ordinary deck) that varied along four dimensions: number of forms printed on them (1, 2, or 3); number of borders (1, 2, or 3); type of form (cross, square, or circle); and color (green, red, or black). Some subjects were asked to discover a deterministic concept that described a particular category, a subset of the 81 cards. For example, a category might be "black crosses" or simply "black." Subjects could do this by pointing to one of the cards and asking the experimenter whether or not the card was in the category. This was called a *selection* experiment, because the subjects selected the cards. In *reception* experiments, the experimenter chose the cards (randomly). The subject guessed whether each card was in the category or not and received feedback from the experimenter.

Bruner and his colleagues discovered a number of *strategies* that subjects used in these two kinds of experiments. One strategy (used by some subjects in both selection and reception experiments) was *simultaneous scanning*. The subject would take all of the features of the first positive instance (or case in which the experimenter said, "Yes, this card belongs to the category") as an initial hypothesis. For example, if this card had "1 red cross with 2 borders," the subject would take the exactly this as the initial hypothesis. With each new positive instance, the subject would eliminate any of these features not present. For example, if the next positive instance was "2 red crosses with 3 borders," the subject would conclude that the number of forms and the number of borders were irrelevant, and the new hypothesis would be "red cross." This strategy is conservative; it never leads to an error in which the subject says that something is in the category when it is not – unless the category is disjunctive, in which case the subject will have a very hard time discovering the category.

A second strategy is *successive scanning*, in which the subject tests one hypothesis at a time. For example, the subject might hypothesize that the concept is "red" and go on to select (in the selection task) red cards that differed on other attributes. The subject would continue, until the hypothesis was shown to be wrong, and would then change the hypothesis in a way consistent with the card that proved it wrong. For example, if a red square turned out not to be a member of the category, the new hypothesis might be "cross." An advantage of this strategy is that it makes few demands on the subject's memory. A disadvantage is that it is inefficient. Unlike the simultaneous-scanning strategy, which effectively evaluates a number of hypotheses simultaneously, the successive-scanning strategy cannot make any use of the information provided by past trials (unless the cards are kept in view).

In the selection task, the subject can vary one feature at a time, after finding a single positive instance. For example, if "2 red crosses with 3 borders" is a positive instance, the subject might try "2 red crosses with 1 border." If the answer is yes, the subject will have good reason to think that the number of borders does not matter. If the answer is no, the subject will have good reason to think that "3 borders" is part of the concept. This strategy was called *conservative focusing*. It is somewhat like Platt's method of strong inference, because each card eliminates one set of hypotheses.

In another strategy, the subject varies all attributes but one. For example, after the same first positive instance, the subject may try "1 red square with 1 border." If the answer is yes, the subject will have good reason to think that the category is "red." This strategy was called *focus gambling*, because the subject was unlikely to get a yes answer; if the answer *is* yes, however, the subject can be pretty confident that the hypothesis is correct. This strategy is analogous to Popper's method of bold conjecture and risky experiment.

Bruner and his colleagues explained the choice of strategy in terms of cognitive load, or cognitive capacity – especially the memory requirements of keeping track of a number of hypotheses at once. They suggested that the less demanding strategies, particularly successive scanning, were used when demands on memory were greatest. In formulating this view of concept learning, the researchers were implicitly making a distinction between normative (ideal – no memory limits) and prescriptive views of how the task ought to be done, and they suggested (again, implicitly) that people generally follow the prescriptive model.

‾| The view of concept learning that lay behind this work has since been largely discredited. Putnam (1975) has pointed out that the concept of "water" has little to do with the *features* that we usually associate with water, such as being liquid, transparent, freezing at 32 degrees Fahrenheit, and boiling at 212 degrees Fahrenheit, having a density of 1, and so on. As noted earlier, if a substance were found that had all of these properties but had the chemical formula XYZ rather than H_2O, we would say that it was not water, because we take the chemical formula as definitive, not the observable properties. Similarly, if a fruit looked and tasted like an orange but came from a tree that was grown from an apple seed, we would say that the fruit was an (unusual) apple, not really an orange. Concepts about *natural kinds* (categories that exist in nature) *are shaped by scientific theories*.

Similarly, Wittgenstein (1958) has pointed out that many other concepts that we have seem to lack defining (deterministic) features altogether. Take, for example, the concept of a game. There is essentially nothing that is true of all games – no defining features. (For every feature you can think of, such as being done for fun, there are games that do not have it, such as jousting.) Games are not united by any features, but rather by what Wittgenstein called a *family resemblance*. Each game shares some features with some other games. Of course, *within* games, many concepts do have simple definitions. For example, a strike, in baseball, has a disjunction of features. Either the batter swings and misses, the batter fouls (except after two strikes), or the ball goes through the strike zone.

In sum, the idea that concepts have defining features applies only to man-made categories such as "forward pass," "resident alien," and perhaps "past participle." The work of Bruner and his colleagues on strategies for discovering such concepts, therefore, seems to tell us little about the learning of concepts in general. It still may say something, however, about the testing of hypotheses in other situations, such as science and diagnosis.

Congruence bias

Although Bruner, Goodnow, and Austin did not set out to look for flaws in human reasoning, they did make one observation that inspired others to look for such flaws (p. 86):

> Human subjects – and the same may be true of other species as well – prefer a direct test of any hypothesis they may be working on. [Suppose that] a subject is faced with deciding whether a white door or a black door is the correct entrance to a reward chamber and adopts the hypothesis that the white door is correct. There are two ways of testing this hypothesis. The *direct way* is to try the white door. The *indirect way* is to try the black door.

Similarly, when subjects use the successive-scanning strategy, they choose examples consistent with their current hypothesis, rather than those that are inconsistent.

Inspired by this finding, Wason (1960, 1968b) told subjects that the sequence 2 4 6 followed a rule, which they were to discover by providing additional three-number sequences as tests. The experimenter would tell the subject whether each of these sequences followed the rule or not. One difference between this procedure and that of Bruner and his colleagues is that both the number of possible hypotheses and the number of possible sequences that could be used to test them were infinite. This fact makes the situation more like those typically faced by scientists.

Typically, a subject would hypothesize that the rule was "numbers ascending by 2" and give sequences such as 3 5 7, 1.5 3.5 5.5, 100 102 104, and −6 −4 −2 as a series of tests. If the subject followed this strategy – basically the successive-scanning strategy with direct tests – the experimenter would keep saying yes in response to each test. Subjects always got the yes answer they expected, and they never questioned their favored hypothesis. Many subjects, after several trials like this, concluded that their hypothesis must be correct, and they announced that they had discovered the rule. The experimenter then told them that they were incorrect and that they could continue. At this point, some subjects attempted to make changes in the wording of the rule without changing its meaning: For instance, "The first number is 2 less than the middle number, and the third number is 2 more." Other subjects finally attempted an indirect test, such as 2 3 5, got a yes answer once again, and then went on to produce a complex hypothesis such as this: "The first two numbers are random, and the third is the second plus 2." The "correct" rule (the rule that the experimenter followed in giving feedback) was simply "ascending numbers." Many subjects did discover this rule. To do so, however, they had to use an indirect test of their original hypothesis.

Wason's point was not just that subjects had difficulty discovering his rule (which, because of its simplicity, might be considered a kind of trick). Instead, he suggested that many subjects failed to consider alternative hypotheses, such as "numbers ascending by a constant" or even "ascending numbers." Wason's result, however, is not entirely clear. Wason may have been mistaken in concluding that subjects were violating a normative or prescriptive model. Subjects may have been trying to test alternative hypotheses for which the answer would be no (for example, ascending even numbers; numbers ascending by 2 but less than 100; positive numbers ascending by 2; and so forth), but they may have failed to mention these hypotheses. Nonetheless, Wason's experiments inspired a host of similar efforts.

Mynatt, Doherty, and Tweney (1977) examined subjects' behavior in a simulated research environment involving figures displayed on a computer screen (see Figure 7.1). The subject was to try to account for the motion of a particle, which was fired from the position marked by the plus (+). The rule was that the particle stopped moving when it was near any gray figure. Subjects were presented with an initial display consisting of a gray triangle and, on a separate area of the screen, a black triangle next to a gray (shaded) circle. Subjects were then given a series of choices in which they had to choose one display, out of two, in order to test their hypothesis about what

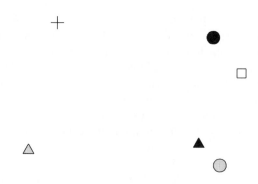

Figure 7.1: Display like that used by Mynatt, Doherty, and Tweney (1977), adapted from C. R. Mynatt, M. E. Doherty, and R. D. Tweney, "Confirmation bias in a simulated research environment: An experimental study of scientific inference," in *Quarterly Journal of Experimental Psychology* (1977): *29*, 89.

caused the particle to stop moving. Subjects whose initial hypothesis was "triangle" consistently chose displays that showed gray triangles rather than displays showing other gray figures. It appeared that they did not consider the alternative hypothesis, "gray figures," and they, therefore, did not choose tests that would distinguish this alternative from their favored hypothesis.[6]

Snyder and Swann (1978) asked each subject to interview another "target" subject, supposedly to determine whether the target subject was an "extrovert" (or, for other subjects, an "introvert"). The subjects tended to ask questions for which a yes answer would support the hypothesis that they were asked to test ("Do you like to go to parties?") or questions that assumed that the hypothesis was true ("What would you do to make a party more lively?").

The term "confirmation bias" has been used for this kind of behavior (Mynatt, Doherty, and Tweney, 1977). The idea is that subjects were trying to confirm their hypothesis rather than to test it or falsify it. This suggestion cannot be correct, if taken literally. Most responses in these tasks could potentially falsify the hypothesis. In the 2 4 6 problem, the test sequence 100 102 104 would falsify the hypothesis "ascending even numbers" if the experimenter's answer were no (meaning, "No, this does not follow my rule").

The subjects' error is supposed to be that they fail to give sequences that don't fit their hypothesis, such as 2 3 5. This may be an error, but producing such sequences is no more "trying to falsify" than is producing a sequence that fits. The sequence 2 3 5 could *support* the hypothesis, if the answer were no, since the hypothesis predicts

[6]These subjects might, however, have considered and rejected the hypothesis "gray" on the basis of the initial display, because they might have attributed the cessation of motion to the black triangle rather than the nearby gray disk. In order to correct this mistake later, subjects might have had to recall the display itself. Thus, their difficulties might have resulted from memory problems or misperceptions.

a negative answer for this item. Certainly the subject *expects* her hypothesis to be supported, but this is true no matter what kind of sequence she gives. A sequence that is incongruent with the hypothesis (such as 2 3 5) need be no more expected to support the hypothesis than a sequence that is congruent (100 102 104).

In sum, if subjects have a problem here, it is not in "trying to confirm." They may have no problem at all. Subjects may well be trying to test alternative hypotheses (such as ascending even numbers less than 100). The hypotheses they have in mind may seem unlikely to us, but nothing in the experiment tells the subject what probabilities to assign to various alternative hypotheses.

What subjects do in these studies is to provide tests that are congruent with their favored hypothesis. As noted, these studies have not shown that this violates any normative model. But perhaps it results from the use of a heuristic that might lead to such violations. We might call this a *congruence heuristic*: "To test a hypothesis, think of a result that would be found if the hypothesis were true and then look for that result (and do not worry about other hypotheses that might yield the same result)."

To show that this heuristic leads to nonnormative tests, we need to set up experiments that allow a normative model to be applied. One suggestive study is that of Shaklee and Fischhoff (1982), who gave subjects (1) an event such as "Diane rode her bike to work"; (2) some possible causes for the event, such as "Diane's car wouldn't start" and "There were no parking places on campus"; (3) a fact supporting one of the causes, such as "Even in bad weather, she rode her bike"; and (4) some questions that might be asked, such as "Had Diane's car been giving her trouble lately?" and "Did Diane ride her bike for convenience?" Subjects were asked which question they "would most like to have answered in trying to explain" the initial event. Subjects usually chose the question most likely to yield a yes answer if the suggested cause were true. This by itself might not be a bias, for the chosen question might still have been the best one. In another experiment, however, the researchers labeled one cause as already known (and omitted the supporting fact). Subjects were told that the alternative causes were not mutually exclusive. Subjects still tended to ask the question corresponding to the known cause. This is such an extreme form of congruence bias that one wonders whether the subjects understood the instructions.

Baron, Beattie, and Hershey (1988) extended the Shaklee and Fischhoff experiment in a variety of ways, finding that subjects did indeed seem to use a "congruence heuristic" in which they favored tests or questions that gave a yes answer if their favored hypothesis was true. Here is one of their test questions:

> A patient has a .8 probability of having Chamber-of-Commerce disease and a .2 probability of Elks disease. (He surely has one or the other.) A tetherscopic examination yields a positive result in 90% of patients with Chamber-of-Commerce disease and in 20% of patients without it (including those with some other disease). An intraocular smear yields a positive result in 90% of patients with Elks disease and in 10% of those without it. If you could do only one of these tests, which would it be? Why?

The "tetherscopic" examination yields a yes answer if the favored hypothesis ("Chamber-of-Commerce disease") is true. Many subjects chose the tetherscopic examination for this reason, even though the "intraocular smear" is a better test in this case. (To see why it is better, note that one could interpret a negative result on the intraocular smear as a positive indication of Chamber-of-Commerce disease; looking at it this way, the test has a 10% false-positive rate, instead of the 20% rate for the tetherscopic examination.)

In another procedure, subjects were given problems much like those of Shaklee and Fischhoff, except that the hypotheses were most easily seen as mutually exclusive (only one being true) rather than compatible. Here is an example:

> You are at your friend's house. Their young son is sent off to run his bath. Later you notice that water is dripping through the kitchen ceiling. You suspect that the child let the water overflow.
>
> Question 1. "Was the bathtub over the kitchen?"
>
> Question 2. "Was it raining?"
>
> Question 3. "Was the drip present before the child went upstairs?"

Subjects were asked to imagine themselves in the situation, knowing nothing more about it than they were told here but in possession of their general knowledge. They were asked to evaluate each question (with a numerical rating) as a test of their hypothesis. They were later asked to give their own probability judgments for the hypothesis (the child had let the water overflow) and for a yes answer to each question, first assuming the hypothesis to be true, and then assuming it to be false. In this example, which was typical, subjects gave the highest rating to Question 1, which yielded a yes answer if the hypothesis was true. The probabilities that the subjects provided, however, indicated that Question 3 would have been the most informative, because it had such a *low* probability of providing a yes answer if the hypothesis was true; a positive answer would essentially rule out the hypothesis. (Skov and Sherman, 1986, obtained similar results.)

In sum, it does appear that subjects asked questions designed to yield yes answers if their favored hypothesis was true, even when these were not the best questions. (Sometimes, or perhaps most of the time, these were the best questions.)

Another experiment that seems to show the use of a congruence heuristic is one that Jane Beattie and I designed (1988). Every subject was given an envelope with four cards inside it. Each card had a letter (A, B, or C) and a number (1, 2, or 3) printed on it. The task was to determine whether a certain rule was true of all four cards in the envelope. The rule, for example, might be "If there is a B, then there is a 2." The subject could ask to know whether certain cards were in the envelope, naming the card by *both* letter and number (B1, B2, B3, and so forth). For the hypothesis just given, the correct answer would include B1 and B3. However, many subjects asked only for B2. Of course, if the rule was true, B2 would be in the envelope, but if the rule was false, B1 or B3 would be present, and B2 could still be present. Apparently the subjects' choice of card was made without thinking about what card would be found if the rule was false.[7]

Two prescriptive heuristics can be used to avoid the negative effects of the congruence heuristic. In the first, we ask, "*How likely is a yes answer, if I assume that my hypothesis is false?*" A good test is one that has a high probability of some answer if the hypothesis is true and a low probability if it is false. We need not have a specific alternative hypothesis in mind; rather, we can estimate the latter probability on the basis of general background knowledge. For example, in the case just given, we might be able to estimate the probability of a yes answer to question 3 if the hypothesis is false without actually thinking of all the other possible hypotheses. Or, in medical diagnosis, we would choose a test that would be unlikely to be positive unless that patient had the disease that we suspect; if the patient has appendicitis, for example, the white blood cell count would be high.

The second heuristic advises, "*Try to think of alternative hypotheses; then choose a test most likely to distinguish them – to make some less probable and others more probable.*" For example, in medical diagnosis, before thinking about what test to do, we would think about what diseases ought to be considered. We would not just consider the most likely or the most dangerous but would look for alternatives as well. The advantage of this heuristic over the first is this: If we fail to consider alternatives, we may end up asking a question or doing a test that would have the same answer for several different hypotheses. For example, the white blood cell count may be high for other infections besides appendicitis, so this test may not distinguish appendicitis from some of the major alternative hypotheses. By thinking of *specific* alternative hypotheses, we may get a better idea of the probability of a result if the favored hypothesis is false. It may even be useful when we do not have a favored hypothesis. These heuristics are both candidates for prescriptive models for any situation in which one is evaluating hypotheses.[8]

What are the causes of congruence bias, when it occurs? I have discussed some of them elsewhere (Baron, 1985b, ch. 4). They are not mutually exclusive; several causes may be at work. One cause involves conflict of goals. Subjects who are asked to test hypotheses may be trying to achieve a different goal as well. They behave as though their goal was to get positive results – to hear the answer "yes" – rather than useful information. Tschirgi (1980) gave subjects problems like the following:

John decided to make a cake. But he ran out of some ingredients. So:

- he used margarine instead of butter for the shortening
- he used honey instead of sugar for the sweetening

---

[7]In Chapter 4 (in "Logical errors in hypothesis testing"), we examined a similar task, in which the subject named only the letter *or* the number. In that task, almost all subjects chose the B card, so they always could have gotten a result (1 or 3) that could disprove their hypothesis. In our task, the subjects who chose only the B2 card could not possibly get such a result.

[8]They are modeled loosely on the prescriptions of Popper and Platt, respectively. Popper and Platt, however, would both want some results to rule out some hypotheses with certainty, and this is not always possible.

- he used brown wholewheat flour instead of regular white flour.

The cake turned out great; it was so moist.

John thought the reason the cake was so great was the honey. He thought that the type of shortening (butter or margarine) or the type of flour really didn't matter.

What should he do to prove this point?

The subjects were given three choices: Use sugar instead of honey; keep the honey, but change everything else; or change everything. Most subjects who were given this version of the problem chose to keep the honey. In another version, subjects were told, "The cake turned out just terrible. It was so runny." In this case, when subjects were asked what test they would carry out, most said that they would use sugar instead of honey.[9]

Both of these tests are equally informative and equally valuable (Baron, 1985b, p. 143). If we keep the honey and change everything else, the cake will most likely turn out as it did the first time (whatever way that was), if our hypothesis is true, and the cake will turn out differently if our hypothesis is false. If we change only the honey, the cake will turn out differently if our hypothesis is true, and the cake will turn out as it did the first time if our hypothesis is false. The situations are completely the same except for the reversal of "as it did before" and "differently."

The reason the subjects choose different tests in the two cases is that they quite legitimately are pursuing two goals: information and a *good cake* at the end of their experiment. The effect of their desire for a good cake on their choice of how they will test their hypothesis is harmless, in this case; either choice is a good one. In other situations, the conflict of goals may not be so harmless. This is particularly true when there is no real value in a "positive" result. For example, in the 2 4 6 task, the desire to obtain yes answers may inhibit subjects from thinking of tests that would yield no as the answer if their favored hypothesis is true, which would in this case be more informative. Subjects may like to hear the word "yes," and physicians may like to hear that a test result was "positive," but these words have no value in themselves. If we seek to hear them at the expense of obtaining real information, we are very likely subverting the achievement of our goals.

Schwartz (1982) demonstrated the detrimental effects of seeking reward by asking one group of subjects to try to earn rewards (nickels) by pressing two buttons (*L* and *R*, for *Left* and *Right*) in a certain pattern. Pressing the button moved a light through a 5-by-5 matrix of squares, starting in the upper left-hand corner; pressing L moved the light down one square, and pressing R moved it one square to the right. A second group of subjects was asked to discover the *rule* that leads to reward (although they were not given monetary rewards for correct sequences of button presses). The rule itself was based simply on the relative number of L's and R's; any sequence of four L's and four R's could produce it (probabilistically). Such a sequence moved the light from upper left to lower right without running off the edge.

[9]Note that these two strategies correspond, respectively, to conservative focusing and focus gambling.

Subjects in the reward group usually developed "stereotyped" sequences, such as LLLLRRRR. At the end of the experiment, when they were asked to give the rule, these subjects stated exactly the pattern they had been using, and they often felt that this pattern was necessary, the only one that would work. The discovery group usually did discover the rule. When the reward group took part in a second experiment with the same instructions as the discovery group, they were less likely to discover the rule than was the discovery group. Apparently their ability to discover the rule was inhibited by their tendency to work for reward rather than information. The reduction of the motivation to discover rules seems to have carried over to a new task.

In a later experiment, Schwartz (1988) examined the finding that stereotypy led to the confusion of sufficiency with necessity. After pretraining in either the "reward" or "rule" condition, subjects were asked to solve problems analogous to the four-card problem discussed in Chapter 4 but using the same apparatus that Schwartz had used earlier (the matrix and buttons). Subjects were asked to test rules concerning either the necessity or the sufficiency of some condition, in order to get a "point" toward their total score. For example, a rule about necessity was "I get a point only if the light goes through the shaded square." Here, if the rule were true, going through the shaded square would be *necessary* in order to get a point. A rule about sufficiency was, "If the light goes through the shaded square, I get a point." Here, going through the square is *sufficient*, but there may be some other way to get a point. Subjects in the rule condition did well at testing both kinds of rules. Subjects in the reward condition, however, did well at testing the rule about sufficiency but poorly at testing the rule about necessity. Statements about necessity require tests with sequences that do *not* move the light through the shaded square (to see whether there is any other way of getting the reward). Subjects in the rule condition made far fewer such tests than those in the reward condition, as though they were still interested in getting the reward.

These experiments probably are analogous to real situations – for example, in classrooms – in which people are induced to work for extrinsic rewards such as grades. The reward may be effective in encouraging the work in question, but it may reduce the commitment to other valuable goals – such as satisfying one's curiosity – that could otherwise motivate the same behavior. Once students find a way of getting the reward of grades, they may be less inclined to try other ways of thinking that might teach them something about the real world that would ultimately enable them to obtain rewards much more important to them than good grades.

Information bias and the value of information

The value of information can be calculated. In essence, what we want to calculate is the extent to which specific information that we have or can get will help us to decide correctly among actions, such as which disease should be treated or which scientific hypothesis should be accepted as a basis for further experimentation. Let me suggest how this might be done, in the context of some examples from medical diagnosis. Medical diagnosis is useful for this purpose because probability is obviously involved. Only rarely can a physician diagnose a disease with absolute certainty. Scientific reasoning, I have argued, is also probabilistic, but it is more difficult to analyze many scientific situations in this way, because it is more difficult to determine what are the possible hypotheses.

Consider the following diagnostic problems (Baron, Beattie, and Hershey, 1988) for a group of fictional diseases:

1. A patient's presenting symptoms and history suggest a diagnosis of globoma, with about .8 probability. If it isn't globoma, it's either popitis or flapemia. Each disease has its own treatment, which is ineffective against the other two diseases. A test called the ET scan would certainly yield a positive result if the patient had popitis, and a negative result if she has flapemia. If the patient has globoma, a positive and negative result are equally likely. If the ET scan was the only test you could do, should you do it? Why, or why not?

2. A [different] patient has a .8 probability of umphitis. A positive Z ray result would confirm the diagnosis, but a negative result would be inconclusive; if the result is negative, the probability would drop to .6. The treatment for umphitis is unpleasant, and you feel it is just as bad to give the treatment to a patient without the disease as to let a patient with the disease go untreated. If the Z ray were the only test you could do, should you do it? Why, or why not?

In their answers to both problems, many subjects said that it would be worthwhile to perform the test in question, even if it was somewhat costly, and even though they understood that this test was the only one that could be done before a decision about treatment was made. (In the first problem, they also assumed that the three diseases were equally serious, and equally treatable, so that we would treat only the most likely disease.) In neither case, however, can the test affect the action to be taken. In the first problem, because the probability for globoma is so high (.8), we will treat globoma no matter what the test says; globoma will be the most likely disease before and after treatment. Likewise, in the second problem, we will treat the umphitis, no matter what the test says. The tests, which would give inconclusive results, are worthless for the purpose of deciding what to do. They cannot affect our decision.

Sometimes we want information because we are simply curious. In treating patients, however, we clearly should not spend money or take risks simply to satisfy our own curiosity: Our goal is to help the patient get well. Subjects who feel that the tests are worth doing may be pursuing an inappropriate goal (satisfying their curiosity or seeking information for its own sake), which, on reflection, they would decide not to pursue. In fact, when we interviewed and presented this argument to them, all of them admitted that the tests were worthless.[10]

[10]Anecdotes suggest that physicians make the same error. In one case, a physician wanted to do a CAT scan (an expensive test) for a woman with acute lower-back pain. An X ray had already been done

We can think about these problems more formally in terms of the concept of "expected utility" (described in detail in Chapter 10). *Utility* is, in essence, a measure of the degree of achievement of goals. In these problems we have been considering, we can assume that there is some utility in treating the right disease (in problem 1) or making the correct decision (in problem 2), and no utility in treating the wrong disease or making the wrong decision. The units for measuring utility are arbitrary, so we can say (to allow us to calculate) that the utility of a correct decision is 1, and the utility of an incorrect decision is 0.

Expected utility applies to a choice with probabilistic (uncertain) outcomes. It is the average utility we would obtain if we made the same choice repeatedly and the outcomes occurred with their respective probabilities. It is therefore the utility we can *expect* on the average. In these problems, there are two choices: test or no test. (There are also essentially two outcomes, correct treatment or incorrect treatment.) To calculate expected utility, we consider all of the outcomes of a given choice, such as not testing. We multiply the probability of each outcome (given the choice) by its utility, and we add up these numbers across the outcomes. For example, in problem 1, for no test the probability of a correct treatment is .8 (assuming we treat globoma), and the probability of an incorrect treatment is .2. The utility of a correct treatment is (we have assumed) 1, and the utility of an incorrect treatment is 0. The expected utility of this choice (no test) is thus $.8 \cdot 1 + .2 \cdot 0$, or .8. Because we have defined the utility of a good outcome as 1 and the utility of a bad outcome as 0, the expected utility is equal to the probability of a good outcome.

Note that the utility of the other choice, testing, is the same. The probability of correct treatment is still .8, with or without doing the test. This is because doing the test cannot change the overall probability that the patient has globoma. Table 7.1 may make this clear. The top two rows of Table 7.1 shows ET scan test results for 100 patients, indicating how many patients with each disease had each test result. The bottom row, the sum of the other two rows, shows the overall prevalence of the three diseases. If no test is done, the figures in the row for "all patients" allow us to calculate the probability of the three diseases: .8 for globoma and .1 for each of the others. If the test is done and is positive, the top row indicates that the probability of globoma is still .8. The same is found for a negative result. Therefore the test outcome cannot affect our judgment of the probability of globoma, the most likely disease, and we should treat globoma with or without knowledge of the test result.

Table 7.2 gives similar information for problem 2. In this case, the test can affect the probability of the most likely disease, but it again cannot affect our decision about treatment. If we do not do the test, we will have an 80% chance of giving the correct treatment, so the expected utility of this choice would be $.8 \cdot 1 + .2 \cdot 0$, or .8. If we do the test and it is positive, the expected utility would be higher. Likewise, if the test

and had ruled out essentially all of the likely conditions that would require any treatment other than bed rest. When the woman asked the physician why he wanted to do the CAT scan, he said that he wanted to "confirm a diagnostic impression." When the woman asked whether any test result could possibly affect treatment, the physician could not think of any way in which it might. The test was not done, and the woman recovered. Reuben (1984) provides other anecdotes like this one.

Table 7.1: ET scan results and incidence of three diseases in 100 patients.

Test result	Globoma	Popitis	Flapemia
Positive ET scan	40	10	0
Negative ET scan	40	0	10
All patients	80	10	10

Table 7.2: Z ray test results and incidence of umphitis in 100 patients.

Test result	Umphitis	No umphitis
Positive Z ray	50	0
Negative Z ray	30	20
All patients	80	20

is negative, the expected utility would be lower: but we must decide whether or not to do the test *before we know what the outcome will be*. Therefore, we must think of what we will do for each outcome of the test. We realize that, for either outcome, we will treat umphitis. Regardless of the outcome of the test, we will treat the same 80 patients correctly that we would have treated otherwise.

The test would have some value if the situation were as shown in Table 7.3. Here, if we do the test and it is positive, we would treat umphitis and be correct every time. If we do the test and it is negative, this time we would *not* treat umphitis, and we would be correct 60% of the time (30 out of 50 patients). Overall, if we do the test, we would treat 80 out of 100 patients correctly. If we do not do the test, however, we would treat umphitis, and we would be correct only 70% of the time; we would treat correctly only 70 out of 100 patients. Therefore, in a group of 100 patients, we would treat 70 correctly if we do not do the test, and we would treat 80 correctly if we do the test. This is because the test result makes a difference; it affects the action we would take. Overall, the expected utility of the *test* is .8 − .7, or .1. This corresponds to the 10 extra patients out of 100 who would be treated correctly only if the test is done.

In sum, a test has some expected utility only if it can affect the action we would take. Subjects in experiments, however, show a bias in which they seek information even when it cannot affect action. This *information bias* can occur elsewhere: in medical practice, in organizations, and in daily life. What is not worth knowing is not worth knowing.

Table 7.3: Z ray test results and incidence of umphitis in 100 patients.

Test result	Umphitis	No umphitis
Positive Z ray	50	0
Negative Z ray	20	30
All patients	70	30

Table 7.4: Test results and incidence of two diseases for 100 patients.

Test result	Disease A	Disease B	
Positive	64	8	72
Negative	16	12	28
	80	20	

Utility and alternative hypotheses

We can use this approach to understand the value of considering alternative hypotheses, as discussed earlier in this chapter. Suppose that we think that the probability that a patient has disease A is .8. We know of a test that yields a positive result in 80% of the patients with disease A. Is the test worth doing?

Many would say yes. I suggest that we would need to know more before we decide. A good heuristic is to ask what other disease the patient may have if she does not have disease A. Suppose the answer is disease B. Then we would want to know what the probability of a positive result from that same test would be if the patient had disease B. Suppose the probability is .4. Then, for 100 imaginary patients, we would have a table like Table 7.4. Even if the test is negative, disease A will be our best guess. Therefore, the test has 0 utility. The problem is that the test has too high a "false-positive" rate (8 out of 20 patients, or .4). Perhaps we could find a more useful test, with a much lower false-positive rate than .4, even if it also has a lower hit rate than .8. We will not think of looking for such a test, however, if we do not ask how likely we are to observe the same results if the alternative hypothesis is true.

The same need to consider whether a result is consistent with alternative hypotheses – before looking for the result – occurs in science. As we can see from the present example, this heuristic can be justified by a normative theory based on the idea of expected utility, a theory we shall explore in Chapter 10.

Conclusion

Actively open-minded thinking can avoid one of the main biases in hypothesis testing, the failure to consider alternative hypotheses (possibilities). In addition, more careful search for goals can help us avoid confusing of the goal of seeking information that is useful in decision making with other goals, such as the goal of seeking information in general, or that of obtaining positive results. These applications of the prescriptive theory of actively open-minded thinking can bring us closer to the normative theory of hypothesis testing as specified by probability and expected-utility theory.

There is more to science than hypothesis testing, however. In formulating hypotheses to test, the scientist must not only consider whether they are testable but also whether they are likely to be true. To meet the latter requirement, we must think well about what we already know (and the better we know it, the better we can think about it). We must make sure that our hypotheses are consistent with the evidence already available before we bother to collect new data.

The rigorous standards of science are often put in opposition to the idea of "learning from experience." In the next chapter, we ask just how good we are at learning from experience about the relation between one variable and another.

Chapter 8

Judgment of correlation and contingency

Many of our beliefs concern the relation between one quantity and another. We may ask whether the speed at which galaxies move away from us is related to their distance from the earth or whether IQ is related to income. Often we are concerned with such relationships because we want to decide whether to manipulate one thing in order to affect another. What is the relationship between the amount of studying we do and the grades we get? between our appearance and the way other people respond to us? between the amount of sleep we get and our ability to pay attention? Over the long term, how do the foods we eat affect our health? How does the way in which children are disciplined affect their behavior as adults?

This chapter is concerned with the inferences that people make concerning such relations. The normative theory is provided by statistical definitions of correlation. Like probability theory, the statistical theory of correlation is widely used in science and is valued for its mathematical clarity. (Unlike probability theory, however, the assumptions behind it are not assumed to apply to every situation. It is therefore normative only when certain assumptions are true.) Descriptively, we shall see that many people systematically violate the normative theory. Prescriptively, we may be able to come closer to the normative model by considering all of the relevant evidence, including the evidence against what we already believe.

Correlation, cause, and contingency

Typically, such inferences are made from data (evidence) in which the two quantities in question have both been observed for a number of items. Thus, for a group of children, we might have the data concerning height and weight given in Table 8.1. In this instance, the two columns of figures are obviously *correlated*. The greater the child's height, the greater the weight. When we say that height is *positively*

Table 8.1: Height and weight for five children

Child	Height (in.)	Weight (lb.)
A	48	45
B	43	35
C	51	55
D	46	44
E	45	40

correlated with weight among people, we mean that taller people tend to weigh more than shorter people. As one figure goes up, so does the other, and vice versa.

We can measure the association between two different quantities on a scale of 1 to -1 by a *correlation coefficient*, abbreviated r. (The formula for r is found in most statistics texts.) The coefficient r measures the extent to which one variable can be predicted as a linear function of the other. A correlation coefficient of 1 indicates that one measure is a perfect linear function of another, or has a *perfect* positive correlation with it. An example is the relationship between degrees Fahrenheit (F) and degrees Celsius (C): if we know one of these, we can calculate the other exactly by a simple linear formula, $F = 1.8 \cdot C + 32$. A correlation of 0 indicates no linear relationship at all. In a long sequence of dice rolls, for example, there ought to be no correlation between the number thrown on one roll of the dice and the number thrown on the next roll. A correlation of -1 indicates a *perfect negative correlation*; for example, there is a perfect negative correlation between a person's height and the distance of the person's head from the ceiling of the room I am now in. The correlation coefficient for the height column and the weight column in Table 14.1 is 0.98, very close to 1. (Again, consult a statistics book for the formula for r.)

The correlation coefficient is only one among many reasonable measures of correlation. It has certain convenient mathematical properties, and it can be shown to be the best measure for achieving certain goals. These issues are discussed in statistics books. For our purposes, the most important property of the correlation coefficient is that it treats all observations equally. For example, it does not weigh more heavily those pairs of numbers that are consistent with the existence of a positive correlation, as opposed to a negative or a 0 correlation.

We can investigate correlations, or associations, when each variable concerns membership in a category. (Such variables are called *dichotomous* because membership and nonmembership constitute a dichotomy.) We may ask, for example, whether "presence of blue eyes" (membership in the category of blue-eyed people) is correlated with "presence of blond hair" in a population of people. To calculate the correlation, we can assign a 1 to "presence" of each variable (blue eyes or blond hair) and a 0 to "absence" of each variable for each person and then calculate the correlation by using the resulting numbers. (This yields a "ϕ (phi) coefficient.") Another reasonable way to measure the association between two dichotomous variables is to subtract conditional probabilities. For example, we can subtract the conditional probability of blue eyes given blond hair from the conditional probability of blue eyes given nonblond hair. If the first conditional probability is higher than the other, knowing that a person has blond hair makes it more probable than otherwise that the person has blue eyes. If the two conditional probabilities are equal, then whether a person has blond hair tells us nothing about whether the person has blue eyes, and it makes sense to say that the two variables are unrelated. (We shall discuss more examples of this measure later in this chapter.)

Correlations are sometimes confused, in scientific analysis and everyday reasoning, with *causal* relationships. It is important to realize that they are not the same. Establishing a correlation does not establish causation, though it often provides *evidence* about causation, because causation is one reason that correlations can exist. (To establish causation, other reasons must be ruled out.) For example, the use of marijuana and the use of heroin may be *correlated*, but it is not necessarily true that one *causes* the other. There may be some third factor, such as exposure to drug dealers or rebellious attitudes, that is a more likely cause of both. If this third factor explained the correlation, then stopping the use of marijuana would not necessarily reduce the use of heroin. When we ask whether use of marijuana *causes* use of heroin, we are asking what *would* happen to heroin use if marijuana use were changed. A correlation between marijuana use and heroin use provides evidence for some causal relationship, but it does not establish one with certainty. Often, a more conclusive way to find out about causal relationships is to do an experiment. For example, correlations between diets with high amounts of saturated fat and heart disease provide evidence that the former causes the latter. Experiments in which some people have been induced to eat less fat would show that the relationship is indeed a causal one, if heart attacks become less frequent in these people (and not in others).

When we speak of correlations in a situation in which causal relationships are assumed, we can use the term *contingency*. A contingent relationship exists if one variable causally affects another. If smoking causes lung cancer, then lung cancer is, to some extent, *contingent* upon smoking. Our perception of contingency is an important determinant of our success at achieving our goals. Does Japan respond favorably when the United States threatens it with trade restrictions? If I drink three cups of coffee after dinner, will I be able to get to sleep tonight? If I try listening to people more, will they like me better? Of course, getting the answers to these kinds of questions does not always involve trial and error. There are ways of understanding such things that allow us to make reasonable guesses without any experimenting at all. We do not experiment, for example, in order to find out whether strong acids are really dangerous to drink. (Those who do, at any rate, are probably not around to argue with me.) Some of our learning, however, does involve observation.

Accuracy of judgment

How good are people at intuitively judging correlations, and where do we tend to go wrong? Jennings, Amabile, and Ross (1982) asked this question in the most straightforward way. Subjects (who had not studied statistics) were asked to study lists of number pairs. For each list, the subjects estimated the strength of relationship on a scale of 100 to -100. The true correlation coefficients of the numbers in each list differed from list to list; the range was from 0 to 1. Subjects gave ratings near 100 for correlations of 1, and ratings near 0 for correlations of 0. For correlations of .5, subjects gave ratings of about 20. These results tell us that the naive idea of "degree of relationship," although it resembles correlation, is not quite the same as the relationship measured by the correlation coefficient r. The subjects' deviation from mathematical correlation was not an error, for r is only one of many possible measures of association, and there is no reason subjects should use this particular measure. (Their judgments were closer to r^2, and closer still to $1 - (1 - r^2)^{.5}$; both of these measures are perfectly reasonable measures of the correlation, because they treat all observations equally, just as r does.) The data from this study also suggest that people have greater difficulty seeing the difference between a correlation of 0 and one of .5 than they do seeing the difference between .5 and 1. Again, this is not an error; it is simply something that might be useful for us to know.

Attentional bias

Attentional bias in judging correlation

Inhelder and Piaget (1958) examined the concept of correlation in 10–15 year old children, using dichotomous variables. Each child saw several cards. Each card had a face with blue or brown eyes and with blonde or brown hair. The subject was asked about the relation of eye color to hair color. The subject could manipulate the cards, put them in piles, et cetera. Most younger children did not consider all four combinations in making their judgment (blue eyes with blond hair, blue with brown, brown with blond, brown with brown). Some children based their response on the proportion of blue-eyed faces that had blonde hair, but they ignore the proportion of brown-eyed faces with blonde hair.

Smedslund (1963) found similar results for adults. In one study, a group of nurses looked through 100 cards supposedly representing "excerpts from the files of 100 patients." The nurses were asked to find out "whether there was a relationship (connection)" between a particular symptom and a particular disease. Each card indicated whether the symptom was present or absent and whether the disease was ultimately found to be present or absent in each case. Table 8.2 shows the number of cases of each of the four types: symptom present and disease present; symptom present and disease absent; symptom absent and disease present; and symptom absent and disease absent.

Table 8.2: Incidence of symptom (S) and disease (D) for 100 patients

	Disease present	Disease absent
Symptom present	37	17
Symptom absent	33	13

From such a table, it is possible to determine whether a correlation exists between the symptom and the disease. In this case, the symptom is not correlated at all with the disease. Out of 54 patients who have the symptom, 37 have the disease, about 69%. Out of 46 patients who do not have the symptom, 33 have the disease, about 72%. A given patient has about a 70% chance of having the disease, whether this patient has the symptom or not. The symptom is useless in determining who has the disease and who does not, in this group of patients.

Nonetheless, 85% of the nurses said that there was a relationship between the symptom and the disease. Smedslund presented the subjects with other kinds of relationships. For example, by switching the 17 and the 13, a real (if weak) relationship between symptom and disease was created. Here, the nurses were no more likely to think there was a relationship than they were in the original case. Smedslund found that the best predictor of the subjects' judgment of relationship was the proportion of the total number of cases in the upper left-hand cell. If the symptom and disease were both frequently "present" (as indicated by high figures in that cell), subjects tended to think that there was a relationship. Subjects seem to attend largely to this cell, when they should (normatively) have been attending to the whole table.

As Nisbett and Ross point out (1980, p. 92), the reasoning exhibited by these subjects is much like that of many laypeople when they discuss a proposition such as "Does God answer prayers?"

> "Yes," such a person may say, "because many times I've asked God for something, and He's given it to me." Such a person is accepting the data from the present/present cell as conclusive evidence for the covariation proposition. A more sophisticated layperson may counter this logic by asking for the data from the present/absent cell (i.e., prayers present, positive outcome absent): "Have you ever asked God for something and not gotten it?"

In fact (Nisbett and Ross point out), even these two cells are not enough. If positive outcomes are just as likely to occur when we do *not* pray for them as when we do, there is still no relationship. We need to know the absent/present and absent/absent cells, the ones at the bottom of the table, as well as the two others.

Many other experiments have supported Smedslund's general conclusion that subjects tend to ignore part of the table. In asking whether a symptom predicts a disease, subjects attend most consistently to the present/present cell (see, for example, Shaklee and Tucker, 1980; Schustack and Sternberg, 1981; Shaklee and Mims, 1982; Arkes and Harkness, 1983). Many subjects, however, behave like the "more sophisticated laypeople" described by Nisbett and Ross, paying attention to the present/absent cell (that is, symptom present and disease absent) as well as the present/present cell. In essence, when these subjects want to know whether the symptom (S) predicts the disease (D), they pay attention most often to the probability of D given S, that is, $p(D/S)$, but they neglect $p(D/\tilde{\ }S)$. Other subjects compare the present/present cell to the absent/present cell. In essence, these subjects attend to $p(S/D)$ and neglect $p(S/\tilde{\ }D)$, the probability that subjects would have the symptom even without the disease.

A consequence of the lack of attention to the "symptom absent" or to the "disease absent" part of the table is that people who have the chance do not *inquire* about the half of the table to which they do not attend. For example, Beyth-Marom and Fischhoff (1983), following Doherty, Mynatt, Tweney, and Schiavo, 1979) asked subjects to determine whether "Mr. Maxwell," a fictitious person whom, they were to imagine, they had just met at a party, was a professor. The subjects were told that Mr. Maxwell was either a professor or an executive and that he was a member of the Bear's Club. The subjects were asked which of several additional pieces of information they would want to have in order to determine his profession. They were asked, for example, whether they would rather know "what percentage of the professors at the party are members of the Bear's Club" or "what percentage of the executives at the party are members of the Bear's Club." Although 89% of the subjects thought the first item was relevant (because it came from the "disease present" part of the table – the "disease" in question being "professor"), only 54% thought that the second item was (because it came from the "disease absent" part of the table). In fact, both pieces are relevant (as is the percentage of professors at the party).

In a similar study, Doherty and Falgout (1986) gave subjects an opportunity to keep or throw away various pieces of data in making an inference about whether cloud seeding causes rain. Subjects varied greatly in their choice of data, but the dominant pattern was to keep data only from the present/present and present/absent cells, that is, those cells in which cloud seeding was done (and rain occurred or did not occur).

Kuhn, Phelps, and Walters (1985) asked children and adults to judge whether a fictional product called EngineHelp makes cars run well. The experimenter told the subjects, "Six people I talked to said they use EngineHelp and they all said their cars run well." A majority of the children, and one-third of the adults, concluded from this single cell that EngineHelp did help. Most of the others said, correctly, that there was not enough information. Then subjects were told, "Two other people I talked to said that they use EngineHelp and that their cars run poorly." The responses were about the same as after the first cell, even though subjects still knew nothing about the absent/absent and absent/present cells.

Attentional bias can be understood as failure to look for evidence against an initial possibility, or as failure to consider alternative possibilities. If there are many observations in the present/present cell (or – as we shall see shortly – if we already think a correlation is present), we may just stop there. If you think that God answers your prayers, it stands to reason that some piece of good fortune is a result of prayer. Further thinking might involve looking for alternative possibilities (such as the possibility that the good fortune would have occurred anyway) and looking for evidence that might distinguish these possibilities from our favored possibility (what happens when you do not pray). Attentional bias can therefore be correctable by actively open-minded thinking.

Attentional bias in judging contingency

The underweighing of the "absent" cells has its parallel in the judgment of contingency. An especially important contingency judgment for decision making is a situation in which we try to judge whether certain outcomes are contingent upon some action of our own: that is, whether we can "control" such outcomes, in the sense of making them occur or not, according to our goals. Jenkins and Ward (1965) asked subjects to push one of two buttons on each trial of a learning experiment. After each response, the subject saw either a "Score" or a "No Score" light on a panel. The experiment was set up so that the subjects received the Score light with a certain probability P after one button was pushed and another probability Q after the other button was pushed. (Expressed as conditional probabilities, $P = p(\text{Score}/\text{one button})$ and $Q = p(\text{Score}/\text{the other button})$.) After 60 trials, the subjects were asked how much control they had over the outcome.

Jenkins and Ward argued that the subjects' actual degree of control – the normative model for this judgment – was the difference between the probability (P) of scoring with one button and the probability (Q) of scoring with the other. That is, control would be $|P - Q|$, the absolute value of the difference. If pushing the first button led to the score with a probability of .7 and the second led to the score with a probability of .2, then the degree of control would be $|.7 - .2|$, or .5.[1]

Subjects judged their degree of control almost entirely in terms of the frequency with which the Score light appeared. Subjects thought they had the greatest control in a condition in which they "scored" with probability .8 no matter which button they pushed. In general, subjects thought they had about as much control in this condition as in a condition in which they scored with probability .8 with one button and with probability .2 with the other. (Although Jenkins and Ward suggested that subjects were attending to the probability of scoring with *either* button, the results are not exact enough to rule out another interpretation: Subjects might have been attending to the probability of scoring with the *one* button most likely to produce the score light. If this interpretation is true, the results would agree completely with the findings about attentional bias, in which subjects typically attend to the probability of the outcome given the "present" cue only.) The fact that subjects think they have

[1] Other reasonable measures of association, such as the ϕ coefficient described earlier, give very similar results, which are quite different from the subjects' judgments.

Table 8.3: Incidence of response and outcome for 120 trials

	Outcome	
Response	Score	No score
A	48	12
B	48	12

some control over the outcome even when they have no control at all has come to be called the *illusion of control*.

These results were obtained despite the fact that subjects were explicitly instructed that "*control* means the ability to produce the No Score light as well as to produce the Score light." Subjects were also explicitly warned that there might be no relation at all between their responses and the outcomes. The same results were obtained in the judgments of subjects who merely watched other subjects do the experiment. Therefore, we cannot explain the results in terms of some effect of the choice itself; the "spectator" subjects made no choices. The results were also obtained when subjects were explicitly asked to try to "control" the outcome rather than to "score"; these "control" subjects had to say aloud, in advance, which light they were trying to produce.

In a questionnaire given after the experiment, subjects were shown tables of outcomes similar to Table 8.3. The figures in this table reveal that the Score light came on with a probability of .8 regardless of the response. Once again, even with the tables before them the subjects judged their degree of control in terms of the probability of success rather than in terms of the difference in results produced by the two buttons.

Part of the subjects' difficulty seemed to result from the fact that they had to press one button on each trial. When they were asked how much "control" they had over the outcome, they tended to assume that they had a fair amount, because, they reasoned, if they had not pushed any button, there would have been no outcome. Allan and Jenkins (1980) tried the procedure with a single button. The subjects could press or not press on each trial, and after 100 trials the subjects were asked to estimate the degree of influence they had, or the degree of connection between pressing the button and the outcome. In this procedure, subjects still showed the illusion of control. They still said they had some control (influence or connection) over the outcome, even when they actually had none. The illusion was smaller with one button than with two, however. Subjects tended to give lower ratings of their degree of control. In this study, subjects' ratings were affected by the actual amount of control; subjects estimated that they had more control in a .9 − .1 condition (outcome appears with probability .9 when they press, .1 when they do not press) than in a .9 − .5 condition. With either one button or two, however, they thought they had more control in a

.9 − .7 condition than in a .3 − .1 condition; the degree of control in these conditions is the same, but the Score outcome is much more frequent in the former.

Effect of goals on illusion of control

Alloy and Abramson (1979) gained more insight into the control illusion by designing a variation on this experiment. They tried the experiment using (relatively) depressed and nondepressed college-student subjects. Depression was measured by the Beck Depression Inventory, a self-rating questionnaire that asks subjects about feelings of sadness, hopelessness, and other negative feelings. Many college students show scores on this measure that are as high as those of patients who seek psychotherapy for their feelings of depression. The very interesting result of this experiment was the discovery that whereas students who were not depressed showed the illusion of control when they received a reward of 25 cents that was not contingent on their pressing a button, depressives did not show the illusion of control in this situation. The depressive students tended to say that they had no control in this case. When the reward *was* contingent on their pressing a button, however, the depressed subjects rated their control just as high as did the nondepressed subjects. (This shows that the difference between the groups was not just a tendency to say "No control," regardless of the facts.) Even nondepressives showed no illusion of control when the outcome in question was a loss of 25 cents rather than a gain of 25 cents. This narrows the illusion of control down to a specific circumstance. The illusion of control was found only in nondepressed subjects working for a *gain* rather than a *loss*.

What was the difference between the depressives and nondepressives? Alloy and Tabachnik (1984) speculated that nondepressives *expect* to have control over outcomes and that this expectation biases their perception of the correlation between their responses and the outcomes. Nondepressives are more inclined to believe that they have discovered a way of controlling the outcome, even when they have very little evidence for such control. For example, they may think that if they follow the rule "Press the button if the desired outcome occurred on the trial before last or did not occur one trial before that," that outcome would occur. Using such rules becomes an increasingly difficult task over the course of 40 trials. The subject cannot recall the entire sequence of presses and outcomes in order to test new rules. Nondepressed subjects may have been forever trying new rules, and forever optimistic that *this* new rule would be the right one. Depressed subjects, on the other hand, may have engaged in this sort of behavior less often.

Schwartz (1988) has questioned this explanation. Schwartz looked for an illusion of control in a task similar to that used by Allan and Jenkins and by Alloy and Abramson. The subjects were not selected for depression, but they were divided into two groups that received different training for the experiment. Both groups first performed Schwartz's confirmation bias experiment (described in Chapter 7), in which they learned how to get a reward by pressing a button to make a light perform a sequence of movements through a matrix. One group of subjects was given the "reward" condition, in which they were told that the task was to obtain a reward. The other was given the "rule" condition, in which the task was to discover the rule relating the sequence to the reward. You will recall that the reward condition made subjects less successful at discovering rules in a subsequent task of the same type, presumably because they were less inclined to look for rules.

After the training, Schwartz had both groups of subjects do a button-pushing experiment similar to the ones done by Allan and Jenkins and by Alloy and Abramson. The subjects in the rule group did *better* at learning that there was no contingency than had the subjects in the reward group. The illusion of control was found in the reward group, but not in the rule group. It seems that those who do not fall for the illusion are those who look for rules. It is possible that depressed subjects did look for rules in the Alloy and Abramson experiment, perhaps because they were not interested in reward.

Further evidence for the role of different goals comes from a study in which the basic one-button task (Allan and Jenkins, 1980) was done under two instructional conditions (Matute, 1996). In one condition, subjects were told to try to avoid aversive sounds (computer beeps or noises). In the other, subjects were instructed to press the button half the time and try to find whether they had control over the same outcomes. The good outcomes occurred 75% of the time regardless of the response. The first group showed a strong illusion of control, and the second group showed no illusion. Interestingly, the first group, with the illusion, pressed the button most of the time, so they never had a chance to learn what would happen if they did not push it. They still thought they had control, even though they had no way of knowing.

Effects of prior belief

A second bias in the judgment of correlation concerns the effect of prior belief about what the correlation ought to be. People tend to find in the data what they think (before they look) will be there.

The most dramatic example is a series of studies done by Chapman and Chapman (1967, 1969). They wondered why clinical psychologists continued to use certain projective tests in psychological diagnosis, particularly the Draw-a-Person Test, even though these tests had been shown to be useless. In the Draw-a-Person Test, patients are asked simply to draw a human figure on a blank sheet of paper. It was thought that patients "project" various aspects of their personalities into their drawings. For example, suspiciousness of others was thought to be associated with atypical eyes, and concerns about manliness were thought to be associated with broad shoulders.

Many studies have shown that these ideas are simply wrong. When drawings made by paranoid patients (who are suspicious) are compared with drawings by people who are psychologically normal, no differences are found in the eyes. What puzzled Chapman and Chapman was the fact that clinical psychologists continued to use the test although they knew about the findings. Informally, many of them said that they simply did not believe the negative results. One commented, typically, "I know that paranoids don't seem to draw big eyes in the research labs, but they sure do in my office" (Chapman and Chapman, 1971, pp. 18–19).

Illusory correlation

To find out whether people were really capable of detecting such correlations, the Chapmans collected a number of these drawings and labeled each drawing with a psychological characteristic, such as "suspicious of other people" or "has had problems of sexual impotence." The labels for each picture were carefully chosen to ensure that there was absolutely no correlation, within the set of pictures, between each label and the features of the human figure thought to be associated with it. For example, human figures with elaborated sexual features were as likely to occur when the label did not indicate sexual concerns as when it did. These drawings, with the labels, were shown to college-student subjects who had never heard of the Draw-a-Person Test. When they were asked to *discover* what features of the drawing tended to go with what labels, the students "discovered" exactly the correlations that most clinicians believed to be present – for instance, suspiciousness and abnormal eyes – even though there was no statistical correlation. Note that the subjects were asked to describe what characteristics of the drawings went with what labels for the drawings they were shown; they were not asked what they thought was true in general.

The same kinds of results were found for the Rorschach ink-blot test, in which patients describe the images they see in a series of ink blots. When students were given a number of blots together with the responses made to them by patients with various diagnoses (which the students were also given) and asked to discover what features of Rorschach responses correlated with homosexuality, they once again "discovered" the correlations that most clinical psychologists believed to be present (for example, homosexuals were thought to be more likely to see a woman's laced corset in one of the blots). Once again, these features were not actually correlated with homosexuality. Research had shown, in fact, that other features tended to be correlated with homosexuality (for example, interpreting a certain blot as a giant with shrunken arms). Subjects did not discover the real correlations, however, even though they were actually present in the information given to them. In sum, subjects' expectations about what ought to correlate with homosexuality led them to perceive the correlations that they expected, but they failed to perceive the correlations that were present.

Personality traits

Prior belief can also distort our perception of correlations among personality traits. It has been well known for a long time that people who fill out questionnaires about other people's personalities are subject to a "halo effect." If, for example, a teacher thinks that a child is intelligent, she will also tend to rate this student as well behaved, even if the child is no better behaved than average. This is presumably the result of the teacher's belief that intelligent children also tend to be well behaved. Because the teacher expects such a correlation, she tends to perceive it in children's behavior. The correlations that people expect to see, however, are not always the ones that are present.

This was demonstrated in a study done by Shweder (1977; further discussed and reanalyzed by Shweder and D'Andrade, 1979). Shweder reanalyzed the data from a much earlier study of introversion and extroversion in children in a summer camp (Newcomb, 1929). The counselors at the camp provided daily ratings of the behavior of each child, on such items as "speaks with confidence of his own abilities," "takes the initiative in organizing games," and "spends more than an hour a day alone." Because the daily ratings were made as soon as possible after the occurrence of the relevant behavior, the ratings were presumably as accurate as possible. From these data, it was possible to measure the correlation of every type of behavior with every other type of behavior over the entire summer. For example, the correlation between "gives loud and spontaneous expressions of delight or disapproval" and "talks more than his share of the time at the table" was .08, indicating a very weak relationship between these two behaviors; children who tend to exhibit the first behavior are not much more likely to exhibit the second behavior than children who do not exhibit the first. Shweder made a list of all of these correlations, one correlation for each pair of behaviors. (The correlations concerned children. All judgments made of a given child were averaged before the correlations were computed.)

At the end of the summer, when the details of day-to-day happenings had been forgotten, the counselors filled out ratings of the same children on the same items. This situation is more like the questionnaires used in personality measurement, where ratings are based on long-term memory rather than specific day-to-day events. Once again, a list of correlations was made, one correlation for each pair of behaviors. Shweder then looked at the correlation of the two lists (of correlations). If the correlation of the two lists was high, those behavior pairs that had high correlations in one list would have high correlations in the other, and likewise for low correlations. For the two items described earlier, the correlation based on memory was .92 (rather than .08); thus, in this case, a *high* correlation in one list went with a *low* correlation in the other. Although the degree of difference observed for these two items was extreme, the two lists of correlations were, in general, not themselves correlated. The correlation between the daily-rating correlations and the memory-based correlations was only about .25.[2]

Why is there such a weak relationship between the correlations of daily ratings and the correlations of the memory ratings? Perhaps because of a sort of halo effect. People think that certain traits ought to go together, so when they give a high rating on one, they tend to give a high rating on the other as well, and vice versa.

To get a better idea of what people *think* ought to go with what, in personality, Shweder asked a number of University of Chicago undergraduates to rate all of the pairs of behavioral descriptions from the summer-camp research for "conceptual similarity," thereby creating a third list. These conceptual-similarity ratings corre-

---

[2]This was the average over several studies of this type (Shweder and D'Andrade, 1979, p. 1081).

lated strongly (about .75) with the memory-based correlations, but not very strongly (about .26) with the daily-rating correlations. In short, the conceptual similarity of a pair of behaviors was strongly related to the correlation between the two traits in the memory ratings, but neither conceptual-similarity nor memory-rating correlations were strongly related to the actual daily-rating correlations. When people make inferences based on memory, they tend to remember what they think they ought to remember; they do not remember accurately what actually happened.

Shweder looked at the correlation of personality traits with each other. Other researchers have examined the correlation of other individual characteristics (including personality traits) and membership in particular groups. Much of this research concerns social stereotypes, such as those of Jews or blacks. A stereotype can be seen as an opinion about what correlates with being Jewish, black, female, or male.

McCauley and Stitt (1978) examined white Americans' stereotypes of black Americans from this point of view. The subjects answered questions like, "What percent of of adult Americans have completed high school?" and "What percent of black Americans have completed high school?" The ratio of these two answers serves as a rough measure of correlation. A ratio of 1 means no correlation. When the study was done, the ratio of these questions was .65: Blacks were less likely to have completed high school. Mean ratios inferred from the responses of different groups of white Americans ranged from .60 (social work students) to .74 (social workers). For this question and most of the other questions (illegitimate children, unemployment, victim of crime, on welfare, four or more children, female head of family), the average ratios of the respondents were in the same direction as the true ratios based on census data and somewhat less extreme — closer to 1.0. In other words, this kind of "stereotype" is fairly accurate, and people judge the correlation correctly between (for example) being black and having completed high school.

Ryan (1996) extended the McCauley and Stitt study by including black subjects — college students — as well as whites. She asked about positive and negative stereotypical traits of blacks and (by comparison) whites, such as "athletic," "sexually aggressive," "academically intelligent," and "self-centered." She assessed accuracy by comparing subjects' estimates of percentages to the subjects' own self-ratings on the same traits. She found, contrary to McCauley and Stitt, that both blacks and whites exaggerated the magnitude of group differences and that blacks did this more than whites. Her findings suggest that some illusory correlation may operate to exaggerate the degree of belief in stereotypes. The McCauley and Stitt results, however, indicate that such exaggeration is not always present.

It is unclear why correlation judgments are sometimes illusory and sometimes accurate. One possibility is the belief in some strong naive theory — like the theory that semantically similar personality traits should correlate — that turns out to be misleading.

Prior belief and attentional bias

Kuhn, Amsel, and O'Loughlin (1988) found a type of illusory correlation – another effect of prior beliefs – in the evaluation of hypotheses about dichotomous variables like those used in the study of attentional bias. Their results suggest that attentional bias can be increased by prior belief. Specifically, when prior belief is present, we tend to focus on the evidence that supports our belief and ignore the evidence against it. This mechanism could explain some of the results of experiments concerning biased attention. For example, if subjects in the contingency experiments had a prior belief that they could control the outcome, they would tend to ignore evidence against this belief.

Although Kuhn and her colleagues used both children and adults as subjects, the results were much the same for both, except for a group of graduate students in philosophy (who did not show illusory correlation).

Subjects were told about some experiments in which children in a boarding school were deliberately given different combinations of foods (at each table in the dining room) by researchers, in order to determine whether the foods affected the probability of the children's getting a cold. Before seeing the data, each subject stated her own hypotheses about which of the foods would cause or prevent colds. Then subjects were shown the data (table by table) and were asked to describe what the data showed. When subjects were asked whether the data showed that the food made a difference, they interpreted the evidence in a way that was colored by their hypotheses. For example, one subject thought that the type of water (tap or bottled) would make a difference but that the type of breakfast roll would not. The evidence presented was identical for both variables, since tap water was always given with one type of roll and bottled water with another, yet the subject interpreted the evidence as showing that water made a difference and rolls did not. When another subject believed that mustard caused colds, she looked selectively for cases in which mustard had been eaten and colds had occurred, and she ignored cases in which mustard had been eaten and colds had not occurred.

Note that subjects in this experiment and in the Chapmans' experiment were asked to describe the evidence, not to *use* the evidence to draw a conclusion (as in the other experiments discussed in this section). Kuhn and her colleagues actually asked subjects both to say what they thought *was true*, after seeing the evidence, and to say what they thought *the evidence indicated by itself.* Many of the subjects failed to distinguish these two questions. They gave the same answer to them, and they seemed surprised if the experimenter asked the second after the subjects had answered the first. The researchers suggest that a basic problem may be the difficulty of putting aside one's prior belief in order to evaluate the evidence on its own. The problem certainly seems to be analogous to that discussed in the chapters on logic, in which we saw that people cannot always put aside their doubts about the truth of premises in order to decide whether a conclusion would follow *if* the premises *were* true.

Understanding theory and evidence

These results suggest that subjects do not understand the relation between theory and evidence. In a sense, they have naive theories about how knowledge is justified. Kuhn (1991) explored people's attitudes to knowledge more deeply by asking adolescents and adults for their own theories about three social issues: "What causes prisoners to return to crime after they're released?", "What causes children to fail in school?", and "What causes unemployment?" After subjects were asked for their theory, they were also asked for evidence to support it; for alternative theories, views that someone else might hold, for evidence (possible or real) in favor of the alternatives; and for a rebuttal of such counterarguments.

In general, subjects with more education (and college-bound adolescents) gave more adequate answers than those with less education. Inadequate answers about evidence failed to distinguish the evidence for a theory from a restatement of the theory itself. For example, a subject who believed that school failure was caused by problems at home, when asked for evidence, said that "when the mother and father are divorced they [the children] can have psychological problems, you know, and they can't really function in school" (Kuhn, 1991, p. 66). Interestingly, most of the subjects said that the "evidence" they provided did prove the correctness of their theory, and their level of confidence was unrelated to the quality of this evidence. Many subjects were also unsuccessful in generating alternative theories to their own. The most common failure was that the response overlapped or coincided with the subject's own theory, often even using the same words. Some subjects denied that anyone would propose an alternative or indicated that, although they could not think of an alternative, they would reject it if it were presented to them. Likewise, some subjects rejected the possibility of any counterargument – for example, because both the antecedent (such as family problems) and consequent (school failure) were present. Finally, "in extreme cases ... the subject exhibits a kind of proprietorship over the theory that undermines its independent existence, rendering it incontestable. To challenge the theory is to challenge the subject's own self" (p. 144).

At the end of the interview, subjects were asked to interpret two kinds of evidence on the crime and school issues. *Underdetermined* evidence simply presented a scenario about one individual person, without mentioning any causal factors. The *overdetermined* evidence reported a study of 25 prisoners or pupils, with no control group, in which one expert found evidence for each of three possible causes (for example, a school psychologist found evidence of learning problems in children who failed at school).

Despite the fact that both sets of evidence were essentially useless, many subjects tended to interpret them as supporting their theories. For the underdetermined evidence, many subjects simply asserted that their theory was correct for the case. For the overdetermined evidence, subjects tended to focus on the parts consistent with their view. Most subjects (especially the noncollege group) interpreted the evidence as agreeing with or supporting their theories. As in the study of food and colds, subjects often answered questions about the *evidence* as if they had been asked about the truth of their own *theories*. If this response is typical of subjects' thinking, then they are unable to evaluate evidence independently of their theories. If the evidence disagrees with the theory, they will not note the disagreement. Instead, they will either neglect the disagreement or eventually change their theory without acknowledging the role of the evidence. This failure is important: In order for people to learn to evaluate evidence correctly, it helps to be able to say what the evidence would imply in the absence of any prior commitment to a particular theory.

Subjects were also interviewed directly about their theories of knowledge. They were asked how confident they were in their own theories; whether experts could or did know the truth; and whether different theories could be correct for different people. Responses to these questions seemed to reflect three kinds of implicit theories of knowledge. "Absolutist" theories hold that experts can be certain of the truth and that the subject could be certain of the truth too. "Multiplist" theories of knowledge hold that experts cannot be certain and that conflicting theories can be simultaneously correct. Responses in this category often referred to personal experience or emotion as the grounds for belief. Subjects owned (or possessed) their beliefs, as indicated by the following responses to the question, "Would you be able to prove this person wrong?": "No, I would just be able to say I disagree with you and this is why and you can't tell me that my experience is wrong because this is what my experience was" (p. 182); "You can't prove an opinion to be wrong, I don't think. ...an opinion is something which somebody holds for themselves. You can't change their opinion or alter it. They have their own opinion" (p. 182). "Evaluative" theorists held themselves to be less certain than experts. They held that "viewpoints can be compared with one another and *evaluated* with respect to their relative adequacy or merit" (p. 188), even if certain knowledge is impossible. Only 14% of the college group fell into this category, and only 5% of the non-college group did. Subjects in this category were less likely than others to be sure, or very sure, that their theory was correct; absolutist subjects were the most likely.

Kuhn argues that opinions held unreflectively are more likely to be incorrect or poorly supported. Reflection involves considering at least one alternative and finding evidence that favors one's own view more than it favors the alternative(s), or evidence that impugns the alternatives more than one's view. These are the same moves that are required when people defend their views in dialogic arguments with others. In order to engage in such reflection, "Individuals must also hold the implicit epistemological theory that treats argument as worthwhile, as a fundamental path to knowing. In other words, people must see the point of argument, if they are to engage in it" (p. 201). People who hold that everyone's opinion is equally valid have no incentive to learn the standards of argumentation and belief formation. Many of Kuhn's subjects seemed unfamiliar with the idea that an argument can be good or poor in some way that is more objective than simply whether or not it succeeds in changing someone's mind. That objectivity, of course, comes from these standards.

Conclusion

Illusory correlation and attentional bias distort our perception of the evidence available to us. We think evidence weighs more heavily on the side of beliefs we already hold than it actually does. Because of this distortion, our beliefs are likely to be less sensitive to counterevidence than they ought to be. In part, this insensitivity may result from our own naive theories of the relation between beliefs and evidence. In the next chapter, we shall take a broader look at the resistance of beliefs to counterevidence.

Chapter 9

Actively open-minded thinking

The human understanding when it has once adopted an opinion draws all things else to support and agree with it. And though there be a greater number and weight of instances to be found on the other side, yet these it either neglects and despises, or else by some distinction sets aside and rejects, in order that by this great and pernicious predetermination the authority of its former conclusion may remain inviolate.

Francis Bacon

The search-inference framework implies that thinking can go wrong for three reasons.

1. Our search misses something that it should have discovered, or we act with high confidence after little search.

2. We seek evidence and make inferences in ways that prevent us from choosing the best possibility.

3. We think too much.

The second of these problems seems to be the most serious. People tend to seek evidence, seek goals, and make inferences in a way that favors possibilities that already appeal to them. For example, we often ignore evidence that goes against a possibility we like.

The same favoritism for a particular possibility may cause us to prematurely cut off our search for alternative possibilities or for reasons against the one we have in mind. This favoritism therefore leads to insufficient thinking or to overconfidence in hasty conclusions — the first reason for poor thinking. This problem is especially great when something is worth thinking about, such as the choice of our personal goals or moral beliefs.

Poor thinking, therefore, tends to be characterized by too little search, by overconfidence in hasty conclusions, and — most importantly — by biases in favor of the possibilities that are favored initially. In contrast, good thinking consists of (1) search that is thorough in proportion to the importance of the question, (2) confidence that is appropriate to the amount and quality of thinking done, and (3) fairness to other possibilities than the one we initially favor.

These three principles are also the standards we apply when we criticize each other in academic settings. When I read a student's paper, or a colleague's, or sometimes even my own, the things I look for are omissions of relevant evidence, omissions of statements about goals or purposes, omissions of alternative possibilities, other answers to the question at issue, and unqualified assertions not supported with evidence. I also look for partiality to the thesis of the paper, partiality that may itself cause the omissions just mentioned. When students take these kinds of criticisms to heart and try to become more thorough and more impartial, they are becoming more intelligent thinkers. They are acquiring abilities — in the form of habits and values — that will increase their effectiveness just as surely as would an improvement in their memory or their mental speed.

Thinking that follows these principles can be called *actively open-minded thinking*. It is "open-minded" because it allows consideration of new possibilities, new goals, and evidence against possibilities that already seem strong. It is "active" because it does not just wait for these things but seeks them out. These are the features of what I regard as "good thinking."

A good prescriptive model of thinking, I shall argue, is one that advises and helps people to become more actively open-minded. It counteracts the major biases in thinking, and it serves as a reminder of the normative theory. Advice of this type is an important part of a good prescriptive model. The rest of a prescriptive model consists of many detailed heuristics, or rules of thumb, some of which will be discussed in this book.

Examples of actively open-minded thinking

Here is an example of actively open-minded thinking. Students in a class on thinking and decision making were asked to think about the following problem and transcribe their thoughts. The problem concerned the "best" way to allocate, among the nations of the world, the mining rights to minerals on the ocean floor, a resource not yet developed. One student's transcribed verbal protocol read as follows:

> Wealth must be divided among nations fairly. What does "fairly" mean? Should allocation be based on the *size* of the country? Some nations are significantly larger than others. But some countries have more people per unit area. Should allocation be based on overall population size? It would be *very* difficult to get all nations concerned to agree their shares were fair. Wait, the United Nations has a certain number of representatives from each country. They would be the ideal group to handle this. Total wealth should be divided by overall number of representatives, then allocated according to number of representatives per country.

But some nations would be better able to *use* the mineral wealth. These would be nations with greater technology. Therefore, underdeveloped nations would be unable to benefit as well as nations that are financially more secure. That would be unfair. [The protocol continues for several more pages.]

This student (who earned an A+ in the course) searched for goals, considered several possibilities. After each possibility, she looked for counterevidence and then tried to modify or replace the possibility to meet the objection she had thought of.

By contrast, the following protocol, handed in by another student, shows no evidence of actively open-minded thinking (although it is always possible that some such thinking went on beforehand):

I believe that the most logical way of allocating the mineral wealth beneath the ocean is to allocate the ocean floors by extending national borders outward along the ocean floors. In effect, this plan would treat the ocean floor in the same way as exposed land surfaces. The water above the floor should still remain international territory, except where it is already considered national property.... Establishing boundaries in this manner is fairly simple, but it will favor nations with long coastlines along large bodies of water, but is no less fair than the rules for establishing national air space. [This protocol also went on for a page or two.]

It must be remembered that this kind of prescriptive model advises moderation, a middle course. More thinking, as we have already noted, is not always better. The search for counterevidence and alternative possibilities reaches a point of diminishing returns — often quickly. We can compare active open-mindedness to a virtue such as thriftiness. Thriftiness, too, must be practiced in moderation. We think of thriftiness as a virtue because most people usually do not have enough of it, but some people are *too* thrifty, penny-pinchers unable to enjoy the fruits of their labor. Similarly, active open-mindedness is a virtue because most people do not have enough of it, but too much of it can lead to intellectual paralysis.

Here is another example of two thinkers, C and S, sixth-grade students in Alberta, Canada, who were asked to report their thoughts after reading each segment of the following story (Norris and Phillips, 1987):

1. The stillness of the morning air was broken. The men headed down the bay.

2. The net was hard to pull. The heavy sea and strong tide made it even more difficult for the girdie. The meshed catch encouraged us to try harder.

3. With four quintels aboard we were now ready to leave. The skipper saw mares' tails in the north.

4. We tied up to the wharf. We hastily grabbed our prongs and set to work. The catch was left in the stage while we had breakfast.

5. The splitting was done by the skipper. The boys did the cutting and gutting.

6. Catching fish is filled with risk.

C's response to segment 1 was, "The men are going shopping. [Why do you say that?] They're going to buy clothes at The Bay [a Canadian department store]. [Any questions?] No." Notice the lack of qualification, the high confidence in this statement. C continues the interpretation of a shopping trip through the story, forcing the subsequent details to fit; at the end, C concluded, "Like I said before, they went shopping and got some fish, met some horses and then went to a show."

S, on the other hand, said, "I think they might be going sailing." S states a possibility, but qualified, so that it can be easily revised with subsequent evidence. S's response to segment 3 illustrates well the potential of actively open-minded thinking: "I wonder what quintels are? I think maybe it's a sea term, a word that means perhaps the weight aboard. Yes, maybe it's how much fish they had aboard. [So you think it was fish?] I think fish or maybe something they had found in the water but I think fish more because of the word 'catch'. [Why were they worried about the mares' tails?] I'm not sure. Mares' tails, let me see, mares are horses but horses are not going to be in the water. They are out in a boat on the bay so there's nothing around except sky and water. The mares' tails are in the north. Here farmers watch the north for bad weather, so maybe the fishermen do the same thing. Yeah, I think that's it, it's a cloud formation, which could mean strong winds and hail or something which I think could be dangerous if you were in a boat and a lot of weight aboard. [Any questions?] I am curious now about whether I'm right about the mares' tails." S considers and rejects possibilities (horses), actively searches for evidence, finds the analogy with local farmers, but remains unsure, awaiting confirmation.

The last example suggests that active open-mindedness can be measured by asking people to think aloud and by subjectively scoring the result for various signs of active open-mindedness, such as considering reasons against a tentative view. Indeed, several measures of this sort have been developed, often on the basis of theoretical schemes very similar to the one I have just presented, although the terms employed are usually different. Ordinarily, some training is required in order to learn to score the results. After the training, the reliability of the scoring can be checked by looking at the correlation between the responses of different judges. One scoring technique is the measure of "integrative complexity" described in Chapter 2. Another scoring system, developed by Perkins, Bushey, and Faraday (1986), scores subjects' written responses to questions such as whether a state should have a compulsory returnable-bottle law. Responses are scored for whether or not they consider both sides of the question.

One general problem of these sorts of measures is that certain issues, for some people, do not lend themselves to two-sided thinking. If most people today were asked to comment on the question "Is slavery wrong?" or "What do you think of the character of Adolph Hitler?" they would probably not have much to say on the "other side." In other cases, people have already thought through some position even though others remain on the opposite side. A devout Christian is unlikely to produce a two-sided discussion of the existence of God. Yet such people are not necessarily poor thinkers in general, or even about these issues.

Even the presence of two-sided discussions does not necessarily indicate actively open-minded thinking, however, when the topic is truly a difficult one. Most people initially consider both sides of an issue when making a decision that they find hard. True active open-mindedness shows itself only after some tentative commitment to one side has been made. Those who still seek out the other side before jumping to a conclusion are the real actively open-minded thinkers. In sum, tests that look at whether people spontaneously consider both sides of an issue are imperfect indicators of the propensity to think well. Perhaps better measures would assess the understanding of the *need* to consider the other side, in general, before reaching a conclusion. This can be done by asking people to evaluate examples of the thinking of others.

Myside bias and irrational belief persistence

An important part of actively open-minded thinking is fairness to possibilities, regardless of their initial strength. People tend to favor possibilities that are already strong, both in search (particularly search for evidence) and in making inferences from evidence at hand. People tend not to look for evidence against what they favor, and, when they find it anyway, they tend to ignore it. David Perkins has named these two characteristics "myside bias" (Perkins et al., 1986). The term refers to "my side" of the issue at hand rather than one side of an argument with another person. (Of course, it happens there, too.)

Irrational belief persistence may result from myside bias in the search for evidence and use of evidence. As a result of these biases, incorrect beliefs are slow to change, and they can even become stronger when they ought to become weaker. Hence, their persistence is irrational.

The irrational persistence of belief is one of the major sources of human folly, as many have noted (Bacon, 1620/1960;   Janis and Mann, 1977; Nisbett and Ross, 1980; Kruglanski and Ajzen, 1983). We tend to hold to our beliefs without sufficient regard to the evidence against them or the lack of evidence in their favor.

Irrational belief persistence affects our lives in many forms in addition to its effect on the judgment of probability and correlation. Good students, for example (like good scholars), must remain open to counterevidence and criticism, willing to be persuaded of alternative views and willing to criticize their own efforts so as to improve them; poor students often seem to be rigid in defending their mistaken beliefs about what they are learning in school (Baron, Badgio, and Gaskins, 1985).

Certain forms of psychopathology, such as delusions, are essentially defined by irrational persistence of belief. A delusional patient is not just someone who believes (wrongly) that her sneezing and coughing mean that she is dying of an incurable disease; she is someone who continues to believe this even after five reputable physicians tell her that her symptoms are caused by a simple allergy to ragweed.

Depressives, Beck has argued, maintain their depression by ignoring evidence that could cheer them up and by taking seriously only the evidence consistent with their gloomy outlook (Beck, 1976). Beck's cognitive therapy of depression tries to teach the patient to treat the relevant evidence more impartially.

Irrational belief persistence has also been implicated in faulty decision making by individuals and governments alike. In any war in which one side clearly loses, the loss is apparent before it occurs, but both the government and people of the losing side continue to believe that they can see victory just around the corner. Moral beliefs that underlie political controversies, such as the controversies concerning abortion, sex, or racial inequality, also seem particularly resistant to arguments or evidence.

Irrational belief persistence can cause serious difficulties in personal matters such as relationships and business ventures, too. In romance and in business, confidence is usually a good thing, because it inspires us to undertake difficult ventures, to initiate relationships, to pursue lofty goals, but when the evidence tells us that a particular endeavor — whether a love affair or a new company – is not getting off the ground after several attempts, we need, for our own sakes, to be responsive to the evidence, and sometimes we are not.

Irrational belief persistence involves two types of biases that we have frequently encountered earlier in this book:

1. The _overweighing_ of evidence consistent with a favored belief or the _under-weighing_ of evidence against it; for example, a general's attending to reports of enemy casualties and ignoring reports of their troop strength.

2. The _failure to search impartially_ for evidence: For example, when supporters of U.S. intervention in Nicaragua searched for historical analogies, they were likely to discover the Munich agreement with Hitler, and opponents, when they searched for analogies, were likely to discover U.S. support of Batista in Cuba or the unsuccessful Bay of Pigs invasion.

Some belief persistence is not irrational. Often the evidence against a belief is not strong enough to make a convincing case for giving it up. Michael Faraday persisted in believing that electrical currents could be induced with magnets despite several failures to produce such currents experimentally and finally, of course, succeeded (Tweney, 1986). If we all gave up beliefs as soon as there was evidence against them, we would hold very few beliefs with any certainty, and we would give up many beliefs that were true.

The amount of belief persistence that is _rational_ is whatever best serves the goals of the thinker. In most cases, the goal is to adopt beliefs that provide the best basis for decisions that achieve those goals. We cannot judge the rationality of persisting in a belief by knowing the truth in hindsight. Although rationally formed beliefs are, on the whole, more likely to be true than irrationally formed beliefs, we cannot assume that false beliefs are always irrationally formed. For example, many efforts have been made to show that it was irrational of President Roosevelt and his advisers not to suspect that the Japanese would attack Pearl Harbor. Such critics claim that the president and his policymakers possessed much evidence that favored such an attack but explained it away or ignored it. Some evidence must always be "explained away" or considered less important, however, even when beliefs are true. Evidence is not always consistent. The question is, how much explaining away is *too* much? For every failure to predict something that happened, Jervis asserts that, "we could look at an event that did not take place, and, acting as though it had occurred, find a large number of clues indicating the event's probable occurrence which the officials had ignored or explained away" (1976, p. 175).

If we want to find out if, when, and why irrational persistence of belief occurs, we need some normative standards for belief persistence itself. We cannot typically use probability theory as a normative model. Some of the beliefs include strongly held personal commitments that shape a person's moral, social, and political attitudes. Many of these things are really goals (in the sense of ch. 1). A person who says that she believes strongly that abortion is wrong (or not wrong) may be willing to spend some time every day campaigning for her views. It is worthwhile to bear in mind, though, that people think about their goals in much the same way in which they think about their beliefs. For example, we think about goals by asking whether they are consistent with other goals, and we think about beliefs by asking whether they are consistent with other beliefs. Probabilities apply to propositions that are either true or false, but goals are not propositions of this sort, and the beliefs of interest here are difficult to study in this way.

The order principle, the primacy effect, and total discrediting

How can we tell whether people are weighing evidence in a way that is normatively correct? We have discussed the difficulties in using probability theory as our normative standard. A good alternative might be to focus on the process of weighing evidence itself and to look for general normative principles that a *rational response to evidence* would have to obey. Once we find such constraints, we can ask whether people violate them.

One such principle is the *order principle*: *When the order in which we encounter two pieces of evidence is not itself informative, the order of the two pieces of evidence should have no effect on our final strength of belief.* Or, put more crudely, "When the order doesn't matter, the order shouldn't matter." Suppose I want to find out which of two political candidates is better, and I start out with no opinion at all. I run into a trusted friend, who tells me that Candidate X is better. Later, another equally trusted friend tells me that Candidate Y is better, but by this time I have already formed an inclination to vote for X, so I question the second friend very carefully. It was simply chance that made me run into X first, so the order of the evidence does not matter, yet I might end up favoring X because that evidence came first.

Such an effect is called a *primacy effect*, because the first piece of evidence is weighed more heavily than it should be. One explanation of the primacy effect is that the initial evidence leads to an opinion, which then biases the search for subsequent evidence, as well as the interpretation of that evidence when it is found. This would be *normatively* irrational. If this kind of response to evidence can easily be avoided, we can say that it is *prescriptively* irrational as well.

Many psychological studies have reported primacy effects in judgment (see, for example, Hovland, 1957; Anderson, 1981, ch. 3), as well as *recency effects*, in which the judgment is more affected by evidence presented later. Recency effects might be taken to indicate the opposite bias of oversensitivity to evidence (relative to prior belief). Many of these studies have used a method devised by Asch (1946) in which the subjects were given a list of adjectives describing a person, such as "intelligent, industrious, impulsive, critical, stubborn, envious" or "envious, stubborn, critical, impulsive, industrious, intelligent." The impressions of the person were more favorable given the first list than the second, even though one list is simply the reverse of the other. The term "intelligent," in the first list, seemed (to Asch) to color the interpretation of the later terms; of course, "envious" would have the opposite effect.

Although Asch and others found primacy effects in this type of experiment, others, such as Stewart (1965), found recency effects. Recency effects do not necessarily imply that subjects were too open-minded. Another explanation is that subjects did not follow the instructions to consider all of the evidence equally. Stewart had to exclude the data from many subjects because they responded only to the most recent item rather than to all the items. Even subjects who tried to respond to all the items could have had difficulty suppressing the tendency to respond to the most recent item alone. This tendency can make primacy effects difficult to discover.

Most studies that show primacy effects are not relevant to the question of rationality in belief persistence. There are two general reasons why not. First, often a great deal of evidence is presented, and later (or earlier) evidence is differentially forgotten at the time a judgment is made. Although violation of the order principle would be normatively irrational for someone with perfect memory, it would not be irrational when we take memory into account. We must do that, for our prescriptive perspective, because a prescriptive guideline must reflect what is *humanly possible*. Second, the subjects might have had reason to believe that earlier (or later) evidence was actually more informative. In natural situations, the most important evidence is presented first (or last, depending on the situation), and it would take at least a little effort to convince subjects that this was not true in the laboratory as well.

Peterson and DuCharme (1967) designed an experiment that minimizes both problems. Subjects were told that a sequence of poker chips would be drawn at random from one of two urns, urn C or urn D. The subject's task was to estimate the probability that the chips were drawn from urn C (or from urn D). Urn C contained 3 red, 2 blue, 2 yellow, 1 green, and 2 white chips. Urn D contained 2 red, 3 blue, 1 yellow, 2 green, and 2 white chips. After each chip was drawn, subjects provided a probability judgment about which urn was more likely to have held the chip. The most recent chips are surely freshest in the subject's mind, so a primacy effect cannot be explained in terms of forgetting the most recent evidence. The experimenter arranged in advance the exact order in which the chips would be drawn. The color frequencies of the first 30 chips favored urn C. The next 30 were the mirror image of the first 30, with red and blue switched, and yellow and green switched. At the end of 60 trials, then, the subject should have thought the two urns to be equally likely. In fact, it took about 20 more chips favoring urn D before subjects reached this point. They seem to have become committed to their initial favoritism toward urn C. Because they still favored urn C after 60 trials, when the evidence was equal for both urns, they showed a primacy effect.

There is some reason to think that irrational primacy effects, and irrational persistence in general, are found only when subjects make some *commitment* to the belief suggested by the earliest evidence they receive. If they simply note the evidence and its implications, without forming a desire that its implications be true, they may remain open-minded until all of the evidence is in; they will effectively be using all of the evidence simultaneously, and irrational persistence will not occur. For example, Dailey (1952) found that subjects were less sensitive to new evidence when they made inferences after receiving early evidence in an impression-formation task (with information presented in paragraphs rather than as adjectives) than when they did not need to make any inferences.

Another experiment that suggests a similar phenomenon is that of Bruner and Potter (1964). Each subject was shown a series of pictures on slides. Each slide was presented several times. The first presentation was very much out of focus, but focus became gradually clearer over the series. After each presentation, subjects were asked to state their best hypothesis about what the picture represented. Subjects began stating hypotheses early in the series. They tended to stick to these hypotheses even after the slide came into focus. Their early hypotheses seemed to inhibit their recognition of what was actually on the slide. This was demonstrated by giving the same slides to other subjects but beginning only slightly out of focus. These subjects had little difficulty recognizing the pictures, even though the original subjects, given this degree of focus, could not recognize the pictures — presumably because they were committed to their original hypotheses, and these hypotheses guided their search for and use of evidence from the slide.

A different type of experimental design, called *total discrediting*, has been used to demonstrate irrational belief persistence (Anderson, Lepper, and Ross, 1980). The idea is to present some evidence that induces a particular belief. For example, subjects are given questionnaire responses of two different firefighters, one rated as better than the other at the job. Some subjects are given evidence indicating that risk taking is positively associated with fire-fighting performance, other subjects are given the reverse. The evidence is then discredited by telling the subject that the evidence was totally fabricated, and the belief is then assessed. The direction of the initial belief manipulation continues to influence the belief, even after discrediting. Those who were initially led to believe that risk taking is associated with success continued to believe it. This is technically a violation of the order principle, but it is a special case, since the second piece of evidence is meaningless without the first.[1]

In another demonstration of the same type, high school students were given either

---

[1] In addition, Wegner, Coulton, and Wenzlaff (1985) point out that part of this effect is due simply to the difficulty of "wiping out" any information from one's memory. Some measures of belief are affected by evidence even when the subject is warned in *advance* that the evidence is false.

a good or a poor film instructing them in how to solve a certain kind of problem, and they were then given four problems of this kind to solve (Lepper, Ross, and Lau, 1986). Their success or failure depended on the film they saw, but they tended to attribute it to their own fixed ability. This attribution persisted even after they were shown the film given to the other subjects. Merely being given an explanation of one's success or failure in terms of the quality of one's instruction did not remove the tendency to attribute it to one's ability.

These effects of discredited information seem to be the result of the subject's searching memory, at the time when the initial belief is created, for other evidence consistent with the belief. Later, despite the discrediting, the additional evidence remains and continues to affect belief. If there is "irrationality" here, it may be in the initial effort to bolster the belief by searching memory for evidence in favor of the belief but not for evidence against it.

Should we regard this effect as truly irrational, for the purpose of designing our prescriptive guidelines? At the time when the initial evidence is presented, I suggest, the bolstering may occur by *automatic* elicitation of associated memories rather than by an intentional search for supporting evidence. This effect might be very difficult to avoid. Later, at the time when the final belief is tested, the subjects may simply be unable to distinguish which evidence for their current belief was elicited by the original manipulation and which they would have thought of in any case. If they were to be more cautious, they might end up dismissing everything that they could think of as potentially biased. Prescriptively, then, this effect might not be irrational, because it might not be avoidable without unreasonable effort. This issue seems to have been largely settled by C. A. Anderson (1982), who found that asking subjects to use a heuristic designed to avoid bias — considering whether one could argue for the other side — substantially reduced the basic effect. Therefore, the original bias is one that can be overcome, if only we think in a way that is fairer to alternative possibilities.

In sum, beliefs created in an experiment seem to affect the search for and use of subsequent evidence in a way that maintains the beliefs. This is the basic mechanism that leads to violations of the order principle.

The neutral-evidence principle

The *neutral-evidence principle* might be stated like this: *Neutral evidence should not strengthen belief.* By "neutral evidence" I mean evidence that is, on the whole, equally consistent with a belief and its converse. Neutral evidence might consist of mixed evidence, that is, some evidence in favor of a belief and equal evidence against it.

The neutral-evidence principle would be violated if we tended to interpret ambiguous evidence as supporting a favored belief. For example, each side of an international conflict often believes that the other side is up to no good. An offer of concessions may be interpreted as a sign of weakness or trickery rather than as evidence against the favored belief. Likewise, if the evidence is mixed, one side may attend only to the evidence that supports its initial belief, so that the belief is strengthened by this part of the evidence but *not* weakened by unfavorable evidence.

The neutral-evidence principle was clearly violated by subjects in experiments that Pitz and his colleagues carried out, using Bayesian probability theory as a normative standard (Pitz, Downing, and Reinhold, 1967; Pitz, 1969). Subjects observed a series of balls drawn from one of two "bingo baskets" — devices for the random selection of balls. The proportion of balls of different colors in the two baskets differed. For example, one basket had 60% red balls (and 40% black), and the other 40% red. The subjects knew that all the balls were drawn from one of the two baskets, and they knew the proportions, but they did not know which basket was used. After each draw, the ball drawn was returned to the basket, so that the proportion of red balls in the basket stayed the same for all draws. After each draw, the subject made a judgment of the probability that the balls were drawn from one of the baskets. When two successive balls were of different colors, the normative model (Bayes's theorem) specifies that no overall change in probability of the subject's hypothesis should occur, yet subjects usually *increased* the probability assigned to their more likely hypothesis after seeing two balls of different colors. If they thought the balls were from the first basket, for example, they counted a red ball as evidence in favor of this hypothesis, but they failed to count a black ball as equally strong evidence against it.

This "inertia effect" was present only when subjects were asked to make a judgment after each draw; when the judgment was delayed until the whole series was over, confidence was a function of the difference between the number of red and black balls drawn, just as Bayes's theorem says it should be. (When an inertia effect was present, confidence increased with the number of draws, even when the difference was constant.) Pitz (1969) suggests that subjects need to commit themselves to a judgment in order to display resistance to evidence against that judgment.

Lord, Ross, and Lepper (1979) showed a violation of the neutral-evidence principle in a situation where such errors in daily life have deadly serious consequences. They selected subjects who had indicated that they favored, or opposed, capital punishment in responses to a questionnaire. Each subject was then presented with mixed evidence on the effectiveness of capital punishment in deterring crime. Each subject read two reports, one purporting to show effectiveness and the other purporting to show ineffectiveness. (Although the reports appeared to be actual journal articles, they had been fabricated by the experimenters.) One report compared murder rates in various states in the country before and after adoption of capital punishment. The other compared murder rates in states with and without capital punishment. The results were manipulated so that only the first report showed deterrence for half the subjects and only the second report showed deterrence for the other half.

The effect of each report on the subject's belief was stronger when the report agreed with the belief than when it did not. Each subject rated the report that agreed with the subject's opinion as "more convincing," and found flaws more easily in the reports that went against the subject's belief. (Of course, neither kind of report is conclusive evidence, but both kinds are better than no evidence at all.) In the end, subjects *polarized*: that is, they became stronger in their initial beliefs, regardless of their direction. If anything, mixed evidence should have made subjects less sure of their beliefs.

This study is disturbing, because it suggests that evidence is useless in settling controversial social questions. Of course the results may be limited to certain types of cases. People do not always have a chance to find flaws in evidence, and the result could be dependent on the greater effort to find flaws in arguments on the other side. Also, attitudes toward capital punishment may be as much a function of basic moral beliefs as of beliefs about its effectiveness as a deterrent. Opponents of capital punishment tend to feel that "two wrongs do not make a right" (even if the second wrong *does* prevent other wrongs), and proponents tend to feel that "the punishment should fit the crime" (even if it *does not* prevent other crimes). Counterevidence is therefore easily resisted, in this case, by simply attending to the moral reasons for or against capital punishment, but such an attention shift is unnecessary when the evidence on deterrence is favorable to the choice consistent with one's moral belief.

It is important to note that this "polarization effect" can be detected only when the bias against counterevidence is extreme. Normatively, we might expect that beliefs would move toward the middle of the range when people are presented with mixed evidence. If people have stronger (or more) evidence for the side they favor, then mixed evidence, which is equally strong on both sides, would add proportionately more strength to the other side. If we could apply a precise normative model to belief revision, it might specify some exact amount of movement toward neutrality. When beliefs do not move toward neutrality at all, they may move *less than they should* according to such a model. When we cannot apply such a model — as we cannot, in the case of the capital punishment experiment — we cannot detect such resistance to evidence unless it leads to polarization. However, the effect can be found in other cases aside from beliefs about capital punishment. For example, it is found with attitudes toward pertussis vaccination, which produces serious side effects as well as preventing potentially deadly disease (Meszaros et al., 1996).

Note that the illusory correlation effect (described in Chapter 8) could lead to violation of the neutral-evidence principle. If people interpret 0 correlation as consistent with their belief in a positive correlation, they will maintain that belief more tenaciously than they should. The experiments on illusory correlation, together with the experiment by Lord and his colleagues in which subjects tended to find flaws only in the evidence that went against them, suggest that a major mechanism of irrational persistence involves distortion of one's perception of what the evidence would mean to an unbiased observer.

An extreme example of the violation of the neutral-evidence principle was found by Batson (1975). In his study, the evidence presented was not even neutral, but was entirely against the belief in question, for the relevant subjects. Fifty female high school students who attended a church-sponsored youth program were given a questionnaire that included items concerning the divinity of Jesus. For example, "Jesus actually performed miracles," and "Jesus was only human." The students were then divided into two groups, according to their answer to the question, "Do you believe

Jesus is the Son of God?" (Of the 50 girls, 42 answered yes; 8 answered no.) Subjects in the two groups were then asked to read, discuss, and evaluate some material purportedly "written anonymously and denied publication in the *New York Times* at the request of the World Council of Churches because of the obvious crushing effect it would have on the entire Christian world" (p. 180). The writings claimed to show, on the basis of newly discovered scrolls, that the New Testament was fraudulent. Of the 42 believers, 11 accepted the veracity of the article. This group became even more convinced of the divinity of Jesus than they had been before reading the article. (The believers who did not accept the veracity of the article did not change their belief, and the nonbelievers also strengthened their disbelief in the divinity of Jesus, even though most of them did not accept the article either.) The believers who accepted the article had the greatest need to strengthen their belief in the divinity of Jesus, and they did so despite being given nothing but negative evidence.

Effect of active open-mindedness on outcomes

These are some of the basic demonstrations of irrational belief persistence. Before looking more closely at how it works, let us ask whether it matters. Does actively open-minded thinking help produce better decisions?

Several studies have looked for a correlation between good thinking and good outcomes. Herek, Janis, and Huth (1987) examined the thinking of U.S. presidents (and their advisers) about how the United States should respond to nineteen international crises from the Greek civil war in 1947 to the Yom Kippur war in 1973. Historical records of decisions were evaluated for several symptoms of defective decision making, including "gross omissions in surveying alternatives" (inadequate search for possibilities); "gross omissions in surveying objectives" (inadequate search for goals); "failure to examine major costs and risks of the preferred choice" (inadequate search for evidence); and "selective bias in processing information at hand" (biased interpretation). Outcomes were assessed by experts in international affairs, from the point of view of taking into account the best interests of the United States and (separately) the best interests of the world. The symptoms of poor decision making correlated with poor outcomes (from either point of view). It is possible that the judgments of symptoms were influenced by the judges' knowledge of the outcome, but the correlations were high, and some of the crises were quite obscure, so the effect is probably a real one. Good thinking does seem to correlate with good outcomes.

Another type of study has examined correlations between measure of actively open-minded thinking and measures of the ability to solve various problems. Some of these problems are of the sort given in school, and others are of the sort used throughout this book to illustrate biases in thinking. I shall suggest that actively open-minded thinking helps to reduce some of these biases, and these studies provide first-blush evidence for that suggestion. They show that people who think in a way that is actively open-minded are better at solving the problems, or less biased.

In one study, Stanovich and West (1998) reported several experiments, involving the presentation of several tasks to each of hundreds of college students. One task, the Argument Evaluation Test, measured myside bias in the evaluation of arguments. Each item began with Dale (a fictitious person) stating an opinion about a social issue, for example, "The welfare system should be drastically cut back in size." The subject indicated agreement or disagreement (to indicate the subject's side). Dale than gave a justification, for example, "because welfare recipients take advantage of the system and buy expensive foods with their food stamps." A critic then presented a counterargument, for example, "Ninety-five percent of welfare recipients use their food stamps to obtain the bare essentials for their families." Finally, Dale rebuts the counterargument, for example, "Many people who are on welfare are lazy and don't want to work for a living." The subject then evaluated the strength of the rebuttal on a four point scale. The subject's answer was compared to answers given by experts — philosophy professors at the University of California, Berkeley, and Stanovich and West. To estimate myside bias, the authors tried to predict the subject's ratings from both the expert ratings and the subject's own opinion about the issue. Myside bias was defined as a positive effect of the subject's beliefs. That is, subjects showing myside bias were those who tended to deviate from the expert ratings in the direction of their own opinions, rating arguments as better when they agreed with that opinion. Most subjects showed some myside bias, but some were more biased than others. The question is whether the less biased subjects do better on other tasks (compared to the more biased subjects).

This happened for several tasks, but not for all the tasks used. Myside bias may be a common problem in reasoning, but it isn't the only problem. Students with less myside bias did better on a test of logical syllogisms and the Wason four-card problem (Chapter 4), a test involving attention to statistical evidence rather than anecdotes, a measure of efficient hypothesis testing, and a measure of the perception of correlations. No measure of myside bias correlated with inappropriate extreme confidence or correct use of Bayes's theorem in probability judgment (Chapter 6). Subjects low in myside bias also got better scores on tests of general ability, such as the Scholastic Achievement Test and the Ravens Progressive Matrices (Chapter 2).

Determinants and related phenomena

Let us now consider some possible determinants of irrational belief persistence.

Beliefs about thinking

General beliefs about thinking itself can play a role. People have their own standards for thinking, some of which encourage poor thinking. The heuristics that we use to form our beliefs are maintained by certain explicit beliefs about how thinking should be conducted — beliefs transmitted through the culture (Perkins, Allen, and Hafner, 1983; Baron, 1991). People differ in their beliefs about how one should draw conclusions. Some think that changing one's mind is a sign of weakness and that a good thinker is one who is determined, committed, and steadfast. Such people, if they followed their own standards, would be more likely to persist in beliefs irrationally. Others believe that good thinkers are open-minded, willing to listen to the other side, and flexible. Most of us probably subscribe somewhat to both of these beliefs. Whatever our beliefs, most of us desire to be good thinkers, so we try to follow our own standards.

The last chapter discussed the work of Kuhn on the kinds of standards that people apply to their own thinking. Other evidence for a role of beliefs about thinking comes from the study of Stanovich and West (1998), just described. They found that subjects with less myside bias had beliefs about thinking itself that tended to favor active open-mindedness. They endorsed items such as, "People should always take into consideration evidence that goes against their beliefs," and they disagree with items such as "Changing your mind is a sign of weakness."

My own research has found similar results (Baron, 1989). I measured subjects' beliefs about good thinking, in two different ways. First, subjects were asked how they thought people ought to respond to challenges to their beliefs. How, for example, should college students respond when they meet new ideas about religion or politics? Subjects were classified according to whether or not they thought people ought to think further, with a view to revising their beliefs if it is warranted. Second, subjects were asked to give grades (A through F) to hypothetical thinking protocols for the quality of thinking. Some protocols considered arguments on only one side of an issue (for example, on the question of whether automobile insurance rates should be higher for city dwellers than for suburbanites: "My first thought is that each group of people should pay for its own accidents. City dwellers surely have more accidents, and their cars get broken into and stolen a lot more"). Other arguments presented evidence on the opposite side as well (for example, "On the other hand, it doesn't seem fair to make people pay for things they can't help, and a lot of people can't help where they live"). Subjects' thinking itself was also measured by looking at whether they themselves produced two-sided or one-sided arguments when asked to consider some question, such as the question about ocean-floor minerals described in chapter 3. Those thinkers who gave higher grades to two-sided protocols, and who thought that we should be open-minded when our beliefs are challenged, were more likely than other subjects to produce two-sided thinking themselves. It appears that people's beliefs about thinking affect the way they themselves think.

Why do some fail to realize that two-sided thinking is better than one-sided thinking? It is possible that belief in one-sided thinking is the result of the evolution of institutions, such as organized religions and nations. To keep its adherents from one generation to the next, each of these institutions must convince them that its views are correct, even though many outsiders will argue otherwise. Those institutions that inculcate an ideology in which defense of one's belief is a virtue and questioning is a vice are the ones most likely to overcome challenges from outside.

Another possibility is that people confuse two different standards for thinking, which we might call the "good thinker" (active open-mindedness) and the "expert."

Because experts *know* the answer to most questions, they usually do not have to consider alternatives or counterevidence. If we admire experts, we may come to admire people who are "decisive" in the sense of being rigid. When a news commentator criticizes a political candidate for waffling and being unsure (as might befit a good thinker faced with many of the issues that politicians must face), the implication is that the candidate is not expert enough to have figured out the right answer. Similarly, a person who adopts a know-it-all tone — speaking without qualification or doubt — is giving a sign of expertise. Some parents (perhaps because they *are* experts about the matter under discussion) talk this way to their children, who come to think of it as a "grown-up" way to talk.

This confusion of expertise with good thinking may reinforce the institutional pressures. Those who are considered wise and respected members of the institution or group may talk like experts, encouraging their followers to "know" rather than to think. And how are the followers supposed to "know"? By listening to the experts, of course.

A third possibility is that people confuse the standards of the thinker with those of an *advocate*. A good lawyer is an advocate for her client. She tries to defend her own side, and she considers the other side of the case only for the purpose of rebutting it. It is inconceivable that she would change her mind, at least in court. She deliberately takes sides, knowing that there is another lawyer on the other side, and a judge to ensure that the opponent is treated fairly. Similarly, in democratic groups, public-spirited people often advocate a point of view they do not necessarily accept but feel is neglected, knowing that the other side of the issue will be well defended. Thus the individual can approach an issue in a one-sided way with the comfort of knowing that the group as a whole will "think well," in the sense of considering alternatives and counterevidence. There is room for one-sided advocacy as part of a larger process of two-sided (or many-sided) group thinking. Even in groups, however, respect and tolerance for the other side is required if the group is to function well. The danger is that people's standards for thinking may be confused with standards for skill as an advocate. That is why debating teams do not necessarily encourage good thinking.

Distortion of beliefs by desires

We now consider the ways in which beliefs are affected by desires (long-term personal goals or temporary goals). These effects may help to explain irrational belief persistence, and they are also of interest in their own right. They have long been known to psychotherapists as types of bias that can seriously interfere with personal functioning, but they are probably just as insidious in the realm of politics.

Self-deception and wishful thinking. Persistence in an irrational belief can be a kind of self-deception in which we make ourselves believe something through the use of heuristics or methods of thinking that we would know (on reflection) are incorrect. By this view, if we were aware that our thinking was biased when we did it, we would not accept its results. This account assumes that irrational persistence occurs even in people who can recognize good thinking in general when they see it.

The best evidence for self-deception as a phenomenon in its own right comes from a study that has nothing to do with belief persistence. Quattrone and Tversky (1984) first asked each subject to take a cold pressor pain test, in which the subject's arm was submerged in cold water until the subject could no longer tolerate the pain. After that, the subject was told that recent medical studies had discovered two types of hearts, one type being associated with longer life and fewer heart attacks than the other. The two types could be distinguished by the effect of exercise on the cold pressor test. Some subjects were told that exercise would increase tolerance in the good type of heart; others were told that it would decrease tolerance in the good type. Subjects then repeated the cold pressor test, after riding an exercycle for 1 minute.

In general, subjects' tolerance changed in the direction that they were told was associated with a good heart. If they were told that exercise increased tolerance in people with good hearts, they managed to tolerate the cold water a bit longer, and vice versa. Only 9 of the 38 subjects indicated (in an anonymous questionnaire) that they had purposely tried to change in the direction associated with a good heart. The remaining 29 showed just as large a change in tolerance (in the good direction) as the 9 who admitted that they tried to change. In general, the 9 who admitted trying to control their results did *not* believe that they really had a good heart, but the 29 who did not admit to "cheating" did believe it. The 9 admitters therefore failed in their attempt to deceive themselves, because they were caught in the act (by themselves, of course), and therefore they could not accept the results of the deception. The 29 others were successful in keeping from themselves what they had done to create their beliefs.

This experiment illustrates the essential features of all self-deception (see Elster, 1979, 1983): the presence of a desire to have a certain belief; an action or inaction designed to create or strengthen that belief; and an unawareness of the relation between the ultimate belief and the motivated action that gave rise to it. If you neglect to mention disturbing symptoms to your doctor, you must forget that you have done this, if you want to be cheered up when she pronounces you to be in excellent health.

Psychologists have found other examples of beliefs distorted in the direction of desires. McGuire (1960) showed wishful thinking in a complicated task involving syllogisms. Svenson (1981) found, for example, that most drivers believe that they are safer and more skillful than average, and Weinstein (1980) found that most people believe they are more likely than average to live past 80. Babad and Katz (1991) found that people who bet on sports events are more likely to bet on a win by their favored team, the team they hope will win. Some betting arrangements allow odds to be set by the bets made (rather than, say, expert opinion). In such cases, it should theoretically be possible to make money by betting against the team or outcome that most bettors favor.

Wishful thinking can affect decisions. Weeks and her colleagues (1998) looked at the decisions of patients who had colon cancers that had spread to their livers or who had advanced lung cancer. All the patients had a very short life expectancy. Patients and their doctors estimated each patient's probability of surviving for six months. Doctors were accurate on the whole, but patients overestimated their probability of

survival, sometimes drastically. These patients were all faced with a choice of pal-
liative therapy to relieve their pain and discomfort or aggressive treatment designed
to extend life, such as chemotherapy. The aggressive treatment typically makes life
worse and has little benefit in these patients. The patients who disagreed the most
with their doctors in overestimating their chance of survival were the most likely to
choose aggressive therapy.

Some wishful thinking is not irrational, however, as we noted in Chapter 3, for
certain unpleasant beliefs may themselves make us unhappy or unable to carry out
our other plans. The prescriptive difficulty is to set policies for ourselves that will
permit wishful thinking and self-deception only when they are harmless or useful.

Dissonance resolution: eliminating conflict among beliefs. A related phenomenon occurs when we make a difficult decision. Often there are reasons favoring the
path not taken. After the decision, we seem to give these reasons less weight than
we gave them before the decision. Festinger (1962) asked adolescent girls to rate
a number of popular records for attractiveness. The experimenter then asked each
girl to choose one of two records that she had rated as moderately attractive. When
the records were rated again, the record chosen was rated higher than before, and
the record rejected was rated lower than before. Presumably the subjects were more
convinced, the second time, that they had good reasons for their original decisions.

In a similar experiment (Festinger, 1962), subjects were paid to write an essay
advocating a position (in politics, for example) with which they disagreed. Those
paid only a little to do this tended to change their opinion in the direction of the
essay they wrote. Those paid a lot did not change. Those paid only a little desired to
believe that they had written the essay for a good reason. Because they did not do it
for the money, they apparently convinced themselves that they had done it because
they really agreed with the position more than they initially thought.

In another classic study, Festinger and Carlsmith (1959) induced subjects to participate in a psychology experiment that they deliberately made boring and tedious.
After the experiment, each subject was asked to convince the next subject (actually
a confederate) that the experiment was interesting and fun. Half of the subjects were
paid $1 for their participation in the experiment; the other half were paid $20. After
this, the subjects were interviewed about their true opinion of the experiment. The
group paid $1 had a more favorable opinion of the experiment.

Festinger (1962) explains these results as a process of "reduction in cognitive
dissonance." When the choice is difficult, the reasons for one decision are "disso-
nant" with the reasons for the other, and the dissonance can be reduced by playing
down the reasons for the choice not made or inventing reasons for the choice made
(for example, that the dull experiment was really interesting).

Surely we try to eliminate conflict among our beliefs. Most of our attempts to do
this, however, are completely rational. When we find evidence against a belief that
we favor, for example, we often reduce the strength of the belief, so as to "reduce the
dissonance." These experiments, however, seem to show some sort of *irrationality.*
What is irrational here? The idea of "dissonance reduction" does not by itself seem
to capture it.

The reason for this sort of postdecisional change could be that people like to believe that they are "good" decision makers — both morally good and intelligent. They change their beliefs about their reasons for *having made* a decision so that their beliefs fit their desire that they be good in these ways. When they write an essay opposing their real view for only a small amount of pay, it is easiest to justify that decision (a bad financial deal) by thinking that they truly have some sympathy for that position. Likewise, they may justify doing a boring task for a small amount of pay by thinking that they actually liked the task. Similarly, when they make a difficult decision between two choices, they may later have doubts about whether they made the best decision unless, in retrospect, they see the decision as not so difficult at all; they therefore play down the value of the rejected choice. These experiments seem to illustrate a form of wishful thinking, where the "wish" is the desire to have been a good decision maker, and the beliefs that are affected are those about reasons for having made a decision.

A number of experiments support this view. Cooper (1971), for example, found that the effect of past decisions on beliefs was larger when the outcome of the decision could be foreseen than when it could not. The decision in question involved agreeing to work with another subject (a confederate) in a task in which the amount of payment depended on the performance of both subjects. In order to receive high payment, both subjects had to solve aptitude test problems and, after doing each problem, indicate accurately whether they had answered it correctly or not. The subject was told that her partner was either "too timid to publicly state that she had [the problem] correct" or else was "a little too sure of herself." In fact, the partner did (always) lower the score for both subjects by being either too timid or too overconfident, but half of the time the source of the difficulty was the opposite of what the subject expected. The interesting result was that the subject liked the partner more (thus justifying her own decision to take part in the experiment) when the difficulty had been foreseen than when it had not. When the difficulty was the opposite of what was expected, the subject could not have foreseen it and therefore had less reason to convince herself that her decision had been a good one.

Another study (Aronson, Chase, Helmreich, and Ruhnke, 1974) showed that subjects can even feel responsible for *unforeseen* (but potentially foreseeable) outcomes and that this responsibility can lead them to justify their decision in hindsight. Subjects were asked to make a videotape recording in which they made arguments (from an outline the experimenter gave them) advocating government regulation of family size — a position with which they disagreed — ostensibly for use in another experiment. In one condition, subjects were told, *before* they agreed to make the tape, that those who would watch the tape would be either highly persuadable (other students who were unsure of their opinion) or not at all persuadable (students who were strongly against government regulation). Subjects who thought that their audience was persuadable changed their opinion more in the direction of favoring government regulation than the other subjects. Presumably, this is because the subjects who thought that they might persuade their audience thought that they would be doing a bad thing to convince someone else of a totally erroneous view, so they convinced themselves that the view was acceptable, and thereby also maintained the belief that they themselves were good people.

In another condition, the subjects were told nothing about the audience until after they had made the tape. The same effect was found, although it was smaller. That is, subjects changed their own attitude more in the direction of favoring regulation when they were told, after making the videotape, that the audience was persuadable, even though they had known nothing about the persuadability of the audience when they agreed to make the tape. Apparently these subjects blamed themselves for being duped. The effect was not found when the subjects were told initially that the tape would not be shown to anyone and were later told that it would be. In this condition, subjects were able to let themselves "off the hook" because the experimenter's lie had been so blatant.

In another experiment, Scher and Cooper (1989) asked college students if they were willing to write essays either for or against an increase in student fees (a proposal that most students opposed). The essays would be shown to the "Dean's Committee on Policy" as part of a study of the decision-making process of that committee. After writing the essay, each student was told either that the essay would be one of the first shown to the committee or one of the last (picked at random). Subjects were also told — and here is the trick — that previous research indicated that the first few essays had a "boomerang effect," that is, "they tend to convince the committee to take the other side." Subjects whose essays would be read early thus thought that their essay would move the committee in the opposite direction from the position advocated in the essay.

The results were clear: The effect of the essay on the student's own opinion depended on the effect that the essay was supposed to have on the committee, not on what the essay said. In particular, subjects who wrote against the fee increase but whose essays would be read early changed their opinion about the fee increase just as much as subjects who wrote against the increase and whose essays would be read late. This study shows clearly that the effect of writing the essay is not in the "dissonance" between the content of the essay and the student's original belief. The results are easily explained by the hypothesis that subjects wanted to avoid self-blame for moving the committee in the wrong direction. If the direction were not so wrong, less self-blame would be needed.

In general, then, people do not like to think of themselves as liars or bad decision makers, and they manipulate their own beliefs so as to convince themselves that they are not, and were not in the past. This appears to be a type of wishful thinking, possibly also involving self-deception.

What is the relation between the effects we have been discussing and the general phenomenon of the irrational persistence of belief? For one thing, the "dissonance" experiments are a type of irrational persistence in their own right. What seems to persist is each person's belief that he is a good decision maker, moral and intelligent. This belief is maintained, however, in a peculiar way. When a person runs into evidence against the belief, evidence suggesting that a bad decision may have been made, the person changes his beliefs about his own desires ("I must really have wanted it, or I wouldn't have done it for so little money," or "put in so much effort," and so forth). These beliefs about desires, in turn, may influence the desires themselves, as we have just seen.

Just as we want to think of ourselves as good decision makers, we want to think of ourselves as good belief formers. When a belief is challenged, our first impulse is often to bolster it (Janis and Mann, 1977), in order to maintain our belief in our earlier intelligence. We want *to have been right all along* — whereas it would be more reasonable to want to be right in the present (even if that means admitting error). This is what makes us into lawyers, hired by our own earlier views to defend them against all accusations, rather than detectives seeking the truth itself.

Related results

Two other results show essential mechanisms underlying irrational persistence. Selective exposure is the tendency to search selectively for evidence that will support current beliefs. Belief overkill is the tendency to deny conflicting arguments, even if they do not need to be denied.

Selective exposure

People maintain their beliefs by exposing themselves to information that they know beforehand is likely to support what they already want to believe. Liberals tend to read liberal newspapers, and conservatives tend to read conservative newspapers. Those who voted for George McGovern for president of the United States in 1972 watched eagerly as the winner, Richard Nixon, was raked over the coals in the Watergate affair of 1973, while those who had supported Nixon were relatively uninterested (Sweeney and Gruber, 1984).

In an experiment conducted during the 1964 election campaign, subjects were given an opportunity to order free brochures either supporting the candidate they favored or supporting his opponent (Lowin, 1967). Subjects received samples of the contents of each brochure. When the arguments in the sample were strong and difficult to refute, subjects ordered more brochures supporting their own side than brochures supporting the other side. When the arguments in the sample were weak and easy to refute, however, subjects tended to order more brochures on the other side. People can strengthen their own beliefs by convincing themselves that the arguments on the other side are weak or that their opponents are foolish, as well as by listening to their own side. Many other studies have found this sort of bias toward information that can strengthen desired beliefs (Frey, 1986).[2]

Selective exposure can lead to self-deception. Imagine that you want to believe that some course of action is correct, so you ask a friend to tell you all the reasons why it is good. If you then say to yourself, "This must be a great plan, because it has

---

[2]Early studies of selective exposure failed to find an overall preference for information on the subject's side, but the arguments on the other side in these studies were often easy to refute, so subjects who chose information on that side might have done so in order to refute it (Freedman and Sears, 1965).

only good points and no bad points," you are neglecting the fact that you have not asked for the bad points. People who select biased information and then believe it as though it were unbiased are manipulating their own beliefs.

This kind of manipulation is particularly easy, because people tend to change their beliefs in response to one-sided evidence even when they know it is one sided. They under-compensate for their knowledge that there is another side. Brenner, Koehler, and Tversky (1996) presented subjects with one side of the evidence concerning a legal dispute. The subjects predicted that other subjects given the role of jurors, who would hear both sides, would favor the side presented. This effect was sharply reduced if the subjects were asked, "Recall that the 'jury' subjects read both the plaintiff's arguments and the defendant's arguments. On the basis of what you've read above, do you expect the defendant's arguments to be weaker or stronger than the plaintiff's arguments?" Evidently, the subjects did not ask themselves this question when they heard only one side.

Belief overkill

A second related phenomenon is belief overkill. Many controversial issues are controversial because there are good arguments on both sides. A rational decision would involve balancing the arguments in a quantitative way, a way that takes into account their relative strengths. But people find ways to avoid this balancing. Through wishful thinking, they convince themselves that all the good arguments are on one side. Robert Jervis (1976, pp. 128–142) provides many examples of this kind of overkill in judgments about foreign policy. In discussions of a ban on testing nuclear weapons, "People who favored a nuclear test-ban believed that testing created a serious medical danger, would not lead to major weapons improvements, and was a source of international tension. Those who opposed the treaty usually took the opposite position on all three issues. Yet neither logic nor experience indicates that there should be any such relationship. The health risks of testing are in no way connected with the military advantages, and a priori we should not expect any correlation between people's views on these questions."

Attitudes about capital punishment provide a good example of overkill (Ellsworth and Ross, 1983). It is possible in principle to believe that capital punishment is morally wrong yet effective as a deterrent against serious crimes, or morally acceptable yet ineffective. Yet almost nobody holds these combinations of belief. Those who find it morally wrong also think it is ineffective, and vice versa.

Here is an example of the process at work, from a subject in a study of reasoning, asked his opinion about animal experimentation: "We actually have no right to do such things. It's not even necessary. If it was necessary, maybe there would be a reason for it, but, there's no need for it, I don't think. We're sort of guardians here." The subject's intuition was that animals have a right to our protection. He could believe this and still also think that we could gain some benefit from experimenting on them, a benefit that we ought to forgo. But, instead, he convinced himself that no benefit exists (dos Santos (1996).

Factors that moderate belief persistence

We have been discussing the major causes of irrational belief persistence. Several other factors have been shown to increase or decrease the amount of this bias that subjects show — or the extent to which thinking is actively open-minded — although none of these factors could provide a sufficient account of the existence of the bias.

Elastic justification

Desires affect beliefs more easily when other determinants of belief are weaker. Hsee (1996), for example, gave American subjects a test of "language intuition" in which they had to pair 20 Chinese symbols with their meanings. The subjects scored their own tests. Hsee told the subjects in the "inelastic" condition to count only the odd-numbered items. He told the subjects in the the "elastic" condition that some of the symbols looked "yin" and others looked "yang," that the meaning of these terms was a matter of individual perception, and that their score should be computed from the 10 items that looked most yang (which subjects could, if they wanted, determine with the scoring key in view). The subjects were paid through a lottery in which the number of dollars they could win was their score on the test (0–100). The subjects wrote their scores on a separate sheet for submission to the lottery, so that nobody could check the honesty of their scoring.

The subjects in the inelastic condition were quite honest and gave the actual mean score of the group as their average score (despite the fact that cheating could not be detected). The subjects in the elastic condition, however, gave themselves higher scores than the mean, and higher than those of the inelastic group. In other words, they cheated. But they may not even have known they were cheating, because the cheating took the form of selecting the "yang" items in a way that achieved the highest score. Hsee suggests that this phenomenon can occur whenever people are conflicted between a "should" response and a "want" response. They will tend toward the "want" response when it is easier to search in a biased way for evidence that supports that response, that is, when justification is elastic.

Value conflict

People think in a more actively open-minded way when they must make a judgment or decision involving values (goals) that are both strong and conflicting. Tetlock (1985) showed this effect by asking college students to write down their thoughts about questions that involved conflicting values, such as "Should the [Central Intelligence Agency] have the authority to open the mail of American citizens as part of its efforts against foreign spies?" — a question that pits national security against individual freedom. Each subject was asked to rank all the values that were pitted against each other by the various questions. Tetlock measured "differentiation" of the response, which was, in essence, the tendency to consider both sides. The differentiation of subjects' thinking was higher when the values underlying the question were ranked close together (and when they were both highly ranked). Subjects thus tended to give a differentiated answer to the question about opening mail if they valued *both* national security and individual freedom. Subjects who ranked only one of these values highly found the question easy to answer and were less prone to consider evidence on both sides.

Accountability

When we express our beliefs to others, we usually have the goal of being liked by those people. We therefore tend to accommodate our statements to the beliefs of our audience. When we must justify our views to an unknown audience, we are inclined to imagine various possible audiences, so that we try to accommodate our statements to many different points of view. In this way, *accountability* for one's judgments increases active open-mindedness.

Tetlock (1983b) found that accountability reduced the primacy effect in a judgment task. Subjects read evidence concerning the guilt or innocence of a defendant in a criminal case. When subjects did not need to justify their judgments, they showed a strong primacy effect: They judged the defendant as more likely to be guilty when the evidence pointing toward guilt came first than when it came second. (Subjects had no reason to think that the order of the evidence mattered, so this experimental condition demonstrates a clear violation of the order principle, described earlier in this chapter.) When subjects were told (before reading the evidence) that they would have to justify their judgments to an associate of the experimenter, they showed no primacy effect at all.

In a similar study, Tetlock and Kim (1987) gave each subject another person's answers to some items of a personality questionnaire and asked the subject to predict the person's answers to other items and to give confidence ratings. When the experimenter told the subjects that they would have to justify their judgments in a tape-recorded interview after the experiment, their judgments were more accurate, their overconfidence was reduced, and their thinking was more "integratively complex." These beneficial effects of accountability on the quality of thinking imply that thinking will be best (and irrational belief persistence minimized) in situations that require such accountability — such as a judge writing a legal opinion — and worst in situations that do not require it — such as a citizen voting by secret ballot.

In general, making people accountable to unknown audiences tends to reduce some biases and increase others (Tetlock, 1992). We may understand these effects by noting that accountability makes people think of more arguments on both sides. When a bias results from failing to take something into account — such as base rates in probability judgments — accountability helps to reduce the bias. However, if subjects think that other people tend to be biased in one direction more often than in the opposite direction, then accountability may increase the amount of bias in that direction. People's theories about the biases of others — whether these theories are correct or not — may sometimes cause accountability to increase biases rather than reduce them. In sum, accountability to unknown others usually leads to an increase in actively open-minded thinking and a reduction in biases, but it can also lead to a tendency to accommodate to the real or imagined biases of others.

Stress

Janis and Mann (1977) proposed that the quality of decision making is affected by "stress," which occurs when it is difficult for the decision maker to see how to avoid extremely negative outcomes. According to their "conflict theory model," decisions are easy, involving little stress, when doing nothing (not changing from the status-quo or default) involves little risk, or when there are serious risks of *not* changing but no risk of changing. These patterns are called "unconflicted adherence" and "unconflicted change." When either option (change or no change) has risks, and when it is realistic to hope to find a better solution and sufficient time to do so, this yields a style of "vigilant" decision making, in which the decision maker seeks information and weighs the options. Vigilant decision making occurs under moderate stress. If it is not realistic to hope to find a better solution, that is, either option will be worse than the status-quo (although one might still be better than the other), the most common pattern is "defensive avoidance," not thinking about the decision at all. Finally, if there is time pressure, a condition of frantic and disorganized search called "hypervigilance" may result, in which the decision maker considers one option after another, with little search for evidence. When the decision maker does seek evidence, the search is unsystematic, and the most useful evidence is often overlooked. Defensive avoidance and hypervigilance are both examples of high-stress decision making. A unique feature of the conflict-theory model, for which much support exists, is the claim that decision making is highly influenced by situational factors. The same person may make rational, methodical decisions in one situation and awful decisions in others.

In some cases, the effect of stress results from time pressure alone. When time is short, decision makers are forced to restrict their search. Kruglanski and Freund (1983) have found that several biases, including the primacy effect, are increased by time pressure.

Keinan (1987) found that stress can impair thinking, even when time pressure is absent. Subjects were asked to solve analogy problems, such as "Butter is to margarine as sugar is to ... beets, saccharin, honey, lemon, candy, chocolate" (p. 640). The problems appeared on a computer display. The subjects had to examine each of the six alternative answers, one at a time, by pressing the corresponding number on the computer keyboard. The computer recorded the number of alternatives that were examined and the order in which they were examined for each problem.

When subjects were told to expect painful electric shocks during the experiment, they often responded before examining all of the alternatives (on the average, on about 5 of the 15 problems). Other subjects, who expected no shocks, rarely did this (on the average, only once out of 15 problems). Subjects who expected shock were less likely to scan the alternatives in a systematic order (for example, 1, 2, 3, 4, 5, 6), and they were less likely to answer correctly (36% correct versus 59% for the group that did not expect shocks). (In fact, no subject received any shocks.) These negative effects of stress occurred even when subjects thought they would receive shocks only if they answered incorrectly too often, so that the threat of shock provided an incentive to answer correctly. Keinan suggests that stress — in the form of fear — can distract our attention and cause us to search less thoroughly.

Groupthink

Biases such as irrational belief persistence are found when thinking is done by groups as well as by individuals. Since much important thinking is done by groups, this field is important. As we noted in Chapter 1, the thinking of groups has analogies with the thinking of individuals. Possibilities and goals are suggested; evidence (arguments) is brought forward; and conclusions are drawn. If, when the group first starts its work, everyone already has a fixed belief, it will be hard to give a fair hearing to other possibilities. There are "hanging juries" as well as "hanging judges."

To a certain extent, the factors that operate in group thinking are the same as those that operate in individual thinking. After all, a group is simply a collection of individuals, and if the individuals making up a group tend to show a certain bias, then the group tends to show it as well.

In other ways, group thinking differs from individual thinking. Groups have an opportunity to overcome some of the biases shown by individuals, because it is possible to choose the members of the group so as to represent a variety of points of view. On the other hand, the individual members may be too willing to assume that this has been done when it has not been done. A group consensus sometimes seems much more obviously "right" than the same conclusion reached by an individual, even though the members of the group are all alike in sharing the characteristics that lead to the consensus. Would it be any surprise if a group of automobile workers in the United States "agreed" that importing of Japanese cars should be stopped, or if a group of Toyota dealers agreed that importing should not be stopped?

Janis (1982) studied the rationality of group decision making and the biases that distort group decisions by reviewing the history of major foreign-policy decisions made by the president of the United States and his advisers. Some of these decisions displayed poor thinking, and others displayed good thinking. As it turned out, the former led to poor outcomes and the latter led to good outcomes. It is to be expected that better thinking will lead to better outcomes on the average, but Janis is aware that the correlation is not perfect. He tried to select his cases according to the kind of thinking that went into them rather than according to the outcome. The examples include what he regarded as the poorly made decision of President Kennedy and his advisers to attempt the Bay of Pigs invasion in Cuba in 1961; the well-made decisions of practically the same group during the Cuban missile crisis in 1962; the poorly made decisions of President Johnson and his advisers to escalate the Vietnam War over several years; and the poorly made decisions of President Nixon and his advisers to withhold information concerning White House involvement in the Watergate break-in from 1972 to 1974.

Janis's selection of cases was supported by Tetlock's study (1979) analyzing the "integrative complexity" of public statements by prominent decision-making groups. Tetlock found that the poorly made decisions were associated with statements at or near the lowest level, but the well-made decisions were associated with well-differentiated statements. (Other recent studies of groupthink include those of Mc-Cauley, 1989, and Tetlock, Peterson, McGuire, Chang, and Feld, 1992. These studies deal with the nature of conformity in groupthink and with its causes, respectively.)

Janis characterized poor group thinking as "groupthink" (borrowing the term from George Orwell). He identified three major causes of groupthink, presented here in outline form:

> *Type I. Overestimation of the group*
>   *1. Illusion of invulnerability*
>   *2. Belief in the inherent morality of the group*
> *Type II. Closed-mindedness*
>   *3. Collective rationalization*
>   *4. Stereotypes of out-groups*
> *Type III. Pressures toward uniformity*
>   *5. Self-censorship*
>   *6. Illusion of unanimity*
>   *7. Direct pressure on dissenters*
>   *8. Self-appointed mind-guards*

By contrast, when good thinking occurs in groups, there is a commitment of the group to a friendly (and sometimes not so friendly) interchange of arguments pro and con, not to a decision already tentatively made. Loyalty to the group is defined in terms of loyalty to the process of making the best decision, not loyalty to a decision already made. Visitors to President Kennedy's inner circle during the Cuban missile crisis were often surprised at the freedom that members had to bring up seemingly irrelevant ideas and suggestions. (Kennedy apparently had learned something about group decision making from the Bay of Pigs.) Information was sought out from a variety of sources, especially people expected to disagree with the group, and these people were questioned thoroughly. (Janis suggests that assigning one member of the group to be devil's advocate can help to prevent groupthink.)

Janis does not deny that there were other causes of poor decision making in his examples. For instance, he noted an excessive concern not to appear "soft on communism," for domestic political reasons. Had presidents Kennedy and Johnson considered the possible outcomes of their poor decisions motivated in this way, Janis argues, they would have realized that they were ultimately undercutting even this goal. One of the advantages of Janis's analysis is that it can explain poor decision making while allowing that very good decision making could occur in similar circumstances. Decision makers are not simply the victims of their political biases, and the purported existence of these biases does not provide a full explanation of poor decisions. In good decision making, questioning is always possible.

Conclusion

This chapter has provided the main evidence for my claim that we tend to be biased in favor of our initial ideas. I showed this by comparing our responses to evidence with normative principles such as the order principle and the neutral-evidence principle. The prescriptive policy to avoid these biases is actively open-minded thinking. We have explored some of the factors that facilitate and inhibit such thinking.

Many of the biases discussed in this chapter are prevalent in conflict situations between two groups: for example, the Bosnians and the Serbs, the Israelis and their Arab opponents, each nation and its trading partners (or would-be partners), and the advocates and opponents of abortion, free trade, and many other public policies.[3] If people learned to think more rationally — to consider counterevidence and to form their ideologies with more sympathy for the variety of goals that people pursue — such conflicts could be reduced. We often suppose that only the other side thinks poorly, that they, not us, are the ones in need of education. Even if this is true, no harm is done by making sure that our own house is in order. Careful attention to the quality of our own arguments can even uplift — by example — the reasoning of our opponents.

Are the biases discussed in this chapter an inevitable part of nature? Apparently not. First, we have discussed the evidence for individual differences. Some people show these biases a lot more than others, and it may be that some people do not show them at all in some situations.

Second, some evidence suggests that people can be taught to think in a more actively open-minded way. Beginning with Selz (1935), several studies have shown that something resembling actively open-minded thinking can be trained and that it transfers to new situations (Baron, Badgio, and Gaskins, 1985; Perkins, Bushey, and Faraday, 1986). Such training does not need to be outside of regular courses. It can often be done by changing the design of traditional course, often in ways that even facilitate the learning of the course content (Baron, 1993).

---

[3]For those interested in further reading on biases and conflict, Jervis (1976) provides an excellent discussion.

Part III

DECISIONS AND PLANS

Part II was concerned with thinking about beliefs. Part III is about decision making, the thinking we do when we choose an action, including both the decisions that affect only the decision maker and the decisions that affect others, that is, decisions that raise moral questions. We shall also examine long-term planning, with special emphasis on the choice of personal goals. Part III is concerned mostly with inference rather than search — in particular, with how we infer a course of action from our goals and from evidence concerning the consequences of our options for achieving them.

Chapter 10 describes the fundamental normative model of decision making, the idea that utility — or desirability of outcomes — should be maximized. This model serves as a theoretical ideal that we can use to justify prescriptive models, and it is also the basis of decision analysis, a set of formal yet practical methods used by decision makers in business, government, and medicine. Chapters 11 and 12 review some descriptive models of decision making. These models are considerably more elaborate than any descriptive models we have encountered so far, and some of them raise questions about how we should interpret the idea of utility maximization itself. Should we, for example, take into account our feeling of regret that results from our having made a decision that happened to result in a bad outcome (aside from our feelings about the outcome itself)? Chapters 13 and 14 discuss the applications of utility theory to medical and other decisions, and the problem of estimating utility from judgments. Chapter 15 examines further our ability to make consistent quantitative judgments without the aid of formal theories.

Chapters 16 through 18 extend the analysis to moral aspects of decision making. I argue that the fundamental normative basis of decision making does not change when these considerations are brought in: We still should try to maximize the utility of outcomes, but we must consider outcomes for others as well as for ourselves. Chapter 19 discusses planning and the potential conflict between goals for future outcomes and goals for immediate outcomes. These conflicts are roughly analogous to those between self and others: We can think of our future selves as somewhat different people from our present selves. The book ends with a discussion of risk policy, which brings together many of the issues discussed in this part.

Chapter 10

Normative theory of choice under uncertainty

This chapter begins the discussion of the normative theory of decision making: that is, the theory of how we should choose among possible actions under ideal conditions. The best decision, I argue, is the one that best helps us to achieve our goals. This idea follows directly from the definition of rationality introduced in Chapter 3.

The application of this criterion, however, is not always so clear. Decisions often involve conflict. There may be conflict between the desirability of an outcome and its probability: The job at Harvard appeals to Ellen more, but the chances of obtaining tenure are better at Yale. The conflict may be between goals: The Yale job is better for her career, but the Boston area is a nicer place to live than New Haven. The goals involved can be those of different people: The Harvard job is better for Ellen, but her husband will have a better chance of finding a job in New Haven. How do we resolve such conflicts?

Normatively, the best answer would depend on the extent to which each consequence of each option (for example, Harvard or Yale) achieves each goal for each person. This measure of extent of goal achievement is called *utility*. Our goals, of course, are what we want to achieve. The normative model states that we should try to "maximize total utility," that is, choose the option that will yield the greatest total utility. When outcomes are uncertain, we take this uncertainty into account by multiplying the utility of each outcome by its probability. (We shall consider the arguments for multiplication later.) This theory of how we should measure and maximize utility is called *utility theory*.

Utility is not the same as "pleasure." The concept of utility respects the variety of human goals. It represents *whatever* people want to achieve. Some people do not want "pleasure" as much as they want other things (such as virtue, productive work, enlightenment, respect, or love — even when these are painful things to have). The utility of an outcome is also different from the amount of money we would pay to

223

achieve it. Money is not a universal means to achieve our goals. As the Beatles said, "Money can't buy me love," and there are many other things that money cannot buy. Utility is also not quite the same thing as "happiness," for we are happy, in a sense, if we expect to achieve our goals, even if we are not now achieving them (Davis, 1981).[1] Finally, utility is not the same as "satisfaction," which is the feeling that comes from achieving our goals. We do not experience the achievement of many of our goals, but that makes them no less important in our decision making. Many composers, for example, strongly desire that their music be played and enjoyed long after they are dead. Those who have achieved this important goal have not had the satisfaction of achieving it.

"Utility" is a bad word. It means "usefulness," as if outcomes had value only because they were useful for something else. But utility is supposed to be a summary measure of how consequences realize our ultimate values or goals. The word "good" would probably be better. Utility is the amount of good or goodness (Broome, 1991). But most people use "utility," so I will stick with it.

At the very outset, you may wonder whether this thing exists, or whether asking about the goodness of consequences is like asking about the redness of musical sounds. People can probably agree, more often than not, that one sound is redder than another, but that does not imply any reality. Consequences differ in ways that make them difficult to compare: they are of different kinds, and they affect different people. Perhaps they have no property of goodness that can be compared in the way required. One answer to this objection is that our choices reveal our utilities, so utilities must be real as explanations of what we choose. (Many economists say this.) For example, if we choose to pay a dollar for an apple, then the apple must have more utility than the money, and if we then choose to keep the second dollar rather than buy a second apple, then the second apple must have less utility than the first (or the second dollar, more). This answer is not fully satisfactory, because it assumes that our choices *do* maximize our utility, yet we do not want to assume this if we want to use the theory to evaluate choices. A normative model should be able to tell us when our choices do *not* maximize utility. Still, the idea that utility should determine our choices helps give the idea meaning, in ways that go beyond the redness of sounds, a judgment that has no implication for what anyone should do.

We shall consider utility theory in four parts: The first part, *expected-utility theory*, is concerned with making a "tradeoff" between the probability of an outcome and its utility. Should you spend time applying for a fellowship that you may not receive? At issue are both how likely you are to receive the fellowship and how desirable it would be if you did. To decide what to do, we analyze choices into outcomes that can occur in different states of the world. To compute the utility of each choice, we multiply the utility of the outcome by the probability of the state that leads to it, and we add across the states. This chapter is mainly about expected-utility

---

[1] Happiness in this sense — the feeling that comes from the *expectation* of achieving our goals — can be, but need not be, a personal goal. We can want to achieve our goals yet not care whether or not we *expect* to achieve them. If we try to pursue this kind of happiness as a goal, we can achieve it all too easily by *deceiving* ourselves into believing that our other goals will be achieved.

theory. The other parts are discussed in subsequent chapters.

The second part of utility theory, *multiattribute utility theory* (MAUT, discussed on p. 335), is concerned with making tradeoffs among different goals. In buying a computer, for example, the relevant goals might be price, portability, speed, ease of repair, and disk capacity. In MAUT, we calculate the utility of an option by breaking each consequence into attributes (each attribute corresponding to a goal), measuring the utility of each attribute of each option, and adding across the attributes. Each option is weighted according to the weight of the relevant goal. If, for example, portability is of little concern, it would get a low weight and have little effect on the choice. We can use MAUT to determine the utility of outcomes in an expected-utility analysis.

The third part of utility theory concerns decisions that involve conflict among the goals of different people. When we make such decisions by maximizing utility, we are following *utilitarianism*, a moral philosophy first developed by Jeremy Bentham (1789) and John Stuart Mill (1863) and defended recently (in a modified form) by Richard M. Hare (1981), John Broome (1991), and others. I discuss utilitarianism in Chapter 16. Modern utilitarianism is basically the claim that *the best action*, from a moral point of view, *is one that maximizes utility over all relevant people*. We may think of this statement as a *normative model for moral decisions*. Many of our personal goals concern other people, and some of our decisions — particularly those that concern the policies of governments or other institutions — have consequences mainly for other people. The desires of other people can therefore be treated as if they were our own goals.

The fourth part concerns conflict among outcomes that occur at different times (Chapter 19).. We tend to discount future outcomes, and we have both good and bad reasons for doing this. The future outcomes can affect the decision maker or others, perhaps even people not yet born.

Utility theory is concerned with inference, not search. We assume that we have already before us our possible choices, our goals, and all the evidence we need; we do not need to search for these. If the decision involves buying a car, for example, we already have a list of possible cars and the strengths and weaknesses of each. If the decision concerns whether to undergo (or perform) surgery, we know as much as we can about the possible consequences, and we assume that their probabilities have already been estimated. Utility theory therefore provides, at best, only part of a normative standard of decision making. The rest of the standard has to do with thorough search for alternative actions, goals, and evidence about consequences and their probabilities. The theory of probability (Chapter 5) provides an additional normative theory, which tells us whether probabilities of consequences are coherent.

Utility theory began in the seventeenth century, and its modern form began in 1738 (Bernoulli, 1954). Its development since that time was largely associated with economic theory, where it became part of the descriptive theory of the behavior of buyers and sellers in markets. Psychologists became interested in utility theory in the early 1950s, soon after the publication of von Neumann and Morgenstern's (1947)

Theory of Games and Economic Behavior.[2] In 1953, the economist Maurice Allais argued that expected-utility theory fails as a descriptive model of decision making. Allais — and many others to follow — also questioned the normative status of the theory. Many scholars (especially economists, but also some psychologists and philosophers) have been reluctant to admit that people are sometimes irrational, so they have tried to develop criteria of rationality that are consistent with our behavior.

The years since 1953 have seen constant tension between the attackers and defenders of expected-utility theory as normative. Both camps have engaged in efforts to develop better descriptive models of decision making. The attackers, who assume that people are generally rational, argue that better descriptive models will lead to better normative models. The defenders, who acknowledge the existence of irrational decision making, argue that the descriptive models will tell us where we fall short according to the normative model and will allow us to ask what, if anything, we can do about it. I take the view that our decisions are often irrational, and I shall defend utility theory as a normative model. I shall also point out, however, that there is room for various interpretations of utility theory as a normative model. The best interpretation of utility theory is still an open question even for those who believe, as I do, that the theory is essentially correct and that the descriptive violations of it are real examples of irrationality. The problems are what to count as "utility."

Utility is a number, but numbers have different functions. Is utility part of nature, in the way that mass and acceleration are? Is it something we discover? Or is more like something we make up, like the number of points in gin rummy? I think the best way to look at it is that it is in between. It is a tool that is useful in thinking about decision making, but it is fundamentally an invention. In this regard, it is more like latitude and longitude than like mass and acceleration. These are concepts that we impose on the earth, but they are extremely useful. We could analyze our position differently, but any other way would be translatable into this way.

Utility is like longitude in another way. The zero point is arbitrary. (We chose the Royal Observatory in Greenwich, England.) And the units are abitrary. We could have 360 degrees or 3, but once we choose the zero point and the units, we have no more freedom. I will explain this shortly.

Can we be so precise about assigning numbers to amounts of good or goal achievement? In the early days of navigation, estimation of longitude was imprecise, but now it can be done within centimeters. Can we ever be this precise about utility? Probably not. Still, it is useful to suppose that there is a reality to it, just as their is to your longitude as you read this. We might try to escape this assumption by imagining that we could really only measure utility within some interval. Within that interval, any two points would be indistinguishable. This won't work. Consider the following points:

A B   C   D   E   F

Suppose that A, B, and C, abbreviated A–C, were within the interval that makes them indistinguishable. And the same for B–D, C–E, and D–F. But if this were true, we

---

[2]Edwards and Tversky (1967) reprint some important papers from this period.

could in fact distinguish A and B, because A would be outside of the interval B–D and B would be in it. Likewise for distinguishing B–C because of the interval C–E. Thus, there would in fact be no interval within which we could not distinguish one point from another. It is difficult to think of how such intervals could exist (Broome, 1997).

As in the case of any judgment, of course, when two outcomes are very close together, we will find it difficult to judge which is better, just as we find it difficult to judge which of two different colored patches is brighter or more saturated (less gray). If we make such judgment repeatedly (after forgetting our previous answers), though, we will find that we tend to favor one more than the other. In sum, the idea that utility is as precise as longitude — and as difficult to judge as longitude was to the early navigators — is not as unreasonable as it might seem to be at first.

Expected-utility theory

We have seen that some of the tradeoffs we must make involve conflicts between utility and probability. Simple examples are choices such as whether to live with a disturbing health problem or risk surgery that will probably help but that could make the condition worse; or whether to put money into a safe investment or into a risky investment that will probably yield more money but could result in a big loss. A decision of this sort is a *gamble*. Expected-utility theory deals with decisions that can be analyzed as gambles. The problem with gambles is that we cannot know the future, so we must base our decisions on probabilities.

↗ When a simple gamble involves money, the *expected value* of the gamble can easily be computed mathematically by multiplying the probability of winning by the monetary value of the payoff. For example, suppose I offer to draw a card from a shuffled deck of playing cards and pay you $4 if it is a heart. The probability of drawing a heart is .25 (because there are four equally likely suits), so the expected value of this offer is .25·$4, or $1. If we played this game many many times (shuffling the cards each time), you would, on the average, win $1 per play. You can therefore "expect" to win $1 on any given play, and, on the average, your expectation will be correct. To calculate the expected value of a more complex gamble, with many possible outcomes, simply multiply the probability of each outcome by the value of that outcome, and then sum across all the outcomes. For example, if I offer you $4 for a heart, $2 for a diamond, and $1 for anything else, the expected value is .25 · $4 + .25 · $2 + .50 · $1, or $2. This is the average amount you would win over many plays of this game. Formally,

$$EV = \sum_i p_i \cdot v_i \qquad (10.1)$$

where EV stands for expected value; i stands for all of the different outcomes; p_i is the probability of the "ith" outcome; v_i is the value of the ith outcome. $p_i \cdot v_i$ is

Table 10.1: Decision table for Pascal's wager.

Option	State of the world	
	God exists	God does not exist
Live Christian life	Saved (very good)	Small inconvenience
Live otherwise	Damned (very bad)	Normal life

therefore the product of the probability and value of the ith outcome; and $\sum_i p_i \cdot v_i$ is the total of all of these products.

The use of expected value as a way of deciding about money gambles seems reasonable. If you want to choose between two gambles, it would make sense to take the one with the higher expected value, especially if the gamble you choose will be played over and over, so that your average winning will come close to the expected value itself. This rule has been known by gamblers for centuries. (Later, we shall see why this might not really be such a good rule to follow.)

The same method can be used for computing expected *utility* rather than expected monetary *value*. The philosopher and mathematician Blaise Pascal (1623–62) made what many regard as the first decision analysis as part of an argument for living the Christian life (Pascal, 1670/1941, sec. 233). His famous argument is known as "Pascal's wager" (Hacking, 1975). The question of whether God exists is an ancient one in philosophy. Pascal asked whether, in view of the difficulty of proving the existence of God by philosophical argument, it was worthwhile for people to live a Christian life — as though they were believers — in the hope of attaining eternal life (and of becoming a believer in the process of living that life). In answering this question Pascal argued, in essence, that the Christian God either does exist or does not. If God exists, and if you live the Christian life, you will be saved — which has nearly infinite utility to you. If God exists, and if you do not live the Christian life, you will be damned — an event whose negative utility is also large. If God does not exist, and if you live the Christian life, you lose at most a little worldly pleasure compared to what you would get otherwise. The basic argument was that the expectation of living the Christian life was higher than that of living otherwise, almost without regard to the probability of God's existence. Not to live the Christian life is to take a risk of an eternity in hell, in exchange for a little extra worldly pleasure. The expected utility of this choice is low.

We can express this situation in table form (Table 10.1). If we wanted to assign numerical values to the various utilities expressed in the table, we could assign them using an appropriate scale. For this table we could assume, for example, that the utility of a "normal life" is 0; the utility of a small inconvenience is a small negative number; the utility of being damned is a large negative number; and the utility of being saved is a large positive number.

Zero utility can be assigned to any one of the outcomes (it does not matter which);

this then becomes our reference point. For example, in the table, we could assign a utility of 0 to "normal life" and a small negative number to "small inconvenience," or we could assign 0 to "small inconvenience" and a positive number to "normal life." Likewise, the units of utility are arbitrary, but once we choose a unit, we must stick with it. We could take the difference between "normal life" and "small inconvenience" as our unit, or we could, just as reasonably, call that 10 units.

In these respects, the measurement of utility resembles the measurement of longitude on the earth's surface. We take zero longitude to be the position of the observatory at Greenwich, England, but we could just as well take it to be Greenwich, Connecticut. Nothing in nature prefers one to the other. And we define the unit of longitude as a degree, but we could also define it as a radian, or a mile on the equator. We would still have a scale of longitude. The measurement of utility is unlike the measurement of length or weight, where there is only one natural zero point (although the units are still arbitrary). Of course, once we choose a zero point and a unit, we must stick with them when we compare things. Utility is like longitude in another way. Both are human inventions imposed on reality for our own convenience. Neither existed before we invented them. We use longitude for navigation, et cetera, and we use utility for evaluating choices.

The concepts and relationships displayed in tables of this sort lie at the heart of most utility analyses of decisions that must be made under uncertainty. Given our limited ability to predict the future, this includes most decisions. The outcome depends not only on which option we choose (live the Christian life or not) but also on which of various propositions — called unknown "states" — are true (the Christian God exists or not). Such tables have three elements: *states, options,* and *outcomes*. The *states* represented in the table are arranged so that they are mutually exclusive: Only one *can* be true. They are also exhaustive: One of them *must* be true. When we assign probabilities, it is to these states. In the gambling example used earlier, the relevant unknown "state" of the world is whether the card will be a heart or not. The states correspond to the column headings ("God exists," "God does not exist").

Options are the possible courses of action we are considering. In the table, they correspond to the row headings ("Live Christian life," "Live otherwise"). They must all be feasible. For example, one could argue that "Live Christian life" is not a feasible option; rather, the proper expression of this choice would be "*Try* to live Christian life." In this case, success or failure at living a Christian life would distinguish the uncertain future states. We would then expand the list of states to include "God exists, and I succeed," "God exists, and I fail," and so forth.

The entries in the middle portion of the table are the *outcomes*. Outcomes are simply the descriptions of whatever would occur if an option is taken and a certain state comes about. Outcomes can themselves include other options, other states, and so on. For example, "normal life" surely includes many other choices, some of which might involve more inconvenience than the Christian life. We could, if we like, expand the analysis to include these, or we could treat the outcome as a whole, using some sort of expectation as a substitute for all of the other choices and their consequences. There is no single right answer to the question of how much detail to include in an expected-utility analysis. There may be such a thing as an outcome that cannot be analyzed further, but such elemental outcomes play no special role in this theory.

Each outcome has a utility assigned to it, which represents the extent to which it achieves the decision maker's goals. If this utility is expressed as a number, and if each state is assigned a numerical probability, we can calculate the *expected utility* of each *option* by multiplying the probability of each outcome by its utility and by summing across the outcomes in the row. The mathematical formula for calculating expected utility is as follows:

$$EU = \sum_i p_i \cdot u_i \qquad (10.2)$$

Here, EU stands for *expected utility*, and $u(i)$ stands for the utility of the ith outcome. In the next section, we shall explain why formula 2 is normative, why it ought to serve as a standard for good decision making.

To rephrase Pascal's argument in the language of modern utility theory, Pascal argued that the expected utility of living the Christian life was higher than that of not living it. For example, suppose that the probability of God existing is .50. In this case, it is obvious that EU (live a Christian life) is greater than EU (live otherwise), since $.50 \cdot u$ (being saved) $+ .50 \cdot u$ (the small inconvenience of living a Christian life if God does not exist) is greater than $.50 \cdot u$ (being damned) $+ .5 \cdot u$ (a normal life). Even if the probability of God's existence is very small, say .01, the differences in utility are still sufficiently great that $.01 \cdot u$ (being saved) $+ .99 \cdot u$ (the small inconvenience of living a Christian life if God does not exist) is greater than $.01 \cdot u$ (being damned) $+ .99 \cdot u$ (a normal life).

Another way of looking at this is to say that the *utility difference* between being saved and being damned is so great that it is worthwhile to live the Christian life, even if the probability of God's existence is very small. We can use the difference between outcomes to determine expected utility. When we compare two options, we can compare them within each column in a utility table. We then multiply the difference between the two utilities by the probability of the state. The following table shows this in a general form, with two options, A and B.

Option	State of the world 1	2	3
A	$u_A(1)$	$u_A(2)$	$u_A(3)$
B	$u_B(1)$	$u_B(2)$	$u_B(3)$

Here, the expected utility of option A is

$$EU_A = p(1)u_A(1) + p(2)u_A(2) + p(3)u_A(3)$$

and the utility of option B is

$$EU_B = p(1)u_B(1) + p(2)u_B(2) + p(3)u_B(3)$$

so the difference between the two utilities is

$$EU_A - EU_B = p(1)[u_A(1) - u_B(1)] + p(2)[u_A(2) - u_B(2)] + p(3)[u_A(3) - u_B(3)]$$
(10.3)

It is the difference that determines which option is better. If the difference is positive, option A is better, and, if it is negative, B is better.

You can see here why it does not matter which outcome is selected as the zero point. If we add a constant to everything in the same column, that constant gets multiplied by the probability and then added to the utilities of both options, and the difference between them is unchanged. For example, if we add C to both $u_A(3)$ and $u_B(3)$, then the rightmost term in equation 10.3 becomes $p(3)[(u_A(3) + C) - (u_B(3) + C)]$, and the C's cancel out to give back the same term that was there before. Naively, we tend to think of some outcomes as being favorable and others as unfavorable *in themselves*; however, outcomes are all relative. Thus, a well-known decision theorist, asked, "How's your wife?" answered, "Compared to what?"

The units do not matter either, provided that the same units are used throughout the whole table. Multiplying everything in the table by the same constant (and thus changing the unit) would just multiply the difference between EU_A and EU_B by the same constant, but its direction would not change. If A were higher (better) than B, it would still be better.

Pascal advocated this sort of analysis as what we would call a normative theory of decision making in general. Implicit in his approach is the decomposition of decisions into states, options, and outcomes (or consequences). To each state we can assign a number expressing our personal probability judgment, and to each outcome we can assign a number representing its utility. Once we have made these assignments, we can calculate the expected utility of each option (or compare the expected utilities of two options, as in 16.3) by a method completely analogous to the calculation of the expected value of gambles.

A numerical utility estimate, as used in this kind of analysis, is not something that exists in the head, to be read off as if from a thermometer. It is, rather, a *judgment* of the desirability of an outcome, made (ideally) as if the judge knew all relevant facts about the outcome. Utility judgments are useful for making important decisions. We must remember, however, that expected-utility theory is a normative model, not a prescriptive one. If we tried to calculate expected utilities for every decision we make, we would spend our whole lives making calculations. Instead of doing this, we adopt prescriptive rules of various sorts, including rules of personal behavior and rules of morality. If these rules are good ones, they will usually prescribe the same decisions that we would make if we had time to carry out a more thorough analysis.

Why expected-utility theory is normative

Why should we use expected-utility theory as an ideal standard of a rational decision? Why, in particular, should we *multiply* utilities of outcomes by their probabilities?

The long-run argument

One "argument" for this "design" concerns the long-run effects of following expected-utility theory. This rule for decision making is the one that helps us achieve our goals to a greater extent, in the long run, than any other rule. Although this argument turns out to be weak, it may help to explain the immediate appeal of expected-utility theory.

To see this, consider the analogy between expected *value* (formula 1), and expected *utility* (formula 2). In both cases, we are trying to maximize something. In one case, it is wealth; in the other, it is utility. In both cases, we will do better *in the long run* by making all of our decisions in agreement with the formula than by any other method at our disposal. (Remember, we cannot see into the future.)

If, for example, I have a choice between $4.00 if a heart is drawn and $1.00 if any red card (heart or diamond) is drawn, the expected value of the first option ($1.00) is higher than that of the second ($0.50). In the long run — if I am offered this choice over and over — I am bound to do better by taking the first option every time than by any other policy. I will win 25% of the times when I choose the first option, so I will average $1.00 each time I choose it. I will win 50% of the times when I choose the second option, but my average winning will be only $0.50. Any way of playing that tells me to choose the second option on some plays of the game will lead to a lower total payoff on those plays. In a sufficiently large number of plays, I will do best to choose the first option every time.

The same reasoning can be applied if I am faced with many different *kinds* of decisions. Even if the amount to be won and the probability of winning change from decision to decision, my total wealth will be highest at the end if I choose the larger expected value every time.

Similarly, if utility measures the extent to which I achieve my goals, if I can add up utilities from different decisions just as I can add up my monetary winnings from gambling, and if I maximize expected utility for every decision I make, then, over the long run, I will achieve my goals more fully than I could by following any other policy.

The same reasoning applies when we consider decisions made by many people. If a great many people make decisions in a way that maximizes the expected utility of each decision, then all these people together will achieve their goals more fully than they will with any other policy. This extension of the argument to many people becomes relevant when we reflect on the fact that sometimes the "long run" is not so long for an individual. Decisions like that described in Pascal's Wager are not repeated many times in a lifetime. Even for once-in-a-lifetime decisions, the expected-utility model maximizes everyone's achievement of his goals, to the extent to which everyone follows the model. Moreover, if we give advice to many people (as I am implicitly doing as I write this), the best advice is to maximize expected utility, because that will lead to the best outcomes for the group of advice recipients as a whole.

Can we add utilities from the outcomes of different decisions, in the same way that we add together monetary winnings? Three points need to be made. First, this idea requires that we accept a loss in utility at one time — or for one person — for the sake of a greater gain at another time — or for another person. If I am offered the game I have described, in which I have a .25 chance of winning $4.00, I ought to be willing to pay some money to play it. If I have to pay $0.50 each time I play, I will still come out ahead, even though I will lose the $0.50 on three out of every four plays.

Similarly, if many people choose to have a surgical operation that they know has a .0001 probability of causing death, in order to achieve some great medical benefit, some of these people will die, but, if the utility of the medical benefit is high enough, the extent to which all the people together achieve their goals will still be greater than if none of them chooses the operation. When we add utilities across different people, we are saying that the loss to some (a few, in this case) is more than compensated by the gain to others (a great many, in this case).

The second point about adding utilities is that sometimes it does not make sense to do so, because the utility of one outcome depends on the outcomes of other decisions. To take a simple example, suppose I enter two lotteries, one with a prize of a vacation in the Caribbean next month and the other with a prize of a vacation in the Caribbean two months hence. The utility of the second vacation would be lower if I won the first lottery as well. I would have had enough vacation for a while. To avoid this problem of utilities not being constant as a function of the outcomes of decisions, I can redescribe my decisions. Rather than thinking of this as two separate decisions — whether to enter one lottery and whether to enter the other — I can think of it as one decision. For this decision, there are four options — enter neither, enter both, enter the first only, and enter the second only — and four possible outcomes — win neither, win both, win the first only, and win the second only. The long-run argument applies only to decisions that have been described in a way that makes the utilities of outcomes independent of other outcomes. Because the long-run argument applies across people, as we have seen, this can often be done.

The third point is that this whole approach is weak because it is true only if the long run is very very long indeed, that is, infinitely long. Even when the argument is applied to groups of people, the groups must be infinite in size. It may be possible to save this sort of argument, but we do not need to do so.

The argument from principles

Another argument applies to each decision, rather than a series of decisions. It turns out that expected-utility theory is implied by certain principles, or "axioms," that are closely related to the idea of rational decision making as whatever helps us achieve our goals. These axioms create an internal consistency among the choices we would make at a given time — something like the idea of coherence discussed in Chapter 5. This rather amazing fact was discovered by Ramsey (1931),[3] and the theory was developed more formally by de Finetti (1937), von Neumann and Morgenstern (1947), Savage (1954), and Krantz, Luce, Suppes, and Tversky (1971). The two main principles are called *weak ordering* and *the sure-thing principle*.

I shall present these principles first in terms of "choice," but the point of them is that they are about utility or what Broome (1991) calls "betterness." Think of "we should choose X over Y" as meaning "X is better than Y." In particular, X is better than Y for our achieving our goals. The tricky part of the theory is that X or Y can consist of two or outcomes that happen in different states of the world. In some states, the outcome of Y might be better than X. But we want to compare X and Y in terms of their overall betterness.

The *weak ordering* principle simply asserts that we can do this, that it make sense, even when X is a mixture of different things. It is an idealization. Sometimes we feel we cannot do this in real life, but that doesn't matter. This is the framework that we impose. The principle of weak ordering has two parts. First, our choices must be *connected*: For any two choices X and Y, we must either prefer X to Y, Y to X, or we must be indifferent between them. In terms of betterness, either one is better than the other or they are the same. We are not allowed to say that they cannot be compared, although in real life we may sometimes feel that way. The idea that two things can always be compared in betterness is part of the idealization imposed by the normative framework, just like the idea of addition that we discussed in Chapter 2 in connection with raindrops. At the beginning of this chapter, I argued that this was a reasonable idealization.

Second, our choices must be *transitive*, a mathematical term that means, roughly, capable of being placed in order. More precisely, if we prefer X to Y and Y to Z, then we must prefer X to Z. I cannot simultaneously prefer apples to bananas, bananas to carrots, and carrots to apples. In other words, in terms of achieving our goals, we cannot have X better than Y, Y better than Z, and Z better than X. Weak ordering clearly is required if we are to assign utilities to our choices. The rule we adopt is that we should choose the option with the highest expected utility, so we must assign a number to every option representing its expected utility. (Numbers are connected and transitive.)

In sum, connectedness and transitivity are consequences of the idea that expected utility measures the extent to which an option achieves our goals. Any two options either achieve our goals to the same extent, or else one option achieves our goals better than the other; and if X achieves our goals better than Y, and Y achieves them better than Z, then it must be true that X achieves them better than Z.[4]

---

[3] Frank Plimpton Ramsey was a philosopher and mathematician who died at the age of 26, while he was still a graduate student at Cambridge University, after making major contributions to scholarship.

[4] Another way to understand the value of transitivity is to think about what happens if one has fixed *in*transitive choices over an extended period. Suppose X, Y, and Z are three objects, and you prefer owning

An apparent counterexample may help to understand utility theory more deeply (Petit, 1991). Consider the following three choices offered (on different days) to a well-mannered person:

1. Here is a (large) apple and an orange. Take your pick; I will have the other.

2. Here is an orange and a (small) apple. Take your pick; I will have the other.

3. Here is a large apple and a small apple. Take your pick; I will have the other.

It would make sense to choose the large apple in Choice 1 and the orange in Choice 2. But a polite person who did this would choose the small apple in Choice 3, thus (apparently) violating transitivity. It is impolite to choose the large apple when the only difference is size, but it is acceptable to choose the larger fruit when size is not the only difference.

Is transitivity really violated? Here is why not. Choice 3 is not just between a large apple and a small apple. It is between "a large apple plus being impolite" and a small apple. The impoliteness associated with the large apple reduces its utility and makes it less attractive. Now a critic might say, "Can't you always make up a story like this, whenever transitivity seems to be violated?" We could, in fact, *make up* such a story all the time. But the story would not always be true. Here, the story is true, so transitivity is not violated. The polite person really does have goals concerning politeness. More generally, utility theory is not something we try to impose onto a decision by making up goals that make the decision seem consistent with the theory. Rather, utility theory is a way of deriving choices from our beliefs and our utilities (which reflect our goals). The example is not really a counterexample, because the polite person has real goals that violate the assumption that "large apple" means the same thing in Choices 1 and 3.

The *sure-thing principle* is a little difficult to understand, even though it sounds easy. It says that: if there is some state of the world that leads to the same outcome no matter what choice you make (the "sure thing"), then your choice should not depend on that outcome. For example, suppose you are planning a trip, and there are two lotteries you can choose, 1 and 2. Lottery 1 will give you a trip to Europe if your birthday number is drawn from a hat, and lottery 2 will give you a trip to the Caribbean if your birthday number is drawn (in the same drawing). If you lose, you will take some local vacation, V. The choice is shown in Table 10.2. The point is that it does not matter what V is; V is irrelevant. If lottery 1 is better for you than lottery 2, when V is a trip to the beach, then 1 is better 2 when V is an expedition exploring caves.

X to owning Y, Y to Z, and Z to X. Each preference is strong enough so that you would pay a little money, at least 1 cent, to indulge it. If you start with Z (that is, you own Z), I could sell you Y for 1 cent plus Z. (That is, you pay me 1 cent, then I give you Y, and you give me Z.) Then I could sell you X for 1 cent plus Y; but then, because you prefer Z to X, I could sell you Z for 1 cent plus X. If your preferences stay the same, we could do this forever, and you will have become a *money pump*. Following the rule of transitivity for stable preferences avoids being a money pump. This money-pump argument, of course, applies only to cases that involve money or something like it.

Table 10.2: The sure-thing principle

	State	
Option	Win	Lose
Lottery 1	Europe	V
Lottery 2	Caribbean	V

This principle is, once again, a consequence of the basic idea of a rational decision as one that best achieves our goals. It is a matter of logic. There are two possible
states, "win" and "lose." If the state "lose" occurs, then the nature of V does not affect the difference between the options in goal achievement, for we have assumed
that V is the same for both options. If the state "win" occurs, then the nature of V
does not affect the difference between the options in goal achievement, for V does
not occur, and what does not occur cannot affect goal achievement. Therefore, the
nature of V cannot affect goal achievement, since it cannot affect goal achievement
in each of the two possible states. If we base our decisions on goal achievement, then
we must ignore the nature of V, that is, the nature of anything that occurs in a state of
the world that leads to the same outcome regardless of what we choose. It is important to remember this argument later when we run into violations of the sure-thing
principle. These violations either violate the principle of basing decisions on goal
achievement or violate logic. Notice that the logic begins once we have imposed the
idea of analyzing decisions into states, options, and outcomes. That was the critical
step.

The sure-thing principle has implications about what matters as well as what
does not matter. If two options have different outcomes only in certain states (in
the example, the state in which you win the lottery), then your preference between
the *options* should depend on your preference for the *outcomes* in those states only.
If you do not follow this rule, you will fail to do what achieves your goals best,
whenever these states occur.[5]

The sure-thing principle is also a consequence of the expected-utility formula, so
it must apply to our decisions if we make them in agreement with this formula. By the
formula, the utility of lottery 1 in the example is $p(\text{win}) \cdot u(\text{Europe}) + p(\text{lose}) \cdot u(V)$,
and the utility of lottery 2 is $p(\text{win}) \cdot u(\text{Caribbean}) + p(\text{lose}) \cdot u(V)$. The choice
depends on which utility is larger. For comparing the two utilities, we can ignore the

[5]This argument for the sure-thing principle assumes that our goals are fixed. If our goals change as
a function of what outcomes can occur, the principle can be violated even though we still choose what
best achieves our goals in each case. For example, if my goals change so that my *desire* to go to Europe
exceeds my desire to go to the Caribbean only when the "lose" state of both lotteries leads to a vacation in
Mexico, I will violate the sure-thing principle. This fact does not undercut the argument for the sure-thing
principle, however, because we have assumed all along that utility theory is a model of inference, taking
our goals and beliefs as given and therefore fixed. We must, however, be aware of possible changes in
desires or goals when we ask whether the sure-thing principle is descriptively true of our decisions.

common term $p(\text{lose}) \cdot u(V)$.

If weak ordering and the sure-thing principle — plus some other axioms of lesser importance — have been adhered to in a person's choices, it can be proved that this person will follow expected-utility theory. That is, it is possible to assign a utility to each outcome (or option) and a probability to each state, such that the choice that is made will maximize expected utility. Mathematicians use many different proofs for this (see Krantz, Luce, Suppes, and Tversky, 1971, ch. 8), so that a proposition that appears as an "axiom" in one proof may be presented in another proof as a "theorem" that follows from other axioms. In all of these proofs, some form of the sure thing principle and weak ordering are regarded as the most essential of the axioms. Other axioms that mathematicians have identified are less essential for our purposes. For example, one is, roughly, that if you are indifferent between the two outcomes, you can replace one outcome with the other in a more complex decision and you will not change the decision.

Many writers regard the last paragraph as the most important point. They think of utility theory as a set of conditions for constructing a utility function. A utility function is an assignment of numbers to outcomes; each number is the utility of its respective outcome. If the conditions are met for a set of choices, then the numbers can be assigned, and utility is this assignment. By this view, utility is something we infer from choices. (The choices may be real or hypothetical.) I have taken a somewhat different view. My view has been that utility is, in a sense, already there. It is the amount of good that the outcome does, according to all the relevant goals. By this view, utility theory is a way of inferring choices from utilities (and from probabilities). My view leaves us with the problem of how to discover the utilities. But we have that problem anyway, because, in fact, people do not follow the theory. So we cannot use people's choices to discover their utilities. The next chapter chapters will explain why people do not follow expected-utility theory, and Chapter 13 will explain how we might measure utility anyway.

Note that following expected-utility theory means following probability theory as well. The probabilities we assign to the states must be additive and must add up to 1 (because the states are assumed to be mutually exclusive and exhaustive). The arguments for expected-utility theory therefore provide additional support for probability as a normative model of belief. (This is not obvious. See, for example, Krantz et al., 1971, for proofs.)

An alternative principle: Tradeoff consistency

We can replace the sure-thing principle with another principle, which implies the expected-utility formula with no other principles except weak ordering, tradeoff consistency (Wakker, 1989; Köbberling and Wakker, 1999). A slightly simplified version of the idea concerns two states of the world, A and B and two options at a time, such as the following two choices, in which the numbers represent amounts of money.

Option	State	
	A	*B*
U	200	100
V	310	0

Option	State	
	A	*B*
W	400	100
X	540	0

Suppose you are indifferent between U and V, and you are indifferent between W and X. And suppose you make your decisions in terms of goal achievement. These assumptions imply that the difference between 200 and 310 in state A just offsets the difference between 100 and 0 in state B, in terms of achieving your goals. This takes into account both your utility for the money and your personal probability for states A and B. Now suppose that you are also indifferent between the two choices in the second table, W and X. This would imply that the difference between 400 and 540 in state A just offsets the difference between 100 and 0 in state B. If, as assumed, you are basing these judgments on goal achievement, then we can conclude that the difference between 200 and 310 matters just as much as the difference between 400 and 540 in terms of your goals, because they both offset the same thing. We are, in essence, using the 100–0 difference in B as a measuring stick to mark off units in state A.

Now suppose that we increase the outcome of X in state A a little, from 540 to 550. This would then favor option X. In fact, this must always happen. The idea of tradeoff-consistency is that we can never have a situation in which one difference (like 400–540 in A) and a necessarily larger difference (like 400–550 in A) offset the same difference (like 0–100) in another state (B). We know that the larger difference is larger because it is the same at the low end (400) and slightly better at the high end (550 versus 540). Again, tradeoff consistency says that this sort of thing never happens. If this never happens, then we can always assign utilities to outcomes and probabilities to states in a way that is consistent with expected-utility theory.

Note that we are also assuming that the idea of differences in goal achievement is meaningful. But it must be meaningful if we are to make such choices at all in terms of goal achievement. For example, if states A and B are equally likely, then any choice between U and V must depend on which difference is larger, the difference between the outcomes in A (which favor option V) or the difference between the outcomes in B (which favor U). It makes sense to say that the difference between 200 to 310 has as much of an effect on the achievement of your goals as the difference between 0 and 100.

The utility of money

Let us apply expected-utility theory to gambles that involve money. In analyzing money gambles, we may think that we ought to choose on the basis of expected (monetary) value, for we may assume that the utility of money is the *same* as its monetary value. This, as we shall see, is not true, since it neglects an important factor; but let us assume, for the moment, that the expected utility of a gamble is simply its expected value.

If I offer you a chance to win $4 if a coin comes up heads on two out of two tosses, the expected value of this gamble is $1 (since there is a .25 probability that both tosses will be heads, and .25 · $4 is $1). Therefore, you ought to have no preference between $1 and this gamble. Taking this argument one step farther, you even ought to be willing to *pay* me any amount less than $1 for a chance to play the gamble. If you have a ticket allowing you to play the gamble, you ought to be willing to *sell* it for any amount over $1.

Most people would not pay anything close to $1 to play this game, and many would sell it for less than $1, given the chance. It does not seem to be the case that we evaluate gambles by their expected value.

Daniel Bernoulli, in 1738, reported a more dramatic demonstration of this point (which he attributed to his cousin Nicholas Bernoulli). Because his paper was published in a journal whose title translates roughly as *Papers of the Imperial Academy of Sciences in Petersburg*, this demonstration has come to be called the *St. Petersburg paradox*. It is as follows:

> Peter tosses a coin and continues to do so until it should land "heads" when it comes to the ground. He agrees to give Paul one ducat if he gets "heads" on the very first throw, two ducats if he does it on the second, four if on the third, eight if on the fourth, and so on, so that with each additional throw the number of ducats he must pay is doubled. Suppose we seek to determine the value of Paul's expectation. (Bernoulli, 1738/1954, p. 31)

The *expected value* of this gamble is infinite. To see this, note that there are infinitely many possible outcomes: heads on the first throw, heads on the second, and so on. The higher the number of tosses required, the less likely the outcome, but the higher its value. The probability of the first outcome is $1/2$ and its value is 1 ducat, so it contributes an expectation of $1/2$ ducat. The probability of the second outcome is $1/4$, and its value is 2 ducats, so it contributes $\frac{1}{4} \cdot 2$, or $1/2$ ducat again. The contribution of the third outcome (heads on the third throw) is likewise $\frac{1}{8} \cdot 4$, or $1/2$ ducat again. Using the formula for expected value (formula 1),

$$
\begin{aligned}
EV &= \frac{1}{2} \cdot 1 + \frac{1}{4} \cdot 2 + \frac{1}{8} \cdot 4 + \frac{1}{16} \cdot 8 + \ldots \\
&= \frac{1}{2} + \frac{1}{2} + \frac{1}{2} + \frac{1}{2} + \ldots = \infty
\end{aligned}
$$

Bernoulli concludes, however (p. 31), "Although the standard calculation shows that the value of Paul's expectation is infinitely great, it has … to be admitted that any fairly reasonable man would sell his chance, with great pleasure, for twenty ducats." If we present the problem in dollars rather than ducats, most people whom I have asked will pay no more than $3 or $4 to play and will sell their chance to play for not much more.

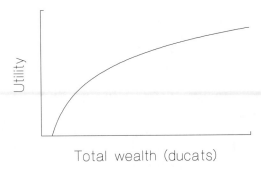

Figure 10.1: Utility of a person's total wealth, according to Bernoulli.

To explain this reluctance, Bernoulli suggested that the utility (in Latin, *emolumentum*) of wealth is not simply its money value. Rather, the value of an *additional* ducat to Susan decreases as Susan's wealth (or income) increases. An extra dollar meant a lot to her when she was making $10,000 a year, but now that she earns $60,000 a year an extra dollar does not seem so important. As our wealth increases, it becomes more difficult to achieve our personal goals by spending money, because we are already spending it on the most important things. (The utility of goods other than money is even more sharply dependent on the amount we have. If you love oranges, you will achieve your goal of eating oranges much better with 1 orange per day than with none, and better with 2 than with 1, but if someone is already giving you 5 oranges per day, an additional orange would probably make no difference at all — unless you treated the orange like money and tried to trade it for something else. Money is less like this than most goods, because it is so versatile.)

Bernoulli suggested that the utility of wealth, for most people, is roughly proportionate to its logarithm.[6] If this were true, the difference in utility between a total wealth of 1,000 ducats and a total wealth of 10,000 ducats would be about the same as the difference between 10,000 and 100,000. The graph in Figure 10.1 shows the relationship between utility and wealth in Bernoulli's theory. As shown in the graph, the value of each additional ducat declines as total wealth increases. Economists call this the *marginal utility* of wealth, that is, the utility of wealth at the "margin" of growth in wealth. The idea of declining marginal utility (with the logarithmic function) does explain the reluctance of people to spend very much to play the St. Petersburg game. The extra utility of the high winnings from the very improbable outcomes (for example, heads on the tenth toss) is no longer high enough to compensate for their low probability.

The idea of declining marginal utility can explain why people are reluctant to

[6]Specifically, Bernoulli argued that "it is *highly probable that any increase in wealth, no matter how insignificant, will always result in an increase in utility which is inversely proportionate to the quantity of goods already possessed.*" This assumption yields a logarithmic function. Bernoulli gave no other justification for this function.

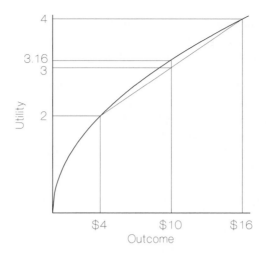

Figure 10.2: Graph illustrating the fact that the expected utility of a fair bet is less than the utility of not betting when the utility function is concave.

gamble on even bets. Very few people will accept a bet with "fair" odds. For example, few people would be willing to give up $10 for a bet in which they win $16 if a coin comes up heads and $4 if it comes up tails. Of course, $10 is the expected value of the bet, the average value if the bet were played many times. Figure 16.2 shows the utility of each outcome of this bet, assuming that the utility of each outcome is its square root. This function is marginally declining; that is, its slope decreases. Notice that the utility of $10 is 3.16 (which is $\sqrt{10}$), but the expected utility of the bet is 3, which is the average of the utilities of its two, equally likely, outcomes (with utilities of 2 and 4, respectively). The expected utility of the bet (3) is lower than the utility of the expected value (3.16) because the slope of the curve is decreasing. In other words, the curve is *concave* (as seen from the bottom; convex curves bow in the other direction). Such concavity of the utility curve explains why, in general, people are averse to taking risks. This desire to avoid risks is called *risk aversion*. Although we shall see in Chapter 17 that there are other causes of risk aversion aside from the concavity of the utility curve, some concavity is present.

The idea of declining marginal utility makes sense if we think of utility in terms of goal achievement, as we are doing. If you have very little money, you should use it in the most efficient ways possible to achieve your goals. To do this, you will buy essential food, clothing, housing, and medical care. If you have much more money, in the form of more income, you will have enough of these things. You will look for ways to use money to achieve other goals. You may spend money on entertainment, and your expenditures on clothing and food may be based on fashion and taste rather than survival. These things are not as important to you per dollar spent as were the other things, or else you would have bought them first. With still more money, you will find yourself looking for ways to spend the money to achieve your goals. You may have to develop new goals, such as a taste for expensive wine or philanthropy. Again, if these things were as important per dollar as other things, you would have bought them first.

Note, though, that the use of declining marginal utility to explain risk aversion — the aversion to "fair" bets — is a descriptive theory that might not be the whole story. People may behave as though their decisions were determined by expected utility, but the "utility" involved in this case is a hypothetical influence on decisions, not necessarily a true measure of future goal achievement. This kind of "decision utility" (in the terms of Kahneman and Snell, 1992) may obey different rules than true utility, a point we shall return to later.

When individuals make decisions concerning amounts of money that are very small relative to their total lifetime income, they will do best in the long run if they essentially ignore their risk aversion and think about expected *value*. For example, suppose you have a choice of two automobile insurance policies. One policy costs $100 more per year than the other, but the less expensive policy requires that you pay the first $200 of any claim. If your probability of making a claim in a given year is .4, your choice each year is between a sure loss of $100 and a .4 probability of a $200 loss, an expected loss of .4 · $200, or $80. Over many years, you will save an average of $20 per year by purchasing the less expensive policy, even though it involves a greater risk. (The same reasoning applies to maintenance contracts.) Because your savings account will have $20 more in it each year (or you will owe your creditors $20 less), your savings will add together over time. The declining marginal utility of money is more relevant when we are considering large amounts of money accumulated over a lifetime.

The fact that the marginal utility of money is generally declining has implications for the distribution of income and wealth in society. If $1,000 means more to *me* when I have only $2,000 in my bank account than when I have $200,000, then it seems reasonable to assume that, in general, $1,000 would mean more to poor people *in general* than to rich people in general. Accordingly, in designing a system of taxation, it makes sense to require the rich to pay more. Such an uneven distribution of the *monetary* burden makes the distribution of the *utility* burden more even. It also allows the government to impose the smallest total utility burden across all taxpayers in return for the money it gets. In fact, most systems of taxation operate on some version of this principle. Similar arguments have been made for directly redistributing wealth or income from the rich to the poor. We must, however, consider the effects of any scheme of redistribution or unequal taxation on *incentive to work*. In principle, it is possible to find the amount of redistribution that will strike the ideal compromise: In this state, any increase in redistribution would reduce total utility by reducing incentive, and any decrease in redistribution would reduce total utility by taking more utility from the poor than it gives to the rich in return.

Exercises on expected-utility theory[7]

[7] Answers to selected problems are found at the end of the chapter.

Assume that someone's utility of receiving an amount of cash X is $X^{.5}$.

1. Make a graph of this function. (It need not be exact.)

2. What is the utility of $0, $5, and $10?

3. What is the expected utility of a .5 chance of winning $10?

4. Compare the expected utility of the gamble with the utility of $5. Which is greater?

5. Compare the expected value of $5 with the expected value of the gamble.

6. Compare the expected utility of $5 with the expected utility of the gamble if the utility of X were X^2 instead of $X^{.5}$.

7. On the basis of your answers to questions 4 and 6, what is the relation between the curvature of the utility function and risk attitude (risk seeking versus risk averse), according to expected-utility theory?

8. Assume that the utility of yearly income X is $X^{.5}$. If you have $50,000 in income to divide between two people, what division will maximize their total utility? Show your work. (You can do this graphically, if you do not know calculus.)

Conclusion

Utility theory as a *normative* model tells us what it means for a decision to be best for achieving our goals. The theory has been widely applied as the basis of decision analysis. It plays another important role, however, in justifying the *prescriptive* model of actively open-minded thinking. Actively open-minded thinking about decisions helps us to achieve our goals because it helps us to maximize utility. The expected utility of a neglected possibility (option) could be higher than that of any option that was considered, so we do well to search thoroughly for options. Likewise, neglecting a possible piece of evidence (possible consequence) or goal (attribute), or weighing the evidence in a biased way, could lead us to choose an option with less utility than the best option we could choose. Parallel arguments can be made for the importance of actively open-minded thinking in belief formation. Beliefs formed after a thorough search for evidence and an unbiased evaluation of that evidence are the most useful for decision making. They reflect the evidence available most accurately and correspond to better-calibrated probability judgments, so they help us to maximize utility in the long run.

Utility theory also justifies my claim that thorough search is a virtue to be practiced in *moderation*. The utility of search is negative, and the compensating expected benefits decline as search continues: There is a point of diminishing returns in the expected utility of thinking itself.

Utility theory in general can also serve as a prescriptive model for decision making, as well as a normative model. When we make real decisions, it may usually be helpful to ask ourselves what produces the best expected outcome. This heuristic — and it is a heuristic — may lead us to make decisions that produce good outcomes.

In the next chapter we shall look at the descriptive theory of decision making. Departures from utility theory, we shall discover, provide further reasons not to trust decisions made without adequate thought or formal analysis.

Answers to exercises

1. The line plotted on the graph should pass through the origin and be curved downward.

2. $0, \sqrt{5}, \sqrt{10}$

3. $.5 \cdot \sqrt{10}$

4. $EU(\$5)$ is greater, thus showing risk aversion.

5. These are the same. $EV(\$5) = \$5$.

6. $EU(\$5) = 25$. $EU(\$10, .5) = .5 \cdot 100 = 50 > 25$. This shows risk seeking when the utility function is convex.

7. Concave implies risk aversion; convex implies risk seeking.

8. If X is the amount for person 1, then $\$50K - X$ is the amount for person 2. Total utility $U = u(X) + u(\$50K - X)$. $\frac{dU}{dX} = .5 \cdot X^{-.5} - .5 \cdot (\$50K - X)^{-.5} = 0$, so $.5 \cdot X^{-.5} = .5 \cdot (\$50K - X)^{-.5}$, so (multiplying by 2 and squaring both sides), $X = \$50K - X$, $2X = \$50K$, $X = \$25K$. (If we graph these functions, the sum of the two curves should have a smooth peak in the middle.)

Chapter 11

Descriptive theory of choice under uncertainty

Don't gamble. Take all your savings and buy some good stock and hold
it till it goes up. If it don't go up, don't buy it.

Will Rogers

Although the normative principles of choice appear reasonable enough to most people, psychological research has shown that we violate these principles systematically
when we make decisions. That is, the violations are not just a consequence of the
random variation to be found in any difficult judgment; rather, they are usually in a
particular direction.

On the face of it, the descriptive models presented in this chapter differ considerably from the normative models presented in Chapter 10. This raises a familiar
question: Is the normative model really normative? I shall argue that it is still normative but that some of the descriptive findings raise interesting and complex questions
about how the model should be interpreted in certain situations, particularly those in
which decision makers have, or expect to have, emotional responses to the decision
itself (as distinct from the consequences of the option chosen). We shall also explore
the reasons why people deviate from the normative model, and I shall suggest that
most deviations are caused by misleading heuristics.

This chapter concerns the way in which we respond to uncertainty about the outcome of an option. Uncertain, or risky, options are those that could lead to outcomes
much better (or much worse) than the outcomes of less risky options. Examples of
risky options are speculative investments, the decision to have dangerous surgery,
and bluffing in a high-stakes poker game or during a military confrontation. We
tend to be averse to risks when the alternative is a gain that is certain (a gain with a
probability of 1), even when the expected utility of the risky option is high. Bernoulli
thought that such risk aversion for gains was rational — given our declining marginal

utility for gains — but psychological research has found determinants of risk aversion that cannot be explained this way. We are therefore biased in making decisions when outcomes are uncertain, just as we are biased in the various ways we examined in Part II.

Some writers make a distinction between risk and uncertainty. They use the term "risk" when the probabilities of outcomes are known. A Bayesian view of probability, however, tends to downplay this distinction, and I shall give other arguments against its importance later in this chapter. For the purpose of talking about experimental results, though, we can take "risk" to refer to experiments in which subjects are given numerical probabilities and "uncertainty" to refer to experiments in which they are not. Most of the experiments are about risk.

Bias in decisions under uncertainty

A number of findings indicate that we systematically violate expected-utility theory when making decisions under uncertainty. These demonstrations often use hypothetical decisions. Sometimes, researchers gave these decisions to subjects, but in other cases the author of a paper simply presents the examples to the reader, hoping that the reader will at least understand how people are inclined to respond in a certain way. I shall do the same here. If you are not inclined to make the choice that others make, try to understand why they might make it. In all the cases I shall discuss, subjects do yield the choice patterns of interest, even when investigators have used small amounts of real money in place of hypothetical outcomes.

Neglect of probability

Perhaps the simplest bias in decision making under uncertainty is to fail to consider probability at all. Baron, Granato, Spranca, and Teubal (1993) gave children the following question:

> Susan and Jennifer are arguing about whether they should wear seat belts when they ride in a car. Susan says that you should. Jennifer says you shouldn't. . . . Jennifer says that she heard of an accident where a car fell into a lake and a woman was kept from getting out in time because of wearing her seat belt, and another accident where a seat belt kept someone from getting out of the car in time when there was a fire. What do you think about this?

One subject responded to this question:

> A: Well, in that case I don't think you *should* wear a seat belt.
> Q (interviewer): How do you know when that's gonna happen?
> A: Like, just hope it doesn't!
> Q: So, should you or shouldn't you wear seat belts?

A: Well, tell-you-the-truth we should wear seat belts.

Q: How come?

A: Just in case of an accident. You won't get hurt as much as you will if you didn't wear a seat belt.

Q: OK, well what about these kinds of things, when people get trapped?

A: I don't think you should, in that case.

Another subject said:

A: If you have a long trip, you wear seat belts half way.

Q: Which is more likely?

A: That you'll go flyin' through the windshield.

Q: Doesn't that mean you should wear them all the time?

A: No, it doesn't mean that.

Q: How do you know if you're gonna have one kind of accident or the other?

A: You don't know. You just hope and pray that you don't.

These subjects, and many others, did not spontaneously realize that the probability of the different outcomes was relevant to the decision. They therefore found the decision much more difficult than it would have been if they had explicitly considered probabilities. Similar neglect of probability may occur in adults, for instance, when making a medical decision under uncertainty. Probabilities matter, and sometimes asking about them can lead to a clear resolution of what would otherwise be a difficult decision.

Preference reversals

Even when probability is not neglected, the weight given to it in a decision may depend on the kind of decision problem that is faced. Lichtenstein and Slovic (1971, 1973) asked subjects to choose between two gambles: one gamble (called the P Bet) featured a high probability of winning a modest sum of money; the other gamble (called the $ Bet) featured a low probability of winning a relatively large sum of money. Here is an example (from Tversky, Sattath, and Slovic, 1988):

> P Bet   29/36 probability to win $2
>
> $ Bet   7/36 probability to win $9

Most subjects preferred the P Bet. Subjects were also asked how much money each bet was worth to them. (For example, subjects were asked the lowest amount for which they would sell the opportunity to play one of the bets, or, in other experiments, they were simply asked what amount of money was just as valuable to them as the bet. The method used did not affect the main findings.) Most subjects gave higher monetary values to the $ Bet, thus "reversing their preference." For example, a subject says that the P Bet was worth $1.25 and the $ Bet was worth $2.10.

Table 11.1: The Allais paradox. Each option is a gamble described in terms of the possible outcomes and the probability of each.

Situation X		
Option 1	$1,000,	1.00
Option 2	$1,000,	.89
	$5,000,	.10
	$0,	.01
Situation Y		
Option 3	$1,000,	.11
	$0,	.89
Option 4	$5,000,	.10
	$0,	.90

This result has been replicated in a variety of situations, many of which involved real money rather than hypothetical gambles (for example, Grether and Plott, 1979; Tversky, Sattath, and Slovic, 1988).

The main explanation for this effect is that people overprice the $ bet when they are asked how much it is worth (Bostic, Herrnstein, and Luce , 1990; Tversky, Slovic, and Kahneman, 1990). In particular, when a subject makes a choice between the $ Bet and what the subject said was its cash equivalent (or even a little less than this), the subject chooses the cash equivalent. This result, in turn, seems to result from paying too much attention to the dollar amount in the pricing task. In process-tracing studies, subjects anchor on or near the dollar amount in pricing tasks, but not in choice tasks (Schkade and Johnson, 1989).

The Allais paradox

Allais (1953) proposed the following hypothetical decision: Suppose you were offered the choices (between different amounts of money) given in Table 11.1. You are to make one choice in Situation X and one in Situation Y. Notice that the table also gives the probability of each outcome.

Most people are inclined to choose Option 1 in Situation X and Option 4 in Situation Y. In Situation X, they are not willing to give up the *certainty* of winning $1,000 in Option 1 for the chance of winning $5,000 in Option 2: This extra possible gain would expose them to the *risk* of winning nothing at all. (If you do not happen to feel this way, try replacing the $5,000 with a lower figure, until you do. Then use that figure in Option 4 as well.) In Situation Y, they reason that the difference between the two probabilities of winning is small, so they are willing to try for the larger amount.

Now suppose (as suggested by Savage, 1954) that the outcomes for these same

Table 11.2: The Allais paradox as a lottery.

	Ball numbers		
	1	2–11	12–100
Situation X			
Option 1	$1,000	$1,000	$1,000
Option 2	$0	$5,000	$1,000
Situation Y			
Option 3	$1,000	$1,000	$0
Option 4	$0	$5,000	$0

choices are to be determined by a lottery. Balls numbered from 1 to 100 are put into an urn, which is shaken well before any ball is drawn. Then a ball will be taken out, and the number on the ball will, together with your choice, determine the outcome, as shown in Table 11.2. The dollar entries in the table represent the outcomes for different balls that might be drawn. For example, in Option 2, you would get nothing if ball 1 is drawn, $5,000 if ball 2, 3, 4, . . . or 11 is drawn, and so forth. This situation yields the same probabilities of each outcome, for each choice, as the original gambles presented in Table 11.1. For example, in Option 1, the probability of $1,000 is .01 + .10 + .89, which is 1.00.

It is apparent from Table 11.2 that Options 1 and 2 are identical to Options 3 and 4, except for the outcome for balls 12 through 100. Moreover, the outcome in the rightmost column does not depend on the choice made in each situation. In Situation X, whether you choose Option 1 or Option 2, you would get $1,000 if the ball drawn is numbered between 12 and 100. Situation Y is the same, except that the common outcome for the two choices is $0.

By the sure-thing principle, described in Chapter 10, we should ignore these common outcomes in making such a decision. We should choose Options 1 and 3, or Options 2 and 4. When choices are presented in this tabular form, it becomes easier for us to see what is at issue. Many subjects do in fact change their choices to make them consistent with the expected-utility axioms when they are shown in the table (Keller, 1985). Other subjects stick to their choices of Options 1 and 4, even after being shown the table (Slovic and Tversky, 1974). As the economist Paul Samuelson put it (1950, pp. 169–170), they "satisfy their preferences and let the axioms satisfy themselves."

Because the choice of Options 1 and 4 violates the sure-thing principle, we cannot account for these choices in terms of expected-utility theory. The expected utility of each choice (using data from Table 11.1) is calculated in Table 11.3. If we prefer Option 1 to Option 2 and if we *did* follow expected-utility theory, then the expected utility of Option 1 must be higher than that of Option 2, so, from Table 11.3,

Table 11.3: Expected utilities of options in the Allais paradox.

Situation X			
Option 1	$.01\,u(\$1,000)$	$+\,.10\,u(\$1,000)$	$+\,.89\,u(\$1,000)$
Option 2	$.01\,u(\$0)$	$+\,.10\,u(\$5,000)$	$+\,.89\,u(\$1,000)$
Situation Y			
Option 3	$.01\,u(\$1,000)$	$+\,.10\,u(\$1,000)$	$+\,.89\,u(\$0)$
Option 4	$.01\,u(\$0)$	$+\,.10\,u(\$5,000)$	$+\,.89\,u(\$0)$

$$.01\,u(\$1,000) + .10\,u(\$1,000) > .01\,u(\$0) + .10\,u(\$5,000)$$

since the term $.89\,u(\$1,000)$ may be dropped from each side. Exactly the opposite inequality,

$$.01\,u(\$1,000) + .10\,u(\$1,000) < .01\,u(\$0) + .10\,u(\$5,000)$$

is true if we prefer Option 4 over Option 3 (because $u(\$0)$ is dropped). There is therefore no way of assigning numbers to $u(\$0)$, $u(\$1,000)$, and $u(\$5,000)$ so that both inequalities will be true. Prospect theory will enlighten us about the nature of this paradox.

Lopes (1987) and Shafer (1986) have suggested that the *context of possible outcomes* affects our utilities, so that when the chance of winning something is high, the utility difference between $1,000 and $0 seems larger to us than when the chance of winning something is low. As we shall see, however, the choices that we make in the Allais paradox are consistent with a more general descriptive theory — prospect theory.

Prospect theory

In 1979, psychologists Daniel Kahneman and Amos Tversky proposed a *descriptive* theory, which they called prospect theory, that accounted for almost all of the available data concerning decisions under risk. It has inspired many other similar attempts. It is important to remember that prospect theory is descriptive, not normative. It explains how and why our choices *deviate* from the normative model of expected-utility theory. Kahneman and Tversky's guiding idea, however, was to take expected-utility theory and modify it as little as possible, in order to make it account for the observed violations of expected-utility theory, such as those observed in the Allais paradox. Prospect theory applies directly to situations — like the Allais paradox — in which we choose among options that are described to us in terms of their possible outcomes and the numerical probabilities of these outcomes.

Prospect theory, as a modification of expected-utility theory, has two main parts, one concerning probability and one concerning utility. The theory retains the basic idea that we make decisions as though we multiplied something like a subjective probability by something like a utility. The more probable a consequence is, the more heavily we weigh its utility in our decision. According to prospect theory, however, we distort probabilities, and we think about utilities as changes from a reference point. The reference point is easily affected by irrelevant factors, and this fact leads us to make different decisions for the same problem, depending on how it is presented to us. Let us look at the probability part first.

Probability: the pi function

Pi and the certainty effect. In essence, prospect theory begins with the premise that we do not treat the probabilities as they are stated. Instead, we distort them, according to a particular mathematical function that Kahneman and Tversky named the "pi function," using the Greek letter π instead of the usual p for probability. Instead of multiplying our utilities by p, the researchers proposed, people multiply by $\pi(p)$.[1] The function is graphed in Figure 11.1. For example, in a gamble some people prefer ($30) to ($45, .80), but they prefer ($45, .20) to ($30, .25). Here ($30) means $30 for sure; ($45, .80) means $45 with probability .80 and $0 with probability .20, and so forth. If you prefer ($30) to ($45, .80), this would imply — using the expected-utility formula — that

$$u(\$30) > .80\, u(\$45)$$

If you prefer ($45, .20) to ($30, .25), this implies that

$$.25\, u(\$30) < .20\, u(\$45)$$

Both inequalities cannot be true. Each side of the second inequality can be derived from the corresponding side of the first by multiplying by .25. This pattern of choices is called the *certainty effect*, because subjects appear to be attracted by the absolute certainty of the $30.

The π function explains the certainty effect, because of the fact that $\pi(1.00)$ is much higher than it ought to be relative to $\pi(p)$ for other values of p (except for very low values, which are not used in this problem). Certainty is overweighed. Put another way, it appears that other values of p are *under*weighed relative to $p = 1.00$.[2]

---

[1] In Chapter 6, we examined distortions of probability judgments. These distortions can operate when we judge the probabilities of the outcomes ourselves, but in the situations described by prospect theory, the probabilities of the outcomes are given to us. We distort the probabilities when we use them to make decisions. If the probabilities are not given to us, both kinds of biases — those discussed here and those discussed in Chapter 6 — can occur.

[2] It is not simply that certainty is *desired* for its own sake or that uncertainty is avoided. The certainty effect is also found in the domain of losses. People seek to *take* risks to *avoid* a certain loss, just as they seek to avoid risks to *obtain* a certain gain.

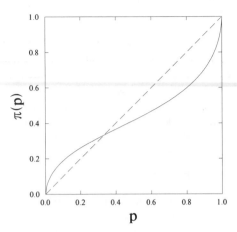

Figure 11.1: π, the weight applied to the utility of each outcome, as a function of p, the probability of the outcome, according to prospect theory (based on Tversky and Kahneman, 1992).

More generally, we can describe the π function by saying that people are most sensitive to changes in probability near the natural boundaries of 0 (impossible) and 1 (certain). Sensitivity to changes diminishes as we move away from these boundaries. Thus, a .1 increase in the probability of winning a prize has a greater effect on decisions when it changes probability of winning from 0 to .1 (turning an impossibility into a possibility) or from .9 to 1 (turning a possibility into a certainty) than when it changes the probability from, say, .3 to .4, or .6 to .7 (turning a smaller possibility into a larger possibility). Imagine a raffle for a trip to Hawaii in which 10 tickets are being sold. Most people would pay more for a first ticket if they had none (in order to give themselves a possibility of winning the prize) or the tenth ticket if they had already had nine (in order to guarantee winning the prize) than they would pay for, say, a fourth ticket if they already had three (which would only increase an intermediate possibility of winning).

An interesting consequence of the π function is shown in the following problem (based on Tversky and Kahneman, 1981, p. 455):

> Consider the following two-stage game. In the first stage, there is a .75 probability of ending the game without winning anything, and a .25 chance to move into the second stage. If you reach the second stage, you have a choice between ($30) and ($45, .80). However, you must make this choice before either stage of the game is played.

Most subjects think about this problem in the same way as they thought about the choice of ($30) versus ($45, .80). They therefore choose ($30). These are the same subjects who chose ($45, .20) over ($30, .25), however. Think about the two-stage gambles for a moment, though. If you calculate the overall probability of $30, assuming that that option is chosen, it is .25, the probability of getting to the second stage. Likewise, the probability of $45, if that option is chosen, is (.25)(.80) (the probability of getting to the second stage multiplied by the probability of winning if you get there), or .20. Therefore, the probabilities of the outcomes in the two-stage gambles are identical to the probabilities of the outcomes in the gambles ($30, .25) and ($45, .20), yet the common pattern of choices is reversed.

Subjects who show this kind of reversal (as many do) are violating what Kahneman and Tversky (1984) call the *principle of invariance*. The invariance principle asserts that *one's choices ought to depend on the situation itself, not on the way it is described*. In other words, when we can recognize two descriptions of a situation as equivalent, we ought to make the same choices for both descriptions. Subjects seem to violate this principle.[3] The invariance principle would seem to be a principle of rational choice that is at least as fundamental as other principles we have assumed as part of utility theory, such as transitivity and the sure-thing principle. Violations of the invariance principle are also called *framing effects*, because the choice made is dependent on how the situation is presented, or "framed."

Note that $\pi(p)$, unlike p itself, is not additive. In general, $\pi(p) + \pi(1 - p) \leq 1$. Therefore, we cannot assume that the 1.00 probability of $1,000 in the Allais paradox can be psychologically decomposed (as in Table 11.2) into .01 + .10 + .89. At least part of the bias shown in the Allais paradox is caused by the certainty effect operating on Option 1.[4]

Is the certainty effect rational? Why should we not weigh certain (sure) outcomes more than uncertain ones? One reason why not is that it leads us to more inconsistent decisions, decisions that differ as a function of the way things are described to us (or the way we describe things to ourselves). Second, our feeling of "certainty" about an outcome is often, if not always, an illusion, or, to put it more precisely, another sort of artifact of the way things are described (as we noted in Chapter 16). For example, you may think of ($30) as a certain outcome: You get $30. Unless having money is your only goal in life, though, the $30 is really just a means to other ends. You might spend it on tickets to a football game, for example, and the game might be close, and so exciting that you tell your grandchildren about it — or it might be a terrible game, with the rain pouring down, and you, without an umbrella, having

---

[3]The different patterns of choices in the Allais paradox, depending on whether the situation is presented in a table or not, are another example of violation of the invariance principle.

[4]Quiggin (1982), Segal (1984), and Yaari (1985) have shown that the major results ascribed to the π function, including the certainty effect, can be accounted for by other transformations of p. These transformations avoid the following problem: According to prospect theory taken literally, a person might prefer ($5.01, .05; $5.02, .05) to ($5.03, .10), even though we might think of ($5.03, .10) as ($5.03, .05; $5.03, .05), which is clearly better than the first option. This preference is possible if $\pi(.05)$ is sufficiently large compared to $\pi(.10)/2$. It is called a violation of stochastic dominance. The way to avoid violations of stochastic dominance is to rank the outcomes in order of preference and calculate, for each outcome, the probability Q of doing at least as well as that outcome. These Q's can be transformed freely, as long as Q is 1 for the worse outcome. Reviews of other recent developments of this sort are found in Fishburn (1986), Sugden (1986), Machina (1987), and Weber and Camerer (1987).

to watch your team get slaughtered. You might use the money to buy a book that enlightens you more than a year of college — or a book that turns out to be a lot of trash. In short, most, if not all, "certain" outcomes can be analyzed further, and in doing so one finds, on close examination, that the outcomes are themselves gambles. The *description* of an outcome as certain is *not* certainty itself.

An important consequence of the certainty effect (McCord and de Neufville, 1985) is the conclusion that people do not conform to the assumptions underlying the method of gambles when this method is used to measure utility. When people say that they are "indifferent" between ($5) and ($20, .5), we cannot assume that their utility for $5 is literally halfway between that of $0 and that of $20. They underweigh the .5 probability of winning $20 relative to the 1.0 probability of winning $5. Most likely, the true halfway point is higher than $5.[5]

Overweighing and underweighing probabilities. Another property of the π function is the *over*weighing of very low probabilities. This may also contribute to the Allais paradox. The .01 probability of winning nothing looms larger in our minds than it ought to. The fact is that the .01, in Option 2, is the same as the *difference* between the probability of winning nothing in Option 3 and Option 4. In Option 2, the .01 seems quite significant, but in Options 3 and 4 it seems like a small difference. Normatively, of course, a difference of .01 is the same whether it is between 0 and .01 or between .89 and .90.

Likewise, part of the effect in the Allais paradox may be that we overweigh the .01 probability of winning nothing in Option 2. This effect may remain, even when the problem is presented to us in the form of a table.

Our tendency to overweigh very low probabilities may explain why some of us buy both insurance (such as life insurance for an airline flight) and lottery tickets, even though these are *opposites* in terms of assumption of risk. When we buy insurance, we are paying someone *else* to accept risk; when we buy a lottery ticket, we are paying someone to let *us* take the risk. Both choices are reasonable, if the low-probability event is overweighed. We probably focus too much on the very low chance of winning the lottery or of being killed in a plane crash.[6]

In the laboratory (and the real world), the overweighing of low probabilities is again shown in people's willingness to buy tickets in a "fair" lottery (one in which the seller of the tickets pays out in prizes an amount equal to the receipts from ticket sales). Many people are willing to spend a dollar for a .001 probability of winning $1,000. The same people, however, avoid fair gambles with larger probabilities of winning. People in general appear to be risk-averse, yet they take risks that offer very low probability of gain.

[5] There is no simple solution to this problem except to use other methods for measuring utility, such as difference measurement. The shape of the curve of the π function makes it very difficult to choose gambles that mean what they seem to mean in terms of utilities.

[6] Bernoulli, of course, can explain why people buy insurance. The disutility to the purchaser of very large losses (damage to property and so forth) is very great because of the shape of the utility curve for wealth. Bernoulli cannot, however, easily explain playing the lottery, except through a convex utility curve, which would predict that people would not buy insurance.

When probabilities of some outcome are sufficiently small, we tend to disregard that outcome completely in our decisions. We behave as though we had a *threshold* below which probabilities are essentially zero. Schwalm and Slovic (1982), for example, found that only 10% of their subjects said they would wear seat belts when they were told that the probability of being killed in an automobile accident was about .00000025 per trip, but 39% said they would wear seat belts when they were told that the probability of being killed was about .01 over a lifetime of driving. The second probability is derived from the first, using the average number of trips per lifetime. People treat a probability of .00000025 as essentially zero, so it does not matter to them how many trips they take when the probability is so low.

A similar "threshold effect" for money can provide another explanation of people's willingness to buy lottery tickets. People may perceive the $1 spent for the lottery ticket as trivial compared to the prize, and therefore essentially not worth considering at all. (Such people do not apparently think about the low probability of winning.) Of course, for those who play the lottery every week over a period of years, the dollars add up.

Utility: The Value function and framing effects

Let us now look at the part of prospect theory that concerns utility. According to prospect theory, individuals evaluate outcomes as *changes from a reference point*, which is usually their current state. Because we take different conditions as the reference point, depending on how a decision is described to us, we can make different, inconsistent decisions for the same situation, depending on how it is described.

The Value function. As noted in Chapter 10, Bernoulli viewed the utility of financial gains or losses to an individual as a function of the person's *total wealth after the gain or loss occurred*. Therefore, if one already has $10,000, the added utility of winning $30 would simply be $u(\$10,030) - u(\$10,000)$. Kahneman and Tversky, by contrast, suppose that we evaluate the utility of the $30 gain by itself, as $u(\$30)$, essentially without regard to our total wealth. They propose that we make decisions as if we had a *Value function* for gains and losses, with the curve depicted in Figure 11.2. The horizontal axis is not wealth, but rather monetary gain (to the right), or loss (to the left), compared with one's reference point (the middle). The vertical axis is essentially utility, but these authors use the letter $v(.)$, for Value, instead of $u(.)$ to indicate the difference between their theory and standard utility theory. They acknowledge that this Value function might change as a person's total wealth changes, but they suggest that such effects of total wealth are small. (Do not confuse this v with the v used to represent monetary value in ch. 10, even though the two v's look alike. Note also that Value is capitalized to distinguish it from "value" in "expected value." Value in prospect theory is a form of utility.)

The Value function shows that we treat losses as more serious than equivalent gains. We consider the loss in Value from losing $10 is greater than the gain in Value from gaining $10. That is why most of us will not accept a bet in which we have an even chance of winning and losing $10, even though the expected value of that bet

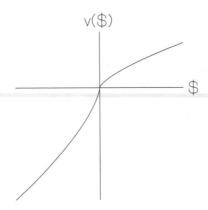

Figure 11.2: The Value, v, of a monetary gain or loss as a function of the amount of gain or loss, according to prospect theory.

is $0. This property is called *loss aversion*. It plays a large role in explaining several other phenomena in decision making.[7]

A glance at the graph shows that a second property of the Value function is that it is convex for losses (increasing slope as we move to the right, as shown in the lower left of Figure 11.2) and concave for gains (decreasing slope, as shown in the upper right). This means that, for simple gambles, subjects tend to avoid risks in the domain of gains and tend to seek risks in the domain of losses, when gains and losses are defined in terms of expected monetary change from their reference point. Because of the concavity in the domain of gains, people usually decline to pay $10 in return for a chance to win $20 with a probability of .5. They prefer the safer option here, because the Value of $10 is higher than the expected Value of $20 with a probability of .5, which is $.5\,v(\$20)$.[8] In other words, $v(\$10)$ is more than half of $v(\$20)$: A $10 bird in the hand is worth two $10 birds in the bush. In the domain of losses, however, the same people might prefer a loss of $20 with a probability of .5 to a loss of $10. They prefer the riskier option here, because the expected Value of a loss of $20 with a probability of .5 is higher (less negative) than twice the Value of $-\$10$.[9] Here, $v(-\$10)$ is "less negative" than half of $v(-\$20)$, and "less negative" would be preferred.

The differently curved Value functions for gains and losses result in what is called the *reflection effect*. As we have just seen, the choice reverses when the signs of the

---

[7] The principle of declining marginal utility also implies that losses from some point on a utility function will be weighed more heavily than gains from that point. Loss aversion, however, implies a kink at the reference point. Also, by manipulating the reference point, we can make a subjective gain into a subjective loss and vice versa.

[8] Let us put aside, for this example, the π function, which would make people behave as though the probability was lower than .5.

[9] We again ignore the π function.

outcomes are changed. If we choose the risky option for losses, we tend to choose the safe option for gains, and vice versa.[10]

Framing effects for Values. Using the Value function in decision making is not necessarily irrational. If people's goals are to avoid losses and to seek gains, well, that is reasonable enough. It is a little more difficult to understand how people can care proportionately more about small financial losses than about large ones, but there is no accounting for taste. The function *can* lead to irrationality, however, when we are able to lead people into adopting different reference points by describing the situation differently.

As Thaler points out, for example (1980), a "cash discount" on a purchase and a "credit card surcharge" are different ways of describing the fact that there are two prices, one for cash and one for credit. Purchasers, however, perceive a "cash discount" as a gain compared to the credit card price, and they perceive the "credit card surcharge" as a loss compared to the cash price. Because, in the Value function, the slope of the loss function is steeper than the slope of the gain function, consumers, if given the choice, are more willing to use their credit card when they perceive it as giving up a "cash discount" (forgoing a small gain in Value) than when they perceive it as accepting a "credit card surcharge" (accepting a larger loss). If merchants profit more from the higher of the two prices, they will do well to call the difference a "discount."

Tversky and Kahneman (1981, p. 251) gave the following problem to a group of subjects:

> Imagine that the U.S. is preparing for the outbreak of an unusual Asian disease, which is expected to kill 600 people. Two alternative programs to combat the disease have been proposed. Assume that the exact scientific estimate of the consequences of the programs are as follows:
>> Program A: (200 saved)
>> Program B: (600 saved, .33)

Most subjects chose Program A, presumably because they did not want to take the substantial risk (probability .67) that nobody would be saved at all. Other subjects, however, were presented with the same problem, except that the choices were as follows:

> Program A: (400 die)
> Program B: (600 die, .67)

When the problem was presented this way, most subjects chose Program B, presumably because 400 deaths seemed almost as bad as 600 and because it seemed worthwhile taking a chance that nobody would die at all.

Note that the two versions of the problem are identical. The situation is merely described differently, the first emphasizing the saving of life (a gain) and the second,

---

[10]These predictions are only approximately supported by subsequent research (Hershey and Schoemaker, 1980; Schneider and Lopes, 1986).

death (a loss). In the first version, the reference point is the expected future if nothing is done: 600 dead. Subjects see the outcomes as gains (people saved), compared to this "worst case." Subjects chose Program A because they are risk-averse in the domain of gains. Because the curve of the Value function is concave, $v(200$ lives$)$ is higher than the expected value $.33\,v(600$ lives$)$.

In the second version the reference point is shifted to the present state, in which nobody has died; the outcomes are described as losses (deaths). The curve is convex, and subjects are risk-seeking: $.67\,v(-600$ lives$) > v(-400$ lives$)$.[11]

We have here an excellent example of a framing effect, a violation of the invariance principle. Subjects give different judgments, depending on whether outcomes are *described* as gains or losses.

To summarize this description, prospect theory predicts two kinds of deviation from expected-utility theory. One type concerns distortion of stated probability. At the very least, subjects do not deal with stated probabilities as they ought to. The second type of distortion concerns the Value function. There is nothing necessarily wrong with the function itself, but once we start thinking of outcomes by comparing them to some imagined reference point, it becomes relatively easy for our perception of that point to be manipulated. We end up making different decisions depending on how the reference point is described to us or how we describe it to ourselves.[12] We could, as an antidote to this sort of error, try hard to use a constant imagined state for all decisions. As yet, no research has been done to determine whether such corrective heuristics work.

Prospect theory is a formal, mathematical theory of decision making under uncertainty. As noted, it began as an attempt to modify expected-utility theory so that it could serve as a descriptive model. (For other attempts along this line, see Weber and Camerer, 1987.) But prospect theory can also be seen as giving us hints about the heuristics that people use to make decisions under uncertainty: People tend to simplify their thinking about probability into categories of sure thing (certain), possible, or impossible. The distinction between certain and possible is salient even when "possible" corresponds to a very high probability. This distinction could cause the certainty effect. A similar distinction between impossible and possible could cause the overweighting of low probabilities, or the "possibility effect" (Fox and Tversky, 1998). Another possible heuristic is "Avoid risks, but take risks to avoid losses." We shall see other examples of heuristics in decision making. Prospect theory can be a valuable theory whether or not it can be explained in terms of heuristics.

---

[11]One may well wonder whether it makes sense to have anything other than a linear utility function for lives saved or lost. If the function is curved, the six-hundredth person to die is "worth less" than the first person. This seems highly unfair to the six-hundredth person. If we accept the view (advanced in Chapter 16) that everyone's utilities are equally important, we are inconsistent if we do not worry as much about each individual death, when many people die at once, as we worry about individual deaths, when people die one at a time.

[12]Unlike the part of prospect theory dealing with probabilities, to which several alternatives have been proposed (as we noted earlier), the part dealing with the role of the reference point has not been seriously challenged.

Exercises on prospect theory[13]

Assume that someone's Value function for receiving or losing an amount of dollars X is $X^{.5}$ if $X \geq 0$ and $-2(-X)^{.5}$ if $X < 0$. Assume that the π function is 0 if $p = 0$, 1 if $p = 1$, and $.75 \cdot +.05$ if $0 < p < 1$. (This isn't quite right, but it makes calculations simple.)

1. Make a graph of this Value function. (It need not be exact.) Make a graph of the π function.

2. Calculate the expected (prospect theory) Value of the four gambles ($30), ($45, .80), ($30, .25), and ($45, .20).

3. Calculate the expected utility of these gambles assuming that the utility of X is $X^{.5}$. Notice that the two models order the gambles differently.

4. Calculate the expected Value (according to prospect theory) of the four gambles in exercise 2, but assume that the outcomes are losses. Notice the difference between this and the answer to exercise 2.

5. What amount of money would be indifferent to a 50–50 gamble between $0 and $10, i.e., (X) versus ($0, .5; $10, .5), according to prospect theory and according to expected-utility theory with $u(X) = X^{.5}$? What implication do these results have for measuring utility or Value with standard gambles?

Extending prospect theory to events without stated probabilities

In all the experiments described so far, the subject sees numerical probabilities. They are about risk rather than uncertainty. Numerical probabilities are, however, rarely available in real life. Much more often, we must make decisions based on descriptions of the events themselves. When you decide whether to put in the effort to compete for a prize, or whether to bet on a sports event, you cannot ask anyone for your numerical probability of winning. Prospect theory can be extended to these cases (Fox and Tversky, 1998; Tversky and Fox, 1995). The idea is that people think about decisions by analyzing them into beliefs and values, just as the theory specifies. People make decisions as if they assigned probabilities to the beliefs. The probabilities are subadditive (as discussed in Chapter 6).

Subadditive probability means that, for two mutually exclusive events A and B, the probability assigned to the union of the events, "A or B," is lower than the sum of the probability assigned to A and the probability assigned to B. (It should be the same as this sum, since A and B are mutually exclusive.) Subadditivity leads to diminished sensitivity to changed in probability. For instance, consider an upcoming football game. Let event A be "the home team wins by more than seven points," and let event B be "the home team wins by 1–7 points," so that the union of these events, A or B, is "the home team wins." Adding A to the null event (neither) has more effect on judged probability than does adding A to B, since the judged probability $p(A \text{ or } B)$ is less than $p(A) + p(B)$, so $[p(A \text{ or } B)] - p(A)$ is less than $[p(A) + p(B)] - p(A)$

The subadditivity of implicit probability is seen when subjects indicate their certainty equivalents for bets on various propositions. For example, Fox and Tversky

---

[13] Answers to selected exercises appear at the end of the chapter.

(1998) asked basketball fans to make a series of choices between various amounts of money and various bets. Each bet paid $160 if the winner of the 1995 National Basketball Association Championship was a particular team or if the team came from a particular division or conference. From these choices, the researchers could infer the value that the subjects placed on the bets, their certainty equivalents. At the time of the study, eight teams could win, representing two conferences.

According to expected-utility theory with risk aversion, certainty equivalents for the two conferences should sum to less than the prize of $160. Certainty equivalents for the eight teams should add up to an even smaller amount. The principle of subadditivity, in contrast, allows for the opposite ordering between teams and conferences because subjects will overweigh the probabilities of individual teams winning. Indeed, Fox and Tversky observed median certainty equivalents that summed to $152 for the two conferences and $290 for the eight teams, far greater than the $160 prize.

For low probabilities, this subadditivity effect works in the same direction as the π function itself. As explained earlier, the π function leads to a "possibility effect," in which people are more sensitive to changes in probability near zero. As a result, the possibility effect is larger for uncertain events than for risk (stated probabilty), even if the stated probabilities for the risk correspond to those that subjects would assign to uncertain events, if they were asked.

Rank-dependent utility theories

If we view prospect theory as a way of expressing various heuristics mathematically, it fails to capture all the heuristics that people seem to use. This is particularly apparent when decisions involve many possible outcomes. Table 11.4 shows two lotteries. Each **I** represents a ticket. Lopes (1996) asked subjects to choose between these two (and other pairs) and to explain their reasons.

One subject chose Peaked because, "I like to be able to count on getting a moderate amount rather than choosing to get much higher or much lower." Another made the same choice because there were "too many chances of getting a lower prize" in Rectangular. Another because "it offers a majority of chances of at least an amount somewhere between $40 and $159. The odds of winning are best between these dollar amounts, and the odds indicate an excellent chance of winning an amount between $80 and $119." Lopes (1996) notes that subjects tend to think in terms of the chances of getting a large amount, or a very low amount, or "at least as much as" some amount. The latter statement refers to an aspiration level, and the idea of "at least as much" implies that the subject is thinking about the sum of all the probabilities of that amount or larger.

Lopes (1996) argues that a good approximation of risky decisions can be achieved by considering how people think about *security, opportunity,* and *aspiration*. Security is reflected in terms of the attention people pay to the worst outcome. Opportunity is reflected in attention to the best outcome, and aspiration is the attention they pay to whether a certain desired level is achieved. This is somewhat different

Table 11.4: Examples of lotteries used by Lopes (1996). Each **I** represents a ticket.

Peaked		Rectangular	
$200	**I**	$200	**IIII**
$186	**I**	$189	**IIII**
$172	**III**	$178	**IIII**
$159	**IIIII**	$168	**IIII**
$146	**IIIIIII**	$158	**IIII**
$132	**IIIIIIIII**	$147	**IIII**
$119	**IIIIIIIIII**	$136	**IIII**
$106	**IIIIIIIIIIII**	$126	**IIII**
$93	**IIIIIIIIIIIII**	$116	**IIII**
$80	**IIIIIIIIIII**	$105	**IIII**
$66	**IIIIIIIII**	$94	**IIII**
$53	**IIIIIII**	$84	**IIII**
$40	**IIIII**	$74	**IIII**
$26	**III**	$63	**IIII**
$13	**I**	$52	**IIII**
$0		$42	**IIII**
		$32	**IIII**
		$21	**IIII**
		$10	**IIII**
		$0	**IIII**

from prospect theory, which roughly divides outcomes into those above and below the status quo.

Lopes's theory is a member of a broader class of theories called "rank dependent."[14] The idea is that people evaluate prospects (possible outcomes of choosing an option) in terms of their rank, such as best, second best, third best, ... worst. Rank-dependence is usually combined with another idea, that people treat probabilities as *cumulative*. That is, when people evaluate prospects with several outcomes, they behave as if they thought of the probability of doing "at least as well as" some outcome (or, "no better than"). This contrasts with the view of prospect theory that people think of the probability of each individual outcome. People still apply a utility function to the outcomes one by one, as assumed by prospect theory.

The difference between cumulative and non-cumulative models has to do with the way in which probabilities are transformed. The π function applies to individual probabilities. In cumulative rank-dependent theories, some other function applies to the cumulative probability, the probability of doing at least as well as some outcome. An example of such a function is shown in Figure 11.3 (adapted from Birnbaum and

[14]The first published theory of this type seems to be that of Quiggin (1982).

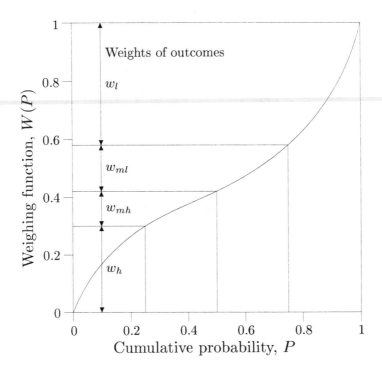

Figure 11.3: Example of a cumulative weighing function. P is the probability of doing as well or better than an outcome. The four outcomes are abbreviated h for high, mh for medium high, ml for medium low, and l for low.

Chavez, 1997). This figure applies to a gamble with four outcomes. P is the probability of doing at least as well as that outcome, and $w(P)$ is a weighing function that distorts P. $W(P)$ is like $\pi(P)$, but it applies to cumulative probability rather than to probability itself. The decision weight assigned to each outcome is the *difference* between $W(P)$ for that outcome and and $W(P)$ for the next higher outcome. (For the best outcome this difference is just $W(P_{best})$, since the probability of doing better is zero. In Figure 11.3, the difference is represented with w.) For the function shown in Figure 11.3, the decision weight is highest for the worst outcome and next highest for the best outcome. A person with this function would be somewhat risk averse but would not pay much attention to outcomes other than the worst and the best.

One property of this function is that the decision weights necessarily add to 1. This is not true of prospect theory in its original form. Strictly speaking, a person could regard a gamble consisting of a .5 chance of \$101 and a .5 chance of \$100 to be inferior to a 1.00 chance of \$100. Because the first two outcomes are not the same, they would be evaluated independently, and the π function would cause their weights to be considerably below .5. Of course, people would not think this way, but the need for additional assumptions about how people "edit" gambles struck some theorists as an unparsimonious feature of prospect theory. (These included Tversky and Kahneman, who developed a cumulative version of prospect theory itself, 1992).

If the weighing function W is linear, then cumulative theories are equivalent to expected-utility theory. This is almost true of prospect theory if the π function is linear, except that prospect theory (and cumulative prospect theory) treat gains and losses differently.

There are many versions of cumulative rank-dependent theories and many related experiments (Birnbaum and Chavez, 1997; Lopes, 1996; Tversky and Kahneman, 1992; Weber and Kirsner, 1997). The theory has inspired a great deal of interesting research. For those interested in learning about how people actually make decisions, the idea of rank-dependence is a real addition to the inferences we might make from the original version of prospect theory.

Emotional effects of outcomes

Prospect theory may not capture all of the interesting departures from the simplest form of expected-utility theory. The rest of this chapter will consider other effects on decision making. The first kind of effect concerns our reactions to outcomes. Expected-utility theory, in its simplest form, assumes that the utility of an outcome does not depend on what other outcomes *might* have occurred. In fact, though, we react emotionally to comparisons between what happens and what might have happened. (We shall see other examples of this in the next chapter.)

We may compare outcomes to what would have occurred in different states of the world, that is, to events in the same row but different columns of the utility table. We may also compare outcomes to what would have occurred if a different option had been chosen, that is, events in different rows but the same column. These comparisons lead to emotions of regret, rejoicing, disappointment, and elation. If these emotions are going to occur, we should anticipate them and count them as part of the utility of the outcomes that we experience, for we have goals concerning these emotions. Some emotions are desired, and others are undesired. Expected utility as a normative theory must include these emotional effects in order to maintain its connection with its purpose, maximizing goal achievement. Descriptively, too, people may anticipate these emotions and take them into account.

Regret and rejoicing

According to *regret theory*, we *regret* our decision if we learn that the outcome would have been better if we had chosen differently: for example, if we decide to carry an umbrella and find that it does not rain or if we decide not to carry an umbrella and find that it does rain. We *rejoice* in our decision if we learn that the outcome would have been worse if we had chosen differently: for example, if we carry an umbrella and it rains, or if we do not carry an umbrella and it does not rain. When

Table 11.5: Analysis of "inconsistent" choices according to regret theory

First pair	Probability		Second pair	Probability			
	.80	.20		.05	.20	.15	.60
Option 1	$30	$30	Option 3	$30	$30	$0	$0
Option 2	$45	$0	Option 4	$45	$0	$45	$0

we make a decision, we anticipate these feelings and take them into account (Bell, 1982; Loomes and Sugden, 1982).

This anticipation in itself does not necessarily lead to any departures from expected-utility theory. (We noted in connection with Table 10.1 that we can compare options column by column in the utility table.) According to regret theory, however, we overweigh these anticipated feelings of regret and rejoicing when the difference between outcomes is large. For the umbrella decision, the large differences between outcomes probably occur if it rains. In this "state of nature," we rejoice greatly if we have an umbrella but regret our decision if we do not. If it does not rain, the difference between outcomes is relatively small (carrying an umbrella needlessly or not), so here we do not take our feelings into account. In this case, our anticipation of regret and rejoicing would make us more inclined to take the umbrella than would an analysis of expected utility that ignored these feelings.

Both regret and rejoicing apply to our decision making itself. It is as though we pride ourselves on a well-made decision, if the outcome is good, and blame ourselves for a poorly made decision if the outcome is poor. Perhaps we anticipate our own confusion between the quality of our decision making and the quality of its outcome (Baron and Hershey, 1988).

Regret theory can explain in principle many of the phenomena that are explained by the π function in prospect theory. Consider the inconsistency observed by Kahneman and Tversky between the choice of $30 as opposed to $45 with a probability of .80 and the choice of $30 with a probability of .25 as opposed to $45 with a probability of .20. Many people choose the first option in the first pair but the second option in the second pair. According to regret theory, we can represent these two pairs as in Table 11.5. The table for the first pair of options (1 and 2) represents outcomes of these options in two states of the world (with probabilities .80 and .20, respectively). We think about this decision by comparing $v(\$45)$ to $v(\$30)$, in the first column, and by comparing $v(\$30)$ to $v(\$0)$ in the second column. The former difference is smaller, and we tend to neglect it. Specifically, we think about our regret if we chose option 2 and receive $0 (knowing that we would have received $30 if we had chosen option 1), or our rejoicing if we chose option 1 and received $30 (knowing that we would have received $0 from option 2). The difference between $v(\$45)$ and $v(\$30)$ is not great, so the feelings of regret and rejoicing in this state of nature play little role in our decision.

For the second pair of options (3 and 4), the situation is more complicated. We can think of each gamble as being played (or "resolved"), whether we choose it or not. We see that there are four possible states of the world, corresponding, respectively, to the four columns: win if either gamble is played; win with option 3 but lose with option 4; win with option 4 but lose with option 3; and lose with either. The table is constructed on the assumption that the two gambles are independent; therefore, the probability of winning with option 3 is the same, whether or not option 4 wins.

Here, we have two main sources of regret, corresponding to the second and third columns. If we take option 3 we might experience regret because we could lose that gamble but would have won if we had taken option 4. Exactly the opposite could happen if we take option 4. Further, the potential regret, in both cases, is about equally strong. (The smaller difference, between $30 and $0 in the second column, is a little more likely, so the two effects are about equal, if we take probability into account.) The small difference in the first column (between $30 and $45) does not induce much anticipated regret, because regret depends more heavily on large differences. In this pair of choices, anticipated regret does not lead strongly to either choice. Because of this, the potentially greater winning in the first column is likely to determine the choice made. Subjects will therefore be likely to choose option 1 in the first pair but option 4 in the second, the pattern we previously noted to be inconsistent (in the section on the π function of prospect theory).

Although regret theory can explain such effects in principle, and early evidence (for example, Loomes, 1987) suggested that this explanation was correct in some cases, more recent evidence (Starmer and Sugden, 1993) suggests that anticipated regret plays essentially no role in those phenomena ascribed to the π function of prospect theory. This does not mean that anticipated regret plays no role in decision making, however. The assumptions required to get regret theory to work in the example just described were quite elaborate. Some of these assumptions could be incorrect, for instance, the assumption that small differences in outcomes within a column are neglected.

Disappointment and elation

Most people are risk-averse. They avoid a 50–50 gamble, if given a choice of a certain (sure) outcome with equal *expected utility* (not just equal monetary value). For example, *if* your utility for money can be expressed as a linear function in the range from $0 to $10, you will prefer $5 for sure to a .5 chance to win $10. Regret theory cannot explain this effect: As shown in Table 11.6, regret theory would concern itself with the differences in the columns, and the utility difference between $10 and $5 is the same (we have assumed) as that between $5 and $0. Therefore, the potential regret would be the same with either option.

Another explanation of risk aversion is that we make comparisons within the rows as well as within the columns. If you take option 2 in Table 11.6, for example, you will experience *disappointment* if you win $0, comparing it with the $10 you

Table 11.6: Representation of a fair bet

	$p = .5$	$p = .5$
Option 1	$5	$5
Option 2	$10	$0

might have won, and you will experience *elation* if you win $10, compared with the $0 you might have won. In general, if the anticipated disappointment effect is larger for you than the anticipated elation effect, you will tend to avoid risks. Any risk involves the possibility of losing, and if you focus on how you will feel if you lose — more than on how you will feel if you win — you will avoid the risk.

The following example (based on Quinn and Bell, 1983) illustrates the disappointment phenomenon: Person A goes to the movies and turns out to be the theater's one-thousandth customer. She is given a check for $100. Person B goes to a different theater and turns out to be the one-millionth customer. He is given a chance to spin a spinner. He has an 80% chance of winning $50,000, and a 20% chance of winning $100. As luck would have it, he wins the $100. Which person do you think is happier with the $100? Most people say that A is happier; B is disappointed that he did not win the $50,000.

Disappointment and elation (Bell, 1985a) are the counterparts of rejoicing and regret. Disappointment and elation involve comparisons of different outcomes caused by different states within a single choice. Regret and rejoicing involve comparisons caused by different choices within a single state.

The role of regret in decisions

Although regret does not explain the results of prospect theory, it does play a major role in decisions. We can study the role of anticipated regret by looking at the effects of "resolution" of the uncertainty, whether the decision maker finds out what would have happened if another option were chosen. The original theory assumes that the decision maker always imagines the consequences of all options and compares them to each other in every possible state of the world. This could be true, but it turns out not to be true. It matters whether people think they will know (Josephs et al., 1992; Boles and Messick, 1995; Ritov and Baron, 1995; Zeelenberg et al., 1996).

For example, Zeelenberg and his colleagues (1996) gave subjects a choice between a "risky" gamble and a "safe" gamble. The gambles were chosen to be equally attractive (as determined in a matching task). An example of a risky gamble is a 35% chance to win 130 Dutch Guilders (versus nothing), and a safe gamble is a 65% chance to win 85 Guilders. When subjects expected to learn the outcome of the risky gamble, 61% of them chose that gamble. When they expected to learn the outcome of the safe gamble, only 23% chose the risky gamble. What subjects tended to avoid was losing the gamble they chose and learning that they would have won if they had chosen the other gamble. This result indicates not only that people pay attention to resolution but also that regret has a larger effect than rejoicing. Attention to rejoicing would lead to the opposite result. Subjects would think that they might win the gamble they had chosen and lose the other gamble.

When we make decisions, we often can compare the outcome to several different reference points. We can say "it could have been worse" or "it could have been better." The former response would lead to rejoicing, the latter, to regret. Research on the choice of reference points suggests that regret and rejoicing have two functions and that we have some control over them. Rejoicing improves our mood. Other things being equal, most of us tend toward the "could have been worse" way of thinking. Regret, however, teaches us a lesson. We use regret to learn from experience. We thus tend to allow ourselves to experience regret when we have a chance to learn, and when we can control the outcome through our choices, despite the short-term negative effects on mood. Our control is not perfect, of course, and some people experience pathological regret over events they cannot control.

Markman and his colleagues (1993) had subjects play a card game, like blackjack, on a computer. The computer was rigged so that every subject won $5 (by tieing the dealer). The subject could have won nothing (if the dealer won) or $20 (if the subject beat the dealer). After the outcome was revealed, subjects thought aloud. The question was whether subjects would think "if I had chosen differently I might have won" (upward counterfactuals) or that they might have lost (downward counterfactuals). Subjects either thought they would play the game again or not. When they thought they would play again, they imagined more upward counterfactuals (might have won) than when they thought they would not play again. And, when they thought they would play again, they expressed less satisfaction than when they thought they would not play again. The knowledge about whether they would play again or not thus affected their choice of counterfactuals and their emotional response. They paid the price of momentary dissatisfaction when they thought they could do better the next time.

Rationality of regret and disappointment in decision making

Is it rational to be sensitive to such factors as disappointment and regret, when making decisions? The question is not as easy to answer as it seems. We could argue, on the one hand, that by being sensitive to these feelings, we fail to maximize our expected utility, because we act in ways that are contrary to those specified by expected-utility theory. This is true, if we assume that feelings such as disappointment and regret have no utility for us. We could argue, however, that these feelings do have utility, because they reflect our personal goals, and that they should therefore be included as part of our analysis of any decision. If we consider them as consequences of the decision, then it is obviously rational to take them into account.

In my view, this last argument, though correct, is somewhat too simple an answer (Baron, 1985, Chapter 2). These feelings, although real, arise specifically from our attitudes (*beliefs and goals*) concerning decision making and risk themselves, or even from conscious decisions we make that affect our emotions. If we could control our emotions, we might be able to achieve our other goals more effectively, since we would not have to limit our choices by trying to avoid regret and disappointment, as if they were beyond our control. The results on upward and downward counterfactuals just described suggest that we do have some control over our emotional responses.

Suppose, for example, that you are considering purchasing a particular stock. On the basis of everything you know about this stock, a simple calculation of expected utility leads you to the conclusion that it is, overall, a better bet than some safer investment (such as a Treasury bond) might be. Still, you are held back by your fear that the price of the stock will go down and that you will blame yourself for a bad decision (feel regret) or will be disappointed that the price did not go up. If you are sure that you will experience these feelings *in addition* to the simple loss of utility from losing money (which you have already included in your calculations), you would be rational not to buy the stock. If you think you could put these feelings aside, however, you ought to go ahead and buy the stock. To put these feelings aside is to take a "philosophical" attitude toward the outcomes of decisions. You must be able to tell yourself, if you end up losing, that you knew that this could happen, and you made the best decision you could; you lost anyway, but there is nobody to blame, and it is no use crying over what might have been. Anyone who is used to taking risks (for example, a surgeon or a stock portfolio manager) probably is able to handle feelings of regret in this way. You learn to put your losses behind you and move on.

Of course, control of emotions is likely incomplete, and it has a cost in terms of effort. The upshot is that we need to expand the analysis of decisions that involve emotion. We need to include not just the options that we are given but also the combinations of these options with other options concerning efforts to control our emotions. These efforts may sometimes be worth their cost, and, at other times, they may not be worthwhile, and then we must accept our emotions as a fact of life. This is a highly general issue, of course. It concerns anger and fear as well as regret and rejoicing. Do we give in to our fear of flying and cancel the trip? Or try to control that fear? The right answer to such questions is bound to differ from person to person.

The ambiguity effect

Another phenomenon concerning decisions under uncertainty was discovered by Daniel Ellsberg (of "Pentagon Papers" fame) in 1961. Ellsberg found that subjects violate the axioms of expected-utility theory by seeking to avoid risks associated with situations in which the probability is (or appears to be) "unknown." Suppose there is an urn containing 90 balls. Thirty of them are red, and 60 of them are either black or yellow — we do not know which. A ball is to be drawn from the urn, and we can win some money, depending on which ball is drawn and which option we take.

Table 11.7: Demonstration of the effect of ambiguity. (The relative number of black and yellow balls is unknown.)

	30 balls	60 balls	
	red	black	yellow
Option X	$100	$0	$0
Option Y	$0	$100	$0
Option V	$100	$0	$100
Option W	$0	$100	$100

Ambiguity and "unknown probability"

Consider first a choice between options X and Y, whose payoffs are shown in the top half of Table 11.7. You get the choice once. It is not repeated. Most subjects lean toward option X. They "know" that they have a 1/3 chance of winning $100 in this case (30 out of 90 balls). They do not like option Y because they feel that they do not even know what the "real probability" of winning is. It appears to them that it could be as high as 2/3 or as low as 0. Note, however, that if the principle of insufficient reason (p. 100) is adopted, we can assume that the probability of winning is 1/3, given either option, and we conclude that we ought to be indifferent between the two options.

Now consider options V and W, whose outcomes are shown in the bottom half of Table 11.7. Here, most subjects prefer option W, because they "know" that their chance of winning is 2/3, whereas their chance of winning with option V could be as low as 1/3 or as high as 1. (Again, the principle of insufficient reason would dictate indifference.)

Together, this pattern of choices violates the sure-thing principle. Subjects reversed their choices merely because the "yellow" column was changed. By the sure-thing principle, this column should be ignored when choosing between X and Y, or when choosing between V and W, because it is identical for the two options in each pair.

Many of us, nonetheless, feel a strong temptation to make the choices as Ellsberg's subjects (mostly economists) did, choosing X, and Becker and Brownson (1964) have even found that subjects will pay money to avoid making choices in which the probabilities seem to be "unknown." Ellsberg used the term *ambiguity* for this kind of unknown risk. A situation in which the "probability is unknown" is called *ambiguous*.[15]

Effects of ambiguity can influence our responses to real risks in the world (Slovic, Lichtenstein, and Fischhoff, 1984). Some risks, such as those of nuclear power and

[15]Ellsberg cites a distinction that economists (such as Knight, 1921) made between "risk" and "uncertainty," the latter term covering what Ellsberg meant by "ambiguity."

DNA technology ("genetic engineering"), are perceived as ambiguous, and others, such as the risk of accidents in coal mining (which is very high), are perceived as known. If ambiguity affects our social choices, we will opt for the known risks over the unknown ones — perhaps wrongly.

Another real-life example concerns the risk calculations used to set the rates for insurance premiums. Insurance companies base these premiums on statistics — for example, for automobile insurance, statistics about the frequency and cost of car accidents among various groups of drivers. Insurance companies are always reluctant to cover unknown risks, such as the risk of military attack for the tanker ships that were bringing oil out of Iran during the early days of the Iran–Iraq war (without insurance, the tankers would not attempt the voyage). When policies to cover unusual risks like that are provided (often by the famous Lloyds of London consortium, which pools capital from several sources), subjective probability estimates are used instead of observed frequencies. These subjective estimates are felt to be ambiguous, and Lloyds charges higher premiums than they would if the same probabilities were based on frequency data. (This principle may also be involved in the high cost of medical malpractice insurance in the United States, reflecting the insurance industry's feeling that there is "ambiguity" about national trends in the size and fairness of damage awards.) Hogarth and Kunreuther (1984) have shown how such factors can lead to the total breakdown of markets for insurance.

Rationality of the ambiguity effect

As argued already, ambiguity effects violate the sure-thing principle. In Chapter 10, I argued that this principle is normative, since outcomes that do not depend on our choice and that do not occur (such as the outcome determined by "yellow," if the ball is not yellow) should not affect our utilities for outcomes that do occur (such as the outcomes determined by red or black balls).

The personal theory of probability (Chapter 5) implies that the idea of "unknown" probabilities makes little sense. Because probabilities are properties of the person, not the world, the only way in which a probability could be "unknown" is for a person not to have reflected enough about the situation. To say that a probability is "unknown" is to assume that probabilities can be known only if relative frequencies have been observed or if the possibilities can be analyzed logically into exchangeable alternatives.

Let us reexamine the ambiguity effect described in the Ellsberg experiment. Looking more carefully, we can see that any argument for Option X (or W) can be matched by a comparable argument for Option Y (or V). Yes, it *could* be the case (in deciding between Option X and Option Y) that the urn has 60 yellow balls, and this is an argument for Option X, but it could also turn out that the urn contains 60 black balls, and this is an equally strong argument for Option X. We conclude that there is no good reason to prefer Option X over Y. If we are not indifferent, we seem to be contradicting a very fundamental principle of decision making: When there are equally strong reasons in favor of two choices, then there is no overall reason to prefer one option or the other. (Likewise, if we must pay extra in order to make Option X, we would be irrational to choose Option X, because there is one reason to favor Option Y that is not matched by an equivalent reason for Option X — namely, the need to pay.)

Ultimately, I would argue, the ambiguity effect is another kind of framing effect, dependent on the way a problem is described. If we were given a great many choices like X and Y, but with *different urns*, we could assume that red and black would be drawn equally often over the whole sequence of choices. (If we do not assume this, then we must have some reason to think that one color is more likely than the other, and we would always bet on that color — choosing X and V, or Y and W, consistently and therefore not violating the sure-thing principle.) Therefore, a choice between X and Y is just a choice between one member of a sequence in which the red and black are equally likely. It would not do any injustice to describe the situation that way. If the situation were described this way, there would be no difference between the Ellsberg situation and one in which the probabilities were "known" (Raiffa, 1961).

On the other hand, consider an apparently unambiguous case, in which an urn has 50 red balls and 50 white ones. It would seem that the probability of a red ball is .5, but think about the top layer of balls, from which the ball will actually be drawn. We have no idea what the proportion of red balls is in that layer; it could be anywhere from 100% to 0%, just like the proportion of black to yellow balls in the original example. By thinking about the situation in this way, we have turned an unambiguous situation into an ambiguous one.

In sum, ambiguity may be a result of our perception that important information is missing from the description of the decision. In the balls-and-urn example, we brought out the missing information by focusing attention on the top layer of balls. Information is always missing in any situation of uncertainty, though, and so we can make any situation ambiguous by attending to the missing information. Conversely, we can make any ambiguous situation into an unambiguous one by imagining it as one of a sequence of repeated trials.

Aversion to missing information

Ritov and Baron (1990) found direct evidence for the view that the appearance of missing information makes people reluctant to chose an option with uncertain outcomes. Subjects were told about a hypothetical strain of "flu" that would kill 10 out of every 10,000 children. Vaccination against the flu would remove this risk, but the vaccine itself could kill children. Subjects were asked how much risk from the vaccine they would tolerate before they would refuse to give it to their child (or to all children, if they were policy makers). In the missing-information condition, subjects were told that children would not die from the vaccine unless they were with a "risk group," but the test to determine who was in the risk group was not available. Subjects were more reluctant to tolerate risk from the vaccine when they were told about the risk group. Notice that this could be seen as a kind of framing effect, if we imagine that any effect of this sort involves unknown risk factors.

When people feel knowledgeable about a subject, they may feel that they have very little missing information, so they may be strongly inclined to bet on their own probability estimates. Heath and Tversky (1991) asked subjects for their confidence in their own answers to questions about history, sports, geography, and other topics, as was done in the studies of confidence described in Chapter 6. Subjects were carefully instructed in the meaning of confidence. Then the subjects were given a choice between betting on their answers or on a lottery with a probability equal to their confidence. When subjects expressed little confidence, they preferred betting on the lottery. When subjects expressed high confidence (but less than 100%, where the lottery was a sure thing), they preferred to bet on their own judgment, especially when they considered themselves to be knowledgeable about the topic. These results may be explained in terms of the feeling of missing information. When confidence was low, subjects tended to feel that information was missing about their judgment. When confidence was high, subjects may have felt that more information was missing about the lottery!

Why, if the ambiguity effect conflicts with normative models, is it so compelling to some people? Slovic and Tversky (1974) found that many subjects stuck to their (nonnormative) choices of X and W even after they read an explanation of the sure-thing principle. One explanation hinges on our feeling that there is something we would very much like to know before we make the decision.[16] Of course, in any risky decision, we would like to know what the outcome will be, but in the "ambiguous" cases, there are more specific things we would like to know, such as the proportion of black balls in the urn, the intentions of the Iraqis, or the intentions of legislators concerning tort reform.

Perhaps, then, we avoid ambiguous options because we really want to exercise another option: that of obtaining more information. When this other option *is* available — as it often is — it is perfectly rational to choose it, providing that the information is worth obtaining (see the discussion of the value of information in Chapter 13). When the information is not available, however, or not worth the cost, we would do better to put aside our desire to obtain it and go ahead on the best evidence we have, even if it is "ambiguous" and even if we must use the principle of insufficient reason. More generally, we can think of our tendency to avoid ambiguous decisions as a useful heuristic that points us toward the option of obtaining more information. From a *prescriptive* point of view, we probably do well to follow a rule of thumb that tells us to avoid irreversible commitments when information is missing. If we can learn to put this rule aside when the missing information is truly unavailable, however, we shall achieve our goals more fully in the long run.

The feeling of missing information may be limited to cases in which the existence of that information is salient. Ambiguity effects appear to be limited to situations in which the ambiguous and nonambiguous conditions are both presented together to the same subjects. This is the usual way of doing experiments on ambiguity. Fox and Tversky (1995) looked for ambiguity effects when subjects got either an ambiguous

---

[16]See Frisch and Baron (1988) for other explanations of ambiguity effects.

bet or a non-ambiguous bet, but not both. For example, subjects said how much they would pay to bet on a color of their choice with an urn containing 50 black chips and 50 red ones, or on an urn containing an unknown number of black chips and the rest red ones. When the amount to be won was $100, subjects averaged $24.34 and $14.85, respectively, when the urns were both presented, thus showing the usual effect. When each subject saw only one urn, the responses were indistinguishable: $17.94 versus 18.42, respectively.

Ambiguity and adjustment of probability

The ambiguity effect described so far can be seen as a direct effect of ambiguity on decisions. Ambiguity has a second effect that is more easily understood as an effect on personal probability, which, in turn, affects decisions. Consider two urns with 1,000 balls each. In Urn 1, the balls are numbered from 1 to 1000. In Urn 2, each ball has a number, chosen at random from the numbers 1–1000. If you get a prize for drawing the number 687, which urn would you choose? (The example, attributed to Daniel Ellsberg, is from Becker and Brownson, 1964, fn. 4.) Many people choose Urn 2, which seems ambiguous, despite the fact that the the probability of the number 687 being on the ball you draw is .001 in either case. The probability seems higher in Urn 2, though, because you can easily imagine that Urn 2 could contain 2, 3, or more balls with the number 687, and these possibilities seem to outweigh the possibility that it has no such balls. Einhorn and Hogarth (1985) argued that people adjust subjective probabilities on the basis of such imagined possibilities. In general, extreme probabilities will be adjusted so that they are less extreme, because it is easier to imagine less extreme possibilities (e.g., 2 or 3 balls with 687) than more extreme ones (only 0 balls with 687). As a result, people prefer ambiguous options when probabilities of winning are low.

In an Ellsberg-type urn problem with one urn containing 50% winning balls and the other anywhere from 0% to 100%, people prefer the non-ambiguous option even when the outcomes are losses rather than gains (Einhorn and Hogarth, 1986). Interestingly, this effect becomes even stronger when the probability of a loss is .001 (rather than .5) as in the two urns just described. Presumably, people can imagine how the probabilities could be higher, so they fear that the loss in the ambiguous, low-probability, urn is even higher. Thus, for losses, pure ambiguity aversion — the direct effect on decisions — and the effect of ambiguity on subjective probability work in the same direction.

Uncertainty and reasons for choice

Uncertainty can affect our reasons for acting. We may be reluctant to act without some clear reasons, and reasons may be unclear if we do not know the outcome. If we are uncertain about the reasons, we may prefer to defer the decision. Consider the following scenario (Tversky and Shafir, 1992a): "Imagine that you have just taken a tough qualifying examination. It is the end of the fall quarter, you feel tired and run-down, and you are not sure that you passed the exam. In case you failed you have to take the exam again in a couple of months — after the Christmas holidays. You now have an opportunity to buy a very attractive five-day Christmas vacation package to Hawaii at an exceptionally low price. The special offer expires tomorrow, while the exam grade will not be available until the following day." Subjects were asked whether they would buy the package, not buy it, or "pay a $5 nonrefundable fee in order to retain the rights to buy the vacation package at the same exceptional price the day after tomorrow — after you find out whether or not you passed the exam." Sixty-one percent chose to pay the $5. Only 32% would buy the package. When asked what they would do if they knew that they had passed or knew that they had failed, however, most subjects would buy the package in each condition, and only 31% would pay $5 to delay the decision for two days. It seems that people would take the vacation to celebrate, if they passed, and to gather their strength if they failed, but, if they did not know their reasons, they preferred not to decide until they did.

A similar tendency to defer decisions or to "do nothing" results from conflict, that is, from having reasons to choose or reject more than one option (Tversky and Shafir, 1992b). For example, in one experiment, subjects had filled out a questionnaire and expected to be paid $1.50. Half of the subjects were offered a metal pen worth about $2 instead of their payment, and only 25% of these subjects took the $1.50, the rest taking the pen. The other half of the subjects were offered a choice of the same pen or two plastic pens. Now 53% of these subjects took the money instead of either of the other options. As in the vacation study just described, people need clear reasons to abandon the default option: delaying the vacation decision or taking the money. The heuristic of not acting without reasons is, of course, generally a good one. But if you would take the same action in all possible states of the world — despite the reasons being different in different states — then you might as well decide to take it. You *do* have reasons, although your reasons may not be known yet.

Conclusion

We have seen in this chapter that several factors — not all fully understood — lead us to violate expected-utility theory in its simple form. Some apparent violations, such as those caused by regret or disappointment, are not necessarily violations at all. In these cases, an overly simple analysis could have neglected real emotional consequences of decisions. (It is also possible, however, that we sometimes fail to consider the option of trying to control our emotional responses in order to achieve our remaining goals.)

Other violations of the theory, such as ambiguity effects, might result from our using generally useful heuristics in situations in which they are harmful rather than helpful in achieving our goals. Prescriptively, we would do well to learn to distinguish the different kinds of cases. (In the case of ambiguity, I argued that what matters is whether it is worthwhile to wait until we can obtain the information we see as missing.) If we thought more about the heuristics that govern our decisions, we might be able to learn when these heuristics are helpful shortcuts and when they are self-made blinders that prevent us from achieving our goals.

Certain violations concern neglect of goals when several attributes are relevant to a choice. These illustrate a kind of single-mindedness that can result from insufficient search for goals. In other violations, we seem to attend largely to the most important difference, as in regret effects. A failure to search for evidence may be involved here.

These last violations of the theory, as well as the framing effects and probability distortions we discussed, provide additional arguments for the use of decision analysis as a tool for making important decisions. All of the violations in question occur in holistic judgments, but they can be avoided if utility theory is used to provide a "second opinion" for holistic decision making. The same violations, however, make it more difficult to use decision analysis: The method of gambles, in particular, can yield invalid measurements of utility, because it is distorted by the certainty effect.

The violations of utility theory discussed in this chapter indicate clearly that the options we choose are often not the ones that best achieve our goals in the long run. In view of these findings, we can no longer assume — as many economists do – that we always know what is best for us and express this knowledge in our choices. The question of how we should deal with these violations is not fully solved. I have suggested that actively open-minded thinking and the judicious use of decision analysis are parts of the answer to this question, but we may also need to learn new heuristics specifically for making decisions.

Answers to selected exercises:

2. $V(30) = 30^{.5} = 5.48$
$v(45, .8) = \pi(.8) \cdot v(45) = .65 \cdot 45^{.5} = 4.36$
$v(30, .25) = \pi(.25) \cdot v(30) = .2375 \cdot 30^{.5} = 1.30$
$v(45, .2) = \pi(.2) \cdot v(45) = .20 \cdot 45^{.5} = 1.34$

3. $u(30) = 30^{.5} = 5.48$
$u(45, .8) = .8 \cdot u(45) = .8 \cdot 45^{.5} = 5.37$
$u(30, .25) = .25 \cdot u(30) = .25 \cdot 30^{.5} = 1.37$
$u(45, .2) = .20 \cdot u(45) = .20 \cdot 45^{.5} = 1.34$

Prospect theory overweighs $p = 1$ but otherwise underweighs differences in probabilities, such as the difference between .25 and .20. Hence the reversal of the ordering of the third and fourth gambles, according to the two theories. Utility theory must order the second pair of gambles by analogy with the first pair.

4. All values are negative and twice those in question 2. The ordering of the gambles is reversed, because the preferred gamble is the one that is *less* negative. This is the "reflection effect."

5. $v(X) = \pi(.5) \cdot v(\$10)$
$X^{.5} = .425 \cdot \$10^{.5}$
$X = .425^2 \cdot \$10 = \$1.81$

$u(X) = .5 \cdot u(\$10)$
$X^{.5} = .5 \cdot \$10^{.5}$
$X = .5^2 \cdot \$10 = \$2.50$

Prospect theory makes people seem more risk averse here because of the π function, which changes the .5 into .425. If gambles were used to measure the utility of money, the obtained function would be too concave.

Chapter 12

Choice under certainty

This chapter and the next are concerned with decisions made under certainty, that is, decision in which we analyze as if we knew what the outcomes would be. Many of these decisions can be analyzed normatively by MAUT (p. 335. We shall find heuristics and biases in these decisions, too. The present chapter concerns decision making proper. The next chapter concerns judgments made of one "option" at a time, a task that has been studied extensively.

Biases in decisions under certainty can usually be understood in terms of heuristics that are useful much of the time but are applied mechanically even when it is easy to see why they fail to produce the best outcome. One such heuristic is making decisions in terms of the most important goal (ignoring other goals). A second set of heuristics are those concerning the keeping of "mental accounts" of gains and losses. Finally, other heuristics concern the resolution of explicit conflict or tradeoffs between goals.

Single-mindedness, prominence, and noncompensatory strategies

Many biases found in decisions made under certainty can be described as involving incomplete search for goals. In the extreme form of this bias, the decision maker makes a decision by considering the extent to which the options achieve a single goal: the "bottom line," the defeat of communism, the downfall of capitalism, the protection of abstract "rights," and so on, disregarding all other goals. Such single-mindedness — in its extreme and less extreme forms — is often brought about by situational factors that encourage attention to a certain goal, but, regardless of its cause, it can be cured by actively open-minded thinking.

When we consider more than one goal, we often find that different options are better when evaluated according to different goals. Montgomery (1984) suggested that we generally try to avoid making such tradeoffs between goals. When faced with a clear conflict between goals, he asserts, we try to think of reasons why one goal can be completely ignored in decision making. Often, these single-minded arguments involve social roles. A good soldier must obey his commander (even if his commander tells him to kill innocent people); a good scholar must seek and publish the truth (even if someone will use it to promote racist doctrine); a good politician must defend the interests of her constituents (even if she must trample on the interests of others); a lawyer's duty is to his client (even if he must help his client commit perjury). This is not to say that a good soldier should *not* obey his commander, and so forth: It is just to say that in doing so he ought to be aware of what goals he may be sacrificing. Soldiers, scholars, politicians, and lawyers are people, and they have goals other than those associated with their roles. On some occasions, these other goals may outweigh the main one stemming from the work role. Such single-minded arguments reflect insufficient search for goals, or neglect of goals even after they are found.

An interesting practical example of the effect of single-mindedness comes from a study by Gardiner and Edwards (1975). In California, proposals for "developing" the Pacific coastline (housing developments, for example) are controversial. Some Californians favor them, focusing on the economic advantages of increased employment and the like. Others oppose them, focusing on the environmental disadvantages of increased demands on resources and physical unattractiveness. The California Coastal Commission, which had the task of approving or disapproving such proposals, was often completely polarized, with members who held these opposite views constantly at each other's throats. Gardiner and Edwards were aware that each proposal could be ranked as better or worse on the two dimensions. Some proposals had relatively great economic advantages combined with relatively little environmental disadvantages, and these proposals, they felt, clearly ought to be given priority.

Gardiner and Edwards asked twelve knowledgeable subjects, including two members of the Coastal Commission, to rank order several proposals like the ones the commission normally considered. The subjects, like the commission, fell into two groups — prodevelopment and proenvironment. These holistic ratings showed very little agreement between the two groups of subjects. Members of each group were paying attention only to the dimension that was most important to them. Then the researchers asked subjects to carry out a MAUT (multiattribute) analysis (p. 335, in which subjects individually rated each proposal on each of the major dimensions and then assigned a weight to each dimension. Of course, the prodevelopment subjects gave greater importance to the economic dimensions, and the proenvironment subjects gave greater importance to the environmental dimensions. Nonetheless, each group now gave *some* weight to the *other* group's favored dimension. When new rankings were calculated from these analyses, there was now very good agreement between the two groups. Some proposals apparently were fairly satisfying to both groups. This became readily apparent only when the decision procedure forced attention to dimensions that each group had considered unimportant, as well as those that it initially considered important.

We conclude that attention to a single, dominant dimension can lead both to unnecessary disagreement between groups and to violation of each individual's true preferences. Making tradeoffs helps — when we have the time to do it.

The tendency to neglect goals that seem less important may be at work in the *prominence effect*. Tversky, Sattath, and Slovic (1988) compared subjects' choices in the following problem to other subjects' responses in a numerical matching task based on the same problem (p. 373):

> About 600 people are killed each year in Israel in traffic accidents. The ministry of transportation investigates various programs to reduce the number of casualties. Consider the following two programs, described in terms of yearly costs (in millions of dollars) and the number of ca-sualties per year that is expected following the implementation of each program:

	Expected number of casualties	Cost (millions)
Program X	500	$55
Program Y	570	$12

When subjects were asked to *choose* which program they favored, 67% favored Pro-gram X, which saves more lives but at a higher cost per life saved than Program Y. Subjects in the matching task were given the same situation but with one of the num-bers missing. They were asked to fill in the missing number so that the two programs would be equally desirable, that is, to *match* the two programs. From the response to this question, we can infer what they would have chosen in the choice task (assuming they would have been consistent). For example, suppose that the cost of Program X was missing, and a subject wrote down $40 million. We can infer that this subject would have preferred Program Y: If X and Y are equal when the cost of X is $40 million, then X must be worse than Y when the cost of X is raised. When the rela-tive desirability of the two programs was inferred in this way from responses on the matching task, only 4% of the subjects favored Program X; 96% favored Program Y, the more economical program that saved fewer lives.

Clearly, subjects regard casualties as more important, or more *prominent*, than cost. When they choose between the two programs, many subjects base their choice largely (or entirely) on the single most important attribute: number of casualties. In the matching task, they are forced to attend to both attributes and to make an explicit tradeoff between them. The conflict between the two tasks is the prominence effect. The most plausible explanation of this effect is that in making a choice subjects often attend only to the most important goal, but in matching they express something closer to their true tradeoff between the two goals.[1] If this interpretation is correct, it argues for the use of something like matching, rather than choice, in the measurement of values. It also suggests that many choices in the real world are inconsistent with people's underlying goals.

[1] An alternative interpretation is that choice is closer to the true tradeoff and matching leads to excessive attention to less important goals. We have no reason to think that this is true. We have other evidence, however, for neglect of less important attributes in choice.

Compensatory decision strategies are those in which one dimension can compensate for another. Use of a single dominant dimension is thus a *noncompensatory* strategy. Individuals seem to differ in the tendency to use these strategies and in their beliefs about the nature of good decision making. Zakay (1990) developed a questionnaire to measure these beliefs. Sample items were: "It is essential to compare rival alternatives across all their attributes" (compensatory); "A good decision maker is able to reach a decision on the basis of one or two important attributes only" (noncompensatory). Nurses completed this questionnaire. They were then asked to make hypothetical nursing decisions where outcomes possessed several attributes. For example, in a decision about which patient to help first when two patients call for help in the middle of the night, the attributes were age, type of call (e.g., ringing bell, shouting), physical condition, and mental condition. Items were designed so that compensatory strategies would lead to one choice and noncompensatory strategies would lead to another. The most important dimension (age, in this example, as judged by expert nurses) conflicted with all the others. Nurses who attended only to this dimension would help the older patient first, but the other dimensions (and all the dimensions together) favored the younger patient. Responses to these hypothetical cases correlated strongly with the subjects' attitudes as measured by the questionnaire. Nurses who thought that noncompensatory strategies were better tended to use them in the cases.

Other preference reversals:
Compatibility and evaluability

A preference reversal is a kind of experiment, in which the implied ordering of two options changes as a function of some experimental manipulation. The last section described a preference reversal that depended on choice versus matching. People choose on the basis of the more prominent attribute, but their matching responses imply the opposite choice. Chapter 11 described another preference reversal for gambles, between choice and willingness to pay. People prefer the gamble with the higher probability of winning, but they are willing to pay more for the gamble with the greater maximum win. In principle, we could try to devise experiments of this sort whenever some factor distorts preference as assessed by one method but not by another method. We use the second method as a control for the first. (We can show that the methods yield inconsistent results, which implies some bias, but we cannot infer from the result alone which method is biased.)

In the recent history of our field, though, preference reversals have been used largely to illustrate three kinds of effects: prominence, compatibility, and evaluability. We have just discussed the prominence effect. Let us turn now to the other two.

Response mode compatibility

The method of indicating preference seems to call attention to dimensions that are "compatible" with that dimension. This is the usual explanation of the pricing versus choice result for gambles described in Chapter 10. When subjects indicate how much they are willing to pay for a gamble, they respond with a monetary amount. This monetary mode of responding calls attention to the monetary dimension of the gambles, as opposed to the probability-of-winning dimension. The general term "contingent weighting" describes this result. That is, the relative weights of dimensions are contingent on something, not fixed. One possible cause of contingent weighting is response-mode compatibility. People weigh more heavily those dimensions that seem similar to the mode of responding.

In one study 41% of the responses involved reversals between choice and pricing in gambles of this sort (Slovic et al., 1990). When goods were used instead of monetary amounts, the proportion of reversals dropped to 24%. The goods were things like a one-week pass for all movie theaters in town , or a dinner for two at a good restaurant. For goods such as these, pricing resposes (maximum willingness to pay) were more often consistent with choice. That is, subjects were willing to pay more for the one they preferred.

In another study that did not involve probabilities at all, most subjects preferred "$1,600, 1.5 years from now" to "$2,500, 5 years from now," but they expressed greater willingness to pay for the latter (Tversky et al., 1990).

Direct evidence for compatibility effects comes from a study of Schkade and Johnson (1989), who used a computerized process-tracing method (see Chapter 2), in which the subject used a mouse to open windows on a screen. When subjects made pricing responses, they spent more time looking at the monetary amounts. They kept those windows open longer. This result implies that compatibility effects are, at least in part, related to subjects paying more attention to the more compatible attribute. We can think of these effects as biases if we assume that subjects should pay equal attention to both attributes, although it is not always clear what "equal attention" means. These results suggest that more neutral response modes, such as choice or ratings of attractiveness, should be less biased. We cannot test this hypothesis easily, though, because we have no clear criterion of equal attention.

Evaluability and joint versus separate evaluation

One of the big lessons of utility theory is that everything is relative. When we evaluate an option with two or more dimensions, we must establish some value for each dimension. Suppose you are considering the purchase of a secondhand music dictionary with a torn cover and 20,000 entries (Hsee, 1996). It is easy for you to evaluate the torn cover, but not the 20,000 entries. You would probably think badly of this option. If, later, you are presented with another option without a torn cover but with only 10,000 entries (and you have forgotten the 20,000), you might take it. But if you evaluated the two options side by side, you would probably take the one with the torn cover. It would then be easier for you to evaluate the number of entries, because you would have a comparison point.

Another experiment illustrates how evaluation can be made easy or difficult (Hsee et al., 1999). Subjects gave their maximum willingness to pay for two compact-disk changers:

	CD capacity	THD
CD changer J	holds 5 CDs	.003%
CD changer S	holds 20 CDs	.01%

Subjects were told that THD stood for "total harmonic distortion" and meant better sound quality when the number was lower. When subjects priced the two changers separately, they priced S higher than J, but they priced J higher than S when they priced them jointly, that is, side by side. In the joint condition, subjects had some idea how to evaluate THD. When subjects were told the overall range of THD (.002% to .012%), however, they could evaluate THD more easily even with separate presentation, so they gave a higher price for J. In sum, either telling subjects the range or presenting the two changers side by side made THD easier to evaluate.

In general, it is better to be able to evaluate relevant attributes. Decisions will achieve goals better when they are made with explicit comparisons available or with information about the ranges and effects of relevant attributes. One possible exception to this principle is a selection of a single good that is valued mainly for the experience it provides. You might notice a difference in THD when you listen to two CD changers one after the other, but when you take one home, THD may not affect the quality of your experience very much, if at all. You might do better to evaluate the changers in the mode like that in which you experience them (Hsee et al., 1999). More usually, this does not happen. When you buy a car, for example, you care about such features as braking speed because this is a means to another end, prevention of crashes. The ultimate experience involved here is one you hope you never have, a crash. The braking speed is not evaluable in ordinary driving, but it is still very important.

Effects of the options available on choice

The last section described the discrepancy between choice and matching. Other non-normative effects are found in choices alone. Choices typically involve tradeoffs of two or more attributes. In a tradeoff, one option is better on one attribute and another is better on another attribute. If this kind of tradeoff were not involved, the choice would be easy, a "no brainer." Because tradeoffs are difficult, people often use simplifying heuristics. Sometimes these heuristics shown themselves in the form of inconsistencies that depend on which alternatives are available.

Table 12.1: Ratings of five applicants on three dimensions.

Applicant	Dimension I	Dimension E	Dimension S
a	69	84	75
b	72	78	65
c	75	72	55
d	78	66	45
e	81	60	35

Intransitivity of preferences

Tversky (1969) decided to test the idea that the axiom of transitivity is violated because of overweighing and underweighing of differences in utility. In one experiment, he asked subjects to choose which of two applicants for college to accept. The applicants were described in terms of three numerical ratings, one for intelligence (I), one for emotional stability (E), and one for social facility (S). The numbers were carefully chosen to reflect the subjective weights that individual subjects placed on each of these attributes. One subject was given the set of profiles shown in Table 12.1, which presented ratings for five applicants, a through e. The applicants were presented to the subject in all possible pairs (along with other pairs), and the subject was asked to judge, on the basis of the ratings, which applicant was better qualified. For the pairs a-b, b-c, c-d, and d-e, the typical subject favored applicants higher in the list: a over b, b over c, and so forth. The difference within each pair in I, for intelligence, seemed too small to matter. For the a-e comparison, however, subjects typically favored e over a. For these extreme pairs, the difference in the ratings for intelligence was great enough to outweigh the differences in the other two dimensions. (Subjects were instructed to consider intelligence as the most important attribute.)

The result was a violation of transitivity. Applicant a was preferred to b, b to c, c to d, d to e, but then e was preferred to a. It was impossible to assign numbers to the five applicants so that the applicant with a higher number would be consistently chosen over an applicant with a lower number. Tversky (1969, p. 45) suggests that similar violations occur outside the laboratory:

> Consider . . . a person who is about to purchase a compact car of a given make. His initial tendency is to buy the simplest model for $2,089.[2] Nevertheless, when the salesman presents the optional accessories, [the purchaser] first decides to add power steering, which brings the price to $2,167, feeling that the price difference is relatively negligible. Then, following the same reasoning, he is willing to add $47 for a good car radio, and then an additional $64 for power brakes. By repeating this process several times, our consumer ends up with a $2,593 car, equipped

[2]The $2,089 is not a misprint; Tversky was writing in 1969.

with all the available accessories. At this point, however, he may prefer the simplest car over the fancy one, realizing that he is not willing to spend $504 for all the added features, although each one of them alone seemed worth purchasing.

A general principle of decision making seems to be at work in this example. People tend to underweigh or ignore small differences, such as those between applicants a and b in intelligence, as opposed to large differences. Of course people *should* weigh small differences less than large ones, but they overdo it. Therefore, relatively large differences, such as those between applicants a and b in emotional stability and social facility, or between applicants a and e in intelligence, play a larger role than they ought to. It is as though we simplified our decisions by ignoring small differences altogether.

Elimination by aspects

Tversky (1972) developed a descriptive theory to explain why some decisions are apparently more difficult to make than others. When decisions are difficult, Tversky says, we shift back and forth, favoring now one option and now another, as we think about the decision, until we make our choice. If we are asked what we favor at a given time, then, it is fairly probable that at various times we will mention each of the options as our preference. This process could produce violations of utility theory, under certain conditions.

Suppose you are indifferent between a trip to Paris and a trip to Rome. Since you are attracted to both cities, this is a difficult choice. Now you discover that the airline that would fly you to Rome offers a free bottle of wine on the flight. Would this tip the balance? Surely not, for most people. You would still find it difficult to choose. If you were asked, on various occasions, where you planned to go, you would probably say "Paris" half the time and "Rome" half the time, and the bottle of wine would not matter.

The bottle of wine probably *would* matter, though, if there were two airlines with flights to Rome that were *identical*, except that one offered the wine and the other did not. This would induce a consistent preference for the flight with the wine; you would (assuming that you have any interest in wine at all) then be likely to prefer this airline 100% of the time.

As Tversky puts it (p. 284), "Choice probabilities ... reflect not only the utilities of the alternatives in question, but also the difficulty of comparing them." Rome and Paris differ in a great many attributes or "aspects." A single bottle of wine is one attribute in favor of Rome, but so many others must be weighed that this one gets lost. The bottle of wine makes a big difference, however, when everything else is the same.

In another example, suppose that you are indifferent between receiving a record of a Beethoven symphony and a record of some piano pieces by Debussy. You might even slightly prefer the Beethoven. Your probability of favoring the Debussy at any given time would then be about .50, or a little less. Now suppose you are given a choice among three records: the Debussy, the Beethoven symphony, and a different, but equally attractive, recording of the same Beethoven symphony. What would be your probability of choosing the Debussy now? Most people think it would still be about .50, or maybe a little less — but still a lot more than .33, which is what your choice probability would be if you were considering three equally attractive but very different choices. Tversky suggested, however, that the probability of choosing each Beethoven would be much lower, about .25. It is as though we had first made a decision between Beethoven and Debussy, and then, if we had decided on Beethoven, we decide which Beethoven we prefer.

Tversky provides a general descriptive model that accounts for these examples, as well as the data from several experiments. He suggests that we make complex decisions by looking for favorable aspects (attributes), one aspect at a time, across all of the choice alternatives. For example, in comparing Paris with Rome, you would search your memory for attractive aspects of each city: You might think about the Louvre in Paris, or St. Peter's in Rome, or the fact that you do not speak Italian.[3] Whatever attribute you find, you *eliminate* all of the options in the choice set that lack this single attribute. If you think of the Louvre first, you eliminate Rome, and the decision is made. You might, of course, think of some aspect of these cities that does not distinguish them for you, such as "good food." In this case, you simply continue the search for aspects. When there are more than two options, you may find an aspect that allows you to eliminate one of them but leaves others for you to consider. Tversky also assumes that you tend to think of the more important aspects first, but the order of thinking of aspects is not fixed. Because the order is not fixed, the choice you would make is somewhat unpredictable, especially when two options each have many different but attractive aspects.

In the Rome-Paris example, we can think of many different attributes that distinguish Rome and Paris. Your chance of finding one of these before hitting on the bottle of wine as the decisive attribute is quite high — so high that the wine is unlikely to affect your choice. (For it to do so, you would have to hit on it before any other distinguishing attributes.) When the choice is between Rome with wine and Rome without, however, there are no other distinguishing attributes. You would go through all the attributes and find them identical for the two choices before you hit on the wine, so you would choose the trip with wine with probability 1.

In the record example, many people are likely to think of attributes that make us favor Debussy or Beethoven in general. If we think of an attribute that favors Beethoven, this will probably eliminate the Debussy. If there are two Beethoven records to choose from, however, we will then have to continue the search for more attributes to distinguish them. We are unlikely to discover an attribute that allows us to eliminate *one* of the Beethoven records *and* the Debussy all at once. This is why we appear to make the decision in two steps, first between Beethoven and Debussy, then, if we decide on Beethoven, between the two Beethoven recordings.

[3] In this analysis, an "attractive aspect" could be identical to the *absence* of an unattractive aspect.

This elimination-by-aspects model need not be used all the time in order for it to have its effect. We might think of it as a *heuristic* for making decisions, a heuristic that is used some of the time. (It has actually been observed in think-aloud protocols of decision making on such decisions as choosing an apartment; see Payne, Braunstein, and Carroll, 1978; Svenson, 1979.)

Tversky points out that this heuristic is encouraged by advertisers who try to induce people to focus on certain attributes of the products they are promoting. Producers of products with a low share of the market — let us say a particular soap — want people to see their soap as quite distinctive and not easily compared to others, so that the consumers' attention is focused on the attributes that are favorable to their product. On the other hand, the makers of inexpensive aspirin try to induce people to see all of the competing pain killers as practically identical to each other as medicines (equally effective, and so forth), so that the only relevant attribute becomes the price: "All aspirins are the same. Why pay more?" (Tversky, 1972). Here is another example from a television commercial for a computer-programming school:

> "There are more than two dozen companies in the San Francisco area which offer training in computer programming." The announcer puts some two dozen eggs and one walnut on the table to represent the alternatives, and continues: "Let us examine the facts. How many of these schools have on-line computer facilities for training?" The announcer removes several eggs. "How many of these schools have placement services that would help you find a job?" The announcer removes some more eggs. "How many of these schools are approved for veterans benefits?" The announcer continues until only the walnut remains. The announcer cracks the nutshell, which reveals the name of the company, and concludes: "This is all you need to know in a nutshell." (Tversky, 1972, p. 287)

Use of the "elimination-by-aspects" heuristic is a way to avoid searching for goals (attributes). The decision maker simply searches for *any* goals that will eliminate options. This heuristic can therefore lead to less than optimal decisions. When we make a decision on the basis of a single outstanding attribute, we may ignore a host of smaller differences in other dimensions that would, taken together, favor some other option. For example, in deciding whom to vote for as our U.S. senator, we might base our decision on a single issue that we care greatly about or on the candidate's party. If we were to consider all of the issues and qualifications of all of the candidates, we would often want to vote differently.

Although this heuristic leads to departures from the normative model of decision making, it may be prescriptively sensible, especially for the simpler decisions of daily life, where little is at stake. When we attend to single attributes for more important decisions, however, we may make more serious mistakes.

Asymmetric dominance

Suppose that there are only two brands of beer. Brand X sells for $1.80 per six-pack and has a "quality rating" of 50, on a scale of 0 to 100; brand Y sells for $2.60 and has a rating of 70. Some beer drinkers will prefer X, others Y. Now suppose we introduce brand Z into the market, with a rating of 50 and a price of $2.00, as shown in the figure below. Brand Z will not get much market share. It is *dominated* by X; that is, Z is no better than X on either dimension, price or quality, and X is better than Z on one. No matter how people weigh the two dimensions, nobody has any reason to choose Z. If everyone chose on the basis of the tradeoff between the two dimensions, then the introduction of Z would not affect the proportion of people who choose X and Y. That is, it would not affect the market share of these two.

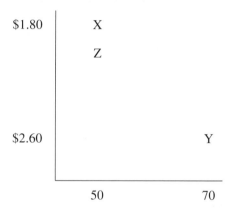

Of course, I would not be telling this story if that always happened. Introduction of Z increases the market share of X (Huber, Payne, and Puto, 1982). That is, when neither of two options (X and Y) dominates the other, introduction of an option that is *asymmetrically dominated* — dominated by one option but not the other — increases the probability of choosing the option that dominates the new option. Why? The best account we have of this phenomenon is that consumers who have trouble deciding between X and Y now have an additional *reason* to choose X. Whatever else can be said about X, it is clearly better than Z. Z serves as a reference point for evaluation of X. Some evidence for this explanation is provided by a study in which certain subjects (students in a class) made decisions anonymously whereas others were *accountable*, told that they might have to justify their decisions to other students in the class (Simonson, 1989). The accountable subjects showed a larger asymmetric dominance effect, presumably because the dominance relation would make it easier for them to justify their choice. Verbal protocols also supported this explanation. Subjects often mentioned the superiority of X over Z as a reason for choosing X.[4]

---

[4] Simonson and Tversky (1992) provide a somewhat different account of the asymmetric dominance effect based on comparison of the X-Y tradeoff with the Z-Y tradeoff. No verbal protocols are cited in

You might wonder why Z would ever be introduced. Sometimes it just happens to be there. But it may be to the advantage of the maker of X to introduce it. In effect, this may happen when an item is sold at a discount: the discounted item dominates the same item without the discount.

Compromise

Another heuristic used for tradeoffs between two attributes is to compromise between extremes. Consider X, Y, and Z, ordered in opposite ways by two attributes (X best on one attribute, Z best on the other), as shown in the following diagram. The probability of choosing Y can be higher when Z is an option than when it is not (Simonson and Tversky, 1992). That may be because compromises are seen as sensible.

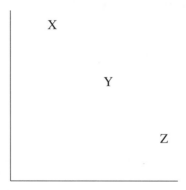

Mental accounting

Many of the characteristic features of decision making can be understood by thinking of people as naive "accountants" (Thaler, 1980). We write down each consequence in black ink or red ink, depending on whether we count it as a gain or loss with respect to some reference point. Sometimes we take shortcuts and combine two gains, or two losses, or a gain and a loss, before writing them down in our mental ledger. When we think about the gains and losses, though, we do not just add them up as an accountant would. Rather, we consider them separately, weighing the losses more.

The status quo (endowment) effect

Recall from the last chapter that the Value function of prospect theory is steeper for losses than for gains (loss aversion), concave for gains, and convex for losses. These properties have implications for decisions involving separate gains and losses.

support of this account, however.

The most direct effect of loss aversion is that people are often unwilling to give up what they already have, their "endowment," for what they would otherwise prefer to it. The loss looms larger than the gain. People are therefore biased toward the status quo, or things the way they are. Consider the following examples, from Thaler (1980, pp. 43–44):

1. Mr. R. bought a case of good wine in the late 1950s for about $5 a bottle. A few years later, his wine merchant agreed to buy the wine back for $100 a bottle. He [Mr. R.] refused, although he has never paid more than $35 for a bottle of wine.

2. Two survey questions:

(a) Assume you had been exposed to a disease which if contracted leads to a quick and painless death within a week. The probability you have the disease is .001. What is the maximum you would be willing to pay for a cure?

(b) Suppose volunteers were needed for research on the above disease. All that would be required is that you expose yourself to a .001 chance of contracting the disease. What is the minimum payment you would require to volunteer for this program? (You would not be allowed to purchase the cure.)

In example 1, Mr. R. will not accept $100 for a bottle of wine, although he would not pay more than $35 for (presumably) the same bottle. In both cases, however, the choice is between wine and money. It might help to think of the true value of the wine as the amount of money that would have the same desirability as the wine *if Mr. R. had to choose between a gift of money and a gift of wine* (having neither at the outset). Most likely, this value would be between $35 and $100, because the endowment effect induces an unwillingness to part with money when one has the money and with wine when one has the wine.

In example 2, the value of not having to risk getting the disease, measured against the price for getting rid of it (a), is far lower (for most people) than the same value measured by the payment required to take it on (b). In general, it appears that there is some value in keeping what we already have. If it is good (as in example 1), we require more payment to give it up than we would spend to acquire it. If it is bad (example 2), we would pay less to give it up than we would require to take it on.

Researchers demonstrated this effect in the laboratory with real goods and real money (Knetsch and Sinden, 1984; Kahneman, Knetsch, and Thaler, 1990). In one experiment in the latter study, members of a group of "sellers" were each given a coffee mug from their university bookstore and were asked to indicate on a form whether or not they would sell the mug at each of a series of prices ranging from $0 to $9.25. A group of "buyers" indicated, on a similar form, whether they were willing to buy a mug at each price. At the end, a "market price" was picked at which there were enough sellers to meet the buyers' demands, and transactions were completed at that price for sellers willing to accept it and buyers willing to pay it, as in a real market. The median values assigned to the mug were $7.12 for sellers and $2.87 for buyers. Although we would expect that half of the buyers and half of the sellers would prefer the mug to the market price (since the mugs were assigned randomly), three-quarters of the sellers ended up keeping their mugs (and three-quarters of the buyers were unwilling to pay enough to get them).

In this study, a group of "choosers" were also asked to choose, for each price in the series, between receiving a mug or receiving the indicated amount in cash. (Most choosers, of course, would prefer the cash if the amount were high enough. The highest amount at which a chooser would still prefer the mug is a measure of her value for the mug.) A random price was then picked from the series, and choosers' wishes were granted for that price. The choosers preferred the mug if the cash amount was $3.12, on the average. This amount was closer to the buyers' willingness to pay for the mug ($2.87) than to the average selling price ($7.12). The important factor causing the endowment effect was whether or not the subject had been endowed with the mug (sellers versus choosers), not whether the cash was gained or lost (choosers versus buyers). The endowment effect seems to operate more for mugs than for cash.

Any of these situations involves a transaction, giving up one thing in exchange for something else. If we suppose that the thing given up (for example, the bottle of wine) and the thing gotten in return (the $100) would have the *same* value if they were both received, we can see why Mr. R. would not want to make the trade. The thing given up (the wine) would have a larger (absolute) value when it is perceived as a loss, because losses are valued more than gains. Therefore Mr. R. would require even more money in order to trade. On the other hand, when asked how much he would pay for the wine, the value of the money is increased, because the money is now seen as a loss. Therefore he would not be willing to pay as much. The negative value of $35 would be greater than the value of the wine, because the $35 is now seen as a loss. Put mathematically, $v(\$100) < -v(-\text{wine})$, but $v(\text{wine}) < -v(-\$35)$. The absolute value of the loss is greater than the value of the gain.

The status quo bias has several practical implications. One is that markets in which people buy and sell goods can be "sticky." In the mugs experiments, far fewer than half of the mugs changed hands, even though we would expect that half of the buyers would place higher values on the mugs than half of the sellers, if there were no endowment effect. Only when the good in question is seen as a commodity, something like a form of currency that has value only because it can be bought and sold, would we expect trades to take place at the expected level. Thus, the status quo bias may reduce the amount of buying and selling in markets in which trades occur rarely and in which individuals, rather than professional traders, make the decisions. The housing market is a good example.

Another example is the choice of health plans by employees. Between 1980 and 1986, Harvard University offered its employees four new health plans, in addition to the four available in 1980. In 1986, employees who were hired before 1980 tended to stick with the plans they had originally chosen, and the new plans were chosen mainly by new employees, regardless of the age of the old and new employees

(Samuelson and Zeckhauser, 1988). The most plausible explanation of these results is that employees simply tend to stick with the status quo each year, even though they might choose something else if they were choosing for the first time.

A second practical implication concerns the use of hypothetical questions to measure the economic value of public goods. In a technique called "contingent valuation," people are asked how much they are willing to pay for various goods that cannot be bought and sold because they are "consumed" freely by everyone, goods such as clean air, public wilderness areas, or transportation safety (Mitchell and Carson, 1989). This technique has been used by governments to decide whether to invest funds in projects such as one to reduce air pollution from a power plant. Subjects may be shown two pictures of an area, showing different levels of haze in the air, and asked how much they would be willing to pay in increased electricity bills in order to reduce the haze from the higher level to the lower level. The average answer to this question (in dollars), multiplied by the number of people affected, may be compared to the actual cost of reducing the pollution, in order to decide whether the change is worthwhile. The technique has even been used to decide on how much a company should pay in penalties for pollution. When a huge tanker ship, the *Exxon Valdez*, spilled oil along the coast of Alaska in 1989, the U.S. and Alaskan governments planned to evaluate the damage to fish, wildlife, beaches, and plants by asking people how much they were willing to pay to prevent such a spill. The method of measurement was to be a major issue in the court case against Exxon, but the parties settled out of court.

Instead of asking people how much they are willing to pay for an improvement (or to prevent a harm), we could ask how much people are willing to *accept* in order to forgo the improvement or to allow the harm. Typically, what is called "willingness to accept" (WTA) is two or three times "willingness to pay" (WTP). This WTA/WTP difference — a form of the status quo bias — seems to be somewhat greater for environmental goods than for consumer goods such as coffee mugs (Irwin, 1992). It may be that people do not like the idea of benefiting personally by allowing harm or preventing improvement of a public resource that affects others. The large difference between WTA and WTP has raised questions about the true nature of "economic value" and about the possibility of measuring this value with much accuracy. On the other hand, the contingent-valuation method may yield results that are correct within an order of magnitude, and this may be better than alternative methods for making decisions about whether public goods should be provided. (For other criticisms and defenses of the method, see Kahneman and Knetsch, 1992, and Jones-Lee, 1989.)

Omission bias

The status quo bias involves an asymmetry between two options: One option is taken as the "reference point," because it is the present state. Another way to create an asymmetry is to designate one option as the *default* — what will happen if the decision maker does nothing. An interesting natural experiment occurred when, in 1988, motorists in the state of New Jersey were given a choice between two kinds of automobile insurance. The new kind of insurance had lower rates than the old kind, because the right to sue was limited. The idea was to save money by reducing lawsuits. Pennsylvania motorists were given essentially the same choice in 1990. In both states, the status quo was the same (higher price, full right to sue), but the default was different. In New Jersey, motorists were given the new policy unless they explicitly said that they wanted the old one. In Pennsylvania, the default was the old policy. In New Jersey, 83% chose the new option, the default. In Pennsylvania, the majority chose the old option, again, the default (as predicted by Hershey and Johnson, 1990). People seem to be biased toward the default.

Behavior in this case could also be affected by the effort involved in reading the options and returning an envelope, or by people's belief that the state recommends the default by choosing it as the default. Laboratory studies, however, support the existence of a bias toward the default, toward *omission* as opposed to action. In a study of hypothetical vaccination decisions, many subjects were unwilling to vaccinate children against a disease that could kill 10 out of 10,000 children when the vaccine itself would kill 5 out of 10,000 through side effects (Ritov and Baron, 1990). Some subjects would not tolerate any deaths from the "commission" of vaccinating. We shall examine other examples of omission bias in Chapters 16 and 20.

Emotional effects of the reference point

Our emotional reactions are stronger to events produced by action than to those produced by inaction. In the following scenarios (from Kahneman and Tversky, 1982), Paul and George experience the same outcome, but it results from action in George's case and from inaction in Paul's.

> Paul owns shares in Company A. During the past year he considered switching to stock in Company B, but he decided against it. He now finds that he would have been better off by $1,200 if he had switched to the stock of Company B. George owned shares in Company B. During the past year he switched to stock in Company A. He now finds that he would have been better off by $1,200 if he had kept his stock in Company B. Who feels greater regret?

Most subjects think that George will be more upset than Paul.

Kahneman and Miller (1986, p. 145) suggested that "the affective response to an event is enhanced if its causes are abnormal" and that actions are considered abnormal because "it is usually easier to imagine abstaining from actions that one has carried out than carrying out actions that were not in fact performed." We have a tendency to see the omission as the reference point. Actions leading to the worse outcome are seen as more blameworthy than any omission. Conversely, actions leading to the better outcome are seen as better than any omission. Landman (1987), and Gleicher et al. (1990), found that anticipated joy in response to positive outcomes was stronger when the outcomes were the result of action rather than inaction. For example, if Paul and George would both have been *worse* off by $1,200 from the forgone option, then we think George would be happier. The emotional effects of outcomes are *amplified* when the outcomes result from actions.

When we evaluate outcomes, we often look for points of comparison, or "norms," even when no decision was involved. Our reactions depend on the comparison that comes to mind most easily. Consider the following case (from Kahneman and Tversky, 1982):

> Mr. C and Mr. D were scheduled to leave the airport on different flights, at the same time. They traveled from town in the same limousine, were caught in a traffic jam, and arrived at the airport 30 minutes after the scheduled departure time of their flights. Mr. D is told that his flight left on time. Mr. C is told that his flight was delayed, and left only 5 minutes ago. Who is more upset?

Most people agree that Mr. C is more upset. It is easier for Mr. C to imagine how things could have been otherwise. These mental simulations of alternative outcomes function as reference points to which the real outcome is compared.

Opportunity costs

Economists and accountants use the term "opportunity cost" to refer to the *benefit* of a forgone option relative to the status quo. Consider two business ventures. Both cost $10,000. Venture A is expected to return $11,000 in a year. Venture B is expected to return $11,500 in a year. Venture B uses some materials that you already own, which you could sell for $1,000 if you don't use them. It is tempting to decide in favor of venture B because it yields a larger profit, and many people do indeed make this choice (Becker, Ronen, and Sorter, 1974). But this is a mistake. Venture B will "cost" an additional $1,000 because the materials cannot be sold. This is the opportunity cost. We can also think of this as a benefit of A: If we undertake A, we gain an additional $1,000 from selling the materials. It does not matter how we think of it: Venture A is still better.

It is easy to neglect opportunity costs when considering whether to make a transaction or do nothing. For example, suppose that you are buying a car and you are offered a low-interest loan. If you have sufficient cash to buy the car outright, you may reject the loan, thinking, "Why should I pay interest if I don't have to?" But if you spend your cash, you also lose the interest that you could make by investing that cash. If the investment interest is higher than the interest you must pay on the loan, then you should take the loan. (In real life, the decision is more complex because of taxes.) In making decisions like this, it is often useful to focus on the differences between the options rather than on the gains or losses of one option relative to a reference point.

Positive and negative attributes

We sometimes think of decisions negatively as dilemmas in which we must choose the lesser evil, as when we must choose between two unpleasant medical treatments. At other times we think of decisions positively as opportunities for achieving a good, as when we must choose between two attractive job offers. This perception is a matter of framing. We could think of the medical treatments as good things, if we compared them to no treatment at all. Grouches will think of the job choice as a question of which job they will have to give up, as if their reference point were all the attractive features of both jobs. Normatively, all that matters is the relative position of the options, the differences between them. It is not the decision that makes the options good or bad relative to some other reference point. It is fate, and our own frame of mind in choosing the reference point.

The reference point can be manipulated, too. Houston, Sherman, and Baker (1991) asked subjects to choose between two options, each described in terms of a number of features, some positive and some negative. In one type of decision, the negative features were all common to both options, and the positive features were unique. For example, in a choice between two automobiles, both had such negative features as "hard to find service outlets" and "poor warranty." But the positive features were different for the two options. If one had the feature "doesn't need repairs often," the other would have some other positive feature, such as "good financing available." This method of presentation encourages subjects to ignore the common negative features and make the decision in terms of the positive features. Other choices were devised in which the positive features were shared and the negative features were unique. Each option had as many positive as negative features in all choices. Subjects took longer to make decisions when the negative features were unique than when the positive features were unique. Decisions with unique negatives seemed more difficult. If the unique features were positive, subjects were more satisfied with the decision when they focused on the chosen option (and less satisfied when they thought about the rejected option) than when unique features were negative.

Another way to manipulate attention to positive and negative features is to ask subjects either to "choose" an option or to "reject" an option. We tend to choose options because of their positive features but reject them because of their negative features. If option A has more positives and more negatives than option B, we will choose A when we are asked to choose and reject A when asked to reject (Shafir, 1992). For example, subjects read descriptions of two vacations. One was described as "average weather, average beaches, medium-quality hotel, medium-temperature water, average nightlife." The other was described as "lots of sunshine, gorgeous beaches and coral reefs, ultramodern hotel, very cold water, very strong winds, no nightlife." When asked to choose, most subjects chose the second. When asked which vacation they would cancel if they had reservations for both at the same time, most chose to cancel the second, thus choosing the first.

Integration and segregation

In the early 1980s, many automobile manufacturers in the United States started to offer rebates to customers who purchased their cars. Why rebates? Why not just reduce the price of the car by the "rebate" amount? It seems like a dubious sales technique, since there is an obvious economic disadvantage to it for purchasers. If the state has a sales tax, they have to pay sales tax on the full price of the car.

Thaler (1983) argues that the rebate program seemed more attractive to consumers than a simple price reduction because consumers keep separate *mental accounts* for the price of the car and the rebate. If the price of the car was simply reduced from \$8,000 to \$7,500, the buyer would, according to Kahneman and Tversky's value function, gain a subjective value of $v(-\$7,500) - v(-\$8,000)$. This is a small gain, because the curve of the function for losses is convex and has a low slope in this range. If, on the other hand, the buyer codes the \$500 separately, the gain would be $v(\$500)$, a large gain, because the Value function is steeper near zero.

Thaler suggests that we either *integrate* or *segregate* multiple outcomes (gains or losses) of a single option. If we integrate outcomes, we add them together before we apply the Value function. They are considered as part of the same mental account. If we segregate different outcomes from each other, we apply the Value function to each gain or loss and then mentally add or subtract the derived values to find the total gain or loss. In general, segregation appears to be irrational, but integration can be difficult when the goods in question are not monetary. Indeed, multiattribute utility theory (MAUT) assumes that we do not integrate dimensions that are expressed in different units (for example, the salary of a job and its consistency with our personal goals).

Despite the rationality of integration in most circumstances, by segregating outcomes at appropriate times we can deceive each other — and even deceive ourselves — into thinking that we are getting more for our money. One simple principle here for a seller (including the person who wants to sell something to himself) is the motto "*Segregate the gains, integrate the losses.*" The late-night television advertisements for kitchen utensils offer a long list of (segregated) gains from buying the product, as does the car dealer who wants to add many options (for only a "small" additional cost). In the latter case, each option alone may not be worth it if considered separately, but if its price is integrated with the loss already taken in deciding to purchase the car, the additional decrease in value is slight (because the value curve is not steep at this point). The options themselves are mentally segregated, because they are different sorts of things: They cannot simply be added. The subjective value of each option does not change as new options are added, but the subjective value of the *price* of each option does decrease, because it is integrated with the price of everything else.

We sell things to ourselves as well. Some of us would not pay \$5 for a dessert or \$15 for a \$5 bottle of wine, if we bought them in a bakery or liquor store, but are quite willing to pay that much if they are added on to a restaurant bill that is already over \$50. The dessert or the wine is segregated, but the loss of the \$5 or the \$15 is integrated with the total price of the dinner. As an addition to the bill, the extra price does not seem so much. In general, integration of losses reduces their effect on our decision. Segregation of gains increases their effect. This combination, therefore, encourages any *transaction* in which someone suffers a loss to obtain a gain — for example, when someone pays money to obtain a combination of goods or services.

Mental accounts affect the effort we make to save money when we buy things. The degree of effort seems to depend on the subjective value of the money saved, not the amount of the money. Many of us are willing to spend as much effort to save $1 on a $10 purchase as we would to save $100 on a $1,000 purchase. Here is a good example:

> Imagine that you are about to purchase a jacket for $125, and a calculator for $15. The calculator salesman informs you that the calculator you wish to buy is on sale for $10 at the other branch of the store, located 20 minutes' drive away. Would you make the trip to the other store? (Tversky and Kahneman, 1981, p. 457)

Most subjects asked were willing to make the trip to save the $5. Very few subjects were willing to make the trip to save $5 on the jacket, though, in an otherwise identical problem. In both cases, the "real" question is whether you would be willing to drive 20 minutes for $5. If the savings is part of your mental account for the calculator, the savings is subjectively greater than it is if it is part of your account for the jacket, because of the convexity of the curve of the Value function for losses.

More generally, whenever we spend money in order to buy something or in order to make an investment, we are in effect "mixing" gains and losses. We lose whatever money we pay and we gain the purchase or investment. If we mentally segregate these gains and losses from each other, the losses will appear to be greater than if we integrate them, because of the curves of the Value function for losses and gains.

As a result, monetary losses appear more acceptable if they are integrated with gains. For example, most employees are not as upset by the deduction of taxes, insurance, investments, charity contributions, and union dues from their paychecks as they would be if they had to pay each of these things separately. Deduction practically ensures mental integration, because many employees do not bother to think about what their take-home pay would be without the deductions. Separate payment would permit the employees to mentally segregate the accounts. It is not necessarily wrong to think about a paycheck in this integrated way. In fact, one can argue that this is the right way to think about things, if we want to approach expected-utility theory. The deductions might be worthwhile, when seen as a reduction in our total income. The problem arises when we do *not* integrate gains and losses for other purchases, such as books or common stocks, which we are therefore less likely to purchase than we would be if they, too, were deducted from our paychecks.

Integration and segregation can be manipulated, as in the *extra cost effect* (Tversky and Kahneman, 1981). "Imagine that you have decided to see a play where admission is $10 per ticket. As you enter the theater you discover that you have lost a $10 bill. Would you still pay $10 for a ticket for the play?" Most subjects asked this question said that they would. "Imagine that you have decided to see a play and paid the admission price of $10 per ticket. As you enter the theater you discover that you have lost the ticket. The seat was not marked and the ticket cannot be recovered." In this case, most would *not* spend $10 on another ticket. Apparently, these subjects think of the cost of the ticket as $20. Larrick, Morgan, and Nisbett (1990) succeeded in convincing most subjects that this was an error and that decisions should be made on the basis of future consequences only. The choice in both cases is whether to spend $10 for a ticket, given one's current wealth, which is already $10 less than it was thought to be.

The sunk-cost effect

Sometimes people act as though the very commitment they have made requires them to keep going. This is like "throwing good money after bad." Another name for it is the *sunk-cost effect*: Once funds have been "sunk" into a plan, the only way not to waste them, it seems, is to sink still more. We see this sort of rationale operating in public policy making as well as in our personal lives. It figured, many now think, in such possible misadventures as the Vietnam War and the Tennessee-Tombigbee Waterway project. A senator expressed sunk-cost thinking when he said, about the latter project, "To terminate a project in which $1.1 billion has been invested represents an unconscionable mishandling of taxpayers' dollars" (Senator Jeremiah Denton, November, 1981, quoted by Arkes and Blumer, 1985).

Such a position is irrational; it subverts one's own (or society's) goals. Once you have determined that the best course of action for the future is to change plans — having weighed the effect on others and all of the relevant factors — the time, effort, and money you have spent in the past does not matter one bit. Sticking to a futile plan will not make your earlier decision the right one, if it was really wrong. When we concern ourselves with sunk costs, we are basing a decision on the past, not on its consequences.

This effect was demonstrated experimentally by Arkes and Blumer (1985). If you had been a subject in one experiment of theirs (p. 126), you would have been told to imagine that you had paid $100 for a ski trip to Michigan and $50 for another ski trip to Wisconsin. Money considerations aside, you would prefer the trip to Wisconsin. If you then discover that the trips are on the same weekend and that you cannot sell either ticket, which trip would you choose? Most subjects picked the less preferred trip to Michigan.

This result shows a kind of framing effect, a result of segregating the mental accounts for the two ski trips. Subjects felt that they would "waste less money" by taking the $100 trip. If they had integrated the two accounts, they would have realized that $150 had been irretrievably spent and that the choice was between the more preferred and the less preferred trip.

Another of Arkes and Blumer's experiments (pp. 132–133) shows this clearly:

> On your way home you buy a TV dinner on sale for $3 at the local
> grocery store.... Then you get an idea. You call up your friend to ask
> if he would like to come over for a quick TV dinner and then watch a
> good movie on TV. Your friend says, "Sure." So you go out to buy a
> second TV dinner. However, all the on-sale TV dinners are gone. You
> therefore have to spend $5 (the regular price) for a TV dinner identical
> to the one you just bought for $3. You go home and put both dinners in
> the oven. When the two dinners are fully cooked, you get a phone call.
> Your friend is ill and cannot come. You are not hungry enough to eat
> both dinners. You cannot freeze one. You must eat one and discard the
> other. Which one do you eat?

Although most subjects said it did not matter, over 20% said that the $5 dinner should
be eaten. If these subjects integrated the costs, they would have seen that $8 was
already lost, and that the dinners were identical.

In another experiment, subjects were told:

> plane
>
> As the president of an airline company, you have invested $10 million of
> the company's money into a research project. The purpose was to build
> a plane that would not be detected by conventional radar .... When the
> project is 90% completed, another firm begins marketing a plane that
> cannot be detected by radar. Also, it is apparent that their plane is much
> faster and far more economical than the plane your company is building.
> The question is: Should you invest the last 10% of the research funds to
> finish the radar-blank plane? (p. 129)

In this condition, 41 out of 48 subjects said they should. In another condition, in
which the $9 million had not been invested and the only issue was whether to invest
$1 million, only 10 out of 60 said they should. This effect was not changed much by
changing the story so that the subject was in the role of an outside observer rather
than president of the company. Personal involvement does not seem to be crucial.

One explanation of the sunk-cost effect is that people are applying a heuristic
against waste. People often endorse this argument as a justification of responses that
show a sunk-cost effect (Bornstein and Chapman, 1995). This heuristic also affects
decisions about changes of plans. Arkes (1996) presented subjects with the following
story:

> Mr. Munn and Mr. Fry each live in an apartment near the local movie
> theater. Mr. Munn can go to the movies only on Monday night. Mr.
> Fry ...only on Friday night. Each movie costs $5 .... Each movie is
> generally shown for a whole week. ...The manager of the theater offers
> a package to those who to do the movies on Mondays. Although tickets
> are $5, the manager will sell a three-pack for $12. The three-pack can be

used on any three Mondays during the next month. Mr. Munn looks over the schedule ... and sees only two movies he is interested in seeing. So he decides not to buy the three-pack. Instead, he pays $5 on each of the first two Mondays of the month to see a movie. Then there is a change in the schedule. ... The manager substitutes a new movie that both Mr. Munn and Mr. Fry are somewhat interested in seeing.

The subjects felt that Mr. Fry would be more likely to see the new movie. Both could see it for $5, but Mr. Munn would see the extra expenditure as wasteful. Arkes also cites a real example: "While I was writing this manuscript, someone offered to take three of us to the movies .... When we arrived at the theater, he was aghast at the ticket prices — $7.25 each! The four tickets would cost him $29. Someone pointed out that he could buy a strip of six tickets for only $25. He refused. 'What would I do with the two extra tickets' he asked. 'They'd just go to waste.' "

Another reason for the sunk cost effect is that people feel that they ought to punish themselves, to teach themselves a lesson for making a bad decision (Bornstein and Chapman, 1995). Of course, they could learn the lesson without making a second bad decision — the decision to continue with a project that should not be continued. (How should they punish themselves for *that*?)

Thaler (1980, pp. 47–50) explained the sunk-cost effect in terms of prospect theory's Value function for gains and losses combined with his idea of integration. When $9 million has already been invested, the additional $1 million is perceived as a small *additional* loss of value, because the Value function for losses has a low slope at this point. The extra $1 million is *integrated*, in subjects' thinking, with the $9 million already spent. The additional "benefit" — a nearly worthless plane — seems to outweigh the small *additional* loss. In other words, the value of the plane appears greater than the difference between the value of losing $9 million and the value of losing $10 million:

$$v(\text{plane}) > v(\$9 \text{ million}) - v(\$10 \text{ million})$$

When the $9 million has not been spent, the value of $1 million is much greater than when it is added to $9 million already spent, because the Value function is steep near zero. Hence,

$$v(\text{plane}) < v(-\$1 \text{ million})$$

The sunk-cost effect could also be explained in terms of regret, in the sense of self-blame (Arkes and Blumer, 1985, p. 137). If we spent the $9 million "for nothing," we might regret it more than if we "at least got something."

Larrick, Morgan, and Nisbett (1990) explained to subjects, with some examples, why the sunk-cost effect was an error. Specifically, decisions should be made on the basis of future consequences. (Past expenditures — such as paying for an indoor tennis court — should not affect choices when they do not affect their future consequences: If the weather is better for playing outside, then we should play outside, regardless of the past.) In a telephone survey conducted four to six weeks after the training, subjects in the training condition were slightly more likely to say that they had bought an object and not used it. People who rent a videotape, find it dull, and then force themselves to watch it all so that they "don't waste money" are victims of this effect, and it appears that training can reduce the number of such victims.

Mental budgets and underinvestment

In the sunk-cost effect, people overinvest resources because of prior investments. People also exhibit a reverse sunk-cost effect when they can think in terms of a fixed budget. Heath (1995) asked subjects about hypothetical investment decisions for commercial real-estate projects. For each project, the subject saw the amount of prior investment, the future investment required to complete the project, and the sales forecast. For example, $9.07 million had been invested in Project A, $2.57 million was required to finish the project, and, if the project is finished, it will pay off $9.16 million (and nothing if it is not finished). Project B was the same except that the prior investment was $6.33 million. (The money could earn 15% if the project were not completed, in either case.)

Eighty-six percent of the subjects said they would complete Project B, but only 64% said they would complete Project A, despite the similarity of the two projects. Other differences in the experiment were larger, but these two projects are interesting. Notice that the total expenses for Project A ($9.07 + $2.57 = $11.64, in millions) exceed the total sales ($9.16), but the total expenses for Project B ($6.33 + $2.57 = $8.90) are less than total sales ($9.16). Thus, Project B makes a profit and Project A does not. Subjects were reluctant to invest when the total expenses exceeded the income. The ones who did not invest in Project A had, in effect, used the sales forecast as a limit on what they would invest.

Notice also that both investments were equally profitable in terms of the decision to be made. Putting past expenses aside, in each case an investment of $2.57 yields a return of $9.16, far better than the 15% yield from not making the investment.

In a second study, subjects played an investment game (like the game Monopoly) with real money. On each play, they could invest in a project with a certain chance of paying off. They could invest repeatedly in the same project, or switch to another project. For example, "Boardwalk" had a payoff of 400 cents, a probability of success of .42, and an investment fee of 147. The subject thus had to decide whether to invest 147 for a .42 chance of winning 400 (a good deal in terms of expected value, since the expected value of the investment is 168). Most subjects invested repeatedly in a project until they won or until their *total* investment would have exceeded the total payoff. In this case, they invested twice. After this, they would switch to another project, possibly one with a worse payoff.

In these experiments subjects seem to confuse total value and marginal value. Marginal value of an investment is the expected return on the next increment, which is actually the decision to be made, for example, whether to invest 147 in Boardwalk this time, regardless of how many previous investments had been made in it. That is the normative basis for this decision, since it concerns the future payoff of the option under consideration.

Notice that this kind of reasoning is difficult in the typical sunk-cost experiments because the payoff is not provided. Subjects do not have the total payoff at hand, to compare to the total investment. This reasoning can, however, explain the lost-ticket problem described earlier. The subjects seem to think of the value of the ticket as $10 or a bit more, so they are not willing to make a total investment of $20 for the ticket. Of course, the result in the lost-ticket example still requires that the money be integrated when the ticket is lost but not when the money is lost (because the money is not seen as part of the cost of the ticket).

The reference price

We have already seen that subjects tend to evaluate outcomes by comparing the outcomes to their reference point. A number of other reference points seem to be involved in decision making. In purchasing behavior, one common reference point is the idea of a fair price, or market price, or what Thaler (1985) calls a reference price. Consider the following scenario:

> You are lying on the beach on a hot day. All you have to drink is ice water. For the last hour you have been thinking about how much you would enjoy a nice cold bottle of your favorite brand of beer. A companion gets up to go make a phone call and offers to bring back a beer from the only nearby place where beer is sold, a small run-down grocery store. He says that the beer might be expensive and so he asks you how much you are willing to pay for the beer. (Thaler, 1985, p. 206)

Your friend will buy the beer only if it is less than the price you state. The median price that subjects given this description were willing to pay was $1.50. When "fancy resort hotel" was substituted for "run-down grocery store," though, the median price went up to $2.65.

Thaler argues that subjects took into account the idea of a fair price for the beer, given the type of establishment that was selling it. (Note that the consumer of the beer would not consume any of the "atmosphere" of the fancy hotel — presumably the factor that permits the hotel to charge more.) In addition to considering the value of the money lost and the beer gained, we seem to take into account an additional value having to do with the extent to which the price is above or below the reference price.

This hypothesis explains a number of otherwise curious phenomena of the marketplace, such as "discount prices" advertised as being below the "suggested retail price." When certain rather expensive goods are purchased once every few years, at most, many consumers do not know what the price "ought" to be, so it is possible to make them think that they are getting a 50% discount on a new camera, stereo system, or set of silver flatware by mentioning a "suggested retail price" of twice the asking price.

Another common device is to change the goods in some way so that the reference price is unknown. Have you noticed that movie theaters sell unusually large candy bars? This is handy for pricing, since we cannot recall what the price would be elsewhere.

Conclusion

If our decisions were made by trying to maximize utility, they would not depend on the way we are asked about the decision or on the presence of options that we would reject. We may in fact try to maximize utility much of the time. But some of the time we use various heuristics instead. For example, we ignore small differences among options, integrate outcomes when doing so increases the attractiveness of an option, make decisions according to the most "important" dimension, weigh losses more heavily than gains, look for simple reasons for choosing (such as dominance), and compare outcomes to convenient reference points such as the status quo or the default. Because we do not attend to all relevant attributes, our attention can be manipulated.

Most of these heuristics are reasonable ones, because they save time. If we use them knowingly for that purpose, we can avoid real trouble. When decisions are important, we can check to see that they are not misleading us. For example, we can try framing the decision in a different way. (Would I still refuse the second job offer, if I weren't using the earlier offer as a reference point?) Or we can try to carry out a rudimentary decision analysis. Or we can develop heuristics to counter the ones that get us into trouble. Can you think of heuristics to avoid the endowment effect for goods, the certainty effect (Chapter 11), and the effects of framing and mental accounting?[5]

Heuristics become especially perilous when we become overconfident of their value, so that we reject superior procedures, or when we become committed to them as methods in themselves, without understanding that they are tools of convenience and not normative standards in their own right. We shall consider examples of these dangers in later chapters.

---

[5] Here are some suggested answers: For the endowment effect, imagine a choice between the good in question and the money, assuming you had neither. For the certainty effect, think about *un*certainties lying behind apparent certainties. For the effects of framing, compare everything to the status quo. For mental accounting, integrate everything possible.

Chapter 13

Utility measurement

The normative theory of decision making is closely related to several applied fields. These include *decision analysis*[1] and cost-effectiveness analysis. This chapter and the next discuss the problem of measuring utility for such applied purposes. This chapter is about measurement, and the next is about a particular type of decision analysis that emphasizes values.

Decision analysis and related methods

Decision analysis is the attempt to apply utility theory directly to decisions. Utility theory is normative, but decision analysis treats it as a prescriptive theory. If you use expected-utility theory in this way to decide between two uncertain prospects, you would estimate the probability and utility of each outcome and multiply them. This procedure will make the best decision, according to utility theory as a normative model, if you estimate probabilities and utilities with sufficient accuracy. These estimates require judgment. They require that a judge or subject, or you, try to answer certain questions. You then infer your probabilities and utilities from the answers to these questions. On p. 132, I discussed how you can estimate proabilities by asking yourself questions about conditional probabilities.

This chapter and the next concern the kinds of questions you could use to estimate utility of outcomes. This chapter concerns basic comparisons of the utility of two outcomes. The next chapter concerns the decomposition of utility into independent attributes (price, quality, et cetera), each corresponding to some goal or subgoal. With such a decomposition, you can measure the utility of each outcome on each attribute separately and combine these attribute-utilities. This is called multiattribute analysis. Decision analysis also includes many practical (prescriptive) techniques for searching for options (possibilities), evidence, and goals.

[1] Excellent texts on this field are: Raiffa, 1968; Brown, Kahr, and Peterson, 1974; Keeney and Raiffa, 1976; Behn and Vaupel, 1982; and von Winterfeldt and Edwards, 1986.

Most of the methods I describe are used in practice. Some are used more than others, but practices vary over time and region, and all these methods are closely related, so any practitioner should understand all of them. One major application is in medicine. The methods discussed in this chapter are used mostly in medicine. Estimation of utility is becoming more common because of two factors. One is the increasing adoption of new medical technology, from magnetic resonance imaging (MRI) in rich countries to polio vaccination in poor ones. The more technology available, the more likely that some of it will raise questions about whether the benefits are worth the costs. The second factor is that more people around the world have their medical costs paid by someone else, either the government or a private health-insurance plan. These payers often realize that they cannot afford to pay for every potentially beneficial application of every technology. They must set policies about which technologies to cover. A useful approach is to cover those methods that do the most good for the money available. This requires measurement of good, and this is, of course, something like utility.

Multiattribute analysis has been applied to a greater variety of decisions. It has been applied to such practical questions as where to put the Mexico City airport; where to locate a national radioactive-waste disposal site in the United States; which school desegregation plan the city of Los Angeles should accept; and hundreds of other problems in business and government.

The Oregon Health Plan

The State of Oregon lies .just north of California. As one of the states of the United States, it had to grapple with the problem of providing medical care to the poor. In the 1980s, the U.S. government provided funding for Medicaid, a government insurance Program available to children and to those with incomes below the official poverty line. The benefits provided by Medicaid were comparable to those provided by private health insurance. But the program was not given enough funding to provide these benefits to all who could qualify, let alone to the millions of others who were just above the poverty line but still found ordinary medical insurance too expensive. Those without insurance hoped they would not get sick. When they got sick, they went to the emergency room. This was expensive for hospitals, but hospitals did not turn needy people away. In the mid 1980s, Oregon found itself unable to cover more than half of those technically eligible.

John Kitzhaber was a state legislator who had been an emergency room doctor. (At the time I write, he is governor.) He led a movement to revise the state law to provide Medicaid benefits to more people. In order to free up money for this extra coverage, the plan was to stop covering health services that were expensive and relatively ineffective, such as liver transplants that were unlikely to work anyway in people whose life expectancy was short, that is, older people. Thus, many more people would get coverage for basic health care, even perhaps more than basic health care, but some people would do without very expensive procedures that did little good. Total utility would increase because the utility of the basic services provided to people would be very great, and the loss to those who did without would be relatively small.

The benefit of a health treatment is not something that comes in units like acres or dollars. Health has value because people value it. Nor can we consult the market price to determine how much people value health. There is no store where you can buy a cure for migraines or a bad back. You can buy treatments that might help, but their price is not determined by the free market. Most people who get these treatments have insurance, so they do not pay the cost. Ultimately, the best way to assign values to treatments is to ask people to judge their utility.

This is just what the state did. It appointed a commission to elicit utility judgments from the public. The idea was to measure the benefit of various treatments. Then the benefit would be divided by the cost, and each treatment would be assigned a number representing its benefit per dollar, that is, its utility per dollar. The treatments would then be ranked by this measure. Those with the highest benefit per dollar would be at the top. The state would then go down the list, one by one, figuring out how much money it would have to spend per year on each treatment. When it ran out of money, it would draw a line. It would not cover anything below the line. This way, the state would get the most total benefit for the dollars availalble. Notice that any switching above and below the line would make things worse. If some treatments below the line cost the same as some above it, then switching the two groups would mean that less benefit was obtained for the same cost. (The estimates were not exact, so it would not be possible to "cheat" by moving a rare treatment above the line, on the ground that it just used up the small excess left over.)

Initially, opponents saw the plan as another way to pick on the poor, who were already picked on enough. Indeed, the very poor who qualified for Medicaid got a reduction in coverage. In 1987, Coby Howard, a seven-year-old boy, died of leukemia after being denied a bone-marrow transplant under Medicaid because the legislature had already decided not to cover such transplants. This was not part of the Oregon Health Plan, but it raised fears of more of the same. This kind of treatment is exactly what would be cut off. It was very expensive and very unlikely to succeed. (Now the plan covers such transplants routinely.) But Kitzhaber and others rallied support for the plan, and it went ahead.

The commission made up a list of 709 condition-treatment pairs. Each pair was evaluated in terms of alleviation of symptoms, quality of life, and cost. To rate the utility of the symptoms, the commission did a telephone survey of Oregon residents. Each respondent rated 23 symptoms on a scale from 0 to 100, where 0 represents "as bad as death" and 100 represents "good health." The symptoms included such things as "burn over large areas of face, body, arms, or legs" (rated about half as bad as death), "trouble talking, such as lisp, stuttering, hoarseness, or inability to speak," and "breathing smog or unpleasant air" (rated closest to good health). The respondent also rated descriptions of limitations in mobility, physical activity, and social activity, such as health related limitation in some social role.

Experts then used these ratings to determine the average benefit of each treatment-condition pair. They took into account the duration and probability of the benefits of treatment, compared to what would happen without the treatment under consideration. Then these benefits were divided by the cost to get the average benefit per dollar. Highest on the list were medical therapy for pneumonia and heart attacks. The lowest single item was life support for babies born without brains. The initial cutoff was set at 587. That is, the first 587 out of 709 items on the list would be covered. Items just above and below the cutoff, respectively, were treatment of cancer of the esophagus and breast reconstruction after mastectomy for cancer.

Public hearings led to major revisions in the list. People were disturbed to see that surgical treatment for ectopic pregnancy and for appendicitis were ranked about the same as dental caps for "pulp or near pulp exposure" in the list (Hadorn, 1991). In fact, the expected benefit of tooth capping was 8 (on the scale of 0–100) and that of surgery for ectopic pregnancy was 71. The surgery is often life saving. People wanted a higher priority for potentially life saving treatments, and the list was revised in that direction. However, "If you want to check the results against your intuition, you should compare the *volumes* of different services that can be offered with a particular amount of resources. In this example, the appropriate comparison is not between treating a patient with dental caps for pulp exposure and treating a patient with surgery for ectopic pregnancy but between treating 105 patients with dental at $38 each versus treating one patient with surgery for ectopic pregnancy at $4,015 $(4,015/38 = 105)$" (Eddy, 1991). On the other hand, the 8 versus 71 was the result of human judgment. If judgments are not as extreme as they should be, then the 8 was still too high, and the surgery should have ranked much higher. The problem of eliciting such judgments is the main topic of this chapter.

In the end, the state implemented the plan, but the cutback in coverage was very small, only 2% of the total cost of the program (Jacobs et al., 1999). Medicaid was extended to cover more poor people, but largely because of extra money from a cigarette tax and from other cost-saving measures. Many of the poor remain without coverage, although fewer than in other states. One fear of the critics was the treatments below the line would still be highly beneficial for some patients, even though they are not beneficial on the average. These treatments are mostly provided, despite the rules.

Decision analysis versus cost-benefit analysis

Decision analysis has much in common with cost-benefit analysis, a technique used by business organizations and government agencies for the same purposes as decision analysis. A cost-benefit analysis reduces everything to money rather than utility. It attempts to place a monetary value on all outcomes and then to choose the option that maximizes expected monetary gain or minimizes loss. The problem with cost-benefit analysis is that money is not the same as utility. We saw in Chapter 10 that the utility of money is typically marginally declining for each person. In Chapter 16, we shall see that this makes sense when comparing people, too. Cost-benefit analysis recognizes this problem, and has various ways of dealing with it, but none is quite as direct as doing the analysis in utility rather than money. The cost-benefit analyst might argue that money is easier to estimate. This is not obvious, though. Have you ever tried to predict your expenditures on basic expenses? The prediction problem might be even more difficult for governments and large institutions. It is not clearly easier than estimating utility, although, of course, it may be. Even so, accuracy of estimating the input is not the only criterion of a good decision-making scheme.

Consider how it would work to apply simple cost-benefit analysis to a question of life or death. Suppose a very wealthy patient is trying to decide whether or not to have a coronary bypass operation. The operation promises to relieve his pain and weakness and perhaps reduce the risk of death from a heart attack some years hence, but the operation is itself dangerous and may cause immediate death, with some probability, P. We could analyze this decision by asking how much money the patient would pay to avoid the "loss" of immediate death ($\$L$). The risk of the operation would then be the loss of $\$L$. We also ask how much he would pay for the beneficial effects of the operation (if these could be assured) ($\$B$). We could then suppose that the patient is presented with a gamble and should make the decision on the basis of the *expected value* of the gamble. By this weird reasoning, the expected value of the operation would be $(1-P) \cdot \$B - P \cdot \$L$, since $(1-P)$ is the probability of actually getting the benefit $\$B$, and the equivalent of $\$L$ would be lost with probability P. If the expected value is greater than the cost of the operation, the patient should have the operation.

What is wrong with this method? We cannot assume, in this situation, that the utility of money is a linear function of the amount. Our patient would probably be willing to part with his entire fortune in order to avoid immediate death. Therefore, even if P were quite small, this calculation would tell him to avoid the operation, when in fact the risk of death may truly be worth taking to improve the quality of his remaining life. Because of the declining marginal utility of money, the utility of avoiding death has been overestimated by this method. (Another problem with cost-benefit analysis is that when we try to convert everything to money values, there is a danger that we will confuse the market value of something with its subjective value to those affected, as pointed out by Schwartz, 1986, and by Baron, 1993a.)

Decision analysis reduces everything to a common coin of expected utility. We are assuming that once we have measured the utility of some outcome (or of some attribute of an outcome), we know everything that we need to know about it, for the purpose of making the decision. Outcomes can be fully represented by their utilities — by *how much they help us achieve our goals*.

A decision analyst may use her own utility estimates, or she may try to estimate the utility for other people by putting herself in their position, or she may ask them for their own utilities. Asking the people involved is not always best. Because medical patients, for example, often lack experience with the consequences that they must consider, a physician or nurse may do a better job of deciding on their behalf than the patients themselves.

We can think of decision analysis as a "design" (see Chapter 1). The structure is that of utility theory (including both expected-utility theory and multiattribute utility theory, which I shall discuss later in this chapter), plus a number of prescriptive techniques for thinking of options, consequences, and goals. The *purpose* of decision analysis is to make decisions. The *arguments* for decision analysis consist of the reason why the theory is normative, which we just considered, and the fact that we depart systematically from the normative model when we make decisions without analyzing them, a matter that we shall examine in the next chapter.

Because decision analysis is an approximate standard for rational decision making, it is also used to evaluate decisions after they are made. For example, it has been used as a standard in medical malpractice cases — specifically, to explain why decisions were reasonable risks to take, even when they turned out badly (Forst, 1974; Bursztajn, Hamm, Gutheil, and Brodsky, 1984). Of course, it would be best in such cases to carry out the analysis *before* the decision is made and to pay attention to its results. Decision analysis can also be used to understand and resolve conflict among different decision makers. If the disagreement is about the probability of outcomes, more information might be sought. If it is about utilities, some sort of average might be appropriate, or the parties might discuss their images of the outcomes to find out why their utilities differ. More generally, decision analysis can be used in the early stages of thinking about a decision, before all the possibilities and evidence are available, as a way of finding out what sort of possibilities or evidence are needed or of discovering what our goals are. We must remember that utility theory itself is only a method of inference. If it is to be useful, it must be coupled with sufficiently thorough search for possibilities, evidence, and goals.

We noted earlier, in connection with Pascal's Wager, that the amount of detail used in a decision analysis is arbitrary. The least amount of detail is none at all. One could simply assign a utility to a whole option (for example, living the Christian life), just as we assigned a utility to "normal life." This is essentially what is done when decisions are made "holistically," or without analysis. In the light of this fact, what should we do when the result of a decision analysis disagrees with what we are inclined to do without it? Suppose you are deciding whether to accept a certain job. You want to accept it, but you carry out a decision analysis (concerning the probability of receiving an offer of a better job), and the analysis says that you should wait. What should you do? Should you always follow the analysis?

My answer is — not necessarily. If you know that you have carried out the analysis perfectly, you ought to do what it says — but you can never be sure. In fact, you do not have one analysis, but two, one being your original intuition, which is essentially an assignment of utility directly to your two choices (Brown and Lindley, 1985). You should try to understand why the two analyses differ. (Some of the problems discussed in the Chapter 12 may be at fault.) It may be that the analysis has left out some important factor, such as your admiration for the people with whom you would be working. In the end, you have to ask yourself how good each analysis is, how well it serves its purposes. Perhaps the best way to think of a decision analysis is as a *second opinion*. As in medical decisions, it can be reasonable to ignore a second opinion, but in some cases the second opinion calls your attention to an important factor that you had ignored before.

A method closely related to decision analysis is *cost-effectiveness analysis*. This term is used to cover many things. They all involve decisions about spending money (or time). The goal is to get the most benefit for the money spent. So they need a measure of benefit. Sometimes the measure is obvious because there is only a single goal. UNICEF, for example, sometimes carries out cost-effectiveness analysis in terms of the number of children's deaths prevented per dollar spent on vitamins, oral rehydration, vaccinations, etc. Sometimes, a report of a cost-effectiveness analysis includes more than one measure (deaths prevented and cases of malaria prevented), leaving it to the reader to decide on their relative importance. Cost-effectiveness analysis becomes more like decision analysis when some effort is made to represent different outcomes on a common scale, like utility.

In health fields, this measure is often "health-related quality of life" or simply "health utility." It is the part of utility that is attributable to changes in health. This is difficult, because medical decisions often involve life versus death, and the utility of life may be affected by other things aside from health, such as relationships with others or even wealth. Health professionals usually do not think it is their business to make judgments about such things or even take them into account in deciding on policies, such as whether an insurance policy should pay for heart bypass surgery after a certain age.

Utility measures in medical decision analysis are often converted to Quality Adjusted Life Years (QALY; Pliskin, Shepard, and Weinstein, 1980). The idea is health utility adds up over time, so we can multiply the utility per year times the number of years to get a total measure of QALYs. A QALY is the total utility of a year in normal health. If some condition reduces health utility to three quarters of its normal value, then living with that condition for 4 years provides a total of 3 QALYs, the same as three years in normal health. A cure that lasts for 4 years would improve a person's life by 1 QALY, the same as extending that person's life by one year. QALYs are widely used as a standard measure of treatment effectiveness. They allow comparison of treatments that extend life with treatments that improve it. In cost-effectiveness analysis, it is convenient to think about cost per QALY as a standard measure. In the U.S. treatments that cost over $100,000 per QALY are considered extremely expensive and are routinely questioned on the grounds of cost. Many treatments are far more cost-effective than this, and, when resources are limited, we can improve matters on the whole by taking money from the less effective treatments and spending it on the more effective ones. Note, however, that this kind of argument is useful only when costs are limited and can be redirected in this way. This argument does not tell us how much a QALY is truly worth. From a decision-theoretic point of view, that would depend on the alternatives available for spending the money, and the utility that those provide.

We will begin the discussion of utility measurement with the kind of measures used in health. The basic problem is to elicit judgments about health-related quality of life, but we will speak of utility. The methods are useful elsewhere, outside of the health domain.

The measurement of utility

The problem of measuring utility has both a theoretical and a practical aspect. The theoretical problem is to state the conditions under which utility can be measured using each of the methods that have been devised. What would it mean for each method to be internally consistent? The practical problem is to state the conditions under which each method should be used. Which methods are easiest to use? Most internally consistent? Most sensitive to factors that should affect them and most insensitive to factors that should not affect them? How can we improve each method in these respects? Before dealing with the various methods for measuring utility, let us consider some general aspects of the problem, the nature of utility measurement, and the distinction between direct and indirect measures.

Utility measurement as prediction

When we try to measure utility in any way, we are, in essence, making a prediction about the utility of an outcome. We do not know everything relevant that would allow us to judge the outcome in the light of our goals. Even putting aside the uncertainty about which variants of an outcome will occur, we might be unaware of the extent to which factors will affect the achievement of our goals.

Kahneman and Snell (1992) explored some prediction failures in cases in which the main goals were purely hedonic: experiencing pleasure and avoiding pain. In one study, subjects were asked to predict how much they would like eating a serving of plain low-fat yogurt while listening to a piece of music on each of eight successive evenings. Subjects initially tended to dislike the yogurt, and they predicted (on average) that they would dislike it more and more with repetition. Contrary to their expectations, however, they tended to like the yogurt more — or dislike it less — over the eight days, as indicated by ratings they made after each experience. The latter ratings correspond most closely to true goal achievement in this case, because they were made with something closer to full knowledge. It is not clear just what psychological mechanisms accounted for the change in liking, but it seems that the subjects' naive theories concerning changes in taste did not include them.

Part of the reason that we cannot predict our experiences well is that we cannot remember them well. Our memories of the quality of experiences are excessively influenced by their endings and by their best or worst points, and we tend to ignore their duration. In an experiment done by Kahneman, Frederickson, Schreiber, and Redelmeier (1993), each subject was given two unpleasant experiences: holding his hand in very cold water for a minute; and holding his hand in the water for a minute and a half, with the last half minute slightly less cold, but still unpleasant. Most subjects chose to repeat the longer experience rather than the shorter one, and they remembered the longer one as being less unpleasant, although it contained a greater total amount of unpleasantness. Of course, this kind of experiment is relevant to utilities of events that we value because of the experiences they provide, but it suggests more generally that we may have trouble learning what achieves our goals.

Utility measurement is not always prediction. Some of our goals do not concern experiences, or things that happen at a given point in time. (For example, we can want the house we build to last for a long time after our death, or want our great grandchildren to have good lives.) It is still helpful to suppose that utility is real and that we are trying to judge it. We can be more accurate or less accurate in our judgments, just as we can predict our experiences accurately or inaccurately. The judgment from which we infer utility is not the same as the utility itself. All along, we have assumed that the question "which option is best" has a right answer (which might be that two are equally good). We have thus assumed that utility is real. We can try to judge what it is, and our judgments will be inaccurate to varying degrees, but we can meaningfully ask how we can minimize this error. We shall thus distinguish here between Judged Utility and True Utility.

Direct versus indirect judgments

The simplest methods for measuring utility are *direct*. In these methods, the subject simply makes a judgment of the utility of one object as a proportion of the utility of another, or adjusts the end of one interval so that it is equal to another. Note that such matching responses need not involve hypothetical decisions. Another way to do this, which we shall examine later, is to make rating responses to stimuli that vary on several dimensions. For example, subjects can rate the badness of situations involving combinations of health states (X) and monetary losses (Y). We can compare the utility of X and Y by asking how much Y is needed to compensate for a given loss of X, so as to make the average rating the same.

Indirect judgments are based on hypothetical decisions. For example, in the time-tradeoff (TTO) method, the subject indicates how many years of future life with normal vision is just as good as 50 years with blindness. The idea here is to assume that the subject makes decisions based on utility and to infer the utility from the decision. If the subject says 40 years, and if we assume that utility adds up over time, then we can conclude that the subject's utility for blindness is .8, on a scale where death is 0 and life with normal vision is 1. This is because $.8 \cdot 50 = 1 \cdot 40$. Or, in the person-tradeoff (PTO) method, we can ask how many cases of blindness is just as bad as 10 deaths. If death is 5 times as bad as blindness, and if the judgment is based on adding utility across people, then the answer should be 50.

When subjects make indirect judgments, they do it in two ways. In one way, they make a direct judgment and then infer their indirect judgment from that. For example, when they are asked (in the person tradeoff method) how many people losing a finger is equivalent to ten people losing an arm, they may ask themselves, "How many times worse is it to lose an arm than a finger," and then they multiply this by ten. In the other way, they think about the people, not the badness of the losses.

We may summarize the situation as follows:

Here, True Utility represents the actual outcome evaluated in terms of the subject's ultimate criteria. Decision Utility represents what is inferred from decisions. Judged Utility is the internal representation of True Utility. Arrows represent possible cause-effect relations. Although most discussion of utility measurement is based on an assumed path from True Utility to Decision Utility and from there directly to the judgment, it seems likely that several biases affect the link from True Utility to Decision Utility, such as risk aversion in standard gambles. It is possible the best way to remove these biases is to concentrate on the use of Judged Utility. Decision Utility then becomes a way of informing that judgment, through the downward arrow: for example, a person who was considering a very extreme utility judgment could imagine a hypothetical decision (PTO or TTO) as a way of checking it.

Direct judgments are those based on Judged Utility. Direct judgments suffer from biases too, and it may just turn out that these are larger than the biases introduced by some corresponding indirect task. However, if we want to eliminate all biases, then we may do better to start with direct judgments. We cannot expect to eliminate biases by finding tasks with several different biases that just happen to cancel each other out, and it is clear that direct judgments suffer from several biases inherent in the nature of the tasks.

This argument is against the spirit of current economic theory, which gives behavior a privileged place in the definition of value. For example, if we want to find out the average tradeoff between commuting time and money for some group of people, the best way to tell is to ask how much those people actually pay for reduced commuting time in a free market. If no real market is available, then we ask hypothetical questions about what people would be willing to pay, if they could.

An alternative view is that, in order to decide rationally what to do in a market or anywhere, people should consult their values and make judgments about their application to the case at hand. When people ask themselves what they would do in a hypothetical situation, they either consult their values in this way, or they distract themselves with irrelevant considerations (such as trying to figure out a fair price, as found by Baron and Maxwell, 1995). Thinking about hypothetical behavior adds an extra step to the process, with additional opportunity for error to intervene. Moreover, even real behavior may be fallible as an indicator of value, because people can go against their deepest values and regret their behavior, for example, saving too little money, engaging in unhealthful habits, or failing to do enough for others in need or for environmental protection.

Of course, *real* behavior adds a kind of discipline by forcing people to ask hard questions about tradeoffs, questions they may try to avoid when they make judgments of values. Judgments alone, taken at face value, are not an absolute criterion of value, for they may be distorted by such careless thinking. But this proposal is about cases in which real behavior cannot be used. *Hypothetical* behavior – making judgments about hypothetical decisions – need not impose this kind of discipline.

One problem with indirect judgments is that they tend to be difficult. When a subject is asked "How many cases of blindness is as bad as 100 cases of blindness plus deafness?", the temptation is to think of this as an analogy problem. Subjects often get it backward. They think, "Blindness is about 40% as bad as blindness plus deafness, so I will say 40." But blindness is not as bad, so the number should be higher. The most direct methods do not suffer from this kind of difficulty.

Simple direct judgment and the analog scale

The simplest way to estimate utility is to assign numbers to the various outcomes. For example, suppose you must decide whether to accept a job or to refuse it and hope for a better offer, which you expect with a probability of .5. There are three possible outcomes: the job you have been offered (B); the better offer (A); and the job you would have to take if the better offer does not come through (C). To assess your expected utility, you might assign a value of 100 to job A, and a value of 0 to job C, and ask yourself where job B falls on this scale. Clearly, if the value of job B is greater than 50, the expected utility of accepting job B is higher than that of waiting.

A visual aid like the following is often used to help subjects make judgments like this. The ends of the line are labeled with the extreme conditions (A and C), and the subject is asked to mark the line where the other condition falls (B). This is called the *visual analog scale*. We have no evidence that the visual aspect of it helps in any way, but also no evidence that it hurts.

A   B   C
_____

The direct approach has the virtue of simplicity, but it has a couple of defects. First, you (the judge of your utilities) have not been told much about what the numbers you assign are supposed to mean. The only requirement that is obvious to you is that higher numbers should correspond to higher utilities. You are free to assign ratings that express the square of the utility (or some other function) rather than the true utility. If you did this, a rating of 36 for job B would correspond to a true utility of 6, and a rating of 100 would correspond to a utility of 10. Although the analysis would say that you should decline job B (because 36 is less than 50, which is half the assessed utility of A), the true utilities would say that you should take job B (because 6 is greater than 5, which is half the true utility of job A).

Another problem with direct scaling (and perhaps with other methods) is that psychological experiments suggest the relative ratings chosen depend on the set of stimuli used. For example, if subjects are asked to rate the length of rods that are respectively 1, 3, 5, 7, 8, 9, and 10 inches long, they tend to rate the longer rods as more different in length and the shorter rods as closer in length than they really are. If, on the other hand, subjects are given rods with lengths 1, 2, 3, 4, 6, 8, and 10 inches, the reverse is found (Poulton, 1979). The same may be true for rating utilities. This effect might be avoidable by selecting stimuli carefully (on the basis of preliminary studies) or by presenting only three stimuli at a time.

A form of this effect still happens even with three stimuli, however. Suppose you are asked, "On a scale where 0 is being blind and deaf and 100 is normal health, where is being blind?" You say 40. Being blind, you think is 40% as bad as being blind and deaf. This is your judgment. Then, you are asked, "On a scale where 0 is normal and 100 is being blind, where is being blind in one eye?" You say 25, because you think that being blind in one eye is only a quarter as bad as being blind in both eyes. Now you are asked, "On a scale where 0 is normal and 100 is being blind and deaf, where is being blind in one eye?" You should say 10, because that is a quarter of 40. Most people say more. It is as if they move their judgments away from the extremes, so that they can spread them out evenly. Although this effect, called *ratio inconsistency*, is found in many kinds of judgments, it can be reduced by training (Baron et al., 1998). In general, it may be helpful in any utility judgment to include checks for consistency and to ask the subject to resolve any inconsistencies that are found. It may also be helpful to use a logarithmic scale, marked off with units like "1/3 1/10 1/30 1/100" and so on, for the relative badness of one interval compared to another.

Difference measurement

The first problem can be solved by giving the rater a clear conception of what it means to rate utility, rather than some function of utility such as the square. Perhaps the most important requirement of an accurate utility scale is that it should reflect *differences* between utilities, as well as the utilities themselves. The idea of difference measurement is to ask the rater to compare differences between outcomes, rather than outcomes themselves. If you say that the utility *difference* between A and B is equal to the difference between B and C, then we can safely assign a utility to B that is halfway between the utility of A and C. If A is 100 and C is 0, then B would be 50.

Suppose I want to measure my own utility for various levels of total wealth. I might begin by picking a lower and an upper limit on the range that I shall consider, say $0 and $1 million. I then ask myself to cut this interval in half subjectively. I seek an amount of wealth (x), such that the subjective difference between $0 and x is the same as the subjective difference between x and $1 million. If I cannot do this right away, I might pick some value arbitrarily, such as $500,000, and ask whether it is too high or too low.[2] If the value is too high (as it is), I might adjust

---

[2]This method exposes me to the risk of an anchoring-and-adjustment bias, however (see Chapter 15).

it downward by half the difference, to $250,000, and so on, going up and down by half of the difference each time, until I come close to the value I seek. For me, this would be about $150,000. That is, the subjective difference in utility between $0 and $150,000 is about the same as the subjective difference between $150,000 and $1 million.

If I have trouble thinking about differences in utility directly, I might ask myself which *change* would be subjectively greater: the change from $0 to $x or the change from $x to $1 million. Again, I might ask which would be a more pleasant surprise: expecting $0 and finding that the truth was actually $x, or expecting $x and finding that the truth was actually $1 million.

I could continue in this manner, dividing the utility interval in half each time. If I assigned a utility of 0 to $0 and a utility of 8 to $1 million, I would assign a utility of 4 (halfway between 0 and 8) to $x, once I discovered what $x was. I could then divide the interval between $0 and $x in half in the same way, and assign this wealth a utility of 2, and so on. In my case, I might assign a utility of 2 to $50,000, since this would be subjectively halfway between $0 and $150,000.

Notice that the bottom and top values of the scale could be chosen arbitrarily. To use utilities in decision analysis, we need only *relative* values. For example, suppose that I have $50,000 in savings and I want to know whether I ought to invest it in a real estate deal that has a .5 probability of netting me $1 million and a .5 probability of losing everything. The expected utility of the deal is $.5 \cdot u(\$1 \text{ million}) + .5 \cdot u(\$0)$. The way I have scaled utility, this would be $.5 \cdot 8 + .5 \cdot 0$, or 4. This is higher than the utility of my current wealth, which is 2, so I ought to go for it.

Suppose I had used a different scale, though, so that I had assigned a utility of 100 to $0 and a utility of 200 to $1 million. When I cut this interval in half, I would have discovered that the utility of $150,000 is 150, halfway between 100 and 200, and the utility of $50,000 is 125. In this case, the expected utility of the real-estate deal is 150, and the utility of my current wealth would be 125, still less than 150, and by the same proportion of the total range as before.

In order for difference measurement to be used, the utilities of outcomes must be related by a condition called *monotonicity*. Consider the following outcomes, laid out in order of desirability. The letters A through F might stand for different amounts of money, or different jobs.

A   B   C   D E   F

Suppose that the difference between A and B is subjectively equal to the difference between D and E, and the difference between B and C is subjectively equal to the difference between E and F. It must be the case, then, that the difference between A and C is also equal to the difference between D and F (Krantz, , Luce, Suppes, and Tversky, 1971, ch. 4). If this monotonicity condition is not met, inconsistencies will arise in the scale. To see how that might happen, imagine that F is directly *above* E, rather than to the right of it. Then the distance between E and F could still be the same as that between B and C, yet the distance between A and C would be greater than that between D and F. The outcomes would not lie along the same line.

Note that the difference method can be used directly, as in the examples just given, or it can be used as a check on the direct-rating method. If the rater understands that the differences between ratings are supposed to be meaningful, this may be enough to correct distortion of the scale. Either way, the monotonicity condition can serve as a check. As yet, no one has asked experimentally whether monotonicity applies either to direct ratings or to difference measurement. Perhaps this question has not been asked because no one has thought of a reason why the monotonicity condition would ever be violated systematically. Checks seem to be a good idea, however.

One problem with the difference method is that it requires a large number of possible outcomes (as is the case when we are rating some continuous quantity like wealth), so that it is possible to find outcomes halfway between other outcomes. If it is to be used for a decision analysis with only a few outcomes, we can add hypothetical outcomes to the set being rated.

Difference measurement may not escape from the prediction problems discussed earlier. Varey and Kahneman (1992) told subjects that A must carry a 30-pound suitcase for 200 yards, B must carry it for 550 yards, and C must carry it for 900 yards. When subjects were asked whether B's "overall physical discomfort for the task as a whole" is closer to A's or C's, most subjects thought it was closer to C's. The answer implies that disutility for this task is marginally declining, like the negative side of the Value function of prospect theory. The same subjects were asked directly whether an individual who carried the suitcase for 900 yards would suffer greater discomfort while walking the interval from 200 to 550 yards or the one from 550 to 900 yards. Here, most thought that the second interval would have greater discomfort, so that disutility was marginally increasing. Either way of asking the question could be used in difference measurement. It seems that, in this case, the second way of asking induced subjects to think about the experience, but the first way of asking evoked a general heuristic or naive theory that we generally adapt to experiences (which is usually correct, but surely not in this case). In sum, even if difference measurement leads to consistent judgments of utility, these judgments need not be correct predictions of true utility (in this case, experienced utility).

Standard gambles

Suppose we accept Bernoulli's idea that we choose gambles according to the principle of expected utility. If we do, then this leads to yet another method for measuring utility. We can decide how we would gamble and then *work backward* from our choice of gambles to determine our utilities.

For example, suppose I want to discover my utility for wealth, in the range between $0 and $1 million. I could ask myself this: At what amount x would I be indifferent between x and a gamble in which I have a .5 chance of gaining $1 million and a .5 chance of losing everything? If I judge gambles as Bernoulli says I do (and as expected-utility theory says I ought to), I would say that x is $150,000, the same point yielded by the difference method. (In fact, very few people give the same results with the two methods. Most people are more averse to risks than the theory says they ought to be, for reasons discussed in Chapter 11.) In a similar manner, we could use 50–50 gambles of this sort to bisect utility intervals, exactly as we did with the method of differences. In this way, I could discover $y such that I would be indifferent between $y and a gamble in which there was a .5 chance of $x and a .5 chance of $0, and so on.

We might ask how this method could possibly be valuable, since the usual reason for wanting to discover utilities in the first place is to make decisions about gambles (for example, the job choice described earlier). One answer is that the method might be useful for measuring utilities for the purpose of formulating public policy. For example, we might want to determine the disutility of having chronic chest pain from heart disease, so we know how important it is to cure such pain (for example, through by-pass surgery). We can describe such pain to a subject, or test a subject who is experiencing the pain. Our comparison point is death. We thus ask, "Suppose you have two choices. One is a probability P of normal health and $1 - P$ of imminent death. The other is chest pain of the sort described. At what value of P would you be indifferent between these two choices?" If the subject says .75, then we infer that the utility of the pain is .75, on a scale where normal health is 1 and death is 0. We assume that the subject follows expected-utility, so $.75 \cdot U(normal) + .25 \cdot U(death) = U(pain)$. In this case, the subject thinks that getting rid of the pain is worth taking a 25% chance of death. This is called the standard-gamble method of utility elicitation.

If we take this result seriously, we would conclude that curing the pain is 25% as valuable as preventing death (assuming that the remaining life expectancy is the same in both cases). If we were trying to maximize the benefit from expenditures on health care, and if we could save a life for (say) a million dollars, then we should not spend more than a quarter of a million on curing chest pain. If we had to spend more than that per cure, we would do more total good by using the money to save lives.

Another value of this standard gamble method is for breaking down complex decisions that involve a few possible outcomes. Consider, for instance, the decision that many couples face about whether a woman who is expecting a baby should have amniocentesis. That is a test that determines whether a fetus has Down's syndrome, a condition that usually means that the child will be severely mentally retarded and have other serious medical problems. Parents who have the test done should be willing for the mother to have an abortion if the test is positive. The test itself can cause a miscarriage, so there is no reason to do it unless one is prepared to act on the results. Amniocentesis is usually done in women over 35, because the probability of Down's syndrome increases with the mother's age. However, this is an arbitrary cutoff point. From a decision-analytic point of view, the choice of whether or not to do the test depends on the parents' relative utilities for the four possible outcomes: normal birth, Down's syndrome, miscarriage, and abortion.[3]

---

[3] In the present discussion, based on Hill et al. (1978, ch. 10), I ignore conditions other than Downs, complications other than miscarriage, and the possibility that the test is fallacious. All of these factors must be considered in a full analysis. I also ignore many recent advances in prenatal testing.

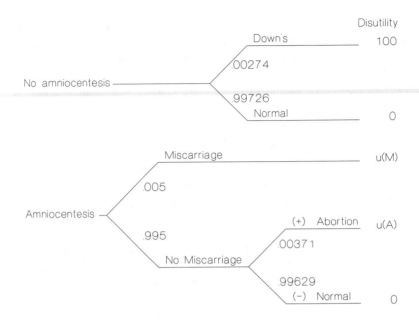

Figure 13.1: Tree for outcomes and probabilities of amniocentesis decision.

The situation can be represented in a tree diagram, as in Figure 13.1. Here, the plus (+) and minus (−) branches represent the outcome of the test. The probabilities given in the diagram are chosen for illustrative purposes only. We have assigned a *dis*utility of 100 to a Down's syndrome birth and a utility of 0 to a normal birth. To make the decision, we must know the two missing utilities, $u(M)$, the utility of a miscarriage, and $u(A)$, the utility of an abortion, on this 0 to 100 scale. To assess $u(M)$, the couple can imagine a simpler decision in which they must choose between a miscarriage for sure and a gamble between a Down's syndrome child with probability p and a normal child with probability $1 - p$. The question is, at what value of p will the couple be indifferent between the miscarriage and the gamble? Suppose it is .02. Then we know — again making the usual assumption that the couple chooses as Bernoulli says they will — that the expected utility of the gamble is the utility of the miscarriage. The expected utility of the gamble is $.02 \cdot 100 + .98 \cdot 0$, or 2. Hence, $u(M) = 2$. In the same manner, we can assess the utility for an abortion. For example, if p for an abortion is .03, then $u(A)$ is 3. We can then replace $u(M)$ and $u(A)$ with their estimated values to calculate the *overall* expected utility of the choice of amniocentesis, and we can compare this to the expected utility of not having amniocentesis, which, in this case, is .274. In this case, the expected utility of the test is $.005 \cdot 2 + (.995 \cdot .00371) \cdot 3 + (.995 \cdot .99629) \cdot 0$, or about .011. In this case, the expected disutility of the test is less than that of not having the test, so the couple should have it.

This example shows how the method of gambles allows us to break down a complex decision into a set of simpler ones. Of course, each of the "simple" ones could also be analyzed into more outcomes, each with its own probability. Down's syndrome, for example, has many manifestations, and miscarriages may be harmful to the mother or less harmful, and have fewer or more numerous implications for future births. In this example, we have treated such outcomes as miscarriage and abortion as holistic entities, not to be analyzed further. We could have treated amniocentesis itself as a holistic outcome and made the decision without analysis at all. (This is what most people do.)

Of course this method of measuring utility is valid only if Bernoulli's assumption that people choose gambles according to their expected utility is correct. In fact, we do not always choose in this way (Chapter 11). For example, people may prefer a gamble (such as a Down's syndrome child with probability p and a normal child with probability $1 - p$) to a quite certain outcome (such as a miscarriage with probability 1), even though the gamble would have the same "true" expected utility (see Chapter 11). The knowledge that a particular bad outcome is certain to occur apparently interferes with making decisions consistent with expected-utility theory; the hope of avoiding any bad outcome seems to take control.

More generally, the π function of prospect theory (Chapter 11) implies that judgments made in this way will be inaccurate and inconsistent with each other. Such inconsistency happens (de Neufville and Delquié, 1988). For example, a subject is indifferent between $70 with probability 1 and $100 with probability .5, so the utility of $70 is .5 (if $100 has utility 1). But the utility of the $70 is inflated by the π function. Suppose we cut both the probabilities in half. The subject now says that a .25 chance of $100 is equivalent to a .5 chance of $60, not $70. The same subject might say that a .125 chance of $100 is equivalent to a .25 chance of $55. The $70, $60, and $55 would be the same if the subject followed expected-utility, but this sort of difference is typical. The inconsistency gets smaller (in terms of ratios) as probabilities are reduced, but it does not go away.

Another problem is that different utility estimates result from asking people to fill in the probability than from asking them to fill in the value of the certain option (Hershey and Schoemaker, 1986). Suppose you ask, "What probability of $100 is just as good as $50 for sure?", and the subject says .7. Then you ask, "What amount of money is just as good as a .7 chance of $100?", and the same subject says $60. Several psychological factors are at work in explaining this discrepancy (Schoemaker and Hershey, 1992). One effect (but not the only one) is that, when subjects are given a choice with probability 1, they regard that as the reference point, so that they demand a higher chance of winning to compensate for the fact that they might "lose " (for example, the .7 probability just described). They are less likely to do this when they must name the amount of money, so they are not so risk averse (as in the $60 response — a risk-neutral subject would say $70).

In sum, the use of standard gambles to infer utility is seriously flawed. No way has been found of compensating for these flaws. The method may still be useful when we need only a rough answer, and this is often all we need. For example, the amniocentesis decision, for most couples, is not close at all. One option has several times the utility of another, depending on the couple's utility for avoiding Down's syndrome, miscarriage, and abortion. The method is difficult to use, though, and, if all we need is a rough estimate, direct rating might be quicker and easier, or the difference method, if we can use it.

Time tradeoff and person tradeoff

We can compare the utility of outcomes by using duration or number of people, instead of probability, to modify the utility of one outcome so that it becomes equal to another. Suppose we want to assess your judged utility of curing a persistent but not very serious cough, compared to that of curing persistent and excruciating headaches. We can describe each to you in some detail. Then we ask, "How many days of headaches is just as bad as 10 days of cough?" If you say 2, we can conclude that the headaches, as described, are 5 times as bad as the cough. We infer this by assuming that duration multiplies the utility per day. You are thus telling us that 2 times the daily disutility of headache equals 10 times the daily disutility of cough, in your judgment. This method of utility assessment is called the time-tradeoff.

We could use this method to evaluate chest pain of the sort described in the section on standard gambles. We could ask, "Imagine you have a choice of living 10 years with chest pain or some shorter period T in normal health. You die at the end. What is T so that you are indifferent?" An answer of 7 years implies a willingness to sacrifice duration of life for quality. Again, we assume that the total utility of some condition, compared to death as 0, is constant over time, so that we can add up the utilities year by year (or day by day). This amounts to multiplying the utility per year by the duration in years. In this case $7 \cdot U(normal) = 10 \cdot U(pain)$. If the utility of normal health is 1, then the utility of pain is .70.

$\nearrow$ Notice that we left death out of the last equation. We can do that because it has a utility of 0. The full equation would be $7 \cdot U(normal) + 3 \cdot U(death) = 10 \cdot U(pain)$. In other words, 7 years of normal health followed by 3 years of death is just as bad as 10 years of pain. Putting it this way calls attention to a strange feature of using death to anchor one end of the scale, as usually done when eliciting health utilities. We assume that the states of interest exist over time, and we multiply the duration of a state by its utility per unit time to get the total utility. But death is not exactly a state. It is more like an event. The badness of being dead does not so clearly accumulate as a result of being dead for a longer time. On the other hand, the reasons that we have to avoid death are much the same reasons that we have for wanting to live, and many of these involve what we can do with our lives — including both accomplishment and enjoyment. Poor health is bad because it limits what we can do, so life in poor health is truly not as valuable as life in good health. We can do the same amount in a shorter period with good health as we can in a longer period of poor health. The time-tradeoff method, used with death at the end, is a way of asking people to make this judgment very explicitly.

Empirically, judgments made this way do not conform to the assumption that the utility of health is constant over time. When durations are very short, many people give absolute priority to living as long as possible (Miyamoto and Eraker, 1988). They will say, for example, that 10 weeks in pain (followed by death) is equivalent to 10 weeks in normal health (followed by death), but if the units are changed to years, rather than weeks, they might say that 7 years in normal health is equivalent to 10 years in pain. This leads to inconsistent utility assessments, but it may be perfectly rational. It may be that the things that people want to do with their lives when death is imminent are different things than they want to do when they have longer to live. People with a few weeks to live may focus more on getting their affairs in order for the benefit of their survivors — insofar as they can focus on anything — and this may not depend much on the state of their health. For practical purposes of measurement, this problem may be avoidable by using longer durations.

Even with longer durations, though, some people claim to be unwilling to make any sacrifice of duration of life for quality of life, even when the quality difference is large, as determined by direct rating (O'Leary et al., 1995). Such people may be following a simple rule of giving priority to life rather than thinking of what they (or others) might do with their lives over the periods at issue.

Another result that is disturbing for the time-tradeoff method is a kind of preference reversal (Stalmeier, Wakker, and Bezembinder, 1997). When people are given a choice between living 10 years with 5 days per week of migraine headaches (described thoroughly to them) and 20 years with 5 days per week of migraine, they prefer the shorter life span. This might be a rational choice if you thought that the 10 years would give you a chance to tie up various projects and prepare for death but that, from a strictly experiential point of view, this condition would otherwise be worse than death. Yet, the same people were asked how many years of good health was equal to these two situations, and they gave longer durations for the 20 years than for the 10 years, as if asking about years called attention to the duration of the two states rather than the severity of the condition. The time tradeoff may induce people to to attend to duration more than would be consistent with their overall goals.

A closely related method counts people instead of time intervals. Suppose you have a choice of curing 100 people of cough or X people of headache. At what number X would you be indifferent? If you say 25, then we infer that the utility of curing cough is a quarter of that utility of curing headache, in your judgment. Or, you have a choice of curing 100 people of chest pain or saving Y people from imminent death. At what value of Y are you indifferent. If you say 30, then we conclude that chest pain is .3 of the distance between normal health and death, so that it would have a utility of .7 on the scale we've been using. This method is called the person tradeoff.

This method assumes that we can add utility across people. This is the assumption of utilitarian philosophy. We shall examine this idea in Chapter 16. Part of the problem with the person tradeoff is that people do not accept the assumption. For example, many people think that is equally good to save the life of 100 people who will be paralyzed after they are saved as it is to save the life of 100 people who will be normal after they are saved Ubel, Richardson, and Pinto Priades, 1999). This implies that paralysis has a utility of 1 on the usual scale: It is as good as being normal. When the subjects are asked to compare saving 100 people from paralysis and saving X people from death, they give intermediate values for X, around 50. These responses imply that paralysis is half way between death and normal health. The trouble seems to be that some people do not think that it is fair to consider people's future handicaps in deciding whether to save their lives.

What counts in health utility?

Should we consider handicaps? What is the difference between handicaps and health states? This question applies generally to all methods of eliciting utility judgments. Part of the problem is that health utility is not the same as total utility or well being. In assessing health utility, we must draw some line between what we count as health and everything else. For example, we do not usually consider people's economic well being or their personal ties. Yet, we do more good by restoring rich people to health than by restoring poor people to health. The rich have more resources to enjoy their health. Likewise, we do more good by helping people with many other people dependent on them — whether in their family or their work — because we help the dependents as well as the patients. The problem is that the health system is not supposed to be concerned with such issues in most countries. Governments have divided up responsibility for various tasks, and the health system is usually responsible for health alone. Handicaps are a borderline case. It is reasonable to think of them as health conditions, but it is also reasonable to think of them as more like income or family status, things that affect people's well-being but that are outside the bailiwick of health decisions.

More generally, in assessing health utility, we need to distinguish health's contribution from other effects of our decisions on utility. Notice the wording here. Utility is relative. It is always meaningless to compare absolute levels of utility. In health, we can compare health state to death, but that is not the same thing as absolute level, because we cannot assume that death has the same significance to everyone. The only thing we ever need to know is how our choices affect utility. Still, our choices may affect utility by affecting health or in other ways.

The problem is difficult. Health is not always a fundamental value. Like life, health is something we use for other things, like enjoying ourselves or contributing to projects. The utility of health for a person will thus depend on the circumstances of that person's life. A tennis player might resort to risky and painful knee surgery that has a chance of restoring her to top form, where most people would decide that a minor knee ailment is something to live with. It is difficult to draw the line between health and nonhealth effects.

We have no general solution to this problem. We should and do define health differently for different purposes. For public policy concerning what health procedures must be available to all, it might make sense to think in terms of health functions that essentially everyone would want. Decisions made by and for individual patients should take into account more information about the person's entire life.

Adaptation and point of view

Another general problem in assessing health utility is who does it. Health professionals know more about the conditions in question. Patients know more about how their health affects their own lives. When we ask patients about their utility, we can ask them either before or after they experience the health state in question. For example, in using the standard gamble to assess the utility of chest pain, we can ask patients who have chest pain what probability of death they would accept in order to be rid of it, or we can describe chest pain to those who do not have the pain and then ask the same questions.

Several studies have asked whether patients who are experiencing some condition evaluate it differently from those who simply imagine it. Some studies find no difference (for example, O'Connor et al., 1987; Llewellen-Thomas et al., 1993), but other studies find that those in a condition assign it a higher utility (that is, closer to normal health) than those not in it (for example, Boyd et al., 1990; Gabriel et al., 1999). Researchers must, and often do, make sure that the descriptions given to those not in the state are accepted as accurate by those in the state.

One possible reason why evaluations might differ is that patients adapt to their conditions over a long period. This is especially true when conditions can be described as handicaps rather than illnesses. Such adaptation may occur for two kinds of reasons. One reason is that people not in the condition do not imagine all the ways of adapting to it. For example, voice-dictation software is now available for those with arm problems that prevent typing or writing. The condition is still bad, but less bad than would be apparent to someone who did not know of this possibility.

The other reason is that people may change their goals to adapt to what they can do (Elster, 1983). People who become blind can lose their interest in the visual arts and in the beauty of nature, thus being less frustrated by their handicap. Is this rational? Should we take it into account in evaluating the utility of a disorder such as blindness? These are very deep questions, and this short discussion cannot do justice to them, but a couple of suggestions are in order.

It may well be rational for people to change their goals to adapt to reality. As we shall discuss in Chapter 19, some of our decisions affect the existence of goals (in ourselves and others). One property of a goal that we might consider, in deciding whether to bring it into existence or increase its strength (or the reverse) is whether it can be achieved. If we favor goals that are achievable, we can increase total utility. Changing goals can also be irrational. People sometimes "give up too soon." They convince themselves that something is unachievable and stop wanting it, when, in fact, they could achieve it. For example, with effort, people with severe handicaps can work.

When we decide how much money to spend on the prevention of blindness, for example, it may not be correct to consider the fact that blind people will change their goals to adapt to their handicap. We may do better to honor the goals of the people who have not yet become blind, before adaptation. Arguably, these are the people who matter. We should, however, make sure that, when they evaluate blindness, they consider the pressure to change their goals as part of what blindness means. This consideration can make blindness seem less bad, because of the adaptation of goals, but worse because of the need to change the goals. This need may itself be undesired.

If the question is cure rather than prevention, then the people affected are those with the condition. If their goals are rationally chosen, then we should honor them. We may find ourselves placing a higher value on the prevention of a condition than on its cure, because those with the condition have rationally adapted to it. This need not be as crazy as it sounds. If the adaptation is irrational, a "sour grapes" effect, then we should ignore it and treat both groups equally, those who do not have the condition yet and those who have it.

Other methods involving matching and comparison

The time tradeoff and person tradeoff methods ask the subject to equate two situations so that they match. The subject does this by changing the amount of time or the number of people in one of the two situations. In the time tradeoff method, we assume that utility per time is constant, so we assume that the total utility is the product of the duration times the utility per unit time. Likewise, in the person tradeoff, we multiply utility per person by the number of people in each situation.

We can do this in other ways, even when the units in the two situations are different, so long as there are units. We can compare any two dimensions of situations by matching the quantity of one of them that has has just as much utility as a given quantity of the other. For example, we could compare two medical treatments of an infection in terms of their cost and speed of recovery (in days). We could ask how many days is equivalent to a cost of $50.

We do not need to assume that the utility of days or dollars is constant. We can specify the numbers involved. Let us, for the moment, assume that the utility of dollars is linear (within the range of interest) but the utility of days is not. Suppose, for example, that you are sick and missing work. You can afford a day or two, but after that things get increasingly difficult. So the utility difference between 2 and 3 days recovery time is greater than that between 1 and 2. The question then might be to match the following two situations:

    A. 2 days recover time, for $50.
    B. 1 day recovery time, for $X.

If you said $70, we would infer that the difference between 2 days and 1 day has a utility equal to that of $20. We could ask the same question using 3 days and 2 days, and you might give a larger number of dollars, say $80. If we defined the utility of money as 0 for $100 and 1 for $0, and if we assume that this utility is linear, then we can assign utilities to days of recovery time. If 1 day had a utility of 1, then 2 days will have a utility of .8 and 3 days will have a utility of .5. This is because the difference of 1 and .8 is .2, which is the utility of the $20 value assigned to the difference between 1 day and 2 days, and the difference between .8 and .5 is .3, which is the utility of the $30 value assigned to the difference betwen 2 and 3 days.

We can also use direct judgments to compare any two intervals (Edwards and Newman, 1982). When we compared being blind with being blind and deaf, we were actually judging the utility *ratio* of two intervals. One interval is the difference between having no deficit and being blind. The other interval is the difference between no deficit and being blind and deaf. It is like comparing the length of the following two lines:

No deficit _____ Blind
No deficit _____ Blind and deaf

We can use the same method for any two intervals with the ends defined. For example, we ask, "How large is the difference between 2 and 3 days recovery time, compared to the difference between spending $0 and spending $100?" So we would be comparing the following two lines:

2 days _____ 3 days
$0 _____ $100

This ratio should be .3, if the last example is correct. Notice that this method no longer assumes that the utility of money is linear. It just uses the difference between $0 and $100 as the unit. It ignores what happens in between. On the same scale, you might judge that the difference between $0 and $50 is .4 of the difference between $0 and $100. Of course, this method has all the difficulties of direct judgment. Consistency checks are needed to insure accuracy.

You can use this kind of method to assign weights to attributes of options when we are considering several options and several dimensions (Edwards and Newman, 1982; von Winterfeldt and Edwards, 1986; Keeney, 1992). For example, in choosing a car, you might consider such dimensions as cost, expected frequency of repair, driver safety, and environmental effect. You would first define the ends of each dimension by choosing the highest and lowest values you might consider. Cost might range from $0 (a hand-me-down) to $40,000. Driver safety might range from that of a motorcycle to that of a tank. You could first choose the largest dimension by asking yourself, "Which is more important to me, the difference between $0 and $40,000 or the difference between the safety of a motorcycle and that of a tank?" Suppose you thought safety. Then you would compare the safety difference to all the other dimensions in the same way.

Once you had found the dimension with the biggest difference, you would ask yourself how large each difference is, as a proportion of that. For example, you might judge that the price difference between $0 and $40,000 is .8 of the safety difference between a motorcycle and a tank. You could do this again, using another dimension as the standard, in order to check your consistency. If you think the price difference is .8 of the safety difference and the environmental difference is .2 of the safety difference, then you should think that the environmental difference is .25 of the price difference.

You could use these weights to convert the utility of one scale into the units of another. For example, suppose you assigned 100 "price-utility points" to the difference between $0 and $40,000, so that $0 had 100 points and $40,000 had 0. And you assigned 100 safety-utility points to a tank and 0 to a motorcycle. But now you want to decide between:

   A. A car that has 50 price-utility points (because you think that is the
      right number for $20,000, its cost) and 60 safety-utility points (be-
      cause it is a bit closer to a tank than a motorcycle) and,
   B. A car that has 31 price-utility points (instead of 50) and 80 safety-
      utility points (instead of 60).

If you just look at the points, you would choose car B, because the total is higher (31 + 80 versus 50 + 60). But the price points aren't worth as much. So you convert the price points into safety points. You know that 100 price points is the same as 80 safety points. That was your judgment. So each price point is worth .8 safety points. To convert everything to safety points, you multiply the safety points by .8 before you add. Then car A is better, because it is 50 + 48 safety points instead of 31 + 64. It doesn't matter which scale we use, since utility has no particular unit. We just have to use the same scale for everything.

This chapter will provide another example of this later, in discussing multiattribute utility theory. In that theory, the relative difference is called a "weight."

It is very important to notice here what we are *not* asking. We are not asking "How important is recovery time relative to money?" (Or price relative to safety.) That question has no meaningful answer. The answer depends on how much money and how much time. The utility difference between 2 and 3 days recovery time is smaller than that between $0 and $100 but larger than that between $0 and $5. This point is not widely understood. People who make up attitude questionnaires — professionals as well as amateurs (such as politicians) — often ask such questions as "Which is more important to you, controlling crime or protecting the environment?" Or they ask you to rate several issues for "importance." The right answer is, "It depends on how much of each you are talking about. Preventing a single mugging is not as important as eliminating all cases of pollution-caused illness, but reducing crime by 50% is more important than eliminating pollution from a single stream."

The problem here is related to the prominence effect discussed in Chapter 12. People seem to have a concept of "importance" that does not depend on quantities. This is what influences choice in the prominence effect. It is also what allows people to answer questionnaires that ask about importance but do not specify quantity. It is not clear what importance means. In particular, it is not clear how we use importance judgments to make concrete decisions, which involve quantities. If we are really deciding between spending money on crime or the environment, we can usually estimate the effects of the alternative programs. Someone who said that crime is more important might still prefer a very cost-effective program to clean up the environment over an ineffective program to fight crime.

It is difficult to avoid the prominence effect even when comparing utility differences. Respondents do not pay enough attention to the ranges given, the differences between one end and the other of each dimension. Keeney (1992, p. 147) calls underattention to range "the most common critical mistake." Subjects in experiments on weight assignment are often undersensitive to the range (Weber and Borcherding, 1993). Doubling the range of money, for example, should approximately double its relative importance, but this rarely happens.

Underattention to range can be reduced. Fischer (1995) found complete undersensitivity to range when subjects were asked simply to assign weights to ranges (for example, to the difference between a starting salary of $25,000 and $35,000 and between 5 and 25 vacation days – or between 10 and 20 vacation days – for a job). When the range of vacation days doubled, the judged importance of the full range of days (10 vs. 20) relative to the range of salaries ($10,000) did not increase. Thus, subjects showed inconsistent rates of substitution depending on the range considered. Subjects were more sensitive to the range, with their weights coming closer to the required doubling with a doubling of the range, when they used either matching or direct judgments of intervals. In matching (as described earlier in this section), the subject changed one value of the more important dimension so that the two dimensions were equal in importance, for example, by lowering the top salary of the salary dimension. In direct judgment, subjects judged the ratio between the less important and more important ranges, for example, "the difference between 5 and 25 vacation days is 1/5 of the difference between $25,000 and $35,000." (This is also called the method of "swing weights.")

Contingent valuation (CV)

One form of matching involves willingness to pay or accept money. This is called contingent valuation (CV; Mitchell and Carson, 1989). The idea was to create a contingent or hypothetical market to determine the market value of goods that could not be bought or sold in markets, such as clean air or a pristine wilderness. For example, in 1989, the tanker *Exxon Valdez* spilled about 11 millions gallons of crude oil into Prince William Sound on the coast of Alaska. The oil killed birds, fish, seals and sea otters. It spoiled the beaches and the vegetation. Under the law, Exxon was required to pay a penalty equal to the value of the damage it caused, including damage to the environment, and including environmental damage that had no effect on commercial activity. Although Exxon finally reached a settlement with the governments of Alaska and the United States without an actual determination of the value of the damage, a preliminary study had already begun the process of evalating the damage with the CV method (Carson et al., 1992).

The study involved a personal interview with each respondent. The interviewer used words and pictures to describe the damage done by the spill and how spills could be prevented by using escort ships and other means. The most critical parts of the interview included the following:

If the program was approved, here is how it would be paid for.

All of the oil companies that take oil out of Alaska would pay a special *one* time tax .... Households like yours would also pay a special *one* time charge that would be added to their federal taxes ....

Because everyone would bear *part* of the cost, we are using this survey to ask people how they would vote if they had the chance to vote on the program. ...

Of course, whether people would vote for or against the escort ship program depends on how much it will cost *their household*. *At present*, government officials estimate the program will cost *your* household a total of $X ....

If the program cost your household a total of $X would you vote for the program or against it?

The value of $X was either $10, $30, $60, or $120 for different respondents. Respondents who said yes were then asked about a higher amount (for example, $30, if the respondent would pay $10), and those who said no were asked about a lower amount. The method of asking for a yes-no vote does not actually tell how much each respondent is willing to pay. It can only tell whether the amount is more or less than each of the two values used. With many respondents, the researchers could estimate the median (middle) critical value, which ranged from $27 to $46 depending on how the estimate was made. In other CV studies, respondents are often asked outright how much they would be willing to pay, at most, for some program or good.

The CV method is expensive. Even when respondents provide a number, the time required is large. Of course it is possible to modify the method and ask about several goods in one interview, but this is rarely done in practice. Researchers feel that they must specify each good with great care, and that takes as much time as most respondents are willing to spend. When, after half an hour, the respondent specifies only a vote, so that we do not even know the number she would provide, the method is more expensive still. Even more respondents are required in order to estimate the median. CV has still other problems, some of which are common to other methods too.

Insensitivity to quantity

For one thing, CV responses are insensitive to quantity. People are not willing to pay much more to prevent ten oil spills per year than to prevent one. Unless their price is very high, so that it dents significantly into their wealth, they should be willing to pay about ten times as much for ten as for one. Some studies of quantity effects are unable to detect any difference at all, and those that find differences find them to be much smaller than this. We thus cannot use CV responses to determine the value of preventing an oil spill, which is what we want to know.

One reason for insensitivity to quantity seems to be the prominence effect. Even when the task involve matching, subjects assign dollars according to the importance of the issue rather than its quantity, as if these were separate dimensions and the importance was more important. Subjects do not really mean to be insensitive to quantity; they just ignore it. When the question asks how much they would pay *per unit* of the good, responses are about the same as those to questions about paying for one unit or paying for 10 units, which are also about the same (Baron and Greene, 1996).

Another possible reason for insensitivity is that a single good evokes points of comparison like itself. For example, CV responses to saving endangered Australian mammals are higher than CV responses to reducing skin cancer among farmers, but subjects prefer reducing skin cancer when the two programs are presented side by side. When each program is evaluated alone, it may be compared to other programs of the same type. Skin cancer is relatively low on the ladder of important diseases (except to those who have it, of course), but Australian mammals are unique and well known, hence high on the ladder of animals worth saving. But when the choice is between people and animals, people seem more important.

Sensitivity to cost

Users of CV typically assume that the value of the benefits is a function of the effects of the good in question, not its cost. Although cost is usually a good guide to value, excessive attention to cost as a guide can cause trouble. For example, suppose that government program X has a little more benefit than program Y, so that willingness to pay (WTP) for X would be a little higher if the costs of the two programs were the same. But suppose that respondents would express higher WTP for Y than for X if they learned that Y was more costly for the government to implement. Then, if the government used WTP as an index of preference, and if cost were not a major issue, it would assume that people preferred program Y. A government that acted on this information would choose Y over X. The citizens would pay more and get less benefit.

Reported WTP increases with cost of the good even when benefit is constant. This was shown in the study of beer on the beach (Thaler, 1985, described in Chapter 12): WTP was higher if the beer came from a fancy resort hotel than if it came from a mom-and-pop store. Because the beer was to be consumed on the beach, none of the atmosphere of the hotel would be consumed. Baron and Maxwell (1996) asked WTP questions concerning hypothetical public goods, such as removing harmful chemicals from drinking water. When the project was described in a way that made it seem more costly, respondents were willing to pay more. The results can be understood as overextension of a somewhat useful heuristic: things that cost more often yield more benefit. The findings suggest that contingent valuation methods may be improved by eliminating information from which costs could be inferred, so that respondents can focus more easily on benefits alone.

WTA (willingness to accept) is larger than WTP

A general result in CV is that willingness to accept (WTA) is larger than WTP
(Mitchell and Carson, 1989). For example, the minimum WTA for a change in the
pollution level from 10 to 20 units is about twice the WTP for a reduction from 20 to
10. This is an example of the status-quo bias (Chapter 12).

Several studies have succeeded in manipulating the effect. Irwin (1994) found
that this kind of effect was greater for environmental goods than for market items,
and she presented evidence that the difference was the result of respondents' moral
concerns about making the environment worse. Marshall et al. (1986) found that
WTA versus WTP effects do not occur for advisers (as opposed to decision makers).
A possible explanation of this result is that the norm prohibiting accepting money in
return for losses (even personal losses) might be "agent relative," that is, dependent
on the role of the decision maker rather than the outcome alone (Chapter 16).

In sum, CV responses are affected by several factors that should not affect the
utility of the good being evaluated — cost and WTA versus WTP — and they are not
affected enough by factors that should affect the utility of the good, particularly its
quantity.

Disagreement among measures

Methods of utility measurement disagree with each other. In health judgments, for
example, the standard-gamble and time-tradeoff methods tend to yield higher utilities
than other methods (closer to normal, farther from death) for intermediate health
states (see Baron, 1997). The standard gamble is usually highest of all. When asked
how much risk of death they will take for the sake of avoiding various conditions,
people tend to give small probabilities, which imply high utilities for the conditions.

What should we conclude from these disagreements? Scholars have proposed
many answers to this question. One general answer seems initially promising but
runs into problems when we examine it. This is the idea that different methods
measure different kinds of utility. Scholars often say that standard gambles (SGs)
measure "von Neuman-Morgenstern utility," which differs from utility measured in
other ways. This provides a simple explanation of the fact that utilities measured by
SGs differ from those measured in others. (They are higher for good outcomes that
occur with probability 1, relative to uncertain outcomes, for example.)

Similarly, we might imagine PTO utilities that differ from utilities estimated in
other ways. In all these cases, the idea is to use different utilities depending on
the kind of decision at issue. If the decision involved risk, we use utilities elicited
from SGs. If the decision involves tradeoffs across different people, we use the PTO
utility. By this proposal, each outcome has a fixed utility for each kind of decision.
Thus, once in the domain of gambles, the probabilities or alternative outcomes do
not affect the utility assigned to each outcome, and, once in the domain of tradeoffs
among people, the numbers of people and the conditions of each do not matter, just
the fact that the decision involves this kind of tradeoff.

This proposal runs into several difficulties. The main one is that utility is supposed to be a summary measure of goal achievement. It is difficult to see what goals could lead to systematic changes in utility of this sort. These changes must affect the utility of an outcome only according to the type of decision involved, and not any of the other properties of that decision. In any choice between $50 for sure and some other amount with some other probability, the utility of the $50 would have to increase by the same amount, just because it had a probability of 1 and the other outcomes did not, regardless of what these other outcomes are, or their probabilities. What sort of goals could do that? Certainly not the goals concerning how you would spend the money, because those goals are relevant only after the money is in hand.

We can imagine various other goals that might matter. Responses to SGs are clearly affected by anticipated regret and disappointment, and we have goals concerning our emotions. But, as we have seen in Chapter 11, such emotions are usually handled by treating them as outcomes in their own right. When this is done, it becomes clear that they do not simply change the utility of an outcome to some new utility, the minute we know that the outcome is sure and that other possible outcomes are uncertain. Likewise, tradeoffs among people are affected by other emotions, such as envy (Chapter 17). Again, envy would seem to depend very much on utility differences among different people. It would not simply add or subtract some amount from each outcome depending only on the outcome and whether a person tradeoff was involved. In sum, it is difficult to maintain that utility measures goal achievement, that the normative standard for decision making is to maximize the achievement of goals, and that utility (hence goal achievement) depends on the type of decision being made, with everything else held constant.

The second problem with the idea of different utilities for different methods is that we can imagine real decisions that combine the situations used in different methods. These combinations yield implausible results. For example, we can combine PTO and SGs. We can imagine gambles for which the outcomes are distributions, or distributions for which the outcomes are gambles.

Suppose we measure the SG utility of money for a group of people and find that $50 has a utility of .8, if $100 has a utillity of 1. People regard $50 for sure as equal to a .8 chance of $100. Now these people are asked about a PTO in which the choice is between giving $50 to 100 people or $100 to X people. They say that they would be indifferent if X were 60. The PTO utility of $50 is therefore .6. The same people have a linear utility function using direct judgments (DJ), so the utility of $50 is .5. In other words, to get the PTO utility of $50, we multiply the DJ utility by 1.2 (to get .6), and to get the SG utility we multiply by 1.6 (to get .8).

What happens when we now say that the outcomes of the PTO are not fixed amounts of money but gambles? In particular, the choice is now between giving 100 people a .99999 chance of winning $50 (versus nothing, if she loses) and giving Y people a .99999 chance of winning $100. To be consistent, we would have to apply the SG utilities before applying the PTO utilities. The PTO utility of $50 would now be approximately $1.2 \cdot 1.6 \cdot .5$, or .96. A subject who said that X was 60 would say that Y was 96. That is, 96 people would have to have a .99999 chance of $100 in order to make the outcome equivalent to 100 people having a .99999 chance of $50. Yet, if we simply replace .99999 with 1, then the answer suddenly changes to 60, rather than 96. The problem here is that utilities change simply because outcomes are embedded in gambles, regardless of the probabilities of the gambles. A probability of 1 is no longer a gamble. (We could, of course, extend this argument by adding 9's to the right of the decimal point as far as we like.)

A third problem is that the creation of different utilities depending on the measure can lead to framing effects, when we can describe the same decision in terms of different measures. Consider the tradeoff between 100 people getting $50 and X people getting $100. We can approximate this with a standard gamble given to all 100 people. The gamble is a choice between $50 for sure and $100 with probability P. By the assumptions we just used, P would be .8, yet X would be 60. Yet the gamble offered to each person could be exactly the mechanism by which X people win the $100, if all get the gamble. We can often describe tradeoffs across people as gambles for individuals.

Another way of stating the third problem is that decisions made according to one measure can sometimes make everyone worse off according to another measure (Kaplow and Shavell, 1999). According to the PTO, in the last example, it would be better to give everyone a gamble with a .7 chance of winning $100 than to give everyone $50. Yet the $50 is better for each person according to the standard gamble method (which we could assume to be a measure of individual utility). So, by following the results of the PTO, we make everyone worse off.

A fourth problem is that the suggested solution does not work. This is a mere fact, however. The other reasons would apply even if it worked. The solution does not work because methods of utility assessment are internally inconsistent. The internal inconsistencies also seem to have a lot to do with the disagreements between methods.

For example, we have seen (in Chapter 11) that the distortion of utilities in SG can be explained in terms of the π function of prospect theory. This produced a certainty effect, which makes the utility of money more sharply declining than it would otherwise be. The same function can explain internal inconsistencies within gambles.

The PTO shows other kinds of internal inconsistency. Subjects are unresponsive to changes in the ratios of conditions being compared. For example, a subject will say that 40 people becoming blind and deaf (BBDD) is just as bad as 100 people becoming blind (BB). The subject will also say that 20 people becoming BB is just as bad as 100 people becoming blind in one eye (B). These judgments would imply that BB is .4 as bad as BBDD, and B is .2 as bad as BB. Thus, B should be .08 as bad as BBDD. If we ask how many people becoming BBDD is as bad as 100 people becoming B, we should get an answer of 8. In this kind of task, the answers are usually much higher, for example, 16. It is impossible to know which judgment is best from this information alone, but we know the three judgments, 40, 20, and 16, are inconsistent with each other. Consistency could be restored either by moving the 40 up to 80 or the 16 down to 8, or other ways. The problem is that the judgments are not far enough apart (Ubel et al., 1996). Depending on which conditions are used, this effect could make the PTO disagree in various directions with the results of other methods.

Conclusion

It may seem that utility measurement is beset with so many problems that it is hopeless. The various methods of measurement are internally inconsistent and inconsistent with each other. There are two responses to this negative assessment. First, "compared to what?" Alternative methods of allocating resources, which rely on direct intuitive judgments about the decisions in question, are very likely even worse at maximizing true utility. We may usefully think of utility assessment as something like accounting. Accountants surely make systematic errors in evaluating net worth of a business enterprise, for example. They use simplifications that are surely wrong, but they undoubtedly come closer to the truth than the owners or stockholders would do on their own.

The second reply is that all the research on utility measurement has pointed the way to improvements and better methods. For one thing, it seems that the simpler methods — such as direct rating — have no particular disadvantage compared to the more complex methods, such as CV and the person tradeoff. For another, it seems that judgments can be improved in the course of eliciting them by the use of probes and consistency checks.

In the next chapter, we apply some of the methods of this chapter to a major type of decision analysis, involving values. The discussion of values there will also bear on the nature of the inconsistencies in value measurement.

Chapter 14

Decision analysis and values

A promising approach to the problem of measuring utility and making difficult decisions is that of multiattribute utility theory (MAUT). The idea is to separate utility into attributes. Ideally, each attribute should correspond to a goal or value that is separate from those corresponding to the other attributes. This approach allows us to consider all relevant goals in the same way. For policies for the prevention of oil spills, the prevention of the deaths of marine mammals and the saving of money for gasoline consumers are two goals. The problem is how these are to be traded off. How many sea otters for how many cents per gallon. But there are many other goals in the same decision. MAUT considers all of them at once, in the same way.

This chapter discusses the application of MAUT in decision analysis. The main issues concern the examination of values and the weighing of values against each other. So we begin with some discussion of values themselves. Values are, technically, the functions we use to assign utilities to outcomes. They are also what I have referred to as goals. They are the criteria by which we evaluate the outcomes of our decisions.

With all the inconsistency in utility described in the last chapter, we might ask whether utilities are real? Many have asked this question (for example, Fischhoff, 1991), and the idea that "preferences are constructed" has become a part of conventional wisdom. Utilities may be real but difficult to assess.

First, some of the problems that people have are the result of various heuristics or psychophysical distortions. These are peculiar to the tasks we give them. These problems might be overcome with consistency checks. Consistency checks are commonly used in decision analysis.

Second, recall from Chapter 13 the distinctions among predicted utility, decision utility, and experienced utility. Predicted utility is what we get from judgments. Decision utility is what we infer, indirectly, from asking people about hypothetical decisions. Experienced utility is the real thing. But, as I argued, some of our goals do not concern experiences, so we must broaden the concept of experienced utility to include these. We can still assume some reality. Some outcomes are better than

others for each of us, and it is sensible to speak of differences among them in the
amount of good they provide. The problems of consistency are all either in decision
utility or predicted utility. The only conclusion we are compelled to draw is that
people have difficulty judging their own good.

Fundamental versus means values

A third source of difficulty in assessing utilities lies in the useful distinction between
means values and fundamental values (Keeney, 1992). Values, again, are the criteria
that we use to evaluate outcomes. Fundamental values are those that express our most
important concerns. Means values are related to fundamental values through *beliefs*
about the extent to which our satisfying the former will satisfy the latter. If people's
beliefs about the relation between means values and the underlying fundamental values are incorrect, then their expressions of value will be invalid indicators of their
real concerns. If people are unsure of the relation between what they are asked about
and their fundamental values, they may have difficulty answering questions with reference to fundamental values. They may then either make guesses about the missing
facts or else use various heuristics to answer the questions.

For example, suppose I am asked to evaluate the saving of ten sea otters from
death in an oil spill. This event would be a means to other things that I care about: the
pain that the otters would experience; the shortening of their lives and the consequent
loss of the pleasures of existence, such as they are for sea otters; the effects on prey
and predators of sea otters; and the effect (together with other events) on the stability
of ecosystems, which in turn, is a means to the achievement of many other goals.
These *are* some of the important values I have that make me care about sea otters.
Yet I have *almost no idea* how any of these values are affected by the death of ten
sea otters in an oil spill. For example, I do not know how the otters would die, and
how much worse this death is than the normal death of sea otters. Perhaps it is no
worse at all. Perhaps they usually get eaten by sharks. A serious attempt to measure
my values for sea otter deaths would tell me some of these things I need to know. Of
course, we must make decisions even in the absence of complete information, so it is
unreasonable for me to demand that I have all the answers, even the ones that nobody
knows. But it is not unreasonable to demand that I have some expert opinions about
all the major issues.

The usual way of looking at CV and other methods of valuation bypasses questions of this sort. Economists are happy with valuation methods if they predict real
economic decisions. By this view, it does not matter whether responses reflect fundamental values. Yet, even consumer decisions can ignore these values: they are
often made on the basis of easily correctable false beliefs, such as beliefs about the
risks of eating apples that contain small amounts of Alar.

The failure to make respondents consult their fundamental values seriously may
well be the largest source of error in utility measurement as currently practiced. It is
these values that give meaning to the whole enterprise. They are precisely the reasons

why people care about sea otters or anything else. We do not need to measure values just to have a way of making decisions. We already have legislatures, courts, regulatory officials, doctors, deans, our spouses, and our own intuition for that. If methods of utility measurement have any special status compared to these other institutions, it would seem to have something to do with their ability to measure fundamental values.

The problem may sometimes be reduced by providing respondents with summaries of expert opinion. DeKay and McClelland (1996) provided respondents with summaries of various dimensions of ecological importance of endangered species. They found a shift away from more superficial attributes such as similarity to humans, which, they argued, were being used as heuristics in the absence of information about ecological effects, which was the main concern. In general, correcting people's false beliefs, when this is possible, can help them evaluate what they are asked about in terms of what they care about.

It may also be helpful to make explicit diagrams of the relation between means values and fundamental values (Keeney, 1992). I give an example of this in the next section.

Discovering values

The first and most important step in any real application of MAUT is to discover the values to consider. Ralph Kenney, in his book called *Value-Focused Thinking*, argues that this step often leads to solutions to practical problems. Discovery of values is what I have called search for goals. Chapter 12 presented evidence that people sometimes focus single-mindedly on one goal, ignoring others. The conscious search for other relevant goals can avoid this error.

Particularly important is the distinction between means values and more fundamental values. We think we value the means, but when we ask why we care about something we find a deeper goal that is actually easier to achieve. U.S. Senator Daniel Patrick Moynihan tells the story of an apparent impasse between the goal of auto-accident prevention and the goal of minimizing restrictions on drivers Moynihan (1996). The critical insight came when it was understood that accident prevention was not the fundamental goal. Rather, the main purpose of accident prevention was to prevent death and injury to people. With this realization, emphasis shifted from traffic laws and their enforcement to seat-belt laws and the safe design of cars. A diagram of values (objectives) in terms of means-ends relationships is called a *means-ends objectives* hierarchy.

We may also find it useful to break our values down into components, so that we can discover means to the achievement of each. Safe design of cars can be decomposed into ease of control, protection of occupants in a crash, and perhaps other subattributes. A diagram of fundamental values or objective, broken down this way, is called a *fundamental objectives hierarchy*.

Keeney (1992, ch. 3) lists several methods as a way to discover values:

1. Make a wish list. "If you had no limitations at all, what would your objectives be."

2. Consider the advantages and disadvantages of alternative options. These will usually correspond to objectives.

3. Look for problems and shortcomings of current alternatives. This has the same effect.

4. Think of consequences. Consider why they might be good, bad, acceptable, or unacceptable.

5. Look for goals (of the sort that are either achieved or not), constraints, and guidelines.

6. Consider different perspectives on the problem. What would someone else think?

7. Think about your own strategic objectives, the long-run fundamental values for the type of decision at issue.

8. Think of generic objectives, those that anyone would have, not just you.

9. Structure your objectives. Organize them into means-ends relationships and into a fundamental objectives hierarchy. The next example illustrates this process and how it leads to discovery of new objectives.

10. Quantify objectives. Often this will lead to the separation of one objective into two. For example, "optimizing the speed of driving" might break down into "minimize driving time" and "maximize safety."

Here is an example of a combined fundamental-objectives hierarchy and means-ends objectives hierarchy, using the method of Keeney (1992). "Parts" are analyses of the objectives and "means" are objectives that are means to others.

Objectives of hiring a new faculty member in psychology

1. Increase social good through encouraging good research
    Part 1A. Knowledge that leads to new technology
    Part 1B. Knowledge that helps people in their lives and work
    Means 1C. Get basic knowledge that leads to A and B
    Means 1D. Colleagues to help those here and improve their work
    Means 1E. Educate future researchers to do all this
        Part 1E1. Undergrads
            Means 1E1a. Research experience courses
            Means 1E1b. Independent research
            Means 1E1c. Courses to attract student interest in research
        Part 1E2. Grads
            Means 1E2a. Attract grad students

    Means 1E2a1. Have areas that are uniquely good
    Means 1E2a2. Have people doing uniquely good work
   Means 1E2b. Educate them
  Means 1F. Work in a promising field
  Means 1G. Be creative and industrious
2. Provide undergrads with beneficial understanding and knowledge
  Part 2A. Knowledge of psychology and biological basis of behavior
   Part 2A1. For application (clinical psych., medicine)
   Part 2A2. For research preparation (for the students)
   Part 2A3. For enriching knowledge of related fields
   Means 2A4. Cover field broadly
   Means 2A5. Provide research experience
  Part 2B. Knowledge of methodology and data analysis
   Part 2B1. For research in other fields
   Part 2B2. For citizenship
   Means 2B3. Provide research experience (same as 2A2)
  Part 2C. General wisdom and enlightenment
   Part 2C1. As individuals
   Part 2C2. As citizens
   Means 2C3. Present interesting point of view
   Means 2C4. Be wise and enlightened
  Means 2A. Attract educable, interested undergrads to courses
   Part 2A1. Be good teacher
   Part 2A2. Appeal to current interests
   Means 2A3. Increase prestige of Penn (media, etc.)
3. Make our lives better
  Part 3A. Good departmental citizen
  Part 3B. Good colleague
4. Help the university
  Part 4A. Attract good students
  Part 4B. Get money
   Part 4B1. Get grants (overhead)
    Means 4B1a. Do research on fundable topics
   Part 4B2. Attract donations
   Means 4B2a. Do research on popular topics
5. Improve future decision making
  Part 5A. Avoid lopsided majorities in future votes

  I wrote this as a guide to my own thinking about a decision my department was making about which fields to search in over the next five years. I showed it to a few colleagues, and they added the last point. I actually cared about this too. I was worried that, regardless of the other factors, hiring someone in the more scientific parts of psychology might make it harder to get a majority vote for a candidate directed more at "wisdom and enlightenment" (2C). When I realized this, I also realized that we had other options for dealing with this problem, such as changing the voting rules so that the scientific and wisdom parts of the department would have equal say, no matter how many members each area had. We did not do this, but my realization illustrates one of the beneficial side effects of this kind of analysis: it leads us to consider a wider range of possible options, and sometimes one of these will be better than the options in the range we were considering.

Decision analysis sometimes convince a group of people to use a framework like this to make a real decision. The process is time consuming. For our purpose, it would have required much more than the six hours of meetings that we ultimately had concerning this question (150 person-hours, not counting discussion between the meetings). For a more momentous decision, such as which departments to strengthen or weaken, the extra time might be worthwhile. It would require several steps. The initial diagram would be developed by the analyst after preliminary discussion, then presented to the group for their criticism. Everyone should agree that it includes all relevant goals, however important or unimportant they seem to each person. The idea is that people will agree on this list even if they disagree on the weight that each element should receive. This process can lead to increased agreement. It can force each member to give some consideration to goals that are important to others but that she would ignore. She would ignore them because of her single-minded concentration on only the goals most important to her. A listing of attributes is thus an antidote for single-mindedness.

The next step would be to define each attribute so that it can be measured numerically. Then the group might be able to agree on the assignment of numbers to each option (in this case, each field in which the department hire, perhaps) on each attribute. This can be done by averaging individual estimates. Such agreement is more likely when people agree on the meaning of the attributes. No agreement about their importance or weight is needed yet. Finally, each member would assign a weight to each attribute. An analysis for that member would multiply the weight by the number assigned to each option on each attribute and add up across the attributes so as to assign a utility to each option. (Later, I shall give more detailed examples of this process of multiplying and adding.) At this point, the analyses of individual members would be aggregated into an overall analysis. This could be done by averaging the weights assigned to attributes or (equivalently) the utilities assigned to options. Ordinarily, this would be done in a preliminary way, then discussed by the group, then done again.

Conjoint measurement

Before returning to multiattribute analysis, I want to step back to examine its theoretical basis in conjoint measurement. Conjoint measurement is a mathematical idea that justifies multiattribute analysis and that has also led to another method for utility assessment, called "conjoint analysis," which is discussed in Chapter 15.

Conjoint measurement deals with the situation we have been discussing, in which

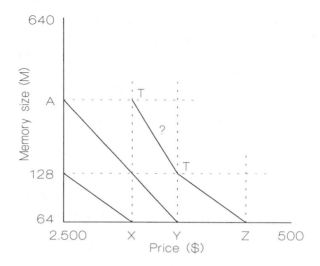

Figure 14.1: The principle of conjoint measurement of the utility of two attributes of a computer: price and memory size. (The lines connect points judged to have equal utility. The question mark indicates an equality that was inferred from the other judgments.)

outcomes can be described in terms of two or more attributes. An "attribute," in this case, is a value on a dimension. The price of a given computer, for example, is an attribute on the "price" dimension. For example, it might make sense to think of your utility for a computer as the sum of your utility for memory size and your utility for price. (The lower the price, the higher the utility. We are assuming all other attributes to be the same, in this example.) The amazing thing about the technique of conjoint measurement is that we can discover *both* utility functions simply by asking you about your preferences among suitably chosen examples of computers. The method assumes that your utility for computers is indeed the sum of the utilities on the two dimensions (price and memory), but this assumption itself can be checked.

The method is called conjoint measurement because of this magical property. It is not used as I shall describe it here. This is a theoretical justification. It is theoretically important because it justifies two other, more practical, methods. The next section describes one of these, multiattribute utility theory, and Chapter 15 describes another, called "conjoint analysis."

The basic idea of conjoint measurement is the use of one dimension to define a *quantitative unit*, which we then use to discover equal-utility intervals along the other dimension. Suppose that the range of memory size was from 64K to 640K, and the range in price was from $2,500 to $500. You can discover the utility of the money by defining a unit on the memory dimension, as shown in Figure 14.1.

Suppose you take the unit of utility as the difference between 64K and 128K. Let us call this 1 *utile*. What price is 1 utile more than $2,500? (Utility increases as price decreases.) To answer this, ask yourself at what price x you would be indifferent between 128K for $2,500 and 64K for x. You can determine x by starting with a value that is clearly too high and lowering it until you are indifferent, and then starting with a value that is clearly too low and raising it. If you encounter a range of indifference, you can choose the middle of the range as your best guess. If you are indifferent between 128K for $2,500 and 64K for x, then it would make sense to assume that $u(\$2,500) + u(128K) = u(\$x) + u(64K)$, or $u(\$x) - u(\$2,500) = u(128K) - u(64K)$. Hence, if $u(128K) - u(64K)$ is 1 utile, then $u(\$x) - u(\$2,500)$ must be 1 utile as well.

We could then mark off another utile on the price dimension by asking at what price x you would be indifferent between 128K for x and 64K for y. For the next utile, we could ask at what price z you would be indifferent between 128K for y and 64K for z, and so on.

Once we have defined 1 utile on the price dimension, we can then use *this* unit to mark off steps on the memory dimension in the same way. For example, we can ask at what memory size A you would be indifferent between A at $2,500 and 128K at x. In theory, the method of conjoint measurement is like the method of differences, except that the differences compared are on various attributes instead of a single attribute.[1]

Once we have gone this far, we ought to be able to check what we have done by asking about the two points labeled T in Figure 14.1. We ought to be indifferent between these two points: A for x and 128K for y. This condition is called the *Thomsen condition* (Krantz, Luce, Suppes, and Tversky, 1971, ch. 6). In order for this scaling method to work, it must be satisfied for all sets of points of this form. The Thomsen condition serves as a check on this method, just as monotonicity does on the difference method.

When there are three or more dimensions, we can replace the Thomsen condition with a simpler condition, called *independence*[2] This means that the tradeoff between any two dimensions does not depend on the level of a third. For example, if you are indifferent between 128K for $2,500 and 64K for $2,000 when the computer has a 10-megabyte hard disk, you will still be indifferent between 128K for $2,500 and 64K for $2,000 when you have a 30-megabyte hard disk. The tradeoff between money and memory is not affected by the size of the hard disk. This condition ensures that the contribution of each dimension to overall utility will be the same, regardless of the levels of other dimensions.

[1] In practice, the method of conjoint measurement can be applied to data in which judges simply express a large number of preferences among pairs of options spread throughout the space in Figure 14.1. The analyst then *infers* the equivalent intervals from these preferences (Tversky, 1967; Keeney and Raiffa, 1976). This is the basis of conjoint analysis, discussed in Chapter 15.

[2] Independence implies the Thomsen condition(Keeney and Raiffa, 1976, sec. 3.5.3). The term "independence" has been used for a variety of conditions, each of which may imply different types of measurement (von Winterfeldt and Edwards, 1986, chs. 8–9). It is also analogous to the sure-thing principle, if we look at states as dimensions of choices. The probability of a state corresponds exactly to the weight of the dimension in MAUT.

MAUT as a type of decision analysis

Conjoint measurement is one of the more amazing "rabbit out of the hat" tricks that mathematicians have been able to show us in utility theory. It provides the theoretical basis for MAUT. Like other forms of decision analysis, MAUT is based on the idea expressed in the motto "Divide and conquer." In this case, the division is into *psychologically independent attributes*: that is, attributes that the decision maker views as being separate and independent. If the dimensions are indeed independent, proper application of MAUT ensures that the decision made will maximize the achievement of our goals. The attribute on each dimension determines the extent to which we achieve the goal corresponding to that dimension, so we can measure the utility of each option on each dimension and add up the utilities on the various dimensions in order to determine the total utility of the option.

If the attributes in the particular decision do not seem to be psychologically independent from the outset, MAUT, in its basic form, has no normative status and should not be attempted. For example, suppose you were using MAUT to decide which computer to buy, and the three dimensions were price, memory size, and hard-disk size. If you regarded these three dimensions as independent, you could use a MAUT analysis. You might think that a large memory makes disk size less important, however, so that you would be willing to pay less extra money for a large disk if the computer had a large memory than if it had a small memory. In this case, the size of the memory would affect the tradeoff between price and disk size. If you tried to use disk size to measure the utility units for price, you would get different results for different memory sizes. You need not go through the whole MAUT analysis to determine whether this is the case. You can just ask yourself directly whether this would occur.

It is also important to make sure that the dimensions really refer to different things. For example, it would not be helpful to add a fourth dimension, "ease of use," to your analysis, because ease of use is affected by memory and disk size. If you did this, you would be counting the effects of memory and disk size more than once. A suitable new dimension would be "keyboard layout."

Although conjoint measurement provides the theoretical basis for MAUT, you do not have to use conjoint measurement to estimate the utilities for a MAUT analysis. Once you have established that the dimensions are independent, you can use any of the measurement techniques described in the last section: difference measurement, direct rating, or any other method, on one attribute at a time.

Suppose you have found that the three dimensions of the computer really are independent for you. You assign a utility of 100 to the most desirable end of each dimension, and 0 to the least desirable end. Suppose that you gather data on four different models, organized as in Table 14.1, with the utilities *on each dimension* shown in parentheses. You cannot simply add up the utilities for each model and compare them to decide among them. If you do, model B will win, but perhaps you do not care very much about memory size. If price is more important to you, you will want model A; if disk size is more important, you will want model C. To use

Table 14.1: Values of 3 attributes for each of 4 computers (with utilities in parentheses).

Model	Memory (Kbytes)		Disk size (Mbytes)		Price	
A	64K	(0)	100M	(0)	$500	(100)
B	640K	(100)	200M	(50)	$1,500	(50)
C	64K	(0)	300M	(100)	$2,500	(0)
D	640K	(100)	200M	(50)	$2,500	(0)

MAUT, you need to determine the *relative* importance of the dimensions.

It is important to understand what is involve here. One way to think about it is to suppose that the difference between the top and bottom of one of the dimension has the greatest effect on the achievement of your goals. Suppose it is price. This means that you would rather pay $500 for a computer with a 100M disk than $2,500 for one with a 300M disk. The price difference is more important to you. Likewise, you would rather pay $500 for 64K of memory than $2,500 for 640K. So the utility difference between $500 and $2,500 is larger than the difference between the top and bottom end of either dimension. Suppose we use the price dimension to define the units of utility. So $500 has utility 100 on the price dimension and $2,500 has 0. You could now rate all the other dimensions on the same scale. You might judge, for example, that, if a 100M disk has a utility of 0, then a 300M disk has a utility of 50. But you have assigned ratings to the disk-size scale so that 300M has a utility of 100 rather than 50. Thus, you must correct for the fact that you used a different scale. You must divide the utility of disk size by 2, in order to make it comparable. This is like translating from one currency to another, or from inches to centimeters, or Fahrenheit to Celsius. This is what we mean when we talk about the relative weight of disk size compared to price. It is simply a correction for the fact that you rated each dimension on a 0–100 scale. You might have used the same scale for everything, but you didn't.[3]

There are many ways to determine relative weight (von Winterfeldt and Edwards, 1986). Conjoint measurement is only one of them. Another, simpler way is to determine your scale for each attribute and to estimate the utility of the extreme of the scale for one attribute on the scale for another attribute. For example, suppose that price is more important than disk size. You could ask yourself, "How much more than $500 would I pay in order to replace a 100-megabyte disk with a 300-megabyte disk?" Suppose the answer is "$1,000 more," so that the total cost is $1,500. You have now found that the scale for disk size should be weighed half as much as the money scale, for the difference between the two ends of it equals only the difference

---

[3]It is usually better *not* to use the same scale, especially when several people are involved. People usually agree more about the assignment of values on a dimension than about the relative weights of dimensions.

between $500 and $1,500, a utility difference of 50 on the price scale.

Suppose you find, on the other hand, that the memory scale is equal to the disk-size scale, so that you are indifferent between a 640K memory with 100-megabyte hard disk and 64K memory with a 300-megabyte disk. Then the memory scale would also get half as much weight as the price scale. To compute the total utility of each model, you would multiply the memory and disk-size utilities by .5 before adding them. (Equivalently, you could multiply the price utility by 2. This would just change the units.) This would yield utilities of 100, 125, 50, and 75 for the four models, respectively. Your analysis would tell you to choose model B after all.

Notice that when you determine the weight of the scales, you need to know what the ends of the scales are. Unless you know the ends, you cannot ask yourself whether the range in memory size is more important than the range in price, or vice versa, and this is the question that you must answer. If the price range is only from $1,500 to $1,600, for example, price would not be very important.

Questions about the relative weights of attributes are not like the usual questions often seen in opinion surveys, which take the form "Which is more important, reducing crime or reducing air pollution?" Such questions do not tell us how much crime and how much pollution are involved in the decision at hand. If policy makers knew that a reduction from 2,000 to 1,900 robberies per year was just as good as a reduction of pollution from 100% to 90% of the maximum allowable level, they could decide how to allocate funds so as to do the most good. If they could reduce air pollution from 100% to 90% for the same cost as reducing robberies from 2,000 to 1,950, they should choose the former. But we do not know what citizens mean when they say that "crime is more important." The reason we need to know the ranges when we compare attributes is so that we can translate the units. If the "robbery attribute" ranged from 2,000 to 1,000, and if someone said that a reduction in pollution from 100% to 90% was 10% of this range, then we would have a good idea how to use that judgment in making decisions. In essence, we convert these measures to a common scale. If we want to measure with money, we convert all the different currencies to a common currency using their rates of exchange. If we want to measure with utility, we must convert to a common scale of utility, and we must determine these rates of exchange.

The attributes or dimensions in a multiattribute analysis work best if each of them corresponds to a fundamental goal or objective (Keeney, 1992). In many analyses, as discussed earlier, each attribute is decomposed into subattributes. For example, in an analysis concerning pollution control, "effects on health" can be decomposed into "causing new cases of chronic lung disease" and "causing temporary coughs and breathing difficulties." Each of these subattributes can be further specified or decomposed; for example, chronic disease can be decomposed into lung cancer, emphysema, asthma, and other diseases. Note that each subattribute corresponds to a *part* of the goal of minimizing harm to health.

It is sometimes also useful to consider *subgoals*, in the sense of Chapter 1, such as minimizing pollution from small airborne particles. Such a subgoal provides a means to the end of minimizing health effects. The trouble with such subgoals is that their relation to the fundamental goals depends on facts (as best determined by expert opinion). If minimizing particles is important because of its effects on health, then expert knowledge is required in order for us to know the health benefits of a given reduction in particles. We therefore need such knowledge in order to assign a meaningful value to particle reduction in comparison with other attributes.

If such subgoals are excluded, we can often specify a full set of attributes for a given type of decision. Each attribute is defined in terms of a best and worst value. The weight of the attribute relative to other attributes is determined from its best-to-worst range. For example, suppose that we are comparing health effects to tax increases. We might consider each health effect separately. If the range of lung cancer cases caused by pollution is from 0 to 100 per year in a given region, and the range of property tax increases is from 0% to 5%, we can ask about the relative importance of these two ranges. We might judge that it is worth a 3% tax increase to prevent 100 cases of lung cancer. (Information about the number of taxpayers and the average amount now paid would of course be relevant.) If the utility functions for cancer and taxes were assumed to be linear, then we would conclude that preventing lung cancer has a weight that is 60% of the weight of preventing tax increases. The weight of "tax increases" relative to "health effects" will depend on the range of each attribute. If the range of tax increases were 0% to 2%, then cancer would be more important. Note especially that it makes no sense to ask, "Which is more important, keeping taxes down or preventing cancer?", unless we have a range of effects in mind.

Once a full set of attributes is specified and their weights provided, subsequent decisions can be analyzed. To do this, we need to know the effects of each option on each attribute. This information can be provided by expert judgment. Expert judgment is not normally required, however, to determine the values or goals of interest and their relative weights. Such an analysis can use public representatives or typical members of the public, for example.

Keeney (1992) describes many ways in which specifying attributes, utility functions, and weights can lead to insights about values or goals. For example, in considering various taxes, we might discover that taxes on businesses and individuals are not independent when a third dimension such as health effects is included. In particular, the level of personal taxes may be more important relative to health when business taxes are low than when they are high. Further examination may reveal that we care not only about the absolute level of taxes but also about the fairness of spreading the tax burden between businesses and individuals. Thus, we are more willing to raise the taxes of one group when the other group is already getting a large tax increase. An additional attribute — equity — may then be included in the analysis.

As an exercise, you might try applying MAUT to a personal decision, such as which apartment to rent, or to a public policy question. A good example of a policy question is the optimal speed limit for motor vehicles. The speed limit affects a number of different dimensions, such as property damage from accidents, injury and death from accidents, gasoline use, pollution, speed of transportation for goods, and speed of transportation for individuals. You do not need to look up the data to see how such an analysis would work. You might try a holistic estimate first, in which you simply give your opinion. Then use your own best guesses for the effect of different speed limits on the various dimensions, and give your own utilities for the dimensions.

MAUT can be modified considerably for the analysis of real decisions. For example, suppose you have one usable eye, and it has a cataract that your doctor must eventually remove. You must decide whether to have the cataract removed now or wait a month. Your vision is getting slowly worse. A successful operation will restore your vision fully, but a failure will leave you blind. The probability of failure is something your doctor can tell you. What you need is an estimate of the relative utility — for the next month — of the three possible outcomes: restored vision, blindness, and your present vision (assuming that it does not change over the course of the month). How can you think about this? One way is to think of the various activities that you can do given some outcome but not another. The activities should be separate and independent. For example, you cannot count both "reading" and "doing your job," if your job involves reading. (You can count "reading for pleasure.") You can assign utilities to these activities by finding groups of them that are equivalent.

Suppose that there are ten activities, all with the same utility. Nine are activities you can do now but would not be able to do if you were blind, but there is one you cannot do now but would be able to do if your vision were restored. If we assign a utility of 100 to restored vision and 0 to blindness, the utility of your present condition is 90. You should have the operation now if the probability of success is greater than .90, since its expected utility would then be at least $.90 \cdot 100 + .10 \cdot 0$, or 90. Of course, after doing an analysis like this, you could decide that the activities were not independent after all, because the loss of the ability to engage in one of them would be much worse if it were the only one left than if there were other alternatives. Nonetheless, an analysis of this sort could help you to think about your decision in a new way. If you repeated this process month after month, eventually you would reach a point at which the activities you would gain back from success would be worth the risk of failure.

Table 14.2 shows another example of a multiattribute analysis. The question is to choose a birth control method. This too is a repeated decision. Let us assume it is made once a year, so the decision concerns the effect of using one method or another for a year. The particular analysis into attributes is one of many ways to do this. A unique feature is the separation of AIDS risk from risk of other sexually transmitted diseases. Some attributes are omitted, such as cost, religious issues, reversibility, and health *benefits*, such as the reduction in the risk of some cancers later in life that results from hormonal methods (pills, Norplant). Many methods are not included, such as Depo Provera, sterilization, the "ryhthm method" and combinations of condom use with hormonal methods.

In order to assign weights to the attributes, we need to know their ranges. Here is how they are defined, in order from left to right:

Table 14.2: Abbreviated decision analysis for birth control

	HIV prev.	STD prev.	Hlth. risk	Preg. prev.	Easy use	Sex pleas.	TOTAL UTIL.
IUD	0	0	0	96	50	100	196.8
Pill	0	0	50	94	80	100	247.2
Norplant	0	0	0	99	100	100	219.2
Condom	99	99	90	84	0	90	377.7
Diaphr.	0	0	90	82	0	95	232.6
None	0	0	90	15	100	100	224.0
Abstain	100	100	100	100	100	0	350.0
WEIGHT	1.00	.50	.80	.80	.40	1.00	

HIV Prevention Range is 0 to 1 in 1,000 chance of infection per year.

STD Prevention Diseases include: chlamydia (pelvic inflammatory disease, which can cause future ectopic pregnancy or infertility); gonorrhea (pain when urinating, in men, and other minor discomfort, sterility in women, arthritis, and blindness in babies who catch it before birth if untreated); syphilis (sore, flu-like symptoms, blindness, paralysis, severe brain damage, birth defects if untreated); genital herpes (sores, recurrent, incurable, affect infants). All except the last are easily cured. The range here is from no protection to perfect protection, for mutually monogamous relationships. We have assumed that the worst case for no protection is a 50% chance of some STD per year.

Health risk. 0 represents unpleasant (and usually short-term) side effects such as irregular menstrual bleeding (the most severe of the common side effects).

Pregnancy prevention. 0 represents the certainty of getting pregnant. Other numbers reflect failure rates per year when used correctly.

Easy use. 100 is nothing to do. 0 is as bad as putting on a condom or inserting a diaphragm. This could have been broken into parts corresponding to use near the time of sex and other things done in advance, such as minor surgery in the case of Norplant. These have been collapsed.

Sexual pleasure. This is present mainly because of abstention as an option, but some methods may reduce pleasure for some people.

   The weights are filled in, but they would vary from person to person. With the weights assigned, condom use is the best, and abstention is second best. Obviously, that is because the risk of AIDS and other STDS combined is more important than having sex at all. This can be true even though the question of birth control might not come up except for the attribute of preventing *pregnancy*. The "reason" for making a decision in the first place need not be the main consideration in choosing among the options at hand.

   If you were to determine the weights for yourself, you would first pick the most important attribute range and then compare other ranges to that. You can pick the most important range in two ways. First, you might just ask yourself which is more important, the difference between the top and bottom of one range (as you have defined the top and bottom) or the difference between the top and bottom of another. Second, you could make up a hypothetical decision, for example, between two methods that were *identical* except that one was as good as abstention on preventing pregnancy (100) and as bad as pills at preventing STDs (0), and the other was as good as abstention at preventing STDs (100) and led to certain pregnancy (0). When you do this, it is important to realize that the two methods are hypothetical and are identical in all other respects. In thinking about pregnancy, you might want to think about how you would respond to pregnancy. Would you have an abortion if you or your partner were pregnant now? Or would you plan to have the baby?

There are also two ways to determine weights. First, you could use the direct judgment method. How big is the difference between the top and bottom of the smaller range, compared to the difference between the top and bottom of the larger range (or vice versa)? Second, you could adjust the top of the larger range (or the bottom) so that the two ranges are equal. (You can't always do this.) For example, if pregnancy prevention is more important than STD prevention, lower the maximum of the pregnancy prevention dimension until the two ranges are equal. If it is 80 (20% chance of pregnancy), then the STD dimension gets a weight of .80 relative to pregnancy dimension. You can put this in the context of a hypothetical decision if you find that helpful, for example, between two methods that are identical except that one has a value of X on preventing pregnancy and 0 on preventing STDs, and the other has a value of 100 on preventing STDs and leads to certain pregnancy (0). What value of X would make you indifferent?

Finally, complete the analysis by multiplying the attribute utility by the weight and summing across rows. For condom, the sum is $1.00 \cdot 99 + .50 \cdot 99 + .80 \cdot 90 + .80 \cdot 84 + .40 \cdot 0 + 1.00 \cdot 90 = 377.7$. The numbers, of course, are arbitrary.

One interesting feature of this analysis is the treatment of AIDS risk. Rather than defining the bottom end of the dimension as getting AIDS, this analysis uses an estimate of the risk of AIDS for a particular person. It is quite possible that the weight given to AIDS is too high because the judge did not properly discount the risk of AIDS for its low probability. If the analysis had defined the bottom of this dimension as AIDS for sure, then the weight of this dimension would have to increase by a factor of 1,000. But the values of the various methods on the dimension would then range from 99.9 to 100 instead of from 0 to 100.

Test your understanding. Would it matter if the values ranged from 0 to .1 instead of from 99.9 to 100 (assuming that abstinence was always assigned the highest value)?[4] What would we do with someone who had the same values but a much lower risk of AIDS?[5]

Decision analysis is often applied to decisions that are difficult because the options appear to be close in utility or expected utility. This appearance is often cor-

---

[4]No. It would just lower all the utilities by a constant.

[5]If the risk were .0001 instead of .001, then we could either divide the weight by 10 or have the values range from 90 to 100 instead of 0 to 100.

rect. A disturbing fact of life is that options are often equally good, insofar as we can determine their goodness, even when the decisions are important and when great uncertainties are present. Von Winterfeldt and Edwards (1986) refer to such situations as "flat maxima" because, when expected utility is plotted as a function of some attribute (for example, the amount of money invested in a project), the function typically does not have a sharp peak: Within a fairly large range, the value on the attribute does not make much difference. Once we determine that we are in such a situation, it is perhaps best not to agonize and to reserve our agonizing for situations in which we can still learn something about which option is best (Elster, 1989b).[6]

Rules and tradeoffs

When it comes to matters of public policy or major personal decisions, some people regard MAUT with a certain suspicion (Schwartz, 1986). MAUT seems to require that people make tradeoffs they think should not be made. For example, some people think that it is wrong to "trade off" human life for anything. They claim to want to follow this rule: Human life comes before anything else — before any other dimension or any other consideration.

Taken literally, they are saying that the weight of the human-life dimension is infinite relative to all other dimensions, so that any two policies (for example, about the speed limit) must be evaluated first on that dimension and then on other dimensions only if they are equal on that one. Such rules are called *lexical rules*, because they give a list of the *order* in which different issues are considered (a "lexicon" is a dictionary, an ordered list). A lexical rule for buying cars might say that reliability comes first and that only when two cars are equally reliable should style be considered. A couple might decide that the wife's job takes priority. Some people try to follow lexical moral rules: "Never kill anyone, except in war or self-defense"; "Never lie"; "Never break the law"; "Never eat pork (unless you are starving)." Notice that exceptions are allowed, but they are spelled out in advance, as part of the rule. When the exception is absent, the rule takes priority over everything else.

Alternatively, when we make *tradeoffs*, we take into account the magnitude of each competing consideration in the case at hand. We may consider a car's reliability to be more important than its style, but if we think the Fiat is *almost* as reliable as the Toyota but *much* more attractive, we will take the Fiat. If Yale is almost as good for the wife as Princeton and is also much better than Princeton for the husband, Yale will probably be chosen. A person who tells "white lies" to save the feelings of others (for example) might have to weigh the possible damage caused by telling the truth against the possible damage that results from telling the lie.

Many of the most controversial and difficult issues that we face as individuals and as a society involve the conflict between tradeoffs and rules. We know, for example, that air pollution kills people (through disease) but that curbing air pollution

---

[6] At this point, it might be useful to carry out a decision analysis of a decision in your own life, using MAUT.

costs money. How much money should be spent, to save how many lives? If we follow a rule that life is more important than anything else, we could end up spending enormous amounts of money. To take another example, we believe in basic human rights, but in some countries governments have argued that certain rights must be denied to preserve the stability of the state. Again, many of us believe that in personal relationships love ought to "conquer all," yet we are often faced with choices that put romance in jeopardy for the sake of one person's job or education.

People who think they want to follow lexical rules, no matter what, may, after reflecting, find that in fact they simply have a very high *subjective weight* for one dimension as opposed to another. They do not really think that one dimension has absolute priority. Consider the claim that life should come before everything else. Suppose that a health insurance company (in determining what treatments its policies will cover) has a choice of saving the life of Mr. Smith by paying for a heroic operation that will cost millions of dollars or else paying for treatment to cure arthritis in 1 million policyholders. (I pick arthritis because it is painful but not usually life threatening.) If we wanted to put life ahead of everything else, we might still balk and decide to pay for Mr. Smith's operation. Now let us suppose, however, that the success of the operation is not a certainty but rather a probability (p). Suppose that p were .001. Would we still prefer the operation? What if p were .000001? It seems that there must be a value of p sufficiently small so that our preference would switch. If such a value of p exists (above 0), then we are, in fact, willing to trade off the two attributes at issue — life and pain. That is, we are willing to say that some finite interval on the pain scale is equivalent to a nonzero interval on the life scale. The nonzero interval on the life attribute is just the interval between no change at all and a p probability of saving a life. This interval is equivalent to (or less than) the interval between the status quo and the arthritis cure, on the pain scale.

Some of our resistance to the idea of making tradeoffs is caused by our attachment to certain *prescriptive* rules of decision making. Lexical rules may prevent us from sliding down *slippery slopes*, in which one decision, justified in its own right, sets a precedent for similar decisions that are not well justified. A decision analysis might tell an official, for example, that the gain from taking a small bribe is greater than the harm that this single act would cause. The slippery-slope rule would tell the official, however, that accepting one bribe might be like trying cocaine "once"; it might become a habit, and then the harm would be much greater. Similarly, people argue that if we allow life to be sacrificed for one reason (mercy killing, for example), we might be more willing to allow it to be taken for other reasons (lack of enforcement of safety regulations, for example).

Instead of invoking the slippery-slope rule, I would argue that the decision analysis that led to taking the bribe was seriously incomplete, because it ignored a major consequence of the choice in question, namely, its effect on later decisions about bribes. Therefore, we do not need the "slippery-slope" argument, if we do a thorough analysis. Also, when we decide to favor one dimension (or goal), such as life, we are always ignoring some other dimension, such as pain, and that bias could lead us down a slippery slope as well. If we insist on taking small chances to save lives when we could be curing pain instead, we might become callous to pain. Slippery slopes can work both ways. To neglect this fact is to fail to be sensitive to evidence on both sides of the question.

Nonetheless, lexical rules can be useful prescriptive devices for self-control. As a rule of thumb, it may be helpful to us to think that certain things always "come before" others — but it is difficult to justify such rules as normative in decision making (Baron, 1986).

The value of human life

Governments must often make decisions that involve a tradeoff between money and human life. Lives are saved by regulation of motor vehicle safety, workplace safety, pharmaceutical sales, nuclear power plant operation, and release of chemicals into the environment. In each of these cases, additional lives could be saved if regulations were strengthened, but more money would be spent by businesses and government agencies. Money could also be saved by weakening the regulations, but more deaths would result. Individuals and insurance companies must make the same tradeoff in deciding whether to purchase additional safety, whether that takes the form of new tires for the family car or a costly medical test that is unlikely to discover anything wrong. How much should be spent to save one human life?

To some, the need for consistency implies that this question has an answer. It seems inconsistent to spend $6 million on a heroic medical procedure to save one life when we could save another life for only $1,000 by vaccinating more children against measles. But inconsistency of this sort may not be a useful guide to decision making. If we can redirect the $6 million to saving six thousand lives instead of one life, that is surely better (other things being equal). If, however, redirecting the $6 million is not an option, then it is not necessarily wrong to spend this on one life. If we do not have a better option, the existence of hypothetical better options is irrelevant. It therefore matters who the decision maker is. An individual physician in private practice cannot direct his patients, or their insurers, to donate money for vaccination in the Third World instead of lung transplants in the United States, even if vaccination saves more lives per dollar than transplants. A government might be able to do this through law, but at the risk of not staying in power to do other good things. Consistency, then, is not the only virtue here.

On the other hand, it may sometimes be useful to attempt to measure the monetary value of human life for certain purposes. For example, the U.S. government sets standards for chemicals in the environment and for food additives. It has been argued that some of these regulations are so costly and ineffective that weakening them could save tens of millions of dollars per life or more, while strengthening other regulations could save lives for a few thousand dollars each (Breyer, 1993; Tengs et al., 1995). The government has the power to bring these regulations into line by specifying a fixed cost per life and then imposing regulations only when the cost of the regulations per life saved is less than that cost (assuming no other effects of the regulation).

Several methods have been used to set a monetary value for life (Schelling, 1968). The most sensible measures are based on the measurement of willingness to pay for reductions in the probability of death (or to accept money for taking risk).[7] For example, if you were exposed to a virus that had a .000001 chance of causing sudden and painless death within a week, how much would you pay now for the cure (if this were your only chance to buy it)? Risk is used because it does not make much sense to ask people how much they would pay to avoid being killed. In this case, if you said that you would pay $10, an estimate of the value you place on your life would be $10/.000001, or $10 million. *only is utility Linear*

Jones-Lee (1989) reviewed a variety of (mostly British) studies of willingness to pay. Some of these studies looked at the effect of job-related risk on wages. Others asked people explicitly, in a great variety of ways, how much they were willing to pay for a certain reduction in the yearly probability of death (from a particular cause, or in general). The various measures showed surprising agreement: The value of life was on the order of $1 million (as opposed to $100,000 or $10 million).

In decision analyses concerning money and life, adjustments are often made to take into account the changing value of life as a function of the age of those affected, as in the use of QALYs (described earlier in this chapter). Comparison of two treatment choices is made in terms of the number of years of life that each choice leads to, with a correction for the quality of the life, a life of pain being counted as some fraction of a life without pain. By this sort of analysis, coronary bypass surgery may be worth its cost largely because it improves the quality of life, not because it lengthens life very much.

A disturbing fact that emerges in most studies of the value of life is that life is worth more to the rich than to the poor. This need not mean what it seems to mean, however. Our concern here is not with the ultimate value of life but rather with the tradeoff between life and money. The root fact may be, then, not that life is worth *less* to the poor but, rather, that money is worth *more*, in utility terms. This follows from the principle of declining marginal utility. In the virus example just described, suppose that a very rich person and a poor person were give a choice between the cure and $10,000. The rich person would take the cure, because it seems worth at least $10,000, given that he does not need the money much for anything else. The poor person might well prefer the money, thinking of what else could be bought with it that is so sorely needed. Of course, it may *also* be true that the lives of the rich are truly better than the lives of the poor, but the differing value of life may be understood in terms of the value of money alone. One implication of this fact is that a given level of government regulation of safety might be too little for the rich but too much for the poor. The rich might want to buy more safety on their own. The poor might prefer that the money be given to them rather than spent on their safety.

Life may also change its value as a function of age and life expectancy. The last

[7]Less sensible methods are based on such indices as production (which makes retired people worthless) or the value of a person to others (which neglects the desire of a person to live).

chapter discussed the idea of quality adjusted life years (QALYs) as a measure of the utility of a medical intervention. By this standard, the death of a person who has a long life expectancy is a greater loss than the death of a person with a short life expectancy. And such a standard is not unreasonable. Your life has value to you — at least in part — because of what you do with it. In general, the longer your life, the more you can do.

What about infants? They have the longest life expectancy of all, on the average, but it can be argued that their death is less serious that that of an older child or an adult. Singer (1993) carries out a kind of multiattribute analysis (although he doesn't call it that) of the value of human life itself. He argues for three main attributes. One concerns experiences, the second concerns personhood — the other things that make human beings special, such as plans, projects, and ongoing relationships with other people — and the third concerns the values the people have for other people's lives, including those that arise from their personal attachments to each other. Infants, non-human animals, and some severely debilitated adult humans lack personhood attributes to some degree. Life for them has value largely because of the experiences it contains. It makes sense to add these up over time. When a normal adult dies, however, more is lost than the stream of future experiences. The persons plans, projects, and relationships are disrupted. This affects the second and third attributes. For infants, the third attribute — the attachment of the parents — is typically involved as well, but not the second. We could thus think of the value of life as rising with increasing age during childhood and then falling again in adulthood, as life expectancy becomes shorter.

In sum, estimates of the monetary value of life are at best crude approximations. The true tradeoff between money and life depends on the duration and quality of the life in question, the age of the person, and also on the feasible alternative uses of the money. If the money to save lives will be taken from expenditures on education for the poor, then life might have a lower value than if the money came from a tax on fountain pens costing over $1,000.

Teaching decision analysis

Decision analysis has been taught routinely to business and medical students and to military officers for several years. Training in basic decision analysis is sometimes included as part of courses in thinking (see Wheeler, 1979). Although few formal evaluations of the effectiveness of decision-making courses have been made, word-of-mouth reports suggest that students of expected-utility theory or MAUT seldom use these methods later in their decision making, unless they become professionals in the field. The study of formal methods, however, may help these students to avoid many of the errors that characterize informal decision making in others. It may also help them understand formal analyses carried out by others, even when these are only reported in the press.

We have evidence that it is possible to teach decision making to children and adolescents. For example, Kourilsky and Murray (1981) reported on a program designed to teach "economic reasoning" to fifth- and sixth-grade children, in part in the classroom and in part through a seminar for parents. Economic reasoning essentially involves making tradeoffs among potential outcomes, considering what one might do with the money other than spend it impulsively. The program increased the use of economic reasoning by parents and children, and they were reported to be satisfied with the economic decisions that they made.

Feehrer and Adams wrote a curriculum for a unit in decision making as part of an eighth-grade program designed to increase intelligence (Adams, 1986). The curriculum deals with the analysis of decisions into possible choices and their probable consequences, consequences that differ in likelihood. Students are encouraged to trade off probability and utility informally, are taught to gather information that will improve probability estimates, and are urged to evaluate information for relevance and credibility. The curriculum also addresses tradeoffs among attributes, in the form of "preference tables." All of the examples are based on detective stories. Other approaches are reviewed in Baron and Brown (1991).

A promising approach to teaching decision making to such students is to give additional emphasis to the types of errors that people make in the absence of decision analysis, such as shortsightedness (Chapter 19); single-mindedness (neglect of relevant goals); impulsiveness (failure to consider alternatives and evidence); and neglect of probability. This emphasis both explains why formal analysis is sometimes useful and also warns the students against the errors themselves. In addition, instruction might be given in heuristics designed to avoid these errors, heuristics that are useful both in informal thinking about decisions and in the construction of a formal analysis. Examples are: "Think about the precedent-setting effect of a choice, as well as the direct effect"; "Ask whether there are future effects"; "Consider alternatives." A useful instructional technique is to discuss a decision and then, as impulsive solutions are suggested ask the class what might be wrong with the idea. It usually turns out to be one of the errors in question (for example, failing to consider alternatives or relevant goals).

Conclusion

Decision analysis would not be useful if our intuitive decisions were always the best. Sometimes decision analysis is useful because it simply gives us another way to think about decisions, even when we do not carry out the whole analysis formally. For example, knowing something about decision analysis can help us see that unintended but foreseeable outcomes of our choices — such as the health-protection benefits of birth-control methods (which are used primarily to prevent pregnancy) — can be important. Decision analysis can also help us to avoid certain systematic errors. These are the concern of the next few chapters. The best option is sometimes a risky one, so it may lead to a poor outcome as well as a good one. The next chapter concerns decisions under risk, and the following chapter, decisions under certainty.

Chapter 15

Quantitative judgment

Quantitative judgment is the evaluation of cases on the basis of a set of evidence and with respect to a set of criteria. Some judgments involve assigning numbers: for example, assigning grades to students' essays, salaries to employees, or sales quotas to sales people. Quantitative judgments can involve ranking people or things: ranking entrants in a beauty contest, applicants for graduate school (to be accepted in order of rank as places become available), or applicants for a job. In some cases, the judgment is basically a matter of determining whether a person or thing is above or below some cutoff point. For example, is this patient sufficiently depressed so as to require hospitalization? Quantitative judgment, then, consists of *rating*, assigning numbers or grades; *ranking*, putting things in order on some dimension; and *classifying*, which in this chapter will mean assigning something to one of two groups.

When we judge livestock, paintings, or automobiles with a view to purchasing, our judgment of each item provides input to a decision that will select one or more of these items. We can think of quantitative judgment as part of a decision process in which each option is first evaluated separately, and the final decision is based on a comparison of the evaluations. (Other decisions might be made by looking only at differences among options.)

In most experiments on judgment, subjects are presented with evidence about attributes of each option and are asked to evaluate each option. For example, subjects might be given a student's test scores, grades, and disposable income and asked to judge the student's worthiness for a scholarship on a 100-point scale. Or the subjects might evaluate a car on the basis of its price, safety record, handling, and other features. Typically the subjects use their goals, so we can infer their utilities from their responses. Judgment tasks are thus another way of eliciting judgments of utility, and we shall discuss that application in this chapter. The study of judgment is closely related to Multiattribute Utility Theory (MAUT) (discussed in Chapter 14). In most judgment tasks that have been studied, the cases to be judged can be described in terms of a set of attributes, just as if MAUT were going to be applied.

Some judgment experiments have the same form but use goals other than the

Table 15.1: Measures used in regression example

Abbreviation	Definition
GPA	High school grade point average on a scale from 0 to 4.0.
SAT	Total Scholastic Aptitude Test score on a scale up to 1600.
REC	A rating summarizing the letters of recommendation on a scale from 1 to 5. This rating is assigned by an admissions officer who reads the letters of recommendation and assigns the number. (Notice that here a judgment is used as input for another judgment.)
ESS	A rating of the student's own essay on a 1 to 5 scale.

subjects' own. We can even ask the subjects to predict some objective criterion. This procedure may involve many of the same processes as evaluation, so we discuss it here too.

A major question in the study of judgment concerns the relative efficacy of unaided holistic judgment — in which the judge simply assigns a number to each case — and judgment aided by the use of calculations, like those done in MAUT. The answers to this question have strong implications for decision making in government, business, and the professions, and in any situation where important decisions are made about a number of cases described on the same dimensions.

Multiple linear regression

Most of the literature on judgment has looked at situations in which each of a number of possibilities, such as applicants for college, is characterized by several numbers. Each number represents a value on some dimension, or *cue*, such as grades or quality of recommendations. The judge's task is to evaluate each possibility with respect to some goal (or goals), such as college grades as a criterion of success in college. Each dimension or cue has a high and low end with respect to the goal. For example, high test scores are assumed to be better than low test scores. In these situations a certain kind of normative model is assumed to apply, specifically, a statistical model called *multiple linear regression* (or just *regression*, for short).

Suppose that we are admissions officers at a college, and our task is to rate several applicants. For each applicant, we have the numerical ratings, scores and other information given in Table 15.1. Suppose also that we have a computer, and we want to discover a formula for predicting the applicant's *college* grade-point average, which we call COL.

We have data on a number of students who are now at the college. For each student, we know the four variables given in the table (SAT, the aptitude test score; REC, a rating of the letters of recommendation; ESS, a rating of the essay; and GPA, high school grades), and we know COL. What we want is a predictive index,

Table 15.2: Data and predictions (PRE) for regression example

| Student | COL | Predictors | | | | PRE | Error |
		SAT	REC	ESS	GPA		
1	3.8	1500	4.0	4.0	4.0	3.910	0.110
2	3.6	1310	4.0	3.0	3.6	2.902	−0.698
3	3.5	1300	5.0	3.0	3.9	3.560	0.060
4	3.2	1280	3.0	5.0	3.7	3.428	0.228
5	3.0	1260	4.0	4.0	3.5	2.921	−0.079
6	2.8	1210	3.0	4.0	3.4	2.631	−0.169
7	2.5	1320	5.0	3.0	3.5	2.807	0.307
8	2.2	1220	4.0	3.0	3.2	2.129	−0.071
9	2.0	1200	2.0	5.0	3.0	1.997	−0.003
10	1.5	1170	3.0	2.0	3.2	1.811	0.311

PRE, a measure that comes as close as possible to predicting COL for the new applicants from the four other variables. Table 15.2 shows, for 10 of the college students, the four variables, the college grades (COL), and the predictive index (PRE). The last column is the error in each prediction, the difference between PRE and COL. PRE was calculated using a computer program for multiple linear regression (a technique described in detail in most modern statistics texts). The numbers in the first five columns were typed into the computer. The regression program was told to assume that COL is a linear function of the four other variables — that is, to assume that the following equation is true:

$$COL = a \cdot SAT + b \cdot REC + c \cdot ESS + d \cdot GPA + e + error$$

The error is a different number for each student, but each of the other coefficients — a, b, c, d, and e — is the same for all students. The coefficients a through d may be seen as weights; they indicate how much each of the variables (SAT, and so forth) affects COL. The coefficient e is a constant that is added or subtracted so that the mean predicted COL comes out right. The computer figures out the values of a, b, c, d, and e so as to make the error as small as possible. (Usually the computer does this by minimizing the mean of the squares of the error values.) Once we know the values of the coefficients, PRE is found by using the same equation but without the error:

$$PRE = a \cdot SAT + b \cdot REC + c \cdot ESS + d \cdot GPA + e$$

PRE would be as close as we can come to predicting COL with this kind of formula, if all we knew were the other four variables. Using the data given in Table 15.2, the values of a through e, respectively, are 0.000175 (for SAT); 0.092 (for REC); 0.217 (for ESS); 1.893 (for GPA); and -5.161 (the constant e added at the end). Therefore, the equation for PRE is as follows:

$$PRE = 0.000175 \cdot SAT + 0.092 \cdot REC + 0.217 \cdot ESS + 1.893 \cdot GPA - 5.161$$

Notice that the constant (-5.161) would not be needed, if all we wanted to do was to compare students with one another. What we are trying to do, though, is to compare the four variables with each other, to determine their relative importance. The four values a through d represent the relative importance of each of the four variables.[1]

Notice that SAT is unimportant in the formula. Notice also, however, that SAT *does* correlate with COL: The student with the highest COL got the highest SAT, and the two students with the lowest COL got the two lowest SATs. How could this happen? The answer is that SAT correlates with GPA in high school, and GPA in high school *also* correlates with COL. The reason that SAT correlates with COL appears to be that it correlates with GPA. Here, SAT seems to measure something like the ability to get good grades, but it does not measure this as well as the grades themselves. If we did not know high school GPA, then the SAT *would* be a useful predictor of COL, in this example.

This example is, of course, overly simple. In deciding whom to admit to college, there are other predictors to consider aside from these four factors, and there are other things to predict besides college grades. Many of these variables can be expressed as numbers, but when we apply a numerical formula of this sort we may always run across unusual cases that require us either to make exceptions or add a variable to the formula for the benefit of a single case. Would it make sense to include a measure of every applicant's criminal record, when probably only a few applicants have any record at all?

Moreover, the idea of a formula might be too simple. The basic idea of the model — that everything is multiplied by a weight representing its importance and all of the values are then added together — might be wrong. One way in which the model could be wrong is that there might be an *interaction* between two variables. This means that the *importance* (or weight) of one variable depends on the *value* of the other. For example, perhaps we should weigh REC more when a student does poorly on the Scholastic Aptitude Test. This would amount to accepting students who did well either on that test or in REC (or both), no matter how badly they might have done on one of the measures. Thus, when one of these two measures was high, the other would not matter.

Another way in which the model could be wrong is that some variables might not have a simply linear effect. The importance of a variable might be different for different parts of its range. For example, the difference between a SAT of 1100 and one of 1200 might be much more important than the difference between a SAT of

---

[1] A better measure of importance would take into account the amount of variation on each variable. In this case, SATs would have even less weight, because they vary by hundreds of points instead of just a few.

Table 15.3: Data for regression example, with judgments (JUD)

Student	COL	Predictors				PRE	Error
		SAT	REC	ESS	GPA		
1	3.8	1500	4.0	4.0	4.0	3.910	4.0
2	3.6	1310	4.0	3.0	3.6	2.902	3.1
3	3.5	1300	5.0	3.0	3.9	3.560	3.8
4	3.2	1280	3.0	5.0	3.7	3.428	3.4
5	3.0	1260	4.0	4.0	3.5	2.921	3.0
6	2.8	1210	3.0	4.0	3.4	2.631	2.7
7	2.5	1320	5.0	3.0	3.5	2.807	3.0
8	2.2	1220	4.0	3.0	3.2	2.129	2.3
9	2.0	1200	2.0	5.0	3.0	1.997	1.9
10	1.5	1170	3.0	2.0	3.2	1.811	2.1

1300 and one of 1400. The effect of the SAT would then be *curvilinear* rather than linear. (We might want to use for our calculations something such as the square root of SAT rather than SAT itself.) We shall return to this question.

The lens model

Suppose we asked an admissions official to predict COL (college grades) without the benefit of the formula. We could then obtain a list of judgments that we could place beside the true values for comparison, as shown in Table 15.3. We could then ask several questions about these judgments. For example, we could ask how close they come to the true values, or whether the judgments themselves could be predicted from the four main variables, and so on.

One useful way to think about this kind of situation is the *lens model*, based on the work of Brunswik (1952), Hammond (1955), and others. This term results from the sort of diagram shown here, which is supposed to look something like light rays being focused by a lens. Each line in the diagram represents a relationship, usually a correlation. (Some possible lines of correlation are left out of my diagram.) Each variable has a particular role. COL is the *criterion*, the thing to be predicted. JUD is the *judgment* provided by the judge. PRE is the value of COL predicted from the regression formula.

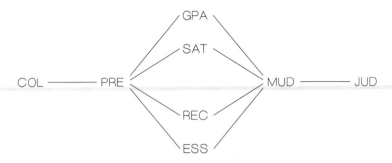

The new idea in the diagram is MUD (the Model of the jUDge). This is what we get if we try to predict JUD from the four main variables, just as we originally tried to predict COL from these variables. MUD is a *model of the judge*, just as PRE is a model of the criterion. In this example, MUD is based on the following equation:

$$MUD = 0 \cdot SAT + 0.1 \cdot REC + 0.1 \cdot ESS + 2.0 \cdot GPA - 4.8$$

Compared to PRE, the judge depends a little too much on GPA (2.0 for the judge versus 1.893 for PRE) and not enough on ESS (0.1 versus 0.217). This leads the judge, for example, to predict too high for student 10, whose ESS rating was very low. On the whole, however, the judge does well, almost as well as the formula for PRE. (Because that formula was chosen to minimize error, the judge cannot possibly do as well on evaluating these students' potential, unless the judge uses the same formula.)

Notice that the correlation between MUD and JUD is perfect (1.00) in this case. MUD is identical to JUD. This is not the usual case. It seems that our judge was calculating, rather than making an intuitive judgment, but the judge was not using quite the best formula for the calculations.

We can use the lens model to answer a great variety of questions about judgment in particular situations. Most of these judgment situations are quite similar to the one in the example just given. A judge is asked to predict some numerical criterion, such as stock prices, success in school or work, livestock quality, or COL, from a set of numerical predictors. The predictors (or the criterion) themselves sometimes represent summaries of other judgments. There is reason to think that each of the predictors might be related to the criterion in a simple way — that is, by either a positive or a negative correlation. Let us consider some of the questions about such judgments, and their answers.

Which does better, the judge or the best-fitting model of the data (PRE)? In practically every study in which this question has been asked, the answer is that the model does better over a set of judgments. When possible, it is always better to use a formula than an individual human judgment (Meehl, 1954; Goldberg, 1970; Dawes, 1971, 1979; Dawes and Corrigan, 1974; Camerer, 1981). This has been found in studies of the judgment of how psychotic people are (from personality-test profiles), graduate student success, success of people in various jobs, and future stock prices.

Which does better, the judge (JUD) *or the model of the judge* (MUD)? Again, in practically every study, the answer is that the model of the judge does better than the judge. Suppose we have a judgment task such as predicting college grades, and we have a judge who claims to be able to do it. Consider two ways we could proceed. The first is to have the judge make judgments of every case. The second is to have the judge make judgments of a number of cases, enough so that we can find a formula that predicts *the judge's judgments*. Then we would tell the judge to go home, and we would use the formula for all the cases, including those the judge already judged. The fact is that the second method is better than the first, even for the cases that the judge already judged. (Note that we are using the formula for predicting the *judgments*, not the formula for predicting what the judge is trying to predict. The latter formula, when we can find it, works even better at predicting the criterion.)

This is a rather surprising result. Why does it happen? Basically, it happens because the judge cannot be consistent with his own policy (unless, like our judge in the example, he calculates on his own). He is unreliable, in that he is likely to judge the same case differently on different occasions (unless he recognizes the case the second time). As Goldberg (1970, p. 423) puts it,

> The clinician is not a machine. While he possesses his full share of human learning and hypothesis-generating skills, he lacks the machine's reliability. He "has his days": Boredom, fatigue, illness, situational and interpersonal distractions all plague him, with the result that his repeated judgments of the exact same stimulus configurations are not identical. He is subject to all those human frailties which lower the reliability of his judgments below unity. And if the judge's reliability is less than unity, there must be error in his judgments — error which can serve no other purpose but to attenuate his accuracy. If we could remove some of this human unreliability by eliminating the random error in his judgments, we should thereby increase the validity of the resulting predictions.

We can, however, think of reasons why the judge might still be better than the model of himself. In particular, there might be interactions or curvilinear relations (nonlinearities) that are not represented in the linear models we have been considering. It might really be true that SATs are more important in the middle range than the higher range, for example. If this were true, the judge would be able to take it into account, and the linear model of the judge would not.

The judge might also have additional information not included in the linear model, such as observations made during a personal interview with the applicant. This gives the judge an unfair advantage over the model, however, since it is possible for the judge to assign numerical ratings to that information and include it in the model.

In the great variety of situations examined so far, interactions and nonlinearities have never been as important as the error to which Goldberg refers. There are

sometimes nonlinearities and interactions in the true situation, and there are sometimes nonlinearities and interactions in the judge's judgments, but the nonlinearities
and interactions expressed in his actual judgments have little to do with the nonlinearities and interactions actually present (Camerer, 1981). (Later in this chapter,
however, we shall consider a case in which subjects make use of interactions among
features when deciding whether a stimulus is a member of a category.)

In general, then, it is better to use the formula than the judge, because the formula
eliminates the error. This method is called *bootstrapping.* We pull ourselves up by
our bootstraps. We improve our judgment by modeling ourselves. A good example
of the successful use of bootstrapping methods is a formula devised by Gustafson,
Tianen, and Greist (1981), which predicts suicide attempts in psychiatric patients on
the basis of variables that can be assessed in clinical interviews (such as extent of
suicide plans and degree of isolation from other people). The predictions are more
accurate than those made holistically by the judges.

When we use bootstrapping to make decisions, we estimate weights from holistic decisions, rather than from systematic considerations of tradeoffs; we calculate
the weights so as to best explain a person's holistic ratings.[2] Although bootstrapping does better than holistic judgments, it is still derived from such judgments. We
noted in Chapter 12 that less important dimensions will be underweighed in holistic
judgments. Bootstrapping does solve the problem of random error, but it does not
remove the effects of this underweighing. Studies have found that in a bootstrapping
procedure the dimensions considered less important in fact receive less weight, relative to other dimensions, than in a MAUT procedure (von Winterfeldt and Edwards,
sec. 10.4). In addition, bootstrapping leads to greater disagreement among judges
than MAUT.

Another way to reduce judgment error is to average the judgment of several different judges. When this is done, the errors of different judges tend to cancel each
other out. Such *composite* judgments are indeed more accurate than judgments made
by individuals. If enough judges are used, they may do as well as a formula based on
the composites themselves. Goldberg (1970) examined the ability of 29 clinical psychologists to predict the diagnosis of mental patients ("psychotic" versus "neurotic")
from test profiles. The best prediction was accomplished by the composite of the 29
judges. A model of the composite did a little worse, but not significantly so. Next
best was a model of the average *individual judge*, and worst of all was the average
individual judge alone. Although use of many judges for prediction may help, it is
much more time-consuming than use of a single judge. The model of the group may
be best of all, taking efficiency into account.

Formulas may do better than judges, even when there is no objective way at all
to measure the criterion. For example, suppose we wanted to judge desirability of
prospective graduate students, on the basis of GREs (Graduate Record Examination
scores), college GPAs, and ratings of letters and essays, for the purpose of admitting
candidates to graduate school. We do not know, in this case, what "desirability"

---

[2]We also assume that the utility scales are linear.

means. It is not the same as grades in graduate school, for nebulous things such as quality of scholarship are important as well. What we do is to take a judge, or a committee of judges, and ask them to rate a number of prospective students. We then find a formula (MUD) that accounts for *their judgments* (JUD). We tell the judges to go home, and we use the formula.

Because of the findings that MUD is better than JUD at predicting an objective criterion, we can assume with some confidence that here, too, MUD would do better, *if there were an objective criterion*. The fact that there is not can hardly be expected to affect the superiority of MUD over JUD. We can be confident that we are doing better with the formula than with the formula derived from the judge's judgments, even when we cannot measure how much better we are doing. Another advantage of a method like this is that it may prevent complex judgments from being reduced to single numbers, such as use of grades alone as a measure of academic success or (in war) body counts of enemy soldiers as a measure of military success.

Do we need the judge at all? Dawes (1979) points out that in most situations of interest the variables we use to make predictions tend to be correlated with each other. For example, grades, SATs, and recommendations tend to be correlated; a student who does well on one measure tends to do well on others. In such cases, the precise weight we give to each variable does not make much difference. If we overweigh one variable and underweigh another, and if the two are correlated, our judgments (in relative terms) will not be very different. In our example, the judge did almost as well as the ideal model, even though he weighed things somewhat differently.

What this implies is that we can often do quite well if we simply know *which* variables to use (and in which direction). For example, in our case concerning admission, an expert might tell us that grades, recommendations, and essays were all important, but SAT were not. (It would not have produced such different results if we had used SATs.) Often, consulting an expert is not really necessary. Of course, there are cases, such as medical diagnosis, in which a nonexpert has no idea what is relevant. Would you know which measures to look at in order to determine whether someone has diabetes? In such cases, an expert can go a long way simply by knowing what is relevant, whether she weighs it correctly or not.

When we use the method of weighing all predictors equally, we must make sure that they are all expressed in the same sort of units. In our COL example, REC, ESS, and GPA have about the same range, but SAT has a much larger range. If we simply added up the predictors, SAT alone would determine the ranking, so the predictors would not be weighed "equally" at all. The way this problem is usually handled is to divide each predictor by the *standard deviation* of that predictor. The standard deviation is — like the range between the highest and lowest scores — a measure of the extent to which that predictor varies across all the cases (here, students).[3] In our COL example, the standard deviations of the predictors are SAT,

---

[3]The standard deviation is essentially the square root of the average difference between each score and the average score.

89; *REC*, 0.90; *ESS*, 0.92; and *GPA*, 0.30.

Dawes (1979) describes a number of cases in which such an equal-weighting method has been used with apparent success. In those cases in which the question can be asked, the equal-weighting model did better than the judge by himself. So great is the judge's unreliability that we can do better than the judge (in most cases) by knowing only which variables are relevant.

Why are people so resistant to the making of decisions by formula? Universities and colleges typically pay an admissions staff substantial amounts to read each application and weigh all of the variables. Faculty members do the same for applicants to graduate school and applicants for jobs. Business managers devote great time and effort to such matters as the setting of sales and production quotas. In all of these cases, there is a need for human judgment, to be sure. Somebody has to read the letters of recommendation and (at least) assign numbers to them, but there is no apparent need for the human judge when it comes to combining all of the various pieces into a single overall judgment. This is done better by formula.

Many people say that they are reluctant to use formulas because they want to be free to use a special policy for special cases. Among graduate-school applicants, for example, the foreigner whose poor command of English keeps test scores down, or the handicapped person who has overcome enormous odds just to meet minimal admission standards, and so on. This is not a good reason to reject formulas altogether. These cases do not have to be ignored when we use the formula. We can include a "special factors" variable in our formula, or omit tainted data (such as a verbal *SAT* score for foreigners), or we can simply scan through the pile of applicants looking for such exceptions and judge just these individually.

Another explanation of the reluctance to use formulas is that the judgment procedure often has other goals besides simply making the best judgment. For example, when my own department admits graduate students, the admissions committee asks faculty members who are likely to get these students in their laboratories to make an overall evaluation of each such applicant. The admissions committee does this not because it believes, for example, that a physiological psychologist is a better judge of physiological applicants than the committee is. Rather, it wants to alert faculty members who are not on the committee to the fact that certain students may end up working in their laboratories. (Technically, a memorandum to this effect would serve the purpose, but it is well known that many of us do not read memos.)

Another objection to formulas is the argument that individuals cannot be (or should not be) reduced to a single number. When we put individuals in rank order for some purpose, however, we are already reducing them to a single scale. The only issue is whether we do it well or badly given all the goals we ought to have.

Many of the people who object to the use of formulas are unaware of a hidden cause for their belief — *overconfidence* in their own powers of judgment. Psychologists have found this overconfidence factor elsewhere, in probability judgments (Chapter 6) and in phenomena such as the overuse of interviews for evaluating applicants. Hiring and admissions personnel often feel that they need a personal interview with each of many applicants, as though the fifteen- or thirty-minute sample of behavior will stack up against the four years of data represented in a student's transcript and recommendations or the ten years in a résumé. Evidence suggests that interviews ordinarily add nothing to the validity of prediction based on all other data that are usually available (Schmitt, 1976). If you were choosing members of an Olympic team, would you set up a thirty-minute tryout or look at each person's track record (literally) over the last few years?[4] An interview, of course, is like a thirty-minute tryout.[5]

Overconfidence in judgment has been found in an experiment by Arkes, Dawes, and Christensen (1986), who asked college-student subjects to choose which of three players had won the Most Valuable Player Award of the National Baseball League in each of the years from 1940 to 1961 (excluding those years in which pitchers won the award). Subjects were given the batting average, the number of home runs hit, the number of runs batted in, and the position of the player's team, for each of the three players listed for each year. Subjects were told — correctly — that the position of the player's team was an extremely useful cue, which would lead to 14 correct choices out of 19 if it was the sole basis for the judgment. Subjects who knew more about baseball (as determined from their answers to a baseball quiz) were more confident in their ability to "beat" the simple rule they had been given concerning team position. As a result of this confidence, they used the position rule less often and were actually less accurate in choosing the award winner (9.4 correct out of 19) than were other subjects with more modest knowledge of baseball (11.4 correct). Neither group of subjects did as well as they could have done by taking the experimenter's advice and attending only to team position. Overconfidence can be exacerbated by expertise.

We are not always, or usually, good judges of our own ability as judges. As a result, we waste effort making judgments that could be made more accurately by formula. The use of a formula guarantees that errors will be made, but we hope, however vainly, that human judgments will be perfect. As Einhorn (1986) puts it, we need to "accept error to make less error."

When we, as applicants, are rejected for a job or a school by a formula, we feel that an error is likely. The formula could not possibly have seen our special attributes (even though the teachers who gave us the grades and wrote the letters of recommendation, whose ratings go into the formula, had every opportunity to do so). When we are rejected by a person, we are more likely to feel that the rejection was based on real knowledge, yet, as we have seen, people make more errors than formulas (if we use people's judgments of specific dimensions as inputs).

A warning is in order lest anyone get carried away with the idea of replacing human judges with computers or even hand calculators. Although many of the objections to formulas are (arguably) mere mystical rhetoric, one is worth heeding. This is that the use of formulas may encourage us to use only the predictors that are easily quantified. For example, in admitting students to graduate school, we might tend to rely too heavily on test scores and grades and not enough on recommendations or

---

[4] Apparently, some nations *do* use tryouts instead of track records.

[5] On the other hand, an interview, even by telephone, may provide important information not usually included in a résumé, such as how serious the candidate's interest in the position in question is.

research papers. If admissions committees do this, then students will overemphasize tests and grades too, as they prepare themselves for graduate school. The solution to this problem is to turn recommendations and research papers into numbers so that they can be included in a formula. Indeed, in most of the examples given so far in this chapter, the *input* to the judgment process has consisted of other judgments, for which human judges are necessary. In many of the situations in which formulas are useful, the numbers are already available. For example, college admissions offices make ratings on applicants' essays, and even on their overall "sparkle," although these numbers are not always included in a formula.

The research that I have been discussing does not suggest that formulas should replace people altogether. It suggests, rather, that formulas should replace people *at the single task of combining a set of piecemeal judgments into an overall summary score*.

The mechanism of judgment

Do people really follow linear models?

Do judges really weigh cues numerically? The question is particularly acute when the task involves classifying stimuli into two categories (such as "neurotic" and "psychotic") on the basis of numerical predictors. A reasonable alternative strategy, it might seem, is to set cutoff points on each predictor. In order to be classified as psychotic, for example, a patient would have to exceed the cutoff point on a certain number of predictors (perhaps one, perhaps all). Although such a strategy would probably not be optimal, since it throws away information about how far from the cutoff point each patient is, we might use it anyway because it is easy. (A patient who is far above the cutoff point on one predictor and just below it on another is probably more likely to be psychotic than one who is just above the cutoff on both, yet the use of a strategy requiring both cutoff points to be exceeded would classify the former patient as neurotic and the latter as psychotic.)

Thinking-aloud protocols have been used to study judgment tasks (as well as other thinking tasks), and these results suggest that individual judges often use some sort of cutoff strategy (Payne, 1976; Einhorn, Kleinmuntz, and Kleinmuntz, 1979). Here are some fictional protocols (from Einhorn et al., p. 473) of a typical judge deciding whether a patient is psychologically "adjusted" or "maladjusted," on the basis of three numerical cues, x_1, x_2, and x_3, which represent scores on various psychological tests:

> *Case 1.* I'll look at x_1 first — it's pretty high ...the x_2 score is also high. This is a maladjusted profile.
>
> *Case 2.* Let's see, x_1 is high but ...x_2 is low, better check x_3 — it's low, too. I would say this is adjusted.
>
> *Case 3.* This person's x_1 score is low. Better check both x_2 and x_3 then — both pretty high. Ummm ...likely to be maladjusted.

Case 4. x_1 is fairly low here ... x_2 is quite high ... this is an interesting case ... x_3 is very low ... I'd say adjusted.

Case 5. x_1 is extremely high — this is maladjusted.

Case 6. x_1 is an iffy score ... let's see x_2 and x_3. Both are mildly indicative of pathology — I guess, that taking all three are pointing in the same direction, call this maladjusted.

Einhorn and his colleagues point out that these protocols can be described in terms of various rules involving cutoffs. For Case 1, it looks as though the judge is applying some sort of cutoff point to the x_1 and x_2 scores. If these are high enough, she does not look at x_3. In Case 2, it looks as though there is a rule instructing her to look at x_3 when the other cues conflict. Case 4 is "interesting," because two cues that are usually correlated conflict. In Case 5, it looks as though the judge is applying another cutoff point to x_1; if x_1 is sufficiently high, she does not look at the other cues at all.

Einhorn and his colleagues point out that these protocols are also consistent with the use of a "compensatory" strategy more in line with the linear model itself. For example, suppose that the scores were all on a 1 to 10 scale, and the judge's linear model was the formula:

$$y = .6 \cdot x_1 + .2 \cdot x_2 + .2 \cdot x_3$$

The patient is called maladjusted if the score y is 5 or greater. The six cases could then be represented like this:

1. $y = .6 \cdot 7 + .2 \cdot 6 = 5.4$ (maladjusted)

2. $y = .6 \cdot 7 + .2 \cdot 1 + .2 \cdot 2 = 4.8$ (adjusted)

3. $y = .6 \cdot 3 + .2 \cdot 8 + .2 \cdot 8 = 5.0$ (maladjusted)

4. $y = .6 \cdot 4 + .2 \cdot 9 + .2 \cdot 1 = 4.4$ (adjusted)

5. $y = .6 \cdot 10 = 6$ (maladjusted)

6. $y = .6 \cdot 5 + .2 \cdot 6 + .2 \cdot 6 = 4.4$ (adjusted)

The reason for not looking at x_3 in Case 1, then, is that the first two cues are sufficient to put the case above the cutoff point. Likewise, x_1 alone does this in Case 5. The judge could be using a compensatory rule, based on a weighted combination of all three attributes, and yet could still appear to be using something like cutoff points applied to individual attributes.

In sum, the use of protocols here may be misleading if it leads us to think that judges are not using some sort of subjective weighing scheme much like the linear model itself. Thus the linear model may be a good description of what judges actually do, even though evidence from protocols appears initially to suggest that it is not. Of course, judges are not entirely consistent in the way they weigh various cues, and they may not be consistent in their protocols either. It is this inconsistency that makes the use of a formula attractive.

Impression formation

Linear models can be applied even when the stimuli to be judged are not presented in the form of numbers. The *impression-formation* task invented by Asch (1946) is a good example. Asch was interested in the basic processes by which we form impressions of other people's personalities. His experimental procedure involved a very simple situation in which some of these processes could be studied. The subject was given a list of adjectives describing a particular person and was instructed to make some judgment about the person on the basis of these adjectives. For example, Asch told subjects in one group that a certain person was "intelligent, skillful, industrious, warm, determined, practical, cautious." Subjects were asked to make judgments about this person on other dimensions, such as those defined by the adjectives "generous versus ungenerous." (Try it.) Another group of subjects was given the description "intelligent, skillful, industrious, cold, determined, practical, cautious" and asked to make the same judgment. Notice that the two descriptions are identical, except for the words "warm" and "cold."

Asch (a Gestalt psychologist) found that the first group tended to make many more positive judgments than the second group. He suggested that the subjects formed impressions of a person as a whole. The parts worked together to create an overall impression, which, in turn, affected the meaning of the various parts. For example, when he asked subjects to give a synonym of the word "intelligent" in the two descriptions, subjects given the second description tended to give synonyms such as "calculating," whereas those in the first group gave synonyms such as "clever." The terms "warm" and "cold" seemed to be *central* to the whole description. They appeared to affect the meanings of the other terms (which Asch called *peripheral*).

Asch's account makes sense intuitively, but it has been questioned by many investigators (see Anderson, 1981, for a review). An alternative explanation (to Asch's) of the findings concerning synonyms (of words such as "intelligent," for example) is that the subjects found it difficult to follow the instructions to give a synonym only of the word to which they were told to attend. The word "calculating," for instance, is in fact an associate of the word "cold." Subjects might have associated to the word "cold" itself, or perhaps to both "cold" and "intelligent" in combination — but without the meaning of "intelligent" changing under the influence of the word "cold" (Anderson, 1981, p. 216).

The rest of Asch's results can be explained by a simple algebraic model, a variant of the linear regression model. Each adjective has a certain weight on each scale. For example, "warm" has a very high weight on the scale from "generous" to "ungenerous," and "cold" has a very low weight. (This is because we generally think that warm people are generous. The reason we think this is not relevant to the controversy at hand.) Anderson (1981) points out that a good account of all the results can be obtained by assuming that the subject *averages* the weights of the separate adjectives on the scale in question. If "generous" has a value of $+10$ and "ungenerous" has a value of -10, "warm" by itself might have a value of $+6$ and "cold" a value of -6. "Intelligent" might have a value of $+1$ by itself. A person described as warm and intelligent would have an average of $(6 + 1)/2$ or 3.5, which would come close to the subject's rating.

The averaging model applies to a great many judgments of the sort we have been discussing, judgments whose stimuli can be decomposed into separate attributes or features. For example, in one study (Anderson and Butzin, 1978), children were asked to play Santa Claus. Their task was to give a "fair share" of toys to other children, each of whom was described in terms of need (how many toys they already had) and their achievement (how many dishes they had washed for their mothers). The subjects were sensitive to both variables, and the number of toys allotted to each child was a linear combination of the two variables (each given a certain weight).

The averaging model is completely consistent with the linear regression model. Of course, "averaging" implies dividing by the number of cues or dimensions. As long as the number of cues is held constant, however, we do not know whether a subject is adding their weights or averaging them. The results obtained in connection with the averaging model therefore provide additional support for the regression model as a description of behavior, and vice versa.

Averaging, adding, and number of cues

As noted, the term "averaging" implies that subjects add up the impression from each cue and then divide by the number of cues.[6] In the experiments described so far, the number of cues is held constant, so, for all we know, subjects might simply be *adding* the impressions from the separate cues. They might then divide (or multiply) by some number that would be the same regardless of the number of cues, merely in order to produce responses that fall within a reasonable range. To find out whether subjects are adding or averaging, we need to vary the number of cues.

The simplest way to do this is to compare the effect of one cue and two cues. When this is done, presentation of two equally positive cues usually leads to a higher rating than either term alone but less than the sum of the two ratings. It would seem that subjects do something in between adding and averaging. For example, if the personality rating (on a scale of "generosity" in which 0 represents neutrality) for "happy" alone were 3 and the rating for "friendly" alone were 3, the rating from the two together might be 4, which is higher than the average of 3 and 3 (which is 3) but less than their sum (which is 6).

To explain such findings (and others) Anderson assumes that subjects have some sort of starting point or initial impression (just from knowing that it was a *person* being described, perhaps) that had to be averaged in. Suppose that "happy" and "friendly" each has a weight of 6, and the initial impression has a value of 0. Given

---

[6] Actually, each *scale* (for example, friendliness, intelligence) is assumed to have a different *weight* for a given judgment. These weights correspond to the coefficients a through e in the regression example. The weight depends on the relevance of the scale (for example, friendliness) to the judgment being made (for example, generosity). The value of each cue (for example, the word "friendly") on its own scale (for example, friendliness) is thus multiplied by this weight before being added. Then this sum is divided by the sum of the weights themselves, rather than just by the number of cues.

one of the terms, the average would be $(0 + 6)/2$ or 3. Given two of the terms, the average would be $(0 + 6 + 6)/3$, or 4.

Another kind of explanation of subjects' behavior holds that they often "fill in" missing values, which they then use to make their final judgment. A subject told that a person is "happy" might fill in the "neutral" value of friendliness, or predict the value of friendliness from the value of happiness (by assuming that happy people are friendly, for example) — or do neither. Following this filling in (if it occurs), subjects might either add or average the values at hand. For example, the hypothetical result just described could be explained if the adding model were true and if subjects took a happiness value of 3 to imply a friendliness value of 1, since $3 + 1 = 4$. People do sometimes fill in missing values on the basis of their knowledge of relationships. When the two attributes are positively correlated, subjects behave more as the adding model predicts (for example, ratings of 3 on either happy or friendly might lead to a generosity rating of 6), but, when they are negatively correlated, then the rating based on one attributed is downgraded (Jagacinski, 1991).

In certain situations, an adding model seems to be normatively correct, and in these situations departures from that model leads to fallacious judgments. The clearest cases are those in which two cues are independent, which means that the value of one cannot be predicted at all from the value of the other. Although the cues are independent of each other, they are both relevant to prediction of a criterion. For example, suppose that in a certain pool of applicants for graduate school (let us say a pool from which applicants who clearly will be rejected have already been removed, perhaps by self-selection), amount of research experience and GRE scores are independent. Within this pool, GRE score and research experience are unrelated. Now suppose that the GRE score is missing for one applicant, and we make a judgment of acceptability on the basis of research experience alone. Since the applicant's research experience is near the top of our scale, we give the applicant a very high rating, compared to others in the pool. Then the applicant takes the Graduate Record Examination, and the scores turn out to be a little better than the average of those in the pool. Should we raise our rating for this person or lower it?

Most people would lower it (Lichtenstein, Earle, and Slovic, 1975), but they should raise it. The lowering of the rating is just another example of subjects behaving roughly as though they were averaging the two cues; the second cue lowers the subjective average of the two. (Any account that explains departures from the adding model can explain this.)

Why should the rating be raised? Before we find out the applicant's GRE, our best guess is that it is at the average of the group. This is what we would guess if we knew nothing at all, and since the applicant's research experience is unrelated to GRE, we should still guess that the GRE is average after we knew about research experience. Therefore, when we find out that the student's GRE is a little better than average, we ought to think that this student is even *better* than we would have predicted when we did not know her GRE. (This argument depends on the cues being independent. If the cues are highly correlated, a moderate level of one should make us suspect the validity of a very high value on another.)

Representativeness in numerical prediction

The representativeness heuristic (discussed in Chapter 6) seems to cause biases in quantitative judgment just as it causes biases in probability judgment. In the example I just gave, we expect the GRE to be above average because that kind of GRE score is more similar to (more representative of) the applicant's research experience than an average GRE score would be. We seem to have made a prediction based on similarity rather than on the normative model, which holds that we ought to ignore research experience — which is useless information because it is unrelated to GRE score — and to guess the average GRE score.

As another example, suppose you are told that a certain student ranked in the 90th percentile in terms of grade point average (GPA) in his first year of college. What is your best guess of the student's GPA? Suppose you say 3.5 (between B and A), because you think that this is the 90th percentile for GPA. (So far, you have done nothing unreasonable.) Now what GPA would you predict for another student, who scored in the 90th percentile on a test of mental concentration? or for another student who scored in the 90th percentile on a test of sense of humor? Many subjects give the same prediction of 3.5 (Kahneman and Tversky, 1973, pp. 245–247). This may be because a GPA of 3.5 is most *similar* to the 90th percentile on the other measures.

In fact — as I shall explain shortly — your prediction should *regress* toward the mean (the average grade for the class, which was judged to be about 2.5 by Kahneman and Tversky's subjects), the worse the predictor is. In the extreme, if the subject were in the 90th percentile on shoe size, that would probably have no relation at all to grades, and your best guess would be that the student would have a GPA at the class mean of 2.5. Sense of humor is probably as useless as shoe size in its power to predict college GPA, so your best guess might be a little over 50% (or a little under, if you think that humor gets in the way of good grades). Mental concentration is probably a better predictor than sense of humor but not as good a predictor as the percentile rank in GPA itself, so the best prediction should be somewhere between 2.5 and 3.5.

To see why we should regress toward the mean, let us suppose a student scores at the 90th percentile on the mental concentration test, and let us ask whether we would expect the student to obtain a GPA of 3.5 (which, let us assume, is the 90th percentile for GPA), or higher, or lower. Mental concentration is not a perfect predictor of grades, so some of the students who score in the 90th percentile on the mental concentration test will do better than a GPA of 3.5, and some will do worse. More students will do worse than will do better, however, because there are more students with a GPA below 3.5 than there are with a GPA above it. There are, for example, more students with a GPA of 3.4 than with a GPA of 3.6, because 3.4 is closer to the mean GPA. It is therefore more likely that a randomly selected student will have a GPA of 3.4 and a mental concentration score at the 90th percentile than a GPA of 3.6 and a mental concentration score at the 90th percentile. The same argument applies to GPAs of 3.3 and 3.7, 3.2 and 3.8, and so on. If we predict that students in the 90th percentile in mental concentration will have a GPA of 3.5, we are, in effect, ignoring the prior probability of their GPA's being above or below 3.5 (as discussed in Chapter 6). We can think of the mental concentration score as a datum, from which we must infer the probability of various hypotheses about the student's GPA. The hypotheses below 3.5 are more likely at the outset, so they remain more likely after the datum is obtained.

Nonregressiveness may be overcome by thinking about missing data. Ganzach and Krantz (1991) gave subjects experience at predicting the college grade-point average (COL) from descriptions that included ACH and SAT (as described earlier in this chapter). When subjects then made predictions on the basis of single predictor (SAT or ACH), they regressed these predictions toward the mean, unlike other subjects who did not have the experience of using more than one predictor. It seems that these experienced subjects thought about the missing predictors and assumed moderate values for them. This heuristic will not always work, however, because it is not always possible to know what are the missing predictors. *n their means*

Another example of nonregressiveness, failure to regress enough toward the mean, is prediction of completion times (Buehler et al., 1994). Projects of all sorts, from massive works of construction to students' papers to professors' textbooks, are rarely completed in the amount of time originally estimated. Cost overruns are much more common than underruns (to the point where my spelling checker thinks that only the former is an English word). In 1957, for example, the Sydney (Australia) Opera House was predicted to cost $17 million and to be completed in 1963. A scaled-down version opened in 1973, at a cost of $102 million! Kahneman and Tversky (1992) argue that we could, in principle, know all this and take it into account in making predictions. We could regress toward the mean based on experience. (The mean completion time might, for example, be about twice the initial estimate, so we could routinely double all our estimates.) We fail to regress toward this kind of mean because we think in terms of "singular" data — facts about the case at hand — rather than "distributional" data, which concern other cases of the same type. Buehler and his colleagues (1994) found that this overprediction phenomenon, for students completing assignments, could be reduced if the students were told to think about past experiences and relate them to the present case.

A final possible example of representativeness is the _dilution effect_ (Nisbett et al., 1981). People use totally useless information. They seem to average it in with useful information, so that it causes a kind of regression effect. For example, when subjects were asked to predict Robert's grade point average (GPA) from the number of hours per week that Robert studies, they reasonably predict a higher GPA when he studies 31 hours than when he studies 3 hours. When they are also told that Robert "is widely regarded by his friends as being honest" or "plays tennis or racquetball about three or four times a month," they make more moderate predictions. It is as thought they take this useless information to predict a moderate GPA, and then they average this prediction with the more extreme prediction derived from the hours per week of studying.

In sum, the representativeness heuristic seems to cause us to neglect the effects of unpredictability. This results in many misinterpretations in daily life. For example, when a person is learning a difficult skill such as flying an airplane, performance on a given maneuver varies unpredictably from trial to trial. If we look at those trials in which performance is exceptionally good, then it is very likely that performance will be worse on the next trial. If we look at trials on which people do poorly, then people are likely to do better on the next trial. Now suppose that we adopt a policy of rewarding student pilots when they do well and punishing them when they do badly. Further, suppose that the reward and punishment have only small effects, compared to the variation in performance from trial to trial. It will *appear* that the reward makes the pilots do worse on the next trial and that the punishment makes them do better (Kahneman and Tversky, 1983).

In ordinary life, we are always asking questions that show that our expectations are based on the representativeness heuristic. Why is it that brilliant women (men) marry men (women) who are not quite as brilliant? Why is it that the food in restaurants tends to be better the first time you go than the second? The answers to these questions have to do with unpredictable variation. Brilliant women (men) marry men (women) who are not quite as brilliant because equally brilliant partners are hard to find, and it just might be that we look for other things in a mate besides equivalent brilliance. Why is the food in restaurants better on the first visit than the second? Because you go back a second time only when the food is very good the first time. Very likely you have gone to that restaurant on a good day (for that restaurant). When you go on a bad day, you are disappointed, and you do not go back.

Anchoring and underadjustment

We often make numerical judgments by anchoring on some number and then adjusting for other things that we know. The *anchoring and adjustment heuristic* affects quantitative estimates of all sorts. In general, people tend to underadjust. They do this even when the anchor is totally irrelevant to the judgment. For example, Tversky and Kahneman (1974) asked subjects to estimate certain proportions, such as the percentage of African countries in the United Nations. "For each quantity, a number between 0 and 100 was determined by spinning a wheel of fortune in the subject's presence. The subject was instructed to indicate first whether that number was higher or lower than the value of the quantity, and then to estimate the value of the quantity by moving upward or downward from the given number" (p. 1128).

The number the subject started with, determined solely by the spin of a wheel, had a marked effect on the final estimate. Subjects who were given high numbers to start with gave higher estimates than those given low numbers. The adjustment was insufficient. This effect is found even when the subject simply was required to attend to the anchor (for example, by rewriting it); it does not require an initial judgment of whether the anchor is too high or too low (Wilson et al., 1996). Of course, when the number is not arbitrary, the effect is even more robust. One practical consequence of this effect is in the domain of liability law. The amount of damages requested by a plaintiff in a lawsuit influences the jury's decision of how much to award (Chapman and Bornstein, 1996), even though, in principle, the size of the damage award should depend only on the facts presented. Apparently, the jury anchors on the request.

There is nothing wrong (in principle) with forming an estimate by starting with one value and then adjusting it successively as each new piece of information comes to mind. The mistake that subjects make is not adjusting enough. Underadjustment, in turn, may result from a failure to look for counterevidence, a failure of actively open-minded thinking. Chapman and Johnson (1999) asked subjects to think of features of the target item that were different from the anchor, and this reduced the underadjustment effect. When the subjects tried to think of features of the target that were similar to the answer, the effect did not change. This phenomenon supports the claim I made (in Chapter 3) that we tend to be biased in favor of our present beliefs, even when these beliefs are induced in an experiment. We do not take sufficient account of evidence against them. In this kind of experiment, subjects could manifest this bias by searching their memories for evidence consistent with the initial estimate, or anchor, even though they know that this estimate is completely arbitrary.

Classification

Suppose we change the task slightly. Instead of looking at a policy already formed over years of experience (as our personal method of assessing personality is), we require the subject to learn to make judgments during the experiment. On each trial, subjects make a prediction and are then given feedback about the actual value of the criterion they were trying to predict. The cue and criterion variables can now be entirely artificial, with labels such as x and y instead of GPA and SAT. When this procedure is used, subjects still make their judgments in terms of linear rules (Klayman, 1984). In general, if the system in question obeys linear rules, subjects will learn them about as well (or as badly) as they do in real life.

Suppose we make one more change. Instead of the variables being continuous quantities, with each variable taking several possible values, we use variables with only two possible values each. For example, let us assume that from such variables as a person's hair color (light or dark), shirt color (light or dark), hair length (short or long), and smile (open or closed) we are supposed to guess whether the person's name is Asch or not (Medin, Dewey, and Murphy, 1983). (Clearly, this is a very artificial task.) Once again, the results do not seem to change much (Smith and Medin, 1981). Subjects' judgments can be predicted fairly well on the basis of a linear combination of features.

In this kind of task, though, certain experiments suggest that something else is going on. The results from these experiments may have implications for judgment research as a whole. The fictional findings from a medical case study given in Table 15.4 were used in an experiment by Medin, Altom, Edelson, and Freko (1981, p. 39). Subjects were presented with these cases as examples, one by one, and were told that the initials represented patients with "burlosis," a fictitious disease. In Table 15.4, 1 represents the presence of a symptom, and 0 represents its absence. Notice

Table 15.4: Case-study data for judgment experiment (1 = symptom present, 0 = symptom absent)

Case study	Swollen eyelids	Splotches on ears	Discolored gums	Nose-bleed
R. C.	1	1	1	1
R. M.	1	1	1	1
J. J.	0	1	0	0
L. F.	1	1	1	1
A. M.	1	0	1	1
J. S.	1	1	0	0
S. T.	0	1	1	1
S. E.	1	0	0	0
E. M.	0	0	1	1

Source: D. Medin, M. W. Altom, S. M. Edelson, and D. Freko, "Correlated symptoms and simulated medical classification," *Journal of Experimental Psychology: Learning, Memory, and Cognition* (1982), 8, 39.

that the last two symptoms, discolored gums and nose bleed, are perfectly correlated. Otherwise, all symptoms are equally useful. The same number of patients has each of the four symptoms.

After studying these cases, subjects were asked to classify new cases. In this particular experiment, the subjects were asked to say which of two matched cases was more likely to have burlosis. For example, the subject might be given the Cases 1101 and 0111. (The order of the ones and zeros corresponds to the order of the four symptoms in the table. Thus the first case has the first two symptoms and the fourth, but no discolored gums.) In these two cases, the second case preserves the correlation between the third and fourth symptoms, and subjects generally said that this person was more likely to have the disease. (This case matched one of the original cases, a person with initials S. T. A subsequent experiment showed that subjects are sensitive to correlated symptoms even without such matching.)

Putting this result in the context of this chapter, it appears that these subjects were sensitive to an interaction between two variables. When discolored gums are present, the cue value of nosebleed is positive; patients with nosebleed are more likely to have the disease than those without it. When discolored gums are absent, the opposite is true; patients with nosebleed are *less* likely to have the disease than those without it. This is an interaction. Moreover, the results indicate that subjects are sensitive to the interaction. This is an exception to the more usual finding that judges are not sensitive to the interactions present.

One explanation of this finding is that subjects classified the new cases on the basis of their similarity to the cases they had seen. Read (1983) found that social judgments were often made on the basis of similar cases, especially when no general rule had been formulated by the person making the judgment. Read asked subjects to predict whether a member of an unfamiliar primitive tribe engaged in a certain behavior, such as drawing symbols on a piece of bark with one's own blood, after giving the subjects information about other members of the tribe who either engaged in the behavior or did not. When the subjects did not understand the rule governing the behavior in the tribe, they based their predictions on the similarity between each new case they were given and individuals they had been informed about who had also engaged in the behavior.

The same mechanism seems to operate in real judgment tasks. Faculty members whom I have worked with on a graduate admissions committee frequently evaluate applicants by comparing them to students already admitted into the program. Similarly, political leaders often make analogies to particular cases, such as the Munich Agreement with Hitler.

The use of similarity to old examples as a basis for categorization of new instances has both advantages and disadvantages. An advantage is that it sensitizes judges to interactions, if they are present. Notice that in the disease experiment, the case with the correlated symptoms is more similar to many of the examples given than is the case without them. (It is identical to one example, S. T., as noted, but this is not necessary for the result.)

The disadvantage of this mechanism of learning is that it "sensitizes" us as well to interactions that are not really there. For example, suppose a particular woman has done very well at a graduate school. This woman had as an applicant (contrary to the usual pattern for women who take the Graduate Record Examinations) a high quantitative GRE score and a low verbal GRE score. A judge admitting new graduate students to that school might tend to think very highly of applicants with the identical pattern, even to the point of favoring such applicants over other applicants with high scores on *both* parts of the GRE. It is extremely unlikely that such a preference would be valid. Most likely, those who do well on everything are more likely to succeed than those who do well on only some things. The problem here may be in using a single, salient exemplar rather than a great many exemplars.

Functional measurement and conjoint analysis

At the beginning of this chapter, and in Chapter 13, I said that judgment tasks could be used to measure utility. One way to do this is apparent from the discussion of linear regression. If we assume that each utility scale is a linear function of the attribute, then the regression weights might correspond to the weights we would use in MAUT. Actually this is not generally true, but it captures the idea.[7]

[7] It is true if prediction of the responses from the dimensions is perfect and the dimensions are never perfectly correlated, or if the dimensions are not correlated at all in the set being judged.

What happens if we drop the assumption that the scales are linear? Let us do this one step at a time. First, let assume that the response is a linear function of utility, so we can use it as a utility measure directly. We made this assumption in discussing direct judgments of utility. We can now plot graphs of how the ratings depend on each level of each dimension. With two dimensions, we can plot the ratings for one dimension as a function of the first dimension, with a second curve for each level of the other dimensions. When we analyzed data in this way, taking the ratings as given and trying to find what functions predict them, we are using *functional measurement*, a set of ideas developed by Norman Anderson and others (for example, Anderson, 1981).

Suppose, though, that the ratings are not direct measures of utility. That is, suppose that the ratings are only monotonically related to utility; that is, they increase when utility increases, but they are not necessarily linear functions of utility. Also suppose that each dimension — price, quality, or whatever — has some nonlinear utility function. So the "input" dimensions are transformed to get their utilities. The dimension utilities are then added. Then, before the summed utilities are expressed as responses, they are transformed again. Can we still discover the utilities on each dimension?

In principle, we could do this by using the ratings to rank all the possible options. Recall the discussion of conjoint measurement in Chapter 14. If we whether each option in a set was ranked, we could figure out the required indifference points. We could then infer the utility of each level of each attribute, as in the computer example on p. 341. All we would need to assume is that the subject is indifferent between two objects that get the same rating, and prefers objects with higher ratings. Once we had these functions, we could compute the utility of each option and then plot the subject' ratings a function of utility, with one point for each option. We would thus know how the rating scale is related to utility.

In practice, this approach has two problems. One is that the subjects are somewhat inconsistent, and most of their inconsistency is the result of random variation. The Thompson condition (p. 342) may be violated repeatedly. This is why formulas are better, when we have them. But the result is that we cannot apply the approach described in Chapter 14, the step-by-step calculation of indifference points. Instead, modern computer programs try to fit all the functions at once, using an iterative procedure. This means that the program starts out with some rough guess about the utility of each level of each attribute and about the relation between each level of utility and the final rating. Then it successively modifies these guesses, one at a time, counting the number of inconsistencies. If a change in one guess reduces an inconsistency, then that is adopted, and the cycle continues until no further reduction is possible (or until some preset low level of inconsistency is reached). It is lucky that nobody tries to do this by hand.[8]

Here is an example of what the method can do. Imagine a subject asked to rate

[8] Recently, this procedure has been incorporated into the standard version of some statistical packages, such as Systat.

a set of products that differ in price and quality. The figure on the left shows a
subject's ratings ratings of several bottles of wine as a function of price ($5, $10,
or $15) and quality (high, medium, and low). The ratings are on a scale from A
to E. Suppose that the ratings are a function of the utility of price and the utility of
quality. The numbers 1–3 on the horizontal axis represent the utility of price. The
prices are evenly spaced in the left graph, but the utilities are unevenly space. The
utilities are not a linear function of price. The ratings A–E are themselves derived
from an internal psychological scale of overall utility (combining price and quality),
represented by the numbers on the vertical axis. The ratings are evenly spaced, but
the overall utility scale is not. This has to do with the way the subject translates
utilities into responses, which is also nonlinear. The figure on the right shows what
happens after conjoint analysis. Instead of curved lines, all the lines are now straight.
Both axes now represent utility. (The ratings and prices are omitted, but they would
now be unevenly spaced if they were included.) The conjoint analysis procedure
essentially figures out what the utility functions would be if the utilities were additive
and the response was some function of the total utility.

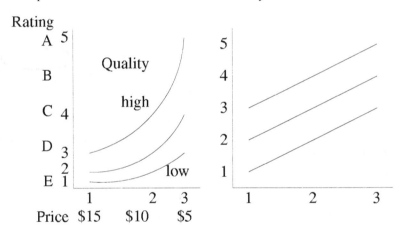

Conclusion

People use various heuristics to make quantitative judgments, such as representativeness, anchoring and adjustment, and averaging. They also attend to different factors
on different occasions. This leads to random variation. As a result, when judgments
of the same type are made repeatedly, and when simple models are possible, then
formulas do better than people, despite the fact that formulas are incapable of considering all possible factors.

People often resist this possibility because they are overconfident about their
judgments. Increased awareness of our limitations as judges and decision makers
ought to improve our mutual tolerance of one another, and it can also lead to increased acceptance of new methods for decision making.

Chapter 16

Moral thinking

I might as well give you my opinion of these two kinds of sin as long as, in a way, against
each other we are pitting them.

And that is, don't bother your head about sins of commission because however sinful, they
must at least be fun or else you wouldn't be committing them.

It is the sin of omission, the second kind of sin, that lays eggs under your skin.

The way you get really painfully bitten

Is by the insurance you haven't taken out and the checks you haven't added up the stubs of
and the appointments you haven't kept and the bills you haven't paid and the letters you
haven't written.

Also, about sins of omission there is one particularly painful lack of beauty,

Namely, it isn't as though it had been a riotous red letter day or night every time you neglected
to do your duty. ...

You didn't slap the lads in the tavern on the back and loudly cry Whee,

Let's all fail to write just one more letter before we go home, and this round of unwritten
letters is on me.

No, you never get any fun

Out of the things you haven't done.

Ogden Nash (from "Portrait of the artist as a prematurely old man")

Moral thinking is important for decision making as a whole, since most real decisions
involve moral issues. We often are not aware that moral issues are involved in our
everyday decisions, but wherever our choices affect the utilities of others, a moral
decision must be made. The choice of one's work, for example, is often considered
to be a purely personal decision, but we can do various amounts of good or harm to
others by choosing different paths through our working lives. The saintly aid worker
who helps the poor in return for poverty-level wages and the Mafia leader who bleeds
the rich and poor alike are only the extremes of a continuum on which each of us has
a place. Likewise, personal relationships are not really so "personal" when they
involve promises that are kept and broken, expectations of loyalty that are set up and
violated, and responsibilities that are fulfilled or neglected. Of course, certain issues

much more obviously involve moral questions, especially those that arouse political passion: abortion, property rights, capital punishment, and aid for the poor.

The most basic moral judgments are statements about what *decision* someone in a certain situation, or a certain kind of situation, should make. Should Susan have an abortion? Should legislators or judges change the law concerning abortions? Should Henry join a political demonstration concerning this issue? Unlike other judgments about what someone should decide to do, moral judgments have a special character: They are universal. They are meant to ignore the identity of the relevant people, so that they apply to anyone in the same situation. If it is wrong for me to steal a book from the library, then it is wrong for you, too, if you are in exactly the same situation.

Moral rules are taught to us as children, and they become some of our most strongly held beliefs. Sometimes these *moral intuitions* come into direct conflict with the beliefs of others. In these cases, and in others in which thinking about moral issues is needed, it is difficult for us to think well, because in this area our prior beliefs are strong, and we tend to be biased in their favor. We do not see moral issues as an area in which actively open-minded thinking is appropriate. The traditional beliefs we are taught may represent the conclusions of good moral thinking that was done by others in the past, but when they are passed on to us in the form of beliefs that we cannot question, we do not learn the details of the normative theories that stand behind them, if any.

The general philosophy that underlies utility theory — utilitarianism — is one such normative theory that has been used to justify moral decisions and prescriptive moral rules. It is not possible, within the scope of this chapter, to present a defense of the entire position of utilitarianism. My aim has to be more modest. I shall simply argue that utilitarianism provides a way to understand and analyze moral issues in terms of the consequences of decisions. It also provides a way for us to think critically and constructively about our basic moral intuitions, the beliefs we acquired as children. When we think in this way, we find that many of our intuitions are good ones, but some — like other heuristics that we use for judgments and decisions — are misleading or are applied in inappropriate situations.

Morality and utility

Does being moral conflict with maximizing expected utility? Some have argued that the idea of personal utility, by its very nature, implies seeking one's own "pleasure" or "satisfaction," so that the use of the maximization of utility as a normative criterion tends to make us selfish (Schwartz, 1986). Surely many economists think of people as pure "self-interest maximizers," and certainly such cynical views tend to become self-fulfilling. If theorists tell you that your fellows *are* self-interest maximizers, and you believe it, you may argue, "Why should I care about them when they do not care about me?"

Nothing inherent in the idea of utility leads to this conclusion. Utility is a measure of goal achievement, and some of our goals are that the goals of others be achieved. In this way, our utilities are linked with theirs. People are altruistic, then, *in the sense that they often have goals that others' goals be satisfied*. I, and most other people, would rather see *you* get what you want than not, other things being equal. If I act on this goal and do something for you, you may say that I am just indulging my *own* goal for your welfare, so I am being selfish after all. But this is a generous kind of "selfishness" that should not bother us much. More serious is the kind of selfishness that leads people to neglect, or even frustrate, the desires of others.

The logic and illogic of moral judgments

We can begin to understand morality by asking about the functions that it serves. Morality involves *telling each other* what we should do, or otherwise trying to influence each other's decision making. We can express morality, as a way of influencing others, in several ways: teaching principles directly by explaining them or by expressing moral emotions; setting examples of how to behave; gossiping (and thereby expressing principles by presupposing them when we criticize others – see Sabini and Silver, 1982); rewarding behavior that follows the principles and punishing behavior that violates them; supporting or violating institutional (family, governmental) laws or rules (depending on what we think of their morality); supporting or opposing such laws or rules, making or repealing them; or justifying them in hindsight by referring to norms, which are then supported by the appeal. The concept of morality can be seen as arising as an abstraction from all of these situations (Singer, 1982). Although "morality" may have other meanings, this is the meaning that is relevant to decision making.

From this analysis of the functions of morality, we can derive a couple of principles.

Imperatives and the naturalistic fallacy

The philosopher Richard M. Hare (1952, 1963, 1981) points out that a moral statement is like an imperative statement. Logically, the statement "You should not steal" resembles, in usage, the statement "Do not steal." Moral statements tell us to do (or not do) something. It would be inconsistent to say, "You should be kind to animals — but don't be."

Moral conclusions do not follow, as an inference, from a set of premises unless at least one of the premises is also of this imperative form (Hare, 1952). For example, the argument, "It would be helpful to me if you opened the door; therefore, open the door" is not valid without the added premise "Do whatever would be helpful to me."[1]

---

[1] If we adopt Toulmin's theory for extended logic, described in Chapter 4, we might say that this inference is valid, but the warrant or backing must involve a statement such as, "Do whatever would be helpful to me."

This has an interesting consequence. We cannot draw moral conclusions (logically) from facts alone. From the fact that Harry's father says that Harry should not marry a gentile, it does not follow that Harry should not marry a gentile, unless we also assume that he ought to do what his father says. From the fact that the Bible says to keep the sabbath, we cannot conclude that we ought to keep the sabbath, unless we assume that we ought to do what the Bible says. From the purported fact that males evolved to spread their seed widely whereas females evolved to seek the protection of a single male, we cannot conclude that infidelity in marriage is more excusable for males than for females, unless we assume that people should do what they (purportedly) evolved to do. From the purported fact that people were not made to reproduce by artificial means, we cannot conclude that artificial insemination is immoral, unless we assume that people ought to do only what is "natural."

All of these mistaken inferences are examples of the *naturalistic fallacy*. To commit the naturalistic fallacy is to *draw a conclusion about what ought to be true solely from what is true.* It reflects a kind of confusion about the origin of moral rules themselves.

In many cases, people who commit the naturalistic fallacy would be quite willing to accept the premise they need — for example, that one should do what the Bible says or that one should not do what is unnatural — but simply have not given the matter much thought. Their acceptance of such principles is unreflective. A person who says that artificial insemination is wrong because it is "unnatural," for example, may have no objection at all to our using telephones, automobiles, and railroads, and may not notice that these things also violate the principle that whatever is unnatural is wrong.

The fallacy of relativism

Moral statements are more than just imperative in this way. As Hare (1963) points out, the difference between the moral statement, "Tell the truth!" and the ordinary imperative statement "Open the door!" is that the former is impersonal: That is, it is meant to apply to anyone who is in certain circumstances.[2] An impersonal rule need not be very general, for the "circumstances" may be very precisely defined, as, for example, in this moral statement: "Residents should turn off their record players on weekdays during exam period, when people nearby are trying to study and are disturbed by the music." Although precisely these circumstances do not arise very often (considering mankind as a whole, at any rate), this moral prescription applies to *anyone* in these circumstances.

The requirement of impersonality comes from one of the reasons we want moral rules in the first place. We want them to *regulate conduct concerning issues that concern us all.* A moral rule or judgment is a type of premise to which anyone can appeal. Moral advice giving goes beyond specific cases. When we try to influence

[2] Hare (1963) uses the term "universal" instead of "impersonal," but "universal" invites misunderstanding, so I avoid it.

people morally, we try to influence some standard they hold for how they should behave in a class of cases. We thus try to influence the principles they follow, not just their behavior in a specific situation. And not just one person.

Failure to understand that moral rules are impersonal results in the fallacy of *relativism*. To the relativist, moral questions are simply questions of taste. What is right (or wrong) for one person, the relativist says, may not be right (or wrong) for another person in exactly the same situation. It depends on the person's own moral beliefs. I may think smoking marijuana is wrong, but if you think smoking it is moral, then it is not wrong for you to smoke marijuana. By this view, we can "agree to differ" about morality, just as we agree to differ about whether we like the taste of chili pepper. If moral judgments are impersonal, however, such relativistic judgments are not truly moral judgments at all, for it is in the very nature of moral judgments that they apply to everyone in the circumstances specified by the rule. If Judy and Jane are both pregnant, for example, and if their circumstances are the same in other relevant respects, one cannot think that abortion is wrong for Jane but right for Judy, just because it is Jane's opinion that abortion is wrong and Judy's opinion that abortion is right. If you truly think this, then you have no real moral opinion about abortion at all. If you think that all moral questions are matters of opinion, then you have, in effect, no real moral beliefs at all.

To say that relativism is a fallacy is not, of course, to say that everyone already agrees about moral questions such as premarital sex, euthanasia, or world government. On the contrary, we obviously disagree about such matters very strongly, but the reason our moral disagreements are so vehement is precisely because moral rules are supposed to apply to everyone. Each side believes that its opinion applies to everyone, and that people ought not to differ about moral questions — even though we know that in fact they do.

If moral judgments are not matters of taste, then some answers to moral questions (like some answers to virtually any question) are better than others. People often reject this idea, claiming that "we all have a right to our own opinions" about moral matters. Notice, though, that the question of whether people have a right to their opinions is different from the question of whether some opinions are better than others. We can believe that our opinions are best and still believe that it is morally wrong to try to force people to agree with us (for example, by prohibiting publication of opposing arguments). Aside from the harm done in forcing people to do anything, we cannot be sure that we ourselves have unique access to the right answers. (In this way, morality is no different from science. No scientist can be sure of believing the best theory either, although some theories are better than others.)

Granting that we should not exterminate our moral opponents or prevent them from speaking freely, it seems inconsistent not to try to influence other people. If we are willing to act on our moral beliefs ourselves, impersonality requires that we be willing to try to induce others to act on them as well, within the limits set by our beliefs about tolerance, freedom of expression, and following the law. Again, this requirement stems from the premise that true moral judgments apply to everyone.

Moral judgments can be impersonal without being simple, crude, or insensitive to conditions. It is not inconsistent to think that a legal limit on the number of children per woman is acceptable in China but not in Australia, if one believes that China is more seriously overpopulated and that population is relevant to the "right" to have children. Nor is it inconsistent to think that walking down Main Street in a bikini is acceptable in Monaco but not in Mecca. The expectations of people, and what offends them, can matter too. When we say that a judgment applies to anyone in the "same situation," the description of the situation can be quite rich, so long as it does not include people's names.

In sum, moral judgments can be seen as expressing principles or norms that we want others to follow. These expressions are like imperative statements because they recommend action to others. They are impersonal because they apply to anyone in exactly the same situation. They gain their persuasive power in part from their impersonality. When people recommend rules for everyone, including themselves, these recommendations do not seem to arise from mere self-interest alone. Taken at face value, they are meant to apply to those who make them as well as to others. If we take this restriction seriously, then it would be rational for us to recommend rules that benefit everyone, that is, rules that help all of us — including ourselves — to achieve our goals.

Utilitarianism as the normative theory

The idea of moral principles as intended for everyone to follow can help us decide which principles are worth endorsing. Of course we already have moral principles among our goals for ourselves and others. We might find it useful to start from scratch, putting aside the moral judgments we have already made and the goals that arise from these judgments. We can then ask ourselves what principles we have reason to endorse. By putting aside our current moral views, we make sure not just to endorse the beliefs we have. We can see whether these principles, or some other principles, would be rational to endorse, for someone who as yet had no moral principles at all. Such a person would still have to have some altruism though. The goal of wanting others to achieve their goals is crucial to any moral motivation. Without it, people would probably have no reason to endorse any moral principles at all. (And altruism is not itself a moral principle, but more like a basic motivation.)

Under these conditions, we have reason to endorse the view that the morally best thing to do is whatever achieves everyone's goals the most (Baron, 1993a, 1996). We would want to endorse this principle because it would help to achieve the goals we already have, including our altruistic goals. If we assume that we can somehow add goal achievement, or utility, across people, this view is a form of utilitarianism. This is a major moral theory, although not the only one. It is the one most consistent with utility theory. It simply extends the idea of utility maximization to everyone.

What does this exclude? One thing it excludes is what might be called "moralistic goals." These are goals *for others* that do not arise from *their* goals. They are like making someone drink beer because *you* believe it is good for her, that she ought to want it, that morality demands people to like beer and consume it. Of course, it isn't usually about beer. It is about style, religious piety, aesthetic taste, and life style. Most of these kinds of moralistic principles come from moral principles that people already hold. (Principles of style can be moral if they are endorsed for others.) The argument I have made gives no reason to endorse these goals to someone who does not already have them (unless, of course, they turn out to be means for the achievement of real goals that people do have, but that is another matter).

Utilitarianism excludes other things, as I shall explain, but this first example might help to show that it is not a trivial, empty doctrine.

Maximizing expected utility for everyone

Utilitarianism provides a way of thinking about moral issues in which people have conflicting desires. To think about the best thing to do in such situations, you can try to put yourself in the position of all parties simultaneously. It is easiest to think about such decisions when you are not involved, of course, but this is a theoretical exercise. For example, suppose you are in charge of a college dormitory and you must decide when to allow John to play his stereo in the dormitory (and at what volume) and when he should not. To do this, you would put yourself in the position of John (who wants to hear his records) and also of the person he might be bothering (Judy, who lives in the room below). You would ask whose good (utility) is greater: John's, to hear his music, or Judy's, to get her work done. Because moral judgments are impersonal, it does not matter what particular individuals are involved; the answer should be the same even if John and Judy switched places. (When they switch places, they must switch their utilities too.) Notice that when you do this, we are basically trying to maximize their combined utility, as if we were applying MAUT (Chapter 14), with each person providing one dimension of a decision involving two independent dimensions.

If the decision maker is one of the parties, the decision is more difficult. Suppose that John himself must decide. From a purely moral point of view, the best decision is the same as if it were made by a disinterested third person. When John thinks morally, he tries to put himself in the other person's place as well as his own. Because of its resemblance to the biblical rule "And as ye would that men should do unto you, do ye also to them likewise" (Luke 6:31, also Matthew 7:12), Hare (1963, chs. 6 and 7) calls this sort of thinking a "Golden Rule argument." Notice, though, that this rule conflicts with John's maximizing his own self-interested utility, unless he is a saint (that is, unless he cares about others as much as about himself).

Many moral issues involve consequences of acts for the satisfaction of people's desires (the achievement of their goals). If we take this view of what morality is about, and if we then try to apply expected-utility theory to our decisions, we are led to adopt various forms of *utilitarianism* as our approach to moral questions (Hare, 1981). The basic idea of modern utilitarianism is that we treat each moral decision as a choice among competing acts. Each act has certain consequences, with different probabilities, for certain people. To decide which act is morally best, we simply add up the expected utilities of the consequences for all of the people. The best acts are those with the highest expected utility, across all of the people.

This is essentially what we do when we apply decision analysis to social questions such as medical treatment policies. We assume that the utilities of different outcomes of medical treatment for different people can be measured and added (and, therefore, traded off). For example, if the utility of death from a certain heart operation is -100 (relative to the patients' current painful life), the utility of improvement is 20 (on the same scale), and the probability of death from the operation is .05, then the expected utility from the operation (relative to the current state) is $.05 \cdot (-100) + .95 \cdot (20)$, or 14 per person. For 1,000 people to whom these figures apply, the expected total gain in utility, if all have the operation, is 14,000. On the basis of this analysis, we would decide to advise all 1,000 patients to have the operation, yet 50 of these people will probably die (if all 1,000 accept our advice), so total utility would increase for everyone at the expense of a great loss in utility for some.

Utilitarianism, like decision analysis, attends only to future effects of choices. It ignores the past. Utilitarians seek to punish bad behavior only because punishment deters or prevents future bad behavior, not because of any belief in the inherent necessity of retribution or deservingness. They go out of their way to keep promises, for example, only to support the institution of promise making (because of its future value to all), not because of any binding force inherent in promises themselves.

Older forms of utilitarianism spoke of maximizing total pleasure or happiness, but (for reasons given at the beginning of Chapter 10) more recent versions have tended to emphasize maximizing the achievement of personal goals, just as modern utility theory itself does. Many writers speak of utility as the satisfaction of preferences. The term "preference" suggests a decision, however, and we have found that our decisions are not always the ones that best achieve our goals. It does not do people any good to give them something they "prefer" now but that will in the future prevent them from achieving their goals. Our personal goals, together with our beliefs about the effects of our choices, are the *reasons* for our preferences, as expressed in our decisions.[3] Other writers speak of utility as the satisfaction of desires. The term "satisfaction," however, suggests an emotion that we experience only after our goal is achieved, and, as I pointed out in Chapter 10, for many of our important goals we cannot have this experience (for example, our goal that our children have a long and happy life after we die). I shall therefore continue to assume that our main concern is with the achievement of our personal goals.

When we use utilitarian concepts in our everyday reasoning, however, we do not need to be so precise in our expression. We often speak of "paying attention to other people's feelings" when we are trying to emphasize the basic message of utilitarianism, that what matters in our decision making is the consequences of what

[3] Some forms of utilitarianism consider effects of choices on the satisfaction of *rational* preferences only, those preferences that people would have on reflection. But the form of reflection is not usually specified. An implication of the view I present here is that the relevant sort of reflection is about the distinction between fundamental values and means values. We should try to achieve means values only to the extent to which they are connected to fundamental values by true beliefs (Chapter 14).

we do for people (not just the people near to us but those distant in time and space as well).

Utilitarianism assumes that all people are weighed equally. If we are concerned with maximizing the achievement of goals, then it should not matter whose goals are at issue. We can treat everyone's goals as though they all belonged to the same person.[4]

Utilitarianism is not the view that the right answer to moral questions should be decided by adding up people's moral opinions; in fact, we might even want to exclude such opinions from a utilitarian analysis on the ground that prior belief often does not reflect our best thinking (Baron, 1986). In the nineteenth century, for example, many people favored the institution of slavery so much that they desired that slavery continue to exist, as a moral goal, just the way some of us today desire that other people be prohibited from having (or that they be allowed to have) abortions. If such desires had been considered in a utilitarian analysis of slavery, they might have been strong enough to tip the balance in its favor. Because utilitarian analysis, like decision analysis, is a way of determining what our action should be, both kinds of analysis should exclude prior desires concerning the action itself (as opposed to its consequences). If they include such desires, they are useless for their purpose; they are no longer a "second opinion" but an echo of the first opinion.

Interpersonal comparison

Utilitarianism requires comparison of one person's utilities with another person's, as in the case of John (who wanted to play music) and Judy (who wanted to study). Does this make sense?

Notice that the comparison is of differences or changes, not levels. All we need to decide is whether John's playing his music increases his utility more than it decreases Judy's. We do not need to decide whether John is happier or better off than Judy in general. Likewise, in considering a tax on the rich to help the poor, we should ask whether the decrease in utility for the rich is smaller than the increase for the poor. For making the relevant comparison, we need not consider absolute levels of utility. We are concerned only with the consequences of a particular decision, and we want to know whether the good that results from some option — compared to an alternative option — is greater than the harm.

Comparisons of utility differences are difficult, but we do make them, on the basis of the same sort of information we use to think about tradeoffs within other individuals. It is clear, for example, that the utility that my friend Bill gains from having a $30 bottle of wine with his dinner out, instead of a $15 bottle, is less than the utility gain to someone else from having her malaria cured. (The comparison is even easier if the disease is fatal without the cure.) If I could purchase a cure for $15

---

[4]Singer (1993) discusses the utilitarian view of animals. In brief, utilitarians generally count animals, but the utilities of most animals are different from those of most people, because animals do not have long-term future plans. Many questions remain about how people should treat animals, which I shall not discuss.

by making Bill forgo the more expensive wine, other things being equal, I ought to do it. Other comparisons are more difficult, but the difficulty of making them is only a matter of degree.

The fact that we make such comparisons does not necessarily make them meaningful. Comparisons of utilities across people could be like comparisons of the saltiness of colors. We can make such judgments, and we might even agree somewhat on them. But there is no truth about them.

Can we imagine some kind of yardstick that would have the same utility for two people? That would be a starting point. Let us imagine two identical twins with identical experiences.[5] Suppose each twin is given a 30 volt electric shock lasting for 1 minute. It is reasonable to assume that this has the same utility for both of them. Pure experiences of this sort could serve as the yardstick we are seeking. We have no reason to question the equivalence of the experience for both twins.

We could extend this to cases of people less closely related. We know something about what makes people respond differently to painful experiences, and we could use this knowledge to make reasonable guesses about the utility of the same event for different people. The less similar the people are, the more error our judgment will have, but error is present in all judgments. The point is that we have reasons for our judgments of interpersonal comparison of utility. They are not like judging the saltiness of colors.

. Once we have the yardstick, we can use it to measure other goals, goals that do not involve experiences only. We could do this by asking for judgments within individuals. For example, we could ask such (outlandish, but meaningful) questions as, "Would you accept an hour a day of 100 volt electric shock for a year in order to prevent the Mona Lisa from being defaced?" (We ask this of a person who may well never see the Mona Lisa but who has a personal goal of preserving original art works.) In this way, we could determine the strength of goals that do not involve experiences. If we knew as well the psychological determinants of aversion to electric shock, the problem of interpersonal comparison is in principle solved.

When we make interpersonal comparisons, we accept a great deal of error. Surely many factors affect people's tolerance for pain, their desire to live, their desire for material comfort, and so on, and we are not aware of all of these factors. Once again, the acceptance of error is not an argument that the enterprise is theoretically impossible or that there is no truth of the matter.

The problem of error led many economists to reject the possibility of interpersonal comparison. Robbins (1938), for example, cites "the story of how an Indian official had attempted to explain to a high-caste Brahmin the sanctions of the Benthamite system. 'But that,' said the Brahmin, 'cannot possibly be right. I am ten times as capable of happiness as that untouchable over there.'" Robins goes on, "I had no sympathy with the Brahmin. But I could not escape the conviction that, if I chose to regard men as equally capable of satisfaction and he to regard them as

---

[5]This is not truly possible, but it is approximately possible, and certainly imaginable, and this is all we need for a an argument about normative theory.

differing according to a hierarchical schedule, the difference between us was not one which could be resolved by the same methods of demonstration as were available in other fields of social judgment."

Anyone's estimate of the tradeoff between your utilities and mine could well be off by a factor of ten. But, crucially, it could be off *either way*. In making decisions between the Brahmin and the untouchable, we might just as easily conclude that the *untouchable* is more sensitive (since the Brahmin is jaded, et cetera). Uncertainty about the strengths of goals is just one form of uncertainty about the state of the world. If we follow expected-utility theory, we will made decisions according to our expectation. Although we can be wrong, we can do no better. If our expectations are informed, as I have argued they are, the problem of error is not a decisive objection no matter how great the possible error. For many purposes, we simply assume that people are alike in their utilities. When we make choices that affect life and death — such as choices about how much to spend on medical technology — we do not attempt to determine which of two patients has a greater desire to live.

Utilitarianism is closely related to expected-utility theory (Chapter 10). When a group of people all face the same decision, then the two models clearly dictate the same choice. For example, suppose each of 1,000 people faces a .2 probability of some disease without vaccination, but the vaccine causes an equally serious disease with a probability of .1. The best decision for each person is to get the vaccine. If everyone gets the vaccine, then we expect that 100 will get the disease caused by the vaccine, instead of 200 getting the other disease.

The relationship goes deeper than this. It is possible to show that, if the overall good (utility) of each person is defined by expected-utility, then, with some very simple assumptions, the overall good of everyone is a sum of individual utilities (Broome, 1991). In particular, we need to assume the "Principle of Personal Good" (Broome, 1991, p. 165): "(a) Two alternatives are equally good if they are equally good for each person. And (b) if one alternative is at least as good as another for everyone and definitely better for someone, it is better." This is a variant of the basic idea of "Pareto optimality," named after the economist Vilfredo Pareto (1848–1923). This variant assumes that the probabilities of the states do not depend on the person. It is as though the theory were designed for decision makers with their own probabilities.

To make this argument, Broome (1991) considers a table like the following. Each column represents a state of nature (like those in the expected-utility tables in Chapter 10). Each row represents a person. There are s states and h people. The entries in each cell represent the utilities for the outcome for each person in each state. For example u_{12} is the utility for Person 1 in State 2.

$$
\begin{array}{cccc}
u_{11} & u_{12} & \dots & u_{1s} \\
u_{21} & u_{22} & \dots & u_{2s} \\
\cdot & \cdot & \dots & \cdot \\
\cdot & \cdot & \dots & \cdot \\
u_{h1} & u_{h2} & \dots & u_{hs}
\end{array}
$$

The basic argument, in very broad outline, shows that total utility is an increasing function of both the row and column utilities, and that the function is additive for both rows and columns. Expected-utility theory implies additivity for each row. For a given column, the Principle of Personal Good implies that the utility for each column is an increasing function of the utilities for the individuals in that column. An increase in one entry in the cell has to have the same effect on both the rows and the columns, so the columns must be additive too. [6]

Rights theories

Utilitarianism conflicts with many of our intuitions, the basic moral beliefs we have acquired from our culture. Does the state, for example, have a right to protect us from ourselves by passing laws requiring motorcycle riders to wear helmets, or should citizens be considered autonomous, capable of running (or ruining) their own lives as they see fit? A utilitarian would have no choice but to argue that the state should protect us from ourselves, if the harm avoided is, on balance, greater than the harm from the interference. Utilitarians have been called, with some justice, "moral busybodies." A good utilitarian is a "Jewish mother" to the world.

Other moral theories take autonomy to be more fundamental, so that any violation of autonomy requires special justification. A very popular moral theory of this sort in the United States is based on the theory of moral rights. The "unalienable rights" that Jefferson refers to in the Declaration of Independence, for example, reflect a long tradition of political "rights" theory. The laws of the United States itself are not themselves a moral system, but many have argued that they are based on such a system and that the system that they are based on recognizes the idea of individual rights. (Parts of the law — particularly the laws pertaining to environmental regulation — also recognize utilitarianism.) It is commonplace for political movements in the United States today to base their demands on the idea of rights: the "right" to life (of fetuses, usually); the "right" to control one's own body (that is, have abortions); the "right" to medical care of a certain quality; the "right" to profit from one's good luck. The most sophisticated rights theory formulated in recent years is probably that of the American philosopher John Rawls (1971), which proposes a fundamental right (the right to equal liberty) from which all other legitimate rights are derived. [7]

For rights theories in general, a "right" can be seen as a consequence of a moral rule about what to do — or (most typically) not do — in a given situation: for example, "Do not murder"; "Do not interfere forcibly with a person's control over her body"; "Do not prevent a person from having his say." Each of these rules generates both a right and a duty: for example, a right not to be murdered (or a right to life) and a duty not to murder. Many rights involve some sort of autonomy. In the case

---

[6] For details, see Broome, 1991, particularly, pp. 68, 69, and 202.

[7] I do not mean to suggest that rights theories are uniquely parochial and limited to one national tradition. Jefferson was strongly influenced by the British philosopher John Locke, and, conversely, utilitarianism has been described to me by one American philosopher (Samuel Freeman) as a "British national treasure."

of the first rule, for instance, a right to noninterference and a duty not to interfere in certain ways.

Many rights theories, including Rawls's, justify the idea of autonomy by thinking of morality as a kind of contract or agreement, usually a hypothetical one. By this argument, our moral obligations result from our participation in a society. We take certain benefits from this participation, and, in return, we have agreed to give up to the society certain *limited* parts of our own autonomy. In return for other people honoring and protecting our autonomy (for example, our right to life and property), we agree to honor and protect (through government) the autonomy and rights of others. Beyond the demands of such agreements, however, there are no moral obligations (in the simplest form of these theories), and we can be as selfish as we like.

Rights theorists generally believe that people behave morally if they follow all of the rules concerning the rights of others, but usually that is impossible to do, because in many cases the rules conflict. For example, in deciding whether to allow abortion, the right of the fetus to live conflicts with the right of the mother to make decisions that affect her own health. Rights theories have various ways of resolving such conflicts. One is to conclude that it is impossible to be moral. Another is to set up a lexical order of rules (see Chapter 14), so that certain rules are always given priority (for example, right to life over right to make medical decisions for oneself). Still another is to pare down the list of rights to one or two basic ones (as Rawls did).

As an example of the conflict between rights theories and utilitarianism, consider the case of John, a member of a fraternity, who likes to play his record player very loudly on warm spring days, with his window open. He may think he has a "right" to do this. (There is no rule against it, he thinks.) Jon, who walks through the campus, finds John's taste in music (hard rock) offensive; it bothers him not just to hear it, but to have it going through his head for several hours afterward. (He rushes home after work to wash it out with a dose of Debussy.) Jon may think he has a "right" not to be assaulted in this way. (He would like there to be a rule against it, to protect his right.) A utilitarian would have to weigh Jon's displeasure against John's pleasure. A utilitarian would also have to consider the number of people who are bothered by John's music, and the effect of John's music as a precedent for others and for John himself at other times, which leads to effects on still more people. A rights theorist might ignore the number affected, arguing that violating the rights of even one person is as bad as violating the rights of a million people.

As another example of the conflict of theories, let us consider the question of the amount of income tax (if any) that people with different income levels should pay. A utilitarian analysis usually focuses on two facts: First, the "marginal utility" of income is declining (Chapter 10), which means that total utility increases if we tax those with high incomes and use part of the taxes to subsidize those with low incomes (either by reducing their taxes or by supplementing their incomes). Second, some differences in income are needed to provide incentives for people to work and thereby provide the goods and services that give money its value. Declining marginal utility by itself would lead to equality of income, but the need for incentive, it is argued, justifies economic inequality. By utility theory, the question of the best compromise on the taxation issue becomes a mathematically and empirically difficult, but morally simple, calculation. The solution is simply whatever form of taxation maximizes total utility, all things considered. (Notice that "total utility" here is not measured by such indices as the Gross National Product, for such indices count the monetary value of expensive luxury goods just as much as the value of "necessities." The utility of $3,565 worth of medical care, however, is probably much greater than the combined utility of an $815 wristwatch and a $2,750 fountain pen.)

Rights theorists, on the other hand, take varying positions on this issue, depending on which rights they consider primary. *Libertarian* rights theorists, such as Nozick (1974), argue that people have a basic right to keep what they earn, even if all would benefit if the more prosperous were forced to give up some of their income. (Where this right came from is left unanswered.) *Liberal* rights theorists such as Rawls (1971) argue that the poor have a right to first consideration (lexical priority), so that the sole consideration should be to maximize the benefit of the poor. (This might still allow differences in income, because of the same incentive principle that the utilitarian acknowledges.) The utilitarian solution is roughly in between these two. Unlike the libertarian solution, it permits taxing the rich to help the poor, but, unlike the liberal solution, it does not give the poor absolute priority over everyone else.

Sometimes rights theories are defended by the argument that the utilities of different people cannot be compared. It is true that interpersonal comparisons are often difficult to make. But this is not special to interpersonal comparisons. It is also difficult to compare one's own utilities for very different kinds of outcomes (health, wealth, or wisdom, for example). It is certainly not impossible to compare utilities for different people — and sometimes it is easy. If I could effect a cure of one case of malaria by contributing $5 to a charity, for example, the gain to the person cured would surely be greater than the loss to me. We must remember that we do not need to compare the overall levels of happiness or life satisfaction for two individuals (which might be more difficult) but merely the difference between *outcomes*: my having $5 more or less, and the other person having or not having malaria. Hare (1981, p. 123) even suggests that interpersonal comparisons can be used to measure utility. The basic idea is, in effect, to use each person's outcomes as an independent dimension in a MAUT analysis (Chapter 14).

Deontological rules

Rights theories are part of a broader alternative to utilitarianism, which may be called *deontology*, a term that refers to rules of duty or obligations, or rules that concern what to do and what not to do, rather than the value of consequences. Of course, one way to specify what to do is to say, "Do whatever achieves a certain consequence." This is not a deontological rule. Such rules are described in terms of the conditions, not the consequences, even though conditions may be correlated with consequences. For a pigeon in a Skinner box, a consequential rule is "peck whichever key produces food," and a deontological rule is "peck the red key." If the red key produces food all the time, then the distinction is empty. But if the green key sometimes produces food while the red key does not (and the pigeon has learned this), the rules conflict. Rights theories are deontological because they specify what we can and cannot do to each other regardless of the consequences. Stealing (thus violating the right to property) is wrong, even if a particular act of stealing leads to some very good outcome.

Many deontological rules prohibit actions that cause some harm, even if the action prevents a greater harm. For example, such a rule might say that it is wrong to bomb civilians in order to terrorize an enemy into surrender (thus saving many more lives). Some pacifists oppose fighting in a war, even if the purpose of the war is to prevent someone else from waging a more destructive war. Some pacifists may explicitly argue this position. Others may truly believe that such wars are always ineffective. These beliefs, however, may sometimes arise from the belief-overkill phenomenon discussed in Chapter 9.

Other deontological rules are based on the injunction not to use people as means, but to treat everyone as an end. This would seem to prohibit such terror bombing. Kant's second formulation of the famed Categorical Imperative reads: "Act so that you treat humanity, whether in your own person or in that of another, [1] always as an end and [2] never as a means only" (Kant, 1959). The negative injunction "never as a means only" has been the source of much speculation. Because it contains the word "only," it is fully consistent with the utilitarian view, which simply holds that those used as means must also be considered as part of the overall accounting. But a utilitarian would also find the injunction to be redundant. When everyone is considered as an end, we weigh the interests of some against the interest of others, and often we have no choice but to settle for the lesser harm. Perhaps Kant was drawing on a more common intuition against the idea of using people as means at all.

The same principle may be part of the doctrine of the double effect in Catholicism, attributed to Thomas Aquinas (1947, II–II, Q. 64, art. 7) as part of his explanation of why killing in self-defense can be morally acceptable:

> Nothing hinders one act from having two effects, only one of which is intended, while the other is beside the intention. Now moral acts take their species according to what is intended, and not according to what is beside the intention, since this is accidental.... Accordingly the act of self-defense may have two effects, one is the saving of one's life, the other is the slaying of the aggressor. Therefore this act, since one's intention is to save one's own life, is not unlawful, seeing that it is natural to everything to keep itself in "being," as far as possible. And yet, though proceeding from a good intention, an act may be rendered unlawful, if it be out of proportion to the end.

As later writers attempted to make sense out of this injunction, the role of intention was downplayed and another distinction came to the fore, that between indirect or accidental harm, on the one hand, and direct harm that is a means to an end is another. Quinn (1989), for example, says that, "a new and better formulation of the doctrine [of the double effect] ... distinguishes between agency in which harm comes to some victims, at least in part, from the agent's deliberately involving them in something in order to further his purpose precisely by way of their being so involved ... and harmful agency in which either nothing is in that way intended for the victims or what is so intended does not contribute to their harm." Quinn uses the term "direct" and "indirect" for these two kinds of harm, and we shall use these terms.

Other deontological rules might specify just treatment in terms of balancing or retribution: reward good behavior and punish bad behavior, even if there is no good consequence. Still others concern truth telling or promise keeping. The important aspect of these rules is that they are at least somewhat independent of consequences. A blanket deontological rule concerning truth telling would prohibit white lies to save people's feelings. The rule could be tailored to allow exceptions, but the exceptions would be described in terms of the situation, not the expected consequences. Most laws are of this form. The distinction between deontological and utilitarian rules is often fuzzy. For example, the law distinguishes murder from manslaughter on the basis of intended consquences.

Many modern deontologists trace their roots to Kant's *categorical imperative*. Kant argued that moral principles had to be categorical (required in all cases) rather than "hypothetical" (dependent on other desires). Thus, the reason to keep promises should not depend on the motive of inculcating trust. The justification must come from "reason" alone. One statement of the Categorical Imperative was "Act only on that maxim through which you can at the same time will that it should become a universal law." Thus, making a false promise whenever it suits you to do so (for example, borrowing money without intending to pay it back) would not fit. If it were a universal law to do this, promises would be meaningless. So it is *inconsistent* to follow such a maxim.

Kant's categorical imperative is difficult to understand, and some have argued that it does not imply very much. A more powerful statement is "Do whatever would be best if everyone did it," or "Follow the rule (maxim) that would best for everyone to follow." This is called the *generalization test*. The idea is to evaluate moral principles by asking "What if everybody did that?" Most scholars do not think that this is what Kant had in mind, but it is a popular approach to morality. A problem with it is that each option can be described in terms of many different maxims or rules. For example, one rule that describes many moral actions is "Do whatever does the most good." This is, of course, the utilitarian rule.

Rule utilitarianism

Some philosophers have resolved the conflict between utilitarianism and deontological theories (including rights theories) by arguing that utilitarianism does not apply to specific acts (as we would assume using utility theory), but rather to the moral *rules* that we adopt and try to live by. This approach is called *rule utilitarianism*, as distinct from *act utilitarianism*. Act utilitarianism is the standard form. According to rule utilitarianism, the question is not whether John should play his stereo in a given case, but rather whether utility is maximized if people are, in general, free to play their stereos or not. Rule utilitarians try to show how moral rules generally maximize utility. If it turns out that some rules do not, then they are suspect. But most rules do, compared to their opposite. It is usually better to tell the truth than to lie, for example.

Rule utilitarianism takes as its starting point the fact that most conventional moral rules seem designed to maximize utility, and we might do best to follow them even when we think that breaking them would maximize utility. For example, the rights of autonomy are justified by the fact that each individual generally knows more than anyone else about the nature of his or her personal goals and how to achieve them. (We take away the rights of autonomy in exactly those cases in which this is probably not true: young children and mental patients.) In many cases, by this argument, the assumption that people know what is good for them is not true, but it is true more often than not. Since it is impossible to ascertain (for adults outside of institutions) just when it is true, we maximize utility by assuming that it is generally true of everyone. This argument implies that autonomy is not a fundamental moral principle but rather a generally well-justified intuition, suitable as a guide to daily life but not as the fundamental basis of a moral theory.

The idea that following rules can maximize utility also helps us understand the importance of moral motives and goals. Take the classic dilemma in which a cruel dictator offers you the following choice: Either you shoot one of his political prisoners for him, or he will shoot ten others, as well as the one. There is no way out, and the choice you make will not be known to anyone else. Clearly, the utilitarian solution here is to shoot one prisoner. Losing one life is not as bad as losing eleven; but many would balk. They would stand on (intuitive) principle and refuse to take part. More important, we might admire them for this stand.

Hare (1981) argues that both sides are right, in different senses. If we used true utilitarian thinking, we would conclude that it is right to shoot but that it is also right to develop an intuitive rule against participation in wanton killing. (If more people adhered to such a rule, dictators like the one in question would not so easily come to power.) We admire the person who refuses to shoot for sticking to what is basically a good rule, even though the right *act* goes against the rule in this case. Moral motives are important, even when they go against right acts. In the long run, things work best if people have good motives, even if their acts are occasionally non-optimal as a result.[8]

Why should we follow a rule when we are sure that breaking it would do more good? Why shouldn't John play his stereo when everyone is absolutely sure that all the rock-music haters have cleared out for the summer. At least he and the few others left would enjoy it, and nobody would be harmed.

[8] One could also argue that the refusal to shoot is a kind of self-indulgence, a selfish concern with one's own guilt feelings at the expense of ten lives. Although from Hare's point of view this is true, it is beside the point, which is that the guilt feelings would result from failing to follow a good rule.

The answer may be that trying to follow a utilitarian theory is, sometimes, self-defeating. If utilitarianism is the normative standard, then we might do better, according to this standard, by trying to follow rules, even when the rules seem, at first blush, not to follow the standard. This argument is consistent with several psychological principles discussed in this book.

For example, wishful thinking (Chapter 9) may distort our beliefs. People who are tempted to commit adultery want to believe that their spouses will not find out, that they will not be hurt all that much if they do find out, and so on. If their beliefs are influenced by their desires, they will go ahead, even though they are wrong. People may do better to follow the rule "Do not commit adultery," even when it seems to them to be okay. Notice that people may do this with full understanding. People can simply remind themselves that their perception of the situation is likely to be distorted, just as they do when they refuse to sign contracts while they are drunk.

We may also tend to think in terms of immediate consequences. When we break a promise, we may correctly think that the immediate consequences of breaking the promise are better than those of keeping it. I may, for example, miss an appointment because someone telephones me who seems to need immediate help. But this comparison of utilities does not include the long-run social effects of breaking a rule. If people break appointments more often, then others will think that this is acceptable, and the whole custom of making appointments will weaken. Appointments are a good idea, because they allow people to meet who would not otherwise meet. The long-run harm from breaking a single appointment is difficult to think about. It must happen. There is no critical point at which breaking an appointment first starts to undermine the custom. The more broken appointments, the more the custom is weakened. So every broken appointment does some harm in the long run.

Although this is a good argument, a utilitarian might still resist the dictum: "Always keep appointments, come hell or high water." Sometimes the person who demands immediate attention really *is* more important than all the effects of breaking the appointment. (And these effects can be mitigated by telling the story later.)

Another reason for following conventional moral rules is that people who violate certain rules for moral reasons have turned out to be wrong almost all the time. Political terrorists have often concluded that the harm they do is justified by the greater good, but it is difficult to find a clear case where this was true.

Similar reasons apply to political and social rights. For example, the right of free speech helps us to obtain the information we need to elect our government wisely. Other rights, such as the right to worship (or not worship) as we choose, allow us to pursue the personal goals that are important to us, without the threat of interference from busybodies who think they know what everyone else's goals ought to be. Surely, in some cases, it is better to violate these rights. Should overt or implicit advocacy of violence be included in the protection of free speech? Should religious freedom be allowed when a religion requires parents to withhold medical treatment from their children? or when it prohibits male doctors from seeing the nude bodies of female patients? Yet, any attempt by a government to intervene in such matters is subject to wishful thinking and miscalculation. The moral life is hard.

➤ So far, this discussion has treated intuitive moral rules as if they always disagree with utilitarianism, although they may approximate it. Intuitions need not conflict with utilitarianism, however. The following quotation, from a subject interviewed by Gilligan (1982, p. 67) as part of a study of moral reasoning, illustrates a set of moral intuitions that seem to represent a prescriptive form of utilitarianism itself:

> [What makes an issue moral is] some sense of trying to uncover a right path in which to live, and always in my mind is that the world is full of real and recognizable trouble, and it is heading for some sort of doom, and is it right to bring children into this world when we currently have an overpopulation problem, and is it right to spend money on a pair of shoes when I have a pair of shoes and other people are shoeless? It is in part a self-critical view, part of saying, "How am I spending my time and in what sense am I working?" I think I have a real drive, a real maternal drive, to take care of someone — to take care of my mother, to take care of children, to take care of other people's children, to take care of my own children, to take care of the world. When I am dealing with moral issues, I am sort of saying to myself constantly, "Are you taking care of all the things that you think are important, and in what ways are you wasting yourself and wasting those issues?"

Biases in moral judgment?

If we accept utilitarianism as a normative model, we can identify biases in moral judgment, analogous to the biases that have been found in other sorts of judgments and decisions. Of course, this is a more difficult enterprise, because the normative theory of morality is so controversial. (Controversy about normative models is not unique to morality, though. For example, Ellsberg, 1961, argued that the "ambiguity effect" is rational, and that expected-utility theory is therefore not normative. This sort of controversy persists in utility theory, and even probability theory.) Here, I shall regard utilitarianism as the correct normative theory, but the general idea of comparing moral judgments to *some* normative theory does not depend on the the particular theory we use.

By this analogy, moral judgments arise from various heuristics or naive theories. We become committed to these theories, however, because moral judgments are expressed as recommendations to others through direct statements and through indirect statements such as gossip. After we have expressed principles to others, it is more difficult for us to think that the principles we have stated might be wrong. (Cognitive dissonance research has demonstrated this effect; see Chapter 9.) Our moral principles, therefore, may start as heuristics but end up as firm intuitions. If some of our intuitions are nonnormative — whatever normative theory we adopt — we will resist the normative theory itself. The intuitions may become somewhat systematized, as may occur with other naive theories.

Acts and omissions

A possible example of a nonnormative moral intuition is the distinction often made between acts and omissions, which we identified in Chapter 12 as an example of bias in decision making. The vaccination case in which people do not vaccinate babies even when the vaccine risk is much lower than the disease risk is, however, also a moral example, especially when the decision is made by a policy maker for a large group of people (Ritov and Baron, 1990, see Chapter 12). It is analogous to the question about whether it is right to shoot one person in order to save ten others, although in the case of vaccination the numbers are different, no shooting is required, and the identities of the victims are unknown.

We can argue that this intuition is nonnormative even without defending all of utilitarianism (Baron, 1993a, ch. 7). The simple argument is the Golden Rule. If you were a child, which would you prefer: a 10/10,000 chance of death from a disease or a 5/10,000 chance of death from a vaccine? Would it matter to you whether the chance resulted from an act or omission? More generally, each of us has reason to endorse a principle that others should make decisions so as to minimize our chance of death (other things being equal). The reason we have comes from the fact that we all want to live; this is one of our goals. But we have no reason to limit this principle to certain kinds of options, such as acts or omissions. If we have altruistic goals toward others, then these goals too give us reason to endorse the same principle, and no reason to restrict it. Altruistic goals are goals for the achievement of others' goals, so, if others have reason to endorse a principle, then so does the altruist. Moral principles are empty if we have no reason to endorse them, and they are inferior if we have better principles to endorse.

Spranca, Minsk, and Baron (1991) found a bias toward omissions in situations that were more obviously moral than those discussed so far. In one scenario, John, the best tennis player at a club, wound up playing the final of the club's tournament against Ivan Lendl (then ranked first in the world). John knew that Ivan was allergic to cayenne pepper and that the salad dressing in the club restaurant contained it. When John went to dinner with Ivan the night before the final, he planned to recommend the house dressing to Ivan, hoping that Ivan would get a bit sick and lose the match. In one ending to the story, John recommended the dressing. In the other, Ivan ordered the dressing himself just before John was about to recommend it, and John, of course, said nothing. When asked whether John's behavior is worse in one ending or the other, about a third of the subjects said that it was worse when he acted. These subjects tended to say that John did not cause Ivan's illness by saying nothing. (In reply, it might be said that the relevant sense of "cause" here concerns whether John had control over what Ivan ate, which he did.)

In sum, "omission bias" is the tendency to judge acts that are harmful (relative to the alternative option) as worse than omissions that are equally harmful (relative to the alternative) or even more harmful (as in the vaccination case) (Baron and Ritov, 1994). In any given case, some people display this bias and others do not. In this regard, at least, omission bias is like the other biases described in this book. In some cases, people can be persuaded to consider acts and omissions as equivalent, with an argument like that just made (Baron, 1992).

Omission bias is related to issues of public controversy, such as whether active euthanasia should be allowed. Most countries (and most states of the United States) now allow passive euthanasia, the withholding of even standard medical treatment for those who are judged to be no worse off dead than alive, but active euthanasia is almost everywhere banned even for those who wish to die. Opponents of active euthanasia can, of course, find other arguments against it than the fact that it is "active." But it is possible that these arguments would not be seen as so compelling if the distinction between acts and omissions were not made.

Omission bias could also justify a lack of concern with the problems of others (Singer, 1979). For example, much of the world's population lives in dire poverty today and into the foreseeable future. People — even people who take an interest in social issues — often think that they are not responsible for this poverty and need do nothing about it. It can be argued, however, that with a little effort we can think of all sorts of things we can do that will help the situation immensely at very low cost to ourselves, such as supporting beneficial policies. Failure to do these things can be seen as a harm, but many people do not see it that way.

More generally, omission bias helps people believe that they are completely moral if they obey a list of prohibitions while otherwise pursuing their narrow self-interest. An alternative view is that represented by Gilligan's subject quoted earlier in this chapter. For this subject, the failure to use her life in ways ultimately beneficial to others would count as a moral failure.

Other possible biases

So far very little descriptive work has been done on other non-utilitarian biases in moral judgment. But we may speculate on where such biases might be found, by examining the moral principles that people advocate. Three possible biases are indirectness, agent relativism, and naturalism.

The indirectness bias is illustrated in the doctrine of the double effect, described earlier. We see this in some ethical rules. For example, when a mother's life is threatened by a pregnancy, some Catholic hospitals will permit a hysterectomy to save the mother, but they will not permit an abortion. The fetus dies in either case, but, in the case of the hysterectomy (which of course leaves the mother unable to bear another child), the killing is seen as an indirect by-product (Bennett, 1966; Kuhse, 1987). In the abortion, however, the death of the fetus is the means to save the mother, so the fetus is being harmed directly. In other cases, the idea of harming someone directly to help others is invoked as a reason for moral restraint, as in the treatment of human subjects in research. The principle of informed consent is often justified as a way of making sure that subjects are not treated as means and harmed *directly* in order to help others. The indirectness bias is shown in the following scenario (Royzman and Baron, 1999):

A new viral disease is spreading rapidly in a region of Africa. Left alone, it will kill 100,000 people out of 1,000,000 in the region. X, a public health official, has two ways to prevent this. Both will stop the spread of the virus and prevent all these deaths:

A. Give all 1,000,000 a shot that makes them immune to the first disease. The shot will also cause, as a side effect, a second disease that will kill 100 people.

B. Give all 1,000,000 a shot that gives them another disease, which is incompatible with the first disease. The second disease will kill 100 people.

Most subjects thought that option A was better, since the deaths are a side effect rather than part of the mechanism of the main effect.

Agent relativity illustrated in the following scenario used by Baron and Miller (1999). X is one of 10 people who could save someone's life by donating bone marrow (a painful but relatively risk-free procedure) to Y. Is X's obligation to donate greater when X is Y's cousin then when X and Y are unrelated? Many people think so. Utilitarians even think so, if they think that family cohesion is a good thing that should be promoted for other reasons. Now consider Z, who is unrelated to X or Y. X, the potential donor, asks Z's advice about whether to donate, and Z knows that X will probably follow the advice offered. Does Z have a greater obligation to advise donation when X and Y are cousins than when X and Y are unrelated? A utilitarian who answered yes to the first question would have to answer yes to this one. After all, it is promoting family loyalty that is at issue, and it doesn't matter whose family it is (without knowing more details, of course). An *agent relative* response, however, would say that only Y needs to worry about family obligations. The obligation is relative to the agent. It differs from person to person. Miller and Baron found no evidence for agent relativity in any of their subjects (who were Indian as well as American). However, many philosophers argue that some obligations are agent relative in this way.

Omission bias is agent relative when the omission is the result of someone else's action. In the classic case of shooting one prisoner to save ten from the horrible dictator, the choice of not shooting is implicitly agent relative, because shooting will happen anyway. This is not a pure test of agent relativity, though, because the two options also differ in doing something versus doing nothing.

Naturalism is the bias toward nature. It is also related to omission bias, because "nature" often defines the default situation, the result of inaction, as in the case of the vaccination, where the disease can be assumed to be natural. (Of course, the result of omission is not always natural, as in the case of the dictator just described.) Chapter 20 presents evidence that people regard harms caused by people as worse than otherwise equivalent harms caused by nature. Spranca (1992) found that people would often pay extra to drink "natural water" rather than water that had been distilled and then had exactly the right chemicals added to it so that it was chemically identical to natural water. Baron, Holzman, and Schulkin (1998) found that many doctors would prefer to give "natural" hormones to menopausal women, rather than chemically identical synthetic hormones.

Let me emphasize again that the term "bias" here, as elsewhere in this book, is not pejorative. A finding of bias in judgment does not mean that the judge should be punished or condemned. It does mean that she should be educated if that is possible, *and* if we have sufficient confidence in our normative model. We must bear in mind that we can make both kinds of errors: mis-educating someone who doesn't really need it and failing to educate someone who does need it. In real prescriptive situations, you might want to take some small risk of mis-education errors. Note also that education here means persuasion not indoctrination. Without understanding, utilitarian moral principles are far less likely to be used correctly, and understanding can be achieved only by giving reasons.

In sum, then, we have two different reasons for looking for nonutilitarian biases. First, from the perspective of psychological theory, utilitarianism serves as a kind of null hypothesis. Judgments that we should do the most good are easy to explain in many ways and do not enlighten us much about the psychology of moral judgment. If everyone said that only the amount of harm mattered and not whether it was indirect or direct, this would be easy to explain in terms of a general principle that moral intuitions are designed to prevent harm. If this were the only principle that people used, it could be explained in so many ways as to be uninformative.

Second, intuitions that oppose producing the best overall consequences might actually lead to worse consequences (Baron, 1994, 1998). Those people who are concerned with why the outcomes of human decisions are not as good as possible might find it useful to know that some of the explanation lies in our moral intuitions. Utilitarians will ask why anyone should suffer harm or forgo benefit because of someone else's moral intuitions. Perhaps others can provide an answer, in which case utilitarianism will not turn out to be the ultimate normative theory.

Can intuitions be values?

Sometimes people say that the intuition is itself a value, so these biases are not really biases at all, even in utilitarian terms. For example, people say that they personally find it worse to harm others through an act than through an omission. They say that this is one of their values. So, when we carry out a utilitarian calculation of costs and benefits, we must count the individual's disutility arising from performing the harmful act. The problem is how we distinguish a value from a deontological moral intuition. Such a moral intuition is a kind of opinion about what should be done, not a judgment about the consequences.

Note that this is part of a more general problem. When people allow greater harm because they do not act to prevent it, they are causing harm to others because of their own personal values. The others do not value this harm. (If they did, we wouldn't call it harm.) The more general problem is whether we should consider values or utilities that cause harm to others.

This issue has many manifestations. One is the question of whether we should count the anti-Semite's attitude toward Jews as a value that counts, or the racist's attitude toward blacks. It may seem that the values of those who will not inflict harm to prevent greater harm are quite different from these. From the inside, though, the values of the racist may feel much the same. Racists may think of their values as moral ones, even though those who bear the brunt of these values, and most other people, certainly do not seem them (his) as moral.

A more acceptable example is the intuitions that people have about allocation of resources. Suppose that a government health program has decided not to pay for bone-marrow transplants for certain types of cancer, because the transplants are expensive and very rarely effective. Paying for such transplants would require denying other people services that are more effective, even at preventing death. An analysis of utilities supports this decision. But public attitudes go against this analysis and want the transplants paid for, even at the expense of more beneficial services to others. If the government decides to give in to these attitudes (because, for example, it sees itself as democratic), then some people will get marrow transplants and others will be hurt, perhaps even die, as a result of the denial of other services. In this case, a moral opinion or value has caused harm to some people and benefit to others, but the benefit is, we have assumed, less than the harm. We cannot justify the harm by pointing to greater benefits. The harm results from people's values or intuitions.

Other examples are values that are simply moralistic. Some people are offended by nudity (for example, at private beaches), homosexuality, or women in public with bare faces or legs. They want the government to ban these things. Again, they have a value that seems moral to them but actually goes against the values of others. Should we count these moralistic values as something worth considering in a utilitarian calculation? The term "moralistic" is a good one for the whole class of values or intuitions. They are moral opinions about what should be done, or values.

If they are moral opinions and not values, then we can safely ignore them in making our own utilitarian calculation about what to do. How do we distinguish values from intuitions? In theory, people could ask themselves how they would evaluate states of affairs, if it were impossible to affect these states. These are values rather than intuitions about action, because no action is involve. The states could include other people's actions, however. Very likely, the prude who opposes nudity will think that it is bad when other people go naked, whether the people who do it think it is bad or not. This is a value. The prude will also support legislation banning the practice. The latter is an opinion about action. We separate these two components of attitude. In practice, this is difficult, at best. But we must do it when we think theoretically about these issues.

When moralistic opinions are values, they do not necessarily win. We must count the harm we do to people who hold these values when we ignore the values. This harm is not necessarily greater than the harm caused to others when we pay attention to these values. The harm suffered by the prude when people go naked may be less than the harm suffered by those who cannot go naked because the prude has gotten a law passed banning nudity. Sometimes, though, moralistic values may tip the balance. For example, in Islamic countries, enough people may hold these values so that the affront to them may count more than the harm done to women who must cover themselves in public (and to the men who might otherwise wish to see women with less covering). Is this right?

From a utilitarian point of view, it seems difficult to find a good reason to ignore these moralistic values (Hare, 1963, 1981). So we must count them. There are problems in how much to count them. People who hold these values often say that they are absolute, more important than anything. If that were true, we should not violate them at any cost, unless the values of those who were harmed were just as absolute. Let us assume that we can resolve this problem. But I will not try to resolve it here.

On the other hand, we might well try to discourage people from having values that lead to behavior that is harmful to the values of others. Moralistic values are of this sort. One way to discourage such values is to ignore them.

Another possibility is that some of these values are actually means values in the sense of Chapter 14. That is, they are not fundamental values. They are held because people believe they are means to the achievement of something else, such as the good society. One way to deal with these values is to increase the level of public discussion about the beliefs in question. Does nudity really lead to other, clearer, kinds of immorality? It may be too late to affect people who are committed to one side or the other of such questions. In the long run, though, people may respond to evidence, whichever side it is on. The same may be true of racist values, or to come back to the beginning, values concerning harmful acts versus omissions. We might persuade people that their fundamental value behind their dislike of harmful acts is their altruism, their concern for the goals of others. If this is true, then they may come to see that omissions can be just as harmful as acts.

To the extent to which we are sure that people are acting on the basis of false beliefs about the relation between their expressed values to their fundamental values, we might try to satisfy their fundamental values when we, as citizens, create public policy.

Conclusion

Here is a summary of the argument for utilitarianism as the normative theory. First the act-omission distinction by itself is normatively irrelevant because we would not want to endorse moral rules that hurt the achievement of our goals by favoring harmful omissions over harmful acts. The "harm" refers to our goals, and they are what matter to us. Second, more generally, whenever we violate the utilitarian rule we make outcomes worse, by definition. They may be worse for someone and better for nobody, thus violating Pareto optimality (p. 391). Or they may be worse for someone and better for someone else, but the former must outweigh the latter (or else utilitarianism would agree). Utilitarianism poses a skeptical challenge. How can we justify harm to someone, if nobody else gets equal or greater benefit? It holds, however, that the even-more-skeptical question of how we can justify harm to anyone at all, ever, has an answer in terms of the irrelevance of the act-omission distinction. If you *fail* to harm person B in order to help person A, then, really, you are hurting A in order to help B. ("Hurt" and "help" are, by this view, relative.) So you must decide, and you have at least *some* reason if you decide in favor of the person who is more affected. Finally, what about cases in which we apply utilitarian reasoning narrowly, for example, to the inhabitants of our nation only? If we maximize the good of people within a group at the expense of greater harm to those outside, we lose the opportunity to endorse a principle that would do even more good, which takes everyone into account.

Much more work remains to be done on the subject of moral reasoning, including clarification of the normative model. A search for biases, of the sort that we have found in other decision making, would be a worthwhile approach. Once departures from a normative model are discovered, we could go on to ask whether the normative model is wrong and, if not, whether there are some prescriptive heuristics that could bring people's reasoning closer to it than the heuristics they use.

The first task, then, is to discover and understand biases in moral thinking and to study ways of correcting these biases. Of course, some of the biases in moral thinking are exactly the biases that occur in all thinking: failure to consider goals (in this case, moral goals), biased search for evidence and biased inference — particularly those biases that favor our beliefs that we are morally good people and do not need to improve — and failure to examine critically our own intuitive rules.

The next task is prescriptive. Education is one approach. An approach to moral education that I have defended (Baron, 1989), which to my knowledge has not been tried, is to regard moral thinking as an extension of decision making. The errors that people commit in moral thinking are much like those that they commit in other decision making. Some errors in moral thinking include failure to recognize the precedent-setting effects of choices; neglect of consequences of a choice for the feelings of others; neglect of consequences for those far away or those in the future; failure to recognize the conflict between self-interest and the interests of others (thoughtlessness); and the omission–commission framing effect. Discussion of such errors need not imply acceptance or rejection of any particular moral code. All moral codes recognize the relevance of the effect of our choices on others. People who support some codes may feel that morality is not limited to such effects, but they can hardly object to more systematic instruction in thinking about them.

Education in moral thinking may not reduce the crime rate, for some crimes result from simple overweighing of self-interest; people would still want to do these things even if they were aware of the effects of their actions on others' feelings. It is possible, however, that some blatantly immoral behavior *is* the result of failure to think through the effect of one's choices on others and would be prevented by moral education. Bad effects can also result from good intentions; some of this is just bad moral luck. At other times the intentions result from poor thinking about what is the right course of action. When this occurs in the decisions of government leaders or in the decisions of those who choose them, many people feel the bad effects. Moral education might do some good after all, if it helped to prevent this.

Chapter 17

Fairness and justice

This chapter and the next concern two common kinds of moral decision problems that have been studied extensively, both normatively and descriptively. The next chapter concerns decisions made by several people, each facing a conflict between what is best for the self and what is best for others. The present chapter is about the allocation of rewards and punishments: who gets what. Examples of such allocation decisions are these: How should a university allocate financial aid to its students? When organs for transplantation are scarce, who should get them? How should criminal penalties depend on the crime? When a product injures a customer or the environment, how much should the company pay as a penalty, if anything? How should salary levels be determined within an organization, within a country, across the world? How should taxes be levied? We call such questions matters of fairness, justice, or equity. I shall use these terms interchangeably.

Sometimes these decisions are made by people who are not directly involved in the allocation — judges who assign penalties to criminals or professors who assign grades to students. At other times, allocation decisions are made by the affected parties, as in treaties between nations, agreements between buyers and sellers, or plans among roommates or family members on the division of the housework.

As usual, we shall be concerned with both normative and descriptive accounts. At issue is what it means to be fair, and how real decisions compare to the normative standard of fairness. Utilitarianism — a normative theory introduced in the last chapter — holds that fairness is whatever yields the best overall consequences in the long run, summed across everyone. Alternative normative theories hold that fairness is an extra consideration, beyond consequences. These alternatives often work better than utilitarianism as descriptive accounts, in many cases. This is not surprising, because quite a few of the alternative theories were derived by philosophers consulting their own intuitions about such cases ("To each according to his contribution," for example).

Following our intuitions about justice often helps to maximize utility. For example, the principle "Grades should be based on the quality of work done" embodies the idea of incentive. Students will learn more if they are rewarded for it, so this principle will increase utility (assuming that learning has utility, etcetera). Principles of distribution would tend to receive little cultural support if their good effects on utility did not usually outweigh their bad effects. Utilitarians also argue that some intuitive principles should be followed, prescriptively, even when they *seem* not to maximize utility in a given case: for instance, when a poorly performing student needs a better grade in order to play on a team. The law is notorious for such reasoning.

I shall argue here, however, that people can learn such principles without understanding how the principles increase utility. As a result, people can apply principles of fairness even when the principles cannot be justified — normatively or prescriptively — in terms of utility maximization. In such cases, intuitions about fairness can work against the greater good. If people understood the relation between fairness and utility, I argue, they would at least be in a better position to understand how this can happen. If they made decisions against the greater good, they would at least know what they were doing.

The study of fairness and justice

Studies of justice are usually divided into those concerned with *distributive* justice — who gets what — and those concerned with *procedural* justice — the methods by which decisions about distribution should be made. Questions about distributive justice are relatively simple: They concern judgments or decisions about different principles of allocation: equality, need, proportional to contribution, and so forth. Questions about procedural justice are more complex because they involve judgments about the design of entire institutions. These judgments, in turn, are influenced by expectations based heavily on history and culture. This chapter is limited largely to questions about distribution, except that one of the things to be distributed is procedural power, such as the right to vote. At the end, we shall examine cases in which those involved must negotiate among themselves about a distribution.

Many studies of distributive justice have been carried out in the laboratory. Typically, subjects are asked to divide some reward or punishment among the members of a group, which may or may not include the subject doing the dividing. The group may be as small as two people. The members of the group may differ in such characteristics as how much each one contributed to a group project or how needy each one is. In many laboratory studies, the task is hypothetical, and subjects are asked what is fair rather than being asked to apportion outcomes. In other cases, the rewards or punishments are real, especially when the researchers are interested in people's willingness to sacrifice in order to see that justice is done.

Distributive justice is also easy to study outside of the laboratory, perhaps easier than other topics in this book. Laws and institutional rules often embody people's judgments of how outcomes should be apportioned (Elster, 1993). Examples are policies for college admissions, receiving donated organs, salaries and promotions (within some institutions), immigration, office space (within a department, for instance). Even when the rules are not written down, we can observe how various things are apportioned. When it is not clear whether a distribution resulted from any-one's conscious decision (for example, the distribution of income in a country), we can also ask people whether they approve of the distribution. Any general descriptive statement concerning how people make decisions about distribution must therefore meet a much more severe test of adequacy than in other fields where only laboratory data are available.

Equity theory: the desire for justice

According to *equity theory* (Walster, Walster, and Berscheid, 1978), people desire to see that outcomes are just or equitable. (They come to desire this because they are rewarded for it, supposedly, but no evidence for this supposition is presented.) Be-cause of this desire, people try to restore equity when outcomes are inequitable. They therefore reward those who have been underrewarded and punish those who have been overrewarded. They do this even when they must sacrifice some of their own reward. More interestingly, when people cannot restore equity, they try to deceive themselves into believing that the winners deserved to win and the losers deserved to lose.

An example of the restoration of equity is a study by Adams (1965), in which three groups of subjects did a proofreading task for pay. One group was told that they were qualified to be paid at the usual rate per page, and they were paid at that rate. A second group was told that they were not qualified, but they were paid at the usual rate anyway. A third group was "not qualified" and paid at a lower rate. The second group worked harder than the other two groups, as evidenced by a lower error rate, apparently because they were making up for the inequity that resulted from their "excessive" pay.

Willingness to sacrifice for the sake of equity is also found in simple laboratory games involving money. In a *dictator game*, one subject — the dictator — is asked to divide an amount of money between herself and another subject. The other subject has no choice about whether to accept the offer or not; hence the first subject is the "dictator." In an experiment on this game, Kahneman, Knetsch, and Thaler (1986a) asked each student in a class to divide $20 with an anonymous other student in the same class. There were only two options: an equal division of $10 each, and an unequal division of $18 for the "dictator" and $2 for the other. The other student could not reject the offer. The subjects knew that after they made their decisions only some of them would be chosen at random for actual payment. Out of the whole group of subjects, 76% divided the money equally.

In a second part of the experiment, each subject who was not selected to be paid was told that she would make a second decision about sharing some money among herself and two other students. One other student, called E (because he had divided equally), had decided on an equal division of the $20 in the first part of the experiment, and the third student, called U, had decided on an unequal division. The subject had two options: She could allocate $5 to herself, $5 to E, and nothing to U, or she could allocate $6 to herself, nothing to E, and $6 to U. The question here was whether the subject would sacrifice $1 of her own money in order to punish another subject who had been unfair and reward another subject who had been fair. Out of the whole group of subjects, 74% chose to make this sacrifice (81% of those who had themselves chosen equality in the first part, but only 31% of those who chose inequality).

In sum, subjects are, once again, willing to sacrifice their narrow self-interest for the sake of fairness, but this sort of fairness involved reward for prior fairness and punishment for prior unfairness. We could say that the subjects who do this get more utility from punishing unfairness than from receiving an additional dollar, so they are selfish after all. But this sort of utility depends on a commitment to a moral principle. The important point is that they follow this principle, even when their behavior *otherwise* reduces their utility.

Another case in which subjects sacrifice narrow self-interest in order to punish unfairness is the *ultimatum game*. Suppose you are told that you and a student in a different class have a chance to divide up $10. The other student, the offerer, will offer you some part of the $10. If you, the receiver, accept the offer, you will get the amount offered, and the offerer will get the rest. If you reject the offer, you will each get nothing. Would you accept an offer of $5.00? $2.00? 1 cent? Offers much below $5 are often rejected. The receiver prefers to see both subjects get nothing rather than tolerate such unfairness. The receiver therefore is willing to sacrifice in order to punish unfairness. (This is the negative side of fairness motivation, the desire to hurt others, even at one's own expense, in order to restore equality.) Notice that if receivers were concerned only with their self-interest, they would accept an offer of 1 cent, and the offerers, knowing that, would offer only 1 cent. Most offerers offer $5, or only a little less — perhaps out of a desire for fairness, perhaps out of fear of rejection, perhaps for both reasons (Thaler, 1988).

Notice that the receiver is following a principle of equal division (when there is no reason for unequal division). This principle normally helps to maximize utility, because of the principle of declining marginal utility (Chapter 10): the total utility of $5 for each person is higher than the utility of $8 for one and $2 for the other (other things being equal). In this case, however, the principle fails to maximize utility when the offer is rejected. Both players would be better off (in terms of narrow self-interest) if even a low offer were accepted.

When others cannot be given their due, people often change their perception of the situation. Students who watched another student receive electric shocks when trying to learn nonsense syllables tended to give that student low ratings on social attractiveness (Lerner and Simmons, 1966). The ratings were not low when the subjects thought they could ensure that the learner would be placed in a second condition in which she would be rewarded instead of shocked. Thus, the subjects "derogated the victim" only when they could not restore equity themselves. Lerner and Simmons suggest that we desire to believe that the world is orderly and fair, lest we fear that we ourselves will become victims of unfairness. This "just world" hypothesis has been supported by many other experiments. If this is generally true, it makes us less concerned with victims of all sorts whom we feel we cannot help: victims of rape, of other crimes, of disease, of poverty, of having the wrong parents, of being born in the wrong country.

In sum, people desire to see fairness. They will try to bring about fairness, even when utility is not maximized, and even when they must sacrifice to bring it about. When they cannot bring it about, they will try to deceive themselves into thinking that things are fair.

Utilitarianism and fairness

Equity theorists also maintain that people want rewards and punishments to be proportional to "inputs." It is often unclear what the inputs are, though. Colleges in the United States typically allocate financial aid according to need, but graduate schools typically do not. Should need be an input? In assigning grades, should a teacher consider ability, effort, or just the end result? What is the input here? If some citizens contribute more than others, why should each citizen have one vote? Why doesn't each stockholder have only one vote? Is the size of an investment an input? Should criminal penalties depend only on the magnitude of the crime? If so, are we wrong to excuse people who are insane?

I suggest that it is useful here, as elsewhere, for us to consider the normative theory — to ask ourselves, "Just what is the ultimate goal we are trying to achieve?", before we ask about people's actual judgments. We may want to consider prescriptive theory as well. Although the philosophical accounts of fairness are rich and varied (for example, Rawls, 1971; Nozick, 1974), I shall concentrate here on the utilitarian account (Baron, 1993a,b), mentioning in passing where other accounts disagree with it.

Utilitarians have both a simple answer and a complex answer to the problem of fairness. The simple answer is that we should strive to maximize utility. When asked how to do that, another simple answer is that it depends on the details of the case at hand. This is not very helpful guidance. The more complex answer is to present several principles that need to be considered. Let us look at some of these.

Declining marginal utility. If you are asked to distribute $1,000 between two anonymous people, neither of whom you would ever see again, what would you do? Most people would divide the money equally. According to utilitarianism, this is normatively correct if we assume that the utility of money is marginally declining (Chapter 10). If two people have the *same* marginally-declining utility function for money, and if we consider changing away from a 50–50 split, the utility benefits for one person that result from having a greater share will be more than outweighed by the utility of the losses for the other person.

Even if the two people have different utility functions, equal division is still the best solution, as long as we do not know which utility function is which, and as long as both are marginally declining. We would want to make the division in order to maximize *expected* utility, and, since we have the same information about both people, the expected-utility functions for both people would both be the same — the average of the two possible utility functions — and the same argument would apply. Notice that this argument still applies, even if one person is a "utility monster" who has 100 times the utility of the other for everything, as long as we do not know *which* one is the monster.

Moreover, by the same reasoning, a division that is close to 50–50 is better than one that is farther away. We can generally increase total utility by taking from the rich and giving to the poor, provided that this transfer of resources has no other effects. (We shall see that it does have other effects.) In general, the utility of money is greater for the poor than for the rich.[1]

Incentive and deterrence. Why, then, don't we just make sure that everyone has the same income? The utilitarian answer is that we use differences in income to provide incentive for people to contribute to the welfare of others by working. Productive work increases utility because it produces things that increase the achievement of goals. If doctors make more money than other people, then young people will compete with each other for the chance to become doctors, and this will lead to more competent doctors, who provide better medical care, thus helping to achieve the goals we all have concerning health. If we systematically take from the rich and give to the poor until everyone has the same income, this incentive effect will be lost. Utilitarians can thus be found on both sides of the political spectrum, depending on their beliefs about the optimal balance between the incentive principle and the redistribution principle. (Of course, at least one side must either be wrong or overconfident.)

Alternative normative theories emphasize one side or the other as normatively fundamental. Nozick (1974), for example, asserts that the right to keep one's income is fundamental. Utilitarians reply that this "right" is just a device that we have adopted to provide incentive. Even the idea of property rights is a device used in part to maintain incentive.

On the other side, some theorists (such as Rawls, 1971) want to divide certain primary goods as equally as possible, subject only to the constraint that the least well-off group of people is as well off as it can be. Theorists in this tradition often make some sort of distinction between needs and wants. Thus, certain goods, such as education, police protection, food, basic housing, and basic medical care, would be available equally to all, while other goods, such as televisions, automobiles, and luxury items, would provide the incentive for people to earn the money to buy them.

Utilitarians would again say that the "right" to the fulfillment of needs is not fundamental but is, rather, a means to maximize utility. The distinction between needs and wants can be justified in at least two ways. One is that the "needs" provide the prerequisite to participate in the incentive system. In essence, without food, health, and education a person cannot be a good worker. The other justification is

---

[1] Within a nation, this claim would be less true to the extent to which the rich became rich *because* they had a greater utility for money than did those who remained poor. This mechanism, however, seems far less likely to apply across nations.

that the desires for primary goods are not controllable, while the desires for luxury goods are acquired tastes. Moreover, the effort to satisfy these tastes may reduce the satisfaction of less controllable desires. It may be helpful for a society not to give too much encouragement to the development of the taste for good wine, for example, since the capacity to produce wine is limited by available land, some of which is also usable for growing crops that all can enjoy.

Just as incentive can be used to encourage certain behavior, punishment can be used to deter it. Utilitarianism holds that two wrongs do not by themselves make a right. That is, punishment is a harm, so it is not justified unless it prevents even greater harm. It must do that by deterring the person punished, by deterring others from harmful behavior, or by expressing a standard of behavior that affects what people do even if they do not fear the punishment itself. Utilitarian arguments about the death penalty are therefore concerned with whether it prevents as much harm as it causes. (It may even increase the number of killings by making killing seem like a legitimate means of revenge.) In principle, such an issue can be decided by research, although, in this case, it is difficult to do the research that is needed. (As we saw in Chapter 9, though, the difficulty of finding an answer does not stop people from holding strong opinions on this topic.)

Some nonutilitarian views hold that retribution is justified even without deterrence. Thus, capital punishment might be justified even if it is a poor deterrent, because it is a just punishment for some crimes. Other nonutilitarian views hold that some punishments, such as capital punishment, are never justified even if they prevent greater harm: Punishing one person in order to deter others amounts to using the former as a means rather than an end, according to some of these views, and that is morally prohibited.

The line between incentive and deterrence is often hard to draw, and we may have no reason to draw it. For example, the government of China has tried to control population growth by "giving benefits to those families with one child or none." We might say that this amounts to punishment of those families with two children or more. From a utilitarian point of view, all that matters is that people would rather have the benefits than not have them, so the law does affect their behavior. On the other hand, it is worth noting that incentives typically involve allocation of limited resources (as in the Chinese example). More reward for one person usually means less for someone else, while deterrence may involve punishment that is not limited in this way. Use of this form of punishment may thus be a less expensive way to control behavior than the use of reward.

Incentive and deterrence are relevant to questions about *responsibility*. We sometimes say that people are not responsible for their actions, or that they should not be *held* responsible. We often mean that we should not punish them for a harmful act (or, less often, reward them for a good act). For example, we do not punish criminals so severely when they are judged to be insane. For utilitarians, such leniency is justified if the insane are less sensitive to deterrence.[2] It does not do any good to punish

---

[2] Another justification is that sane criminals are more difficult to catch, so that those who are caught

people for things that they and others like them would do anyway, regardless of the punishment. More generally, utilitarians might take "responsible" to mean "sensitive to reward and punishment." It is not clear how most people use the term, however, and experiments that ask subjects about responsibility are difficult to interpret.

Tastes and needs. If we have 6 avocados and 6 grapefruits, and you like grapefruits but hate avocados, and I like avocados but hate grapefruits, then we maximize our utility by giving all the avocados to me and all the grapefruits to you. This plan maximizes utility (plan) even if we have only 3 grapefruits, or none. This principle of "tastes" works against equal division of goods. It also applies to "needs." If my desire for avocados depends on a vitamin deficiency, rather than my liking their taste, the principle is unchanged. One institution that satisfies this principle is the market. People can use money to buy what they particularly want. Even without money, they can trade.

Envy. A reason for equal division, especially among people who are similar in some way, is to avoid envy, which sometimes amounts to a desire to restore equity by hurting those who have more than they seem to deserve (Sabini and Silver, 1981; Frank, 1988; Elster, 1989). People seem to evaluate their situation by comparing what they get to what those around them get. Students who get B's are often envious of those who get A's, especially if the A is seen as a reward for being a teacher's pet.

Envy is (like anger) a moral emotion. It arises out of beliefs about how goods should be distributed (although these beliefs may also be distorted by self-deception based on self-interest). Thus, it may be possible to avoid envy by convincing those who are envious that they and others have received what is fair. As we shall see, though, people's view of fairness may depend on what is good for them. The B student who does not talk in class may think it unfair that class discussion was part of the grade. Avoidance of envy can conflict with incentive: Some students say that they try not to get good grades for fear of becoming unpopular.

Expectations and rights. Groups or governments often set up rules of distribution in order to solve practical problems. For example, governments have tax laws and laws concerning criminal penalties. Such rules are clearly inferior to what could be achieved by an all-knowing and benevolent dictator sending just the right tax bill to every household, taking into account everyone's utilities for money. But the rules are often close to the best that can be achieved in practice, far better than anarchy. Once stated, the rules define rights and expectations that people use for making decisions. If the rules are violated, people lose confidence in them, and the benefits of the rules over anarchy are lost. For example, part of the incentive system deals with inheritance laws: People work, in part, to provide for their survivors after their death. A sudden and large increase in inheritance taxes might make people more reluctant to save money, even if the increase were repealed the next year. Many of the rules that we call "rights" have this character too, such as the rights associated with property. From a utilitarian point of view, these are not absolutes, and cultures could be (and are) designed without them, but removing them can have a large cost in stability.

need to be punished more severely in order to deter others from taking the same risk.

Error, power, and bright lines. Organs for transplantation are in short supply, and elaborate rules have been set up to determine who gets them (Elster, 1993). The rules often consider such factors as time spent waiting, compatibility with the donor, and age (with younger people having priority). A utilitarian might argue that the social value of the recipient should also be considered. Recently, Governor Robert Casey of Pennsylvania received a heart and a liver, only a few days after his doctors found that he needed them. Several letters and editorials suggested that he was given "unfair" priority because he was a governor. This charge was vigorously denied, but would it have been so bad to give him such priority?

What is the problem here? One problem with considering the value of the recipient is, "Who decides?" Unlike judgments of tissue compatibility, age, and even medical condition, judgments of the social value of individuals are highly dependent on who makes them. They are "subjective." They are bound to be full of error. This in itself might not be so bad, so long as the utilitarian value of considering social value was positive. But when judgments are subjective, the judge entrusted with making them is bound to be criticized by those who lose as a result of her judgments — for example, those who did not get the organs. (In Casey's case, there were no others in the queue for double organs.) Few will want to be in this position. The psychological cost of the procedure itself may not be worth the benefits. On the other hand, the desire to avoid making such subjective life-and-death judgments may not always be rational (Beattie, Baron, Hershey, and Spranca, 1994).

When judgments are prone to error and disagreement, it is often better to adopt some simple rule or formula that approximates a utilitarian outcome. Such rules avoid the need for case-by-case judgment (Baron, 1993, ch. 12), which takes time and provokes disputes. Lawyers often call such rules "bright lines." When two countries have a territorial dispute, there may be nothing special about putting the boundary at longitude 30 except that this seems "brighter" (more salient) than putting it at 29 degrees 53 minutes or any other similar line. The next section presents some examples of simple rules that people often adopt.

In sum, the application of utilitarianism in practice need not involve the calculation of expected utility for each option. Instead, it often involves the use of rules or general principles that can be justified because they increase utility in some cases. Often these rules conflict, and a compromise between them is struck, as in the case of tax laws, which frequently are intended to strike a balance among several of the principles listed here.

Intuitions

When people make judgments about what is fair or just, they rely on various heuristics, or naive theories, or intuitions, or moral principles or rules, such as the rule "To each according to his contribution." In many situations, these rules do serve utilitarian functions. Such simple rules, however, correspond to utilitarian principles only approximately, and at times the departures from utilitarian outcomes are extreme.

We can thus find cases in which people's intuitions about fairness — when followed — lead predictably to worse outcomes than could have been achieved by some other option.

Even when the rules clearly lead to poor outcomes, though, people are sometimes attached to them. People have nonutilitarian intuitions about morality. It is not clear where such intuitions come from. They may be "innate," the result of biological evolution. They may be the result of cultural evolution, passed on from each generation to the next. Or they may be discovered in the course of development, as each individual tries to make sense of the social world. Or these mechanisms could work together: for example, Simon (1990) suggests that people evolved biologically to be "docile," that is, to learn from each other, and such docility would make us more susceptible to the effects of cultural evolution. Whichever process led to the rules we use, it can occasionally lead to errors, if only because things change too fast. Biological evolution, after all, produced birds without wings and gave us spinal columns that lead to endless trouble for many people. Some of our favorite moral intuitions might be in this category, when viewed from the perspective of the consequences they produce.

Such attachments to moral principles might also have served as the basis for alternative moral theories, such as the Kantian view that people should be "ends, not means." In other cases, though, the rules really are seen as rules of thumb, to which people are not so strongly attached. Let us look at some of these rules.

Equality, need, contribution, and maximization. When people are asked to distribute rewards or punishments among other people — in experiments or real life — four types of principles seem to predominate. All of these principles can approximate utilitarianism in some situations. Prescriptively, they might be the best that can be done in some situations. In other situations, the same principles might clearly violate utilitarianism. The principle might be wrong for the situation. Or people might rely on only one principle when a more complete analysis would require a compromise between two or more of them, as in the case of the "poll tax" (a tax based on equality) that threatened to bring down the Conservative government of the United Kingdom in 1990.

By the principle of *equality*, each person gets the same. This principle is widely used in most cultures for division of all sorts of things, from voting rights ("one person, one vote") to allocation of work in group projects. The similar principle of *need* distributes more of a good to those who have less of it, even if equality cannot be achieved in the end. Both of these rules are justified, in typical cases, by declining marginal utility. One case in which need conflicts with utilitarianism is in organ donation: The sickest person is often the most "needy," but frequently the one most likely to benefit from the transplant is not so sick.

By the principle of *contribution* (or "equity"), people are paid (or punished) in proportion to their relative input to an overall enterprise. This input may be positive or negative. Many variants of the contribution rule have been devised. For example, relative contribution can be defined partly in terms of rank order as well as absolute amount (Mellers, 1986). Compromises between equality and contribution are also sometimes found: Reward can be a linear function of contribution with a slope less than 1 and a positive intercept, so that even those who contribute nothing get something (Ordóñez and Mellers, 1993). The contribution principle approximates the utilitarian principle of incentive. It conflicts with utilitarianism when incentive is absent, as when people are punished for outcomes that they could not have prevented.

The principle of *maximization* (or "efficiency") is applicable only when the options differ in the total of some quantity. For example, if the two options are (A) $100 for you and $1 for me and (B) $10 for you and $10 for me, then the total amount of money is higher in (A). If the options are (C) $100 for you and $100 for me and (D) $190 for you and $10 for me, then maximization of money cannot decide between them, although maximization of utility would probably favor (C). The possible distributions of wealth or income need not involve dividing up a "fixed pie," since the creation of inequality in the form of incentive might increase the total wealth to be divided.

Bar-Hillel and Yaari (1993) studied the conflict between equality and maximizing in cases in which a shipment of fruit had to be divided between Jones and Smith. One case concerned a shipment of 12 grapefruit. "Jones's metabolism is such that his body derives 100 mg of vitamin F from each grapefruit, whereas Smith derives 20 mg from each grapefruit." Both Smith and Jones are interested in the fruits only for the vitamin F (and the more the better); and, after the fruits are divided, Jones and Smith will not be able to trade, or to transfer fruits to any third person. Subjects typically gave 2 grapefruit to Jones and 10 to Smith, thus applying an equality heuristic to the vitamin but failing to maximize. If, however, Smith's ability to extract the vitamin declines enough (in other cases), most subjects gave all the fruit to Jones, thereby maximizing the vitamin extracted. Subjects thus applied a kind of "triage" heuristic, in which the goods were given to those who could benefit the most, regardless of need. A tendency to maximize was also found when "Jones is crazy about grapefruit, it's his favorite fruit, [but] Smith just sort of likes it." Here most subjects gave more fruit to Jones rather than dividing the fruit equally. Thus, tastes are treated differently from health needs.

An extreme example of the preference for equality over maximization is the ultimatum game described earlier in this chapter. Recall that receivers prefer equality — both subjects getting nothing — to inequality, even though the inequality is maximizing for both subjects. At face value, this is a clear conflict with utilitarianism.

The equality principle can conflict with itself, because different quantities can be equated, such as income and costs of a business. Harris and Joyce (1980) told subjects about various situations in which a group of partners had opened a business (for example, selling plants at a flea market). The partners took turns operating the business, so different amounts of income were generated while each partner was in control, and different costs were incurred. (Costs for one partner were extremely high because of an accident.) When subjects were asked how the *profits* should be divided among the partners, many subjects favored equal division. When subjects were asked how they would divide up the *expenses*, they tended to divide *these* equally, even though they understood that the resulting division of profits would be unequal (because each partner would keep what was earned during her turn, after paying her share of the expenses). Judgments of fairness seem to exhibit framing effects like those we encountered in Chapter 11.

⌐ What determines the choice of these various principles? Deutsch (1975) suggested that contribution will be used when "economic productivity is a primary goal," equality will be used when "the fostering or maintenance of enjoyable social relations is the common goal," and need will be used when "the fostering of personal development and personal welfare is the common goal." (He did not discuss efficiency.) Such suggestions are roughly consistent with the utilitarian justifications of the principles in question, and the evidence both from laboratory studies and real life is roughly consistent with Deutsch's suggestions. But, as I have noted, these principles are sometimes used when they violate utilitarianism. It is also clear that cultural and political differences — and even sex differences — affect the choice of principles. These differences lead to disagreements.

For example, Leung and Bond (1984) asked students in Hong Kong and in the United States to allocate payment to themselves and another subject whom they never saw (and who really did not exist) on the basis of performance of both subjects in a copying task. They were told that the "other subject" did either twice as much or half as much work as they themselves did. Male students in the United States and female students in Hong Kong tended to allocate payment in proportion to contribution; female students in the United States and male students in Hong Kong tended to allocate equally, regardless of contribution.

Another study asked students in India and the United States how they would divide a bonus — or a pay cut — between worker A, who contributed more, and worker B, who was needier (Murphy-Berman et al., 1984). When a bonus was to be allocated, most Indian students allocated according to need, and most U.S. students divided the bonus equally. Many subjects in both countries allocated according to contribution. (Female students in India did this only rarely.) When a pay cut was to be allocated, most Indian students allocated according to need (cutting the pay of A more than that of B), and U.S. students divided it equally. In sum, then, Indians seemed to be more sensitive to need in both cases. In general, too few studies of this sort have been done for us to have a clear picture of the range of cultural and sex differences, let alone the source of these differences.

Within the United States, political liberals tend to favor public policies that allocate according to need or equality, and conservatives tend to favor allocation according to contribution (Rasinski, 1987). Of course, this difference almost defines the U.S. political spectrum: Liberals want to tax the rich more to help the poor; conservatives want to tax less and provide less help directly.

Compensation. Compensation for misfortunes is often provided by insurance — including social insurance, such as government medical insurance or aid for the poor — or by the tort system (liability). The main utilitarian justification of monetary compensation is that losses increase the utility of money. If your house burns down, you now have a way to use money to achieve your goals that you did not have before: obtaining a new house. This argument concerns the compensation alone, not the punitive effects on whoever provides it. (For discussions of the theory of compensation, see: Calabresi, 1970; Friedman, 1982). Compensation should depend only on the nature of the loss for the victim. Any departure from this utilitarian standard implies that some victims will be overcompensated or others undercompensated, or both.

One intuition is that compensation for a misfortune should be greater when the misfortune might have been avoided easily. This does not affect the utility of money for the victim. Miller and McFarland (1986) found that subjects would provide more compensation for a harm suffered in unusual circumstances (a person shot while going to a store that he did not usually go to) than for a harm suffered in the normal course of events (a person going to a store he often went to).

A possible utilitarian justification for this difference is that victims were more emotionally upset in the former case than in the latter. Ritov and Baron (1994) found the same sort of result when subjects understood that the victim did not know the cause of the injury or the alternatives to it. In all cases, subjects were told that a train accident had occurred because a fallen tree blocked the railroad tracks. In one case, the victim was injured by the train's sudden stop to avoid hitting the tree. In another case, the same injury was caused by an unexpected collision with the tree. Subjects judged that more compensation should be provided (by a special fund) when the train's unexpected failure to stop caused the injury than when the suddenness of the stop was the cause. The results were found whether the failure was that of an automatic stopping device or of a human engineer. If the person who caused the accident, the injurer, were required to pay the victim, then it would be reasonable to make the injurer pay more when the accident was more easily avoided, because the injurer would be more likely to be at fault in this case. But the compensation was paid from a fund, not by the injurer. Subjects might have been using an intuitive rule that is consistent with utilitarianism in some cases but not in the case at hand.

A similar sort of misapplication of a rule might be at work in another phenomenon, the person-causation bias. Here, subjects judge that more compensation should be provided by a third party when an injury is caused by human beings than when it is caused by nature (Baron, 1993b; Baron and Ritov, 1993). For example, subjects provided more compensation to a person who lost a job from unfair and illegal practices of another business than to one who lost a job from normal business competition. (Neither victim knew the cause.) The same result was found for blindness caused by a restaurant's violation of sanitary rules versus blindness caused by disease spread by a mosquito.

This effect might arise from a desire to punish someone, despite the fact that this desire cannot be satisfied. Ordinarily, punishment and compensation are correlated, because the injurer is punished by having to compensate the victim (or possibly even by the shame of seeing that others must compensate the victim). But when this correlation is broken, subjects seem to continue to use the same heuristic rule. This sort of reasoning might account in part for the general lack of concern about the discrepancy between victims of natural disease, who are rarely compensated (beyond their medical expenses), and victims of human activity, who are often compensated a great deal (if they sue), even when little deterrence results because the compensation is paid by liability insurance.

Punishment. People often ignore deterrence in making decisions about punishment or penalties. Baron and Ritov (1993) gave a questionnaire to retired judges, law students, other students and other groups. The questionnaire asked respondents to imagine that the United States had a legal system (much like New Zealand's), in which separate decisions were made about penalties against injurers and compensation for victims (Baron and Ritov, 1993). In one case, a child died from a vaccine against a disease. The disease is far more likely than the vaccine to kill the child, and the company was not clearly negligent. The case had two versions. In one version, "The company knew how to make an even safer pill but had decided against producing it because the company was not sure that the safer pill would be profitable. If the company were to stop making the pill that the woman took, it would make the safer pill." In the other version, "If the company were to stop making the pill that the woman took, it would cease making pills altogether." Of course, the deterrent effect of the penalty in this case would be the reverse of its usual effect, because it would provide an incentive for undesirable behavior rather than more desirable behavior. Most of the respondents, including judges, did not think that this made any difference. They thought that the penalty should depend on the harm done, not on its effect on anyone's future behavior. For example, some subjects argued, "We are dealing with solely what happened to the woman." "The damage was already done to that woman." "It should have to pay damages if it was at fault." "[The company] should pay for its previous actions on account of those actions."

In another test of the same principle, subjects assigned penalties to the company even when the penalty was secret, the company was insured, and the company was going out of business, so that (subjects were told) the amount of the penalty would have no effect on anyone's future behavior. Such a situation would remove the usual deterrent effect of penalties. Baron, Gowda, and Kunreuther (1993) likewise found that subjects, including judges and legislators, typically did not want to penalize companies differently for dumping of hazardous waste as a function of whether the penalty would make companies try harder to avoid waste or whether it would induce them to cease making a beneficial product. Some writers have suggested that companies have in fact stopped making certain beneficial products, such as vaccines, exactly because of such penalties (for example, Inglehart, 1987).

Subjects who want injurers to be punished even when the punishment has no benefit could be applying a rule of retribution, a rule that prescribes punishment as a function of the cause of the harm rather than the effect of the punishment. Such a rule normally yields the same result as does the utilitarian deterrence principle: Punishment for causing harm usually deters. In these cases, retribution does not deter. Because the retribution rule and the deterrence rule normally agree, it may be difficult for people who adopt the retribution rule ever to learn about its problems. Other possible sources of a retribution rule may be a perception of balance or equity (Walster, Walster, and Berscheid, 1978) and a generalization from the emotional response of anger, which may operate in terms of retribution.

A second bias in judgments of punishment is that people seem to want to make injurers undo the harm they did, even when some other penalty would benefit others more. Baron and Ritov (1993) found that (in the secret-settlement case described earlier) both compensation and penalties tended to be greater when the pharmaceutical company paid the victim directly than when penalties were paid to the government and compensation was paid by the government. Baron, Gowda, and Kunreuther (1993) found that subjects preferred to have companies clean up their own hazardous waste, even if the waste threatened no one, rather than spend the same amount of money cleaning up the much more dangerous waste of a defunct company. Ordinarily, it is easiest for people to undo their own harm, but this principle may be applied even when no such justification is available.

It might be argued that these biases are harmless in the long run. The heuristics of retribution and "Clean up your own mess" might be the best that people can do, even though these rules sometimes lead to a choice of inferior options. Judges who must interpret the law, such as those on the U.S. Supreme Court, often choose simple rules of interpretation that they know will lead to occasional errors, because they believe that the attempt to implement a more detailed rule may lead to even more errors. Thus, the use of simple, "overgeneralized" rules may itself have a utilitarian justification. In reply, it could be that people just apply these heuristics blindly, without knowing that alternative principles are available. Do people know of the alternatives?

Baron and Ritov (1993) asked subjects if they had heard of the deterrence principle as a justification of punishment and, once it was briefly explained, whether they agreed with it. Some subjects had not heard of it: Of these, about equal numbers accepted and rejected it once it was explained. Other subjects had heard of it: Of these, some rejected it, and some accepted it. Those who rejected the principle did not give a utilitarian justification for doing so; they just thought that retribution was a better way to apply the law. In sum, many people who apply nonutilitarian principles do not know what they are rejecting. A brief explanation of the utilitarian approach will be persuasive to some of these people, but not to others. If utilitarianism is to be rejected, it should be rejected on the basis of understanding, and such understanding is by no means widespread.

Ex post *versus* ex ante *equity*. Keller and Sarin (1988) gave subjects hypothetical options like the following:

Option 1:	100% chance:	Person 1 dies, Person 2 lives.
Option 2:	50% chance:	Person 1 dies, Person 2 lives.
	50% chance:	Person 2 dies, Person 1 lives.
Option 3:	50% chance:	Person 1 dies, Person 2 dies.
	50% chance:	Person 1 lives, Person 2 lives.

Let us suppose that the chance is determined by the flip of a coin. In that case, we say that Option 1 has no equity at all. The two people are treated differently from start to finish. Option 2 has *ex ante* equity, that is, equity before the coin is flipped but not *ex post* equity. After the coin is flipped, the situation is just as inequitable as Option 1. Option 3 has both *ex ante* and *ex post* equity. People generally prefer Option 3 to Option 2, and Option 2 to Option 1. That is, people are concerned with equity before the resolution of uncertainty as well as after. [3]

Typically, *ex post* equity can be justified by the principle of declining marginal utility. If we can redistribute the outcomes to make them more equal by taking from one person and giving to another, we generally improve the situation (except for incentive effects). In this particular case, however, that reasoning does not apply, because only two outcomes are possible. *Ex ante* equity has no simple utilitarian justification. Subjects may (again) be extending an intuitive principle about equity to cases in which it has no justification.

This is not to say that a more complex utilitarian justification is impossible. For example, Option 2 leaves both people with some hope, for a longer period of time. In Option 3, one person cannot grieve for the other. We could modify the situation to remove these justifications. We could say that the people do not know each other, and that they do not know of their risk. This would probably not change people's judgments. Another utilitarian justification is that an actual choice of Option 1 or 2 would set a precedent for ignoring equity more generally, even in cases in which it is justified. We would have to specify that nobody would ever know of the decision.

Preferences for *ex ante* equity can have a cost. Suppose I have two nephews. I can give ten lottery tickets to one nephew or one ticket to each nephew. To get envy out of the picture while they are waiting for the results, suppose that they will never know that I have given them the tickets, and that, if one of them wins, he will simply be told that some unknown person gave him the winning ticket. Many people might still think that it is wrong to give more tickets to one nephew, because *ex ante* equity is important in its own right, even though *ex post* equity is impossible here. In the end, though, only one nephew can win, and giving one of them ten tickets makes such an event more likely. The expected achievement of my nephew's goals — and mine, insofar as I care about theirs — is greater with the unequal division. If I were to choose one ticket for each, I must deprive one nephew of an additional chance to win, and I could not justify this by saying that I had given the other a *compensating* gain.

Chances to win are not the same as winnings. An equal-division rule for winnings is justified by the declining marginal utility of winnings themselves. But the utility of *chances* to win is not marginally declining. People may nevertheless apply the equal-division rule, because they do not know its justification. The same issue may arise in policy disputes concerning the distribution of risk, such as risk of illness from pollution. The simple utilitarian approach says that we should minimize overall risk.

---

[3] A similar example (from Petit, 1991) violates the sure-thing principle (Chapter 10). Consider the following options:

1. Heads Mary wins; tails John wins.
2. Heads John wins; tails John wins.
3. Heads Mary wins; tails Mary wins.
4. Heads John wins; tails Mary wins.

Most people would prefer Option 1 to Option 2, because it is fair *ex ante*. And they would prefer Option 4 to Option 3 for the same reason. But the outcome of "tails" is constant in both choices.

We should not be so concerned with equity.

"Do no harm." Baron and Jurney (1993), asked subjects if they would vote for various reforms. In one experiment, 39% of the subjects said they would vote for a 100% tax on gasoline (to reduce global warming). Of those who would vote against the tax, 48% thought that it would do more good than harm on the whole. They were therefore not using a maximization principle. Of those subjects who would vote against the tax, despite judging that it would do more good than harm, 85% cited the unfairness of the tax as a reason for voting against it (for instance, the burden would fall more heavily on people who drive a lot), and 75% cited the fact that the tax would harm some people on the whole (for instance, drivers). These subjects are apparently unwilling to harm some people — relative to the status quo or relative to an ideal of fairness — in order to help others, even when they see the benefit as greater than the harm (Baron, 1993b, presents further evidence). This effect may be related to the "omission bias" discussed in Chapter 16.

The perception of harm can be manipulated by framing. Kahneman, Knetsch, and Thaler (1986b) told subjects, "A company is making a small profit. It is located in a community experiencing a recession with substantial unemployment but no inflation. There are many workers anxious to work at the company. The company decides to decrease wages and salaries 7% this year." Most subjects (62%) thought that the company's action was unfair. Different subjects saw the same story, except that "no inflation" was replaced with "inflation of 12%" and the last sentence read, "The company decides to increase salaries only 5% this year." Of course, the "5% increase" amounts (with inflation) to a 7% cut in income, but here only 22% of the subjects thought that the company was unfair.

Local fairness. Ophthalmologists in Norway (and probably elsewhere) provide high-quality care to their patients, but there are too few ophthalmologists, waiting lists are long, and some patients never get seen at all (Elster, 1993). The overall result would be better if care were a bit less thorough but more patients were seen. Elster refers to a "norm of thoroughness" to describe the heuristic that justifies the present system. Another way to look at the present situation is that those who operate the system want to be fair to all the patients who get into it, giving each patient the same high-quality care that the most demanding patients would get, according to an equality principle. But this equality is *local*, in the sense that those outside of the system are ignored. The same could be said for nations that provide extensive (and expensive) equal rights for their citizens (or residents) but not for noncitizens (or nonresidents). Could the cost of such provisions do more good if spent otherwise? Singer (1982) presents an interesting discussion of the arbitrariness of group boundaries.

Heuristics and self-interest

When people are affected by the choice of distributional rules, and when several different rules or heuristics may be used, people tend to prefer the rule that favors them.

This effect is illustrated in an experiment done by van Avermaet (1974; reported in Messick, 1985). Subjects were instructed to fill out questionnaires until told to stop. They expected to be paid, but they did not know how much. Each subject was given either three or six questionnaires (depending on the experimental condition) and was told to stop after either 45 or 90 minutes. When the subject finished, she was told that there had been another subject who had had to leave before he could be told that he was supposed to be paid. The experimenter, who also said he had to leave, gave the original subject $7 (in dollar bills and coins) and asked her to send the other subject his money (in the stamped, addressed envelope provided). The subject was told that the other subject had put in either more, the same, or less time and had completed more, the same, or fewer questionnaires.

At issue was how much money the original subject would send to the "other" subject (actually a confederate). Subjects who *either* worked longer *or* completed more questionnaires than the "other" gave the other *less* than $3.50. It just cannot be true that, if they had been asked before the experiment, the subjects who worked longer would have thought that time was more important and subjects who did more would have thought amount was more important. Subjects apparently seized on any excuse to see themselves as deserving more. When the original subjects were equal to the other on *both* dimensions, they sent almost exactly $3.50, on the average. Only when subjects did worse on *both* dimensions (time and number of questionnaires) was there a slight tendency to send more than $3.50 to the other.

This experiment may tell us something very interesting about human nature. People are not simply selfish. They want to do what is right. Almost all subjects took the trouble to give the other subject half of the money, when they had no reason to do otherwise. When people behave selfishly, then, it is likely because they have deceived themselves into the belief that they are behaving justly. We know about this. We have developed a prescriptive heuristic to counter it, "Give the other person the benefit of the doubt." We need to remember this heuristic, because we tend to do the opposite.

Negotiation

So far, the judgments and decisions discussed in this chapter have largely been made by one person. In many situations involving fairness, all the affected parties discuss among themselves how something should be distributed. These cases raise special problems, because the parties have an incentive to exaggerate their own needs. Interpersonal comparison of utility, normally difficult, becomes essentially impossible. In these situations, the parties *negotiate* (or bargain) over the distribution. Examples of negotiations are setting the price of a house, making a treaty between two or more nations, making a contract between labor and management, or deciding when to have dinner. Other parties may also be involved: A *mediator* tries to help the parties reach agreement but has little or no power; an *arbitrator* has some power to impose a distribution. Arbitrators thus make judgments like those discussed earlier.

The study of negotiation is a field in its own right. Here, I shall simply introduce some of the most essential concepts. For good introductions, see Raiffa (1982), Neale and Bazerman (1991), and Bazerman and Neale (1992). Many concepts of this field are drawn from microeconomics, so textbooks in this area are also helpful.

Much can be understood about negotiation from a set of simple representations. Let us first consider negotiations in which two parties are bargaining over division of a single good, a "fixed pie." If it is literally two people splitting up a pie, and if both people agree that equal division is fair, then the problem is easy. One person cuts the pie, the other chooses first. The first person has an incentive to cut the pie into equal parts.

More typically, things are not this clear. When one person sells a house to another, the question is not (usually) how the house will be divided between the two but rather what the price will be. What is being divided here? One way to represent this situation is on a line, with position on the line representing the price, as shown in the following diagram. Let us suppose that each party has a *reservation price*. That is the price at which the party is indifferent between the sale happening and not happening. (The term was first used in auctions for the price below which the seller "reserved" the right not to sell to the highest bidder.) In the diagram, the seller's reservation price is $100,000. The seller would rather keep the house (for the time being, anyway) than sell it for $99,999. The buyer's reservation price is $120,000. That is the most that the buyer is willing to pay.

One way to think about this is that the negotiation is about the division of the gains from trade, which in this case comes to $20,000. If the house sells for $105,000, we can say that the seller has "gained" $5,000 and the buyer has gained (saved) $15,000. Note that we are talking about money here, not utility. This sort of fixed-pie representation — in which one person's gain is another's loss, exactly — would not usually apply to utility. We might think that a fair division would result from the house selling for $110,000. But how is this going to happen? Neither party has any reason to reveal her reservation price. In fact, we have no guarantee that the parties will even arrive at a price in the *zone of agreement*, which in this case is between $100,000 and $120,000.

In a typical negotiation of this type, one of the parties — typically the seller — begins by stating a price. The other party makes a counter-offer. The offers converge until a final offer is accepted by one of the parties. The series of offers and counter-offers is often called the "dance of negotiation." There is no simple normative theory for the steps in this dance. The significance of the steps is dependent on culture and on the expectations of the parties. In some markets, it is expected that the initial offer will be far from the reservation price. In other markets, there is little room for bargaining. This is clearly dependent on culture: U.S. residents rarely bargain over the price of jewelry, so they often pay more than they need to for jewelry sold in Mexican markets, where bargaining is expected. Likewise, the size of the steps can be a matter of custom. If the buyer's steps are small ($90,000, $91,000, $91,500), the seller might well assume that the buyer is approaching her reservation price and end the negotiation — even when a zone of agreement exists — unless patience and long negotiations are expected.

Even when both parties are making offers within the zone of agreement, they have no way of knowing that. If one party is "too tough," the other party can end the negotiation in order to punish unfairness, as people do in the ultimatum game. According to Benjamin Franklin, "Trades would not take place unless it were advantageous to the parties concerned. Of course, it is better to strike as good a bargain as one's bargaining position permits. The worst outcome is when, by overreaching greed, no bargain is struck, and a trade that could have been advantageous to both parties does not come off at all."

A second sort of representation — shown in the following diagram – is suitable for two parties when the quantity to be divided is not fixed. We represent the possible outcomes for one party on one axis of a two-dimensional graph and the possible outcomes for the other party on the other axis. The axes can now represent utilities, or amounts of money, or any other quantities. The diagram represents a hypothetical case in which two brothers bargain over an inheritance that they must divide among themselves and that is their main wealth. The axes are the utilities. Brother A lives in a country that taxes inheritances above a certain amount.

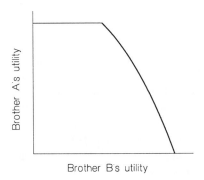

An important set of outcomes is shown as a dark line. These are "best possible" outcomes, in a certain sense: Each outcome cannot be improved upon for one party without making the situation for the other party worse. These outcomes are Pareto optimal (p. 391). The set of Pareto-optimal outcomes is called the "Pareto frontier." For any outcome not on the Pareto frontier, we can find another outcome that is better for at least one of the two parties and worse for neither. Nonoptimal outcomes cannot maximize utility, so we can say something about utility maximization, even when we cannot compare precisely the utilities of the parties.

A body of theory has developed to help choose among Pareto-optimal outcomes (see and Raiffa, 1957, ch. 6, and Elster, 1989). Although utilitarian theory specifies that the outcome chosen must have the highest total utility, the parties cannot find that outcome unless they trust each other and know enough about each other to compare their utilities. (Married couples can sometimes approximate this situation, but strangers or adversaries typically cannot.) Nash (1950) suggested maximizing the *product* of the two utilities rather than their sum. This yields the same solution, even if one of the axes is multiplied by a constant, and it has other neat properties. It does not make the task of negotiation much easier, however.

A third representation of negotiation is possible when two or more dimensions are at issue. For example, in the sale of a house, the parties often negotiate about both the price and the time when the transfer will occur. If the seller needs the money in a week to pay for a new house but the buyer is in no hurry, the speed of the sale can mean much more to the seller. Unless she gets the money right away, she will have to take out a loan at high interest in order to buy her new house. We can represent this situation in the following graph (which economists call an Edgeworth Box, after Edgeworth, 1881). The curves are indifference curves. Each curve joins points that have the same utility for one of the parties. It is apparent here that the seller is willing to sacrifice much about the price in order to make the selling date earlier. (This is analogous to the conjoint-measurement example in Chapter 14, except that the indifference curves for both parties are represented.) The dotted line represents the Pareto frontier. Any possible agreement not on this line can be improved upon for one of the parties (or both) without hurting the other. Once on the line, an improvement for one party requires a loss for the other.

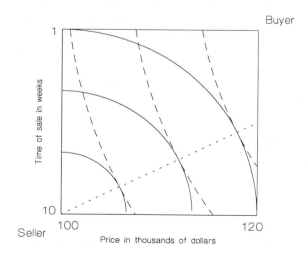

Negotiations with two or more dimensions are called "integrative." These are the most common situations, and, happily, the ones we can say the most about. In particular, we can say that it pays to negotiate about everything at once and to be honest about your tradeoffs. The danger in integrative bargaining is to arrive at a result that is not Pareto optimal. The trouble is that people tend to view integrative negotiations as "fixed pies" (Neale and Bazerman, 1991). They think that what is good for the other side is bad for them, and vice versa. People therefore try to strengthen their bargaining position by pretending to care a lot about something they do not care about much. The buyer might pretend to be unable to move for months, once she hears that the seller is interested in moving quickly. The risk here is that the buyer will win, at the expense of something else that the seller would have been willing to give up more readily, like the sale price. If the buyer had been honest in saying that "the price is much more important to me than the time of sale," then each side would have been more willing to concede what it cared least about, especially if the seller, too, was candid about what was important. The same nonoptimal outcome can result if the parties negotiate about each dimension separately. The possibilities for trades that benefit both sides would simply not be recognized.

The more specific you can be about relative importance, the better. If, for example, two roommates are negotiating about doing the housework, it helps to be able to say, "Two hours of cleaning are equivalent to one hour of cooking, for me, since I hate cleaning so much." If the other roommate feels the opposite, then the optimal solution is for one to do all the cooking and the other all the cleaning. This is far better than splitting everything equally.

Note that it is still possible to bargain hard while being honest about the *relative* importance of the dimensions to you. The point of honesty about relative importance is to make sure that you get to the Pareto frontier. The hard bargaining is about where on that frontier you wind up.

The danger here is real. Many laboratory studies show that college students left to their own devices will not arrive at Pareto-optimal solutions, unless they are given specific advice about how to talk about their tradeoffs or unless they have experience in the same situation (Pruitt and Lewis, 1975; Bazerman, Magliozzi, and Neale, 1985). Even in international negotiations (such as the Uruguay round of the General Agreement on Tariffs and Trade), experienced negotiators make the mistake of "settling one issue at a time" — first agriculture, then telecommunications, and so forth — when it is possible that these could be handled integratively. (An exception to the usual muddling was the Camp David negotiation mediated by President Carter, as described by Raiffa, 1982.)

Negotiations of all sorts — simple and integrative — often founder on differences between the parties in their perception of what is fair. Nobody wants to accept an unfair deal. Much of the discussion in negotiations is about fairness. Even when selling a house, the parties can quibble about the price of similar houses on the market. They assume here that the fair price is the market price. In more complex negotiations, the parties may have different conceptions of fairness. In a labor negotiation about the salary increases of workers, for example, several standards of fairness are available

— wages of similar workers in other companies, wage *increases* of other workers (in dollars or percentages), the rate of inflation, the income of the firm, and so forth — and each side can be expected to choose the standard that gives it a better outcome (Elster, 1989, ch. 6).

When the parties learn more about their situation, a kind of polarization effect (Chapter 9) can occur, in which each party uses every new piece of information that provides a favorable view of what is fair, while ignoring information favoring the other side. As a result, provision of information to the parties increases the difficulty of reaching agreement (Thompson and Loewenstein, 1992; Camerer and Loewenstein, 1993).

Conclusion

People's concepts of justice and fairness are not utilitarian, and these concepts differ greatly as a function of culture, political affiliation, and sex. Some intuitions about justice have a utilitarian justification in certain cases. If we think of utilitarianism as an elephant, then each of these intuitions (or naive theories, or heuristics) is based on one of the limbs, or the trunk, or the tail. Like blind men, each conflicting view has got hold of some part of the whole. This must be true, even if utilitarianism is not the ultimate answer (as I think it is).

Perhaps the most important problem is that people do not understand the justifications of the principles that they endorse, whether this justification is utilitarian or through some other theory. They are not aware of the theories they are implicitly rejecting. Without such understanding, disputes about the nature of justice can amount only to contests to see who can scream the loudest.

Chapter 18

Social dilemmas: cooperation versus defection

The best chance for gains comes through cooperation.

Fortune cookie message

This chapter focuses on a specific type of moral decision problem: decisions involving situations in which the narrow self-interest of each person in a group conflicts with the interest of the group as a whole. Retired people who have medical insurance that covers all expenses stand to gain (from extra medical attention and reassurance) if they visit their doctor weekly, sick or not, but if everyone in their group did this, their insurance premiums would skyrocket. People who watch viewer-supported television can save their money by not contributing to support the station they watch, but if everyone did this the station would be off the air, and all who like to watch it would suffer. Each farmer stands to gain from letting the family cows graze on the commons, the common pasture for the town, but if everyone did this the pasture would disappear (Hardin, 1968).

Such situations are called *social dilemmas*, or *commons dilemmas* (by analogy with the common-pasture example).[1] In a simple social dilemma, each person is better off doing one sort of thing (given what others do), but all are better off if all do something else. The action that is best for all is called *cooperation*; the action best for the self is called *defection*.[2] It is best for all (cooperative) not to overgraze the common pasture but best for each to do so.

---

[1] Other terms used for the same idea, or variants of it, are: public goods problem; prisoner's dilemma; externalities; and free-rider problem.

[2] The basic theory of cooperation and defection comes from the mathematical theory of games, which was developed largely by the mathematician John von Neumann as early as the 1920s. This theory first attracted the attention of social scientists and philosophers in the early 1950s, after the publication of von Neumann and Morgenstern's *Theory of Games and Economic Behavior* (1947), the same book that called attention to utility theory.

Because so many situations can be analyzed as social dilemmas, much of the philosophy and psychology of morality is contained in this problem. The following or breaking of many moral rules can be seen as cooperation or defection, respectively. If everybody lies, we will not be able to depend on each other for information, and we will all lose. Likewise, if nobody keeps promises, it will be impossible to make agreements unless they are consummated immediately. Cheating on one's taxes (making the government spend more money on enforcement), building up arms stocks in the context of an arms race, accepting bribes, polluting the environment, and having too many children are all examples of defection.

Social dilemmas also lie at the foundation of all economic systems. If people are sufficiently selfish, each person benefits most by consuming the fruits of others' labor and laboring himself as little as possible — but if everyone behaved this way, there would be no fruits to enjoy. All economic systems can be seen as ways of inducing people to do their share of the labor and moderate their consumption — in comparison to this dreaded state of anarchy. An effective way to induce people to do these things is to require monetary payment in return for consumption and to require labor in return for money. (Both capitalist and communist systems rely largely on this principle.) As we shall see, however, this is not the only solution people have thought of. Other solutions to social dilemmas try to reduce selfishness itself, to encourage motives that promote cooperation (such as the motive to do useful work), or to induce cooperation with other sorts of sanctions.

Research from social psychology reveals that we often fail to recognize that we are behaving selfishly (or inappropriately deciding to defect) because of motives such as envy or greed. Another cause of defection, which has not been much researched, is simply failure to think about the needs of other people (especially people far removed from us by geography or by time — people of foreign lands or the people of the future who have not yet been born). To avoid such biases and make good decisions about social dilemmas, individuals need a way of deciding whether to cooperate or defect in a given situation. Continuing the utilitarian approach introduced in Chapter 16, I consider the implications of utilitarianism as a normative decision theory for social dilemmas. Prescriptively, we can approximate this theory by drawing on traditional modes of cooperative behavior that have developed and by using certain heuristics that counteract the most common causes of defection and insufficient thought.

Laboratory versions

Psychologists have invented a variety of laboratory games for studying cooperation and defection. The games are used to study the circumstances in which subjects cooperate with fellow subjects or defect and to establish the motives for these behaviors.

Table 18.1: Effects of cooperation (C) or defection (D) on prisoner's jail terms (years).

	Bob chooses C		Bob chooses D	
	Art's term	Bob's term	Art's term	Bob's term
Art chooses C	2	2	8	0
Art chooses D	0	8	6	6

Prisoner's dilemma

The *prisoner's dilemma* is a laboratory task that has been extensively used, in a number of versions, to study cooperation and defection. The name comes from the following story, on which "prisoner's dilemma" tasks are modeled:

Two people, Art and Bob, suspected of having committed a certain crime, are taken into custody by the police. The district attorney is convinced that they are guilty of the crime but does not have enough evidence to convince a jury. The district attorney separates the suspects and offers each a choice between two actions: The suspect can confess and provide evidence concerning the involvement of both suspects (act *D* — for Defect) or not confess (act *C* — for Cooperate — with each other, of course, not with the police). The outcomes for both players depend on what they both do, as shown in Table 18.1. If both choose D (confess), they will both be sent to jail for 6 years. If both choose C (not confess), they will be sent to jail for 2 years on a lesser charge. If only one confesses, however, that one will be set free, and the other will have the book thrown at him and receive the maximum sentence of 8 years.

Putting aside the morality of trying to get away with a crime, C is the *cooperative* act. If both suspects choose C, they will both be better off than if both choose D, yet no matter what Bob decides to do, Art will get 2 years less by choosing D than by choosing C, and the same reasoning applies to Bob's choice. Both suspects appear to be better off by choosing D, given what the other does, but together they would be better off choosing C. This is because the choice of D, while gaining 2 years for the suspect who makes it, forces the other suspect to *lose* 6 years.

In laboratory experiments modeled after this case, the outcomes for subjects are usually designed to be positive rather than negative. Table 18.2 shows a case in which each subject (Art or Bob again) gains $2 by defecting, no matter what the other subject does, but both subjects are $6 better off if they both cooperate than it they both defect. In other words, by choosing D rather than C, each player gains $2 for himself and causes the other player to lose $6.

Table 18.2: Effects of cooperation (C) or defection (D) on subjects' pay.

	Bob chooses C		Bob chooses D	
	Art's pay	Bob's pay	Art's pay	Bob's pay
Art chooses C	$8	$8	$2	$10
Art chooses D	$10	$2	$4	$4

Effects of repetition

In the typical prisoner's dilemma laboratory task (and in some real-world analogues of it, such as arms races) the game is played repeatedly by the same two subjects. This leads to various attempts on the part of each player to make the other player cooperate. Players adopt various strategies to induce cooperation: A *strategy* is a rule that determines which choice a player makes on each play. Axelrod (1984) argues that one of the most effective strategies, both in theory and in fact, is the "tit for tat" approach. You begin by cooperating, but after that you imitate the other player's choice on each successive play, thereby "punishing" uncooperative behavior.

If such a strategy is effective in getting the other player to cooperate, the game is not really a social dilemma at all, for the strategy itself becomes an action that is best for each player. When games are repeated, it is helpful to think not of individual plays but rather of strategies as the choices at issue. When we study performance in laboratory games, then, we must be aware of the fact that repeated games may not actually involve social dilemmas at all. The laboratory studies I shall review, however, use nonrepeated games and are therefore true social dilemmas.

N-person prisoner's dilemma

The basic prisoner's dilemma can be extended to several people, becoming the "*N*-person prisoner's dilemma." (*N* stands for the number of people.) In one form of this game, each choice of Option C — as opposed to Option D – leads to a small loss for the player who makes the choice and a large gain for everyone else overall. In the simplest version of this, imagine a class with 20 students. Each student writes C or D on a piece of paper without knowing what the other students have written. Each student who writes C causes each of the *other* students to receive $1. Each student who writes D gets $1 in addition, but this has no effect on the payoff for others. If everyone writes C, each gets $19. If everyone writes D, each gets $1. But writing D always leads to $1 more than writing C. If you write D and everyone else writes C, you get $20 and everyone else gets $18.

Table 18.3 and Figure 18.1 illustrate a four-person game in which the benefit of cooperation is $4 for each other player and the benefit of defection is $2 for the self. The slope of the lines represents the benefits that accrue to *others* from each person's

Table 18.3: Pay-offs for cooperating (C) and defecting (D) as a function of the number of others who cooperate.

	Number of others who cooperate			
	0	1	2	3
D	$6	$10	$14	$18
C	$4	$8	$12	$16

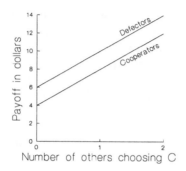

Figure 18.1: Effects of the number of cooperators (those choosing C) on the payoffs of cooperators and defectors (those choosing D), based on Table 18.3.

decision to cooperate rather than defect; each person's decision to cooperate moves everyone one step to the right on their respective line. A decision to cooperate, however, moves the person who makes it from one line to the other, as well as one step to the right.

In general, these laboratory situations present people with a choice of two actions: cooperate (C) and defect (D). Such games are analogous to many situations in daily life in which the interests of individuals conflict with the interests of "society" or, more generally, other individuals. In many of these real-world situations, people do not have a chance to try to make others cooperate. They cannot develop a "strategy," and their behavior does not influence others. It is as though the game was played only once. Both in real life and in the laboratory, social dilemmas do not need to be simple as the examples just given. The benefits provided to others by an additional cooperator may not be constant, for example. They may depend on the number of other cooperators. In some cases, a minimal number may be required for any benefits at all. The benefit to the defector from defecting may also depend on the number of other cooperators.

Normative and prescriptive theory of social dilemmas

The problems caused by the existence of social dilemmas are among the most important that human beings have to solve. If we could learn always to cooperate, wars would disappear and prosperity would prevail. Even without achieving such a utopia, more cooperation would solve many other human problems, from conflicts among roommates and family members to problems of protecting the world environment. These are problems for a prescriptive theory, a theory that takes into account ordinary human behavior. It has been my approach throughout this book, however, to stand back from the immediate problem and try to develop a set of standards that we can apply to evaluate possible prescriptive solutions, that is, a normative theory. Especially in a domain that is so full of prescriptive panaceas as this one — from Marxist revolution to laissez-faire capitalism (at the national level of the problem) — we need to know what makes a prescriptive theory good before we argue about which one is best. We also need a descriptive account of human motives and behavior in social dilemmas. We need to know where the problem is before we try to fix it.

The problem of normative theory is especially difficult because of a clear conflict between two different ways of applying utility theory. First, utility theory is a normative theory of satisfying personal goals. Some of these goals are altruistic (as we have noted throughout), but most of us have other goals that are purely selfish and that sometimes conflict with the goals of others. Second, utility theory, in the form of utilitarianism, has been applied as a normative theory of what is best for everyone, a moral theory that treats all individual goals as equally important, no matter whose goals they are. Because some goals are selfish, these two applications of utility theory cannot give the same answer to every question about what we should do.

To call attention to this conflict, which lies at the heart of the problem of normative theory for social dilemmas, I shall, as an expositional device, discuss only selfish goals. Clearly, if people are sufficiently altruistic, social dilemmas will disappear, since there is no conflict between self and others, but we are not always so altruistic, and that is when the problems arise.

We shall consider the three normative theories that are the obvious candidates for the normative theory of social dilemmas. At the one extreme of altruism, we have what I shall call the *cooperative theory*. Very close to this theory stands *utilitarianism* itself. At the extreme of self-concern, we have what I shall call the *self-interest theory*.

Let us consider these views in the context of a classic example: walking across the lawn instead of on the sidewalk, in a public place. Suppose that everyone prefers to have a nice lawn in front of the college library, but each of us can benefit (save time) by taking a shortcut across the lawn. In this situation, "cooperation" can be defined as staying on the sidewalk (avoiding the shortcut), so that the grass does

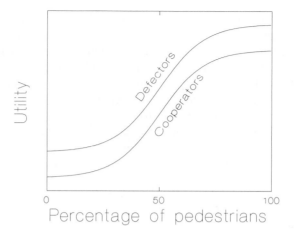

Figure 18.2: Total utility for cooperators (those who do not walk on the grass) and defectors as a function of the percentage of cooperators. Utility comes from both the appearance of the grass and taking the shortcut.

not get trampled to death. A few people could walk on the grass without killing it, however. It takes a fair amount of traffic to kill the grass. If a lot of people have already walked on the grass, though, one more will not make any difference, because it will be too late to save the lawn.

We can diagram the situation as in Figure 18.2. The upper curve is for defectors, because there is always some personal benefit to taking the shortcut. Notice that the slope — the benefit to others from cooperation — changes as a function of the number of cooperators. In the middle region, around 50%, the slope is highest, because at that point an additional defector ruins a little more grass, and so the benefit to all decreases.

The *cooperative theory* states that one should choose whatever would be best for everyone if everyone made the same choice. In all of the examples given so far, it would be better if everyone cooperated, so everyone should cooperate. Indeed, Dawes (1980) defines "social dilemmas" as situations in which defection increases personal benefit (holding constant the actions of others) but the benefit of each is maximized if *all* choose cooperation. In the grass-walking example, nobody should take the shortcut, *no matter how many others did likewise*. The cooperative theory is a natural extension of the contractual view of morality discussed in Chapter 16. It holds that the right question to ask is "If we were all going to agree to do one thing or the other, what would we agree to do?" Of course, given the choice between all cooperating and all defecting, we are all better off if we cooperate, so that is what we would agree to do. Then, by imagining that a hypothetical contract has already been made, it holds that cooperation is what each of us *should* do. If we do not cooperate, we violate the contract.

The problem with the cooperative theory is that following it often leads to harm and no good (Regan, 1980). If everyone has already trampled the grass to death, why should I be the only one to obey the "Keep Off the Grass" sign? I would only decrease net benefit by hurting myself and helping nobody. (Let us put aside such arguments as the fact that by being seen to walk around the grass I might encourage others to do likewise. We have not counted such precedent setting as an outcome in our analysis, and if we did count it, Figure 18.2 would look different.)

Schelling (1978, p. 236) gives another example of the conflict between the cooperative theory and utility maximization. In summer, it is best for everyone if everyone is on daylight saving time. By the cooperative theory, each of us ought to live according to daylight saving time, *even if everyone else around us is on standard time.* This example shows, again, that the effect of what we do depends on what others do. In this case, it is best to conform.

The *self-interest theory* says that I should always do what is best for me and ignore everyone else. Therefore I should always walk on the grass. Two different forms of this theory are often confused. One form says that we should not care about other people. Hardly anyone seriously holds this theory. The second form says that it is best for everyone if individuals look out for their own interest. This theory is, in fact, taken seriously by many as a *moral* theory, because it *is* concerned with what is best for everyone. This theory seems to be the underlying justification for various defenses of free enterprise, for example. It is often argued that the best society for everyone is a society in which all individuals pursue their own self-interest.

The problem with this theory is that it essentially denies the existence of social dilemmas. We may define such dilemmas as cases in which pursuit of narrow self-interest is *not* best for everyone. (We shall make this definition more precise later, but it accounts for all the cases we have encountered so far, and it is consistent both with the definition we shall give and with Dawes's definition.) If there are any such cases — and there surely are many — this theory simply ignores the problem that they create; it gives up on the problem we are trying to solve. As a normative theory, it amounts to saying that morality makes no claims on individual behavior. (It might be more defensible as a prescriptive theory, but later I shall argue against that too.)

If we apply *utilitarianism* to the grass-walking problem, it says that I should cooperate as long as the benefit to others from doing so is greater than the cost to me. Therefore, I should cooperate when the number of other cooperators is about 50%, but not at either end of the percentage range. At the high end, I may not know exactly how many cooperators there are; it would be difficult to determine whether I will be the critical person who starts the decline of the grass. It seems sensible here to compute *expected utility*, given my personal probabilities for the different numbers of cooperators.

Utilitarianism seems to some to be too demanding. It seems to require people to give away money whenever someone else could use the money more than they, for example. (The cooperative theory has the same problem.) But it may not make such impossible demands when it is taken as a theory of an entire life plan rather than individual acts. People who always give their money away may not do as much good in the long run as people who develop their talents in a way that is helpful to others and then put their talents to use, maintaining a life-style that allows them to do this efficiently and wholeheartedly, without begrudging their efforts. Also, utilitarianism is a normative standard that concerns the morality we endorse and try to follow. The closer to this standard, the better, even if we are not very close. That is what standards are for.

Some have proposed that the ideal theory is *weighted utilitarianism,* a consistent compromise between self-interest and utilitarianism, weighing self-interest more than others' interest by a constant factor in all situations, so as to do the most good for others given a constant amount of self-sacrifice (Baron, 1986; Bennett, 1981, p. 78; Hare, 1981, ch. 11; Singer, 1979, p. 181). This may work as a prescriptive theory, but, even for that purpose, it would seem better to take into account the fact that people are much more willing to sacrifice for some people (such as their children) than others, so a more efficient prescriptive system would be one that takes such relationships into account.

But utilitarianism is being proposed as a normative standard, not a prescriptive rule. If we adopted weighted utilitarianism as a prescriptive standard and suddenly discovered a way to increase utility (goal achievement) by increasing the weight given to others' utilities, we would all have reason to endorse adoption of that new standard, as long as the weight for each other person was no higher than the weight for self. So utilitarianism is still the normative standard, even if we must take human nature into account in applying it to real life.

If we accept utilitarianism as a normative standard for social dilemmas, then we will also want to replace Dawes's definition of social dilemmas with one (based on Pruitt, 1967) in which a social dilemma is *a situation in which two or more people are each faced with essentially the same two options, one maximizing total utility over all involved, the other maximizing utility for each individual decision maker.*

Defined in this way, the idea of social dilemmas seems to capture many of the kinds of conflicts that we call "moral," particularly those cases in which self-interest conflicts with the interests of others and in which many people face the same choice. An appropriate normative theory for social dilemmas would seem to require cooperation when cooperation can accomplish some net good. A prescriptive theory for moral educators might take into account the differences from one situation to another in people's willingness to cooperate. It may be too costly to promote cooperation in some situations.

Motives in social dilemmas

With this analysis in mind, let us examine some of the descriptive theory concerning the motives for behavior in social dilemmas that has been developed through psychological research. (Such motives, we shall note later, are not the only cause of defection: Simple thoughtlessness about the needs of others can play a role.) Let us begin with the motives or goals that operate in such situations. These motives can be treated as "dimensions" of utility in a MAUT analysis. If you imagine yourself in a social dilemma (either a real one or a laboratory simulation), it will be apparent that some familiar motives are involved: self-interest, or greed; empathy and altruism; envy of others; the desire for fairness or equity.

    Some of these motives can be represented in the following simple diagram (based on Lurie, 1987). The horizontal axis represents self-interest, and the vertical axis represents altruism. "Cooperation" is roughly equal concern with self and others. Each positive motive has a negative counterpart. Other motives, not represented here, are contingent on expectations of others' behavior. Another important motive, fairness, concerns the distance from an ideal distribution, such as equality between self and other. I shall discuss only the motives about which something may be said. (There is little to say about selfishness.)

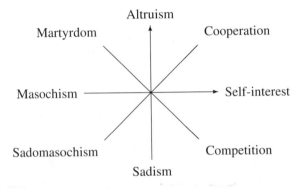

Altruism

Adam Smith, the author of *The Wealth of Nations* (1776), is famed as the theorist of unbridled capitalism, or (supposedly) the self-interested pursuit of profit. How interesting to discover that his first book (1759/1976) was entitled *The Theory of the Moral Sentiments*. In it, he says, "How selfish soever man may be supposed, there are evidently some principles in his nature, which interest him in the fortune of others, and render their happiness necessary to him, though he derives nothing from it except the pleasure of seeing it ... That we often derive sorrow from the sorrow of others, is a matter of fact too obvious to require any instance to prove it" (p. 7). Even today, people contribute to charity and advocate the cause of those less fortunate, and they take pleasure in the good fortune of others. More generally, we can solve social dilemmas by increasing the level of altruism: If our utilities depended heavily enough on each other's gains and losses, no conflict would exist between maximizing the utility of the individual and maximizing the utility of the group. In Table 18.3, where cooperation provides a total of $12 for others at the expense of $2 for oneself, subjects who followed weighted utilitarianism would cooperate if they weighed others more than 1/6 as much as they weighed themselves (assuming utility is proportionate to dollars). If we describe this as a change in the utilities of each subject, then the task is no longer a social dilemma when this weight is exceeded.

As Smith suggested, emotional empathy, the tendency for people to experience emotions that they observe others experiencing, is a source of altruism. This could be the reason why pictures or films of famine victims inspire an outpouring of contributions in the United States and Europe. To measure such empathy in the laboratory, Krebs (1975) asked one subject to watch another subject (actually a confederate) performing a task. In some conditions, the confederate either won money or appeared to receive an electrical shock, as a result of the spin of a roulette wheel. Krebs had convinced the observers that they were either similar (or dissimilar) to the confederate by showing them, in advance, a questionnaire that the confederate had supposedly filled out, which agreed (or disagreed) with the subjects' opinions on various issues. When the confederate was perceived as similar, the observers demonstrated more physiological response (increased heart rate and the like) as a function of the outcome experienced by the confederate. Also, when the confederate was perceived as similar, subjects were more likely to sacrifice some of their own reward for the confederate, when given an opportunity to do so. Krebs concluded that the feelings of empathy made the subjects behave more altruistically.

Cultures seem to differ in their emphasis on cooperation. Parks and Vu (1994) found that cooperation in social dilemmas was much greater in Vietnamese immigrants to the United States than in U.S. college students. Vietnam is thought of as a "collectivist" culture, in which group cohesion is highly valued.

It would seem that empathy and the desire to form and maintain groups are helpful for altruistic behavior (behavior that helps another at one's own expense), but they may not be necessary. Some people apparently act out of a more abstract knowledge that their action is morally right. People who act out of religious convictions often have this sort of motivation, but purely moral behavior is also found in people with no religious belief at all but strong moral beliefs. Nagel (1970) has suggested that the argument "How would you feel if someone did that to you?" appeals to us as an argument that is relevant to our own decisions for very fundamental reasons. This appeal is not based on our having been taught the Golden Rule, nor is it based on our expectation that someone *will* do to us whatever we do to them. Nagel's explanation of the appeal of this argument is obscure and difficult to summarize, so I shall not attempt to give the details. I bring it up just to raise the possibility that there is something like a "pure" motive for concern with others, a motive not tied to empathy, or to the desire for communal relationships, or to anything else we shall discuss. I know of no research on this sort of motivation, but my experience with toddlers suggests that even they can understand this kind of argument. Because very young children have not had time to learn much about morality from their culture, they might be good subjects for the study of such motivation.

Altruism seems to motivate cooperation in social dilemmas, even when strangers are involved. For example, Hershey, Asch, Thumasathit, Meszaros, and Waters (1994) studied subjects' willingness to be vaccinated against a (hypothetical) flulike illness. For some vaccines, vaccination is a cooperative act, because the vaccine prevents the recipient from passing the disease on to others. This is called "herd immunity." (If most animals in a herd are vaccinated, probably none will get the disease.) Other vaccines prevent the symptoms of the disease but do not prevent the vaccinated person from being infected in a way that passes the disease to others. In this case, vaccination does not help others. Subjects were given several hypothetical cases of each type of vaccination. The cases of each type varied in the percentage of others who had decided to get the vaccine (88%, 64%, or 36%). If subjects were interested in helping others, the effect of herd immunity on willingness to vaccinate would be greatest when the fewest other people are vaccinated, because the benefit to others would be greatest here. This result was found.

Outside of the laboratory, it is clear that people often cooperate when they need not sacrifice much, even when those who benefit are strangers. People leave tips for waiters even when they are traveling and have nothing to gain in terms of better service next time. Dawes and Thaler (1988) provide another telling example: "In the rural areas around Ithaca it is common for farmers to put some fresh produce on a table by the road. There is a cash box on the table, and customers are expected to put money in the box in return for the vegetables they take. The box has just a small slit, so that no one can (easily) make off with the money. We think that the farmers who use this system have just about the right model of human nature. They feel that enough people will volunteer to pay for the fresh corn to make it worthwhile to put it out there. The farmers also know that if it were easy enough to take the money, someone would do so."

Competition

In the last chapter, we examined the "fixed-pie assumption" that can hinder integrative bargaining. Each party assumes that his own gain is coupled with the other party's loss. Gains from integrative bargaining are in some ways like gains from cooperation (except that, in bargaining, there is no particular advantage in defection if the other party also defects). More generally, we may sometimes evaluate our own outcomes by comparing them to those of others. Messick (1985, p. 93) tells an anecdote that illustrates this nicely:

> I did an informal experiment with my sons to illustrate this point .... In isolation from each other, I gave them a choice between a dish containing two peanuts and one containing three. With no hesitation, they both chose the three peanuts. The next step was to put one peanut next to the dish containing two, and four peanuts next to the dish containing three. I then asked the boys again to tell me which dish they preferred, with the additional stipulation that the peanuts beside the dish that they chose would be given to their brother: if they chose three, the brother got four; if they chose two, the brother got one.

> Needless to say, making their outcomes interdependent changed the

choice situation dramatically. The younger boy chose the dish with two peanuts and explained that he did not want his brother to get four when he would only get three. The older boy still chose the dish with three but explained that he did not mind giving his brother four peanuts because he was sure that he would ... be able to get some back for himself. He too was not indifferent to relative position.

Of course, competition will prevent cooperation in social dilemmas as elsewhere. It is a motive that is useful only in games. We should not confuse these with real life — either way (Baron, 1985a).

Fairness, equality, and envy

As we noted in the last chapter, people want fair outcomes. This applies to contributions as well as benefits. In simple situations, such as laboratory experiments, fairness often amounts to equality, because there is no legitimate basis for unequal division. People often prefer equal division to a division that gives them a greater share of the benefits or a smaller share of the costs (Lurie, 1987; Loewenstein, Thompson, and Bazerman, 1989). In social dilemmas, this motive is one of several that leads to a desire to do what others do. If all others are following the rules about recycling by putting various kinds of trash in different containers, then it would be unfair for me not to do it too. Unfortunately, social dilemmas in which *all* others are believed to be cooperating are rare. When people see themselves as receiving the low end of an unfair distribution of benefits or contributions, they sometime envy those who are better off. As discussed in the last chapter, envy can lead to a competitive desire to hurt others.

The danger of this sort of social comparison is that the standard of fairness is often ambiguous (Messick, Bloom, Boldizar, and Samuelson, 1985). In a complex society, it is practically always possible to find someone who is treated better than you are *in some way*, no matter how lucky you are. If each of us focuses on aspects of comparisons that make us feel treated unfairly, each will feel justified in demanding (or taking) more at someone else's expense. One professor will feel that she deserves more pay because she is such a good teacher; a second will feel that she deserves more because her research is so important; a third, because she feels that she is an intellectual leader among her colleagues. The residents of a poor country focus on the sheer inequality between them and the residents of prosperous countries; the residents of the latter feel that they "deserve" their prosperity because of their hard work, their superior government, and their other virtues.

Messick (1985) found that envy operates in laboratory games as well as in the real world. Subjects in his experiments chose the "defection" response in order to avoid falling behind another player, even when they knew that they themselves would ultimately get fewer points (and less money) as a result. Like competition, envy is a motive that can be done without. It has no place, even in games.

Fear and greed

Other motives in social dilemmas are contingent on beliefs about what others will do. *Fear* is a tendency to defect when one believes that others will defect — or, conversely, to cooperate when one believes that others will cooperate. The term connotes fear of being a sucker, of cooperating when others are defecting. It is like the equity motive just discussed, but it is more general. It does not require perfect fairness.

Greed may be seen as the opposite, a tendency to defect when others are believed to be cooperating, that is, a motive to take advantage of a cooperative situation by free riding on the efforts of others. The term "greed" makes the most sense in situations in which the benefits of cooperating are not provided unless some minimum number of participants cooperate. Then defection has no benefit when few others cooperate. But the term is used more generally to mean a tendency to do the opposite of what others are thought to be doing.

Dawes, Orbell, Simmons, and van de Kragt (1986) performed an experiment designed to distinguish the roles of fear and greed in causing defection. There were three conditions (see Table 18.4): a standard condition, a condition that eliminated fear, and a condition that eliminated greed. If subjects cooperate more in the condition that eliminates fear than in the standard condition, then we can conclude that fear prevented cooperation, and if subjects cooperate more in the condition that eliminates greed, then we can conclude that greed prevented cooperation. For all three conditions, each of seven subjects was given a note that could be exchanged for $5 at the end of the experiment. Each subject could either keep the note or contribute it to a pool. Subjects were told that if a certain number of subjects contributed to the pool (three out of the seven in one experiment, five out of seven in another), the whole group would receive a $70 bonus — that is, $10 for each person. The subjects all decided individually, at the same time, whether or not to contribute, without knowing what other subjects had decided and without being able to influence anyone. Subjects also knew in advance that they would not see each other as they left the experiment with their winnings and that the game was played only once. This situation is much like the grass-walking example, because in order for the benefits of cooperation to be available, a critical number of cooperators is required. If you know that everyone else is cooperating or that nobody is, you do no harm by defecting (keeping the $5).

In the "money-back guarantee" condition, subjects were told that contributors would get their $5 back if there were too few contributors to produce the $70 bonus. Therefore, subjects had no reason to *fear* that they would contribute while others did not. If defections are caused by fear, we would expect to have fewer defectors — and more contributors — in this condition than in the standard condition.

In the "enforced-contribution" condition, subjects were told that *non*contributors would have to *pay* $5 if there *were* enough contributors to produce the bonus. Greed could therefore play no role in causing defections. Nobody could be tempted to try to get a "free ride" on the contributions of others.

Table 18.4: Experimental conditions used by Dawes and his colleagues to distinguish between fear and greed

	Standard condition		Money-back guarantee		Enforced contribution	
	Bonus	No bonus	Bonus	No bonus	Bonus	No bonus
Contributors	$10	$0	$10	$5	$10	$0
Noncontributors	$15	$5	$15	$5	$10	$5

The proportion of cooperators (averaging across two experiments) was about 58% in the standard condition, 63% in the money-back guarantee condition, and 90% in the enforced-contribution condition. Defections were therefore substantially reduced when greed — the temptation to take a free ride — was eliminated, but reduction of fear had no significant effect.

Although the failure of the money-back guarantee to increase cooperation could imply that fear was not a motivation, Dawes and his fellow researchers provide another explanation. If subjects *believed* that this condition would affect *other* subjects, they would think it more likely that they could get away with defecting without hurting anyone, because enough others would contribute so that the bonus would be provided anyway. This effect would cancel out the effect of reduction of fear itself. On the other hand, if subjects believed that the enforced-contribution condition would encourage others to contribute, they would have no less reason to contribute themselves, since they would probably have to contribute anyway. The experiment therefore provides evidence for greed, but leaves the status of fear in doubt.

It is worth noting, before we leave this experiment, that more than half of the subjects cooperated, even in the standard condition. This behavior is difficult to justify in terms of self-interest, for it is unlikely that the choice made by any given subject would be critical in determining whether the bonus was provided or not.

Other studies provide clearer evidence for both fear and greed. Rapaport and Eshed-Levy (1989) carried out an experiment much like that just described, except that each subject participated in several games. Both greed and fear effects were found, although the greed effect was larger. Bruins, Liebrand, and Wilke (1989) used a simpler N-person prisoner's dilemma like that described earlier in this chapter, played once. In some conditions, the payoff functions for cooperators and defectors were parallel, as in Figure 18.1. That is, the benefit of defecting was constant, regardless of the number of cooperators. In the greed condition, the slope of the line was higher for defectors than for cooperators, and, in the fear condition, the slope was higher for cooperators. That is, in the greed condition, the benefit of defecting was greatest when others were cooperating, and, in the fear condition, the benefit of defecting was greatest when others were defecting. In this study, the rate of defection was increased by both greed and fear.[3]

An experiment done by Yamagishi and Sato (1986) in Japan is particularly interesting, because it provides evidence for individual differences in fear and greed. On every trial, each of five subjects was given a number of points (worth money), some of which the subject could contribute to a common pool. All subjects received bonus points that depended on these contributions.

There were two conditions of interest, which differed in terms of the system used for determining the number of bonus points. In the *minimum* condition, the number of bonus points was determined by the size of the contribution of the subject who had contributed the *least*; if only one subject contributed nothing, there would be no bonus at all. This is analogous to preserving the reputation of a group. One "bad apple," it is said, can spoil things for everyone. Here, fear would be the major cause of defections. If you think that someone else is going to be a fink and give very little, there is no advantage to anyone from your not "finking out" yourself by giving nothing or very little. Greed would play only a small role here, because too much of it would penalize you as well as everyone else.

In the *maximum* condition, the bonus depended on the amount given by the highest contributor. This is like volunteering for a dangerous mission on behalf of a group, when only a few volunteers are required. Here, one is little affected by a few defectors, so fear of someone else's defecting plays little role. One need not fear that one's own cooperative action will be useless to the group, either. Greed, however, may play a larger role, for one's own contribution also matters little, except in the unlikely event that one is the highest contributor.[4]

We can diagram the two conditions roughly as shown in Figure 18.3 (if we think of cooperating as making a large contribution and defecting as making a small one). Note that the curve for the minimum condition resembles the curve for the left half of the grass-walking graph (Figure 18.2) and that the maximum condition resembles the curve in the right half.

Yamagishi and Sato found that friends cooperated more than strangers in the minimum condition but not in the maximum condition. Presumably friends were less afraid that they would cheat on each other by giving less money, but friendship had no effect on personal greed. Subjects were also given a questionnaire about their attitudes toward public questions, with items designed to assess both fear and greed as general motives in the subjects. Here are some "fear" items (pp. 69–70):

Help to developing nations should be limited to the minimum, because it is only exploited by a small group of people.

During the oil shock, people rushed to stores to buy a stock of toilet paper because people are concerned only with their own interest and not with the benefit of society.

[3] Poppe and Utens (1986) found evidence only for greed in yet another kind of study in which subjects could take coins from a common pool that was replenished by a fixed amount on each trial.

[4] Yamagishi and Sato called the two conditions "conjunctive" and "disjunctive," respectively.

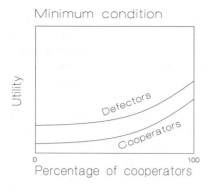

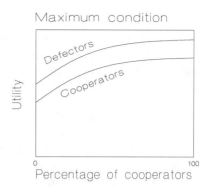

Figure 18.3: Utility for cooperators and defectors as a function of the percentage of cooperators for situations resembling Yamagishi and Sato's minimum and maximum conditions.

> There will be more people who will not work, if the social security system is developed further.

Here are some greed items (p. 70):

> In order to be a successful person in this society, it is important to make use of every opportunity.

> It is not morally bad to think first of one's own benefit and not of other people's.

The score on the fear scale correlated with defection in the minimum condition, but not in the maximum condition. In the minimum condition, where only one "fink" could prevent everyone from getting a bonus, subjects who expressed fear and distrust in the questionnaire were more likely than other subjects to defect. The score on the greed scale correlated with defection in the maximum condition, but not in the minimum condition. In the maximum condition, subjects who were greedy according to the questionnaire were the ones more likely to defect. These results not only indicate the existence of individual differences in the motives in question, but they also suggest that the motives are quite general, affecting attitudes toward public issues as well as behavior in laboratory experiments.

In the minimum condition, subjects' *expectations* about what others would do correlated highly with their own behavior. This was less true in the maximum condition. In the maximum condition, subjects compared their own behavior with the behavior they expected from others. Note that this effect is pretty much in line with the utilitarian model. If others do not cooperate in the minimum condition, then one's contribution will not do much good. The important point here, though, is that subjects differ in their expectations.

Other studies have found that cooperation is correlated with expectations about others, as would occur if people were motivated by fairness or by fear (for example, Dawes, McTavish, and Shaklee, 1977; Dawes et al., 1986). In the 1986 study, subjects cooperated, even when they believed that their own cooperation was redundant, provided that they believed that others would cooperate as well. (The public good would be provided if a minimal number cooperated.) Correlations, however, could result from effects of one's own behavior on beliefs about what others would do, rather than effects of beliefs on behavior. It is important to manipulate expectations experimentally in order to find out whether they affect cooperation.

Experiments in which subjects are given false feedback about the behavior of others in order to manipulate their expectations show conflicting results (Fleishman, 1988). It seems, once again, that subjects are influenced by both fear and greed. Sometimes one predominates, sometimes the other. The relative strength of the two motives may be affected by the framing of the dilemma. Fleishman (1988) used "give some" and "take some" games to study the effects of perceptions of others' behavior. In the give-some game, each subject in a five-person group was given 100 points (each worth 1/3 cent) on each trial. The subject could give any number of those points to a central pool or stock. At the end of each trial, the number of points in the pool was doubled and divided among all the subjects. (Each subject would thus get 200 points per trial, if all contributed all their points.) In the take-some game, 500 units were given to the pool at the beginning of the trial, and each subject could take up to 100 units. Formally, the games are identical, except for the description in terms of giving or taking. Not giving a unit is the equivalent of taking it, and vice versa. To manipulate expectations about others, subjects were told after the first trial that the pool contained either 380 or 120 units.

In the give-some game, subjects *gave less* on subsequent trials when they thought that the pool contained 380 after the first trial than when they thought it had 120. That is, behavior was opposite from what others were perceived as doing. In the take-some game, they *took less* when they thought that the pool had 380. Behavior was the same as what others were perceived as doing. Evidently, give-some subjects reasoned, "If nobody else is giving anything, then I'd better do it, but if others are giving a lot, I can take advantage of them." (Formally, this is what we have been calling greed.) Take-some subjects seemed to reason, "If nobody else is taking, then I'd better not take either, but if others are taking, then I can take too." What we have been calling "fear" seems to operate to prevent harmful actions but not harmful omissions. (These effects were small and should be replicated, but they help to make sense out of previous conflicting results.)

Trust

We can think of trust as the opposite of fear. In the "minimum" condition used by Yamagishi and Sato (1986), the subjects had to trust each other to contribute. If you think that others will not contribute, then your contribution will do no good. In this condition, friends cooperated more than strangers, and fearful subjects (according to the "fear' scale) cooperated less than others.

Yamagishi and Sato used a third condition in which the payoff was based on the average contribution — neither the maximum nor the minumum. In this condition, friends also cooperated more than strangers, and fearful subjects cooperated less. (Parks and Hulbert, 1995, found similar results.) It seems that fear plays a role in ordinary social dilemmas, those in which the benefit of your cooperation (to others) does not depend at all on what the others do. People seem to think of these dilemmas as involving trust, as if their effort would do no good unless it were reciprocated by others.

The existence of trust can be shown in a different kind of experiment. Berg, Dickhaut, and McCabe (1995) had two groups of subjects play a game, each group in a separate room. Each subject started with $10. Each subject in room A could give any number of dollars to an anonymous partner in room B. When the money arrived, it tripled in value. If the A subject gave $5, the B subject would receive $15. The B subject then played a dictator game. He could return any number of dollars in his possession to the anonymous A subject. Of the 32 pairs of subjects in one study, only two of the A subjects gave nothing. Five gave the full $10. And 11 of the B subjects earned the trust that had been placed in them by returning more to the A subject than what the A subject contributed. (Three others returned the same amount.)

This game seems to measure trust. The A subjects who contribute could do so because they expect reciprocation. However, they might contribute simply out of altruism. Their contributions truly expand the size of the pie for everyone, because the contribution triples in value. This is what happens from cooperation in a social dilemma. Likewise, the B subjects seem to be reciprocating, but they are like dictators in a dictator game. They might contribute out of fairness. Indeed, five of the B subjects returned exactly the amount required to make the two subjects equal in the end. Four others split the increase resulting from A's contribution.

In this game, the A subjects seem to behave in a trusting way. What is trust? Is it just the belief that the B subject will reciprocate? Not necessarily. Trust could be a belief, but it could also be a disposition to behave in a trusting way, regardless of belief. Of course, such behavior will be more likely if someone believes that others are trustworthy.

We may thus speak of two kinds of trust. The first is believing something about others. The second is behaving as if you believed this. Although the second sense may be derivative, it is no less real or important. If people behave in a trusting way, even if they are trembling inside out of fear that others will not reciprocate, this will encourage others to believe that trust is usually warranted. Trust is certainly a social good, *if* it is warranted. If we do not trust people to follow the law, do their jobs, and behave morally in general, then we must invest resources in monitoring and enforcement. Such investment is wasteful when people can, in fact, be trusted.

Voters' illusions

So far we have examined those factors that increase or decrease cooperation, and we have seen that poor thinking — particularly distortion of our beliefs — is one factor that works against cooperation. There are other kinds of poor thinking that *promote* cooperation. These are easily seen in the case of voting in political elections. Voting is a simple act of self-sacrifice for the benefit of others. It takes a little effort, but, if enough people put in that effort (including the effort of informing themselves), we are all better off, because, as a society, we will tend to choose the candidates who will be most likely to help us achieve our goals.

One error in people's thinking about voting is the conclusion that self-interest alone makes it worthwhile to vote. (This error has never been formally documented in an experiment, but we can observe it informally by discussing the issue with people who vote.) It is extremely unlikely that one vote is critical in any election, and even if it is the difference one vote would make to the voter who casts it is probably small — too small, given the low probability, to justify voting at all in terms of narrow self-interest alone (Downs, 1957).

It is possible that people vote out of some feeling of moral obligation. From a utilitarian point of view, voting is probably worthwhile. If 50 million voters can, together, make a small improvement in the lives of each of 50 million people (perhaps the voters themselves — but to a utilitarian it does not matter), voting is worthwhile if the benefit (utility gain) to each person is worth the trouble (utility loss) of casting one vote.

It is also possible that people vote because they misunderstand the situation. For one thing, they may believe that they vote out of self-interest. They do not make the calculations required to see that their self-interest is hardly affected. There is a danger in this belief, in that it could inhibit people from voting on the basis of what is best for everyone. They may think that they should vote their own narrow self-interest. If enough people did this, the needs of those who cannot wield power through voting, such as children, minorities, people in the future, or people in other countries, would be neglected. It might be better for everyone if people who voted out of self-interest just decided that voting was not worthwhile — although the rest of us would then have to look out for them.

There is, however, another incorrect reason for voting, which is less insidious. People may think that their own choice affects others' choices. Of course, this is true, in that a vote sets a precedent through example, but the belief in question may go beyond that. Voters may reason, "If people on my side vote, I'll probably vote too. My voting will thus be linked with theirs. Hence, I'd better vote, because if I don't, they won't either." The same reasoning could apply to any social dilemma, of course. The essential confusion here is between *diagnostic* and *causal* relationships. Their own voting is *diagnostic* of the overall turnout on their side, but it does not affect the turnout, except for their own vote. (The same reasoning is involved in the Quattrone and Tversky experiment on self-deception described in Chapter 9.)

Quattrone and Tversky (1984) told subjects about a hypothetical election in a country with 4 million supporters of party A, 4 million supporters of party B, and 4 million nonaligned voters. Subjects were told that they were supporters of party A. Some subjects were told that the election depended on whether more of the supporters of party A or the supporters of party B turned out to vote. These subjects said that their side (party A) was substantially more likely to win if they voted than if they did not vote. They were also quite willing to vote. Other subjects were told that the election depended on whether more of the nonaligned voters voted for party A or for party B. These subjects thought that the probability of their side's winning was not much different whether they voted or not. They were less willing to vote than the subjects who were told that the election depended on the turnout of party supporters. Of course, one vote is one vote; in fact, these latter subjects would have just as much influence on the election whether it was "determined" by the party supporters or by the nonaligned voters. In short, people may think that their vote affects other people, when in fact they are only themselves *affected* by the same factors that affect other people.

A related demonstration of this effect concerns the prisoner's dilemma itself (Shafir and Tversky, 1992). When subjects in a two-person prisoner's dilemma were told that their partner had defected, 97% of the subjects defected too. When they were told that their partner had cooperated, 84% still defected. But when they did not know what their partner had done, 37% cooperated and only 63% defected. Apparently, many subjects did not think through the uncertainty about what their partner had done: "If she cooperates, I will defect; if she defects, I will defect; so I don't need to know what she does, I should defect anyway." Perhaps it is a good thing that people do not think so logically in this case!

A second illusion that makes people vote is the confusion of morality and self-interest. It is as though people resist the very idea of a social dilemma, which is a conflict between self and others. People try to reduce this conflict by convincing themselves that it doesn't exist. They may do this by telling themselves that "cooperation doesn't do any good anyway, so I do not need to sacrifice my self-interest." They may also do the opposite, and convince themselves that cooperation is in their self-interest after all. They may focus on the slight self-interested benefit that accrues to them indirectly from their own cooperation and ignore the fact that this benefit is less than the cost of cooperating. (If it were not less than the cost, then we would not have a social dilemma after all. The necessity for self-sacrifice for the good of others is a defining property of social dilemmas.) This is an example of belief overkill (Chapter 9).

In one study subjects read the following scenario (Baron, 1997): "Suppose you are an ocean fisherman. The kind of fish you catch is declining from over-fishing. There are 1,000 fishermen like you who catch it. The decline will slow down if the fishermen fish less. But, of course, you will lose money if you cut back. Nobody knows how much fish you catch. .... If nobody cuts back, then everyone can keep fishing at roughly their current rate for 2 years and then they will have to stop. Every 100 people who cut back to 50% of their current catch will extend this time for about a year. Thus, if 100 people (out of 1000) cut back this much, fishing can continue for 3 years, and if 200 people cut back, it can continue for 4 years. (It is not expected that many more than this will cut back voluntarily.)"

Subjects were asked whether they would cut back and whether cutting back would "increase your income from fishing over the next few years?" Many of the subjects (29%) saw cooperation as helping them financially in the long run, although it clearly did not. The most common argument referred to the long term versus short term distinction. Examples were: "If I cut back now, I would not have to face the fear of running out of fish to sell and I could keep staying in business for a longer time and everyone else would also benefit." "Because if we cut back, there will be more fish for 4 years of 3 years so it would be a greater profit." The second response was typical of many that explicitly changed the question so that it was about the group rather than the individual.

In a way, this confusion is a good thing. It makes people willing to sacrifice their self-interest for others. The trouble is the group. People may confuse their self-interest with the interests of members of a particular group, when that group is competing with other groups over limited resources such as land or jobs. They may thus sacrifice their self-interest for the benefit of the group, but at the expense of another group, so that the overall benefit of the sacrifice is zero. This is called parochialism.

An experiment by Bornstein and Ben-Yossef (1994) shows this effect. Subjects came in groups of 6 and were assigned at random to a red group and a green group, with 3 in each group. Each subject started with 5 Israeli Shekels (IS; about $2). If the subject contributed this endowment, each member of the subject's group would get 3 IS (including the subject). This amounts to a net loss of 2 for the subject but a total gain of 4 for the group. However, the contribution would also cause each member of the *other* group to *lose* 3 IS. Thus, taking both groups into account, the gains for one group matched the losses to the other, except that the contributor lost the 5 IS. The effect of this loss was simply to move goods from the other group to the subject's group. Still the average rate of contribution was 55%, and this was substantially higher than the rate of contribution in control conditions in which the contribution did not affect the other group (27%). Of course, the control condition was a real social dilemma in which the net benefit of the contribution was truly positive. It seems that subjects were willing to sacrifice more for the sake of winning a competition than for the sake of increasing the amount their own group won. Similar results have been found by others (Schwartz-Shea and Simmons, 1990, 1991).

We don't know fully why the subjects behaved as they did, but it is possible that they saw their own self-interest as tied up more with their group than with the larger group consisting of all six players.

This kind of experiment might be a model for cases of real-world conflict, in which people sacrifice their own self-interest to help their group at the expense of some other group. We see this in international, ethnic, and religious conflict, when people even put their lives on the line for the sake of their group and at the expense of another group. We also see it in strikes and in attempts to influence government policy in favor of one's own group at the expense of other groups. What is interesting about these cases is that we can look at the behavior from three points of view: the individual, the group, and everyone (the world). Political action in favor of one's group is beneficial for the group but (in these cases) both costly to the individual and to the world. Perhaps if people understood that such behavior was not really in their self-interest, they would not be so willing to do this, and we would see fewer of these kinds of conflicts.

Thoughtlessness

Another possible cause of defection in social dilemmas is simple *thoughtlessness*. The person who plays his radio loudly while walking along the sidewalk, rather than expressing social envy, may simply not be *thinking* about whether anyone else is being bothered. Likewise, the woman who buys her twenty-seventh pair of new shoes in the last two years does not *think* about whether someone in Africa might put the $89.95 (plus tax) to better use.

This possibility has not been studied, to my knowledge, but it seems worth studying. Religions try to teach people to be thoughtful of others. Do they succeed? Can children be taught thoughtfulness in school? It seems likely that part of such instruction would involve instruction in good thinking. If we search thoroughly, we are more likely to discover the needs of others than if we do not.

Solutions to social dilemmas

The idea of teaching people to be thoughtful is one of many possible prescriptive solutions to the problems posed by social dilemmas. Let us turn now to a broader consideration of this prescriptive problem. By definition, cooperation is better for all, so it is something that we would want to increase in general. First, it is clear that there is much we can do to maintain moral norms that favor it. We can encourage thoughtfulness and altruism. Moreover, we can discourage some of the motives that work against cooperation and that have little useful purpose, such as competition and envy, when these motivate harm to others or failure to cooperate.

Fear and greed, as we have defined them, are more complex. Although the words suggest that they work against cooperation, we have defined them simply as differences in the tendency to cooperate as a function of expectations about others. The goodness or badness of each may depend on the situation. In some situations, cooperation is most beneficial when few others are cooperating. An example is calling attention to a hazard. In these situations, "greed" is harmless. If all about you are losing their head, you'd do better to keep your own. But fear amounts to keeping your mouth shut just because everyone else is doing the same. In other situations, cooperation is most helpful when many others are cooperating, such as when the goal is to keep a secret. Here, greed is insidious, but fear is harmless. Perhaps people can learn to adapt their motives — or at least their behavior — to the situation.

But we can rely only so much on changes in human motives and habits. When self-interest is too strong, other solutions to social dilemmas must be considered. It is not clear, for example, that altruistic concern for the growth of world population has had any noticeable effect on decisions about childbearing in any countries.

Experimental approaches

Several experimental results provide suggestions about what does and does not affect cooperation. The experiments of Kahneman and his colleagues (Chapter 17) suggest that the utility of fairness to others sometimes outweighs the individual's self-interest. This fact may provide a way out of the typical social dilemma in which all individuals suffer collectively because many (or all) pursue their self-interest. "Contract" theories of social decision making suggest that one way to achieve fairness, with relatively little self-sacrifice, is for people involved in a social dilemma to make an *agreement* to enforce cooperation. Essentially, they agree to assess a penalty of some sort against anyone who defects, a penalty large enough to make defection unprofitable. This can be done through the election of a government, or the delegation of the enforcement power to an existing authority such as a chief, boss, parent, ruler, mediator, or experimenter. People will be inclined to accept such a situation to the extent to which they are sure that fairness will increase as a result of the change.

Interestingly, all of these changes create a second-order social dilemma. Electing a leader or changing the rules often requires that all participants expend a small amount of effort in order to bring about a benefit to everyone, in the form of a better system. If most others make this small effort to bring about change, then I am better off by not making it, that is, by defecting. If most others do not make the effort, then I am still better off, since one person cannot do much. The situation is much like the game described earlier in this chapter in which a certain number of cooperators are required.

Cooperation in this second-order social dilemma need not have the same benefits (to others) and costs (to oneself) as the original dilemma that created the problem. In particular, the individual costs of cooperating might be much lower. If, for example, I think that everyone should use half the amount of fossil fuels that they now use, it might be very costly to me to cut my own use to this extent, but it is easy for me to vote for someone who will force me and everyone else to do it, and the expected benefit to others might be equally great. Why is this? One reason is that "forcing" usually means threatening punishment. Punishment can be inflicted without drawing much on limited resources (see p. 415). If, by contrast, we tried to reward people for cooperation, the cost of the reward would fall on everyone else, so the cost of cooperation would increase in direct proportion to the reward. It would not work.

Yamagishi (1986, 1988) has studied second-order dilemmas in the laboratory. As in the give-some game described earlier, subjects could either contribute to a pool (which was to be doubled or tripled and divided among *other* subjects) or keep points for themselves. Some subjects could also contribute to a "punishment fund."

The total amount in the fund was then subtracted from the points held by the least cooperative member of the group. Subjects contributed more to the fund when the temptation to defect was larger (for instance, when a bonus was promised to the subject with the most points) (Yamagishi, 1988). Subjects also differed: Those who were more trusting of others, as indicated by a short questionnaire, contributed more to the pool than less trusting subjects, but less trusting subjects contributed more to the punishment fund (Yamagishi, 1986). (It is not clear which group was more realistic in their predictions about others.)

Attempts to change the rules may also be affected by the perception of unfairness, that is, by large differences in the amounts that players contribute. Samuelson, Messick, Rutte, and Wilke (1984) studied the effects of departures from fairness in a laboratory game. Six subjects sat at six different computer terminals and watched displays showing the changing levels of a common resource pool. At the outset the pool contained 300 units. On each trial, each player could take up to 30 units for himself. After all players had taken what they wanted, a variable number of units (about 30) was added to the pool. (The units were worth real money.) Each subject saw on the display the amounts that the other players took and the new level of the pool after all players had consumed what they wanted. Subjects knew that if the pool ran out, the experiment was over. Subjects were told both to try to get as many points as possible and to make the resource pool last as long as possible.

In fact, the display was manipulated by the experimenter so that each subject "saw" the other subjects behave in different ways. In some conditions, the other subjects appeared to behave more or less the same way, leading to the appearance of fairness. In other conditions, the subjects' behavior differed drastically. Some behaved like absolute pigs, and others were quite modest in their demands. The average change in the size of the pool was also manipulated so as to make the pool appear to increase, decrease, or stay about the same in size.

Subjects were more likely to take more for themselves when there appeared to be no danger of the pool's running out; when there was danger, subjects moderated their demands, even if their demands had been minimal throughout. Subjects were also asked whether they would like to elect a leader to apportion the resources for the next play of the game. Subjects were more likely to say yes when the pool had run out quickly because units were taken out faster than they could be replenished.

Of greater interest here is the response to the perceived variability among the other players. The researchers ran the experiment in both the United States (Santa Barbara) and the Netherlands (Groningen), and they found that subjects' behavior apparently was affected by their nationality. When the amounts taken by other subjects differed by large amounts, American subjects tended to take more for themselves. It seemed that they did not want to be "suckers." "If some pig is going to lead the whole gang to ruin, well, I might as well share in the spoils," they seemed to reason. Dutch subjects responded differently. In the same situations, they were not more likely to increase their own harvests. When asked if they wanted to elect a leader to apportion the pool on the next play of the game, American subjects were equally likely to want a leader, regardless of whether they saw the other subjects as highly variable in their demands or not. Dutch subjects were considerably more likely to want a leader when the other subjects' demands were variable than when they were all about the same.

In short, Americans tended to respond to unfairness by joining in, by avoiding being "suckers." Dutch subjects responded to unfairness by trying to eliminate it through electing a leader. This study reminds us that the manner in which people weigh moral and social considerations is very often a function of the manner in which they are brought up and educated and of the culture in which they live. The Dutch subjects may have tended to regard large differences among the other subjects as morally outrageous. The Americans seemed to regard such differences as a sign that self-indulgence was acceptable.

The election of a leader is not the only way to solve a social dilemma, and it is possible that Americans may have seen this idea as unnecessarily authoritarian. The parties can simply make an agreement among themselves to abide by certain rules. In a laboratory task, this often occurs when the participants talk among themselves about the situation. Dawes, McTavish, and Shaklee (1977) found that simply giving the subjects a chance to talk about a laboratory dilemma — in which each subject could choose to cooperate or defect — increased cooperation from about 30% to about 70% of responses. (Mere social contact had no effect: When the subjects spent the time discussing another issue, cooperation did not increase.) In such discussion, there is an implicit threat; subjects made it clear to one another that they would each be very angry with anyone who defected (possibly to the point of retaliating outside of the experiment). It is doubtful that this solution could be used in large-scale social dilemmas, because they involve too many people to sit down and talk, but television publicity campaigns for various causes sometimes use a related method. Respected (or ordinary) citizens appear on television and proclaim their intention to perform some socially beneficial action — contribute to the local public television station, clean up their own litter, restrict their fertility (in China). This may have the effect of making people think that an implicit agreement is in force — a thought that can become self-fulfilling.

In a subsequent experiment, Orbell, van de Kragt, and Dawes (1988) found that the beneficial effects of discussion made subjects more willing to cooperate, even with other people who had not been involved in the discussion. In each session, 14 subjects were randomly divided into two groups of 7. Each subject had a note worth $6, which she could either keep or give away (anonymously). Every $6 given away was augmented by $12 from the experimenter. The subject's contribution, plus the bonus, went into a pool that was to be divided up (in one condition) among the other 6 members of the subject's own group or (in the other condition) among members of the other group of 7. Half of the groups in each condition participated in a discussion, and half of the groups did not. Finally, just before the final choices were made, half the groups in each of these subconditions were told that the benefits of their contributions would be switched. Subjects who had been told before the discussion that contributions would go to their own group were then told that the benefits would go to the other group, and vice versa.

When there was no discussion, about 33% cooperated, even when benefits went to the other group — an interesting fact in itself. No beneficial effect of discussion was found when subjects thought, during the discussion, that the benefits would go to the other group. Therefore, the discussion did not promote general altruistic or cooperative motives. Discussion had a beneficial effect, however, when the subjects thought that the benefits would go to their own group; 79% cooperated. In this case, the discussion aroused feelings of general obligation, possibly of a communal sort. The most interesting finding was that when the subjects thought, during the discussion, that the benefits would go to their own group but were then told that the benefits would go to the other group, the discussion still had a beneficial effect: 59% cooperated. It was as though, once the subjects understood the importance of cooperation, they realized that it did not matter much whether others had been involved in the discussion or not. This result is encouraging if we are interested in promoting cooperation among strangers. It suggests that promoting cooperation among people who know each other can be used to teach the benefits of cooperation in general.

Social reform

These experimental results are helpful in designing educational programs to encourage cooperative attitudes and in designing institutions that maximize cooperation. But we must remember that some of the major problems of defection are massive, involving millions or billions of people: overpopulation; excessive use of resources such as oil, land, fisheries, water, and forests; global warming resulting from carbon dioxide; stratospheric ozone depletion; and international trade restrictions. These problems may seem overwhelming, but they are not hopeless. The Montreal Protocol restricting chlorofluorocarbon production has removed much of the threat of ozone depletion. International treaties on trade and the protection of fisheries have been effective. Many nations have substantially reduced pollution within their borders; others have instituted market reforms to improve their standard of living. But these innovations are social reforms resulting from changes in law, not the result of spontaneous cooperation. The production of reforms may be seen as a second-order social dilemma, formally like that studied by Yamagishi, but on a much larger scale. (Past reforms on this scale are the abolition of slavery and the granting of rights to women and minority groups in some countries.)

Elster (1989) has suggested that reforms result through a kind of sequence of actions inspired by different kinds of social norms. The first to act are the "everyday Kantians," idealists who behave as though they accepted the cooperative theory described earlier in this chapter: Vegetarians who object to meat eating on moral grounds; environmentalists who try to adopt a sustainable life-style, despite an economy not designed for it; and so on. Despite the low probability of success and the small immediate benefits, such behavior may be justifiable in utilitarian terms if the long-term benefit of success is sufficiently high. This sort of high benefit may involve recruitment of additional followers, enough to bring about major reform. Elster suggests that such converts might consist of what we might call "everyday utilitarians," those who will join and support a social movement once it is clear that their action can make a difference. Finally, there are those who will cooperate in a social movement when enough others are cooperating, those motivated by what we have called fear, or concern for fairness.

Of course, the path to reform is never smooth, nor assured. Reforms are resisted by those who will lose in order that others may gain. Moreover, as we discussed in the last chapter, other people will object to reforms if the benefits are seen as unfairly distributed, and some will object on principle to the idea of hurting some in order to help others. Other objections to reform (Baron and Jurney, 1993) are expressed in terms of rights violations, that is, removing choices that people think they should be allowed to make freely — such as buying and selling slaves, fishing in traditional fisheries, having children, or refusing medical treatment (such as vaccinations, even when herd immunity is affected).

Conclusion

Defection in social dilemmas can be seen as a paradigm of a great deal of immoral behavior, because defection involves indulging one's narrow self-interest at a great expense to others. Defection seems more obviously immoral when it results from action than when it results from inaction, but this appearance may come from the omission bias discussed in Chapter 16. In general, we have noted three types of poor thinking that cause such immorality. The first is that people hold incorrect theories — accepted without adequate critical scrutiny — about what behavior is right. For example, some people believe that selfishness is a virtue. Second, people fall prey to the temptation to weigh their self-interest excessively, perhaps even more than they would wish to weigh it on reflection. They sometimes do this by self-deception (Chapter 9), convincing themselves that they are not really being selfish, that their behavior is justified, or that they have been treated unfairly. Third, people do not think enough about the effects of their choices on others, possibly because they believe that morality is nothing more than honoring certain prohibitions (Chapter 16).

Incorrect theories, the first cause, can be opposed by discussion and by presentation of arguments for better theories. Perhaps the field of social studies, as taught in elementary and secondary schools, should pay more attention to the normative, descriptive, and prescriptive aspects of social theory of the sort discussed in this chapter. We can oppose the last two causes of immorality by teaching certain prescriptive heuristics. The tendency to overweigh self-interest through rationalization can be opposed by the heuristic: "Give the other guy the benefit of the doubt." The tendency to ignore the effects of choices on others can be opposed by the simpler heuristic — which we try to drum into children's heads almost daily — "Think about other people's feelings."

In the complex world in which we live, these guidelines may need to be supplemented by other heuristics specifically directing our attention to the effects of our choices — for example, our political choices — on people in distant lands, as well as people not yet born. It seems that people are more prone to cooperate when they see their cooperation helping a group to which they belong, such as a nation, even when it hurts outsiders. If they take a broader view, they will cooperate in those projects that benefit more people. This kind of thinking requires active open-mindedness, because such arguments often are not obvious, and even when they are presented clearly we tend to resist them.

Chapter 19

Decisions about the future

But you must bind me hard and fast, so that I cannot stir from the spot
where you will stand me, ...and if I beg you to release me, you must
tighten and add to my bonds.

Homer, The Odyssey

In the last chapter, we examined conflicts between self and others. In this chapter,
we look at a different kind of conflict, that between the present and the future. Many
of our decisions require us to choose between satisfying our goals for the immediate
present and our goals for our futures. Should I do the crossword puzzle or work on
this book? (I will enjoy doing the puzzle now, but if I miss the deadline for this
manuscript, I will be unhappy later.) Should a student go to a movie or get started
on a paper? If she goes to the movie, she may regret it later, when she has to finish
the paper at the last minute. Should Bill take a job he likes now, or should he go to
graduate school and get a job he likes even better later? Should I learn the violin,
putting up with the scratching and sawing in order to play Bach later? We can think
of these kinds of conflicts as analogous to social dilemmas. Instead of a conflict
between self and other, the conflict is between a "present self" and a "future self."

A basic problem we have in such conflicts is that we are biased in favor of our
present self. Our future self, like "others" in social dilemmas, is distant and has
less claim on our attention. We begin to be aware of this problem in childhood, and
we develop methods of *self-control*. Like Ulysses, who had himself bound to the
mast of his ship so that he could hear the song of the Sirens without giving in to the
temptation to visit them, we learn to "bind" ourselves by making decisions before
the temptation occurs, so that we will not succumb to it.

We can think of decisions about the future as *plans* or *policies*. A *plan* is a
decision to do something at a future time. When we cook a meal, we usually have
some plan in mind. We do certain things at one time and put off other things for
the future. The crucial step here is that we decide now to do something at a later
time. There would be no point in planning if we were unable to hold ourselves to

this decision. The study of planning, therefore, is intimately tied up with the study of self-control. A *policy* is a plan that binds us to perform a certain action regularly or under certain conditions. We might establish a policy of practicing the violin for half an hour every day, for example, or a policy of never picking up hitchhikers. A plan is not a policy when it involves only a single, isolated decision, such as planning to go to the movies on a certain day. A policy applies to a whole class of behavior that recurs regularly in our lives.

Some policies are made all at once, but policies also result from individual decisions made without any idea that these decisions will affect the future. Without realizing that we are doing so, we set *precedents* for ourselves(Hare, 1952, ch. 4). Suppose a friend who has missed a class you take together asks to borrow your notes. If you decide to lend them, it will be difficult for you to make a different decision if she asks again. Even if a different friend, who does not even know the first one, asks you for the same favor, you will tend to be bound by your initial precedent.

The same mechanism of precedents applies to the most minute details of our lives, such details as what we eat, when we go to bed, and the way we deal with other people. Practically every decision we make sets a precedent for the same decision in similar cases in the future. In this way, we form policies for the various domains of our lives. At times, of course, we think about these policies and change them. At any given time, however, we can be said to be following certain policies whether we have thought about them or not.

Plans and policies *create new personal goals*, or they change the strength of old ones. If I decide to take up the violin, that gives me a new set of goals right away: finding a good teacher, finding time to practice, obtaining a good instrument. I will also not be surprised if this decision creates or strengthens other goals over time. I will come to like violin music more than I do now, and I will develop certain musical standards. If I start early enough, I could even acquire the goal of being a professional musician. When we make plans and set policies, then, we are making decisions about our own personal goals.

Up until this point, in Part III, we have been concerned to discover the best ways of making decisions that will enable us to achieve our personal goals. We have, on the whole, regarded these goals as "givens." We are now ready to consider how these goals themselves are chosen. These personal goals that we create for ourselves are the most important determinants of our identities as individuals. They are what we stand for, what makes our lives worth living. They are, as noted, chosen through a variety of decisions. Some decisions are apparently trivial: A choice to work on a philosophy term paper instead of one in psychology sets a precedent for similar decisions, which could eventually make the decision in favor of a career in philosophy rather than psychology. Other decisions are made after great agonizing. Should I sacrifice the income I could earn in computer science for a career as a philosophy professor? Is my desire to help others strong enough to make me want to live in a poor country for several years, possibly at the cost of not finding a spouse? Should I retire from working, and what should I do in my retirement?

Most of us, then, are fairly well aware that if we are to have a life plan for the future that will be likely to work for us, we need to search for our major goals and choose among them. Some kinds of decisions, such as those about religious commitments, can be made at any time. We are encouraged to consider other kinds of issues especially seriously at certain times in our lives, particularly at the transition from adolescence to adulthood (with respect to work and marriage), during the childbearing years (with respect to the single decision of bearing children), and at the time of retirement from work. People at these transition points are often encouraged to consider various goals in an actively open-minded manner, seeking evidence from many sources (personal experience, the lives of others, newspapers, works of scholarship, and literature) before making major commitments. Students, at least, tend to be aware of the danger of treating such choices as if they had already been made, without seeking alternatives and counterevidence.

This chapter concerns the theory of plans and policies. The main issue is the extent to which we consider our future interests as we make decisions. Our main problem is a tendency to weigh these future interests too little (compared to what a normative theory would specify), just as we often underweigh the interests of other people. Psychological research has much to tell us about why we have this problem and what we can do about it. Let us begin, however, with a discussion of the normative theory for choosing personal goals.

The choice of personal goals

How should we choose our personal goals? We can either think about decisions that could affect our goals, or we can think about our goals directly. When we think about decisions that could affect our goals, we should be aware of such consequences. For example, psychological researchers who accept military contracts sometimes change their personal goals for their research (ever so slightly) toward the goals of those who support them, and those who study handicapped populations, such as the deaf, sometimes become advocates on behalf of their subjects. Neither of these effects is, by itself, sufficient reason to turn down military funding or to refrain from studying the deaf, for the researchers could have no particular objection to such a change in goals, or they may feel that the risk of such change is worth taking. Anyone who thinks carefully about such decisions, however, must admit that the possibility of such consequences should be considered, along with other consequences. To decide whether we want such consequences, we must ask the next question: How should we think about goals themselves?

When we think about our goals, we must rely on our present goals concerning our future goals. One of these present goals is that we prefer achievable goals to unachievable ones (other things being equal), as suggested by Rawls (1971, ch. VII). This principle argues against choosing such goals as making certain beliefs true ("defending the faith"), for if the beliefs in question are false, the goal is futile. It also argues against choosing goals based on false beliefs. A person who wants to die in order to atone for a horrible sin would be irrational, if the sin were not truly horrible. The same principle tells us that it can be rational to give up a goal that is constantly frustrated and has no chance of being achieved.

On the other side, as Rawls points out, most of us want to develop our talents and to strive for difficult achievements. This too is a rational goal, because developing our talents makes us more effective in doing things for other people, and this is usually one of our goals. Without talent, the musician cannot bring us pleasure, the scientist and scholar cannot enlighten us, our leaders cannot govern us well, teachers cannot teach us well, doctors and nurses cannot care for our illnesses, manufacturers cannot give us affordable goods of high quality, and parents cannot give us the kind of upbringing we should have. Because talents are so important to others, societies develop (to varying degrees) ways of encouraging people to develop their talents, such as rewarding them with respect and money when they have succeeded, so the development of our talents helps us achieve these goals as well. The development of talent, however, is often a risky enterprise. We must strike a balance between the risks of striving for high achievement and the principle that our goals should be achievable.

Another consideration in thinking about personal goals is the relative ease or difficulty of changing our own goals. I heard a story of a music professor who did not like modern atonal music. He tried to "develop a taste" for such music by listening to the complete works of Anton Webern (four long-playing records) daily for several months, but at the end he liked Webern's music as little as he had at the outset. Others, however, claim to have had more success in shaping their own goals. People who have forced themselves to give up smoking often report that (over a period of months) they lose their desire to smoke; those who try to reduce their consumption of saturated fat report learning to like fish; and those who have undergone religious conversions report losing their desire to live in ways they have come to see as sinful. The simplest way of trying to shape our goals is to behave as if we already had them, according to the proverb "Where the hand leads, the heart follows."

More generally, the choice of goals is a decision problem in which we evaluate the consequences of our decision just as we would evaluate the consequences of any other decision, except that the goals we apply to this decision include our goals for our future goals. We must evaluate the total consequence of having a new goal and being able to achieve it to whatever degree we expect. When we think about having a child, we should not ask how much we now care about the welfare of this future child but rather how much we desire to have the child and care about its welfare in the future, as parents tend to do. Similarly, when we make career choices, the relevant question is not how much we now want to do the work of a scientist or teacher but rather how much we want the goals of a scientist and the level of achievement of them that we could expect. We may find that we do not want ourselves to have certain goals in the future, and we can even try to bind ourselves so that we do not develop them, like those scientists who refuse support from the military because they fear that their political goals will change as a result of accepting it. If, however, we become open to changes in our goals, we could realize that many more options are open to us than we previously thought.

The creation of life plans and personal goals is often taken to be a kind of discovery, as though the answer was there all along and our task is only to find it, but what does it mean to say that the answer was "there all along?" As I have argued elsewhere (1985b, ch. 2), the decision to get married, to have a child, to get involved in politics, to learn to play tennis, is usually more like taking on a new set of goals than it is like pursuing goals already present. It is as though we permit another person — the "spouse" in us, the "parent," the "activist" – to share our life. We cannot find our goals simply by asking what they have been or what other people would like them to be, for the goals we would choose in these ways could differ from the goals we would want to have for our own futures.

Many popular ideas about good personal goals are simply attempts to hold up certain ways of living — the fashionable life, competitive success, peace of mind, piety — as better than others. They are not very helpful for planning our personal lives, because they do not provide *reasons* or evidence for choosing these personal goals instead of many other possibilities we could choose.

Good reasons for sticking to plans

Once we have begun a plan or course of action, it is difficult to change. Some of the reasons for this are good, and some are poor. A good reason to stick to our plans is that they usually involve other people, who have, in turn, planned their own lives partly in terms of ours. A music student moves to a new city to study under a great master, who promises to work with the student for two years, but after six months the master decides to have nothing further to do with students. It is good to be a "dependable person," one who can be counted on to carry out plans once they are made.

Another good reason to stick with a plan is that plans very often build their own momentum. If you spend years building up a clientele for your dress shop, you cannot expect to be as successful if you suddenly move it to another town. The same goes for skills and knowledge you have developed. If you spend a long time learning the ins and outs of a certain method of production, you will be valued for your knowledge, but you cannot expect others to value you as much, for quite a while, if you suddenly switch to another line of work. Of course, plans can go bad, and then this kind of reason does not apply. Also, this sort of reason to stick with a plan tends to vary with age. The younger one is, the more one has to gain from thinking about the future rather than the past.

A final reason for keeping a plan is that if we do not, we lose some of our faith in our own ability to make plans and keep them. This reason may not apply when we otherwise have good reason to break a plan. We can make a distinction between trusting ourselves to keep foolish plans and trusting ourselves to keep worthwhile plans. If you give up a foolish plan, you may not lose any faith at all in your own ability to stick to a worthwhile one.

Beyond these four reasons — the interlocking of one's personal plans with others' plans, the value of dependability, the increased chances for success as plans are carried out, and the value of trust in ourselves — there may be no good reasons for sticking to plans. All of these reasons concern future costs and benefits. They may all be overwhelmed by other reasons concerning the future. If a plan is not succeeding, it may be rational to change it, even if the losses just listed are incurred.

Bad reasons for sticking to plans: Biases

Change is difficult. Clinical psychologists are often faced with people who would be happier if they changed their goals or their policies for achieving them. Some of these people know this and still cannot bring themselves to make crucial choices: to decide to quit smoking, to break up with a boyfriend, to go back to school, to retire, to stop bullying other people, or to resist being bullied. Certain types of biases or errors in the way that people think about plans can exacerbate the difficulty of changing them. For example, all the mechanisms of irrational belief persistence discussed in Chapter 9 can cause us to stick to beliefs about the goodness or efficacy of our plans. These biases are usually studied in minor decisions, but they seem to operate in large decisions as well. Of course, we must keep in mind that there are also good reasons to *stick* to plans. Still, some awareness of what makes us stick to them when we should not may help us to decide just *when* to stick to them.

Any change in plans can be thought of as giving up something, a loss, in return for something else, a gain. A change of careers, for example, involves a loss of contact with old colleagues and a gain of new colleagues. In Chapter 12, we examined the status-quo bias. People tend to stick to the old, even when they would choose the new if they were starting afresh. One explanation of this is loss aversion: People may see the losses as greater than the gains, even if this is not the case. A prescriptive heuristic to avoid this effect is to ask what would be chosen if there were no status quo.

Other biases we have examined earlier are relevant to the formation and change of plans. Omission bias leads us to be more concerned about possible harms resulting from action than harms resulting from inaction. When change involves risk, we worry about more about the down side than when our present course involves a similar risk. Finally, the sunk-cost effect (Chapter 12) leads us to carry on with plans only because we have invested in them.

The sunk-cost effect may be exaggerated when the decision maker is responsible for the original decision. People want to believe that they are good decision makers, so they persist in believing that an initial decision was a good one, even when it appears not to be. Arkes and Blumer (1985) found that the sunk-cost effect was somewhat reduced (in one experiment) when subjects were told that the original decision to develop an airplane had been made by someone else; however, the effect was still present.

Staw (1976) found other evidence for a role of commitment to one's own decision. He gave business students a written case study of the recent history of a business firm. Some students were told that, as financial vice president of the firm, they had $10 million to invest and were asked to decide which of two divisions of the business they would invest it in for research and development. Half of these students were told that the division they had chosen did well after the investment; half were told it did badly. They were then asked to divide an additional $20 million between the two divisions. When the chosen division had performed badly, the allocation to that division the second time around averaged about $13 million (out of $20 million), but when the division had done well the allocation averaged only about $9 million.

Other subjects were not asked to make the original decision on the investment of the $10 million; they were told that it had been made by someone else. These subjects allocated about $8 million to the division that had received the $10 million when they were told that the division had done well, and they allocated about the same amount of money when they were told it had done badly. In short, subjects allocated extra money to the division that had previously received $10 million only when *they* had decided to allocate the original $10 million and when the division in question did badly. Presumably this was caused by a desire to believe that their original decision had been a good one, leading to a belief that the original decision had been a good one, leading to additional investment in a cause that seemed likely to succeed (see Chapter 12).

The same results are found when the decision involves hiring people who perform either well or badly (Bazerman, Beekun, and Schoorman, 1982) and when the decisions are made by groups instead of individuals (Bazerman, Giuliano, and Appleman, 1984).

In sum, the status quo bias, omission bias, the sunk-cost effect, and the commitment effect can cause us to stick to our plans, even when the rational reasons listed in the preceding section are not sufficient to keep us from switching, given the greater expected future benefits of a new course. We may stick to our old course because we feel that we have sunk too much into it to give it up – even though putting more into it will only increase the waste. Likewise, by analogy with the endowment effect, we may feel that the loss of the advantages of our current course outweighs the gain from switching to a new course, although we would choose the new course if we looked at the whole situation afresh.

Sometimes we stick to plans irrationally because of our basic aversion to risks, resulting from the certainty effect (Chapter 11). Our present course seems to us to have consequences known with certainty. However (as argued in Chapter 11), this may be an illusion resulting from our failure to consider the true variability of the consequences that might result from our present course.

Finally, a major change of plans, especially when it involves a change of goals, may seem to a person to involve a loss of self, a partial death in which some of the self is replaced with a different person. A change of this sort creates a sense of personal loss that may not be easily compensated for by the creation of a new person inside one's skin. The fear of such a loss, too, is irrational if the new person is otherwise to be preferred (see Parfit, 1984). People who are interested in changing themselves and others must recognize that such changes are far more emotionally involving than a mere calculation of "gains and losses" suggests.

Discounting

Which would you prefer: to get $100 today or $110 a month from now? Many people prefer the immediate reward. Hungry pigeons do too: Faced with a choice between pecking a key that gives them immediate access to food for two seconds and a key that gives them access to food for six seconds — ten seconds later — they repeatedly choose to peck the former, even though the next opportunity to peck will come at a fixed time after their choice is made. Mischel (1984) found that young children, faced with a choice between getting an attractive toy (that they could keep) in five minutes and a less attractive toy immediately, chose the latter. We can, it seems, be unfair to our own futures: We become *temporally myopic* (nearsighted).

The preference for immediate over larger but delayed rewards is one of the most familiar behaviors of the animal kingdom. Human beings are perhaps not as bad as most other species in this regard, but we do seem to have problems. In psychology, the phenomenon is often called *impulsiveness* (Ainslie, 1975) and the attempt to control it is called *impulse control*. Impulsiveness also refers to a tendency to respond quickly in problem solving despite a sacrifice in accuracy (Baron, 1985). The two concepts may be related, because people may respond quickly to gain the reward of removing themselves from a difficult task.

Economic theory of discounting

Giving less weight to the future than to the present is called discounting the future. It is not necessarily irrational and not always excessive. The simplest economic theory of discounting is that people behave as though any gain provides an opportunity to earn interest (or, equivalently, to pay off a debt and avoid paying interest), as though it were a monetary gain. The reason you prefer $100 now to $110 later, the theory goes, is that you behave as though you would begin earning interest on the money when you got it. Therefore, if your subjective rate of interest, your personal *discount rate*, is high enough, the $100 now would be worth more than $100 later. If you were indifferent between $100 now and $150 a year from now, your discount rate would be 50% per year.[1] Note that this is an "as if" theory, meant to explain all behavior of this type: Pigeons do not usually earn interest on their food, even though they prefer two food pellets right away to three after some delay, and people may behave *as if* their personal discount rates were much higher than the interest rate available in the market.

This economic theory suggests that we could think of discounting in terms of a function relating the utility of a reward to the time at which the reward is available.

---

[1] It could be less, if the subjective interest were compounded.

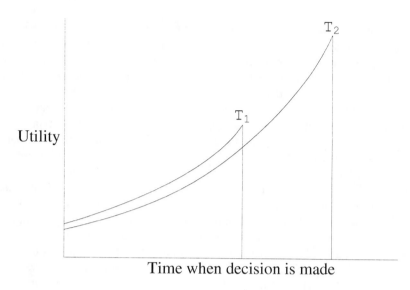

Figure 19.1: Subjective utility of two rewards as a function of the time at which a decision is made. (The utility scale has no units. The reward is available at times T_1 and T_2.)

This is decision utility, in the sense of Chapter 13, not true utility. It is about the power of the reward to motivate a decision, not about the extent to which the reward achieves anyone's goals. This economic theory holds that rewards lose their utility at a constant (percentage) rate over time. If the utility of $100 to you a year from now is 50% of the utility of $100 if you get it today, then 2 years from now the utility of $100 will be 25% of what it is today, and 3 years from now it will be 12.5%.[2]

In psychology, it is customary to plot this function by thinking of the reward as being available at a fixed point in time, T, and by thinking of the *opportunity to choose* that reward (versus some other) as being available at different times before T. As the time approaches T, the decision-utility of the reward increases. Figure 19.1 shows how this works for a small reward available at T_1 and a large reward available at T_2. As the decision is made earlier, the decision utility of each reward decreases. It decreases by the same proportion per unit of time moved. As a result, the two curves do not cross. In the case shown, the decision maker would prefer the smaller reward, because it is sooner. This preference would be independent of delay, that is, independent of the time at which the decision is made.

The economic theory is used in cost-utility analysis and cost-benefit analysis. Future benefits and costs are discounted at some rate of interest. Why do this?

It seems especially odd to discount benefits. For example, suppose you have a choice of two programs that cost the same and that prevent ten (equally valuable)

[2]Mathematically, this amounts to exponential decay.

species of plants from becoming extinct in a given year. In one program, the benefit (saving the plants) is immediate. In the other, it happens in fifty years. For either program, you pay now. Aren't these programs equally valuable? The economic theory says you should favor the first program even if it costs quite a bit more. This is because it assumes that there is a third option available, which is to invest the money, take out your investment in 50 years (when the expectation is that it will be worth much more), and spend it on saving species then. If the cost of saving species has not gone up — and there is no more reason to think it will go one way than the other — then you can do more good with this third option. Thus, if you were going to go for the fifty years, you could do more good with the third option.

Moreover, when 50 years are up, you would be faced with the same choice. If you do not discount the future, you would put off spending the money forever. So the only solution is to discount the future. Of course, there are many assumptions behind this argument, but they are reasonable ones (unless we have good reason to think they are false). Notice that this argument does not assume that you care any less about saving species in the future. It says that you should discount even if you are totally impartial between saving species at one time versus another. Only if you discount would you be indifferent between two programs that saved the same number of species for the same present cost. In particular, the future program would have to save more species, because it would have more money available.

This argument depends on interest being paid on investments. Why is interest paid? First, to make up for uncertainty about getting your money back. That is not at issue in these arguments. Second, inflation. But the theory so far works just as well with no inflation. It could be stated in "constant dollars," adjusted for inflation. Third, investments are often worthwhile: By digging a well, you can get more water, more cheaply than by relying on rain, so investment in the well is worthwhile in the long run. The demand for money for such investments allows investors to get interest.

Two other reasons are more interesting. One is that, psychologically, people are impatient. They favor the present even beyond their concerns about uncertainty or inflation. So, if you want people to lend you money, you have to pay them extra in order to compensate them for delaying the gratification of their desires for immediate reward. Economists call this "pure time preference." We shall see that it exists.

The second reason has to do with declining marginal utility (Chapter 10). The standard of living has been steadily increasing throughout human history. If we assume that this will continue, then people in the future will get less utility from money than people in the present. This is completely analogous to the reasons why the rich should help the poor. But *we* are the relatively poor! And we are making the decisions to soak the rich who will follow us. Strange but, according to the theory, true.

The relative importance of these various justifications for interest is a matter of debate among economists.

[handwritten margin note: More reliably not more cheaply]

Normative theory of discounting

There are good economic reasons to think that this form of the decay curve — of utility as a function of delay — is normative, as long as there is no known reason why the utility of the reward will change.[3] One is the idea of interest rate, already noted. If you have $100 now, you can invest it and end up with somewhat more a year from now, say $110. Therefore, you might be indifferent between getting $100 now and getting $110 a year from now, for this reason alone. Similarly, if you need $100 now, the value of $100 now might be equivalent to $120 a year from now, if you would otherwise have to borrow the $100 at a rate of 20%.

Another reason why discounting makes sense is that unforeseen events can affect the utility of money (or any outcome) to an individual. For example, in the interval between now and when you collect the $100, the economy could be hit by an enormous wave of inflation that makes the money worthless; you could die; or, to end on a more pleasant note, you could become a millionaire and have no need for such a piddling amount. If we make the assumption that each of these events is as likely to happen at one time as at any other, the same curve results. If you think that there is a 1% chance of such an event's occurring in the next year, the expected utility of $100 a year from now would be 1% less than it would be otherwise, because there is a 1% chance that its utility would be zero. The longer you wait, the more likely it is that one of these things will happen, so the lower the utility of the $100.

So far, we have assumed that you care just as much about your utility in the future as you do about your immediate utility, but we do not even need to assume that in order to derive a curve of this form as the normative model. What we do need to assume is that your relative preference for two future outcomes at different times depends only on what the outcomes are and on the time difference between them, but not on the time you make your choice. This is called the principle of *delay independence*.

Consider a simpler case. It is 2:59 P.M. A child has a choice of one piece of candy at 3:00 P.M. or two pieces at 4:00 P.M.. Many children will take the first option. Suppose that such a child is given the same choice at 2:00 P.M. instead of 2:59 P.M.. That is, the choice is still between one piece at 3:00 P.M. or two pieces at 4:00 P.M.. It is easy to imagine that the child will choose the second option. In this case, the child has made different choices as a function of the time alone. (Let us put aside the child's emotions of frustration and anticipation, for now.) This pattern of choices is *dynamically inconsistent, that is, inconsistent over time*. This is nonnormative, because the time at which the decision is made does not affect the extent to which the options achieve the child's goals. If the child's main goal here is to get as much candy as possible, for example, then the second option should be chosen in both cases. Dynamic inconsistency violates the principle of delay independence.

Likewise, your choice between $100 at a certain time and $110 a year later should not change simply as a function of when you make the choice. If one of these options

[3]For example, the utility of a car increases when the owner can obtain a driver's license. Here, we put such predictable changes aside.

achieves your goals better, then you should choose that one, regardless of when you
decide. Unless you learn something that makes a difference between one choice
point and the other — and we have assumed that you do not — such changes are
unwarranted.[4] Note also that this assumption of delay independence does not require
that you value the future as much as the present. It does imply, however, that *if* you
value the future less than the present, you do it in a consistent way. Such consistency
can be shown to imply (barring special events) that in each unit of time (into the
future) the value of a reward will fall off by a constant percentage of its value at the
beginning of the interval (Strotz, 1955; Lancaster, 1963).[5]

For the time being, however, let us assume that one ought to be impartial toward
all times of one's life. If we think of people at different times as though they were
different people, this amounts to the assumption made by utilitarianism that everyone
should be treated equally. (Note that when we apply utilitarianism to decisions about
others, we ought to consider their future preferences as equal in importance to their
present preferences. This often gives us a strong moral reason to go against what
people *say* they want when *they* do not think enough about their own future.) This
assumption of impartiality still implies (except when there are special circumstances)
a discount function like that shown earlier, in which the rate of loss with increasing
delay is constant as a percentage.

Descriptive data on discounting

People often discount too much, and they are dynamically inconsistent. These two
results may be related. Other results have been found repeatedly.

The subjective discount rate

How do individuals discount money? Some economists (for example, Modigliani,
1986) have suggested that the discount rate for money corresponds roughly to the actual rate of interest and that most people try to spread out their income over their lives
so as to achieve a constant income (adjusted for inflation). The fact that many people
put their money in pension funds and other methods of saving is surely consistent
with this view. Pension funds ensure a relatively constant income after retirement;
failure to save for retirement is surely an example of underweighing the future, unless one knows that one will never retire. By this view, people care as much about
their future as about their present.

Thaler and Shefrin (1981) have argued, however, that such saving is not spontaneous. It is, rather, the result of conscious efforts at self-control. When such efforts
are absent — when people do not think about the idea of saving, for example —
Thaler and Shefrin found that consumers had an extremely high discount rate —

---

[4]Of course, you are free to change your mind, but there is no reason why you should change it in any
particular direction — for example, from the later, larger outcome to the smaller, earlier one. This is the
important point.

[5]That is, it will decay exponentially.

much higher than the current rate of interest. When subjects in an income maintenance experiment were asked, "What size bonus would you demand today rather than collect a bonus of $100 in one year?", answers indicated subjective discount rates of between 36% and 122%, far higher than the highest interest rate charged at this time.

The high subjective discount rate (and resulting neglect of the future) is illustrated in the effect of mandatory pension plans (provided by employers) on voluntary saving. If people really looked out for their future, in this case, then those without mandatory pension plans would start their own voluntarily. Other things being equal, people without mandatory pension plans should save more (on their own) than those that have them, yet (before the introduction of government incentives in the form of tax breaks), this was not the case.

Another study reviewed by Thaler and Shefrin examined purchases of home air conditioners. Air conditioners differ, of course, in initial cost and operating expense (including the cost of electricity). The researchers found that people paid most attention to the initial cost. If one calculates the subjective discount rate from such purchase decisions, it is over 25%, well over any interest rate available at the time. (If one wanted to maximize income, one ought to buy the more expensive but more economical model — if necessary, borrowing money to buy it.)[6]

Dynamic inconsistency

It is difficult to draw conclusions about the personal discount rate because this rate is not constant (Chapman, 1998; Kirby, 1997; Loewenstein and Prelec, 1993). Discount rates are higher for shorter delays. This leads to dynamic inconsistency.

Figure 19.2 shows a different function relating the utility of a reward to time. Again, it contrasts a smaller, sooner reward and a larger, later reward. The first reward is available at T_1, and the second at T_2. In this case, the discount rate increases sharply as the time of the reward approaches, so sharply that it cannot be shown on the graph. As a result, the choice between the two rewards will depend on when the choice is made. If it is made far away from both, at the left side of the graph, then it will favor the larger later reward. If it is made soon before the smaller shorter reward is available, it will favor that one. This is like the candy example described earlier. A person with these discount functions would be dynamically inconsistent.

This inconsistency is a clear example of the difference between decision utility and experienced utility, discussed in Chapter 13. We can describe the decision as determined by some sort of hypothetical quantity — decision utility — that is somewhat unrelated to the true utility of interest, the extent to which goals are achieved. In Figure 19.2, decision utility is proportional to the reciprocal of the time between the decision and the reward. The function is a hyperbola. This function cannot be

---

[6]The conclusions of Thaler and Shefrin have been questioned by Modigliani (1986), who has found that many economic data can be accounted for by assuming that people treat all periods of their lives equally. Few of these data, however, directly concern the temporal myopia that Thaler and Shefrin have suggested.

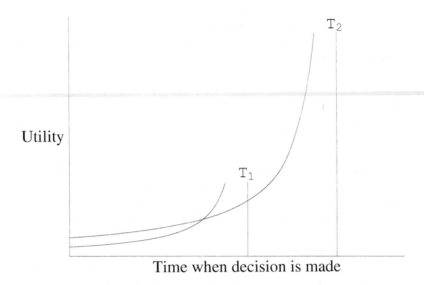

Figure 19.2: Subjective utility of two different rewards as a function of the time at which a decision is made. (The utility scale has no units. Rewards are available at times T_1 and T_2, respectively.)

exactly right, because it would imply that the reward has infinite utility when it is finally available. But this function comes amazingly close to describing the behavior of animals who are faced with repeated choices varying in magnitude and delay over thousands of trials (Chung and Herrnstein, 1967; Herrnstein and Prelec, 1991).

Note that for this effect to occur, the curve on the graph has to have a certain shape. It has to be very steep just as you approach the time of the reward. The economists' idea of a constant discount rate must be incorrect. That idea implies that the utility of a reward increases by a constant percentage for every unit of time; that is, the utility at the end of the time unit is some multiple (greater than 1.00) of the utility at the beginning of the unit. If this were true, any reward with a higher utility at the beginning of each time unit would be higher at the end as well, and there would be no crossover of the sort shown on the graph. Therefore, Ainslie's theory requires a particular shape for the curve relating utility to time.[7]

This theory predicts that preferences will reverse as a function of the time at which they are made (relative to the time the rewards are available). Therefore, delay independence will be violated. Ainslie and Haendel (1983) tested this prediction by asking subjects to choose between two prizes to be paid by a reliable company. The

[7]Ainslie recommends replacing the usual exponential function with a hyperbola. The hyperbola is consistent with a number of experiments discussed under the category of the "matching law" (see Rachlin, Logue, Gibbon, and Frankel, 1986, who also provide an interesting account of the certainty effect by interpreting probability as delay). However, other functions would work.

larger prize always had a greater delay. For example, the choice could be between $50 immediately and $100 in 6 months, or between $50 in 3 months and $100 in 9 months, or between $50 in 12 months and $100 in 18 months. Notice that in this example there is always a 6-month difference between the two prizes. A constant discount rate would imply that either the smaller or the larger prize would be chosen in all three cases. The smaller prize would be chosen if the discount rate was high enough to double the value of the money in 6 months. In fact, most subjects chose the smaller reward, in the first case (0 versus 6 months), and the larger reward in the last case (12 months versus 18 months). Subjects could not wait for the larger reward when the smaller one was available immediately, in clear violation of delay-independence. Kirby and Herrnstein (1992) found similar effects using actual goods. For example, a subject might prefer "a Sony Sports Radio to an Aiwa Cassette Player in 10 days," but the same subject might prefer the cassette player in 5 days to the radio in 15 days. This is what amounts to the same decision made 5 days sooner.

Solnick, Kannenberg, Eckerman, and Waller (1980) tested the same prediction by asking subjects to work on mathematical problems while hearing an annoying noise in the background. When a "choice window" was illuminated on a panel, the subject could press one of two buttons to turn off the noise. One button turned off the noise immediately for 90 seconds, and the other turned it off for 120 seconds, starting 60 seconds after the button press. (The time interval between successive illuminations of the choice window was constant.) Subjects preferred the immediate, smaller reward. If, however, a 15-second delay was added, so that the delays were 15 versus 75 seconds rather than 0 versus 60 seconds, subjects chose the larger, delayed reward.

Herrnstein and Prelec (1991) report a similar experiment that took the form of an intrapersonal social dilemma of sorts. On each trial, a subject received 5 cents after making a choice between two responses, Option A and Option B. The money was given after a delay, which varied between 2 and 8 seconds after the choice was made, as a function of the subject's response and her previous responses. The next trial began immediately. The duration of the session was fixed, so the average delay determined total earnings. Option A always had a delay 2 seconds less than that of Option B, but a choice of Option A increased the delay of each of the next 10 trials by 0.4 seconds, regardless of which option was chosen on those trials. In the long run, the subjects did better if they chose Option B on every trial, and they had 100 practice trials to learn this. Most subjects, though, chose Option A, with the short delay, most of the time. We can think of the next 10 trials as analogous to ten other people in a social dilemma, with the present trial as the decision maker — the present self, as it were, as opposed to ten future selves. The short-delay option is thus a defection: It is better for the present self but worse for each future self. Herrnstein and Prelec suggest that this behavior will arise if subjects always choose the option with the highest immediate expected rate of reward, which in this case means the option with the shorter delay.

These experiments show violations of delay-independence, a violation that is nonnormative even if we do not accept temporal impartiality as normative. Our reasons for being temporally myopic (neglecting the future) seem to go beyond a mere consistent underweighing of our future utility (just as we might underweigh the utility of others). They may instead result from a basic impulsiveness that we should — for our own future good – learn to control.

Decreasing discount rates are found even for public policy decisions that affect others. The declining discount rate may thus result from the way we perceive future time itself, as well as from some sort of impulsiveness. Like the Value function in prospect theory, we may tend to ignore those differences that are farther away from where we are now. Cropper, Aydede, and Portney (1992) did a telephone survey in which they asked such questions as, "Without new programs, 100 people will die this year from pollution and 200 people will die 50 years from now. The government has to choose between two programs that cost the same, but there is only enough money for one. Program A will save 100 lives now. Program B will save 200 lives 50 years from now. Which program would you choose?" The number of lives saved in the future was varied randomly, and the researchers inferred discount rates from the choices. The median discount rates were 16.8% (per year) for 5 years in the future, 7.4% for 25 years, 4.8% for 50 years, and 3.8% for 100 years, a steady decrease. Note that the discount rate continued to decline even after 50 years, a time when few of the respondents would still be alive.

The results showing that people have unusually high discount rates in some situations may be related to these results concerning changing discount rates. The high discount rates may be found when people think about the short term.

Other factors

Other factors affect the subjective discount rate. The discount rate is higher when rewards are smaller, and the discount rate for losses is lower than that for gains. These results are not well understood, but the are pretty clearly not the result of experimental artifact. The loss-gain effect may have something to do with wanting to get bad things over with so that we don't have to dread them (see p. 484).

Discounting may also have something to do with expectation. Chapman (1996) asked subjects to rate their preferences for sequences that described how their health or monetary income could change over their entire lifetime. Total income and average lifetime health quality were held constant. Most subjects preferred to make more money as they got older, and they preferred to have better health when they were young. This result was not found for shorter intervals of a few years, and subjects said that the lifetime pattern was what they expected.

Individuals differ in their tendency to prefer small but immediate rewards to larger delayed rewards, and these differences (at least those in young adolescents) seem to be related to concern with the future and the tendency to imagine it as something real and concrete (Klineberg, 1968). Children who tend to choose the larger delayed reward grow up to be more academically and socially competent in adolescence, and better able to cope with frustration and stress (Mischel, Shoda, and Peake, 1988; Shoda, Mischel, and Peake, 1990). Heroin addicts, too, prefer smaller, shorter monetary rewards in laboratory experiments (Kirby, Petry, and Bickel, 1999): possibly, in order to get addicted to heroin one must put aside one's knowledge that trying it a few times can lead to long-term problems.

The rationality of personal discounting

What should the discount rate be for individuals? We have been assuming that people should be utterly impartial toward all parts of their future lives. They should be just as concerned about themselves a year from now as they are about themselves this minute. Is this right?

We have already noted that temporal impartiality is consistent with some discounting, because of interest rates and unforeseen events. We might also wish to take into account the fact that some goods last so long that time to enjoy them may be shorter if we get them later, because life is finite. Beyond these reasons, there are no additional general reasons to favor the immediate future over the distant future. In many cases, such as those studied by Thaler and Shefrin, it can be assumed that only the interest rate is relevant, to a first approximation. It is therefore fair of Thaler and Shefrin to conclude that we are probably temporally myopic — that is, more concerned about the immediate future than we ought to be if we were impartial toward all parts of our future lives.

What if someone says, "I just don't care about my future. I care only about the present, and I dare you to call me irrational for doing so"? Aren't people free to say this and to ruin their own future lives if they feel like it? Surely they may live to regret this attitude, but just because we regret something does not mean that it is irrational. (We could, for example, regret the rational behavior of others that works to our disadvantage.)

This issue is not settled. Parfit (1984) has argued that rationality does not in fact require impartiality toward all parts of one's future life. He does point out that we have some reasons for being concerned with our future. Interestingly, some of these reasons are the same as those that we have for being concerned with other people. Parfit argues that, in a sense, the "you" that exists ten years from now is not the same person as "you" today — closely related, perhaps, but not the same. Therefore, your concern about yourself in ten years might be the same as your concern with someone very close to you, which might, in turn, not be quite as great as your concern with yourself at the moment.

Despite Parfit's reservations, many of us feel a strong pull toward an attitude of impartiality toward all parts of our future lives. There is certainly nothing *ir*rational about such an attitude in its own right. If we think of our lives as a whole, we may be able to form a better plan for each part than if we merely live for the immediate future, through a kind of cooperation among the different parts for the ultimate benefit of all parts (Elster, 1985). Of course, such planning requires self-control.

In the case of decisions made for other people, impartiality across time is even more attractive. If you are concerned about others, altruistically, then you are probably just as concerned with their future selves as with their present selves. If they are less concerned with their own futures, you may find yourself intervening to protect their future selves from the impulsiveness of their present selves. If you are on good enough terms, you will throw their cigarettes out the window, turn off the television so that they can finish their homework, or stop playing poker so that they (and you) can go to bed.

Some decisions affect different people at different times. Decisions made now about the use of forests, fuels, and birth control will affect future generations. Impartial treatment of all people — as implied by utilitarianism — requires that we do not discount the goals of future people (Broome, 1992). To see this, suppose that we do count future people less. And suppose that we have a choice of when a certain person will live, now or in the future. (She might be a frozen embryo.) Imagine that the person would achieve her goals and those of her contemporaries equally well no matter when she is born. If we discount future people, we would want her to be born now. We would want this even if she would achieve her goals a little better if she were born in the future. We would discount the achievement of those goals. But impartial treatment requires that we would want her to live in the future, if that achieves her goals best (and all else were equal).

Self-control

People are aware of the difficulty of self-control and of their tendency to neglect the future. When they see a situation as one that requires self-control, they often take steps to *bind themselves* to a course of behavior, even if they must pay money in order to do so. So, for example, people join Christmas Clubs in banks — which guarantee them money to spend on Christmas presents, at the expense of receiving only an extremely low rate of interest on these savings.

One mechanism of self-control is the use of more or less categorical rules that people make up for themselves, for example (Thaler, 1985, p. 199):

1. Mr. and Mrs. J. have saved $15,000 toward their dream vacation home. They hope to buy the home in five years. The money earns 10% in a money-market account. They just bought a new car for $11,000, which they financed with a three-year car loan at 15%.

2. Mr. S. admires a $125 cashmere sweater at the department store. He declines to buy it, feeling that it is too extravagant. Later that month he receives the same sweater from his wife for a birthday present. He is very happy. Mr. and Mrs. S. have only joint bank accounts.

In the first case, the J.'s would clearly do better to break into their savings; the effective interest rate would be 10%, not 15%. To do so, however, would be to violate their self-imposed rule. Like the Christmas Club contributor, they pay for their self-control. Similarly, Mr. S. does not allow himself to buy "extravagant" items, even though his pleasure in receiving the sweater indicates that the items are worth the money to him. Because of the joint bank accounts, he ends up paying anyway. A "gift" is often an excuse to break a rule of self-control. Marketers of expensive goods often suggest other kinds of "exceptions" to the rules of self-control: "Here's to good friends. Tonight is something special."

Why we need self-control

It is clear from the examples just given that we take active steps to control ourselves. In a way, the idea of self-control is a paradox. We either want the fourth bottle of beer, or we do not. What could it possibly mean to want it but keep ourselves from having it because four would be too much? If we keep from having it, isn't that because we do not really want it?

A familiar way of looking at this is to say that there are actually two people within each of us, locked in a perpetual struggle for control of our behavior: the id and the superego, the child and the parent, the foolish and the wise. Self-control occurs when the superego (parent, wise) wins. Indulgence occurs when it loses.

Whatever sense such an idea may make, we do not need it to explain the phenomenon of self-control. Ainslie (1975, 1982, 1986) has proposed an account of self-control based on the kind of dynamic inconsistency shown in Figure 19.2. The first reward, T_1 represents the temptation, such as having the fourth beer of the evening; the second, T_2 represents some greater reward that would be received farther in the future, such as not having a hangover the next morning. Now if you make the choice at breakfast that morning (to the far left of the graph), notice that the utility of the second, greater reward (not having a hangover) is higher. As you approach the time at which the first reward (drunkenness) is available (the evening), however, its temptation increases, enough so that its utility surpasses that of the later reward. Therefore, if you make your choice in the morning, well before the temptation, you will choose (relative) sobriety, but if you make it when the temptation is at hand, you will (very likely) give in. Put another way, instead of two people, we can think of one person's preferences at different times. In the morning, the person will decide against the beer; in the evening, the person will decide in favor. Knowing about the conflict, the "morning person" will try to *bind* the "evening person." Of course, they are the same person, so what is really happening is that people try to bind themselves, to control their own future behavior. The paradigm case is Ulysses.

Methods of self-control

Ainslie (1982, 1986) suggests four general ways in which we solve the problem of binding ourselves.

Extrapsychic devices. One way is to remove the choice. We can throw away the bottle of scotch, or throw away the ice cream we are trying to avoid (so that when we want it late at night, it will not be there, and it will be too late to buy any). Christmas Clubs fall into this category. This and other mechanisms of forced saving help people avoid the temptation to spend money. Even some pigeons learn to peck a key to remove temptation: <u>Given a choice between a small immediate reward and a large delayed reward, they choose the former, but if they are given a key that would simply *eliminate* the tempting smaller reward</u> (earlier, before the choice was made), they often peck it (Ainslie, 1975, pp. 472–473).

We can also make contracts with other people. We can agree, for example, to pay a friend $100 if she catches us smoking, thus raising the cost. Some people rely on the sunk-cost effect as a means of self-control, paying large amounts of money for a "cure" of some bad habit (a smoking or alcohol clinic, a "fat farm," a psychotherapist), so that they are then motivated to maintain their new self-control in order to make sure that "all the money does not go to waste." (The additional cost of the self-denial may be integrated with the money already spent, as described earlier.)

Control of attention. One can try to manipulate one's attention so that one is not reminded of the availability of a temptation. A person at a party who is also on a diet may become deeply engrossed in conversation when the hors d'oeuvre tray is passed around. A person who does not want to be sexually tempted may focus on other things, avoiding the issue.[8] Attention control can be revoked at any time, so it may require continued effort (unlike extrapsychic devices, which operate on their own once they are put into effect).

Mischel and his colleagues have examined the use of attention-control strategies in children (Mischel, 1974, 1984; Mischel and Mischel, 1983). In a typical experiment, a child is told that she can receive two marshmallows when the experimenter returns, or she can request and receive one marshmallow at any time before that. At issue is how long the child waits before requesting the single marshmallow. Waiting is easier when the marshmallow is covered up than when it is in view, and when the child thinks about such things as the fluffiness of the marshmallow rather than about the taste. Older children (and children with higher IQs) know these things and make use of these attention-control strategies to help themselves wait. Preschool children choose to keep the marshmallow in view and to think about its taste, almost guaranteeing their failure.

Control of emotion. People can cultivate emotions incompatible with the emotion associated with giving in to the temptation. A person who is afraid of getting angry may cultivate friendliness. (If he is a poor actor, he will be perceived as "sickly sweet.") A woman afraid of being seduced may start a quarrel. Or a person may simply refuse to let an emotion develop.[9]

Personal rules. The most interesting mechanism is to make up rules for ourselves: no more than three beers per evening; no more than one scoop of ice cream per day, and so forth. The effect of these rules is to redefine the situation. Instead of seeing a conflict between a fourth beer tonight and a clear head tomorrow morning, we see a conflict between these two choices repeated over and over for the indefinite

---

[8] Such efforts at attention control correspond to various "defense mechanisms" postulated by psychoanalytic theory, such as repression, suppression, and denial. These defense mechanisms can be understood as attempts at self-control. Indeed, Freudians would see them in similar terms, as the ego's ways of mediating the battle between superego and id.

[9] These mechanisms correspond to the Freudian defenses of reaction-formation and isolation of affect.

future. By defining the situation this way, we ensure that our behavior tonight will set a *precedent* for future behavior in situations that we have defined as the same, as members of the same class. Therefore, if we give in to temptation tonight, we can expect to give in on every other similar night. If we remember this rule when we are offered the fourth beer, we will see it not as a single choice but as a choice for a long string of similar occasions. Because all of the future occasions are far away in time, the utility of not having the beer (on these future occasions) considerably outweighs the utility of having it. This difference in favor of moderation may be large enough to outweigh the difference in favor of indulgence that would otherwise be present.[10]

To some extent, this mechanism can operate even without the conscious formulation of rules. As we noted earlier, each decision we make sets a precedent for making the same decision in similar situations in the future. When we decide to have the fourth beer (the first time we have the opportunity), we are likely to have four beers on similar occasions in the future. If we simply recognize this fact the first time that the decision is presented to us, we may make the decision differently, with more awareness of distant consequences, than if we see the decision as applying to a single case. It is possible that many bad habits, such as smoking, begin in this way, with an apparently isolated decision that sets a precedent. If I try a cigarette that someone offers me at a party, I am likely to make the same decision (to accept one) again later, and soon I will be hooked. What is critical, then, in order for this mechanism to work, is the recognition that single decisions establish patterns over the indefinite future.

We respond to our own violation of our personal rules in two ways. We can rationalize the violations by making up exceptions. The alcoholic trying to reform suddenly discovers an old buddy whom he has not seen for years — a situation that requires a drink — or else it is his half-birthday, or his second cousin's wedding anniversary. If this mechanism is relied upon too much, the rule itself is weakened, but it may never be totally destroyed in the person's mind, even though an external observer would surely think it was. Rationalization of this sort is an example of wishful thinking (Chapter 9).

If we do not rationalize the violation but feel guilty, we may try to compensate for the violations by inventing some sort of self-punishment — in essence, the piling up of rules (concerning penalties) on rules (concerning behavior). The bulimic woman may force herself to fast totally after a day of overeating, leading to the cycles of fasting and overeating that characterize this disorder. This mechanism is often used when the initial rules are too strict.

If personal rules are violated and one of these mechanisms is not used, the person may suffer defeat: A temporary or more permanent inability to exercise self-control (in some area, or in general) may result. In view of the need for self-control, for the sake of both personal welfare (for example, smoking) and making contributions to society (for example, doing one's job responsibly), these topics are of great importance for future research.

[10]This mechanism corresponds to the defenses used by compulsives.

Emotions and time

Ainslie explains violations of delay-independence in terms of the steepness of the discounting curve when a reward is available soon. This is a purely mathematical account, like the economic theories it opposes. Loewenstein (1987) has suggested that several emotional factors play a role in our decisions concerning time, particularly the emotions we feel when we wait for some outcome to occur. Some of these emotions can explain the steepness of the discounting curve, but Loewenstein's theory makes other predictions as well.

When we look forward to pleasant outcomes, we experience what Loewenstein calls "savoring." This emotion is positive, like the experience of the outcome itself. The corresponding emotion for bad outcomes is "dread." Other emotions are derived from the contrast between our current state and a future outcome. When we are unhappy because an expected improvement has not occurred yet, we experience "impatience." When we are impatient, we want to get our current deprived state over with as quickly as possible. (There is a corresponding emotion of being happy because an expected bad outcome has not yet occurred, but it has no common name, perhaps because it is rare compared to the emotion of dread.) Impatience causes impulsiveness, but sometimes, Loewenstein suggests, we avoid impulsiveness through the positive emotion of savoring rather than through self-control. We put off a pleasant outcome, such as a vacation, so that we can gain the pleasure of looking forward to it in addition to the pleasure of experiencing the outcome itself. Conversely, when subjects are given a choice of a painful electric shock immediately or the same shock some time later (minutes, or days), most subjects choose the immediate shock (Loewenstein, 1987). According to Loewenstein, this is because they want to avoid the dread of the shock, in addition to avoiding the shock itself.

In short, some of our emotions are caused by our expectations about outcomes, and we have goals concerning these emotions as well as concerning the outcomes themselves. By Loewenstein's account, these emotions would be absent in decisions we made for other people *who would not know what outcomes would occur until the outcomes did occur.* The situation is similar to that concerning the emotions of regret and disappointment (discussed in Chapter 11): These emotions are real consequences of our choices, but sometimes we would do well to try to suppress them (or even to make them stronger, as when we use savoring as a means of self-control).

Emotions also come about from our looking back on good or bad outcomes after they occur, and still other emotions are connected with uncertain future outcomes, as well as certain ones ("fear" for negative outcomes, "hope" for positive ones). Loewenstein and Linville (1986) proposed that some of these emotions provide incentives for us to deceive ourselves about the probability of an uncertain future outcome, such as whether we will get a good grade on an examination or whether our application for a job will be accepted. Two desires are in conflict: our desire to avoid disappointment if our expectations are too high and the good outcome does not occur, and our desire to savor the outcome before it occurs, which we can do only if our expectations are high enough. When a good future outcome is far away in time, we are better off if we believe that it is likely to occur, because we can savor it for a long time, but when the outcome is imminent we have little time to savor it, and our main concern is to avoid disappointment, so we are better off if we believe it is not likely to occur — if we "don't get our hopes up."

Loewenstein and Linville tested this account by giving subjects a test that the subjects thought was related to intelligence. Half of the subjects were told that they would receive their scores immediately after the session, and the other half were told that they would receive their scores in two weeks. As the researchers predicted, the first group of subjects had lower expectations about their scores than the second group, and, as the end of the session approached, the expectations of subjects in the first group fell even more. (The experimenters did not ask the subjects in the second group about their expectations after the session.) In sum, this experiment suggests that we have desires concerning our hopes and disappointments and that we manipulate our expectations (deceive ourselves) to maximize the utility we derive from them. (Gilovich, Kerr, and Medvec, 1993, report similar results.)

Although this experiment does not concern decision making, it does show that we have emotions concerning future outcomes and that we are concerned with these emotions as well as with the outcomes themselves. Some of these emotions, particularly the impatience that results from the contrast between our present state and a better state that we could choose to have very soon, could cause us to neglect our futures irrationally.

Adaptation, contrast, and heuristics

Psychologists have known for some time that experience establishes a reference point, against which future experiences are compared (Helson, 1964). This works for such sensations as that of heat and cold — a piece of metal at room temperature will feel warm to the touch of a hand just removed from ice water – and it seems to work for pleasure and displeasure as well. Most of us know about this, so we take care not to "ruin" the experience of going to our favorite restaurants or listening to our favorite pieces of music by doing these things repeatedly in quick succession. So we try to spread out good experiences.

Because of the same adaptation effect, we also benefit more from improvement than from slow decline, given the same total level of pleasure averaged over time. With improvement, we benefit from the continuous pleasure to be derived from the contrast of our current state to the preceding state. Thus, although we discount future experiences, most people tend to want to get bad experiences over with. This might be a matter of avoiding dread, but it might also be a matter of preferring improvement.

These two heuristics — spreading good outcomes out and preferring improvement over decline — are like other heuristics in that they are used even when they do not serve their purpose of maximizing the total utility of experiences. They generate some interesting framing effects, as shown by Loewenstein and Prelec (1993).

Given a choice of "dinner at a fancy French restaurant on Friday in one month" and "dinner at the French restaurant on Friday in two months," most subjects preferred the former, presumably because of the usual discounting of the future. But when the choice was between "dinner at the French restaurant on Friday in one month and dinner at a local Greek restaurant on Friday in two months" and the reverse order, most subjects now preferred to delay the French dinner. Interestingly, most subjects also preferred to delay the French dinner when the choice was between "dinner at the French restaurant on Friday in one month and dinner at home on Friday in two months" and the reverse order. For most subjects, this choice was probably identical to the first choice, in which no dinner at home was mentioned. When subjects thought about the dinner at home, they used the heuristic of preferring improvement.

The heuristic of spreading out good things is also affected by framing. Subjects were asked when they would use two $100 coupons to their favorite restaurants. A third of the subjects were given no time constraints; a third were told that they must use the coupons in the next four months; and a third were given two years. The two-year group preferred longer delays than either of the other groups. They wanted to spread out the dinners over the whole interval. Of course, the first group had an even longer interval, but it was not brought to their attention.

Related to the heuristic of spreading out good things is that of seeking variety. Variety seeking is also a way of avoiding adaptation effects. Because we know this, we take it into account in our planning. But perhaps we overdo it. When we plan our choices in advance, we seek more variety than when we make them in succession (Read and Loewenstein, 1995). For example, in one study, children who were going from house to house for "trick or treat" on Halloween were offered a choice between two kinds of candy bars, Three Musketeers and Milky Way. In one condition, they chose one candy bar at each of two neighboring houses. In the other condition, the children chose two at once. All the 13 children who chose two at once picked one candy bar of each kind, thus seeking variety. But 13 of the 25 children who chose one at a time picked the same candy bar.

The more general problem of how to control our experiences so as to avoid the harmful effects of adaptation is an important one (discussed thoughtfully by Ainslie, 1992). It has been argued that improvements in the consumer economy do not really make people happier, because they quickly adapt to whatever new goods are introduced (Brickman and Campbell, 1971), and, indeed, national differences in self-rated "happiness" are small for countries that provide basic subsistence to most of their citizens, even though the differences are large in whether people can afford video recorders or the latest fashions (Strack, Argyle, and Schwarz, 1991). (Self-rated happiness is lower in countries in which nutrition is poor and early death is common.) We must remember, though, that these studies concern only the utility derived from experiences. Other aspects of our goals need not show the same kinds of adaptation effects. We turn now to these other issues.

Morality, prudence, and personal plans

Choosing the basic goals for our lives may be the most important moral choice we make. Why should we consider the interests of others in choosing these goals? First (as we saw in considering the idea of personal utility), it is in our own interest to have moral goals among our goals. The essence of morality is not self-sacrifice but benefiting others, and there are many ways in which it is possible for individuals to "do well by doing good."

Second, moral goals are part of life. To live without a moral ideology and without trying somehow to serve others is, in a way, like living without love, or music. It is missing something good that life has to offer. Moral goals, in general, reinforce other goals rather than conflict with them.

Third, there are reasons for being moral that are more purely logical (Nagel, 1970). If I care about consistency of belief, then I will find it difficult to argue that I ought to want to satisfy my desires, not yours. Some of the properties of "me" that make me want to satisfy my desires (for example, "personhood") are also properties of you, and therefore I ought to want to satisfy yours as well. Such arguments from consistency (admittedly only sketched here) give us a reason to satisfy each other's desires. Such reasons may not be overriding – there may be other reasons for me to want certain things just for myself — but they *are* reasons.

Most of us have the goal of not hurting people. If we combine this goal with the argument (Chapter 16) that the distinction between omission and commission is normatively irrelevant to decision making, then we must conclude that we ought to desire to help people as well. The reasons for not hurting people and the reasons for helping them are the same: We care about the achievement of their goals.

Parfit (1984) offers another argument from consistency. Most of us, he points out, care about our own future. Does it make sense, Parfit asks, to care about your own future — the future "you" who is a different person from the present "you" — but not about someone else's present? Is there a relevant difference? In either case, our concern goes beyond our own immediate welfare. Let us look at an example.

Consider three people: Jill-1, Jill-2, and Jack. Now it just so happens that Jill-2 is Jill-1 as she will be in the future, say ten years from now. Why should Jill-1 care more about Jill-2 than about Bill? Is it because Jill-2 will share memories with Jill-1? Probably not. Imagine that Jill-2 is amnesic (forgot her past), or that Jill-1 could transfer all of her memories to Bill. Would this change Jill-1's reasons for caring about Jill-2?

What about the fact that Jill-1 makes plans for Jill-2? Would this justify her caring about Jill-2? Again, this does not seem relevant. Jill-2 could change the plans that Jill-1 makes, or Jill-1 might neglect to make any, and it would not seem to matter. In fact, Parfit argues, it is difficult to think of *any* reason why anyone ought to care about herself in the distant future that does not also apply to caring about someone else in the present (or future), at least to some degree.

The question "Why be moral?" occurs to many people, but the question "Why care about one's own future?" occurs to few. By showing the similarity of these questions, Parfit helps us to realize that it may not be any more difficult to care about other people than it is to care about our future selves.

The virtues connected with caring about one's own future are often called *prudence*, and *prudential* judgments are those concerned with one's long-term interest (just as certain moral judgments are those involving the interests of others). Both prudence and morality require that we put aside immediate temptation for the sake of some distant good — our own future, or the interests of others. Therefore, self-control is a virtue required for both morality and prudence.

Moreover, prudent behavior and moral behavior usually reinforce one another (as most of our parents told us). If we are good to other people, if we respect their concerns and interests, if we keep our commitments to them, then we, in turn, will benefit in the future, for others will be obliged (usually) to treat us the same way. Similarly, concern for one's own long-term future is likely to motivate certain behavior that turns out to benefit others. For example, the hard work required to become a physician pays off not only in terms of the respect and tangible rewards that physicians earn but also in terms of the good works that physicians accomplish on behalf of others: curing their illnesses.

Conclusion

Decisions that determine the course of our future lives are frightening, for each of us can choose only one of the paths open to us, but we all make these decisions, with or without thinking. Here, as elsewhere, actively open-minded consideration of the options before us can help us achieve our goals. Thinking, however, does not guarantee a good life. Luck, good and bad, is ever-present.

Chapter 20

Risk

Decisions under uncertainty always involve risk, in some technical sense of the term "risk." People use the term differently in everyday speech, though. The term usually refers to some chance of something bad happening. People take risks when they drive recklessly. Nations take risks when they go to war. Investors and entrepreneurs risk losing time and money.

Governments pass laws and make regulations in order to reduce risks. Most governments have standards for food and drugs. Some have standards for air and water, to reduce the risk of disease. Products are regulated by law. One form of law is the law of torts, which allows a person injured by a product to sue the manufacturer. The possibility of such suits leads manufacturers to worry about the safety of their products.

Many of these laws and regulations — or their absence — are controversial. Real estate developers often feel that they are subject to too many bureaucratic regulations, yet building codes may be necessary to prevent damage to life and property. Environmentalists want more regulation of big cars and gasoline-powered tools that pollute the air, putting people's health at risk, yet these regulations raises prices and restrict individual choice. Democratic governments respond to the concerns of their citizens. We can understand much about these controversies by looking at how people in general think about risks.

This chapter will focus on the issues around these controversies. It will review the normative theory and then the empirical findings concerning intuitions about risk. These intuitions lead people to favor systematic departures from the normative theory. These departures express themselves in government policy. These departures lead to a situation in which we could save money, health, and lives by bringing public policy closer to the normative theory. Such movement will have to find support in the judgments of individuals, however.

The present chapter does not discuss the determinants of personal risk taking. People take all sorts of risks that may, or may not, be irrational. They smoke, eat unhealthy food, exercise too little, and ignore good medical advice. Many of the determinants of these problems are rooted more in factors outside of the scope of this book, although some of them were discussed in Chapter 19.

Normative theory

The normative theory of risk, I shall assume, is simply expected-utility theory as developed in Chapter 10. But the theory has some particular applications that are relevant to government regulation, lawsuits, insurance, and investment, which this section will describe.

One thing worth noting right away is that the reduction of risk usually has a cost. Imagine that you can reduce your annual risk of having your house or apartment burglarized from 20% to 5% by locking your door. That is relatively inexpensive. You can reduce it from 5% to 3% by getting a double lock, to 2% by getting a burglar alarm, to 1% by installing an automatic weapon triggered by a motion detector and a sign to advertise it (or maybe just the sign), to .1% by hiring an armed guard, and so on. Note, however, that the cost of reducing each additional percent goes up and up, both in dollars and in other risks (like forgetting to turn off the motion detector after you come home). This is because, when you are spending resources to reduce risk, you would usually spend on the most effective means first. As a general rule, we can assume that the marginal utility of expenditures on risk reduction is declining.

Although the cost of reducing each percent of risk goes up, the benefit, in expected utility terms, of a 1% reduction in risk is the same, whether it is from 20% to 19% or from 1% to 0%. This is because the expected utility of each option is the probability times the disutility of burglary. If the disutility is D, then the difference between 20% and 19% is just $.20D - .19D$, which is $.01D$, the same benefit you get from reducing the risk from 1% to 0%.

One implication of these facts is that there is some optimum amount of risk reduction. When the cost of reducing the next 1% is greater than the reduction in expected disutility, then you should stop. Putting it another way, there is an optimal amount of risk. Consider the example of putting money in a parking meter when you go shopping. If you try to estimate exactly how long you need, you risk getting a parking ticket if your shopping takes longer than you expected. You can avoid this risk by putting extra coins in the meter. But if you always put in so many coins that you never get a ticket, over many years you will end up spending more money. If you never get a ticket, you are spending too much money on parking meters. Likewise, by the same reasoning, if oil tankers never spill their cargo, then they are being too cautious. Unintuitive, for sure, but convincing if you think about it. Of course, on the other side, too few coins in the meter will lead to too many tickets, and you could save money by spending more on the meter.

Another implication concerns the allocation of resources among different risks. In general, we should try to make sure that the marginal benefit of expenditures across different risks is the same. Marginal benefit is the amount of risk reduction gained by spending the next unit of resources (for example, the next dollar). At the individual level, we can measure risk reduction as a decreased probability of some bad event, like death from some cause, happening to a single person in a year. When each individual faces a certain probability of death from that cause in a year, then the number of people who die from that cause each year is approximately that probability multiplied by the number of people in the population at issue. Probabilities translate into numbers of people. Thus, we often measure risk reduction in lives saved, or life years saved, or quality-adjusted life years saved (see Chapter 13).

Suppose we, as a society, are spending $1,000,000 per life year saved by regulating disposal of hazardous waste, and $1,000 per life year saved by vaccinating children against whooping cough. And suppose we could spend more money on vaccinations and vaccinate more children, at this rate. We could save more lives by taking some of the money from the regulation of hazardous waste and spending it on vaccinations. As we move money from hazardous waste to vaccinations, the marginal benefit of each dollar spent on waste will increase and the marginal benefit of each dollar spent on vaccinations will decrease. We might, for example, have to spend more and more money on advertising to induce the last few holdouts to get vaccinated. At some point, we will probably reach a point where the marginal benefits of the two expenditures are equal. Before we reach this point, we can always save more life years by taking money from hazardous waste and moving it to vaccination. The same kind of argument works for other effects aside from life saving.

This is, of course, a normative economic theory, a "first best" approach. We cannot always move money from one category to another in the real world.

Public control of risk

It is simplistic to say "we as a society" are spending such and such. For one thing, a "society" is an arbitrary unit. From the normative economic (or utilitarian) point of view, the appropriate unit is the world, and the future as well as the present. We might, for example, save more lives by reallocating a fixed amount of resources from rich countries to poor countries. However, risk decisions are made at different levels of government, from the town to the world. The following theory applies to whatever level is making the decision.

One mechanism for risk control is direct expenditure of public funds. Examples are police, armies (to protect against the risk of foreign invasion), sewage treatment, monitoring of contagious diseases, water purification, and medical research (to reduce the risks of disease). Some of these activities, of course, have some private support as well.

A second mechanism is regulation. Regulation puts the cost of risk reduction on those who engage in some activity that increases risk. Examples are rules that require catalytic converters for automobiles, require scrubbers to clean the emissions of smokestacks, and prohibit dumping hazardous chemicals in places where they could get into the water. Regulation of this sort is a solution to a social dilemma (Chapter 18): Each driver saves money by not installing the converter, but everyone benefits from the reduced pollution when it is installed.

Regulation can take many forms. Two of them are "command and control," and taxation. Command and control specifies what must be done, backed by the threat of fines or criminal prosecution. It is the most common form of regulation. The idea of taxation is to make people pay for activities that create risks for others. If the tax is set properly, so that it covers the full harm caused by the increased risk, this can lead to an optimal amount of risky behavior. For example, suppose we could calculate the quality-adjusted life years lost from extra air pollution, and the monetary value of those life years. We could then tax the pollution at this rate. Some firms would still find it worthwhile to create the pollution. People would be willing to pay extra for their products, because of some other benefits. These benefits might outweigh the bad effects of the pollution. A regulation that prevented these firms from all such activity could make things worse. For example, sport utility vehicles create more pollution than other cars, and they put other drivers at greater risk, but they are useful for car pools and family camping trips. So long as their owners pay the full costs of operating them, we have no reason to ban them.

A third mechanism of public risk reduction is provision of information. Often the most cost-effective way to reduce risk is for individuals to protect themselves against it. These individuals have an incentive to undertake this protection, but they may not know about its availability. Examples are smoke detectors and fire extinguishers in the home and child safety seats in cars. Governments also inform people about the risks of smoking, lack of exercise, and so on. Penalties and subsidies — for example, no-smoking discounts on health insurance — can also serve to provide information as well as incentive.

Torts

A fourth mechanism is the tort system. This is a function of government, specifically, the judicial branch of government. The tort system is about lawsuits. When a person is injured because of someone else's risk-producing activity, the victim can sue the injurer. Such lawsuits work much like pollution taxes. They give potential injurers an incentive to reduce risks to others. The incentive is reduced risk of lawsuits. This incentive function is how tort law reduces risk. Being found liable sends a message to those in the position of the injurer (including the injurer) to take care because they will be held responsible for the consequences of their recklessness.

A variety of principles govern tort law, and these principles vary from nation to nation and region to region. One common principle is "negligence." If you are negligent, by this standard, you have to pay for damages that you cause. The economic theory of negligence is that negligence amounts to insufficient care, that is, less care than the optimum. In a classic case in U.S. law, Judge Learned Hand ruled that Carroll Towing Co. was liable for damages caused by one of its barges breaking loose from its mooring and running into a ship. Hand argued that the owner of the barge was negligent if the burden of precautions was less than the probability of harm times the gravity of the injury, that is, the expected loss from not taking a certain amount of care (Landes and Posner, 1987). In this case, the care at issue was having an attendant on board the barge (which was not common practice at the time). If such a precaution could be taken and lead to a total net saving, then the amount of care being taken was less than the optimum. The net saving is the cost of the losses prevented, minus the cost of the radios.

Another standard, more rarely applied, is "strict liability." By this standard, you pay for any damages that you cause, whether you are negligent or not. For example, if Carroll Towing was liable under strict liability, it would pay for any damages it caused, whether or not it was worthwhile to have an attendant. Interestingly, strict liability and negligence standards both provide the same incentive to take the optimal amount of care (Landes and Posner, 1987). This would having an attendant only if the cost of the attendant is less than the cost of the damage they would prevent. With a negligence standard, you are not liable if you take the optimal care or more, but it costs you more to take more care than the optimum, so you do best if you take the optimum amount of care, no more and no less. (For example, you would not hire an attendant, because the costs would more than the extra damage prevented.) In the case of strict liability, optimal care is still best. If you take less than the optimum — for example, if you don't hire an attendant — you pay more for the damages. If you take more than the optimum (two attendants), you waste money. This is not to say that strict liability and negligence have all the same effects. Businesses subject to strict liability end up paying more in damages, so they are less attractive as investments. Certain provisions of U.S. environmental law may amount to strict liability, and these provisions may discourage such enterprises as developing businesses in abandoned urban areas (Huber, 1988).

One issue that often arises in tort law is "who is responsible?" A recent example is the litigation in the United States concerning the risk of cigarettes. The cigarette makers claim that smokers are themselves responsible, so the companies should not have to pay for the harm caused by their products. A simpler example is the case of someone who falls off a ladder as a result of positioning the ladder upside down. Should the company be required to put a "this end up" label on the ladder or to make it impossible to put the ladder the wrong way?

From a normative economic point of view, this issue hinges on the question of who can reduce the risk most efficiently, what Calabresi (1960) called the "least cost avoider." If the law makes the companies pay to reduce the risk, and if individuals could reduce the risk more cheaply, then the payment is inefficient. The extra cost required to avoid losing lawsuits will raise the price of the product, forcing consumers to pay more or do without it. It would be better not to make the company pay. Of course, the question of who is the least-cost avoider depends on what the next step is. A warning label would be inexpensive. A device to make sure that ladders cannot be used upside down might be more expensive and not worth the cost.

Tort law has a second function which is compensation of victims. Compensation and incentive are different functions. Compensation, in the form of money, provides resources to those who can put them to good use to recover their way of life — for example, to rebuild a house that burned down or to replace a car that was destroyed in an accident.

When the injurer compensates the victim, as when a child is induced to give back something he has taken or when a victim sues an injurer in court, punishment and compensation are linked. But sometimes these functions are separated. Criminals are punished whether or not their victims are compensated. We can, then, and we sometimes do, think separately about the functions of compensation and punishment.

The normative theory of monetary compensation is that money becomes more valuable after a loss, so that total utility is increased by giving money to those who lose. If your house burns down, you have a way of spending money to increase your utility that you did not have before the fire. You gain more utility from spending money on a new house than you could have gained from any way of spending money before the fire.

Notice that this normative theory yields some strange results. It implies that people in modern societies should probably not be compensated for the accidental death of their children. When children die, parents lose ways of spending money to increase utility. They can no long spend money on the children. Many other ways of spending money to increase their utility are still available to them, but possibly no more than when the child was alive.

Private insurance

Insurance works exactly this way. It is a way of providing compensation for harm. Interestingly, very few people buy life insurance policies on their children. This is consistent with the theory just described, assuming that the death of a child does not increase the opportunity to spend money to increase utility.

Insurance can also provide incentive to take care, just like liability. It does this offering lower premiums to those who take precautions, such as installing air bags or anti-lock brakes in cars (for automobile insurance), or not smoking (for health insurance), or installing smoke detectors (for house insurance). If the reduction in premiums equals the cost saving to the insurer, then people have an incentive to take the optimal amount of care. Note, however, that the use of such incentives is limited by the cost of monitoring compliance. Health insurers do not offer discounts for people who eat healthful diets, because anyone can claim that they do so, and the insurance company would not be able to check such claims very easily.

Investment and entrepreneurs

Most of the study of risk is about losses. Investing, despite its dangers, is mostly about gains. Of course, everything is relative. An investor who makes 10% a year on shares can still envy his friend who bought Microsoft at $10 per share. The study of investing is the main subject of the academic field called finance. The normative theory is in principle simple, although in practice this is one of the most complex parts of applied economics.

In essence, the normative theory is expected-utility theory. The issue is what to do with spare resources, such as money, or, in principle, time, that could be put to some use. Investment has to do with buying shares of stock, buying bonds (essentially lending money at a fixed rate of interest), buying property to rent or sell later, starting small businesses, or joining with others to start a large business or finance a corporate merger. We can also invest time in education, or in building up a business. For each possible investment of time or money, we can gain or lose different amounts, each with some probability. Usually, we can describe the gains and losses in terms of monetary value.

Because the gains and losses can be almost any amount, most analyses of investment treat the outcomes as a continuum rather than a small number. Instead of thinking about "the probability of making exactly $1,414,159" we think instead about the probability of making X or less, as a function of X. Or we can think of the probability density, the slope of this function, or the probability per dollar. Investments are called risky when the probability density function has high variability, that is, roughly, when the range of possible amounts is very great. People who think about investments are used to thinking of them in terms of risk and return (Markowitz, 1959). Return is the expected value. Risk is the probability of getting much higher or lower than that. Note that, here, the concept of "risk" does not refer to losses, but to uncertainty about the amount you will gain or lose.

Prediction is important in any application of the normative theory, because most investments are made in a free market in which other investors can participate. If an investment, such as stock in a certain company, is known to have a high expected value, then people will bid for it in the market. Those who hold it will demand a higher price, until the price goes up. Before the price goes up, it is better than alternative investments. Once the price reaches its "natural" level, then it is not necessarily any better than other investments. Moreover, its price may increase or decrease with various turns of events. If you can predict how others will respond to these events, you can make money by buying before the price goes up or selling before it goes down. An important point here is that investments must always be compared to the alternative, which is not usually putting the money under your mattress.

People are risk averse, as we have seen, if only because the utility of money is marginally declining. (We saw other reasons for risk aversion in Chapter 11.) If two investments have equal expected value for their ultimate payoff but one is riskier than the other (with a wider range of possible outcomes), individual investors will, and should, prefer the safer one, on the average. The possibility of a large loss is not balanced by an equally probable gain of the same amount of money. Thus, in a free market, safer investments have higher prices relative to their expected value, so the expected gain from them is lower.

Risk regulation and the intuitions that support it

When we look at the way that societies regulate risk, we find that it is far from the normative standard. Most studies have been done in the developed countries that have elaborate systems for the regulation of risk. The story is much the same. Taken as a whole, each nation spends far too much money reducing some risks, and far too little reducing others. For example, Breyer (1993) argues that the removal of asbestos from school buildings might, if it were done throughout the United States, ~~would~~ cost about $100,000,000,000 and save about 400 lives over a period of 40 years. This comes to $250,000,000 per life saved. (And it might not save any lives at all in total, because it endangers the workers who do the removal.) Yet if we returned this money to individuals, so that the average person had more to spend, people would spend some of the money on things that reduce their own risk. The evidence suggests that this effect alone leads to one life saved for every $10,000,000 of income in the United States, roughly (Lutter and Morrall, 1994). On the other hand, some increases in regulation could save lives at little or no cost, because the regulations would pay for themselves through savings in efficiency or in reduced medical costs. Examples are improvements in automobile design for safety, and some ways of reducing pollution from coal-burning power plants (Tengs et al., 1995). And this is just in the United States. If we look for ways to save or extend life in poor countries, vaccination and vitamin supplements for children can also save lives for very little cost. But let us stick to the within-nation comparisons, because these expenses, in some sense, are easily exchanged with one another.

These numbers, of course, are full of inaccuracies. But, even if every estimate were off by a factor of 10, the allocation of resources to reduce risk is still far from normative. We could save lives and save money by moving resources from asbestos to pollution control or auto safety.

What causes these discrepancies? Why do we spend so much on some things than others? Early efforts to answer this question tended toward the view that our expenditures reveal our preferences (Starr, 1969). If we spend more per life saved on benzene regulation than on water purification, then we must care more about preventing deaths from benzene-caused cancer than deaths from water-borne bacteria. More recent approaches have tended to take a more empirical approach. Let us ask, first, how the discrepancies can be explained. Then we can examine the reasons and ask whether they really depart from some normative model or, alternatively, whether apparent inconsistencies reflect simplistic applications of the normative model itself.

The psychometric approach

One approach to answering these questions, called the "psychometric approach," is to ask people questions about their beliefs and values concerning risks and their regulation. It may turn out that the risks that are regulated "too much" have certain properties that make people want to regulate them more, and the opposite for those that are regulated too little. The term "psychometric" comes from the analysis of psychological tests and measures, such as IQ tests and personality tests. The analogy is loose, because most of the research is about the properties of the risks rather than the people who evaluate them. It is as if we were looking for personality differences among the risks. Although the analogy is loose, the statistical methods of data analysis are much the same as those used in the analysis of test data. Most of the work on the psychometric approach has been done by a small group of researchers in Eugene, Oregon, including Paul Slovic and Sarah Lichtenstein, but many others have joined this group or carried out similar studies in other countries, particularly in Sweden, Norway, and The Netherlands.

The ideas for the questions often came from other kinds of evidence, particularly studies that attempted to classify risks in terms of the amount of money spent on reducing them. So it is helpful to look at these economic data alongside the psychological data.

In the original series of studies, subjects from various groups (college students and members of public-interest groups such as the League of Women Voters, expert toxicologists and risk analysts) answered several questions about each item in a list of risks (Slovic et al., 1985; also summarized in Slovic, 1987). The list — which ranged from 30 to 90 items for different groups — contained such items as nuclear power, motor vehicles, handguns, motorcycles, skiing, food coloring, and home appliances. Subjects were asked about the fatality rate from the risk itself. They were also asked whether the risk should be more heavily regulated and whether the acceptable level of the risk was higher or lower than its current level (and by what ratio); "acceptable" was defined as the point where further reductions in the risk would not be worth their cost. They were asked other questions about risk characteristics: voluntariness, immediacy of effect, knowledge that we have about the risk, controllability, newness, chronic versus catastrophic, common-dread, and severity of consequences. Each characteristic was described briefly. For example, chronic-catastrophic was described as, "Is this a risk that kills people one at a time (chronic risk) or a risk that kills large numbers of people at once (catastrophic risk)?" and common-dread was described as "Is this a risk that people have learned to live with and can think about reasonably calmly, or is one that people have great dread for — on the level of a gut reaction?" Each answer was on a 7-point scale, for example, from "risk assumed voluntarily" to " risk assumed involuntarily."

The answers to some of these questions correlated with each other across the risks. For example, risks that were rated as being unknown were also rated as being new, and the same risks tended to be rated as involuntary. Risks that were rated as "dread" also tended to be rated as "catastrophic." These correlations were analyzed into factors. The idea of factor analysis is this: When a group of items correlate highly with each other, it is because they are all affected by the same underlying characteristic. This characteristic may be something like a sort of feeling or intuition about the risks in question. It need not correspond to any question that was asked. Factor analysis applies this assumption to a set of correlations (every question with every other question) and, making various assumptions, reports what the underlying characteristics, the factors, might be. Each factor is described in terms of its correlations with the original questions.

There were two main factors. Factor 1 was correlated highly with — and thus explained the correlations among — unknown, new, involuntary, and delayed. Factor 2 was correlated highly with severity of consequences (certainty of being fatal), dread, and catastrophic. Risks judged high on Factor 1 were food coloring, food preservatives, pesticides, spray cans, and nuclear power. (Recall, these studies were done in the U.S. in the early 1980s.) Low items were hunting, motorcycles, fire fighting, and mountain climbing. Risks high on Factor 2 were commercial aviation and nuclear power. Low items were power mowers and home appliances.

Factor 2 correlated most highly with the items concerning need for greater regulation. Factor 1 correlated with these items in one study that used more risk items. Many of the extra items were chemicals that were judged to be both unknown and needing more regulation. Need for more regulation did not correlate with the actual magnitude of the risk. The single item that the subjects (except for the experts) thought needed the most additional regulation was nuclear power.

Voluntary versus involuntary

We spend a lot more money reducing involuntary risks than voluntary ones. We make laws to reduce the level of smoke in the air, but we do not ban cigarettes. Several studies have examined the economic benefits and risks of activities and have calculated a ratio. The economic benefits are calculated either in terms of contributions to the average person's income or in terms of how much the average person spends on it. The risks are the annual fatalities. Among the activities with high risk/benefit ratios were (when these studies were done) motorcycles, smoking, alcohol, hunting, swimming, and air travel (including private planes). For example, air travel (a typical member of this group) had (in 1979) about 1,000 fatalities in return for benefits of about $3,000,000,000 (Fischhoff et al., 1981, p. 85). Among the activities with low risk/benefit ratios were commercial air travel, nuclear power, large construction, home appliance, and railroads, with an average benefit of about $30,000,000,000 for every 1,000 fatalities. These estimates are very loose, of course, and they vary from study to study (Fischhoff et al., 1981). But the point is clear, we spend more money regulating involuntary risks.

In the psychometric study just described (Slovic et al., 1985), involuntary exposure, as judged by the subjects, was correlated with judged need for more stringent regulation, across risks. This seems at first to be a bias. We could save more lives by spending resources more equally on voluntary and involuntary risks.

But, on closer examination, it is not clearly a bias. People may differ in the value (utility) they place on their lives or health, relative to the value the place on other things, such as the excitement of skiing or riding a motorcycle, the cool image of the smoker, or the social benefits and good feeling that comes from alcohol. If this is true to some extent, then — to that extent — people who suffer or die from these activities are just getting what they bargained for. They accepted the risk as part of the deal. At least some of these people made a rational decision to ride a motorcycle, go skiing, or drink. If the decision was rational for them, then any government attempt to prevent them from doing these things would be a harm. By contrast, nobody gets any thrill from the risk of exposure to air pollution or bacteria in the water. Thus, our relative lack of concern for voluntary risks might be rational.

Of course, we might overdo it. Some of these activities affect others, if only because we could not bring ourselves to deny treatment and, if needed, lifetime care to someone who suffered brain damage from not wearing a motorcycle helmet, so we would end up paying for this. It is hard to tell, though, whether our concern with voluntary risk is too much, too little, or about right.

Known versus unknown

Recall that Factor 1 from the psychometric studies includes unknown risk. Most unknown risks are those of new technologies, such as new kinds of crops resulting from genetic engineering. In some studies, people think that risks should be more highly regulated when the level of the risk is unknown. This belief is related to the ambiguity effect discussed in Chapter 11. Ambiguity is the perception that missing information could change our probabilities. People tend to avoid ambiguous options. Attitudes toward risk regulation seem to be based on the idea that allowing the public to be exposed to an unknown risk is an option of this sort.

Government agencies often incorporate this attitude into their policies. When the U.S. government regulates toxic substances, it tries first to establish the frequency of effects (poisoning, death, and other health effects) resulting from each chemical. The frequency is equivalent to the probability for the average person. Each estimate has some uncertainty around it, and this is represented as a 95% confidence interval. For example, the best guess might be "10 cases per year" but the interval might be "a 95% chance that the number of cases will fall between 5% and 20%." Government agencies typically use the upper bound of the 95% confidence interval as their estimate for policy purposes (Zeckhauser and Viscusi, 1990). In some cases, this policy leads to expensive cleanups that would not be done if the decision were based on the expected benefit (Viscusi, Hamilton, and Dockins, 1997).

Such responses to ambiguity can result in too many resources being spent on reducing ambiguous risks, when the same resources could do more good elsewhere. Suppose two risks have 10 expected fatalities per year. For risk A (like auto accidents), we have had extensive experience and we know that this figure is accurate. For risk B, the best guess is 8, but the 95% confidence interval ranges as high as 16. If we think it is equally costly to reduce each risk by 50%, whatever its level, and if we must allocate funds between these two risks, we will allocate all the funds to B. If we go according to the best guess, we will allocate all the funds to A. If we allocate funds according to the upper bound, then we will — on the average, across many decisions of this type — do a little less well than we could do. On the average, we will cut the total fatality rate by 4 instead of 5.

This argument depends on one crucial assumption. This is that the "best guess" is unbiased for unknown risks. If the best guess for unknown risks is systematically too low, then the strategy of using a safety factor is normatively correct. (Of course, it could be that the bias goes the other way.) To my knowledge, this assumption has not been tested.

Catastrophic versus individual

Slovic et al. (1984) found that people are more frightened of risks with potentially catastrophic outcomes, such as nuclear power-plant meltdowns, than of risks that are expected to cause greater harm at a predictable rate, such as air pollution from the burning of fossil fuels. This was also found in the psychometric research described earlier. Public reactions seem to follow the same principle. Every day in the United States, a dozen children are killed by guns, one at a time. The public and its representatives were galvanized into action by a couple of well-publicized incidents in which several school children were shot at once. This was, as several observers noted, a "statistical blip" in the overall problem. But the fact that the deaths happened all at once made people more concerned. Can our concern with catastrophic risks be justified?

One possible justification is that the utility of a life lost increases with the number of lives already lost. A disaster that kills 10,000 people could be 100,000 times worse than an accident that kills 10. But, to a first approximation, the people who matter most are those at risk. To a person faced with death in an accident, or from a disease, the number of other people in the same situation at the same time would not seem to matter much.

There are, however, other effects. Catastrophic disasters cause great fear because they are well publicized. They may cause extra grief because of the loss of communities and institutions as well as individuals. Other factors work the other way, though. The loss of even a single life from an unexpected source, such as a grape laced with cyanide, can have great significance because of its "signal value" (Slovic et al., 1984), that is, the fact that it indicates a previously unknown threat. Additional deaths from the same source would not increase the resulting worry as much as the first death did. So the utility function would decrease with lives lost.

If we take the view that risk estimates are only approximate anyway, and the view that death is much more serious than fear or grief in those who are still alive, then it would make sense to ignore many of these factors and assume that lives are equally valuable.

Proportions versus differences

An opposite effect seems to happen when people consider changes in risk. They worry more about the proportion of risk reduced than about the number of people helped.

This may be part of a more general confusion about quantities. Small children confuse length and number, so that, when we ask them to compare two arrays for length or number, they will answer with little regard to which question we asked (Baron, Lawson, and Siegel, 1975). In general, they tend to answer as if they were asked about length when the number of items in the array is larger than they can count easily, so they are correct when asked which array is longer but incorrect if asked which array has more items. When the number of items is small, for example, three to five items, they are correct when asked which has more but incorrect when asked which is longer. Similar quantitative confusions are found in older children and adults. As noted in Chapter 6, older children and even adults are confused about probability, so that they answer probability questions according to frequency rather than relative frequency.

News media and perhaps even scientific journals confuse other quantities. Newspapers often tell us that "inflation increased by 2.9%" when they mean that prices increased by this much. The literature on risk effects of pollutants and pharmaceuticals commonly reports relative risk, the ratio of the risk with the agent to the risk without it, rather than the difference. Yet, the difference between the two risks, not their ratio, is most relevant for decision making: If a baseline risk of injury is 1 in 1,000,000, then twice that risk is still insignificant; but if the risk is 1 in 3, a doubling matters much more.

Stone, Yates, and Parker (1994) found that relative risk information, as opposed to full information about the two absolute risks involved, made people more willing to pay for safety when risks were small. Fetherstonhaugh, Slovic, Johnson, and Friedrich (1997) found that people placed more value on saving lives when the lives saved were a larger proportion of those at risk. For example, subjects were told about two programs to save Rwandan refugees from cholera by providing clean water. The two programs cost about the same and both would save about 4,500 lives. One program would take place in a refugee camp with 250,000 refugees; the other, in a camp with 11,000. Subjects strongly preferred the program in the smaller camp.

I have suggested that these results were the result of quantitative confusion between relative and absolute risk (Baron ,1997). In one study, subjects expressed their willingness to pay (WTP) to reduce 18 causes of death (heart disease, stroke, chronic liver disease, etc.) by 5% or by 2,600 people, in the United States. The typical (median) responses to these two questions correlated .96. Some causes of death were much more likely than others. For example, heart disease is about 20 times more likely than chronic liver disease as a cause of death. So a 5% should not be a constant number for different causes. Still, subjects almost completely ignored the distinction between number of lives and percent of the problem.

McDaniels (1988) compared subjects' judgments to actual government expenditures for the risks shown in the following table (in abbreviated form). The first column of numbers shows the mean response of a group of U.S. respondents asked how much they would be willing to pay from their household budget to reduce each risk by 20%. The respondents had been told the number of deaths per year shown in the second column, which were approximately true. The third column in the table shows McDaniels's calculation of the total national willingness to pay to prevent one death from each risk, based on the first column and assuming 90 million households at the time of the study. The fourth column shows McDaniels's rough estimates of what the U.S. was willing to spend to prevent one death from each risk, as revealed by its government regulations.

Hazard	Mean WTP in survey	U.S. deaths per year	Implied national WTP	Actual or proposed expenditures
Workplace chemical	$7.95	1	$715 mil.	> $11 mil.
Explosives	$7.68	2	$345 mil.	$3 mil.
Aviation	$46.07	40	$103 mil.	$680,000
Power tools	$15.05	80	$17 mil.	$430,000
Automobiles	$161.30	10,000	$1.3 mil.	$95,000

This table shows several things. In the first column, we see that people are willing to spend more to reduce larger risks. They are willing to spend about $161 to cut the automobile death rate by 20%, a larger amount than other risks that kill far fewer people. But we can also see that the adjustment in willingness to pay is not proportional to the increased size of the risk. If people had a constant value per life saved, they would be willing to pay 10,000 times as much to cut the automobile death rate by 20% than to cut the death rate from the particular workplace chemical by 20%. But the ratio of $161.30 to $7.95 is only about 20, not 10,000. People seem to compromise between thinking about the proportional reduction in risk and the absolute reduction. Or perhaps they are simply insensitive to both. In any case, the implied willingness to pay, in the third column of number, is much higher for smaller risks.

The last column is based on rough estimates, but the differences among the risks in actual expenditures are large. Most interesting here is the parallel between these figures and the results of the survey. Although the implied willingness to pay per life was much greater in the survey, the interesting thing is that the rank ordering is the same. Both the people and the government seem willing to spend more to reduce smaller risks. These results suggest that the government is responsive to what the people want. And what the people want is inefficient. If the government wanted to save more lives for less money, it could change the regulations so that less money was spent on small risks and more money on larger risks. More generally, we can understand the quirks of public policy in part by looking at the quirks of individual judgment.

Individual versus statistical

"There is a distinction between an individual life and a statistical life. Let a 6-year-old girl with brown hair need thousands of dollars for an operation that will prolong her life until Christmas, and the post office will be swamped with nickels and dimes to save her. But let it be reported that without a sales tax the hospital facilities of Massachusetts will deteriorate and cause a barely perceptible increase in preventable deaths — not many will drop a tear or reach for their checkbooks." (Schelling, 1968)

The quote is from an article on the value of life published in 1968. In 1987, eighteen-month old Jessica McClure spent 58 hours trapped in a well. Her family received $700,000 in contributions, mostly in the months after her rescue. Charities that advertise for money to help poor children often feature pictures of individual children. Some even try to associate the donor with an individual child in some far-off land. Why do people seem to place a higher value on individual lives as opposed to statistical lives?

A study by Jenni and Loewenstein (1997) relates this effect to the proportionality effect just described (after failing to find evidence for other explanations, such as vividness). The idea is that saving a single life is seen as correcting 100% of the problem, while a small reduction in the death rate is seen as a small proportion of the problem of "premature" death.

Natural versus artificial

People are more concerned about artificial risks than about natural ones. Synthetic chemicals added to food are often banned because they cause cancer in tests on animals. Yet, if natural foods are broken up into their constituent chemicals, these too cause cancer in test animals (Ames and Gold, 1990). Caffeic acid is a "carcinogen" found in coffee, lettuce, apples, pears, plums, celery, carrots, and potatoes. In one study, 94% of synthetic carcinogens were subject to U.S. government regulation, but only 41% of a sample of natural carcinogens (Viscusi, 1995). Moreover, the average risk to humans of the synthetic chemicals was lower than that of the natural ones. This all assumes that the animal tests themselves are useful in detecting potential carcinogens. Ames and Gold (1990) argue that the animal tests require such high doses of the chemicals that the cancer is often caused by increased cell division, which happens because the chemical starts poisoning cells and the remaining ones start to divide more quickly. At lower doses of the same chemicals, there is no cell poisoning. So the animal tests may be highly inaccurate. In sum, Ames and Gold argue, if you break up carrots into their constituent chemicals and inject the chemicals into rats in high doses, the rats may get cancer, but carrots are still good for you, and all the evidence suggests that people who eat lots of fruit and vegetables are reducing their risk of cancer. And, if the test is no good for natural chemicals, it is probably not good for synthetic chemicals either.

The same consequences are evaluated differently depending on whether or not people bring them about:

> I don't mind natural extinctions, but I'm not too enthusiastic about extinctions that are directly caused by man. I feel that a species has a right to survive and be able to survive on its own and be able to change and evolve without the influence of whatever man does. I don't want to see man kill [any species]. If it's going to happen, it should happen naturally, not through anything that man has an influence on (from a respondent quoted by Kempton, Boster, and Hartley (1995), p. 109).

Questionnaire studies show the same effects. People are more willing to pay to reduce risks when the source of harm is human than when the source is natural (Kahneman et al., 1993; Kahneman and Ritov, 1994). For example, subjects were willing to contribute about $19 to an international fund to save Mediterranean dolphins when the dolphins were "threatened by pollution" but only $6 when the dolphins were "threatened by a new virus." Similarly, subjects (including judges) think that compensation for injuries such as infertility should be greater when the injury is caused by a drug rather a natural disease, even if the penalty paid by the drug maker does not affect the amount of compensation paid to the victim (Baron and Ritov, 1993).

These questionnaire studies are important because they suggest that the observed economic effects depend on psychological properties of human judgment, rather than some unknown economic effects. In particular, people may use a heuristic principle, or naive theory, that "natural is good." This is a reasonable heuristic. Natural selection has endowed biological systems in their natural environments with some stability, that could be disrupted by changes. But this is a crude principle at best. Strict adherence to it would have prevented the development of modern medicine, among other things. People seem to apply this heuristic intuitively, even when it is clearly irrelevant to the decision at hand. We can think of this as a "naturalness heuristic." Another example of it may be the person-causation bias discussed in Chapter 17.

Omission versus commission

Related to the distinction between natural and artificial risks is that between acts and omissions. Artificial risks are, by definition, the result of human action. The act-omission distinction, affects our decisions even when it is normatively irrelevant (as we saw in Chapters 12 and 16). The "omission bias" is the bias that favors harms of omission over equivalent harms from action. This applies to risks as well as outcomes that are certain. An example is the vaccine for pertussis, a bacterial infection that causes whooping cough and that can cause infants and toddlers. Pertussis is the "P" in "DPT," a commonly used combination vaccine that immunizes babies against diphtheria and tetanus as well. Some governments have not required pertussis vaccination in any form because it causes serious side effects and perhaps even death in a tiny fraction of a percent of children vaccinated. The officials responsible feel that the harm from requiring the vaccine is worse than the harm from doing nothing, even if the latter leads to more disease and death.

Before the DPT vaccine, about 7,000 children died each year from whooping cough caused by pertussis infection.[1] The death rate from whooping cough is now less than 100 per year. (Many children are still not fully vaccinated.) Despite this record of success, people do not like the idea of causing a disease with a vaccine. When a few cases of brain damage apparently caused by DPT vaccine were reported in England and Japan in the mid 1970s, requirements for vaccination lapsed and many children were not vaccinated.[2] In Great Britain, rates of vaccination fell from

[1] Harvard Medical School Health Letter (1989).

[2] In fact, the cases of brain damage may not have been by the vaccine at all (Bowie, 1990; Howson and Fineberg, 1992). Infants unfortunately are subject to brain damage from various diseases, and sometimes

79% in 1971 to 37% in 1974. A two-year epidemic that followed killed 36 people. The epidemic ended when vaccination rates increased. Similar epidemics occurred in Japan, also involving 30 to 40 deaths per year. (Joint Committee on Vaccination and Immunization, 1981; Smith, 1988).

Polio vaccine is similar. The Sabin polio vaccine can cause polio. The Salk vaccine can fail to prevent it. The total risk of polio was higher with the Salk vaccine, but some (for example, Deber and Goel, 1990) argued against the Sabin vaccine because it causes polio through the action of vaccinating. (By 1999, polio had largely disappeared from developed countries, so the situation has changed.)

Ritov and Baron (1990, see also Chapter 12) examined a set of hypothetical vaccination decisions modeled after such cases. In one experiment, subjects were told to imagine that their child had a 10 out of 10,000 chance of death from a flu epidemic, a vaccine could prevent the flu, but the vaccine itself could kill some number of children. Subjects were asked to indicate the maximum overall death rate for vaccinated children for which they would be willing to vaccinate their child. Most subjects answered well below 9 per 10,000. Of the subjects who showed this kind of reluctance, the mean tolerable risk was about 5 out of 10,000, half the risk of the illness itself. The results were also found when subjects were asked to take the position of a policy maker deciding for large numbers of children. When subjects were asked for justifications, some said that they would be responsible for any deaths caused by the vaccine, but they would not be (as) responsible for deaths caused by failure to vaccinate. In other studies, mothers who resist DPT vaccination for their children show a lower mean tolerable risk than mothers who accept the vaccination (Meszaros et al., 1992; Asch et al., 1993).

Zero risk

If we can reduce risks to zero, then we do not have to worry about causing harm. This intuition is embodied in the infamous Delaney clause, part of a U.S. law, which outlawed any food additive that increases the risk of cancer by any amount (repealed after 30 years). The clause was inserted by Congressman James Delaney into the 1958 Food Additive Amendment bill, in response to concerns about the use of diethylstilbestrol (DES), a potent carcinogen, in cattle feed to promote growth. It still is not clear whether DES fed to cattle has any effect on human cancer risk, although minute traces of it were occasionally found in beef (Foster, 1996). Other laws favor complete risk reduction, such as the 1980 Superfund law in the U.S., which concerns the cleanup of hazardous waste that has been left in the ground. Breyer (1993) has argued that most of the cleanup expenses go for "the last 10%," but that, for most purposes, the 90% cleanup is adequate. Cleanup costs are so high that it is proceeding very slowly. It is very likely that more waste could be cleaned up more quickly if the law and regulations did not mandate perfection.

these diseases occur right after the child is vaccinated. Even if some of these cases are caused by the vaccine, they are extremely rare.

In one questionnaire study, subjects were asked to imagine a pesticide that causes a harmful toxic reaction 15 times for every 10,000 containers (Viscusi et al., 1987). They were asked how much they would pay for a pesticide with a lower risk. They were willing to pay $1.04 extra to reduce the risk from 15 to 10 times, but $2.41 to reduce the risk from 5 to 0. In another study Baron, Gowda, and Kunreuther (1993) gave subjects the following case:

> Two cities have landfills that affect the groundwater in the area. The larger city has 2,000,000 people, and the smaller city has 1,000,000. Leakage from the landfill in the larger city will cause 8 cases of cancer per year. Leakage from the landfill in the smaller city will cause 4 cases of cancer per year. Funds for cleanup are limited. The following options are available:
>
> 1. *Partially clean up both landfills.* The number of cancer cases would be reduced from 8 to 4 cases in the larger city and from 4 to 2 cases in the smaller city.
>
> 2 *Totally clean up the landfill in the smaller city and partially clean up the landfill in the larger city.* The number of cancer cases would be reduced from 8 to 7 cases in the larger city and from 4 to 0 cases in the smaller city.
>
> 3. *Concentrate on the landfill in the larger city, but partially clean up the landfill in the smaller city.* The number of cancer cases would be reduced to from 8 to 3 cases in the larger city and from 4 to 3 cases in the smaller city.

Although Option 2 leads to a total reduction of 5 cases, and Options 1 and 3 lead to a total of 6 cases, 42% of the subjects (who included judges and legislative aides) ranked Option 2 as better than one of the others.

In sum, the zero-risk bias is found in questionnaires as well as in real life. It may have a normative justification. When risk is completely removed, people may worry less, and the elimination of worry has utility. Note, though, that the worry itself depends on a framing effect. Risk is never reduced to zero. (We all die eventually.) When we think that risk is reduced to zero, it is because we have isolated some particular risk, such as the risk of a certain kind of cancer from a certain hazardous-waste site. The risk of cancer is still not reduced to zero, nor is the risk of cancer from hazardous waste in general. Possibly, if people understood that what matters is the total risk, they would worry more about the bigger risks that they can do something about.

Intuitive toxicology and naive theories

When people think about risks from the ingestion of chemicals, such as pesticides on fruit, they have a set of intuitions similar to the zero-risk idea. Kraus, Malmfors, and

Slovic (1992) introduced the term "intuitive toxicology" for these beliefs. Toxicology is the science of poisons and harmful chemicals. A kernel of wisdom from that scientific field is that, in general, "the dose makes the poison." In other words, most chemicals are not harmful except in high doses. Moreover, most of the chemicals in food, including vitamins and minerals, are harmful if the dose is high enough. And, in general, the larger the dose, the greater the harm. The question of whether even the most dangerous chemicals require some threshold before they do *any* harm is hotly debated and has rarely been settled for any chemicals.

In contrast to this scientific wisdom, people have what amounts to naive theories about harmful chemicals. In a questionnaire study of toxicologists and laypeople, 35% of the public agreed that "For pesticides, it's not how much of the chemical you are exposed to that should worry you, but whether or not you are exposed to it at all." Only 4% of the scientists agreed. Other questions supported the general conclusion that lay people thought that chemical effects were dependent on exposure and were not dependent on the dose (Kraus et al., 1992).

Lay people have similar theories about nutrition and harmful foods. In a survey of students and other groups in the U.S., 20% agreed that, "If something can cause harm to the body in large amounts, then it is always better not to eat it even in small amounts" (Rozin, Ashmore, and Markwith, 1996). Likewise, 26% agreed that a diet free of salt is more healthful than the same diet with a pinch of salt. Rozin and his colleagues have argued that these results are related to a naive theory based on the idea of contagion from contact. The same kind of thinking makes people reluctant to wear a sweater that has been worn by someone who had AIDS, even though they agree that AIDS cannot be transmitted through clothing, and even reluctant to wear something that has been worn by Adolph Hitler. They refer to the laws of "sympathetic magic," which are apparently part of beliefs of many cultures throughout the world. The main idea is, "Once in contact, always in contact." Contagion is thus seen as insensitive to dose.

A similar example comes from a study of attitudes toward radon gas (Morgan, Fischhoff, Bostrom, Lave, and Atman, 1992), which enters houses from the ground and which leaves no residue once it is aired out. One respondent in the study had been persuaded by a contractor to replace all the rugs, paint, and wallpaper in her home, because it was contaminated with radon!

Intuitions about tort law

When many people think about tort law, they tend to treat all cases as if they were a single standard type, in which punishment and compensation are linked and in which the beneficial consequences of punishment are irrelevant. As a result, tort law does not always produce the best consequences. Tort penalties have caused highly beneficial products — such as vaccines and birth-control products — to be withdrawn and have led to a reduction in research and development expenditures for similar products. For example, production of pertussis vaccine (which, as noted earlier, prevents whooping cough but also causes rare but serious side effects) declined drastically in the U.S. as a result of lawsuits and the price increased, until 1986, when Congress passed a law to provide some protection against lawsuits. Likewise, research on new birth-control methods seems to have decreased for the same reason (Djerassi, 1989). Although it is likely that *some* products *should* be withdrawn from the market, or not developed, because their harm exceeds their benefit, these examples suggest that many successful lawsuits do not involve such harmful products.

Why does the tort system sometimes discourage products that are, on the whole, beneficial? Part of the problem may be the intuitions of those involved in the system — judges, lawyers, plaintiffs, defendants, and juries — about what penalties ought to be assessed and what compensation ought to be paid. In particular, two basic intuitive principles may be involved: the desire for retribution against an injurer, whatever the consequences; and the feeling that harms caused by people are more deserving of compensation than those caused by nature. The latter intuition may result from the standard linking of punishment and compensation. Compensation is considered most appropriate when it is connected with punishment. These intuitions are not based on expected consequences, so it is not surprising that they sometimes lead to consequences that we find objectionable. These principles are supported by several findings reviewed in Chapter 17.

Insurance and protective behavior

Expected-utility theory justifies insurance in terms of declining marginal utility of wealth, or, putting it another way, increasing marginal disutility of losses of wealth. Your disutility for losing $100,000 is, probably, more than 100 times your disutility of losing $1,000. So you come out ahead, in expected-utility terms, if you pay $1,000 to insure yourself against a 1% chance of a loss of $100,000. The larger the potential loss, the more this argument holds. For losses that are relatively small compared to lifetime expected wealth, the utility of money is approximately linear, and any small advantage to insurance is more than compensated by the profit made by the insurance company, in most cases. This is why you should not buy insurance for small losses, unless your risk for these losses is much greater than average. Because the insurance company makes a profit, the expected value of such insurance for average consumers is negative. Average drivers, then, should buy auto insurance with the highest possible deductible amount. The same argument applies to maintenance contracts, which can be seen as a type of insurance against small losses. For the average user of an appliance, the cost of the contract is greater than the expected benefit.

In fact, most people prefer insurance that pays off more often, both in laboratory studies and real life (Kunreuther and Slovic, 1978). They often fail to buy insurance against rare events with very high disutility. Flood insurance in the United States is subsidized, so that its cost is below its expected value, yet many people who live in flood plains did not buy it, until they were required to do so in order to get federally insured mortgages. This requirement can be seen as a prescriptive solution to a departure from a normative model.

People also fail to take protective action against natural disasters such as earthquakes and hurricanes. In California, only a minority of homeowners had taken any protective measures against earthquakes, even after the large Loma Prieta earthquake of 1989 (Kunreuther, 1999). These measures include such inexpensive — and clearly cost-effective — steps as strapping water heaters with plumbers' tape, which prevents heaters from toppling during an earthquake and thereby causing gas leaks and fires. The problem is not just that people forget or do not know. In a survey of hypothetical decisions, most subjects were unwilling to pay the expected value of protective measures that paid off over several years in reduced risk (such as bolting one's house to its foundation), even assuming a 10% discount rate, and even when the expected savings were explicitly stated in the question (Kunreuther et al., 1998).

Part of the problem is that people tend to think about low probabilities in one of two ways. Either they exaggerate the probability, thinking that "it could happen" or they treat the probability as if it were zero. McClelland, Schulze, and Coursey (1993) asked laboratory subjects how much they would pay for insurance against losses of $4 or $40 at various probabilities. At the lowest probability, .01, most subjects were willing to pay much more than the expected value ($0.04 or $0.40, respectively), but many subjects (25% for $4, 15% for $40) were willing to pay nothing at all. Few subjects were in between for low probabilities, although many more subjects offered approximately the expected value for higher probabilities.

A prescriptive solution for the problem of inadequate protective measures (such as taping water heaters or buying cars with air bags or other passive restraints) is to charge reduced insurance premiums for those who take them. Although this method is used, it is somewhat ineffective because of people's tendency to integrate the saving with the cost of the insurance (as described in Chapter 12), so that they see it as only a small reduction in the disutility of paying the premium. If, however, the saving is called a "rebate," consumers seem to find it more attractive (Johnson, Hershey, Meszaros, and Kunreuther, 1993). Other prescriptive measures include laws and regulations. Failure of people to do what is clearly in their own self-interest may justify such regulations, but many failures affect others too, as when a fire or gas explosion affects nearby houses.

Willingness to pay for insurance depends on the vividness of the imagined event. This leads to inconsistencies. One study asked subjects (hospital employees) to imagine that they were planning a flight to London and had a chance to buy flight insurance. The subjects were willing to pay an average of $14.12 for insurance against death from "any act of terrorism," $10.31 for death from "any non-terrorism related mechanical failure," and $12.03 for death from "any reason" (Johnson et al., 1993). Of course, "any reason" includes the other two causes, and more, so the willingness to pay for that should have been at least the sum of the other two. For similar reasons, purchases of earthquake insurance increase after a quake, even though another significant quake becomes less likely, and people often cancel their flood insurance after several years with no flood.

The desire for compensation from insurance also depends on factors other than the need for monetary compensation itself. For example, Hsee and Kunreuther (2000) presented the following scenario:

> Suppose that you are visiting Europe now and bought two vases there for $200 each. You ask a shipping company to ship the vases to your home in the U.S. There is some chance that both vases will be damaged in transit. Suppose that the two vases will be packed in the same box so that if one vase is damaged, the other is also damaged, and if one is not damaged, the other is also not damaged.

> The shipping company offers insurance for individual items. If you buy insurance for a given vase and if it is damaged in shipment, then you will receive a check of $200 as compensation.

> Of the two vases, you love one much more than the other. You feel that the vase you love is worth $800 to you and the other one is worth only $200 to you.

> Suppose that the insurance premium for the vase you love is $12, and the insurance premium for the vase you don't love as much is $10. Suppose also that you have enough money to insure only one vase. If you are to insure one, which one will you insure?

Most subjects were willing to pay more the insurance on the vase for which they had affection, even though the cost was greater and the use of the money would be the same. Subjects also thought they would be more willing to spend time collecting a payment when it was for something for which they had affection. People seem to think of compensation as consolation rather than as something that serves a functional purpose.

When loss probabilities are ambiguous, insurers adjust them upward, thus charging higher premiums. This is the result of the effect of ambiguity on subjective probability, described in Chapter 11 (Einhorn and Hogarth, 1985). Specifically, when probabilities are ambiguous, people imagine that they could be higher or lower, and they adjust the probabilities by forming an average of what they imagine. As a result, the probabilities are adjusted toward some central point, such as .5. When probabilities are extreme (near 1 or 0), it is easier to think of ways to adjust them toward the middle than ways to make them even more extreme.

Insurance, by its nature, deals with low-probability events. When experts disagree about the probability of these events, or when the events are new and unfamiliar, they are ambiguous, and people adjust them. Moreover, buyers and sellers of insurance have different incentives to think of probabilities that are higher than what would otherwise be the best guess. The seller must worry about having to pay for a claim, so the seller sees the bad event (for example, a fire) as a loss. The buyer is compensated if the bad event happens, but the premium paid is a loss. Because losses loom larger than gains (Chapter 11), the sellers imagine more ways that a bad event can happen, so, when the probability is ambiguous, they adjust it upward more than the buyers do. As a result, they demand very high premiums, much higher than expected value, whereas the buyers are willing to pay premiums that are only a little higher than expected value. The difference means that insurance will not be sold. The sellers, the insurers, will demand a higher price than the buyers are willing to pay. This effect has been found in questionnaire studies (Hogarth and Kunreuther, 1989; Kunreuther, Hogarth, and Meszaros, 1993).

This effect may explain such real events as the breakdown of the market for environmental liability insurance in the United States in the 1980s, when many retroactive changes in the law had made the future uncertain for everyone (Huber, 1988). People felt a sense of ambiguity because the missing information about future changes in the law was salient.

Investors and entrepreneurs

Normative theory argues that risky investments should pay a bit more than safe ones. Declining marginal utility makes people rationally risk averse, so they will demand greater expected return, a premium, for speculative investments. Some of this effect will be reduced if investments can be pooled in ways that reduce the risk. A fund made up of many different kinds of speculative investments might not itself be so speculative if some of its components make money while others crash. So this kind of pooling would make the expected premium smaller. It is thus a puzzle that the premium for stocks, equities, is huge. From 1889 to 1978, the annual real rate of return on stocks was about 7 percent, while it was about 1 percent on government bonds. ("Real" means after taking inflation into account.) Stocks did better over the long term (30 years) even for people who bought stock before the 1929 stock market crash, so long as they held their stock and did not sell. This is called the "equity premium puzzle" (Mehra and Prescott, 1985). It is a puzzle because it cannot be explained in terms of any plausible story about declining marginal utility.

Benartzi and Thaler (1995) proposed an explanation of this effect in terms of two psychological phenomena, loss aversion (Chapter 11) and myopia (Chapter 17 — myopia means nearsightedness). They called their explanation "myopic loss aversion." The value of stocks goes up and down over time, but the value of "safer" investments such as government bonds changes very little. When the stocks go down, investors see that as a loss. When they go back up, it is a gain, but (as we saw in Chapter 11), "losses loom larger than gains." This loss aversion makes people think of the the entire sequences of gains and losses as a loss. They segregate the ups and downs. If they integrated over time, they would see it as a gain.

Two experiments support this explanation (Gneezy and Potters, 1997; ,, Thaler, Tversky, Kahneman, and Schwartz, 1997). In both experiments subjects made investments involving potential gains and losses. In one, for example, the stake invested could be lost entirely, with probability 2/3, or it could return 2.5 times its value, with probability 1/3. The expected value of this is positive, of course, but most subjects invested very little in it. When the subjects were required, however, to decide on a sequence of three investments in advance, they were more likely to invest. They then realized that the losses were likely to average out, so that an overall gain was fairly likely. The interesting thing is that both sequences went on for some time. The subjects were making these decisions repeatedly. When the decisions were made one at a time, subjects could easily decide to "bind themselves" to invest every time, knowing that, in the long run, they would come out ahead this way.

We might also think of this in terms of disappointment and regret (Chapter 11). When investors see their stock go down, they feel these emotions, more strongly perhaps than the emotions of elation and rejoicing when the stock goes up. The trick to good investing, then, is buy stock and don't look. That is, do not look at the stock market page. Or, if you look, steel yourself to doing nothing. Be warned, though: This argument is now becoming well known among investors. The better known it becomes, and the more people who accept it, the less it will work.

Another piece of the puzzle is inflation. Remember I said that the return on bonds is around 1%. That is a little shocking, when the bonds say things on the front like 4% or 5%. But the bonds that say these things are issued when prices are increasing at the rate of 3% or 4%, so their real value increases very little. Thus, during a period of 4% inflation, the "nominal" return on bonds might be 5% and the nominal return on stocks might be 11%. That ratio of 2.2/1 is nothing like the ratio of 7/1 in the real return (after inflation). If people think about the nominal return instead of the real return, they might think that the additional safety of bonds is worth it. Moreover, investors may not think so much about the uncertainty of inflation itself. A bond that says 5% on its face might yield real returns that vary considerably over time, depending on the rate of inflation. If investors ignore this, they will think of the return as completely certain. Changes in the rate of inflation, however, can make bonds almost as risky as stocks (especially if the value of stocks depends somewhat on the rate of overall inflation).

Shafir, Diamond, and Tversky (1997) found evidence for both of these effects. The first effect is the classic "money illusion," in which people neglect inflation. Consider Adam and Carl, both of whom inherit $200,000, buy a house with the money, and sell the house a year later. When Adam owned the house, there was a 25% deflation, and Adam sold the house for $154,000, or 23% less than he paid. When Carl owned the house, there was a 25% inflation, and Carl sold the house for $246,000, or 23% more than he paid. Subjects were asked to rank Adam and Carl in terms of "the success of their house transactions." A majority ranked Carl higher than Adam, even though Adam made more money in real terms.

The second effect is neglect of the risk of greater or lesser inflation. This was tested in the following scenario, given in 1991:

Imagine that you are the head of a corporate division located in Singapore that produces office computer systems. You are now about to sign a contract with a local firm for the sale of new systems, to be delivered in January, 1993.

These computer systems are currently priced at $1,000 apiece but, due to inflation, all prices ... are expected to increased during the next couple of years. Experts' best estimate is that prices in Singapore two years from now will be about 20% higher, with an equal likelihood that the increase will be higher or lower than 20%. The experts agree that a 10% increase in all prices is just as likely as a 30% increase.

Subjects then chose between two hypothetical contracts:

A. You agree to sell the computer systems (in 1993) at $1200 apiece, no matter what the price of computer systems is at that time.

B. You agree to sell the computer systems at 1993's prices.

Forty-six percent of the subjects chose A, even though its uncertainty was greater about the real value of $1200. In B, the seller bears no risk at all. If inflation is 30%, then the price of the system is $1,300, and if inflation is 10% the price is $1,100. The value of the price to the seller is the same either way. Another group of subjects saw the same choice with these implications explained, and then only 19% chose A. In sum, many people do not think spontaneously about the uncertainty from inflation itself, and this may account, in part, for the equity-premium puzzle.

If the equity-premium puzzle is a form of excessive risk aversion, another phenomenon is a form of excessive risk seeking. Most people who start new businesses fail within five years.

Although people are (it seems) excessively risk averse when they invest their money, many people make the opposite error when they start new businesses. Over half of new businesses in the United States fail in the first five years, and the situation is much worse in poorer countries. The problem is not specific to any one kind of business. It is as true for bicycle repair shops as for biotechnology firms. In a way this is a good thing. We all benefit from the activities of successful businesses. Nobody knows for sure that failure is assured. The more people who try, the more success will accrue to the enterprises most able to provide what consumers want. Altruism alone could justify the risks that people take when they start new businesses. It could also be that risk taking is rational from a selfish point of view. In many countries the bankruptcy laws cushion the loss from failure, and the benefits of success can be very great, even if its probability is low.

Whatever the benefits for others of risk-taking entrepreneurs, some of their behavior results from a sort of overconfidence. Camerer and Lovallo (1999) did an experiment to simulate entry into new businesses. The experiment consisted of a game with 8 players, who were students (mostly business students). On each play of the game, each of the players decided whether or not to "enter." Beforehand, the players were told how many entrants could succeed. This varied from 2 to 8. Those who entered and did not succeed lost $10. (Only one play was paid for real, chosen at random, and all subjects were paid for showing up.) Of those who succeeded, some won more than others. For example, when four could succeed, the players got $20, $15, $10, and $5, according to their respective ranks. If more than four entered, the lower ranked players lost. Rank was determined either by success or by skill, and the players knew which was in effect on each play. Skill was the ability to solve puzzles or answer trivia questions. In some sessions, subject knew that their winnings could depend on their skill, when they were recruited for the experiment.

There were two main results. First, subjects made more money when their winning was determined by chance than when it was determined by skill. It seems that they were more confident when their success depended on their skill. Second, this effect was greatest when the subjects were recruited knowing that skill was involved. Subjects typically lost money in the skill condition. Moreover, they correctly predicted that the average subject would lose money in this condition, but they thought that they would win.

The first effect, the difference between skill and chance, may be an example of the wishful-thinking effect described in Chapter 9. Just as people think they are better-than-average drivers, they also think they are better than average at whatever skill task is involved. They do not, however, think they are luckier than average at the chance task. This yields the difference.

The second effect, the greater overconfidence effect when subjects knew that skill was involved when they volunteered, is what Camerer and Lovallo call "reference group neglect." Apparently, subjects who think they will be good at the skill task agree to play the game, and subjects who are afraid they are not so good do not play the game. What the subjects do not think about, however, is that the others who choose to play have also made the same decision. Some business people know about this. Camerer and Lovallo quote Joe Roth, chairman of Walt Disney studios. Roth, asked why so many big-budget movies were released at the same time on certain weekends, such as Memorial Day), said, "Hubris. Hubris. If you only think about your own business, you think, 'I've got a good story department, I've got a good marketing department, we're going to go out and do this.' And you don't think that everybody else is thinking the same way." Hence, too many enter that particular game, to the delight of movie goers.

Individual and sex differences

Entrepreneurs are often thought to be more tolerant of risk than the average person. More generally, some people appear to be more risk averse or more risk seeking than others. Risk averse people are those who buy smoke detectors and anti-lock brakes. They invest in U.S. Savings Bonds, not stocks or new businesses, they wash their hands before they eat, and they avoid sky diving, mountain climbing, and motorcycling. We can all think of people like this, or the opposite, but are these differences real? We could just be suffering from illusory correlation (Chapter 8). We expect risk aversion in health to correlate with risk aversion in finances, so we perceive the correlation. Is it there?

The answer is yes, but only a little. Many studies yielded zero or small correlations between risk attitude (risk aversion or seeking) in one area and risk attutude in another, or even between two measures of risk attitude for the same options. For example, Slovic (1972) found only a small correlation between preference for risky bets (as opposed to less risky bets) in a choice task and preference for risky bets as inferred from minimum selling prices for the same bets.

Similar small correlations are found between hypothetical questions about risk and actual risk-taking behavior. In one recent study, over 10,000 people (mostly over 50 years old) answered hypothetical questions and reported their behaviors. The main question was, "Suppose that you are the only income earner in the family, and you have a good job guaranteed to give you your current (family) income every year for life. You are given the opportunity to take a new and equally good job, with a 50–50 chance it will double your (family) income and a 50–50 chance that it will cut your (family) income by a third. Would you take the new job?" If the subject said yes to this question, the second question asked about a possible cut of half, and if the subject said no to the first question, the next question asked about a 20% cut. About 13% fell into the highest risk category, those willing to take a 50% cut if they could double their salary. These "risk seekers" were more likely to smoke, more likely to have more than two alcoholic drinks per day (and much more likely to have more than five drinks), more likely to own shares of stock, less likely to have safer investments such as bonds, and less likely to have health insurance and life insurance. But these differences were small. For example, 30.6% of those in the highest-risk category were smokers as opposed to 26.4% of those in the lowest-risk category (no to both questions).

In this study, males were more likely than females to fall into the risk-seeker category. Such sex differences in risk attitude are widely found. Flynn, Slovic, and Mertz (1994), for example, gave subjects a list of various sources of health risk, such as street drugs, suntanning, food irradiation, nuclear power plants, and radon in homes. The subjects indicated the amount of risk from each source on a scale going from "almost no health risk" to "high health risk." Women consistently gave higher ratings than men, thus perceiving greater risk. In this study, white Americans also gave higher ratings than African Americans, and there was some evidence that white men in particular gave especially low ratings. Of course, perception of the risk is one component of risk aversion. Another is willingness to take the risk, even when perception is not an issue. Across many different kinds of studies, men are more likely than women to take risks, whether the risks are selected because they seem worth taking (such as engaging in athletic competitions), because they do not seem worth taking (such as smoking and driving recklessly), or because they are neutral (such as gambles in experiments) (Byrnes, Miller, and Schafer, 1999). The cause of these differences is unknown.

We have examined many sources of risk aversion and risk seeking in decision making: the shape of the utility function, anticipated disappointment and regret, omission bias, the status-quo bias, distortion of probabilities, overconfidence, loss aversion, and framing effects. It is tempting to think that these factors are important in explaining socially important forms of risky behavior, such as crime, abuse of drugs and alcohol, gambling, reckless driving, and violent conflict. Perhaps the same factors can explain pathologies of excessive risk aversion such as anxiety and obsessive behavior. Perhaps these factors play some role. But the studies that describe these effects are about thinking, in which people consider the alternatives and draw conclusions. Much of the harmful behavior of interest is not the result of thinking. If anything, it is rationalized after the fact, but more often it is simply regretted. Behavior is surely affected by factors other than thought (Loewenstein, 1996).

Conclusion

This chapter has presented several examples of parallel findings from laboratory studies and examination of actual public decisions about risk. Societies have several ways of dealing with risk: individual consumer behavior, lawsuits, laws, and regulations. All these ways seem to express common intuitions about risk. These intuitions oppose risks that are involuntary, catastrophic, unknown, caused by action, or artificial. Intuitions favor reducing risks to zero. In the case of involuntary risks, normative theory and intuition are on the same side. In other cases, normative theory seems to be neutral, and people seem to be biased toward one side. These biases are found in laboratory studies with questionnaires as well as in the real world.

We can avoid the deleterious effects of intuitive thinking if we learn to think quantitatively. This does not mean that we must have numbers. It does mean that we realize that a well-made decision requires comparisons of quantities. If we have a feeling for the quantities, we can make a good guess at what the decision would be even if we do not know the numbers themselves. This is what we do all the time in other domains. Tennis players, for example, realize that the intended placement of a shot is based on a tradeoff of the probability of its going out and the probability of its winning the point if it does not go out. They do not know these probabilities as a function of where they aim, although some tennis statistician could, in principle, compile them. They do, however, think in this quantitative way even without the numbers.

When we think this way, we will be able to make everyday decisions in a sensible way, and we will also know when some public decision, such as whether to build more nuclear power plants, requires a more detailed quantitative analysis by experts. We will also understand that it does not matter whether risks arise through action or omission, or whether the cause of a risk is human or natural. We will understand why we should not pay more to reduce risk to zero, if we can use the money better in other ways by reducing some other risk imperfectly.

Quantitative thinking of this sort is not widespread. People do not even notice its absence. Many people, for example, say that decisions such as whether to recommend estrogen replacement are "difficult" because there are costs as well as benefits. Many of these people do not seem to consider the possibility of looking at some overall measure, such as death rates or life expectancy. Or one can even get a more precise measure by weighing each condition (various cancers, heart disease, strokes, hip fractures) by some measure of their seriousness and their duration. It is clear from looking at the evidence now available that this sort of analysis would strongly favor estrogen for most women.

The same goes for government regulation, such as regulation of clean air. If, for example, we ask people how much money they are willing to pay to prevent one person from getting asthma or emphysema, the answer is a fair amount. The same for the time they are willing to spend. They may be telling the truth. Yet when the U.S. Congress passed the recent revisions of the Clean Air Act and the Environmental Protection Administration (EPA) proposed new regulations requiring extra inspections of motor vehicles, people rose up in anger at intrusive government regulation. Exasperated EPA officials think that the public is inconsistent: Their representatives, after all, voted overwhelmingly for this act. But *none* of the public statements of these officials, or news articles about these issues, told us how many cases of which disease would be prevented by how many extra car inspections. It is easy for public opinion to swing wildly from side to side under these conditions.

Another necessary part of quantitative thinking about risk is the need for evidence that risks are worth considering at all. We face too many real risks for us to waste time worrying about ones that do not exist or freak accidents that have happened once. Should we stop going to the dentist after reading that a few patients contracted AIDS from their dentist? At minimum, we need some evidence of a statistical association between a cause and an effect. The mere fact that a cause was associated with the effect in a few people is not enough. We need to know whether the number of people is more than would be expected by chance.

References

Adams, J. S. (1965). Inequity in social exchange. In L. Berkowitz (Ed.), *Advances in experimental social psychology*, (Vol. 2, pp. 267–299). New York: Academic Press.

Adams, M. J. (Coordinator). (1986). *Odyssey: A curriculum for thinking*. Watertown, Mass.: Mastery Education Corporation.

Adams, P. A., & Adams, J. K. (1960). Confidence in the recognition and reproduction of words difficult to spell. *American Journal of Psychology, 73*, 544–552.

Agnoli, F. (1991). Development of judgmental heuristics and logical reasoning: Training counteracts the representativeness heuristic. *Cognitive Development, 6*, 195–217.

Agnoli, F., & Krantz, D. H. (1989). Suppressing natural heuristics by formal instruction: The case of the conjunction fallacy. *Cognitive Psychology, 21*, 515–550.

Ainslie, G. (1975). Specious reward: A behavioral theory of impulsiveness and impulse control. *Psychological Bulletin, 82*, 463–496.

Ainslie, G. (1992). *Picoeconomics: The strategic interaction of successive motivational states within the individual*. New York: Cambridge University Press.

Ainslie, G., & Haendel, V. (1983). The motives of the will. In E. Gottheil, K. A. Druley, T. E. Skoloda, & H. M. Waxman (Eds.), *Etiologic aspects of alcohol and drug abuse*. Springfield, IL: Thomas.

Akerlof, G. A., & Dickens, W. T. (1982). The economic consequences of cognitive dissonance. *American Economic Review, 72*, 307–319

Allais, M. (1953). Le comportement de l'homme rationnel devant le risque: Critique des postulats et axioms de l'école américaine. *Econometrica, 21*, 503–546.

Allan, L. G., & Jenkins, H. M. (1980). The judgment of contingency and the nature of the response alternatives. *Canadian Journal of Psychology, 34*, 1–11.

Alloy, L. B., & Abramson, L. Y. (1979). Judgment of contingency in depressed and nondepressed students: Sadder but wiser? *Journal of Experimental Psychology: General, 108*, 441–485.

Alloy, L. B., & Tabachnik, N. (1984). Assessment of covariation by humans and animals: The joint influence of prior expectations and current situational information. *Psychological Review, 91*, 112–149.

Alpert, W., & Raiffa, H. (1982). A progress report on the training of probability assessors. In D. Kahneman, P. Slovic, & A. Tversky (Eds.), *Judgment under uncertainty: Heuristics and biases* (pp. 294–305). New York: Cambridge University Press.

Ames, B. N., & Gold, L. S. (1990). Too many rodent carcinogens: Mitogenesis increases mutagenesis. *Science, 249*, 970–971.

Anderson, C. A. (1982). Inoculation and counterexplanation: Debiasing techniques in the perseverance of social theories. *Social Cognition, 1*, 126–139.

Anderson, C. A., Lepper, M. R., & Ross, L. (1980). Perseverance of social theories: The role of explanation in the persistence of discredited information. *Journal of Personality and Social Psychology, 39*, 1037–1049.

Anderson, J. R. (1976). *Memory, language, and thought*. Hillsdale, NJ: Erlbaum.

Anderson, N. H. (1981). *Foundations of information integration theory*. New York: Academic Press.

Anderson, N. H., & Butzin, C. A. (1978). Integration theory applied to children's judgments of equity. *Developmental Psychology, 14*, 593–606.

Aquinas, Thomas (1947). *Summa Theologica*. (Translated by the Fathers of the English Dominican Province.) New York: Benziger Brothers Inc. (http://www.newadvent.org/summa/)

Arkes, H. R. (1996). The psychology of waste. *Journal of Behavioral Decision Making, 9*, 213–224.

Arkes, H. R., & Blumer, C. (1985). The psychology of sunk cost. *Organizational Behavior and Human Decision Processes, 35*, 124–140.

Arkes, H. R., Dawes, R. M., & Christensen, C. (1986). Factors influencing the use of a decision rule in a probabilistic task. *Organizational Behavior and Human Decision Processes, 37*, 93–110.

Arkes, H. R., Faust, D., Guilmette, T. J., & Hart, K. (1988). Eliminating the hindsight bias. *Journal of Applied Psychology, 73*, 305–307.

Arkes, H. R., & Harkness, A. R. (1983). Estimates of contingency between two dichotomous variables. *Journal of Experimental Psychology: General, 112*, 117–135.

Aronson, E., Chase, T., Helmreich, R., & Ruhnke, R. (1974). Feeling stupid and feeling guilty – two aspects of the self-concept which mediate dissonance arousal in a communication situation. *International Journal of Communication Research, 3*, 340–352.

Asch, D., Baron, J., Hershey, J. C., Kunreuther, H. C., Meszaros, J., Ritov, I., & Spranca, M. (1994). Determinants of resistance to pertussis vaccination. *Medical Decision Making, 14*, 118–123.

Asch, S. E. (1946). Forming impressions of personality. *Journal of Abnormal and Social Psychology, 41*, 258–290.

Attneave, F. (1953). Psychological probability as a function of experienced frequency. *Journal of Experimental Psychology, 46*, 81–86.

Ausubel, D. P. (1963). *The psychology of meaningful verbal learning*. New York: Grune & Stratton.

Axelrod, R. (1984). *The evolution of cooperation*. New York: Basic Books.

Babad, E., & Katz, Y. (1991). Wishful thinking — against all odds. *Journal of Applied Social Psychology, 21*, 1921–1938.

Bacon, F. (1960). *The new organon and related writings*. New York: Liberal Arts Press. (Original work published 1620)

Bar-Hillel, M., & Yaari, M. (1993). Judgments of distributive justice. In B. A. Mellers and J. Baron (Eds.), *Psychological perspectives on justice: Theory and applications* (pp. 55–84). New York: Cambridge University Press.

Baron, J. (1985). Rational plans, achievement, and education. In M. Frese & J. Sabini (Eds.), *Goal directed behavior: The concept of action in psychology*. Hillsdale, NJ: Erlbaum.

Baron, J. (1985). *Rationality and intelligence*. New York: Cambridge University Press.

Baron, J. (1985). What kinds of intelligence components are fundamental? In S. F. Chipman, J. W. Segal, & R. Glaser (Eds.), *Thinking and learning skills. Vol. 2: Research and open questions* (pp. 365–390). Hillsdale, NJ: Erlbaum.

Baron, J. (1986). Tradeoffs among reasons for action. *Journal for the Theory of Social Behavior, 16*, 173–195.

Baron, J. (1987). Second-order uncertainty and belief functions. *Theory and decision, 23*, 25–36.

Baron, J. (1989). Why a theory of social-intelligence needs a theory of character. In R. S. Wyer & T. K. Srull (Eds.), *Advances in social cognition, Vol. 2: Social intelligence and cognitive assessments of personality*, pp. 61–70. Hillsdale, NJ: Erlbaum.

Baron, J. (1991). Beliefs about thinking. In J. F. Voss, D. N. Perkins, & J. W. Segal (Eds.), *Informal reasoning and education*. Hillsdale, NJ: Erlbaum.

Baron, J. (1992). The effect of normative beliefs on anticipated emotions. *Journal of Personality and Social Psychology, 63*, 320–330.

Baron, J. (1993). *Morality and rational choice*. Dordrecht: Kluwer.

Baron, J. (1993). Heuristics and biases in equity judgments: a utilitarian approach. In B. A. Mellers and J. Baron (Eds.), *Psychological perspectives on justice: Theory and applications*, pp. 109–137. New York: Cambridge University Press.

Baron, J. (1993). Why teach thinking? – An essay. (Target article with commentary.) *Applied Psychology: An International Review, 42*, 191–237.

Baron, J. (1994). Dichotomous choice vs. free-response pricing in CV.

Baron, J. (1994). Do budget constraints explain insensitivity to quantity in valuation of public goods?

Baron, J. (1994). Nonconsequentialist decisions (with commentary and reply). *Behavioral and Brain Sciences, 17*, 1–42.

Baron, J. (1994). *Thinking and deciding* (2nd ed.). New York: Cambridge University Press.

Baron, J. (1997). Biases in the quantitative measurement of values for public decisions. *Psychological Bulletin, 122*, 72–88.

Baron, J. (1997). Confusion of relative and absolute risk in valuation. *Journal of Risk and Uncertainty, 14*, 301–309.

Baron, J. (1997). Political action vs. voluntarism in social dilemmas and aid for the needy. *Rationality and Society, 9*, 307–326.

Baron, J. (1997). The illusion of morality as self-interest: A reason to cooperate in social dilemmas. *Psychological Science, 8*, 330–335.

Baron, J. (1998). *Judgment misguided: Intuition and error in public decision making*. New York: Oxford University Press.

Baron, J., Badgio, P., & Gaskins, I. W. (1986). Cognitive style and its improvement: A normative approach. In R. J. Sternberg(Ed.), *Advances in the psychology of human intelligence* (Vol. 3, pp. 173–220). Hillsdale, NJ: Erlbaum.

Baron, J., Beattie, J., & Hershey, J. C. (1988). Heuristics and biases in diagnostic reasoning: II. Congruence, information, and certainty. *Organizational Behavior and Human Decision Processes, 42*, 88–110.

Baron, J., & Brown, R. V. (1991). Toward improved instruction in decision making to adolescents: A conceptual framework and pilot program. In J. Baron & R. V. Brown (Eds.), *Teaching decision making to adolescents*. Hillsdale, NJ: Erlbaum.

Baron, J., & Brown, R. V. (Eds.) (1991). *Teaching decision making to adolescents*. Hillsdale, NJ: Erlbaum.

Baron, J., & Frisch, D. (1994). Ambiguous probabilities and the paradoxes of expected utility. In G. Wright & P. Ayton (Eds.), *Subjective probability*. Chichester, Sussex: Wiley.

Baron, J., Gowda, R., & Kunreuther, H. C. (1993). Attitudes toward managing hazardous waste: What should be cleaned up and who should pay for it? *Risk Analysis, 13*, 183–192.

Baron, J., Granato, L., Spranca, M., & Teubal, E. (1993). Decision making biases in children and early adolescents: Exploratory studies. *Merrill Palmer Quarterly, 39*, 23–47.

Baron, J., & Greene, J. (1996). Determinants of insensitivity to quantity in valuation of public goods: contribution, warm glow, budget constraints, availability, and prominence. *Journal of Experimental Psychology: Applied, 2*, 107–125.

Baron, J., & Hershey, J. C. (1988). Outcome bias in decision evaluation. *Journal of Personality and Social Psychology, 54*, 569–579.

Baron, J., Holzman, G. E., & Schulkin, J. (1998). Attitudes of obstetricians and gynecologists toward hormone replacement. *Medical Decision Making, 18*, 406–411.

Baron, J., & Jurney, J. (1993). Norms against voting for coerced reform. *Journal of Personality and Social Psychology, 64*, 347–355.

Baron, J., Lawson, G., & Siegel, L. S. (1975). Effects of training and set size on children's judgments of number and length. *Developmental Psychology, 11*, 583–588.

Baron, J., & Maxwell, N. P. (1996). Cost of public goods affects willingness to pay for them. *Journal of Behavioral Decision Making, 9*, 173–183.

Baron, J., & Miller, J. G. (1999). Limiting the scope of moral obligations to help: A cross-cultural investigation. Manuscript.

Baron, J., & Ritov, I. (1993). Intuitions about penalties and compensation in the context of tort law. *Journal of Risk and Uncertainty, 7,* 17–33.

Baron, J., & Ritov, I. (1994). Reference points and omission bias. *Organizational Behavior and Human Decision Processes, 59,* 475–498.

Baron, J., & Spranca, M. (1997). Protected values. *Organizational Behavior and Human Decision Processes, 70,* 1–16.

Batson, C. D. (1975). Rational processing or rationalization? The effect of disconfirming evidence on a stated religious belief. *Journal of Personality and Social Psychology, 32,* 176–184.

Baumeister, R. F., Heatherton, T. F., & Tice, D. M. (1993). When ego threats lead to self-regulation failure: Negative consequences of high self-esteem. *Journal of Personality and Social Psychology, 64,* 141–156.

Bazerman, M. H., Beekun, R. I., & Schoorman, F. D. (1982). Performance evaluation in dynamic context: The impact of a prior commitment to the ratee. *Journal of Applied Psychology, 67,* 873–876.

Bazerman, M. H., Giuliano, T., & Appelman, A. (1984). Escalation of commitment in individual and group decision making. *Organizational Behavior and Human Performance, 33,* 141–152.

Bazerman, M. H., Magliozzi, T., & Neale, M. A. (1985). The acquisition of an integrative response in a competitive market. *Organizational Behavior and Human Performance, 34,* 294–313.

Bazerman, M. H., & Neale, M. A. (1992). *Negotiating rationality.* New York: Free Press.

Beattie, J., & Baron, J. (1988). Confirmation and matching bias in hypothesis testing. *Quarterly Journal of Experimental Psychology, 40A,* 269–297.

Beattie, J., & Baron, J. (1991). Investigating the effect of stimulus range on attribute weight. *Journal of Experimental Psychology: Human Perception and Performance, 17,* 571–585.

Beattie, J., Baron, J., Hershey, J. C., & Spranca, M. (1994). Determinants of decision seeking and decision aversion. *Journal of Behavioral Decision Making, 7,* 129–144.

Beattie, J., & Loomes, G. (1997). The impact of incentives on risky choice experiments. *Journal of Risk and Uncertainty, 14,* 155–168.

Beck, A. T. (1976). *Cognitive therapy and the emotional disorders.* New York: International Universities Press.

Becker, J. W., & Brownson, F. O. (1964). What price ambiguity? Or the role of ambiguity in decision making. *Journal of Political Economics, 72,* 62–73.

Becker, S. W., Ronen, J., & Sorter, G. H. (1974). Opportunity costs — an experimental approach. *Journal of Accounting Research, 12,* 317–329.

Behn, R. D., & Vaupel, J. W. (1982). *Quick analysis for busy decision makers.* New York: Basic Books.

Bell, D. E. (1982). Regret in decision making under uncertainty. *Operations Research, 30,* 961–981.

Bell, D. E. (1985). Disappointment in decision making under uncertainty. *Operations Research, 33*, 1–27.

Bell, D. E. (1985). Putting a premium on regret. *Management Science, 31*, 117–120.

Bellah, R. N., Madsen, R., Sullivan, W. M., Swidler, A., & Tipton, S. M. (1985). *Habits of the heart: Individualism and commitment in American life*. Berkeley: University of California Press.

Benartzi, S., & Thaler, R. H. (1995). Myopic loss aversion and the equity premium puzzle. *Quarterly Journal of Economics, 110*, 73–92.

Bennett, J. (1966). Whatever the consequences. *Analysis, 26*, 83–102 (reprinted in B. Steinbock, Ed., *Killing and letting die*, pp. 109–127. Englewood Cliffs, NJ: Prentice Hall).

Bennett, J. (1981). Morality and consequences. In S. M. McMurrin (Ed.), *The Tanner Lectures on human values* (Vol. 2, pp. 45–116). Salt Lake City: University of Utah Press.

Berg, J., Dickhaut, J., & McCabe, K. (1995). Trust, reciprocity, and social history. *Games and Economic Behavior, 10*, 122–142.

Bernoulli, D. (1954). Exposition of a new theory of the measurement of risk (L. Sommer, Trans.). *Econometrica, 22*, 23–26. (Original work published 1738)

Beyth-Marom, R., & Fischhoff, B. (1983). Diagnosticity and pseudodiagnosticity. *Journal of Personality and Social Psychology, 45*, 1185–1195.

Birnbaum, M. H. (Ed.) (2000). *Psychological Experiments on the Internet*. New York: Academic Press.

Birnbaum, M. H., & Chavez, A. (1997). Tests of theories of decision making: Violations of branch independence and distribution independence. *Organizational Behavior and Human Decision Processes, 71*, 161-194.

Birnbaum, M. H., & Mellers, B. A. (1983). Bayesian inference: Combining base rates with opinions of sources who vary incredibility. *Journal of Personality and Social Psychology, 45*, 792–804.

Boles, T. L., & Messick, D. M. (1995). A reverse outcome bias: The influence of multiple reference points on the evaluation of outcomes and decisions. *Organizational Behavior and Human Decision Processes, 61*, 262–275.

Bornstein, B. H., & Chapman, G. B. (1995). Learning lessons from sunk costs. *Journal of Experiment Psychology: Applied, 1*, 251–269.

Bornstein, G., & Ben-Yossef, M. (1994). Cooperation in intergroup and single-group social dilemmas. *Journal of Experimental Social Psychology, 30*, 52–67.

Bostic, R. Herrnstein, R. J., & Luce, R. D. (1990). The effect on the preference-reversal phenomenon of using choice indifferences. *Journal of Economic Behavior and Organization, 13*, 193–212.

Bowie, C. (1990). Viewpoint: Lessons from the pertussis vaccine court trial. *Lancet, 335*, 397-399.

Boyd, N. F., Sutherland, H. J., Heasman, K. Z., Tritchler, D. L., & Cummings, B. J. (1990). Whose utilities for decision analysis? *Medical Decision Making, 10*, 58–67.

Braine, M. D. S., & Rumain, B. (1983). Logical reasoning. In J. Flavell & E. Markman (Eds.), *Handbook of child psychology: Vol. 3. Cognitive development* (4th ed.). New York: Wiley.

Bregman, A. S. (1977). Perception and behavior as compositions of ideals. *Cognitive Psychology, 9*, 150–292.

Brenner, L. A., Koehler, D. J., & Tversky, A. (1996). On the evaluation of one-sided evidence. *Journal of Behavioral Decision Making, 9*, 59–70.

Breyer, S. (1993). *Breaking the vicious circle: Toward effective risk regulation.* Cambridge, Mass.: Harvard University Press.

Brickman, P., & Campbell, D. T. (1971). Hedonic relativism and planning the good society. In M. H. Appley (Ed.), *Adaptation-level theory: A symposium.* New York: Academic Press.

Brickman, P., Coates, D., & Janoff-Bulman, R. (1978). Lottery winners and accident victims: Is happiness relative? *Journal of Personality and Social Psychology, 36*, 917–927.

Briggs, L. K., & Krantz, D. H. (1992). Judging the strength of designated evidence. *Journal of Behavioral Decision Making, 5*, 77–106.

Broome, J. (1991). *Weighing goods: Equality, uncertainty and time.* Oxford: Basil Blackwell.

Broome, J. (1992). *Counting the cost of global warming.* Cambridge (UK): White Horse Press.

Broome, J. (1997). Is incommensurability vagueness? In R. Chang (Ed.), *Incommensurability, incomparability, and practical reason*, pp. 67–89. Cambridge, Mass.: Harvard University Press.

Brown, R. V. (1993). Impersonal probability as an ideal assessment based on accessible evidence: a viable and practical construct? *Journal of Risk and Uncertainty, 7*, 215–235.

Brown, R. V., Kahr, A. S., & Peterson, C. R. (1974). *Decision analysis for the manager.* New York: Holt, Rinehart, & Winston.

Brown, R. V., & Lindley, D. V. (1986). Plural analysis: Multiple approaches to quantitative research. *Theory and Decision, 20*, 133–154.

Bruins, J. J., Liebrand, W. B. G., & Wilke, H. A. M. (1989). About the salience of fear and greed in social dilemmas. *European Journal of Social Psychology, 19*, 155–161.

Bruner, J. S., Goodnow, J. J., & Austin, G. A. (1956). *A study of thinking.* New York: Wiley.

Bruner, J. S., & Potter, M. C. (1964). Interference in visual recognition. *Science, 144*, 424–425.

Brunswick, E. (1952). *The conceptual framework of psychology.* Chicago: University of Chicago Press.

Buehler, R., Griffin, D., & Ross, M. (1994). Exploring the "planning fallacy": Why people underestimate their task completion times. *Journal of Personality and Social Psychology, 67*, 366–381.

Bursztajn, H., Hamm, R. M., Gutheil, T. G., & Brodsky, A. (1984). The decision-analytic approach to medical malpractice law. *Medical Decision Making, 4*, 401–414.

Byrnes, J. P., Miller, D. C., & Schafer, W. D. (1999). Gender differences in risk taking: A meta-analysis. *Psychological Bulletin, 125*, 367–383.

Calabresi, G. (1970). *The costs of accidents: A legal and economic analysis.* New Haven: Yale University Press.

Calle, E. E., Miricale-McMahill, H. L., Thun, M. J., & Heath, C. W., Jr. (1995). Estrogen replacement therapy and risk of fatal colon cancer in a prospective cohort of postmenopausal women. *Journal of the National Cancer Institute, 87*, 517–523.

Camerer, C. F. (1981). General conditions for the success of bootstrapping models. *Organizational Behavior and Human Performance, 27*, 411–422.

Camerer, C. F. (1995). Individual decision making. In J. Kagel & A. Roth (Eds.) *The handbook of experimental economics.* Princeton, NJ: Princeton University Press.

Camerer, C. F., & Loewenstein, G. (1993). Information, fairness, and efficiency in bargaining. In B. A. Mellers and J. Baron (Eds.), *Psychological perspectives on justice: Theory and applications* (pp. 155–180). Cambridge University Press.

Camerer, C. F., & Lovallo, D. (1999). Overconfidence and excess entry: An experimental analysis. *American Economic Review, 89*, 306–318.

Carnap, R. (1950). *Logical foundations of probability.* Chicago: University of Chicago Press.

Carson, R. T., Mitchell, R. C., Hanemann, W. M., Kopp, R. J., Presser, S., & Ruud, P. A. (1992). *A contingent valuation study of lost passive use values resulting from the Exxon Valdez oil spill.* Natural Resource Damage Assessment, Inc.

Ceraso, J., & Provitera, A. (1971). Sources of error in syllogistic reasoning. *Cognitive Psychology, 2*, 400–410.

Chaitas, S., Solodkin, A., & Baron, J. (1994). *Students' attitudes toward social dilemmas in Argentina, Mexico, and the United States.* Manuscript, Department of Psychology, University of Pennsylvania.

Chambless, D. L., & Gracely, E. J. (1989). Fear of fear and the anxiety disorders. *Cognitive Therapy and Research, 13*, 9–20.

Chapman, G. B. (1996). Expectations and preferences for sequences of health and money. *Organizational behavior and human decision processes, 64*, 59–75.

Chapman, G. B. (1996). Temporal discounting and utility for health and money. *Journal of Experimental Psychology: Learning, Memory, and Cognition, 22*, 771–779.

Chapman, G. B. (1998). Sooner or later: The psychology of intertemporal choice. In *The Psychology of Learning and Motivation, Vol. 38*, pp. 83–113. New York: Academic Press.

Chapman, G. B., & Bornstein, B. H. (1996). The more you ask for, the more you get: Anchoring in personal injury verdicts. *Applied Cognitive Psychology, 10*, 519–540.

Chapman, G. B., & Johnson, E. J. (1999). Anchoring, activation, and the construction of values. *Organizational Behavior and Human Decision Processes, 79*, 115–153.

Chapman, L. J., & Chapman, J. P. (1959). Atmosphere effect reexamined. *Journal of Experimental Psychology, 58*, 220–226.

Charniak, E. (1983). The Bayesian basis of common sense medical diagnosis. *Proceedings of the National Conference on Artificial Intelligence, 3*, 70–73.

Cheng, P. W., Holyoak, K. J., Nisbett, R. E., & Oliver, L. M. (1986). Pragmatic versus syntactic approaches to training deductive reasoning. *Cognitive Psychology, 18*, 293–328.

Chung, S. H., & Herrnstein, R. J. (1967). Choice and delay of reinforcement. *Journal of the Experimental Analysis of Behavior, 10*, 67–74.

Clement, J. (1983). A conceptual model discussed by Galileo and used intuitively by physics students. In D. Gentner & A. L. Stevens (Eds.), *Mental models* (pp. 325–340). Hillsdale, NJ: Erlbaum.

Cohen, L. J. (1981). Can human irrationality be experimentally demonstrated? *Behavioral and Brain Sciences, 4*, 317–331.

Collins, A., & Gentner, D. (1986). *How people construct mental models.* Cambridge, Mass.: Bolt, Beranek, & Newman.

Collins, A., & Michalski, R. (1989). The logic of plausible reasoning: A core theory. *Cognitive Science, 13*, 1–49.

Cooper, J. (1971). Personal responsibility and dissonance: The role of foreseen consequences. *Journal of Personality and Social Psychology, 18*, 354–363.

Cox, B. J., Swinson, R. P., Norton, G. R., Kuch, K. (1991). Anticipatory anxiety and avoidance in panic disorder with agoraphobia. *Behaviour Research & Therapy, 29*, 363–365.

Cropper, M. L., Aydede, S. K., & Portney, P. R. (1992). Rates of time preference for saving lives. *American Economic Review: Papers and Proceedings, 82*, 469–472.

Dailey, C. A. (1952). The effects of premature conclusions upon the acquisition of understanding of a person. *Journal of Psychology, 33*, 133–152.

Davis, D. A. (1979). What's in a name? A Bayesian rethinking of attributional biases in clinical judgment. *Journal of Consulting and Clinical Psychology, 47*, 1109–1114.

Davis, W. A. (1981). A theory of happiness. *American Philosophical Quarterly, 18*, 111–120.

Dawes, R. M. (1976). Shallow psychology. In J. S. Carroll & J. Payne (Eds.), *Cognition and social behavior.* Hillsdale, N.J.: Erlbaum.

Dawes, R. M. (1979). The robust beauty of improper linear models. *American Psychologist, 34*, 571–582.

Dawes, R. M. (1980). Social dilemmas. *Annual Review of Psychology, 31*, 169–193.

Dawes, R. M., & Corrigan, B. (1974). Linear models in decisionmaking. *Psychological Bulletin, 81*, 97–106.

Dawes, R. M., McTavish, J., & Shaklee, H. (1977). Behavior, communication, and assumptions about other people's behavior in a commons dilemma situation. *Journal of Personality and Social Psychology, 35*, 1–11.

Dawes, R. M., Orbell, J. M., Simmons, R. T., & van de Kragt, A. J. C. (1986). Organizing groups for collective action. *American Political Science Review, 80*, 1171–1185.

Dawes, R. M., & Thaler, R. H. (1988). Cooperation. *Journal of Economic Perspectives, 2*, 187–197.

de Finetti, B. (1937). La prévision: ses lois logiques, ses sources subjectives. *Annales de l'Institut Henri Poincaré 7*, 1–68. Translated into English by Henry E. Kyburg Jr., 1980, "Foresight: Its logical laws, its subjective sources," In Henry E. Kyburg Jr. & Howard E. Smokler, Eds., *Studies in Subjective Probability* (2nd edition), pp. 53–118. New York: Krieger.

de Neufville, R., & Delquié, P. (1988). A model of the influence of certainty and probability "effects" on the measurement of utility. In B. Munier (Ed.), *Risk, Decision, and Rationality*, pp. 189–205. Dordrecht: Reidel.

Deber, R. B., & Goel, V. (1990). Using explicit decision rules to manage issues of justice, risk, and ethics in decision analysis. *Medical Decision Making, 10*, 181–194.

DeKay, M. L., & McClelland, G. H. (1993). Errors in estimating outcome utilities: The flip side of outcome bias. Paper presented at the conference of the Judgment and Decision Making Society, Washington, D.C., Nov. 7–8.

DeKay, M. L., & McClelland, G. H. (1993). The effects of additional information on expressed species preferences (CRJP Tech. Rep. No. 354). Boulder, University of Colorado, Center for Research on Judgment and Policy.

DeKay, M. L., & McClelland, G. H. (1996). Probability and utility components of endangered species preservation programs. *Journal of Experimental Psychology: Applied, 2*, 60–83.

Denes-Raj, V., & Epstein, S. (1994). Conflict between experiential and rational processing: When people behave against their better judgment. *Journal of Personality and Social Psychology, 66*, 819–827.

Deutsch, M. (1975). Equity, equality, and need: What determines which value will be used as the basis of distributive justice? *Journal of Social Issues, 31*, 137–149.

Dillman, D. (1978). *Mail and telephone surveys.* New York: Wiley.

Djerassi, C. (1989). The bitter pill. *Science, 245*, 356–361.

Doherty, M. E., & Falgout, K. (1986). *Subjects' data selection strategies for assessing event covariation.* Unpublished manuscript, Department of Psychology, Bowling Green State University, Bowling Green, OH.

Doherty, M. E., Mynatt, C. R., Tweney, R. D., & Schiavo, M. D. (1979). Pseudodiagnosticity. *Acta Psychologica, 43*, 111–121.

dos Santos, C. M. M. (1996). *Good reasoning: To whom? When? How? An investigation of belief effects on syllogistic and argumentative reasoning.* Doctoral dissertation, University of Sussex.

Downs, A. (1957). *An economic theory of democracy.* New York: Harper and Row.

Duda, R. O., Hart, P. E., Barrett, P., Gashnig, J., Konolige, K., Reboh, R., & Slocum, J. (1976). *Development of the Prospector Consultation System for Mineral Exploration.* AI Center, SRI International, Menlo Park, CA.

Duda, R. O., Hart, P. E., & Nilsson, N. J. (1976). Subjective Bayesian methods for rule-based inference systems. In Proceedings of the 1976 National Computer Conference. (pp. 1075–1082). AFIPS, Vol. 45.

Duncker, K. (1945). On problem solving. *Psychological Monographs, 58* (Whole No. 270).

Eddy, D. M. (1982). Probabilistic reasoning in clinical medicine: Problems and opportunities. In D. Kahneman, P. Slovic, & A. Tversky (Eds.), *Judgment under uncertainty: Heuristics and biases* (pp. 249–267). Cambridge University Press.

Eddy, D. M. (1991). Oregon's methods: Did cost-effectiveness analysis fail? *Journal of the American Medical Association, 266*, 2135–2141.

Edgeworth, F. Y. (1881). *Mathematical psychics.* London: Kegan Paul.

Edwards, W., & Newman, J. R. (1982). *Multiattribute evaluation.* Beverly Hills, Calif.: Sage.

Edwards, W., & Tversky, A. (Eds.). (1967). *Decision making.* Harmondsworth: Penguin.

Einhorn, H. J. (1986). Accepting error to make less error. *Journal of Personality Assessment, 50*, 387–395.

Einhorn, H. J., & Hogarth, R. M. (1985). Ambiguity and uncertainty in probabilistic inference. *Psychological Review, 92*, 433–461.

Einhorn, H. J., & Hogarth, R. M. (1986). Decision making under ambiguity. *Journal of Business, 59*, S225–S250.

Einhorn, H. J., Kleinmuntz, D. N., & Kleinmuntz, B. (1979). Linear regression *and* process tracing models of judgment. *Psychological Review, 86*, 465–485.

Ellis, A. (1987). The impossibility of achieving consistently good mental health. *American Psychologist, 42*, 364–375.

Ellsberg, D. (1961). Risk, ambiguity, and the Savage axioms. *Quarterly Journal of Economics, 75*, 643–699.

Ellsworth, P. C., & Ross, L. (1983). Public opinion and capital punishment: A close examination of the views of abolitionists and retentionists. *Crime and Delinquency, 29*, 116–169.

Elster, J. (1979). *Ulysses and the sirens: Studies in rationality and irrationality.* New York: Cambridge University Press.

Elster, J. (1983). *Sour grapes: Studies of the subversion of rationality.* New York: Cambridge University Press.

Elster, J. (1985). Weakness of will and the free-rider problem. *Economics and Philosophy, 1*, 231–265.

Elster, J. (1989). *Solomonaic judgments.* Cambridge University Press.

Elster, J. (1989). *The cement of society: A study of social order.* Cambridge: Cambridge University Press.

Elster, J. (1993). Justice and the allocation of scarce resources. In B. A. Mellers and J. Baron (Eds.), *Psychological perspectives on justice: Theory and applications* (pp. 259–278). New York: Cambridge University Press.

Ericsson, K. A., & Simon, H. A. (1980). Verbal reports as data. *Psychological Review, 87*, 215–251.

Evans, J. St. B. T. (1982). *The psychology of deductive reasoning*. London: Routledge & Kegan Paul.

Falk, R. (1981–2). On coincidences. *The Skeptical Inquirer, 6*, 18–31.

Feehrer, C. E., & Adams, M. J. (1986). *Odyssey: A curriculum for thinking. Decision making*. Watertown, Mass.: Mastery Education Association.

Festinger, L. (1962). Cognitive dissonance. *Scientific American, 107* (4).

Festinger, L., & Carlsmith, J. M. (1959). Cognitive consequences of forced compliance. *Journal of Abnormal and Social Psychology, 58*, 203–210.

Fetherstonhaugh, D., Slovic, P., Johnson, S., & Friedrich, J. (1997). Insensitivity to the value of human life: A study of psychophysical numbing. *Journal of Risk and Uncertainty, 14*, 283–300.

Fischer, G. W. (1995). Range sensitivity of attribute weights in multiattribute value models. *Organizational Behavior and Human Decision Processes, 62*, 252–266.

Fischhoff, B. (1975). Hindsight ≠ foresight: The effect of outcome knowledge on judgment under uncertainty. *Journal of Experimental Psychology: Human Perception and Performance, 1*, 288–299.

Fischhoff, B. (1977). Perceived informativeness of facts. *Journal of Experimental Psychology: Human Perception and Performance, 3*, 349–358.

Fischhoff, B. (1991). Value elicitation: Is there anything in there? *American Psychologist, 46*, 835–847.

Fischhoff, B., Lichtenstein, S., Slovic, P., Derby, S. L., & Keeney, R. L. (1981). *Acceptable risk*. New York: Cambridge University Press.

Fischhoff, B., Slovic, P., & Lichtenstein, S. (1977). Knowing with certainty: The appropriateness of extreme confidence. *Journal of Experimental Psychology: Human Perception and Performance, 3*, 552–564.

Fischhoff, B., Slovic, P., & Lichtenstein, S. (1978). Fault trees: Sensitivity of estimated failure probabilities to problem representation. *Journal of Experimental Psychology: Human Perception and Performance, 4*, 330–334.

Fischhoff, B., Slovic, P., Lichtenstein, S., Read, S., & Combs, B. (1978). How safe is safe enough? A psychometric study of attitudes towards technological risks and benefits. *Policy Sciences, 8*, 127–152.

Fishburn, P. C. (1986). Reconsiderations in the foundations of decisions under uncertainty (Working paper). Murray Hill, N.J.: Bell Laboratories.

Fleishman, J. A. (1988). The effects of decision framing and others' behavior on cooperation in a social dilemma. *Journal of Conflict Resolution, 32*, 162–180.

Flynn, J., Slovic, P., & Mertz, C. K. (1994). Gender, race, and perception of environmental health risks. *Risk Analysis, 14*, 1101–1108.

Fong, G. T., Krantz, D. H., & Nisbett, R. E. (1986). The effects of statistical training on thinking about everyday problems. *Cognitive Psychology, 18*, 253–292.

Forst, B. E. (1974). Decision analysis and medical malpractice. *Operations Research, 22*, 1–12.

Foster, K. R. (1996). Review of *Cancer from Beef. DES. Federal food regulation, and consumer confidence*, by Alan I. Marcus (Baltimore: The Johns Hopkins University Press, 1994). *Minerva, 33*, 398–402.

Fox, C. R., & Levav, J. (2000). Familiarity bias and belief reversal in relative likelihood judgments. *Organizational Behavior and Human Decision Processes, 82*, 268–292.

Fox, C. R., & Tversky, A. (1995). Ambiguity aversion and comparative ignorance. *Quarterly Journal of Economics, 110*, 585–603.

Fox, C. R., & Tversky, A. (1998). A belief-based account of decision under uncertainty. *Management Science, 44*, 879–895.

Frank, R. H. (1988). *Passions within reason: The strategic role of the emotions*. New York: Norton.

Freedman, J., & Sears, R. (1965). Selective exposure. In L. Berkowitz (Ed.), *Advances in experimental social psychology*(Vol. 2, pp. 57–97). New York: Academic Press.

Frey, D. (1986). Recent research on selective exposure to information. In L. Berkowitz (Ed.), *Advances in experimental social psychology* (Vol. 19, pp. 41–80). New York: Academic Press.

Friedman, D. (1982). What is "fair compensation" for death or injury? *International Review of Law and Economics, 2*, 81–93.

Frisch, D. (1993). Reasons for framing effects. *Organizational Behavior and Human Decision Processes, 54*, 399–429.

Frisch, D., & Baron, J. (1988). Ambiguity and rationality. *Journal of Behavioral Decision Making, 1*, 149–157.

Gabriel, S. E., Kneeland, T. S., Melton, L. J. III, Moncur, M. M., Ettinger, B., & Tosteson, A. N. A. (1999). Health-related quality of life in economic evaluations for osteoporosis: Whose values should we use? *Medical Decision Making, 19*, 141–148.

Gal, I., & Baron, J. (1996). Understanding repeated choices. *Thinking and Reasoning, 2*, 81–98.

Galotti, K. M., Baron, J., & Sabini, J. (1986). Individual differences in syllogistic reasoning: Deduction rules or mental models. *Journal of Experimental Psychology: General, 115*, 16–25.

Ganzach, Y., & Krantz, D. H. (1991). The psychology of moderate prediction: I. Experience with multiple determination. *Organizational Behavior and Human Decision Processes, 47*, 177–204.

Gardiner, P. C., & Edwards, W. (1975). Public values: Multiattribute utility measurement for social decision-making. In M. F. Kaplan & S. Schwartz (Eds.), *Human judgment and decision processes* (pp. 1–37). New York: Academic Press.

Gardner, M. (1972). Mathematical games: Why the long arm of coincidence is usually not as long as it seems. *Scientific American, 227*, 110–112B.

Gentner, D., & Jeziorski, M. (1993). The shift from metaphor to analogy in Western science. In A. Ortony (Ed.), *Metaphor and thought* (2nd ed.). New York: Cambridge University Press.

Gilligan, C. (1982). *In a different voice: Psychological theory and women's development*. Cambridge, Mass.: Harvard University Press.

Gilovich, T. (1991). *How we know what isn't so: The fallibility of human reason in everyday life*. New York: The Free Press.

Gilovich, T., Kerr, M., & Medvec, V. H. (1993). Effect of temporal perspective on subjective confidence. *Journal of Personality and Social Psychology, 64*, 552–560.

Gleicher, F., Kost, K. A., Baker, S. M., Strathman, A. J., Richman, S. A., & Sherman, S. J. (1990). The role of counterfactual thinking in judgments of affect. *Personality and Social Psychology Bulletin, 16*, 284–295.

Gneezy, U., & Potters, J. (1997). An experiment on risk taking and evaluation periods. *Quarterly Journal of Economics, 112*, 631–645.

Goldberg, L. R. (1970). Man versus model of man: A rationale, plus some evidence, for a method of improving on clinical inference. *Psychological Bulletin, 73*, 422–432.

Grether, D. M., & Plott, C. R. (1979). Economic theory of choice and the preference reversal phenomenon. *American Economic Review, 69*, 623–638.

Griffin, D., & Tversky, A. (1992). The weighing of evidence and the determinants of confidence. *Cognitive Psychology, 24*, 411–435.

Griggs, R. A., & Cox, J. R. (1982). The elusive thematic-materials effect in Wason's selection task. *British Journal of Psychology, 73*, 407–420.

Gustafson, D. H., Tianen, B., & Greist, J. H. (1981). A computer-based system for identifying suicide attemptors. *Computers in Biomedical Research, 14*, 144–157. (Reprinted in Arkes & Hammond, 1986, pp. 432–445.)

Hacking, I. (1965). *Logic of statistical inference*. New York: Cambridge University Press.

Hacking, I. (1975). *The emergence of probability*. New York: Cambridge University Press.

Hadorn, D. C. (1991). Setting health care priorities in Oregon: Cost-effectiveness meets the rule of rescue. *Journal of the American Medical Association, 265*, 2218–2225.

Hammond, K. R. (1955). Probabilistic functioning and the clinical method. *Psychological Review, 62*, 255–262.

Hardin, G. R. (1968). The tragedy of the commons. *Science, 162*, 1243–1248.

Hare, R. M. (1981). *Moral thinking: Its levels, method and point*. Oxford: Oxford University Press (Clarendon Press).

Harris, R. J. (1969). Dissonance or sour grapes? Post-"decision" changes in ratings and choice frequencies. *Journal of Personality and Social Psychology, 11*, 334–344.

Harris, R. J., & Joyce, M. A. (1980). What's fair? It depends on how you phrase the question. *Journal of Personality and Social Psychology, 38*, 165–179.

Harvard Medical School Health Letter. (1989). Whooping cough: The last gasp? *15* (2), 3 ff.

Heath, C. (1995). Escalation and *de*-escalation of commitment in response to sunk costs: The role of budgeting inmental accounting. *Organizational Behavior and Human Decision Processes, 62*, 38–54.

Heath, C., & Tversky, A. (1991). Preference and belief: Ambiguity and competence in choice under uncertainty. *Journal of Risk and Uncertainty, 4*, 5–28.

Heckerman, D. E. (1986). Probabilistic interpretations for MYCIN's certainty factors. In J. F. Lemmer and L. N. Kanal(Eds.), *Uncertainty in artificial intelligence* (pp. 167–196). Amsterdam: North Holland.

Heckerman, D. E. (1988). An axiomatic framework for belief updates. In J. F. Lemmer and L. N. Kanal (Eds.), *Uncertainty in artificial intelligence* (Vol. 2, pp. 11–22). Amsterdam: North Holland.

Helson, H. (1964). *Adaptation-level theory: An experimental and systematic approach to behavior*. New York: Harper & Row.

Hempel, C. G. (1966). *Philosophy of natural science*. Englewood Cliffs, N.J.: Prentice-Hall.

Henle, M. (1962). On the relation between logic and thinking. *Psychological Review, 69*, 366–378.

Herek, G. M., Janis, I. L. & Huth, P. (1987). Decision making during international crises. Is quality of process related to outcome? *Journal of Conflict Resolution, 31*, 203–226.

Herrnstein, RJ., Loewenstein, G. F., Prelec, D., & Vaughan, W. (1993). Utility maximization and melioration: Internalities in individual choice. *Journal of Behavioral Decision Making 6*, 149–185.

Herrnstein, R. J., & Prelec, D. (1991). Melioration: A theory of distributed choice. *Journal of Economic Perspectives, 5*, 137–156.

Hershey, J. C., Asch, D. A., Thumasathit, T., & Meszaros, J. (1994). The roles of altruism, free riding, and bandwagoning in vaccination decisions. *Organizational Behavior & Human Decision Processes, 59*, 177–187.

Hershey, J. C., & Baron, J. (1987). Clinical reasoning and cognitive processes. *Medical Decision Making, 7*, 203–211.

Hershey, J. C., & Johnson, E. J. (1990). How to choose on auto insurance. *Philadelphia Inquirer*, June 24, 1990, 8A.

Hershey, J. C., & Schoemaker, P. J. H. (1980). Prospect theory's reflection hypothesis: A critical examination. *Organizational Behavior and Human Performance, 25*, 395–418.

Hershey, J. C., & Schoemaker, P. J. H. (1986). Probability versus certainty equivalence methods in utility measurement: Are they equivalent? *Management Science, 31*, 1213–1231.

Hill, P. H., Bedau, H. A., Chechile, R. A., Crochetiere, W. J., Kellerman, B. L., Ounjian, D., Pauker, S. G., Pauker, S. P., & Rubin, J. Z. (1978). *Making decisions: An interdisciplinary introduction*. Reading, Mass.: Addison-Wesley.

Hoch, S. J. (1985). Counterfactual reasoning and accuracy in predicting personal events. *Journal of Experimental Psychology: Learning, Memory, and Cognition, 11*, 719–731.

Hogarth, R. M., & Kunreuther, H. C. (1989). Risk, ambiguity, and insurance. *Journal of Risk and Uncertainty, 2*, 5–35.

Horton, R. (1967). African traditional thought and Western science (pts. 1–2). *Africa, 37*, 50–71, 155–187.

Horwich, P. (1982). *Probability and evidence*. Cambridge University Press.

Houston, D. A., Sherman, S. J., & Baker, S. M. (1991). Feature matching, unique features, and the dynamics of the choice process: Pre-decision conflict and post-decision satisfaction. *Journal of Experimental Social Psychology, 27*, 411–430.

Hovland, C. I. (Ed.) (1957). *The order of presentation in persuasion*. New Haven: Yale University Press.

Hovland, C. I., & Mandell, W. (1957). Is there a "law of primacy" in persuasion? In Hovland, C. I. (1957).

Howson, C. P., & Fineberg, H. V. (1992). Adverse events following pertussis and rubella vaccines: Summary of a report of the Institute of Medicine. *Journal of the American Medical Association, 267*, 392–396.

Hsee, C. K. (1996). Elastic justification: How unjustifiable factors influence judgments. *Organizational Behavior and Human Decision Processes, 66*, 122–129.

Hsee, C. K. (1996). The evaluability hypothesis: An explanation of preference reversals between joint and separate evaluation of alternatives. *Organizational Behavior and Human Decision Processes, 46*, 247–257.

Hsee, C. K., & Kunreuther, H. C. (2000). The affection effect in insurance decisions. *Journal of Risk and Uncertainty, 20*, 141–160.

Hsee, C. K., Loewenstein, G. F., Blount, S., & Bazerman, M. H. (1999). Preference reversals between joint and separate evaluations of options: A review and theoretical analysis. (Manuscript.)

Huber, J., Payne, J. W., & Puto, C. (1982). Adding asymmetrically dominated alternatives: Violations of regularity and the similarity hypothesis. *Journal of Consumer Research, 9*, 90–98.

Huber, P. W. (1988). *Liability: The legal revolution and its consequences*. New York: Basic Books.

Inglehart, J. K. (1987). Compensating children with vaccine-related injuries. *New England Journal of Medicine, 316*, 1283–1288.

Ingram, D. (1971). Transitivity in child language. *Language, 47*, 888–910.

Inhelder, B., & Piaget, J. (1958). *The growth of logical thinking from childhood to adolescence*. New York: Basic Books.

Irwin, J. R. (1994). Buying/selling price preference reversals: Preference for environmental changes in buying versus selling modes. *Organizational Behavior and Human Decision Processes, 60*, 431–457.

Irwin, J. R., McClelland, G. H., & Schulze, W. D. (1992). Hypothetical and real consequences in experimental auctions for insurance against low-probability risks. *Journal of Behavioral Decision Making, 5*, 107–116.

Jacobs L., Marmor T., & Oberlander J. (1999). The Oregon Health Plan and the political paradox of rationing: What advocates and critics have claimed and what Oregon did. *Journal of Health Politics, Policy and Law, 24*, 161–80.

Jagacinski, C. (1991). Personnel decision making: The impact of missing information. *Journal of Applied Psychology, 76,* 19–30.

Janis, I. L. (1982). *Groupthink: Psychological studies of policy decisions and fiascos.* Boston: Houghton-Mifflin.

Janis, I. L., & Mann, L. (1977). *Decision making: A psychological analysis of conflict, choice, and commitment.* New York: Free Press.

Jenkins, H. H., & Ward, W. C. (1965). Judgment of contingency between responses and outcomes. *Psychological Monographs, 79* (1, Whole No. 79).

Jenni, K. E., & Loewenstein, G. (1997). Explaining the"identifiable victim effect." *Journal of Risk and Uncertainty, 14,* 235–257.

Jennings, D. L., Amabile, T. M., & Ross, L. (1982). Informal covariation assessment: Data-based versus theory-based judgments. In D. Kahneman, P. Slovic, & A. Tversky (Eds.), *Judgment under uncertainty: Heuristics and biases* (pp. 211–230). New York: Cambridge University Press.

Jervis, R. (1976). *Perception and misperception in international politics.* Princeton: Princeton University Press.

Johnson, C. (1993). New vaccine technologies boost children's health. *The Reuter Library Report,* July 15.

Johnson, E. J., Hershey, J. C., Meszaros, J., & Kunreuther, H. C. (1993). Framing, probability distortions, and insurance decisions. *Journal of Risk and Uncertainty, 7,* 35–51.

Johnson, E. J., & Tversky, A. (1983). Affect, generalization, and the perception of risk. *Journal of Personality and Social Psychology, 45,* 20–31.

Johnson-Laird, P. N. (1983). *Mental models: Towards a cognitive science of language, inference, and consciousness.* Cambridge, Mass.: Harvard University Press.

Johnson-Laird, P. N. (1985). Logical thinking: Does it occur in daily life? Can it be taught? In S. F. Chipman, J. W. Segal, & R. Glaser (Eds.), *Thinking and learning skills. Vol. 2: Research and open questions* (pp. 293–318). Hillsdale, N.J.: Erlbaum.

Johnson-Laird, P. N., Byrne, R. M. J. & Schaeken, W. (1992). Propositional reasoning by model. *Psychological Review, 99,* 418–439.

Johnson-Laird, P. N., & Bara, B. G. (1984). Syllogistic inference. *Cognition, 16,* 1–61.

Johnson-Laird, P. N., Byrne, R. M. J. & Tabossi, P. (1989). Reasoning by model: The case of multiple quantification. *Psychological Review, 96,* 658–673.

Johnson-Laird, P. N., Legrenzi, P., & Legrenzi, M. S. (1972). Reasoning and a sense of reality. *British Journal of Psychology, 63,* 395–400.

Johnson-Laird, P. N., & Steedman, M. (1978). The psychology of syllogisms. *Cognitive Psychology, 10,* 64–99.

Johnson-Laird, P. N., & Wason, P. C. (1970). Insight into a logical relation. *Quarterly Journal of Experimental Psychology, 22,* 49–61.

Jones-Lee, M. W. (1989). *The economics of safety and physical risk.* Oxford: Basil Blackwell.

Josephs, R. A., Larrick, R. P., Steele, C. M., & Nisbett, R. E. (1992). Protecting the self from the negative consequences of risky decisions. *Journal of Personality & Social Psychology. 62*, 26–37.

Kagel, J. H., & Roth, A. E. (1995). *The handbook of experimental economics.* Princeton, N.J.: Princeton University Press.

Kahneman, D., Frederickson, B. L., Schreiber, C. A., & Redelmeier, D. A. (1993). When more pain is preferred to less: Adding a better end. *Psychological Science, 4,* 401-405.

Kahneman, D., Knetsch, J. L., & Thaler, R. (1986). Fairness as a constraint on profit seeking: Entitlements in the market. *American Economic Review, 76,* 728–741.

Kahneman, D., Knetsch, J. L., & Thaler, R. H. (1986). Fairness and the assumptions of economics. *Journal of Business, 59,* S285-S300.

Kahneman, D., Knetsch, J. L., & Thaler, R. H. (1990). Experimental tests of the endowment effect and the Coase theorem. *Journal of Political Economy, 98,* 1325–1348.

Kahneman, D., & Knetsch, J. L. (1992). Valuing public goods: The purchase of moral satisfaction. *Journal of Environmental Economics and Management, 22,* 57–70.

Kahneman, D., & Lovallo, D. (1993). Timid choices and bold forecasts: A cognitive perspective on risk taking. *Management Science, 39,* 17–31.

Kahneman, D., & Miller, D. T. (1986). Norm theory: Comparing reality to its alternatives. *Psychological Review, 93,* 136–153.

Kahneman, D., & Ritov, I. (1994). Determinants of stated willingness to pay for public goods: A study of the headline method. *Journal of Risk and Uncertainty, 9,* 5–38.

Kahneman, D., Ritov, I., Jacowitz, K. E., & Grant, P. (1993). Stated willingness to pay for public goods: A psychological perspective. *Psychological Science, 4,* 310–315.

Kahneman, D., & Snell, J. (1992). Predicting changing taste: Do people know what they will like? *Journal of Behavioral Decision Making, 5,* 187–200.

Kahneman, D., & Tversky, A. (1972). Subjective probability: A judgment of representativeness. *Cognitive Psychology, 3,* 430–454.

Kahneman, D., & Tversky, A. (1973). On the psychology of prediction. *Psychological Review, 80,* 237–251.

Kahneman, D., & Tversky, A. (1982). Intuitive prediction: Biases and corrective procedures. In D. Kahneman, P. Slovic, & A. Tversky (Eds.), *Judgment under uncertainty: Heuristics and biases* (pp. 414–421). New York: Cambridge University Press.

Kahneman, D., & Tversky, A. (1982). The psychology of preferences. *Scientific American, 246,* 160–173.

Kahneman, D., & Tversky, A. (1982). The simulation heuristic. In D. Kahneman, P. Slovic, & A. Tversky (Eds.), *Judgment under uncertainty: Heuristics and biases* (pp. 201–208). New York: Cambridge University Press.

Kahneman, D., & Tversky, A. (1984). Choices, values, and frames. *American Psychologist, 39*, 341–350.

Katona, G. (1940). *Organizing and memorizing: Studies in the psychology of learning and teaching.* New York: Columbia University Press.

Keeney, R. L., & Raiffa, H. (1993). *Decisions with multiple objectives: Preference and value tradeoffs.* New York: Cambridge University Press. (Originally published 1976.)

Keinan, G. (1987). Decision making under stress: Scanning of alternatives under controllable and uncontrollable threats. *Journal of Personality and Social Psychology, 52*, 639–644.

Keller, L. R. (1985). The effects of problem representation on the sure-thing and substitution principles. *Management Science, 31*, 738–751.

Keller, L. R., & Sarin, R. K. (1988). Equity in social risk: Some empirical observations. *Risk Analysis, 8*, 136–146

Kelly, C. W., III, & Barclay, S. (1973). A general Bayesian model for hierarchical inference. *Organizational Behaviorand Human Performance, 10*, 388–403.

Kempton, W. (1986). Two theories of home heat control. *Cognition, 10*, 75–90.

Kempton, W., Boster, J. S., & Hartley, J. A. (1995). *Environmental values in American culture.* Cambridge, Mass.: MIT Press.

Keren, G., & Wagenaar, W. A. (1985). On the psychology of playing blackjack: Normative and descriptive considerations with implications for decision theory. *Journal of Experimental Psychology: General, 114*, 133–158.

Kirby, K. N. (1997). Bidding on the future: Evidence against normative discounting of delayed rewards. *Journal of Experimental Psychology: General,126*, 54–70.

Kirby, K. N., & Herrnstein, R. J. (1992). Preference reversals due to myopic discounting of delayed reward. *Psychological Science, 6*, 83–89.

Kirby, K. N., Petry, N. M., & Bickel, W. K. (1999). Heroin addicts have higher discount rates for delayed rewards than non-drug-using controls. *Journal of Experimental Psychology: General, 128*, 78–87.

Klayman, J. (1984). Learning from feedback in probabilistic environments. *Acta Psychologica, 56*, 81–92.

Kleinmuntz, D. N., Fennema, M. G., & Peecher, M. E. (1996). Conditioned assessment of subjective probabilities: identifying the benefits of decomposition. *Organizational Behavior and Human Decision Processes 66*, 1–15.

Klineberg, S. (1968). Future time perspective and the preference for delayed reward. *Journal of Personality and Social Psychology, 8*, 253–257.

Knetsch, J. L., & Sinden, J. A. (1984). Willingness to pay and compensation: Experimental evidence of an unexpected disparity in measures of value. *Quarterly Journal of Economics, 99*, 508–522.

Knight, F. H. (1921). *Risk, uncertainty, and profit.* Hart, Schaffner, & Marx.

Köbberling, V. & Wakker, P. P. (1999). A tool for qualtatively testing, quantitatively measuring, and normatively justifying expected utility. Manuscript, Tilburg University.

Kolm, S.-C. (1986). The Buddhist theory of "no-self." In J. Elster (Ed.), *The multiple self*. New York: Cambridge University Press.

Koriat, A., Lichtenstein, S., & Fischhoff, B. (1980). Reasons for confidence. *Journal of Experimental Psychology: Human Learning and Memory, 6,* 107–118.

Kourilsky, M., & Murray, T. (1981). The use of economic reasoning to increase satisfaction with family decision making. *Journal of Consumer Research, 8,* 183–188.

Krantz, D. H., Luce, R. D., Suppes, P., & Tversky, A. (1971). *Foundations of measurement* (Vol. 1). New York: Academic Press.

Kraus, N., Malmfors, T., & Slovic, P. (1992). Intuitive toxicology: Expert and lay judgments of chemical risks. *Risk Analysis, 12,* 215–232.

Krebs, D. (1975). Empathy and altruism. *Journal of Personality and Social Psychology, 32,* 1134–1146.

Kruglanski, A. W., & Ajzen, I. (1983). Bias and error in human judgment. *European Journal of Social Psychology, 13,* 1–44.

Kruglanski, A. W., & Freund, T. (1983). The freezing and unfreezing of lay inferences: Effects on impressional primacy, ethnic stereotyping, and numerical anchoring. *Journal of Experimental Social Psychology, 19,* 448–468.

Kuhn, D. (1991). *The skills of argument.* New York: New York: Cambridge University Press.

Kuhn, D., Amsel, E., & O'Loughlin, M. (1988). *The development of scientific thinking skills.* New York: Academic Press.

Kuhn, D., Phelps, E., & Walters, J. (1985). Correlational reasoning in an everyday context. *Journal of Applied Developmental Psychology, 6,* 85–97.

Kuhse, H. (1987). *The sanctity of life doctrine in medicine: A critique.* Oxford: Oxford University Press.

Kunreuther, H. (1999). Insurance as an integrated polity tool for disaster management: The role of public-private partnerships. *Earthquake Spectra, 15,* 725–745.

Kunreuther, H., Hogarth, R. M., & Meszaros, J. (1993). Insurer ambiguity and market failure. *Journal of Risk and Uncertainty, 7,* 71–87.

Kunreuther, H., Önçüler, A., & Slovic, P. (1998). Time insensitivity for protective measures. *Journal of Risk and Uncertainty, 16,* 279–299.

Kunreuther, H., & Slovic, P. (1978). Economics, psychology, and protective behavior. *American Economic Review, 68,* 64–69.

Lakatos, I. (1978). Falsification and the methodology of scientific research programmes. In I. Lakatos, *The methodology of scientific research programmes* (J. Worrall & G. Currie, Eds.) (pp. 8–101). New York: Cambridge University Press.

Lancaster, K. (1963). An axiomatic theory of consumer time preference. *International Economic Review, 4,* 221–231.

Landes, W. M., & Posner, R. A. (1987). *The economic structure of tort law.* Cambridge, Mass.: Harvard University Press.

Landman, J. (1987). Regret and elation following action and inaction: Affective responses to positive versus negative outcomes. *Personality and Social Psychology Bulletin, 13,* 524–536.

Langer, E. J., & Abelson, R. P. (1974). A patient by any other name ...: Clinician group differences in labeling bias. *Journal of Consulting and Clinical Psychology. 42*, 4–9.

Larkin, J. H. (1981). Enriching formal knowledge: A model for learning to solve textbook physics problems. In J. R. Anderson(Ed.), *Cognitive skills and their acquisition* (pp. 311–334). Hillsdale, N.J.: Erlbaum.

Larrick, R. P., Morgan, J. N., & Nisbett, R. E. (1990). Teaching the use of cost-benefit reasoning in everyday life. *Psychological Science, 1*, 362–370.

Lehman, D. R., & Nisbett, R. E. (1990). A longitudinal study of the effects of undergraduate training on reasoning. *Developmental Psychology, 26*, 952–960.

Lepper, M. R., Ross, L., & Lau, R. R. (1986). Persistence of inaccurate beliefs about the self: Perseverance effects in the classroom. *Journal of Personality and Social Psychology, 50*, 482–491.

Lerner, M. J., & Simmons, C. H. (1966). Observer's reaction to the "innocent victim": Compassion or rejection. *Journal of Personality and Social Psychology, 4*, 203–210.

Leung, K., & Bond, M. H. (1984). The impact of cultural collectivism on reward allocation. *Journal of Personality and Social Psychology, 47*, 793-804.

Lichtenstein, S., Earle, T. C., & Slovic, P. (1975). Cue utilization in a numerical prediction task. *Journal of Experimental Psychology: Human Perception and Performance, 104*, 77–85.

Lichtenstein, S., & Fischhoff, B. (1977). Do those who know more also know more about how much they know? *Organizational Behavior and Human Performance, 20*, 159–183.

Lichtenstein, S., Fischhoff, B., & Phillips, B. (1982). Calibration of probabilities: The state of the art to 1980. In D. Kahneman, P. Slovic, & A. Tversky (Eds.), *Judgment underuncertainty: Heuristics and biases* (pp. 306–334). New York: Cambridge University Press.

Lichtenstein, S., Slovic, P., Fischhoff, B., Layman, M., & Combs, B. (1978). Judged frequency of lethal events. *Journal of Experimental Psychology: Human Learning and Memory, 4*, 551–578.

Lightman, A., & Gingerich, O. (1991). When do anomalies begin? *Science, 255*, 690–695.

Lim, C. S., & Baron, J. (1997). Protected values in Malaysia, Singapore, and the United States. Manuscript.

Lindley, D. V. (1982). Scoring rules and the inevitability of probability (with discussion). *International Statistical Review, 50*, 1–26.

Lindley, D. V., Tversky, A., & Brown, R. V. (1979). On the reconciliation of probability assessments. *Journal of the Royal Statistical Society* A. *142*, 146–180 (with commentary).

Llewellyn-Thomas, H. A., Sutherland, H. J., & Theil, E. C. (1993). Do patients' evaluations of a future health state change when they actually enter that state? *Medical Care, 31*, 1002–1012.

Loewenstein, G. (1987). Anticipation and the value of delayed consumption. *Economic Journal, 97*, 666–684.

Loewenstein, G. (1996). Out of control: Visceral influences on behavior. *Organizational Behavior and Human Decision Processes, 65*, 272–292.

Loewenstein, G., & Linville, P. (1986). *Expectation formation and the timing of outcomes: A cognitive strategy for balancing the conflicting incentives for savoring success and avoiding disappointment*. Unpublished manuscript, Center for Decision Research, Graduate School of Business, University of Chicago.

Loewenstein, G. F., & Prelec, D. (1993). Preferences for sequences of outcomes. *Psychological Review, 100*, 91–108.

Loewenstein, G. F., Thompson, L., & Bazerman, M. H. (1989). Social utility and decision making in interpersonal contexts. *Journal of Personality and Social Psychology, 57*, 426–441.

Loomes, G. (1987). Testing for regret and disappointment in choice under uncertainty. *Economic Journal, 97*, 118–129.

Loomes, G., & Sugden, R. (1982). Regret theory: An alternative theory of rational choice under uncertainty. *Economic Journal, 92*, 805–824.

Loomes, G., & Sugden, R. (1986). Disappointment and dynamic consistency in choice under uncertainty. *Review of Economic Studies, 53*, 271–282.

Lopes, L. L. (1987). Between hope and fear: The psychology of risk. In L. Berkowitz (Ed.), *Advances in experimental social psychology* (Vol. 20, pp. 255–295). New York: Academic Press.

Lopes, L. L. (1987). Procedural debiasing. *Acta Psychologica, 64*, 167–185.

Lopes, L. L. (1996). When time is of the essence: Averaging, aspiration, and the short run. *Organizational Behavior and Human Decision Processes, 65*, 179–189.

Lord, C. G., Ross, L., & Lepper, M. R. (1979). Biased assimilation and attitude polarization: The effects of prior theories on subsequently considered evidence. *Journal of Personality and Social Psychology, 37*, 2098–2109.

Lowin, A. (1967). Approach and avoidance: Alternative modes of selective exposure to information. *Journal of Personality and Social Psychology, 6*, 1–9

Luce, R. D., & Raiffa, H. (1957). *Games and decisions: Introduction and critical survey*. New York: Wiley.

Luchins, A. S. (1957). Primacy-recency in impression formation. In C. I. Hovland (Ed.), *The order of presentation in persuasion*. New Haven: Yale University Press.

Lurie, S. (1987). A parametric model of utility for two-person distributions. *Psychological Review, 94*, 42–60.

Lutter, R., & Morrall, J. F. III. (1994). Health-health analysis: A new way to evaluate health and safety regulation. *Journal of Risk and Uncertainty, 8*, 43–66.

Machina, M. (1987). Decision-making in the presence of risk. *Science, 236*, 537–543.

Markman, K. D., Gavaski, I., Sherman, S. J., & McMullen, M. N. (1993). The mental simulation of better and worse possible worlds. *Journal of Experimental social*

Psychology, 29, 87–109.

Markowitz, H. M. (1959). *Portfolio selection.* New York: Wiley.

Marshall, J. D., Knetsch, J. L., & Sinden, J. A. (1986). Agents' evaluations and the disparity in measures of economic loss. *Journal of Economic Behavior and Organization, 7,* 115–127

Matute, H. (1996). Illusion of control: Detecting response-outcome independence in analytic but not in naturalistic conditions. *Psychological Science, 7,* 289–293.

McCauley, C., & Stitt, C. L. (1978). An individual and quantitative measure of stereotypes. *Journal of Personality and Social Psychology, 36,* 929–940.

McCauley, C. (1989). The nature of social influence in groupthink: Compliance and internalization. *Journal of Personality and Social Psychology, 57,* 250–260.

McClelland, G. H., Schulze, W. D., & Coursey, D. L. (1993). Insurance for low-probability hazards: A bimodal response to unlikely events. *Journal of Risk and Uncertainty, 7,* 95–116.

McCloskey, M. (1983). Naive theories of motion. In D. Gentner & A. L. Stevens (Eds.), *Mental models* (pp. 299–324). Hillsdale, N.J.: Erlbaum.

McCord, M., & de Neufville, R. (1985). *Eliminating the certainty effect problem in utility assessment: Theory and experiment.* Unpublished manuscript, Ohio State University, Columbus, Ohio.

McDaniels, T. L. (1988). Comparing expressed and revealed preferences for risk reduction: Different hazards and question frames. *Risk Analysis, 8,* 593–604.

McGuire, W. J. (1960). A syllogistic analysis of cognitive relationships. In M. J. Rosenberg, C. I. Hovland, W. J. McGuire, R. P. Abelson, & J. W. Brehm (Eds.), *Attitude organization and change* (pp. 65–111). New Haven: Yale University Press.

Medin, D., Altom, M. W., Edelson, S. M., & Freko, D. (1982). Correlated symptoms and simulated medical classification. *Journal of Experimental Psychology: Learning, Memory, and Cognition, 8,* 37–50.

Medin, D., Dewey, G., & Murphy, T. (1983). Relationships between item and category learning: Evidence that abstraction is not automatic. *Journal of Experimental Psychology: Learning, Memory, and Cognition, 9,* 607–625.

Meehl, P. E. (1954). *Clinical versus statistical prediction: A theoretical analysis and a look at the evidence.* Minneapolis: University of Minnesota Press.

Mehra, R., & Prescott, E. C. (1985). The equity premium: A puzzle. *Journal of Monetary Economics, 15,* 145–162.

Mellers, B. A. (1986). "Fair" allocation of salaries and taxes. *Journal of Experimental Psychology: Human Perception and Performance, 12,* 80–91.

Mellers, B. A., & Baron, J. (Eds.) (1993). *Psychological perspectives on justice: Theory and applications.* New York: New York: Cambridge University Press.

Messick, D. M. (1985). Social interdependence and decisionmaking. In G. Wright (Ed.), *Behavioral decision making* (pp. 87–109). New York: Plenum.

Messick, D. M., Bloom, S., Boldizar, J. P., & Samuelson, C. D. (1985). Why we are fairer than others. *Journal of Experimental Social Psychology, 21,* 480-500.

Messick, D. M., & Sentis, K. P. (1985). Estimating social and nonsocial utility functions from ordinal data. *European Journal of Social Psychology, 15*, 389–399.

Meszaros, J. R., Asch, D. A., Baron, J., Hershey, J. C., Kunreuther, H., & Schwartz-Buzaglo, J. (1996). Cognitive processes and the decisions of some parents to forego pertussis vaccination for their children. *Journal of Clinical Epidemiology, 49*, 697–703.

Mill, J. S. (1863). *Utilitarianism.* London: Collins.

Miller, D. T., & McFarland, C. (1986). Counterfactual thinking and victim compensation. *Personality and Social Psychology Bulletin, 12*, 513–519.

Mischel, H. H., & Mischel, W. (1983). The development of children's knowledge of self-control strategies. *Child Development, 54*, 603–619.

Mischel, W. (1984). Convergences and challenges in the search for consistency. *American Psychologist, 39*, 351–364.

Mischel, W., Shoda, Y., & Peake, P. K. (1988). The nature of adolescent competencies predicted by preschool delay of gratification. *Journal of Personality and Social Psychology, 54*, 687–696.

Mitchell, R. C., & Carson, R. T. (1989). *Using surveys to value public goods: The contingent valuation method.* Washington: Resources for the Future.

Miyamoto, J. M., & Eraker, S. A. (1988). A multiplicative model of the utility of survival duration and health quality. *Journal of Experimental Psychology: General, 117*, 3-20.

Modigliani, F. (1986). Life cycle, individual thrift, and the wealth of nations. *Science, 234*, 704–712.

Montgomery, H. (1984). Decision rules and the search for dominance structure: Towards a process model of decision making. In P. C. Humphreys, O. Svenson, & A. Vari (Eds.), *Analysing and aiding decision processes.* Amsterdam: North Holland.

Morgan, M. G., Fischhoff, B., Bostrom, A., Lave, L., & Atman C. J. (1992). Communicating risk to the public. *Environmental Science and Technology, 26*, 2048–2055.

Moynihan, D. P. (1996). *Miles to go: A personal history of social policy.* Cambridge, Mass.: Harvard University Press.

Mumford, M., & Dawes, R. M. (1999). Subadditivity in memory for personal events. *Psychological Science, 10*, 47–51.

Murphy, A. H., & Winkler, R. L. (1977). Can weather forecasters formulate reliable probability forecasts of precipitation and temperature? *National Weather Digest, 2*, 2–9.

Murphy-Berman, V., Berman, J. J., Singh, P., Pachuari, A., & Kumar, P. (1984). Factors affecting allocation to needy and meritorious recipients: A cross-cultural comparison. *Journal of Personality and Social Psychology, 46*, 1267–1272.

Mynatt, C. R., Doherty, M. E., & Tweney, R. D. (1977). Confirmation bias in a simulated research environment: an experimental study of scientific inference. *Quarterly Journal of Experimental Psychology, 29*, 85–95.

Nagel, T. (1970). *The possibility of altruism*. Princeton: Princeton University Press.

Nash, J. F. (1950). The bargaining problem. *Econometrica, 18*, 155-162.

Neale, M. A., & Bazerman, M. H. (1991). *Cognition and rationality in negotiation.* New York: Free Press.

Newcomb, T. M. (1929). The consistency of certain extrovert-introvert behavior patterns in 51 problem boys. *Contributions to Education, 382.* New York: Teachers College, Columbia University.

Newell, A., & Simon, H. A. (1972). *Human problem solving.* Englewood Cliffs, N.J.: Prentice-Hall.

Nickerson, R. S. (1986). *Reflections on reasoning.* Hillsdale, N.J.: Erlbaum.

Nickerson, R. S. (1996). Ambiguities and unstated assumptions in probabilistic reasoning. *Psychological Bulletin, 120*, 410–433.

Nisbett, R. E., & Ross, L. (1980). *Human inference: Strategies and shortcomings of social judgment.* Englewood Cliffs, N.J.: Prentice-Hall.

Nisbett, R. E., & Wilson, T. D. (1977). Telling more than we can know: Verbal reports on mental processes. *Psychological Review, 84*, 231–259.

Nisbett, R. E., Zukier, H. & Lemley, R. E. (1981). The dilution effect: nondiagnostic information weakens the implications of diagnostic information. *Cognitive Psychology, 13*, 248–277.

Norris, S. P., & Phillips, L. M. (1987). Explanations of reading comprehension: schema theory and critical thinking theory. *Teachers College Record, 89*, 281–306.

Nozick, R. (1974). *Anarchy, state, and utopia.* New York: Basic Books.

O'Connor, A. M. C., Boyd, N. F., Warde, P., Stolbach, L., & Till, J. E. (1987). Eliciting preferences for alternative drug therapies in oncology: Influence of treatment outcome description, elicitation technique and treatment experience on preferences. *Journal of Chronic Disease, 40*, 811–818.

O'Leary, J. F., Fairclough, D. L., Jankowski, M. K., & Weeks, J. C. (1995). Comparison of time-tradeoff utilities and rating scale values of cancer patients and their relatives. *Medical Decision Making, 15*, 132–137.

Orbell, J. M., van de Kragt, A. J. C., & Dawes, R. M. (1988). Explaining discussion-induced cooperation in social dilemmas. *Journal of Personality and Social Psychology, 54*, 811–819.

Ordóñez, L. D., & Mellers, B. A. Trade-offs in fairness and preference judgments. In B. A. Mellers and J. Baron (Eds.), *Psychological perspectives on justice: Theory and applications* (pp. 138–154). New York: Cambridge University Press.

Osherson, D. N., Shafir, E., Krantz, D. H., & Smith, E. E. (1997). Probability bootstrapping: Improving prediction by fitting extensional models to knowledgeable but incoherent probability judgments. *Organizational Behavior and Human Decision Processes, 69*, 1–8.

Parfit, D. (1984). *Reasons and persons.* Oxford: Oxford University Press (Clarendon Press).

Parks, C. D., & Hulbert, L. G. (1995). High and low trusters' responses to fear in a payoff matrix. *Journal of Conflict Resolution, 39*, 718–730.

Parks, C. D., & Vu, A. D. (1994). Social dilemma behavior of individuals from highly individualist and collectivist cultures. *Journal of Conflict Resolution, 38*, 708–718.

Pascal, B. (1941). *Pensées* (W. F. Trotter, Trans.). New York: Modern Library. (Original work published 1670)

Payne, J. W. (1976). Task complexity and contingent processing in decision making: An information search and protocol analysis. *Organizational Behavior and Human Performance, 16*, 366–387.

Payne, J. W., Bettman, J. R., & Johnson, E. J. (1988). Adaptive strategy selection in decision making. *Journal of Experimental Psychology: Learning, Memory and Cognition, 14*, 534–552.

Payne, J. W., Bettman, J. R., & Johnson, E. J. (1993). *The adoptive decision maker.* New York: Cambridge University Press.

Payne, J. W., Braunstein, M. L., & Carroll, J. S. (1978). Exploring pre-decisional behavior: An alternative approach to decision research. *Organizational Behavior and Human Performance, 22*, 17–44.

Perkins, D. N. (1986). *Knowledge as design: Critical and creative thinking for teachers and learners.* Hillsdale, N.J.: Erlbaum.

Perkins, D. N., Allen, R., & Hafner, J. (1983). Difficulties in everyday reasoning. In W. Maxwell (Ed.), *Thinking: The expanding frontier* (pp. 177–189). Philadelphia: Franklin Institute.

Perkins, D. N., Bushey, B., & Faraday, M. (1986). *Learning to reason.* Unpublished manuscript, Harvard Graduate School of Education, Cambridge, MA.

Peterson, C. R., & DuCharme, W. M. (1967). A primacy effect in subjective probability revision. *Journal of Experimental Psychology, 73*, 61–65.

Peterson, C. R., & Ulehla, Z. J. (1965). Sequential patterns and maximizing. *Journal of Experimental Psychology, 69*, 1–4.

Petit, P. (1991). Decision theory and folk psychology. In M. O. L. Bachrach & S. L. Hurley (Eds.) *Foundations of decision theory: issues and advances*, pp. 147–167.

Piaget, J. (1929). *The child's conception of the world.* New York: Harcourt, Brace, & World.

Piaget, J., & Inhelder, B. (1975). *The origin of the idea of chance in children.* New York: Norton (originally published 1951).

Pitz, G. F. (1969). An inertia effect (resistance to change) in the revision of opinion. *Canadian Journal of Psychology, 23*, 24–33.

Pitz, G. F., Downing, L., & Reinhold, H. (1967). Sequential effects in the revision of subjective probabilities. *Canadian Journal of Psychology, 21*, 381–393.

Platt, J. R. (1964). Strong inference. *Science, 146*, 347–353.

Pliskin, J. S., Shepard, D. S., & Weinstein, M. C. (1980). Utility functions for life years and health status. *Operations Research, 28*, 206–224.

Polya, G. (1945). *How to solve it: A new aspect of mathematical method.* Princeton: Princeton University Press.

Poppe, M. & Utens, L. (1986). Effects of greed and fear of being gypped in a social dilemma situation with changing pool size. *Journal of Economic Psychology, 7,* 61–73.

Popper, K. R. (1962). *Conjectures and refutations: The growth of scientific knowledge.* New York: Basic Books.

Poulton, E. C. (1979). Models for biases in judging sensory magnitude. *Psychological Bulletin, 86,* 777–803.

Pruitt, D. G. (1967). Reward structure and cooperation: The decomposed prisoner's dilemma game. *Journal of Personality and Social Psychology, 7,* 21–27.

Pruitt, D. G., & Lewis, S. A. (1975). Development of integrative solutions in bilateral negotiation. *Journal of Personality and Social Psychology, 31,* 621–633.

Putnam, H. (1975). The meaning of "meaning." In *Philosophical papers*: Vol. 2, *Mind, language, and reality* (pp. 215–271). New York: Cambridge University Press.

Quattrone, G. A., & Tversky, A. (1984). Causal versus diagnostic contingencies: On self-deception and the voter's illusion. *Journal of Personality and Social Psychology, 46,* 237–248.

Quiggin, J. (1982). A theory of anticipated utility. *Journal of Economic Behavior and Organization, 3,* 323–343.

Quinn, R. J., & Bell, D. E. (1983). *A preliminary test of a reference-point model of risky choice.* Unpublished manuscript, Harvard University, School of Public Health, Cambridge, MA.

Quinn, W. (1989). Actions, intentions, and consequences: The doctrine of double effect. *Philosophy and Public Affairs, 18,* 334–351.

Rachlin, H., Logue, A. W., Gibbon, J., & Frankel, M. (1986). Cognition and behavior in studies of choice. *Psychological Review, 93,* 33–45.

Raiffa, H. (1961). Risk, ambiguity and the Savage axioms: Comment. *Quarterly Journal of Economics, 75,* 690–694.

Raiffa, H. (1982). *The art and science of negotiation.* Cambridge, Mass.: Harvard University Press.

Ramsey, F. P. (1931). Truth and probability. In R. B. Braithwaite (Ed.), *The foundations of mathematics and other logical essays by F. P. Ramsey* (pp. 158–198). New York: Harcourt, Brace.

Rapaport, A., & Eshed-Levy, D. (1989). Provision of step-level public goods: Effects of greed and fear of being gypped. *Organizational Behavior and Human Decision Processes, 44,* 325–344.

Rasinski, K. A. (1987). What's fair is fair – or is it? Value differences underlying public views about social justice. *Journal of Personality and Social Psychology, 53,* 201–211.

Rawls, J. (1971). *A theory of justice.* Cambridge, Mass.: Harvard University Press.

Read, S. J. (1983). Once is enough: Causal reasoning from a single instance. *Journal of Personality and Social Psychology, 45,* 323–334.

Read, D., & Loewenstein, G. (1995). Diversification bias: Explaining the discrepancy in variety seeking between combined and separated choices. *Journal of*

Experimental Psychology: Applied, 1, 34–49.

Regan, D. (1980). *Utilitarianism and co-operation*. Oxford: Oxford University Press (Clarendon Press).

Reuben, D. B. (1984). Learning diagnostic restraint. *New England Journal of Medicine, 310*, 591–593.

Rips, L. (1983). Cognitive processes in propositional reasoning. *Psychological Review, 90*, 38–71.

Ritov, I., & Baron, J. (1990). Reluctance to vaccinate: Omission bias and ambiguity. *Journal of Behavioral Decision Making, 3*, 263–277.

Ritov, I., & Baron, J. (1992). Status-quo and omission bias. *Journal of Risk and Uncertainty, 5*, 49–61.

Ritov, I., & Baron, J. (1995). Outcome knowledge, regret, and omission bias. *Organizational Behavior and Human Decision Processes, 64*, 119–127.

Ritov, I., & Baron, J. (1998). Protected values and omission bias. Manuscript.

Ritov, I., & Baron, J. (1994). Judgments of compensation for misfortune: the role of expectation. *European Journal of Social Psychology, 24*, 525–539.

Ritov, I., Baron, J., & Hershey, J. C. (1993). Framing effects in the evaluation of multiple risk reduction. *Journal of Risk and Uncertainty, 6*, 145–159.

Robbins, L. (1938). Interpersonal comparison of utility: A comment. *Economic Journal, 48*, 635–641.

Robinson, L. B., & Hastie, R. (1985). Revision of beliefs when a hypothesis is eliminated from consideration. *Journal of Experimental Psychology: Human Perception and Performance, 11*, 443–456.

Roncato, S., & Rumiati, R. (1986). Naive statics: Current misconceptions on equilibrium. *Journal of Experimental Psychology: Learning, Memory, and Cognition, 12*, 361–377.

Ross, M., & Sicoly, F. (1979). Egocentric bias in availability and attribution. *Journal of Personality and Social Psychology, 37*, 322–336.

Royzman, E. B., & Baron, J. (1999). The bias toward indirect harm and its relation to omission bias. Manuscript, University of Pennsylvania.

Rozin, P., Ashmore, M., & Markwith, M. (1996). Lay American conceptions of nutrition: Dose insensitivity, categorical thinking, contagion, and the monotonic mind. *Health Psychology, 15*, 438–447.

Ryan, C. S. (1996). Accuracy of Black and White college students' in-group and out-group stereotypes. *Personality and Social Psychology Bulletin 22*, 1114–1127.

Sabini, J. (1992). *Social psychology*. New York: Norton.

Sabini, J., & Silver, M. (1981). *Moralities of everyday life*. Oxford: Oxford University Press.

Salkovskis, P. M., & Clark, D. M. (1991). Cognitive therapy for panic disorder. *Journal of Cognitive Psychotherapy, 5*, 215–226.

Samuelson, P. (1950). Probability and the attempts to measure utility. *Economic Review, 1*, 167–173.

Samuelson, C. D., Messick, D. M., Rutte, C. G., & Wilke, H. (1984). Individual and structural solutions to resource dilemmas in two cultures. *Journal of Personality and Social Psychology, 47*, 94–104.

Samuelson, W., & Zeckhauser, R. (1988). Status-quo bias in decision making. *Journal of Risk and Uncertainty, 1*, 7–59.

Savage, L. J. (1954). *The foundations of statistics*. New York: Wiley.

Scheffler, I. (1965). *Conditions of knowledge: An introduction to epistemology and education*. Chicago: Scott, Foresman.

Schelling, T. C. (1968). The life you save may be your own. In S. B. Chace, Jr. (Ed.), *Problems in public expenditure analysis* (pp. 127–175). Washington, D.C.: Brookings Institution.

Schelling, T. C. (1978). *Micromotives and macrobehavior*. New York: Norton.

Scher, S. J., & Cooper, J. (1989). Motivational basis of dissonance: The singular role of behavioral consequences. *Journal of Personality and Social Psychology, 56*, 899–906.

Schkade, D. A., & Johnson, E. J. (1989). Cognitive processes in preference reversals. *Organizational Behavior and Human Performance, 44*, 203–231.

Schleser, R., Meyers, A. W., & Cohen, R. (1981). Generalization of self-instructions: Effects of general versus specific content, active rehearsal, and cognitive level. *Child Development, 52*, 335–340.

Schmitt, N. (1976). Social and situational determinants of interview decisions: Implications for the employment interview. *Personnel Psychology, 29*, 79–101.

Schneider, S. L., & Lopes, L. L. (1986). Reflection in preferences under risk: Who and when may suggest why. *Journal of Experimental Psychology: Human Perception and Performance, 12*, 535–548.

Schoemaker, P. J. H. (1979). The role of statistical knowledge in gambling decisions: Moment vs. risk dimension approaches. *Organizational Behavior and Human Performance, 24*, 1–17.

Schoemaker, P. J. H., & Hershey, J. C. (1992). Utility measurement: Signal, noise, and bias. *Organizational Behavior and Human Decision Processes, 52*, 397–424.

Schustack, M. W., & Sternberg, R. J. (1981). Evaluation of evidence in causal inference. *Journal of Experimental Psychology: General, 110*, 101–120.

Schwalm, N. D., & Slovic, P. (1982). *Development and test of a motivational approach and materials for increasing use of restraints* (Final technical report PFTR-1100–82–3). Woodland Hills, Calif.: Perceptronics, Inc.

Schwartz, A. (1988). Proposals for products liability reform: A theoretical synthesis. *Yale Law Journal, 97*, 353–419.

Schwartz, B. (1982). Reinforcement-induced behavioral stereotypy: How not to teach people to discover rules. *Journal of Experimental Psychology: General, 111*, 23–59.

Schwartz, B. (1986). *The battle for human nature: Science, morality, and modern life*. New York: Norton.

Schwartz, B. (1988). The experimental synthesis of behavior: Reinforcement, behavioral stereotypy, and problem solving. In G. H. Bower (Ed.), *The psychology of learning and motivation* (Vol. 22). New York: Academic Press.

Schwartz, S. M., Baron, J., & Clarke, J. R. (1988). A causal Bayesian model for the diagnosis of appendicitis. In J. F. Lemmer and L. N. Kanal (Eds.), *Uncertainty in artificial intelligence* (Vol. 2, pp. 423–434). Amsterdam: North Holland.

Schwartz-Shea, P., & Simmons, R. T. (1990). The layered prisoners' dilemma: ingroup vs. macro-efficiency. *Public Choice, 65*, 61–83.

Schwartz-Shea, P., & Simmons, R. T. (1991). Egoism, parochialism, and universalism. *Rationality and Society, 3*, 106–132.

Scribner, S. (1977). Modes of thinking and ways of speaking: Culture and logic reconsidered. In P. N. Johnson-Laird & P. C. Wason (Eds.), *Thinking: Readings in cognitive science* (pp. 483–500). New York: Cambridge University Press.

Segal, U. (1984). *Nonlinear decision weights with the independence axiom.* UCLA Working Paper No. 353, Department of Economics, University of California at Los Angeles.

Selz, O. (1935). Versuche zur Hebung des Intelligenzniveaus: Ein Beitrag zur Theorie der Intelligenz und ihrer erziehlichen Beeinflussung. *Zeitschrift für Psychologie, 134*, 236–301.

Shafer, G. (1976). *A mathematical theory of evidence.* Princeton: Princeton University Press.

Shafer, G. (1981). Constructive probability. *Synthese, 48*, 1–60.

Shafer, G. (1982). Lindley's paradox. *Journal of the American Statistical Association, 77*, 325–351 (with commentary).

Shafer, G., & Tversky, A. (1985). Weighing evidence: The design and comparison of probability thought experiments. *Cognitive Science, 9*, 309–339.

Shafir, E., & Tversky, A. (1992). Thinking through uncertainty: Nonconsequential reasoning and choice. *Cognitive Psychology, 24*, 449–474.

Shafir, E., Diamond, P., & Tversky, A. (1997). Money illusion. *Quarterly Journal of Economics, 112*, 341–374.

Shaklee, H., & Fischhoff, B. (1982). Strategies of information search in causal analysis. *Memory and Cognition, 10*, 520–530.

Shaklee, H., & Mims, M. (1982). Sources of error in judging event covariations. *Journal of Experimental Psychology: Learning, Memory, and Cognition, 8*, 208–224.

Shaklee, H., & Tucker, D. (1980). A rule analysis of judgments of covariation between events. *Memory and Cognition, 8*, 459–467.

Shoda, Y., Mischel, W. & Peake, P. K. (1990). Predicting adolescent cognitive and self-regulatory competencies from preschool delay of gratification: Identifying diagnostic conditions. *Developmental Psychology, 26*, 978–986.

Shweder, R. A. (1977). Likeness and likelihood in everyday thought: Magical thinking in judgments about personality. *Current Anthropology, 18*, 637–648.

Shweder, R. A., & D'Andrade, R. G. (1979). Accurate reflection or systematic distortion? A reply to Block, Weiss, and Thorne. *Journal of Personality and Social Psychology, 37*, 1075–1084.

Simon, H. A. (1969). *The sciences of the artificial.* Cambridge, MA: MIT Press.

Simon, H. A. (1990). A mechanism for social selection and successful altruism. *Science, 250*, 1665–1668.

Simon, J. L. (1990). *Population matters: People, resources, environment and immigration.* New Brunswick, N.J.: Transaction Publishers.

Simonson, I. (1989). Choice based on reasons: The case of attraction and compromise effects. *Journal of Consumer Research, 16*, 158–174.

Simonson, I., & Tversky, A. (1992). Choice in context: Tradeoff contrast and extremeness aversion. *Journal of Marketing Research, 29*, 281–295.

Singer, P. (1982). *The expanding circle: Ethics and sociobiology.* New York: Farrar, Strauss & Giroux.

Singer, P. (1993). *Practical ethics* (2nd ed.). Cambridge: Cambridge University Press.

Slovic, P. (1972). Information processing, situation specificity, and the generality of risk-taking behavior. *Journal of Personality and Social Psychology, 22*, 128–134.

Slovic, P. (1987). Perception of risk. *Science, 236*, 280–285.

Slovic, P., & Fischhoff, B. (1977). On the psychology of experimental surprises. *Journal of Experimental Psychology: Human Perception and Performance, 3*, 544–551.

Slovic, P., Fischhoff, B., & Lichtenstein, S. (1985). Characterizing perceived risk. In R. W. Kates, C. Hohenemser, & J. X. Kasperson (Eds.), *Perilous progress: Technology as hazard.* Boulder, CO: Westview Press..

Slovic, P., Griffin, D., & Tversky, A. (1990). Compatibility effects in judgment and choice. In R. Hogarth (Ed.), *Insights in decision making: A tribute to Hillel J. Einhorn* (pp. 5–27). Chicago: University of Chicago Press.

Slovic, P., Lichtenstein, S., & Fischhoff, B. (1984). Modeling the societal impact of fatal accidents. *Management Science, 30*, 464–474.

Slovic, P., & Tversky, A. (1974). Who accepts Savage's axioms? *Behavioral Science, 14*, 368–373.

Smedslund, J. (1963). The concept of correlation in adults. *Scandinavian Journal of Psychology, 4*, 165–173.

Smith, M. H. (1988). National Childhood Vaccine Injury Compensation Act. *Pediatrics, 82*, 264–269.

Snyder, M., & Swann, W. B. (1978). Behavioral confirmation in social interaction: From social perception to social reality. *Journal of Experimental Social Psychology, 14*, 148–162.

Solnick, J. V., Kanneberg, C. H., Eckerman, D. A., & Waller, M. B. (1980). An experimental analysis of impulsivity and impulse control in humans. *Learning and Motivation, 11*, 61–77.

Solomon, R. L., & Corbit, J. D. (1974). An opponent-process theory of motivation. *Psychological Review, 81*, 119–145.

Spranca, M. (1992). *The effect of naturalness on desirability and preference in the domain of foods.* Unpublished Masters Thesis, Department of Psychology, University of California, Berkeley.

Spranca, M., Minsk, E., & Baron, J. (1991). Omission and commission in judgment and choice. *Journal of Experimental Social Psychology, 27,* 76–105.

Stalmeier, P. F. M., Wakker, P. P., & Bezembinder, T. G. G. (1997). Preference reversals: Violations of unidimensional procedure invariance. *Journal of Experimental Psychology: Human Perception and Performance, 23,* 1196–1205.

Stanovich, K. E., & West, R. F. (1998). Individual differences in rational thought. *Journal of Experimental Psychology: General, 127,* 161–188.

Starmer, C., & Sugden, R. (1993). Testing for juxtaposition and event-splitting effects. *Journal of Risk and Uncertainty, 6,* 235–254.

Starr, C. (1969). Social benefit versus technological risk: What is our society willing to pay for safety? *Science, 165,* 1232–1238.

Staw, B. M. (1976). Knee-deep in the big muddy: A study of escalating commitment to a chosen course of action. *Organizational Behavior and Human Performance, 16,* 27–44.

Stewart, R. H. (1965). Effect of continuous responding on the order effect in personality impression formation. *Journal of Personality and Social Psychology, 1,* 161–165.

Stone, E. R., Yates, J. F., & Parker, A. M. (1994). Risk communication: Absolute versus relative expressions of low-probability risks. *Organizational Behavior and Human Decision Processes, 60,* 387–408.

Strack, F., Argyle, M., & Schwarz, N. (Eds.) (1991). *Subjective well-being: An interdisciplinary perspective.* Oxford: Pergamon Press.

Strotz, R. H. (1955). Myopia and inconsistency in dynamic utility maximization. *Review of Economic Studies, 23,* 165–180.

Suedfeld, P., & Rank, A. D. (1976). Revolutionary leaders: Long-term success as a function of changes in conceptual complexity. *Journal of Personality and Social Psychology, 34,* 169–178.

Suedfeld, P., & Tetlock, P. E. (1977). Integrative complexity of communications in international crises. *Journal of Conflict Resolution, 21,* 169–184.

Sugden, R. (1986). New developments in the theory of choice under uncertainty. *Bulletin of Economic Research, 38,* 1–24.

Svenson, O. (1979). Process descriptions of decision making. *Organizational Behavior and Human Performance, 23,* 86–112.

Svenson, O. (1981). Are we all less risky and more skillful than our fellow drivers? *Acta Psychologica, 47,* 143–148.

Sweeney, P. D., & Gruber, K. L. (1984). Selective exposure: Voter information preferences and the Watergate affair. *Journal of Personality and Social Psychology, 46,* 1208–1221.

Tengs, T. O., Adams, M. E., Pliskin, J. S., Safran, D. G., Siegel, J. E., Weinstein, M. E., & Graham, J. D. (1995). Five hundred life-saving interventions and their cost-effectiveness. *Risk Analysis, 15,* 360–390.

Tetlock, P. E. (1979). Identifying victims of groupthink from public statements of decision makers. *Journal of Personality and Social Psychology, 37,* 1314–1324.

Tetlock, P. E. (1983). Accountability and the perseverance of first impressions. *Social Psychology Quarterly, 46*, 285–292.

Tetlock, P. E. (1983). Cognitive style and political ideology. *Journal of Personality and Social Psychology, 45*, 118–126.

Tetlock, P. E. (1984). Cognitive style and political belief systems in the British House of Commons. *Journal of Personality and Social Psychology, 46*, 365–375.

Tetlock, P. E. (1992). The impact of accountability on judgment and choice: Toward a social contingency model. In *Advances in Experimental Social Psychology* (Vol. 24, pp. 331–376). New York: Academic Press.

Tetlock, P. E., & Kim, J. I. (1987). Accountability and judgment processes in a personality prediction task. *Journal of Personality and Social Psychology, 52*, 700–709.

Tetlock, P. E., Peterson, R. S., McGuire, C., Chang, S., & Feld, P. (1992). Assessing political group dynamics: A test of the groupthink model. *Journal of Personality and Social Psychology, 63*, 403–425.

Thaler, R. (1980). Toward a positive theory of consumer choice. *Journal of Economic Behavior and Organization, 1*, 39–60.

Thaler, R. (1985). Mental accounting and consumer choice. *Marketing Science, 4*, 199–214.

Thaler, R. H. (1988). The ultimatum game. *Journal of Economic Perspectives, 2*, 195–206.

Thaler, R. H., & Shefrin, H. M. (1981). An economic theory of self-control. *Journal of Political Economy, 89*, 392–406.

Thaler, R. H., Tversky, A., Kahneman, D., & Schwartz, A. (1997). The effect of myopia and loss aversion on risk taking: An experimental study. *Quarterly Journal of Economics, 112*, 647–661.

Thompson, L., & Loewenstein, G. (1992). Egocentric interpretations of fairness and interpersonal conflict. *Organizational Behavior and Human Decision Processes, 51*, 176–197.

Toulmin, S. E. (1958). *The uses of argument.* Cambridge: Cambridge University Press.

Tschirgi, J. E. (1980). Sensible reasoning: A hypothesis about hypotheses. *Child Development, 51*, 1–10.

Tversky, A. (1967). Additivity, utility, and subjective probability. *Journal of Mathematical Psychology, 4*, 175–202.

Tversky, A. (1969). Intransitivity of preferences. *Psychological Review, 76*, 31–48.

Tversky, A. (1972). Elimination by aspects: A theory of choice. *Psychological Review, 79*, 281–299.

Tversky, A., & Fox, C. R. (1995). Weighing risk and uncertainty. *Psychological Review, 102*, 269–283.

Tversky, A., & Kahneman, D. (1973). Availability: A heuristic for judging frequency and probability. *Cognitive Psychology, 5*, 207–232.

Tversky, A., & Kahneman, D. (1974). Judgment under uncertainty: Heuristics and biases. *Science, 185*, 1124–1131.

Tversky, A., & Kahneman, D. (1981). The framing of decisions and the psychology of choice. *Science, 211*, 453–458.

Tversky, A., & Kahneman, D. (1982). Evidential impact of base rates. In D. Kahneman, P. Slovic, & A. Tversky (Eds.), *Judgment under uncertainty: Heuristics and biases* (pp. 153–160).

Tversky, A., & Kahneman, D. (1983). Extensional versus intuitive reasoning: The conjunction fallacy in probability judgment. *Psychological Review, 90*, 293–315.

Tversky, A., & Kahneman, D. (1992). Advances in prospect theory: cumulative representations of uncertainty. *Journal of Risk and Uncertainty, 5*, 297–323.

Tversky, A., & Koehler, D. J. (1994). Support theory: A nonextentional representation of subjective probability. *Psychological Review, 101*, 547–567.

Tversky, A., Sattath, S., & Slovic, P. (1988). Contingent weighting in judgment and choice. *Psychological Review, 95*, 371–384.

Tversky, A., Slovic, P., & Kahneman, D. (1990). The causes of preference reversal. *American Economic Review, 80*, 204–217.

Tversky, A., & Shafir, E. (1992). Choice under conflict: The dynamics of deferred decision. *Psychological Science, 3*, 358–361.

Tversky, A., & Shafir, E. (1992). The disjunction effect in choice under uncertainty. *Psychological Science, 3*, 305–309.

Ubel, P. A., Baron, J., & Asch, D. A. (1998). Equity as a framing effect. (Manuscript.)

Ubel, P. A., De Kay, M. L., Baron, J., & Asch, D. A. (1996). Public preferences for efficiency and racial equity in kidney transplant allocation decisions. *Transplantation Proceedings, 28*, 2997–3002.

Ubel, P. A., De Kay, M. L., Baron, J., & Asch, D. A. (1996). Cost effectiveness analysis in a setting of budget constraints: Is it equitable? *New England Journal of Medicine, 334*, 1174–1177.

Ubel, P. A., Loewenstein, G., Scanlon, D., & Kamlet, M. (1996). Individual utilities are inconsistent with rationing choices: A partial explanation of why Oregon's cost-effectiveness list failed. *Medical Decision Making, 16*, 108–116.

Ubel, P. A., Richardson, J., & Pinto Prades, J.-L. (1999). Life-saving treatments and disabilities: Are all QALYs created equal? *International Journal of Technology Assessment in Health Care, 15*, 738–748.

van Avermaet, E. (1974). *Equity: A theoretical and empirical analysis.* Unpublished doctoral dissertation, University of California, Santa Barbara.

Van Lehn, K., & Brown, J. S. (1980). Planning nets: A representation for formalizing analogies and semantic models of procedural skills. In R. E. Snow, P.-A. Federico, & W. Montague (Eds.), *Aptitude, learning, and instruction* (Vol. 2). Hillsdale, N.J.: Erlbaum.

Varey, C., & Kahneman, D. (1992). Experiences extended across time: Evaluation of moments and episodes. *Journal of Behavioral Decision Making, 5*, 169–185.

Viscusi, W. K. (1995). Carcinogen regulation: Risk characteristics and the synthetic risk bias. *American Economic Review, 85*, 50–54.

Viscusi, W. K., Hamilton, J. T., & Dockins, P. C. (1997). Conservative versus mean risk assessments: Implications for Superfund policies. *Journal of Environmental*

Economics and Management 34, 187–206

Viscusi, W. K., Magat, W. A., & Huber, J. (1987). An investigation of the rationality of consumer valuation of multiple health risks. *Rand Journal of Economics, 18*, 465–479.

von Neumann, J., & Morgenstern, O. (1947). *Theory of games and economic behavior* (2nd ed.). Princeton: Princeton University Press.

von Winterfeldt, D., & Edwards, W. (1986). *Decision analysis and behavioral research*. New York: Cambridge University Press.

Vosniadou, S., & Brewer, W. F. (1987). Theories of knowledge restructuring in development. *Review of Educational Research, 57*, 51–67.

Voss, J. F., Tyler, S. W., & Yengo, L. A. (1983). Individual differences in the solving of social science problems. In R. F. Dillon & R. R. Schmeck (Eds.), *Individual differences in cognition* (Vol. 1, pp. 205–232). New York: Academic Press.

Wakker, P. (1989). *Additive representation of preferences: A new foundation of decision analysis*. Dordrecht: Kluwer.

Walster, E., Walster, G. W., & Berscheid, E. (1978). *Equity: Theory and research*. Boston: Allyn & Bacon.

Wason, P. C. (1968). Reasoning about a rule. *Quarterly Journal of Experimental Psychology, 20*, 273–281.

Wason, P. C. (1968). "On the failure to eliminate hypotheses . . . ." – a second look. In P. C. Wason & P. N. Johnson-Laird (Eds.), *Thinking and reasoning* (pp. 165–174). Harmondsworth: Penguin.

Wason, P. C. (1977). Self-contradictions. In P. N. Johnson-Laird & P. C. Wason (Eds.), *Thinking: Readings in cognitive science* (pp. 114–128). New York: Cambridge University Press.

Wason, P. C., & Evans, J. St. B. T. (1975). Dual processes in reasoning? *Cognition, 3*, 141–154.

Weber, E. U., Kirsner, B. (1997) Reasons for rank-dependent utility evaluation. *Journal of Risk and Uncertainty, 14*, 41–61.

Weber, M., & Borcherding, K. (1993). Behavioral influences on weight judgments in multiattribute decision making. *European Journal of Operations Research, 67*, 1–12.

Weber, M., & Camerer, C. F. (1987). Recent developments in modeling preferences under risk. *OR Spektrum, 9*, 129–151.

Weeks, J. C., Cook, E. F., O'Day, S. J., Peterson, L. M., Wenger, N., Reding, D., Harrell, F. E,. Kussin, P., Dawson,, N. V., Connors, A. F., Jr., Lynn, J., Phillips, R. S. (1998). Relationship between cancer patients' predictions of prognosis and their treatment preferences. *Journal of the American Medical Association, 279*, 1709–1714.

Wegner, D. M., Coulton, G. F., & Wenzlaff, R. (1985). The transparency of denial: Briefing in the debriefing paradigm. *Journal of Personality and Social Psychology, 49*, 338–346.

Weinstein, N. (1980). Unrealistic optimism about future life events. *Journal of Personality and Social Psychology, 39*, 806–820.

Wheeler, D. D. (1979). A practicum in thinking. In D. D. Wheeler & W. N. Dember (Eds.), *A practicum in thinking*. Cincinnati: University of Cincinnati, Department of Psychology.

Wilson, T. D., Houston, C. E., Etling, K. M., Brekke, N. (1996). A new look at anchoring effects: Basic anchoring and its antecedents. *Journal of Experimental Psychology: General, 125*, 387–402.

Wittgenstein, L. (1958). *Philosophical investigations* (2nd ed.), (G. E. M. Anscombe, Trans.). Oxford: Blackwell Publishers.

Woodworth, R. S., & Schlosberg, H. (1954). *Experimental psychology*. New York: Holt.

Woodworth, R. S., & Sells, S. B. (1935). An atmosphere effect informal syllogistic reasoning. *Journal of Experimental Psychology, 18*, 451–460.

Wright, G. N., & Phillips, L. D. (1980). Cultural variation in probabilistic thinking: Alternative ways of dealing with uncertainty. *International Journal of Psychology, 15*, 239–257.

Wright, G. N., Phillips, L. D., Whalley, P. C., Choo, G. T., Ng, K. O., Tan, I., & Wisudha, A. (1978). Cultural differences in probabilistic thinking. *Journal of Cross-Cultural Psychology, 9*, 285–299.

Yaari, M. E. (1985). *Risk aversion without diminishing marginal utility and the dual theory of choice under risk*. Research Memorandum No. 65, Center for Research in Mathematical Economics and Game Theory, Hebrew University, Jerusalem.

Yamagishi, T. (1986). The provision of a sanctioning system as a public good. *Journal of Personality and Social Psychology, 51*, 110–116

Yamagishi, T. (1988). Seriousness of social dilemmas and the provision of a sanctioning system. *Social Psychology, 51*, 32–42.

Yamagishi, T., & Sato, K. (1986). Motivational basis of the public goods problem. *Journal of Personality and Social Psychology, 50*, 67–73.

Zakay, D. (1990). The role of personal tendencies in the selection of decision-making strategies. *Psychological Record, 40*, 207–213.

Zeckhauser, R. J., & Viscusi, W. K. (1990). Risk within reason. *Science, 248*, 559–564.

Zeelenberg, M., Beattie, J., van der Pligt, J., & de Vries, N. K. (1996). Consequences of regret aversion: Effects of expected feedback on risky decision making. *Organizational Behavior and Human Decision Processes, 65*, 148–158.

Author Index

Abelson, R. P., 136
Abramson, L. Y., 58, 181
Adams, J. K., 127, 128
Adams, J. S., 411
Adams, P. A., 127, 128
Agnoli, F., 138, 139
Ainslie, G., 470, 476, 481, 482, 486
Ajzen, I., 195
Akerlof, G. A., 64
Allais, M., 226, 248
Allan, L. G., 180, 182
Allen, R., 204
Alloy, L. B., 58, 181
Alpert, W., 127
Altom, M. W., 376, 377
Amablie, T. M., 176
Ames, B. N., 503
Amsel, E., 186
Anderson, C. A., 199, 200
Anderson, J. R., 43
Anderson, N. H., 370, 371, 379
Appleman, A., 469
Aquinas, T., 395
Argyle, M., 486
Arkes, H. R., 146, 178, 297–299, 367, 468
Arnauld, A., 67
Aronson, E., 209
Asch, D. A., 443, 505
Asch, S. E., 198, 370
Ashmore, M., 507
Atman C. J., 507
Attneave, F., 126
Austin, G. A., 156, 157
Ausubel, D. P., 29

Axelrod, R., 436
Bacon, F., 195
Badgio, P., 54, 195, 218
Baker, S. M., 294
Bar-Hillel, M., 419
Bara, P. G., 73, 74, 76
Barclay, S., 122
Baron, J., 54, 57, 61, 77, 120, 122, 139, 140, 162–164, 167, 195, 204, 205, 218, 246, 264, 266, 267, 271, 272, 292, 307, 312, 314, 329, 330, 352, 355, 386, 389, 400–403, 406, 413, 417, 421–423, 425, 441, 445, 453, 460, 470, 500, 501, 504–506
Barrett, P., 120
Batson, C. D., 202
Baumeister, R. F., 65
Bazerman, M. H., 427, 430, 445, 469
Beattie, J., 46, 162, 163, 167, 417
Beck, A. T., 60
Becker, J. W., 269, 273
Becker, S. W., 293
Beekun, R. I., 469
Behn, R. D., 303
Bell, D. E., 266
Bell, D. E., 264, 266
Ben-Yossef, M., 454
Benartzi, S., 511
Bennett, J., 441
Bentham, J., 225
Berg, J., 451
Bernoulli, D., 225, 239
Berscheid, E., 411, 422
Bettman, J. R., 34

Beyth-Marom, R., 178
Bezembinder, T. G. G., 321
Bickel, W. K., 479
Birnbaum, M. H., 46, 146, 262, 263
Bloom, S., 445
Blumer, C., 297–299, 468
Boldizar, J. P., 445
Boles, T. L., 266
Bond, M. H., 420
Borcherding, K., 327
Bornstein, B. H., 298, 299, 376
Bornstein, G., 454
Bostic, R., 248
Bostrom, A., 507
Bowie, C., 504
Boyd, N. F., 323
Braine, M. D. S., 72
Braunstein, M. L., 286
Brenner, L. A., 212
Brewer, W. F., 17
Breyer, S., 352, 496
Brickman, P., 59, 486
Briggs, L. K., 9
Brodsky, A., 308
Broome, J., 224, 225, 227, 234, 391,
        392, 480
Brown, J. S., 27
Brown, R. V., 118, 303, 308
Brownson, F. O., 269, 273
Bruins, J. H., 447
Bruner, J. S., 156, 157, 199
Brunswik, E., 361
Bursztajn, H., 308
Bushey, B., 194, 218
Butzin, C. A., 371
Byrne, R. M., 78
Byrnes, J. P., 515
Calabresi, G., 421, 493
Camerer, C. F., 46, 253, 258, 362, 431,
        513
Campbell, D. T., 486
Carlsmith, J. M., 208
Carroll, J. S., 286
Carson, R. T., 291, 327, 330

Ceraso, J., 73
Chambless, D. L., 61
Chang, S., 217
Chapman, G. B., 298, 299, 376, 475,
        478
Chapman, J. P., 73, 182, 183
Chapman, L. J., 73, 182, 183
Charniak, E., 120
Chase, T., 209
Chavez, A., 262, 263
Cheng, P. W., 41, 83
Choo, G. T., 128
Christensen, C., 367
Chung, S. H., 476
Clark, D. M., 61
Clarke, J. R., 120, 122
Clement, J., 18
Coates, D., 59
Cohen, L. J., 147
Collins, A., 16, 106
Combs, B., 126
Cooper, J., 209, 210
Corbit, J. D., 59
Corrigan, B., 362
Coulton, G. F., 199
Coursey, D. L., 509
Cox, B. J., 61
Cox, J. R., 82
Cox, R. T., 114
D'Andrade, R. G., 184
Dailey, C. A., 199
Davis, D. A., 135, 137
Davis, W. A., 224
Dawes, R. M., 144, 362, 365–367, 444,
        446, 450, 458
Deber, R. B., 505
de Finetti, B., 234
Delquié, P., 319
Denes-Raj, V., 134
de Neufville, R., 254, 319
Deutsch, M., 420
Dewey, G., 376
Diamond, P., 512
Dickens, W. T., 64

Dickhaut, J., 451
Djerassi, C., 508
Dockins, P. C., 499
Doherty, M. E., 160, 161, 178
dos Santos, C. M. M., 212
Downing, L., 201
Downs, A., 452
Driver, M. J., 38
DuCharme, W. M., 198
Duda, R. O., 120, 122
Duncker, K., 26
Earle, T. C., 372
Eckerman, D. A., 477
Eddy, D. M., 109, 306
Edelson, S. M., 376, 377
Edgeworth, F. Y., 429
Edwards, W., 96, 147, 226, 278, 303,
        325, 344, 364
Einhorn, H. J., 37, 273, 368, 510
Ellsberg, D., 268, 399
Ellsworth, P. C., 212
Elster, J., 60, 64, 65, 207, 410, 416,
        417, 425, 431, 459, 479
Epstein, S., 134
Eraker, S. A., 321
Ericsson, K. A., 36, 37
Eshed-Levy, D., 447
Evans, J. St. B. T., 81, 82
Falgout, K., 178
Falk, R., 119
Faraday, M., 194, 218
Faust, D., 146
Feld, P., 217
Fennema, M. G., 133
Festinger, L., 208
Fetherstonhaugh, D., 501
Fineberg, H. V., 504
Fischer, G. W., 327
Fischhoff, B., 126, 128, 130, 131, 145,
        162, 178, 269, 335, 498, 507
Fishburn, P. C., 253
Fleishman, J. A., 450
Flynn, J., 515
Fong, G. T., 41

Forst, B. E., 308
Fox, C. R., 144, 258, 259, 272
Frank, R. H., 60, 61, 416
Frankel, M., 476
Frederickson, B. L., 310
Freedman, J., 211
Freko, D., 376, 377
Frey, D., 211
Friedman, D., 421
Friedrich, J., 501
Frisch, D., 45, 272
Gabriel, S. E., 323
Gal, I., 139, 140
Galotti, K. M., 77
Gardiner, P. C., 278
Gardner, M., 119
Gashnig, J., 120
Gaskins, I. W., 54, 195, 218
Gentner, D., 16
Gibbon, J., 476
Gilligan, C., 399
Gilovich, T., 132, 485
Gingerich, O., 156
Giuliano, T., 469
Gleicher, F., 292
Gneezy, U., 511
Goel, V., 505
Gold, L. S., 503
Goldberg, L. R., 362–364
Goodnow, J. J., 156, 157
Gowda, R., 422, 506
Gracely, E. J., 61
Granato, L., 140, 246
Greene, J., 329
Grether, D. M., 248
Griffin, D., 132
Griggs, R. A., 82
Gruber, K. L., 211
Guilmette, T. J., 146
Gutheil, T. G., 308
Hacking, I., 93, 96, 228
Hadorn, D. C., 306
Haendel, V., 476
Hafner, J., 204

Hamilton, J. T., 499
Hamm, R. M., 308
Hammond, K. R., 361
Hardin, G. R., 433
Hare, R. M., 225, 383, 384, 387, 394,
        397, 405, 441, 464
Harkness, A. R., 178
Harris, R. J., 65, 419
Hart, K., 146
Hart, P. E., 120, 122
Hastie, R., 125
Heath, C., 272, 300
Heatherton, T. F., 65
Heckerman, D. E., 115
Helmreich, R., 209
Helson, H., 485
Hempel, C. G., 150
Henle, M., 73, 74
Herek, G. M., 203
Herrnstein, R. J., 248, 476, 477
Hershey, J. C., 57, 162, 167, 257, 264,
        292, 319, 417, 443, 509
Hill, P. H., 317
Hogarth, R. M., 270, 273, 510, 511
Holyoak, K. J., 83
Holzman, G. E., 403
Horton, R., 14, 150
Horwich, P., 119, 155
Houston, D. A., 294
Howson, C. P., 504
Hsee, C. K., 213, 281, 282, 510
Huber, J., 287
Huber, P. W., 493, 511
Hulbert, L. G., 451
Huth, P., 203
Inglehart, J. K., 422
Inhelder, B., 134, 176
Irsin, J. I., 330
Irwin, J. R., 46, 291
Jacobs, L., 306
Janis, I. L., 38, 61, 195, 203, 211, 216
Janoff-Bulman, R., 59
Jenkins, H. M., 179, 180, 182
Jenni, K. E., 503

Jennings, D. L., 176
Jervis, R., 197, 212
Johnson, E. J., 34, 143, 248, 281, 292,
        376, 509
Johnson, S., 501
Johnson-Laird, P. N., 73, 74, 76, 78,
        79, 82
Jones-Lee, M. W., 291, 353
Josephs, R. A., 266
Joyce, M. A., 419
Jurney, J., 425, 460
Köbberling, V., 237
Kagel, J. H., 42
Kahneman, D., 31, 50, 134–138, 141,
        248, 250, 252, 253, 257, 263,
        264, 289, 291–293, 295, 296,
        310, 316, 373–375, 411, 425,
        504, 511
Kahr, A. S., 303
Kanneberg, C. H., 477
Kant, I., 395
Kaplow, L., 332
Katona, G., 25
Keeney, R. L., 303, 325, 327, 336–
        338, 342, 345, 346
Keinan, G., 215
Keller, L. R., 249, 423
Kelly C. W. III., 122
Kempton, W., 21
Keren, G., 34
Kerr, M., 485
Kim, J. I., 214
Kirby, K. N., 475, 477, 479
Kirsner, B., 263
Klayman, J., 376
Kleinmuntz, B., 37, 368
Kleinmuntz, D. N., 37, 133, 368
Klinebert, S., 478
Knetsch, J. L., 289, 291, 411, 425
Knight, F. H., 269
Koehler, D. J., 144, 212
Kolm, S.-C., 60
Konolige, K., 120
Koriat, A., 131

Kourilsky, M., 354
Krantz, D. H., 9, 41, 139, 234, 237
Kraus, N., 507
Krebs, D., 443
Kruglanski, A. W., 195
Kuch, K., 61
Kuhn, D., 178, 186, 187
Kunreuther, H. C., 270, 422, 423, 506, 508–511
Lakatos, I., 154
Lancaster, K., 474
Landes, W. M., 492
Landman, J., 292
Langer, E. J., 136
Larrick, R. P., 297, 299
Lau, R. R., 200
Lave, L., 507
Lawson, G., 500
Layman, M., 126
Legrenzi, M. S., 82
Legrenzi, P., 82
Lehman, D. R., 41, 42
Lepper, M. R., 199–201
Lerner, M. J., 412
Leung, K., 420
Levav, J., 144
Lewis, S. A., 430
Lichtenstein, S., 126, 128, 130, 131, 141, 247, 269, 372
Liebrand, W. B. G., 447
Lightman, A., 156
Lindley, D. V., 118, 308
Linville, P., 484
Lipman, M., 67
Llewellen-Thomas, H. A., 323
Loewenstein, G., 431, 445, 475, 484–486, 503, 516
Logue, A. W., 476
Loomes, G., 46, 264, 265
Lopes, L. L., 257, 260, 263
Lord, C. G., 201
Lovallo, D., 513
Lowin, A., 211

Luce, R. D., 234, 237, 248, 315, 342, 429
Lurie, S., 442, 445
Lutter, R., 496
Machina, M., 253
Magliozzi, T., 430
Malmfors, T., 507
Mann, L., 61, 195, 211
Markman, E., 74
Markman, K. D., 267
Markowitz, H. M., 495
Markwith, M., 507
Marshall, J. D., 330
Matute, H., 182
Maxwell, N. P., 312, 329
McCabe, K., 451
McCauley, C., 185, 217
McClelland, G. H., 509
McCloskey, M., 19
McCord, M., 254
McDaniels, T. L., 501
McFarland, C., 421
McGuire, C., 217
McTavish, J., 450, 458
Medin, D., 376, 377
Medvec, V. H., 485
Meehl, P. E., 362
Mellers, B. A., 146, 418, 419
Mertz, C. K., 515
Messick, D. M., 266, 426, 444, 445, 457
Meszaros, J. R., 202, 443, 505, 509, 511
Michalski, R., 16, 106
Mill, J. S., 53, 225
Miller, D. C., 515
Miller, D. T., 292, 421
Miller, J. G., 402
Mims, M., 178
Minsk, E., 400
Mischel, H. H., 482
Mischel, W., 470, 478, 482
Mitchell, R. C., 291, 327, 330
Miyamoto, J. M., 321

Modigliani, F., 474, 475
Montgomery, H., 277
Morgan, J. N., 297, 299
Morgan, M. G., 507
Morgenstern, O., 225, 433
Morrall, J. F. III, 496
Moynihan, D. P., 337
Mumford, M., 144
Murphy, A. H., 130
Murphy, T., 376
Murphy-Berman, V., 420
Murray, T., 354
Mynatt, C. R., 160, 161, 178
Nagel, T., 443, 487
Nash, J. F., 429
Neale, M. A., 427, 430
Newcomb, T. M., 184
Newell, A., 43
Newman, J. R., 325
Ng, K. O., 128
Nickerson, R. S., 67, 119
Nilsson, N. J., 122
Nisbett, R. E., 41, 42, 83, 177, 195,
    297, 299, 374
Norris, S. P., 193
Norton, G. R., 61
Nozick, R., 394, 413, 414
O'Connor, A. M. C., 323
O'Leary, J. F., 321
O'Loughlin, M., 186
Oliver, L. M., 83
Orbell, J. M., 446, 458
Ordóñez, L. D., 419
Osherson, D. N., 74, 118
Parfit, D., 58, 470, 479, 487
Parker, A. M., 501
Parks, C. D., 443, 451
Pascal, B., 228
Payne, J. W., 34, 286, 287, 368
Peake, P. K., 478
Pearl, J., 122
Peecher, M. E., 133
Perkins, D. N., 27, 194, 204, 218
Peterson, C. R., 139, 198, 303

Peterson, R. S., 217
Petit, P., 235, 424
Petry, N. M., 479
Phelps, E., 178
Phillips, B., 128
Phillips, L. D., 128
Phillips, L. M., 193
Piaget, J., 134, 176
Pinto Prades, J.-L., 321
Pitz, G. F., 201
Platt, J. R., 154
Pliskin, J. S., 309
Plott, C. R., 248
Polya, G., 50
Popper, K. R., 68, 150, 153
Posner, R. A., 492
Potter, M. C., 199
Potters, J., 511
Poulton, E. C., 314
Prelec, D., 476, 477, 485
Provitera, A., 73
Pruitt, D. G., 430, 441
Putnam, H., 96, 159
Puto, C., 287
Quattrone, G. A., 207, 453
Quiggin, J., 253, 261
Quinn, R. J., 266
Quinn, W., 396
Rachlin, H., 476
Raiffa, H., 127, 303, 342, 427, 429,
    430
Ramsey, F. P., 234
Rank, A. D., 38
Rapaport, A., 447
Rasinski, K. A., 420
Rawls, J., 48, 392, 413, 414
Read, D., 486
Read, S. J., 378
Redelmeier, D. A., 310
Regan, D., 440
Reinhold, H., 201
Reuben, D. B., 168
Riboh, R., 120
Richardson, J., 321

Rips, L., 72
Ritov, I., 266, 271, 292, 400, 421–423, 504, 505
Robbins, L., 390
Robinson, L. B., 125
Ronen, J., 293
Ross, L., 176, 177, 195, 199–201, 212
Ross, M., 143
Roth, A. E., 42
Royzman, E. B., 401
Rozin, P., 507
Ruhnke, R, 209
Rumain, B., 72
Rutte, C. G., 457
Ryan, C. S., 185
Sabini, J., 59, 77, 383, 416
Salkovskis, P. M., 61
Samuelson, C. D., 445, 457
Samuelson, W., 291
Sarin, R. K., 423
Sato, K., 448, 450
Sattath, S., 247, 248, 279
Savage, L. J., 96, 99, 234, 248
Schaeken, W., 78
Schafer, W. D., 515
Schelling, T. C., 353, 440, 502
Scher, S. J., 210
Schiavo, M. D., 178
Schkade, D. A., 248, 281
Schlosberg, H., 35
Schmitt, N., 367
Schneider, S. L., 257
Schoemaker, P. J. H., 40, 319
Schoorman, F. D., 469
Schreiber, C. A., 310
Schroeder, H. M., 38
Schulkin, J., 403
Schulze, W. D., 509
Schustack, M. W., 178
Schwalm, N. D., 255
Schwartz, A., 511
Schwartz, B., 165, 166, 181, 307, 350, 382
Schwartz, N., 486

Schwartz, S. M., 120, 122
Schwartz-Shea, P., 454
Sears, R., 211
Segal, U., 253
Sells, S. B., 73
Shafer, G., 101
Shafir, E., 273, 274, 294, 453, 512
Shaklee, H., 162, 178, 450, 458
Shavell, S., 332
Shefrin, H. M., 474
Shepard, D. C., 309
Sherman, S. J., 163, 294
Shoda, Y., 478
Shweder, R. A., 184
Sicoly, F., 143
Siegel, L. S., 500
Silver, M., 383, 416
Simmons, C. H., 412
Simmons, R. T., 446, 454
Simon, H. A., 36, 37, 43, 418
Simonson, I., 287, 288
Sinden, J. A., 289
Singer, P., 5, 354, 401, 425, 441
Skov, R. B., 163
Slocum, J., 120
Slovic, P., 279, 498
Slovic, P., 126, 128, 145, 247–249, 255, 269, 272, 281, 372, 497, 500, 501, 507, 508, 515
Smedslund, J., 176
Smith, A., 442
Smith, E. E., 376
Smith, M. H., 505
Snyder, M., 161
Solnick, J. V., 477
Solomon, R. L., 59
Sorter, G. H., 293
Spranca, M., 140, 246, 400, 402, 417
Stalmeier, P. F. M., 321
Stanovich, K. E., 204, 205
Starmer, C., 265
Starr, C., 496
Staw, B. M., 469
Steedman, M., 74, 76

Sternberg, R. J., 178
Stewart, R. H., 198
Stitt, C. L., 185
Stone, E. R., 501
Strack, F., 486
Streufert, S., 38
Strotz, R. H., 474
Suedfeld, P., 38
Sugden, R., 253, 265
Suppes, P., 234, 237, 315, 342
Swann, W. B., 161
Sweeney, P. D., 211
Swindon, R. P., 61
Tabossi, P., 78
Tan, I., 128
Tengs, T. O., 352, 496
Tetlock, P. E., 38, 39, 213, 214, 217
Teubal, E., 140, 246
Thaler, R. H., 425
Thaler, R. H., 60, 257, 288, 289, 295,
     299, 301, 329, 411, 412, 444,
     474, 480, 511
Thompson, L., 431, 445
Thumasathit, T., 443
Tice, D. M., 65
Toulmin, S. E., 84
Tschirgi, J. E., 164
Tucker, D., 178
Tversky, A., 31, 50, 101, 118, 132,
     134–138, 141, 143, 144, 207,
     212, 226, 234, 237, 247–250,
     252, 253, 257–260, 263, 264,
     272–274, 279, 281, 283, 284,
     286–288, 292, 293, 296, 315,
     342, 373–375, 453, 511, 512
Tweney, R. D., 160, 161, 178, 196
Tyler, S. W., 85
Ubel, P., 321
Ubel, P. A., 333
Ulehla, Z. J., 139
Van Lehn, K., 27
Varey, C., 316

Vaupel, J. W., 303
Viscusi, W. K., 499, 503, 506
Vosniadu, S., 17
Voss, J. F., 85
Vu, A. D., 443
Wagenaar, W. A., 34
Wakker, P., 237
Wakker, P. P., 321
Waller, M. B., 477
Walster, E., 411, 422
Walster, G. W., 411, 422
Ward, W. C., 179
Wason, P. C., 79, 80, 82, 160
Waters, J., 178
Weber, E. U., 263
Weber, M., 253, 258, 327
Weeks, J. C., 207
Wegner, D. M., 199
Weinstein, M. C., 309
Wenzlaff, R., 199
Wertheimer, M., 22
West, R. F., 204, 205
Whalley, P. C., 128
Wheeler, D. D., 354
Wilke, H. A. M., 447, 457
Winkler, R. L., 130
Wisudha, A., 128
Wittgenstein, L., 159
Woodworth, R. S., 35, 73
Wright, G. N., 128
Yaari, M. E., 253, 419
Yamagishi, T., 448, 450, 456, 457
Yates, J. F., 501
Yengo, L. A., 85
Zakay, D., 280
Zeckhauser, R., 291
Zeelenberg, M., 266
van Avermaet, E., 426
van de Kragt, A., 446, 458
von Neuman, J., 225
von Winterfeldt, D., 96, 147, 303, 325,
     344, 364

Subject Index

absolute values, 405
accountability, 214
accurate judgments, 185
actively open-minded thinking, 55, 62,
    131, 145, 376
   defined, 192
   examples, 192
   outcomes, 203
adaptation, 323, 485
additivity of probability, 104
agent relativity, 330, 402
Allais paradox, 248
alternative hypotheses, 164
altruism, 382, 442
ambiguity, 268, 499
   and insurance, 510
amniocentesis, 317
analog scale, 313
analogy, 16
anchoring, 375
Argument Evaluation Test, 204
artificial intelligence, 43
asbestos, 496
Asian disease problem, 257
aspiration, 260
asymmetric dominance, 287
atmosphere effect, 73
attentional bias, 176
attribute weight, 325, 344
autonomy, 392
availability heuristic, 141
averaging, 146, 371

Bacon, F., 191
Bayes's theorem, 109, 134

beer on the beach, 301, 329
belief overkill, 212, 395
beliefs
   about thinking, 204
   rational, 62
between-subject designs, 44
biases, 147
   ambiguity, 268
   anchoring and underadjustment,
    375
   asymmetric dominance, 287
   attentional, 176
   availability, 141
   averaging, 146
   base-rate neglect, 134
   belief overkill, 212
   certainty effect, 251
   compatibility, 281
   compromise effect, 288
   congruence, 159
   conjunction fallacy, 137
   dilution, 374
   do no harm, 425
   dynamic inconsistency, 475
   evaluability, 281
   ex-ante equity, 423
   fixed pie, 429
   frequency, 134
   gambler's fallacy, 139
   hindsight, 145
   illusion of control, 179
   illusory correlation, 183
   inappropriate extreme confidence,
    127

inertia effect, 201
information, 166
intransitivity, 283
money illusion, 512
morality as self-interest, 453
myside, 195
naturalism, 402, 503
neglect of opportunity cost, 293
omission, 291, 400, 504
outcome, 57
own waste, 422
parochialism, 454
person causation, 421
polarization, 201
probability matching, 139
probability weighing, 254
prominence, 279
proportionality, 500
punishment without deterrence, 422
reference group neglect, 514
selective exposure, 211
status-quo, 288
subadditivity of probability, 144,
    259
sunk cost, 297
underinvestment, 300
voters' illusion, 452
wishful thinking, 206
zero risk, 505
birth control products, 507
blaming the victim, 412
bootstrapping, 364
bright lines, 416

calibration, 106, 127
    improving, 132
California Coastal Commission, 278
cancer therapy, 207
capital punishment, 201, 212, 415
catastrophic risk, 500
Categorical Imperative, 395, 396
certainty effect, 251, 469
chance setup, 103
childbed fever, 150

Chomsky, N., 48
choosing vs. rejecting, 294
classification, 376
cognitive dissonance, 208
coincidences, 118
commons dilemma, 433
compatibility, 281
compensation, 420, 493, 494, 507
compensatory decision strategies, 279
competition, 442, 444
compromise effect, 288
computer models, 43
concept formation, 157
conditional assessment, 132
conditional probability, 104
confidence, 62, 127
congruence bias, 159
congruence heuristic, 162
conjoint analysis, 378
conjoint measurement, 340
conjunction fallacy, 137
    children, 138
connectedness, 234
contingency, 173
contingency judgment, 179
contingent cooperation, 450
contingent valuation, 291, 327
contingent weighting, 281
contrast, 485
contribution, 418
control of risk, 491
conversion of premises, 73
cooperation, 433, 442
cooperative theory, 439
correlation, 173
    judgment, 176
    personality traits, 183
cost overruns, 374
cost-benefit analysis, 306
cost-effectiveness, 309
counterfactuals, 263, 267
culture, 420, 443, 457
    collectivist, 443
    differences in calibration, 128

debiasing
    extreme confidence, 131
    hindsight, 145
decision
    definition, 6
decision analysis, 303, 335
decision utility, 311, 335, 471, 475
declining marginal utility, 239, 307,
        353, 393, 412, 413, 472, 494,
        495, 508, 511
defection, 433
defensive avoidance, 215
delay independence, 473, 476
deontological rules, 394
depression, 181
descriptive models, 31, 49
deterrence, 414, 422, 507
diagnosis, 12
dictator game, 411
diethylstilbestrol, 505
difference measurement, 314
dilution effect, 374
direct vs. indirect judgments, 311
disappointment, 265
discounting, 470
    economic theory, 470
    normative model, 473
    subjective, 474
distributive justice, 410
do no harm, 425
docility, 418
double effect, 395
DPT vaccine, 504
dread, 484
dual processes, 81
dynamic inconsistency, 473, 475, 476

Earle, T. C., 559
earthquake insurance, 509
Edgeworth Box, 429
elastic justification, 213
elimination by aspects, 284
emotion, 263, 292, 416, 421, 484
    and rationality, 59

defined, 59
    time, 484
empathy, 443
endowment effect, 288
entrepreneurs, 494
envy, 416, 445
equality, 413, 418, 445
equality heuristic, 424
equity, 418
equity theory, 411
escalation of commitment, 469
evaluability, 281
evidence, *see* search-inference frame-
        work
ex-ante equity, 423
exchangeable propositions, 98
expected-utility theory, 114, 167, 224,
        227, 490, 494, 508
expert systems, 120
exponential discounting, 471
Exxon Valdez, 291, 327

factor analysis, 497
fairness in negotiation, 430
falsification, 153
family resemblance, 159
Faraday, Michael, 196
fear, 446, 484, 500
fixed pie, 430, 444
flat maximum, 350
flood insurance, 508
four-card problem, 78, 166
framing effect, 253, 257, 271, 419,
        425, 486
Franklin, B., 428
frequency judgments, 126
functional measurement, 378
fundamental values, 336

gambler's fallacy, 139
gambling, 34
generalization test, 396
give-some game, 450
goals, *see* search-inference framework

for thinking, 11
    personal, 6, 11, 464
Golden Rule, 400
greed, 446
group conflict, 454
group loyalty, 454
groupthink, 216

Hand Rule, 492
handicaps (medical), 322
happiness, 58, 223, 388, 486
herd immunity, 443
heroin addicts, 478
heuristics, 49, 272, 286, 418, 423, 425,
    460, 485, 504
    availability, 141
    congruence, 162
    representativeness, 134, 135
hindsight bias, 145
honesty in negotiation, 430
hope, 484
human life, 352
hypervigilance, 215
hypothesis testing, 149
    falsification, 153
    philosophy, 153
    probability, 155

identity, 487
illusion of control, 179
illusory correlation, 183, 202
impatience, 472, 484
imperatives, 383
imprecision, 226
impression formation, 370
impulsiveness, 470, 478, 484
inappropriate extreme confidence, 127
incentive, 393, 409, 414, 492, 494
incentives, 46
independence (probability), 105
indirect harm, 396
individual differences, 204, 280, 448,
    478, 514
individual vs. statistical risk, 502

inertia effect, 201
inference, *see* search-inference frame-
    work
inflation, 425, 472, 512
information, 166
information bias, 166
insensitivity to quantity, 328
insight problems, 13
insufficient reason, principle of, 100,
    269
insurance, 270, 292, 494, 508
    environmental, 511
integration and segregation, 295
integrative complexity, 39
integrative negotiation, 429
interest, 472
internet research, 46
interpersonal comparison of utility, 389
interviews, 38, 366
intransitivity, 283
intuitions, 382, 403, 409, 417, 423,
    495, 507
    defined, 48
intuitive toxicology, 506
invariance, 253
investment, 494, 511
involuntary risk, 498
irrational belief persistence, 195, 468

Jeziorski, M., 16
joint vs. separate evaluation, 281
judgment, 357
    defined, 8
judgments of utility, 311
just world, 412

Kitzhaber, J., 304
knowledge as design, 28, 307

lawsuits, 291, 375, 492
learning, 13
least cost avoider, 493
lens model, 361
lexical rules, 350, 393

liability, 492
libertarianism, 394
Linda problem, 137
linear regression, 358
local fairness, 425
logic, 67
    categorical, 71
    failure to accept the task, 73
    mental models, 74
    predicate, 71
    probabilistic reasoning, 73
    propositional, 70
loss aversion, 255, 288, 468, 511
low probabilities, 509
luck, 56

mammograms, 109
matching, 280, 324
maximization, 418
means values, 336, 405
mental accounting, 288
mental budgets, 300
mental models, 74
methods, 34
missing information, 271
money illusion, 512
money pump, 235
monotonicity condition, 315
Monty Hall problem, 119
moralistic values, 404
morality, 487
    and utility, 382
    impersonal, 384
    logic, 383
morality as self-interest illusion, 453
multiattribute utility theory (MAUT),
    225, 278, 325, 335, 340, 343
multiple regression, 358
multiplication rule (probability), 105
myopia, 470, 511
myopic loss aversion, 511
myside bias, 195

naive theories, 17, 506

natural logic, 72
naturalism, 383, 402, 503
need, 418
needs, 416
neglect of probability, 246
negotiation, 426
neutral evidence principle, 200
news media and risk, 501
Nixon, Richard, 57
nonregressiveness, 373
normative models, 31, 47, 224, 438,
    473
    belief persistence, 197
    hypothesis testing, 155
    neutral evidence principle, 200
    order principle, 197
    risk, 490
norms (reference points), 293
N-person prisoner's dilemma, 436
nuclear power, 498

odds, 94
omission bias, 291, 400, 468, 504
opportunity cost, 293
optimal risk, 490
order principle, 197
Oregon Health Plan, 304
outcome bias, 57
overconfidence, 367
    in entrepreneurs, 513
overweighing and underweighing prob-
    ability, 254
own-waste bias, 422

panic attacks, 61
parallelogram, 22
Pareto optimality, 391, 428
parochialism, 454
Pascal's wager, 63, 228
Pascal, B., 94
person causation, 421
person tradeoff, 320
personal goals, 464, 465
pi (π) function, 251

planning defined, 11
plans, 463, 467, 487
        biases, 468
pleasure, 223
polarization, 201, 431
policies, 463
polio vaccine, 505
positive and negative attributes, 294
possibilities, *see* search-inference frame-
        work
precedent, 483
predicted utility, 310, 316, 335
prediction, 13
preference reversals, 247, 280, 287,
        294
prescriptive models, 31, 50, 164, 460,
        509
        hypothesis testing, 164
pricing, 281
primacy effect, 197
principle of personal good, 391
prisoner's dilemma, 435
probability
        accuracy, 125
        biases, 147
        calibration, 106, 127
        coherence, 104
        conditional, 104
        defined, 94
        frequencies, 115
        frequency theory, 97
        in hypothesis testing, 155
        independence, 105
        logical theory, 98
        multiplication rule, 105
        personal theory, 99
        scoring rules, 107
        subadditivity, 144
probability matching, 139
procedural justice, 410
process tracing, 34
projective tests, 182
prominence effect, 279, 328
proper scoring rules, 108

proportions vs. differences, 500
prospect theory, 250, 299
        pi function, 251
        reflection effect, 256
        Value function, 255
protective behavior, 508, 509
prudence, 487
psychometric approach to risk, 496
punishment, 388, 422
        without deterrence, 422
pure time preference, 472

quadratic scoring rule, 108
Quality Adjusted Life Year (QALY),
        309, 353
quantitative thinking, 516
quantity confusion, 500

range, 327
rank-dependent utility, 260
rationality, 55
        and luck, 56
        of regret and disappointment, 267
real money, 46
rebates, 295
recency effect, 198
reference point, 255, 421
reference price, 301
reference-group neglect, 514
reflection, 13, 68
reflection effect, 256
reform, 459
regret, 263, 266, 292
regulation, 517
        of risk, 491
relative risk, 501
relativism, 384
representativeness, 135, 373
reservation price, 427
response mode, 281
responsibility, 415, 493
retribution, 388, 396, 415, 422
rights, 392, 397, 416
risk aversion, 240, 260, 265, 495, 511

risk regulation, 495
risk vs. uncertainty, 246
rule utiltarianism, 396
rules, 350

savoring, 484
scientific thinking, 12
scoring rules, 107
search, *see* search-inference framework
search processes, 14
search-inference framework, 6, 225
second order social dilemma, 456
security, 260
selective exposure, 211
self-control, 480, 481
    attention, 482
    emotion, 482
    extrapsychic devices, 481
    personal rules, 482
self-deception, 58, 63, 206, 412
self-esteem, 65
self-interest, 425, 442
    social dilemmas, 440
Semmelweis, Ignaz, 150
sensitivity (of medical test), 109
sensitivity to cost in CV, 329
sex differences, 514
signal value, 500
similarity, 377
single mindedness, 277, 280
slippery slope, 351
social dilemmas, 433
    discussion, 458
    motives, 441
    second order, 456
    solutions, 455
sour grapes, 65
specificity (of medical test), 109
St. Petersburg paradox, 239
standard gamble, 316
status-quo bias, 288, 330, 468
stereotyped behavior, 165
strategies, 158
strategy, 436

stress, 215
strong inference, 154
subadditivity of probability, 144, 259
sunk-cost effect, 297, 468
sure-thing principle, 235, 269, 424
Sydney Opera House, 374

take-some game, 450
tastes, 416
taxicab problem, 134
teaching decision analysis, 354
temporal impartiality, 479
temporal myopia, 470
theories of knowledge, 188
theory and evidence, 187
thinking
    aloud, 34
    defined, 8
    types, 6
Thomsen condition, 342
thoughtlessness, 455
threshold for probability, 254
time tradeoff, 320
tit for tat, 436
Tom W. problem, 136
torts, 492, 507
total discrediting, 199
tradeoffs, 350
transitivity, 234
trust, 450
2 4 6 problem, 160

ultimatum game, 60, 412
Ulysses, 463, 481
underinvestment, 300
undersensitivity to range, 327
understanding, 22
unknown risk, 499
utilitarianism, 225, 382, 386
    and expected utility, 391
    social dilemmas, 440
utility
    defined, 223
    measurement, 310

of money, 238
utility theory, 224

vaccination, 271, 400, 422, 443, 504
vagueness of utility, 226
value conflict, 213
Value function, 255
value of human life, 352
variety, 486
verbal protocols, 368
visual analog scale, 313
von Neuman, J., 433

weak ordering, 234
weather forecasting, 106, 130
weighted utilitarianism, 441
weights of attributes, 325, 344
willingness to pay, 291
wishful thinking, 206, 398, 412, 483,
    514
within-subject designs, 44
WTA vs. WTP, 330

zero risk, 505

Syllogism Problems P83